Psychology of the Arts

Psychology of

the Arts

Hans Kreitler and Shulamith Kreitler

Tel Aviv University

Duke University Press

Durham, N. C.

1972

LCC card no. 70–185466
ISBN 0–8223–0269–1
Printed in the United States of
America by Heritage Printers, Inc.

In memory of Wilhelm and Eugenie Kreitler

Preface

The most daring and presumptuous questions are often asked by under-graduates because they do not yet know the difficulties of answering them. Far back in the past, when one of us was still in his junior year, he light-heartedly posed such a question. Why is it that most enthusiasts of one art form, say literature, are also able and inclined to enjoy other art forms, say music or painting? Have we not to conclude that however different the various art experiences may appear to be, they all derive from the same psychological core and share a great many psychological characteristics? If so, why not unify the psychological theories of different art forms into one encompassing theory, general enough to account for painting, sculpture, music, literature, dance and the rest, but still specific enough to explain the experiential impact of Martha Graham's dances, Beethoven's Piano Sonata Op. 110, or Picasso's *Guernica*.

The quest for such a theory seemed so challenging that it had to be tried. The first formulation of hypotheses was exciting. However several years of experimentation and library work had a somewhat sobering effect. Indeed, summing up the theoretical and empirical findings in the form of a doctoral dissertation by one of the authors seemed to show that art experiences shared enough common characteristics to justify the attempt to construct an encompassing integrative theory. But the shortcomings of this thesis demonstrated convincingly that any further progress demanded a frighten-ing amount of detailed expert knowledge in nearly all fields of psychology and in many domains of art. Hence, the project was first delayed for two or three years, then discarded sceptically, and finally even forgotten.

Only when the authors, after cooperating in other fields of psychological research, found out that two psychologists working truly together could do the job done by four psychologists working separately, was psychology of the arts taken up again. This time it remained in the forefront of our work for several years. Finally we felt that our theory had satisfied our curiosity about the art experience and deepened our understanding of the eliciting stimuli, namely, the works of art. But we also realized that the material we had collected more than sufficed for a basic textbook about psychology of the arts. This created an unexpected complication. How could we combine the open-minded objectivity required from textbook authors with the tendency of theory builders to promote mainly, if not exclusively, their own ideas?

In order to solve this problem we postponed the writing of the book and started instead to teach art psychology. In the beginning we did it hesitantly, mainly in seminars with sophisticated graduate students of psychology. In the next stage we proceeded to teach it for several years in lecture courses to undergraduates who had only some knowledge of introductory psychology and an interest in one domain of art or another. Finally, one of us could even accept an invitation of the Friends of the Tel Aviv Museum to teach psychology of the arts to a crowd of art fans who had only a vague idea of what psychology is about.

The lesson learned from these varied teaching experiences was manifold. For instance, we found lack of psychological knowledge in the students to be a lesser handicap in learning psychology of the arts than lack of personal exposure to at least one form of art. In other words, when teaching psychology of the arts it is not too difficult or too time consuming to explain basic psychological terms and processes to students who have no prior knowledge of psychology, and thus also to refresh the memory of those who have already attended an introductory course in psychology. Yet no explanation can serve as a substitute for an art experience; it can only induce students to read a poem, to visit a museum or listen to good music.

Furthermore, classroom discussions as well as oral and written tests demonstrated that presenting competing and unrelated theories and findings sequentially and on equal footing yields poorer results than using one theory as an anchorage point and basic guideline for scanning the field of art psychology. Thus, those students who studied psychology of the arts in the framework of our theory showed more personal involvement and more inclination to apply what they learned regardless of whether they accepted the theory fully or partly or rejected it, than those victims of our educational experimentation who studied theories and findings in art psychology without coordination through an integrative theory such as ours. The latter have remained by and large personally uninvolved and mostly did not gain enough enthusiasm for further work in this field. We tend to believe that the enthusiasm characteristic of the former group reflects mainly the benefits of a comprehensive integrative theory and not just the enthusiasm of those who taught the material.

When we finally got down to writing this book, we still faced two didactic problems. Since psychology of the arts does not yet constitute an integral part in the curricula of departments of psychology or of the arts, it seemed to us imperative to interest teachers and students alike. For the benefit of teachers and sophisticated experts we sometimes had to present more experimental findings than students like to read, while for the benefit of the student we had to discuss central psychological processes and basic techniques of art in greater length than is necessary for the expert. The first problem we tried to solve by relegating to notes much information that may concern mostly the expert. As for the second problem, we made an attempt to concentrate in one place the discussion of basic concepts, even if they are relevant for different domains of art, and to use cross references instead of repetition. This enables the reader to skip in the first part of the book the detailed discussion of the elements of art forms which do not appeal to him or with which he does not wish to be concerned. For example, the laws of gestalt, important for every domain of art, are discussed in connection with painting (Chapter 4). However, if the reader prefers to skip the chapters about color (Chapters 2 and 3) and form (Chapters 4 and 5), he may use the back reference to Chapter 4 when reading about gestalt principles in music (Chapters 6 and 7), dance (Chapter 8), sculpture (Chapters 9 and 10), or literature (Chapter 11). The same goes for rhythm. It is discussed in connection with music (Chapter 7), but is of equal importance for poetry (Chapter 11), painting (Chapters 3 to 6), and other arts. These remarks do not apply to Chapter 1, which serves as an introduction essential for the whole book. Likewise, no provision could be made for skipping chapters or whole sections in Part II of this book. The processes dealt with there are basic for all kinds of art experiences and their functions are best analyzed and illustrated by presenting side by side examples of all the major arts.

It goes without saying that in different stages of our work we received invaluable work and inspiration from many friends, students, teachers, and colleagues. We are especially indebted to the film and theater director Mr. Peter Frye, who suggested to us an inquiry into the different realities presented in art, and to the philosopher Professor Georg Janoska, who together with his Saturday Afternoon Group of philosophers and artists spent a whole term discussing the aesthetic and artistic implications of our concept of tension and relief. Inspiration and constructive criticism we received also from the psychologists Professors Solomon E. Asch, Karl Bühler, and Ferdinand Weinhandl, the composer Professor Walter Klein, the director of the Viennese Albertina Museum Dr. Walter Koschatzky, the painter Mrs. Eva Boiko-Avi-Yona, the assistant director of Duke University Press Mr. Theodore A. Saros, together with the Press staff, the lovers of all the arts Mrs. Genia Kreitler and Mr. Manfred Teicher, and of course from all the many students who challenged our concepts and forced us through their questions and comments to clarify our ideas and prove our theses. Our extraordinary indebtedness to Mrs. Luba Elblinger, M.D., is best expressed by simply stating that she volunteered to plan and arrange the index. Writing the last draft of this book was facilitated by an invitation to the first author to spend a year (1968–1969) as a USPHS Visiting Scholar at the Research Division, Center for Psychological Studies, Educational Testing Service, Princeton, N.J., and through a postdoctoral fellowship (V67–400) granted to the second author by the Foundations Fund for Research in Psychiatry.

Thanks are also due to the institutions and private collectors who kindly gave permission to reproduce the pictures in this book, and especially to Dr. Stella Kramrisch; Mr. and Mrs. William A. M. Burden; the Israel Museum; the Vatican Museum; the British Museum; the National Gallery; the Tate Gallery; the Musée du Louvre; the Museum of Modern Art, New York; the Solomon R. Guggenheim Museum, New York; the Nolde-Stiftung Seebüll; the Art Institute of Chicago; the Minneapolis Institute of Arts; and Van Nostrand Reinhold Company. Our special thanks go also to Mrs. Anna Dvorak for her execution of the black-and-white figures in the text.

July 1972, Tel Aviv   Hans Kreitler and Shulamith Kreitler

Contents

Part I

Plate 1. Victor Vasarely. Composition *Vega II*. [The Israel Museum, Jerusalem]

Plate 2. The color solid: *above*, surface view; *above right*,
horizontal section; *below right*, vertical section. [J. Itten,
The Art of Color. Courtesy, Van Nostrand Reinhold Company and Otto Maier Verlag]

Plate 3. Alberto Giacometti. *Man Pointing*, 1947. Bronze, height 70½ in. [The Tate Gallery, London]

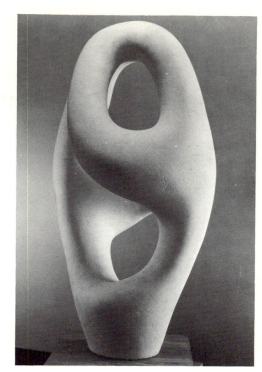

Plate 4. Jean Arp. *Ptolemy*, 1953. Limestone, height 40 in. [The Museum of Modern Art, New York. Gift of Mr. and Mrs. William A. M. Burden, donor retaining life interest]

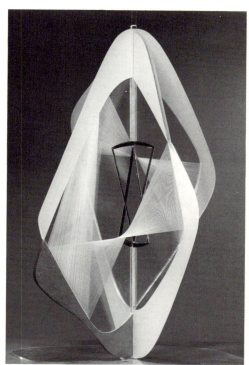

Plate 5. Naum Gabo. *Construction in Space X*, 1952–53. Plexiglas and nylon wire, height 28 in. [Private collection, New York]

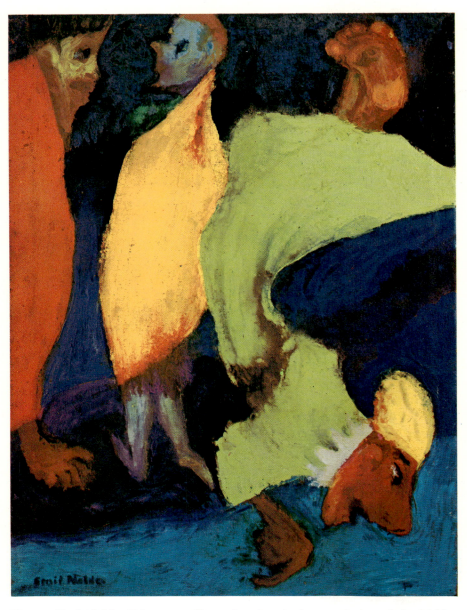

Plate 6. Emil Nolde. *Trio,* 1929. [Reproduced with the permission of the Nolde-Stiftung Seebüll]

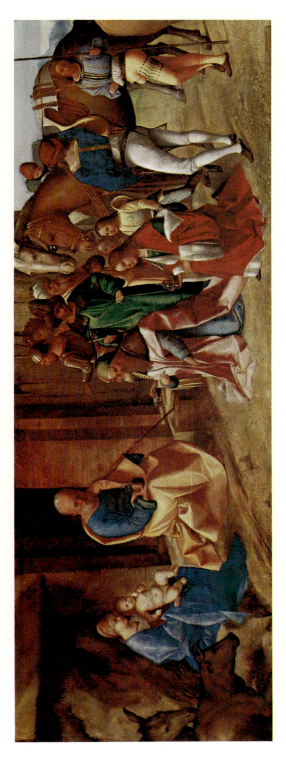

Plate 7. Giorgione. *The Adoration of the Kings* [Reproduced by courtesy of the Trustees, The National Gallery, London]

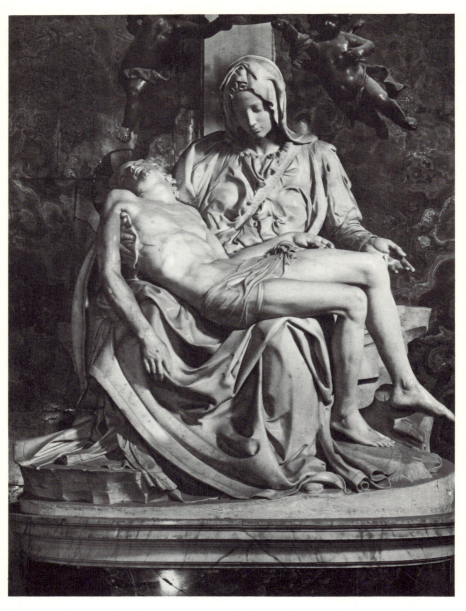

Plate 8. Michelangelo. *Pietà*, 1498–1500, St. Peter's Basilica, Rome. Marble, height 69 in. [Photograph Alinari]

Plate 9. The Birth of the Buddha. Late second or early third century, from Gandhara. Stone, length 20½ in. [Courtesy of the Art Institute of Chicago]

Plate 10. Paul Cézanne. *Chestnut Trees at Jas de Bouffan*, c. 1885–87. [The Minne-apolis Institute of Arts]

Plate 11. Vasily Kandinski. *In the Black Square*, 1923. [The Solomon R. Guggenheim Museum Collection]

Plate 12. Krishna Dancing on the Serpent Kaliya. c. 900, South India. Bronze, height 23½ in. [N. Y. Shastri Collection, Gwalior]

Plate 13. Girl with a Lotus Blossom. Egypt, style of Fifth Dynasty (2750–2625 B.C.). Limestone, sunken relief. [Musée du Louvre, Paris]

Plate 14. Lapith and Centaur. From a metope of the Parthenon, Athens, now in the British Museum, c. 447–43 B.C. Marble. [The British Museum, London]

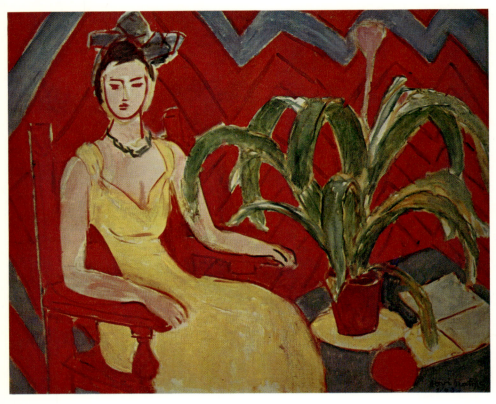

Plate 15. Henri Matisse. *Michaella, Nice, 1943*. [Private collection, photograph Eric Pollitzer; reproduced by permission]

Plate 16. Marc Chagall. *I and the Village*, 1911. [Collection, The Museum of Modern Art, New York; Mrs. Simon Guggenheim Fund]

Plate 17. Jacques Lipschitz. *Mother and Child, II*, 1941–45. Bronze, height 50 in. [Collection, The Museum of Modern Art, New York; Mrs. Simon Guggenheim Fund]

1. Theoretical Background

Psychology of the Arts

What is art? How is it created? And what are its effects on human beings? These are the main questions about art that have fascinated and preoccupied man through the centuries. As a result, a great number of disciplines have grown up around art, ranging from philosophical aesthetics (probably the oldest and richest of them) through the history of art, art criticism, comparative aesthetics of the arts, aesthetic morphology (i.e., analysis of form and style in the arts), to the sociology, anthropology, and ethnology of art and the relatively recent discipline, psychology of the arts. Naturally, these various domains, of which only a sample is mentioned, are further subdivided into specialized fields—by historical period, geographical locus, type of art production, specific problem or preferred approach, methodology, and so on. As is to be expected, the disciplines overlap and interpenetrate.

In this bewildering diversity, there is a place for the psychology of the arts, or "experimental aesthetics" as it is sometimes called, which is characterized by two major features. First, as a scientific discipline it is empirical. Second, as a branch of psychology it concentrates on human beings, on their internal and external behavior and processes as related to art. Both of these features are already evident in the work of Gustav Fechner, whose *Vorschule der Ästhetik* (1876) is generally considered to mark the beginning of the new science, and in the studies of his early followers—Witmer (1893), Cohn (1894), Major (1895), and others.

The empirical approach—the first-mentioned feature—defines psychology of the arts by its methodology. To say that psychology of art has an empirical approach is to say that it treats as findings the products of controlled reproducible observations and regards ideas and insights as hypotheses to be tested or as concepts in a theoretical system designed to account for findings. This methodology sets it apart from philosophical aesthetics, for example, which may deal with similar problems but by the nonempirical tools of logical analysis, deduction from axioms, postulates, or propositions, and other methods typical of theoretical thought.

Concern with human reactions and experiences, the second-mentioned feature, serves to define the subject matter of the psychology of art, the problems with which it deals. These include human beings in the two major roles they may play with regard to art: the role of the creator of art—the artist; and the role of the spectator—the audience or the consumer of art. Each of these two roles forms the basis of a whole set of problems investigated by art psychologists. Concentration on the creator of art might include, for example, investigation of the processes of creativity and expression and of the motivations for artistic expression, comparisons between artistic creativity and other types of creativity in order to determine the special characteristics of art creation, and studies on the development of artistic creativity, the effects of education on it, and even the psychotherapeutic effects of artistic expression for those who have no special training in the arts. On the other hand, concentration on the spectator of art includes investigation of the psychological processes involved in the experiencing of art, the study of the unique and nonunique characteristics of this experience, of its determinants, components, and development, and of the possible less direct long-term effects.

The concentration of the psychology of art on studying human beings as creators or spectators of art helps both to mark off the boundaries of the subject matter of this discipline from other disciplines which deal with art and to define its relations with them. For example, a psychologist in his role as psychologist would not attempt to define value norms and standards for works of art. This problem would belong formally to the domain of aesthetic value theory. But a psychologist would be concerned with the relations between norms that spectators may entertain and their experiencing of art (e.g., Bernberg, 1953; Farnsworth, 1946; Farnsworth & Beaumont, 1929) or with the correspondence between value judgments of experts and non-expert spectators of art (e.g., Bulley, 1934; Child, 1962; D. A. Gordon, 1955). Similarly, a psychologist of art would entrust to the aesthetical morphologist the stylistic analysis of works of art—for example, by means of information-theory concepts—while he himself might undertake to elucidate the effects of various art styles on the experiencing of art (Cerbus & Nichols, 1962; Eysenck, 1941a; Knapp, 1964) or the relations between the personality type of an artist and his style (e.g., Lowenfeld, 1939; Roe, 1946).

The psychology of the arts includes the study of both the creator and the spectator of art. Indeed, some philosophers do not seem to distinguish between art creation and art observation (e.g., Collingwood, 1938; J. Dewey, 1958; Parker, 1939); and even some psychologists (e.g., H. B. Lee, 1947; Kris, 1952; Rogers, 1959) assume that "the creator, the performer, and the audience of a work of art . . . must, at least in some measure, be actuated by common motivational factors and reinforced by common sources of reward value" (Berlyne, 1960, p. 229). Yet, so far as we know there seems to be little correspondence between the process of art creation and that of art experience, even if the spectator is sometimes dubbed a collaborator in the work of art. Moreover, it would be unwarranted to conclude anything about the experience of the creator merely on the basis of knowledge about the experience of the spectator, or vice versa (e.g., Hampton, 1945; Semeonoff, 1940). The enormous diversity of meanings attributed as a rule to one and the same work of art by different individuals and in various historical periods also demonstrates that not even on the level of the general meaning of the product of art is a correspondence to be expected between the artist's possible intention and the spectator's interpretations.

This book concentrates on the spectator of the arts. There are several reasons for this. Spectators of art greatly outnumber creators of art. Moreover, only a few living artists are able and willing to produce works of art under controlled conditions. Yet the group of artists available for study cannot be enlarged by investigating autobiographies and diaries of artists from the past, since such documents are generally so dependent on the writers' uncontrolled introspection that they are of little scientific value. Further, spectators of art can be identified much more easily and by less equivocal criteria than artists in any period.

Again, psychological methods have yielded little information about the processes of creation. Although some headway has recently been made in the domain of general creativity, progress in knowledge about artistic creativity is hampered both by the scarcity of experimentally controlled information about spontaneous activities in general and by the difficulties involved in stimulation of artistic creativity or similar activities under laboratory conditions. Most of the available methods for the study of art production deal with something other than the creative process itself. Thus, for example, investigators who use the psychoanalytic method usually draw from the analysis of the work of art conclusions about processes that precede artistic creation and thus have more to say about the artist's motives than about the dynamics of the creative process.

On the other hand, it seems that much more information is available about processes of perception, elaboration of meaning, identification, and the like, which are intimately involved in the experience of the spectator of art. Moreover, today's methods of experimentation allow us to stimulate aesthetic reactions and experiences by means of art objects in the setting of the laboratory.

The spectator's experience may also prove to be more revealing about the nature of art and art objects than the artist's experiences and creative processes and may better repay investigation. Without plunging into epistemological and metaphysical speculations about the nature of art, there seems to be little doubt—though artists may deplore the fact—that what determines the value, estimation, fate, and survival of a work of art is in the last count the experience it arouses in its perceivers. Thus, if it is spectators who pass the main judgment about what is beautiful and aesthetically enjoyable, it is to spectators that we have to turn if we want a deeper insight into the beautiful in art and its impact.

Summary of Four Main Theories

The approach to art through the spectator's experience is by no means new or peculiar to psychology. It has figured in the aesthetic theories of the greatest philosophers of the past and has been emphasized, sometimes even to the exclusion of other approaches, particularly in the theories of "aesthetics from below" and of modern aestheticians (e.g., Carritt, 1923; Collingwood, 1938; Delacroix, 1927; J. Dewey, 1958; Marshall, 1894; Vivas, 1944).

In the framework of psychology itself, a number of theories have been used to describe and account for the percipient's experience of art. Two characteristics are common to these theories. First, none was developed primarily in order to explain art experience. Rather, they were expounded as general psychological theories—of personality and behavior—and were then applied in the domain of art experience, mainly in order to exemplify their generality and to confirm their validity and soundness as overall psychological theories. Secondly, each concentrates on the elucidation of some special aspect of aesthetic experience, mostly overlooked before. In thus highlighting some particular aspect of this experience, it usually neglects other aspects, which might be highlighted by other theories.

Let us discuss four major theories of the last fifty years or so which have served as central foci for psychological studies of the spectator's experience of art. These are psychoanalysis, the Gestalt theory, behaviorism or neobehaviorism, and information theory.

The basic tenet of *psychoanalysis* is that human behavior is a product of unconscious needs and drives and of superego restraints and norms, all elaborated, compromised, and channeled into overt behavior by the ego. The most characteristic contribution of psychoanalysis to art psychology has been in offering insights into the motivations of the artist and the processes of creation. Starting from the now so famous theory that in his work the artist expresses unconscious desires in a sublimated symbolic form, curbed and inhibited by the superego (Freud, 1930; 1948a, 1948b, 1948c), psychoanalysts have released a flood of studies focusing on the relations between the manifest and latent content of art works and the artists' unconscious motives, traumata, and conflicts.[1] The influence of psychoanalysis in this domain has been so overwhelming that one can hardly find a modern piece of art criticism that does not include an explicit or implicit reference to the ideas of psychoanalysis or its method of approach.

Our interest lies mainly in the contributions of psychoanalysis to the understanding of the spectator's experience. The characteristic question asked here by psychoanalysts is this: What are the sources of the pleasure experienced by art perceivers? The answer is based on the assumption that in every adult person there exist drives and wishes which, owing to fixation and repression, have remained partly infantile or primitive and whose satisfaction is barred either through social rules and standards or through the norms that are internalized in the personal superego. The perception of works of art affords vicarious fantasy gratification for these unsatisfied wishes in a sublimated, that is, socially accepted form. This gratification is made possible by essentially the same mechanisms that account for dreams and daydreams. The latent content of works of art—disguised by symbolizations, displacements, conversions into opposites, and other dreamlike distortions—activates the repressed wishes and thus lets them be gratified in fantasy. The perceiver can identify with this content and project his unconscious strivings onto it with impunity, shielded as he is from the superego by the socially accepted manifest content of the work of art.

The spectator's art experience is thus the sublimated gratification of a drive; hence its pleasurable character. The pleasure attendant upon such satisfaction cannot, indeed, compare with the pleasure in real-life satisfactions. It is in fact merely a mild and temporary narcotic (Freud, 1930). Yet it is undoubtedly superior to the alternatives, to no satisfaction at all, and to neurotic symptoms. Its main asset lies in affording some measure of relief, under conditions inoffensive to the superego and agreeable to the ego, which can sustain control and mastery of the situation. Moreover, the vicarious satisfaction through art reduces for a time the striving for gratification on the level of reality, so that catharsis figures as a "secondary gain" of the art experience.

If psychoanalysis has made a contribution to our domain of interest, it surely lies in the suggested explanation for the impact of specific kinds of latent content and in the method devised for decoding latent contents that underlie the apparently innocent manifest contents. The methodological defects of the psychoanalytic method of investigation in this as in other domains have been discussed all too often (e.g., D. N. Morgan, 1950; Munroe, 1956). Let us just mention that the laxity of the method allows for too many diverse interpretations of the same work of art and of its presumed effects, while the theory leaves us without precise guidelines for reasonable verification procedures. Even apart from this criticism, it is easy to see how incomplete psychoanalysis is as a theory of art experience. The theory is inadequate to explain the function of the cognitive content of art, which it reduces to a conglomerate of defense mechanisms such as rationalization and intellectualization, and completely fails to account for the effects of the formal aspects of the art input. Concerning the latter point, Freud justifiably remarked that psychoanalysis has little more to say about beauty than that it derives from sexual sensations (Freud, 1930, p. 144) and that the nature of the artist's attainment is psychoanalytically inaccessible (Freud, 1948c, chap. 6).

However, concentration on motives and ignoring of cognitive functions —these are assets and failings typical of psychoanalysis in all its applications and lie at the root of its major deficiency to account for and predict the form which behavior will assume. Thus, in the domain of art experience, psychoanalysis leaves us with some puzzling questions. Why should psychotic and neurotic people still be interested in the art experience? Why should people be attracted to art when they can get vicarious satisfactions in their dreams at night and through daydreams in the daytime? Moreover, in line with the psychoanalytic contentions, we should recently have witnessed a decrease in the attractiveness of art and in the enjoyment it affords, as sexual and social taboos grow less rigid. Has such a decrease taken place? The enormous increase in art consumption suggests the contrary.

Although the contribution of *Gestalt psychology* is not as well known, its impact has been no less fruitful than that of psychoanalysis. Gestalt psychology is not primarily a theory of aesthetics, yet it originated in the context of a controversy concerning the perception and recognition of melodies. The main thesis of the theory, formulated first by von Ehrenfels and further developed by Köhler (1929), Koffka (1935), and Wertheimer (1959), states that the whole is more than the sum of its parts or of the relations between its parts. It is a *gestalt* (as it were, a figure, a form, a pattern), a whole with qualities which can neither be reduced to constituent elements nor studied on their level. Gestalt psychologists have traditionally concentrated on demonstrating that there is a striving towards the perception of "good" gestalts (see Chapter 5 below) or at least the best possible in a given situation. They seek to elucidate the conditions under which isolated elements are perceived as gestalts and bad gestalts are transformed into good gestalts through certain mechanisms—"closure," "gestalt pressure." With regard to aesthetics, Gestalt-oriented researchers (Arnheim, 1954; Koffka, 1940; Pepper, 1949; Schaefer-Simmern, 1948; Welleck, 1958) have highlighted the role played by perceptual organizing factors in determining the experience of the spectator of art, what he sees or hears. Their main contribution has been in showing how the various elements of a work of art are transformed into a unified whole in the spectator's experience, how the perception of relatively bad gestalts arouses tension, and how the mutual relations among the various elements in a work of art can best be understood through their role and position in the whole.

Thus the main achievements of Gestalt psychologists in aesthetics lie in unraveling the effects of what may be called the formal aspects of works of art—lines, tones, shapes. Their interest in the content of art has remained closely attached to these formal elements. Their main contribution in this domain, known as "the theory of expression" or "physiognomic perception," consists in showing that perception of expression and emotional meanings is an integral part of the perceptual process, quite as direct and non-mediated as the perception of the line, the color, or the tone as such (Arnheim, 1949, 1958; Köhler, 1938; C. C. Pratt, 1931, 1961; Werner & Kaplan, 1963). But are emotional meanings objective tertiary qualities of the perceptual stimuli? Can Gestaltists show a real isomorphism between the dynamic structure of the external percept and the configuration of forces in the visual cortex? These questions are not always answered in their favor. Colors, lines, and tones may indeed be perceived as excited, joyful, gloomy, or gentle; and these synesthetic and physiognomic qualities are to be sure an integral part of meaning. Yet, such direct impressions constitute but one dimension or level in the overall meaning of the work of art, which probably modifies also the physiognomic impressions by providing for them the appropriate context (Gombrich, 1960). Aside from general statements about "whole" perception, there is nothing in Gestalt psychology which could help us to understand why themes such as the oedipal myth, with its innumerable variations, are so effective, or King Lear's problems, or the representations in paintings and dance; or indeed, why works of art have any content at all beyond the expressive tertiary qualities.

While psychoanalysis and Gestalt psychology have contributed basic theoretical concepts to the understanding of the art experience, work associated with *behaviorism* in this domain has been restricted until recently to experimental studies of narrow scope. Though we should not extend the term "behaviorism" to include all experimental work, we can certainly detect a characteristic inspiration of behaviorism in the bulk of studies devoted to clarifying spectators' preferences among works of art and their elements (e.g., Valentine, 1962), as well as in studies about physiological reactions to works of art (e.g., Dreher, 1948; D. S. Ellis & Brighouse, 1952; Grunewald, 1953). Although both of these directions of study originated before the advent of behaviorism, behavioristic emphasis on experimentation and its methodological sophistication has served to refine and extend such studies on an unprecedented scale. When coupled with an interest in individual differences—for example, along the lines indicated by Bullough (1908) and A. R. Chandler (1934)—studies of this type draw near to the psychometry-inspired tradition of aptitude testing in the domain of aesthetics. Yet the contribution of this work to the understanding of art experience is extremely limited unless one is willing to settle for the implied thesis that art experience is but a taste judgment reflected in a preference statement and that degree of preference for the whole work of art is the summation of preferences for its discrete elements, each considered in isolation.[2]

Within the behavioristic framework, a marked theoretical advance in aesthetics has been made by Berlyne (1960, 1967) in recent years. Berlyne assumes that the most characteristic feature of works of art is that they effect a rise in arousal and afford a subsequent reduction in arousal. The rise in arousal is due to the fact that a work of art contains "collative stimulus variables"—that is, qualities such as novelty, complexity, heterogeneity of elements, and surprisingness, that elicit in the perceiver a conflict among a variety of attention reactions, alternative associations, or possible interpretations. The subsequent exploration of the work of art may lead to patterning of the stimuli and hence to a resolution of the conflict, a reduction of uncertainty, an increase in the perception of redundancy and balance—all these being attended by a drop in arousal. For the first version of his theory, Berlyne (1960, chap. 9) assumes that the art experience consists in mild rises of arousal and is pleasurable because (i) the rise in arousal is soon followed by arousal reduction (the mechanism of "arousal jag") and (ii) the rise in arousal may counteract the low-arousal state of boredom. In the second version of his theory Berlyne (1967) suggests that moderate rises in arousal may be pleasurable in themselves owing to the activation of an assumed "reward system," regardless of whether they are followed by arousal reduction.

Berlyne's main contribution lies in clarifying the relation of the art experience to arousal and to curiosity or exploration evoked by collative stimulus variables. There is little doubt that "interestingness," which he has defined in terms of objective stimulus qualities, i.e., degree of complexity, and distinguished from "pleasantness," is a factor in the experience. However, "interestingness" points to a means for attracting and holding attention and this is only one determinant of arousal rather than the essence of the perceived formal qualities or content of a work of art. Moreover, since Berlyne does not assume aesthetic hedonism and since collative stimulus qualities are not specific to art, it is doubtful whether his theory can account for the particular nature of art and help to distinguish art from humor, play, or science.

Information theory was originally a set of mathematical concepts and rules for the description and study of information-transmitting systems (Shannon & Weaver, 1949). It was soon applied in at least a dozen different fields, including psychology. The main thesis underlying it hinges on the concept of uncertainty and information. Uncertainty, as represented by several equally probable alternatives, is assumed to be an unstable state and thus relatively unpleasant, even frustrating when the perceiver's expectations are disconfirmed by the ambiguity of the situation. Information, which is quantitatively defined in terms of eliminated alternatives or increased probabilities of some alternatives, reduces uncertainty and is therefore assumed to be tension-relieving or a source of pleasure. Information would indeed fulfill this role if it is at all expected and if it is neither too "redundant" nor too great in amount. If there is too high a redundancy, for example, overrepetition of the same element or pattern, the perceiver finds the art product monotonous and is bored. If there is too low a redundancy, the perceiver is overwhelmed and finds the product chaotic.

It is assumed that a work of art evokes in the perceiver certain expectations, both those he has acquired in the past and those he develops on the basis of repeated elements and patterns in the art stimulus. Uncertainty occurs when these expectancies are frustrated, or when new alternatives are established, and may be prolonged by a redundant repetition of the same elements. Confirmation of the expectations, sometimes in an unusual manner, produces pleasure.

In aesthetics, information theory proved to be a challenging tool for the analysis and identification of art styles in terms of redundancies and probabilistic relationships, as well as for the generation of computerized "synthetic" works of art (e.g., Cage, 1959; Hiller & Isaacson, 1959; Knowlton, 1965; Noll, 1967; Pinkerton, 1956; Ulam, 1966; Sowa, 1956; Youngblood, 1960). While these applications are more along the lines of aesthetic morphology, information theory has also been used for the explanation of the art experience, particularly the musical experience (Franke, 1967; Gunzenhäuser, 1962; Kraehenbuehl & Coons, 1959; Meyer, 1956; 1957; Moles, 1956, 1966).

The advantage of information theory lies in the possibility it offers of correlating aesthetic reactions and experience not only with certain stimuli in the work of art—which could have been done without it—but with the sequences and dynamic developments in the art work. Vague descriptions of structure and style can be replaced by operational concepts and by a new quantitative categorization of stimuli in terms of their informational content or redundancy or surprisal value (Cohen, 1962). Its broader theoretical implications, however, rest on the assumption that a work of art is a vehicle for the communication of meaning, as has been suggested in modern times by philosophers such as Cassirer (1953a), Langer (1948), and Morris (1939). Yet it is obvious that information theory provides too limited and unidimensional a measure for the study of meaning, in art as well as in other contexts (Cherry, 1961). At best, its measure of information may be adequate for the analysis of some aspects of the formal structure of works of art, but not for the meanings inherent in thematical contents and developed through their further cognitive elaborations. Like any other percepts, works of art have an informational aspect, but there is more to the evoked experience than the elicitation, frustration and confirmation of expectancies (Meyer, 1959).

In view of the complexity and multileveledness of art experience it should not seem puzzling that the same phenomenon is interpreted so differently by the theories mentioned and many others which could not be mentioned. Rather, it should be emphasized that there is also unity in this diversity. Common to the theories is (i) the explanation of art experience by means of processes and concepts of general psychological validity; (ii) an implicit or explicit reliance on a homeostatic model of behavior; and (iii) the assumption that tension and relief or changes in arousal are an integral part of an art experience.

It seems to us that any psychological attempt to understand the art experience must be based on these three common principles. Yet these principles provide only a sketchy outline for a comprehensive theory of art experience. Such a theory can be formed either by juxtaposing elements from the existing theories or by constructing a new theory which integrates also some of the better-founded hypotheses from the various theories. We have opted for the second possibility not only because it is futile and sterile to combine contradictory theories but mainly because the importance of the domain and the wealth of information about it call for an attempt to structure a new comprehensive theoretical framework.

The Model of Homeostasis

Our own attempt to outline a theory of art experience has its start at the point where most psychological theories of this experience converge with the opinion of the majority of aesthetic philosophers and with the layman's view of the essence of art's attractiveness and meaning. This focal point is pleasure. The close association of the art experience with pleasure is hardly surprising in view of the eagerness with which so many people expose themselves to art, even though art experiences cannot be viewed as indispensable for survival. Recall your own experiences with works of art; you may well find that, whatever else art may mean to you, the component of pleasure is always there. True, human beings derive pleasure from a vast array of objects, activities, and situations. Some may even object that the pleasure afforded by viewing a ballet performance cannot be compared with sexual or gastronomic pleasure, either because they value the pleasure of art more or less than the pleasures of sex and food. The answers are (i) that similar processes may produce dissimilar experiences and (ii) to say that art experiences are pleasurable is not to say that pleasure is the only or major feature of art experiences. A hedonistic aspect of a theory should not be confused with outright hedonism. T. S. Eliot's (1928) remark about poetry can be generalized to all the arts: "Poetry is superior amusement. . . . If we think of the nature of amusement, then poetry is not amusing; but if we think of anything else that poetry may seem to be, we are led into far greater difficulties."

Psychologically and physiologically the evocation of pleasure in nearly all its varied forms is concomitant with a rise in tension followed by a reduction in tension. And "tension and relief" is the kind of thing that can be well studied through the *homeostatic model of motivation*. The homeostatic model is based on the assumption that there are optimal conditions for the existence and survival of organisms, defined by a certain equilibrium between internal and external processes as well as among the various internal processes themselves. Organisms strive to preserve these conditions and to reinstate them whenever a deviation occurs. Any discernible stimulus, external or internal, impinging on the organism can cause a disruption of the homeostatic state in the whole system or in any of its subsystems, and can activate mechanisms for the restoration of equilibrium. The disruption of balance thus puts the organism in an active state of energy mobilization, of tension, which is characterized physiologically by arousal, i.e., activation in a whole set of physiological processes ranging from fast, low-amplitude electroencephalographic waves to heightened muscular tonus, increased heart rate, and so on. When organized in a certain direction or towards a definite goal, the evoked tensions take the form of a "need." The tensions can be relieved through an appropriate action which by gratifying the need serves to restore the balance. Yet restoration of balance does not preclude the possibility of development and evolution, for it implies not only return to a prior state of equilibrium but also the establishment of progressively new and more stable states of balance.

The theory of homeostasis can be traced far back into the history of psychology and biology. Since Plato (1937a, sec. 32) more than 2000 years ago recognized that "pain ensues on the dissolution and pleasure on the restoration of the harmony" in "animated beings," the principle reappears, for example, in Spinoza's (1675) *conatus se conservandi*, in Spencer's (1855) idea of equilibrium as an evolutionary goal, and in Fechner's (1873) principle of stability. Following Bernard's (1859) emphasis on the constancy of the *milieu intérieur*, modern physiologists (Cannon, 1932; C. M. Child, 1924; Selye, 1950) have described the physiological mechanisms involved in maintaining and restoring physiological homeostasis.

Soon the theory was applied to the psychological level of functioning. Thus, by means of the striving for equilibrium, Freud (1922) explained not only the crucial role of the pleasure principle but also the functioning of drives and in particular the origin of the sex drive as a tendency to restore the primary unity of organic matter, and of the death drive as a striving to return to the stability of inorganic matter. Others have identified states of balance and equilibrium-seeking tendencies in psychophysical and perceptual phenomena (Helson, 1964; Köhler, 1929), in thinking operations (Piaget, 1947), in social behavior and perception (Heider, 1958; Newcomb, 1953), in attitudes organization and decision making (Festinger, 1957), etc.

Without unnecessarily multiplying examples, we may state that homeostasis has become a major model in psychology, underlying such rival theories as Gestalt psychology and behaviorism, psychoanalysis and cybernetics. Through its various extensions the main components of the model have undergone theoretical and experimental elaborations. It has become evident that complex behavior sequences, ranging from perverted appetites, defense mechanisms, and psychopathological symptoms, through the seeking of novel stimuli and diversions in a state of boredom, to the hoarding of food and building of houses, may play the role of restoring internal equilibrium and even of anticipating or forestalling situations disruptive of homeostasis. Moreover, the homeostatic state itself was redefined as a dynamic state, characteristic of "open" systems in contrast to static equilibrium with a minimum of energy exchange which may obtain in "closed" systems. As we gain more information about the functions and needs of organisms, "the homeostatic state" has come gradually to denote not only satisfactory physiological conditions but also optimal circumstances as defined by acquired needs, learned habits, sets, expectations, cognitive contents, aspirations, etc. The range of possible balance-disturbing factors has also widened: not only thirst and hunger are disruptive of homeostasis but also such disparate phenomena as facing an unsolved problem, being prevented from concluding an interrupted task, the perception of an unbalanced figure, and awareness of having acted against the dictates of one's conscience.

Though the sensations of pleasure and displeasure are related to the

cycle of tension and relief, the relations are not simple. As a first approximation, sensations of pleasure are the subjective accompaniment of the restoration of balance, while sensations of displeasure are contingent upon the
tension which marks a disruption of balance. There is also a lot of evidence
supporting the generalization that, all other circumstances being equal, the
degree of displeasure varies with the degree of evoked tension. Thus, higher
degrees of tension are accompanied by the experience of more intense displeasure (Schneirla, 1965).

These generalizations about the relations of displeasure and pleasure to
tension and relief should be modified by two further considerations. The
first of these concerns the expectations with regard to the prospects of restoring balance. Regardless of the present state of tension, sensations of
pleasure are evoked when the prospects of satisfaction are regarded as high
and the envisaged reduction in tension seems certain. For example, when a
not too long delay in gratification is demanded or decided upon, tension indeed increases but discomfort does not become unbearable. For by viewing
satisfaction just ahead, one may experience pleasure which sometimes out-
weighs for the moment the amount of concomitant tension and may even be
comparable to the pleasure attending satisfaction (Schueler, 1964). Proximity
to the goal may thus stimulate an imaginary representation of the forth-
coming gratification and pleasure, and this anticipation in fantasy of a future pleasure, particularly if its occurrence is highly probable, may itself be
a source of pleasure.

Freud (1922) coined the term "forepleasure" for this phenomenon, and
explained it by referring to the deposition of libido on the path leading to
satisfaction. The reality of anticipation has been confirmed by studies which
show that certain electric wave patterns in the brain are a rather exact fore-
cast of expected events (John, 1967, pp. 405 ff.). The crucial role played by
expectation in behavior and learning has been recognized even by hard-line
behaviorists like Hull (1943), who elaborated the concept of "fractional
anticipatory goal responses." Some of his major critics and followers[3] have
explicitly posited that it is the anticipation of reinforcement and not its actual
occurrence that directly motivates learning.

Anticipated pleasure may be expected to play a particularly important
role in the very last stages before gratification, when tension is known to
increase,[4] and even in the course of gratification itself, which may necessi-
tate balance-disrupting activities attended by high levels of arousal (Sheffield, 1966; Sheffield & Roby, 1950; Sheffield, Wulff, & Backer, 1951). Yet,
in these situations the probability of gratification is so high that anticipated
pleasure may outweigh the unpleasantness of the high tension levels.

Anticipated pleasure is most prominent in situations when tension is in-

creased by a delay in satisfaction. Such a delay may be used for the enhancement of pleasure, which increases with the increase in tension, both
because the relief is greater and because of "hedonistic contrast" (Beebe-
Center, 1932). The enhancement of both pleasure and forepleasure by delay
in gratification or resolution is an old truth frequently applied by artists
and long recognized by art theoreticians.

The perceived meaning of the situation is the second consideration which
serves to modify the former generalizations that tension is accompanied by
displeasure and tension-reduction by pleasure. Various studies show (Nisbett
& Schachter, 1966; Schachter & Singer, 1962) that the degree of displeasure
accompanying tension increase depends on the interpretation attributed by
the person to the causes of the tension. For example, if a man awaiting his
beloved assumes that she is late because she does not care for him, the tension is much harder to bear than if he assumes that she is late because of a
traffic jam. Similarly, the awareness that tension-inducing painful stimuli
are to some degree under one's control reduces the experienced displeasure
(Champion, 1950; Pervin, 1963). The perceived meaning of a situation is
also involved in the processes which determine whether tension will at all
be aroused and persist. A sudden sharp noise evokes indeed the startle
reaction, but if the noise is identified as that of a car backfiring there will
be no further disturbance, while if the person recognizes that it was a shot
aimed at him, fear and the accompanying tension will develop (Arnold &
Gasson, 1954). Similarly, disruption of homeostasis will take place if an
occurrence is perceived as greatly deviating from one's immediate and general expectations, but not if it is judged as corresponding to one's present
as well as steady expectations (McClelland et al., 1953).[5]

Tension and Relief in Art Experience

Now that we have explored some of the relations of pleasure to tension
and relief, we may venture to suggest, though still in an incomplete form,
one basic principle concerning the pleasure of art experience:

*The art experience is motivated by tensions which exist prior to its onset,
but are triggered through the production of new tensions by the work of art.*

We all know from personal experience that works of art may evoke tension. That the sensation of tension is not a purely subjective impression is
demonstrated, for example, by studies which show that listening to tones
(Davis, Buchwald, & Frankmann, 1955), to melodies (Milerian, 1955), or
to a story (Smith, Malmo, & Shagass, 1954) is accompanied by physiological arousal. However, the principle we have stated immediately provokes

some challenging questions. A problem may have lingered at the back of your mind during our discussion of homeostasis: How can the homeostatic model account for the pursuit of tension-producing situations and activities? If the striving of organisms is towards balance, why do people voluntarily expose themselves to works of art, if these produce tensions? Yet this question is related to an even more puzzling phenomenon suggested by our principle. If an art experience is motivated by already existing tensions, why does a work of art generate new tensions instead of reducing the existing tensions to the optimal level and thus creating pleasure?

The first problem is basic not only to art but to a great many human activities. A person who submits himself to the tensions of a thriller or a movie drama does not differ in this respect from a person who exposes himself to balance-disrupting situations like playing games or gambling adventure. In recent years there has been much talk of the human craving for stimulation and excitement (Berlyne, 1960; Fiske & Maddi, 1961; Hebb, 1949). A host of studies show that people tend to regard as pleasant moderate rises in tension due to various sense stimuli (e.g., Engel, 1928; Haber, 1958; Paffmann, 1960), to novel, complex, or surprising stimuli (Berlyne, 1960; Maddi, 1961), to injections of stimulating drugs (e.g., Frankenhauser & Post, 1964; Hawkins, Pace, Pasternack, & Sandifer, 1961; Lasagna, von Felsinger, & Beecher, 1955), and even to slight pain sensations (Harrington & Linder, 1962; Phillips, 1963; Wohlgemut, 1919).

Within the framework of the homeostatic model several well-known hypotheses have been offered as explanation for this phenomenon. One group of answers is based on the assumptions that there is an optimal level of activation (Hebb, 1955; Fiske & Maddi, 1961) or stimulation (Leuba, 1955) characteristic of normal wakefulness and/or necessary for efficient functioning, and that organisms strive to maintain it.[6] This approach implies that not only very high but also very low levels of arousal are unpleasant, while shifts back to the normal level are attended by pleasure. This hypothesis would lead us to assume that people turn to art when their arousal level is too low, and that exposure to art is pleasurable because it contributes to a restoration of normal arousal level. Even when we disregard the common impression that people tend to indulge in art experiences as a relaxation after days full of excitement, the major difficulty of this hypothesis is that in the best case it could explain the pleasantness of slight tensions produced, for example, by some of the formal elements of art. Since arousal does not usually drop to very low levels, a short and cursory exposure to art would be enough to restore the normal arousal level. In order to understand the prolonged immersion in art and the voluntary exposure to strong tensions evoked by art we would have to assume in defiance of reality that most art spectators approach art in a drowsy, trancelike state of low arousal.[7]

According to a related view, though different in emphasis, organisms are in need of an optimal flow of information from the environment; information is conceived as novelty or reduction of uncertainty, and not as stimulation per se (Glanzer, 1958; A. Jones, 1966; McReynolds, 1956). According to this view people turn to art in order to expose themselves to increased information when information flow has dropped below a certain level. Although works of art undoubtedly are based also on the principle of relative unpredictability and thus may increase information, this view cannot explain in what way the information yielded by art differs from information from other sources which could do as well in restoring the information level. Further, we remain at a loss to understand why people continue to enjoy a work of art a long time after they have come to know it, when novelty can no longer be a factor.

Another set of suggested answers to our problem is that variations as such are necessary physiologically (Platt, 1961) or that slight departures from adaptation level are inherently pleasant (McClelland et al., 1953). Since by virtue of habituation, nonvarying prolonged stimulation ceases to have the effects of stimulation, the tendency to seek moderate variations in stimuli is compatible with the mentioned need to maintain optimal arousal levels. Again the answer fails to account for the attractiveness of exposure to intense and prolonged tensions in art, frequently produced by very strong stimuli, e.g., by a fortissimo of a 120-piece orchestra.

Finally, the third suggestion—that people may expose themselves to rises in arousal only in order to experience the pleasure of return to homeostasis—assumes the craving for pleasure to be a prime motive. A hedonism of this kind is not foreign to psychology, but it has not been a very fruitful hypothesis. Closer analysis usually reveals that a behavior apparently motivated by the desire for pleasure satisfies other needs or drives, and even the proponents of hedonism in psychology have tried to show that what is pleasant is mostly also useful for the maintenance of life (Young, 1955). It is, however, conceivable that pleasure, which is merely an accompaniment of homeostatic processes, a kind of subjective signal for the behaving organism, may become an end in itself, owing to habit formation or to fixation. Yet the tendency to give up stability merely in order to obtain pleasure would be viewed as a pathogenic development. Although the commonness of a behavior is not always identical with its normality, it would be hard to regard attendance at exciting soccer games or the reading of thrillers as deviant.

As mentioned, the problem of exposing oneself to tensions is related to the second problem of relieving tension through tension. Both problems are crucial for the understanding of the art experience, but the range of their importance far exceeds the specific issue of art. It is our contention that a *major motivation for art is tensions which exist in the spectator of art prior to his exposure to the work of art. The work of art mediates the relief of these preexisting tensions by generating new tensions which are specific.*

Our hypothesis that preexisting tensions are involved in the process assumes that tensions may long persist and can be transferred from one domain to another. Both these phenomena are too well known to need detailed discussion. Since all too often a person may be prevented from performing the action appropriate for the reduction of tension, evoked tensions are not reduced and may persist. Obstacles to the performance of the appropriate actions are, for example, superego norms, fear of punishment, and objective barriers. The phenomenon of displacing aggression from the original stimulus to one less dangerous or simply available, i.e., a scapegoat (e.g., Dollard et al., 1939; N. E. Miller & Bugelski, 1948; Levy, 1941), has become almost a paradigm for the flexibility of human beings in transferring tension from one domain to another. Conflicts and other barriers to action have been observed to motivate displacement activities also in animals. When fighting is obstructed in cranes, or copulation in ducks, the birds begin to preen (Tinbergen, 1952). When rats are deprived of food but are not yet weakened by hunger, they seem to engage more in sexual activities than they usually do (Stagner & Karwoski, 1952, p. 65). If conditions allow, tension is discharged through an activity similar to the obstructed one, as has been shown in studies concerning the tension which persists after the interruption of a task (Zeigarnik, 1927; A. A. Smith, 1953). People prefer to resume the original interrupted task, even when not required to do so (Ovsiankina, 1928). But if prevented, they take up other tasks (Lissner, 1933), preferably real and not imaginary ones (Mahler, 1933), as similar to the original as possible (Henle, 1942). When such tasks are not available, the tension sometimes combines with an activity which is available. For example, if the arousal of spectators of a film has been increased through drugs, this arousal seems to summate with the tensions evoked by the film, so that the pleasure they eventually feel is greater than that of spectators whose arousal had not been previously increased (Schachter & Wheeler, 1962).[8]

More often the unresolved tension persists in the form of a *diffuse tension*, whose cause or origin has been forgotten or never clearly identified. Most people are probably acquainted with these diffuse directionless tensions, which take the form of general "emotionality and restlessness" (Barker, Dembo, & Lewin, 1941), overall tenseness, and a readiness to overreact. These are the residuals of frustrated, unaccomplished, interrupted, or merely planned activities which never reached the stage of performance. Stimulation, distractions, and daily disappointments with oneself and others nourish this diffuse tension, which, like general arousal, lacks a specific cause or goal.

More complex is the second part of our hypothesis, which is based on the assumption that the generation of *specific* tensions is necessary in order to dissipate the *diffuse tensions*. Clearly, psycho-logic does not conform in this case to logic, which would lead us to believe that reduction of tension may best be achieved by cessation of all activity. The latter does not seem to be the case. The most common, attractive, and apparently most successful relaxations not only consist in very intense activities but also start with the creation of new and specific tensions. The solution of complex puzzles, playing golf, mountaineering, hunting, and surf riding—these are examples of excitations in which people indulge as so-called relaxing hobbies and activities.

In order to cope with this puzzling yet so common phenomenon,[9] we have to distinguish between arousal and directionality of tension. Both depend upon the stimulus or a constellation of stimuli. Thus, every stimulus has in fact a dual function: it acts as an elicitor of arousal and as a cue (Hebb, 1955). We have already discussed the role of the stimulus in evoking arousal. When homeostasis is disrupted, energy is mobilized for the performance of physiological, mental, and other activities that reinstate balance. The role of the stimulus as a cue—a theme on which we shall dwell later—consists in initiating processes, primarily cognitive, which determine the specific direction of behavior and through feedback serve as a source of further arousal. It is the cue function of the stimulus which enables animals and men to channelize the evoked tension into actions which are expected to reduce tension. When for some reason there are no stimuli with cue function, both humans and animals are hindered in performing the action which would lead to tension reduction.[10]

By means of these concepts we can now diagnose the case of diffuse tensions: There is arousal but there are no specific cues for directing the arousal towards an action adequate for tension-reduction. What is needed in this case is an additional source of stimulation which will be specific enough to serve as a cue for channelizing the tension in a specific direction. Yet this new stimulation, besides providing directionality, is also a source of further arousal. It is thus the source of that tension mentioned as necessary for the resolution of the diffuse tensions. Yet, since the diffuse tensions form the background (or "noise" in terms of information theory), the specific tension can function as the mediator of relief only if it is strong enough to be discernible upon this background. This means that the specific tension must be rather strong, as indeed it very often is as far as art experiences are concerned. But since the spectator is usually assured that this specific tension will be followed by an adequate relief, the displeasure of the tension is mitigated by the anticipated pleasure in the sense of forepleasure. This specific tension, however, may be regarded as the factor mediating overall relief, since it may be assumed to attract and absorb the diffuse tensions by the process of summation, as described earlier.

The argument concerning the reduction of tension by induction of tension can be summed up in two illustrating metaphors. Let us imagine that the diffuse tensions are like toy balloons floating around in a room. We want to clear the room of balloons; yet to catch them one by one and take each outside the room will be time-consuming. But if we can produce a stream of air in the direction of an open window, the air current will carry all the balloons out in a single blast. Or imagine that the diffuse tensions are like many children playing, each separately, in a playground under the window of your study, making a lot of noise. Of course, they can hardly comply with your requests for silence, and to persuade every child separately would demand more patience than you have. But if you can bring in some other kids marching in a row with drums and trumpets, there is a good chance that most of the playing children will join them and march away from your study window, leaving you in comfortable silence after the additional noise of the drums and trumpets dies away.

Metaphors like these, more elaborate and stated in less picturesque terms on a more abstract level, are useful in science and are called models. They serve to explore and explain processes not yet accessible to observation. As a matter of fact, when we speak of specific tensions with a directionality, strengthened by diffuse tensions and pointing towards a behavior which will resolve them summarily, we are alluding to a model, which is simplified as every model is. Terms like tension or arousal are, strictly speaking, mere generalizations used to label a vast array of different processes. Similarly the distinction made above between diffuse residual tensions and tensions endowed with directionality is an oversimplification. These two types of tension denote the poles of a continuum, along which should be placed tensions varying in the degree of their directionality. For example, apart from unconscious wishes which are highly specific but are manifested consciously as diffuse tensions, our inner arena accommodates also strivings pointing only in a general direction, such as a wish to act out anger regardless of object and means, or vaguely circumscribed tendencies, such as a desire to be comforted or to bolster one's optimism, or a longing for something to happen.

These few examples suggest that if tensions differing in specificity and intensity are to be absorbed by the tensions evoked by works of art and thus be summarily resolved, the tensions produced by art stimuli must be variegated and multidimensional. Moreover, the reliefs provided by art must correspondingly differ in nature and specificity. That this is indeed the case can be seen by comparing, for example, the tension elicited by the clash of two colors, possibly resolved through a third color, with the tension produced by the scene of the first meeting between Caesar and Cleopatra in Shaw's play, resolved through a rather diplomatic love affair. Thus, the tension and relief in a story of violence and murder which ends with the balanced distribution of punishments and rewards may be the proper framework for satisfying the specific tendency to act out anger, while following the course of resolution of a complex musical problem may satisfy the wish to buttress optimism. But over and beyond the satisfaction afforded to these partly specific tendencies, the mentioned tensions and resolutions may absorb and relieve other tensions in the observer, the more diffuse as well as highly specific ones.

By way of summary, tying up the various strings of the argument, we propose the following hypothesis:

> A major aspect of the art experience consists in the arousal and the relief of tension in the spectator by the work of art. The work of art is capable of producing tensions, which on the one hand are sufficiently variegated and multidimensional to enable the evoked tensions to absorb and combine with the more and less diffuse residual tensions in the spectator; on the other hand, these tensions are specific enough to be resolved through some other aspects of the art input. Thus, the resolution of the specific tensions implies relief also for the diffuse tensions with which they have combined. The resolution of these tensions is attended by pleasure.

Cognitive Orientation

Just as the homeostatic model spells out a basic motivational principle but is insufficient to account for all human behavior, so the tension-and-relief cycle represents a major aspect but is certainly not the whole of the art experience. A comparison, for instance, of a real boxing match with a dance portraying a boxing match suggests that processes of tension and relief may be equally or more potent in the real match than in the dance. You may remember that even in our earlier discussion, which was designed to deal exclusively with tension and relief, we were led to have recourse to processes which lie beyond this level of analysis—mainly to the meaning from which directionality derives. To our mind, the most prominent weakness of homeostasis is its failure to account for the specific nature and direction of behaviors on any level in any given situation. However, the specificity and directionality of action can be accounted for satisfactorily by the theory of cognitive orientation (H. & S. Kreitler, 1965; Kreitler & Kreitler, 1967, 1969, 1970a, 1970b, 1971b, 1971c, 1972a, 1972b). Many observations suggest that stimuli act not only as elicitors of arousal but also as cues for the evocation of particular actions (Hebb, 1955). The theory of cognitive orientation shows that a stimulus turns into a cue only after it is subjected to a series of processes designed to determine its meaning and the relations of this meaning to the meanings of other concomitant stimuli, external and internal. Every stimulus of sufficient magnitude to be noticed not only disrupts homeostasis but also evokes an orienting response,[11] which is the physiological manifestation of the primary question: What is it? The establishment of meaning constitutes the answer to that question.

In operational terms, meaning can be defined as a set of attributes along one or more dimensions (S. Kreitler, 1965; S. Kreitler & Kreitler, 1968, 1971). Such dimensions are, for example, various sensory qualities of the object or event, causes for its existence or occurrence, consequences which result from its existence or occurrence, its actions or potentialities for action, sensations and feeling it evokes in the perceiver, etc. If the dimensions are conceived as general questions about an object or event, then the attributes fulfill the role of specific answers, although neither is necessarily to be expressed verbally. While the meaning dimensions and some of their attributes may be interpersonally shared as, for example, when we describe "night" as a period without sunlight, other attributes may be much more personal and individual as, for example, when we describe "night" as the primary fruitful womb of life and light.

On the level of reflexes and conditioned responses, the elaboration of meaning is restricted to the determination of just a few attributes which are denotative percepts, such as "red" or "dangerous," along some of the dimensions. But on the level of more complex forms of behavior, meaning includes both percepts and concepts interrelated in the form of beliefs, and is usually much richer in the number of attributes as well as in the meaning dimensions to which they refer. The elicitation of more complex actions or sequences of behavior usually requires the integration of several meanings—for example, those which refer to stimuli in the situation with others which express more steady beliefs of the individual.

The whole set of meanings involved in the elicitation and directing of any action is designated by the term "cognitive orientation." In a simplified form, the theory of cognitive orientation assumes behavior to be directed by what a person knows and believes, by his judgments and evaluations, by his views about himself, others, and the world. These cognitive contents

may not always be verbalizable and may greatly vary in rationality, veridicality, and complexity. In contrast to the behavioristic and psychoanalytic
views, which accord to cognitive processes a secondary subservient role, the
theory of cognitive orientation considers cognition to be as primary as
arousal, with which it interweaves in a permanent sequence of feedbacks
in the determination of behavior on the simplest level above that of the
spinal reflexes, as well as on the more and most complex levels of behavior.

Numerous experiments testify to the crucial role played by cognitive
orientation in the determination of behavior and experience. For example, as
mentioned earlier, the nature and intensity of emotions experienced by a
subject whose arousal has been artificially raised depend on his cognitive
evaluation of the external situation and of his internal state (Schachter &
Singer, 1962). If a man takes a stimulant drug but is led to believe that it
is a sleeping pill, he may fall asleep. But if in taking a sleeping pill, he believes that he is taking a stimulant drug, he may end up being fully awake
and aroused (Storms & Nisbett, 1970). Sensations of hunger (S. Schachter,
1967), intensity of felt pain and of physiological reactions to painful stimuli
(Nisbett & Schachter, 1966; Sternbach & Tursky, 1965), the readiness to
make an effort (Kreitler & Kreitler, 1970b), reactions to stress or annoying
situations (Lazarus, 1966), and even the acquisition of conditioned reflexes
(Dykman, 1965) are influenced to a great extent by what the person believes
about himself, the others, and the world and by the meanings he attributes
to the given situation.

Although cognitive orientation interacts with arousal in codetermining
action and is thus involved in the cycle of tension and relief, the processes
of orientation seem themselves to be subjected to the tension-and-relief
principle. Initial lack of orientation, so characteristic of the first confrontation
with a novel or quasi-familiar or not yet sufficiently elaborated stimulus, is
undoubtedly tension-arousing. The perceiver asks "What is it?" and no clear
answer ensues. Thus the subsequent behavior—exploration and investigation in the external or internal spheres—can be viewed as means for procur-
ing enough information for the establishment of meaning and orientation.
Berlyne (1958a, 1958b) and others (Smock & Holt, 1962; Wohlwill, 1968)
have shown that the more complex and unusual the presented stimuli, the
more exploration they evoke in adults, children, and even infants. When
the stimuli or situation are highly unfamiliar, the lack of orientation may
even lead to fear reactions, distress, or withdrawal, all of which point to
the existence of great tension.[12] Disorientation in animals produced, for
example, by confronting them with difficult tasks or by punishing them for
responses previously rewarded may lead to "experimental neuroses" (Astrup, 1968; Gantt, 1953; Masserman, 1950). In human beings disorienta-

tion has been observed to evoke anxiety (Dibner, 1958) as well as various pathological symptoms (H. & S. Kreitler, 1965).

Further evidence that lack of orientation may be tension-provoking comes from observing people in states of great uncertainty, when they do not know how to act or what to expect, or when they impatiently await news or are otherwise eager and intent on finding out what is going on. In these cases the lack of orientation or of full orientation means insecurity, even possible danger, and is thus tension-arousing, while the attainment of orientation is balance-restoring, relieving, and even pleasurable to a certain degree. Yet, whether it will indeed be pleasurable depends also on the contents of orientation. It is doubtful whether to know the worst is better than not to know at all.

The tension-reducing qualities of orientation depend on contents, as is even more evident for the role of orientation in the stages of a behavior sequence. Orienting processes are involved not only in the initial determination of the stimuli's meaning but also in the selection of behavior(s) from among the available alternatives, in the planning, and in the whole series of feedbacks spanning the performance from beginning to termination (where "termination" is getting the information that the action came out "right"; Bastock, Morris & Moynihan, 1954). However, with regard to none of these stages can it be assumed that the attainment of orientation unequivocally implies reduction of tension and restoration of balance. For example, the initial determination of the meaning of stimuli may be a signal for the undertaking of an action or for withdrawal from action, implying tension reduction. Likewise, the orientative feedback in the course of performance may imply the need for increased or for decreased arousal and effort. Thus, completeness or sufficiency of orientation seems to be a less crucial factor than the contents of the orientation in determining the ensuing tension or relief.

Until now we have viewed orientation as itself subject to the principle of tension and relief and as playing a crucial role in all behavioral and experiential sequences. But there are also other aspects to orientation which testify to its relative independence from the tension-and-relief cycle. Like light, which sometimes behaves in accordance with the laws of waves and at other times in accordance with the laws of particles, orientation is sometimes subject to the stringent rules of homeostasis, but under different conditions it is free from them, functioning according to other laws. For example, stimuli tend to evoke in people many more meaning responses than are absolutely necessary for the guidance or elicitation of behavior. Studies of meaning (S. Kreitler, 1965; S. Kreitler & Kreitler, 1968, 1971; Osgood, Suci, & Tannenbaum, 1957; Werner & Kaplan, 1963) invariably show that meaning structures include many more elements than could ever be applied in any concrete situation.

The attainment of orientation may also be a goal in itself, independent of and transcending the immediate requirements of present behaviors and situations. Since the early demonstrations of latent learning and incidental learning there can be little doubt that solutions are perceived and retained even before a real problem has presented itself, i.e., cognitive orientation is expanded without any immediate requirement. In other words, it may be assumed that the striving for orientation is a basic and autonomous function.

One of the clearest manifestations of this striving is the way that humans and animals not only explore any novel situation with which they are confronted, but actively seek information and opportunities for extending orientation. For example, animals prefer pathways of greater stimulus complexity to familiar ones (Dember, Earl, & Paradise, 1957), and longer or varying routes to food to simpler routes even when they are hungry (Havelka, 1956; Hebb & Mahut, 1955). A copious body of research shows that contact with novel stimuli and opportunity to explore unfamiliar situations may serve for animals as rewards, i.e., as incentives for which they would perform various behaviors and learn new responses.[13] Finally, many studies[14] show that both humans and animals tend to expose themselves voluntarily to stimuli which are at least moderately novel to them and that they prefer stimuli in the intermediate range of complexity or uncertainty to stimuli low or very high in these qualities. Although stimuli of this kind evidently do not present a threat, they affect arousal. Thus, the studies show that the activation of cognitive processes is pursued and the extension of cognitive orientation is undertaken regardless of the tension-provoking impact of the stimuli to which one exposes oneself.

Cognitive Orientation in Art Experience

The discussion above suggests that cognitive orientation processes may be expected to play multiple roles within the framework of the art experience. First, as the processes which are responsible for meaning elaboration, they may be interwoven with the sequence of tension and relief evoked by the work of art. Since meaning elaboration is elicited by the stimuli just as arousal is, orientative functions serve to direct, steer, modify, and specify the tensions and reliefs produced by the work of art. Moreover, meaning processes play a crucial role also in the processes underlying the experiencing of the contents of art, in the course of feeling-into and identification, as well as in the integration of the various aspects and levels of experiencing into the comprehensive unitary art experience.

A second major role of cognitive orientation becomes evident when we consider the process of "understanding" in art and its function for the experience of art. The commonness of the question, What is it?, asked internally and very often also loudly with regard to a work of art, reveals that in spite of the equally common admonition, "One should experience and not seek understanding," spectators are concerned with the meanings of what they perceive. Since general and personal experience has taught them to expect so-called deeper or latent meanings in art, spectators are mostly unwilling to be satisfied with the superficial answer that a work of art depicts a certain object or event. Surface meanings are only a starting point for cognitive search. The frequent use in art of novel or surprising stimuli, with manifold meanings, presented in an unexpected form and in a uniquely structured context, serves to further enhance the tension evoked by the incomplete orientation. This tension elicits external exploration in the form of increased attention and more enhanced perception of the art stimuli, as well as internal exploration in the form of associations and other processes of meaning determination, designed to relieve the tension.

The process of meaning elaboration in the course of perceiving a work of art is affected also by the perceiver's freedom from the necessity to undertake any action in the context of art. As mentioned, stimuli frequently evoke a wider range of meanings than is necessary for the directing of action or for the steering and specification of tensions and relief. In the context of daily life these meaning elaborations are usually subjected to selection in line with the requirements of action and the situation, so that many of the elicited meaning responses are truncated or inhibited. In contrast, exposure to a work of art does not impose any restrictions on the development of these meanings, as they gradually unfold with regard to the relatively small units, such as a line, a color, a chord, or a dancer's movement, encompassing the larger and more comprehensive units and reaching the structure of the whole work of art and beyond. Rather, the development of these multidimensional and diversified meanings is facilitated not only by the absence of demands for action on the part of the perceiver but also by a positive set, the so-called aesthetic attitude.

Finally, the assumption may be offered that experiencing works of art may contribute towards the extension of the perceivers' cognitive orientation. This extension may take the form of perceiving solutions to problems which have once arisen and persisted unsolved or only partly solved, of grasping new problems never before clearly or at all perceived, or of acquiring answers to questions which may or may not ever arise. In our view of the cognitive contents of art, we differ from those who dismiss the contents as of no consequence as well as from those who regard the contents of art as statements of truth and fact, as paraphrases of theories of reality, and even as revelations of ultimate truth otherwise inaccessible. As we shall attempt to show when we deal with these and other views in the course of studying the cognitive contents of art, the possible contribution of art to orientation is of a special nature which renders it different from other contributions deriving from exposure to science, philosophy, or experiences in daily life. The unique nature of the orientative aspect of art depends on the treatment and presentation of contents special to art, on the particular manner of perceiving and experiencing this content in the framework of art, and on the specific truth value of the presented contents. Regardless of the almost infinite range of themes dealt with in art and the even less restricted range of manners of presentation, works of art confront the spectators with special views of reality, the "as if" realities which are mere possibilities, alternative conceptualizations, different in form, substance, fictitiousness, arbitrariness, and temporality from other levels of reality. Thus, when dealing with the contents of art we shall attempt to show the special nature of the insights afforded by art—personal, sometimes compelling, yet not necessarily fully verbalizable—and the implications of these insights for orientation on other reality levels of the self, the others, and the world.

Personal Involvement

A characteristic aspect of art experiences is personal involvement. Involvement implies enhancement of the experiencing of the evoked tensions and reliefs and of the personal relevance of the elaborated meanings. Yet, involvement is mediated by processes other than tensions and reliefs or orientative meanings. Among these the readiness to be involved, or the *set* plays an important role. If you are invited for dinner at six o'clock and are presented instead with two hours of preclassical music, you may find it difficult to worry about the fate of some voices which lag in their rate of correspondence to the others and about identifying the mood of this or that movement. The set of an audience is so important that when, for example, spectators of a film are led to concentrate on observing the technique of the film or on judging its contents in a detached intellectual manner, they fail to experience the tensions involved in the various atrocities presented (Lazarus & Alfert, 1964; Lazarus et al., 1965).

Set is a necessary but not a sufficient condition for involvement. The sufficient conditions depend primarily upon the evocation of *feeling-into* and *identification*, the psychophysiological processes whereby we come temporarily to resonate to external objects and events as if their dynamics, motives, and experiences occurred in us, but without losing the sense of well-delineated self-identity. These processes are evoked not only for the characters of a novel or a drama but also with regard to objects and other dynamic units in the work of art. Through feeling-into and identification the evoked multidimensional tensions, their relief, and the interwoven structures of meanings are channelized into the form of experienced emotions.

In spectators of a baseball game personal involvement may become so intense that the partisans of the teams rush excited to the diamond or fight it out in the bleachers. Spectators of art are rarely observed to act in this way. In some art forms an attempt is made to turn the spectators into more active participants, for example, in extemporaneous psychodramatic theater performances, in the context of sculptural "environments," or through "happenings," but excesses are rarely attained. Moreover, it may also be assumed that if personal involvement progressed beyond certain limits, the elicitation of actions would be hard to restrain, and the processes of tensions, relief, and orientation would be impeded. In aesthetics the limits imposed on the intensity and manifestations of personal involvement are often attributed to the phenomenon of *aesthetic distance* or "detachment." A more detailed analysis in later chapters will help to clarify whether that particular kind of distance is a product of forces inhibiting the degree of involvement or merely a specific form of detached yet intense involvement.

Let us just mention some further factors whose main role we consider to be in mediating the experiencing of the contents of art in a way which renders the contents meaningful to a great many people, yet to each in a unique personal and intimate manner. These are *sublimation, multileveledness, abstraction,* and *symbolization.*

Preview

Each of the mentioned factors as well as those that will be introduced later is meant to designate a region of interaction between certain qualities in works of art and certain processes in the human observer of art. Tension, for example, is a process in the observer, but we assume that it is elicited, enhanced, and steered in a specific manner by certain qualities in works of art. Thus, analysis of the art experience leads to a psychological understanding of the work of art—its characteristic stimuli, its structuring, and import.

However, none of the assumed psychological processes is specific to art. Every single one of them is frequently observed and studied in contexts other than art. Yet we assume that the art experience is endowed with uniqueness and specificity, which set it apart from other experiences. Accordingly, these derive from the *integration* of all the constituent processes as they unfold and interact within the framework of the experience. Thus, uniqueness and specificity are qualities of the whole rather than of the constituent parts.

The interaction among the constituent processes is so close, complex, and dynamic that each abstraction is liable to run the risks of distortion. Nevertheless, for the purposes of analysis we have to single out each of them and to opt for the inevitable presentation in sequence. This we shall do by applying each of our hypotheses separately to the various arts, within the framework of dealing with basic questions about art and art experience.

Certain classical questions have been formulated and analyzed in the course of many centuries of thinking about art and have turned into a kind of touchstone for testing theories in aesthetics (Gilbert & Kuhn, 1939). When we disregard the variety of formulations in which they have been couched and the theoretical systems in which they have been developed, the questions reduce to the following issues: (i) the nature and impact of the formal, nonrepresentational elements of the arts; (ii) the nature and impact of the content, the plot or the narrative-representational elements of the arts; and (iii) the nature and impact of the subject matter or cognitive contents of works of art. In other terms the questions are these: (i) How can colors, forms, tones, movements, or the other elements of the arts, even when considered in detachment from the specific plot of a work of art, often produce an art experience? (ii) How can the plot of a novel, a drama, or a dance, etc., remain exciting even if we already know from previous exposures to it how the dramatic conflict is resolved? And (iii) how can works of art which present remote problems of this or that fictitious personage, or even interwoven colored surfaces or tone sequences, be experienced by millions of different people as providing answers to personal problems and intimate insights of compelling import?

Obviously, each of these questions is a focal point of many more specific and basic questions concerning the stimuli and the experience of art. In this book, Part I discusses the impact of the so-called formal elements in each of the arts, i.e., painting, music, dance, sculpture and architecture, and literature (prose and poetry). In Part II we are led beyond tension and relief to the problems of experiencing the plot and the narrative-representational contents of the arts. We shall dwell on the role of set, feeling-into, and aesthetic distance in experiencing art. This will be followed by a discussion of sublimation, multileveledness, abstraction, symbolization, and the contribution of art to cognitive orientation. Finally, in the epilogue, we shall attempt an integration of the parts of the theory as they apply to the various aspects and levels of the aesthetic experience.

The outlined plan of the book seems to reflect the distinction between nonrepresentational and narrative-representational elements of art. This distinction is reminiscent of the age-long controversy of form versus form-content in aesthetic philosophy. While the so-called formalists—represented in modern times by Bell (1914), Fry (1920), Hanslick (1957), Gotschalk (1941) and Prall (1920) and others—claim that art is basically a composition of formal elements, devoid of connotations and references, the anti-formalists, like Abell (1936), Bradley (1909), Isenberg (1944), Parker (1924) or the "new critics," proclaim the inseparability of form and content and regard the object of art as an organic unity of form-meaning or meaning-in-form. Our theory about the art experience in general and in particular our conception about the dual function of the stimulus as elicitor of arousal and of meaning processes clearly bring us into the camp of the anti-formalists. Thus, we regard form and content as inseparable. Moreover, we find that their effects are often similar and always convergent and complementary on the various levels of experiencing. Yet a partly separate discussion is advisable both for purposes of analysis and in order to do justice to those aspects in which the impact of these two facets of a work of art differ.

And now, what is ART? In an attempt not to follow in the footsteps of those who have tried their hand at the task of defining art and failed, we choose as a starting point a denotational definition. "Art" would thus include works of art regarded in any or all cultures as belonging to any of the domains of art—painting, music, dance, literature, etc. The choice of such a denotational definition suggests an implicit hypothesis that all the products which have been commonly regarded as works of art in any culture at any time are characterized by a series of features which they, at least partly, share and which set them apart to a greater or lesser degree from products which have not been commonly regarded as works of art. This definition serves us only as a point of departure. At the end of our inquiry, when some of the major aspects and levels of the complex phenomenon of the artistic experience have been unraveled, we may be better prepared to approach the formidable task of identifying some of the features common to the paintings of Picasso, the dances of Isadora Duncan, the sculptures of Michelangelo, the music of Schönberg, and the poems of Eliot, which undoubtedly contain the stimuli for the arousal of that which we are about to study—the experience of art.

2. *The Perceptual Impact of Colors*

The Elements of Painting

Painting enjoys a certain advantage which recommends it as a starting point. Unlike music, dance, and literature, which consist of dynamic sequences unfolding along the dimension of time, paintings are static objects, organized visual fields, where "everything is simultaneous, everything spurts forward together, everything operates at once . . . without anything which starts or which ends" (Claudel, 1956).

If a spectator prolongs his observation of a painting beyond the first stage of general scanning, his experience will gradually change. It may deepen, expand, shift in accent, or be deflected into new channels. If we look long enough at even a simple homogeneous patch of color, the color will seem to change—for example, it will appear less saturated and we will notice irregularities in the brightness, saturation, and hue of various spots (J. Cohen, 1946). With prolonged inspection simple line drawings also change and reveal to us unsuspected aspects (Sakurabayashi, 1953). All the more is this true for a painting which includes many colors and highly complex forms. Studies of the manner in which pictures are observed (Brighouse, 1939a; Buswell, 1935) reveal that spectators shift their attention. They look at one detail, then at another, return to the first and so on. Thus, there is reason enough to assume that the experience is highly dynamic. Yet, since the painting itself does not change in time, at least not objectively, the modifications in the experience reflect primarily psychological processes taking place in the spectator in response to the painting. The experience seems thus easier to analyze than the experience evoked by arts which consist of dynamic inputs.

As you may remember, one of our major hypotheses is that works of art produce tensions for which they afford specific reliefs. Thus, our first question with regard to painting is this: How can a picture stimulate tensions in the spectator and afford an adequate relief for these tensions? A painting can do this only by means of the things which are in it, the elements of which it consists. If so, what is there in a picture, in any picture? The obvious answer to this is a story, a scene, a situation. This may be true, but a picture certainly does not consist of a story, although it may suggest one. Let us defer the discussion of the contents of a work of art until later, and so set aside the story.

Now, what remains? In a painting, only colors and forms or, more correctly, colors in a certain organization. Indeed, it is through differences in colors that forms are created at all in our visual field.[1] In daily life we are accustomed to regard forms as the primary constituents of the surrounding world and as the main carriers of meaning, but forms perceptually viewed are secondary phenomena; they are the contours which dis-homogeneities of colors inevitably give rise to. Kandinsky aptly said: "A picture is nothing more and nothing less than organized colors."

If forms are merely a result of the existence of colors (and in most pictures they are also inextricably bound with the representational function, which we are disregarding now) let us approach pictures first from the viewpoint of colors. The definition of colors does not concern us here. It would be misleading for our purposes to define them with the physicists, as light waves of specific length, amplitude, and complexity, as quanta of a certain character, or as electromagnetic radiation; or with the physiologists, as the external stimuli to which the cones together with the rods in the retina of the eye respond. Undoubtedly, the features of waves and the retinal processes help to bring about the perception of colors, but what the spectator sees are not waves and what he feels are not chemical operations of the cones. As our interest lies only in the experience of colors which the human spectator has, it is colors as percepts with which we shall deal, colors as they are phenomenologically seen, felt, and responded to.

In a picture, as in daily life, colors are bound up with forms, objects, meanings, situations, and memories, any or all of which may determine the pleasure or displeasure we feel when seeing colors. Now let us assume, hypothetically of course, that we could experience colors as abstracted from all of these factors. Would certain combinations of colors still have the power to create tension and relief in the spectator, the power to make him feel discomfort and pleasure? As the question is of vital importance in understanding the experience which pictures may evoke, let us attempt to keep in mind this trying, almost impossible abstraction of colors, this platonic concept of them, throughout this chapter and investigate whether the answer can still be positive under these circumstances.

Single colors may indeed be a source of tension or of relief, as we shall see in the following chapter. But since most paintings consist of several colors, while one-color pictures, like Yves Klein's all-blue canvases (*The Monochrome*), represent still the exception, our first concern will be with color combinations. Since we are in search of specific combinations of colors, which may affect spectators as more and less exciting, it would be advisable to represent to ourselves a model from which all of the possible interrelations of colors can be deduced. Such a model, based on a purely phenomenological consideration of colors, is provided by the color sphere (Plate 2).[2] The color solid has the form of a double pyramid, a double cone, or a sphere. Along the circumference of its central slice appear all the hues in medium brightness and maximal saturation, arranged in order, with the purples between red and violet. The vertical axis of the solid represents the continuum of brightness from light to dark, with the achromatic hueless white at the top, black at the bottom, and neutral gray at the midpoint. Saturation is represented as diminishing gradually towards the center of the ball, where the neutral gray lies.

Two types of interrelation among colors will be immediately apparent to any observer of the color solid. On the one hand, there are the graduated passages along any of the three dimensions—hue, saturation, and brightness. On the other hand, there are colors separated by greater or lesser distances. If the distance between two colors is maximal so that they lie on the opposite ends of a straight line crossing the midpoint of the color solid, they are called complementary colors, e.g., red and green. In the purely perceptual and experiential sense, which combinations of colors are felt to be more stimulating and less stimulating, tension-provoking or tension-relieving?

Experiments on the Tension and Relief of Color Combinations

A series of experiments performed by H. Kreitler (1956) in the years 1940–1942 and pursued in 1960 (Kreitler & Elblinger, 1961) was designed to find out which color combinations are experienced as tension-provoking and which as tension-relieving. In these experiments the materials were not paintings, but colored cards representing samples of colors from various segments and cross sections of the color solid.

You may wonder why the tension-and-relief aspect of color combinations was studied by using colors outside the context of art and not more directly within the framework of paintings. There are two main reasons for this procedure. Both derive from the obvious fact that a picture usually contains many colors in one limited visual field. The colors thus give rise to forms. Forms are spontaneously grasped, and the spectator can hardly be expected to liberate himself from the compelling impact of the figures and devote himself to pure color experience. This applies equally whether the colors are bound to representational or to non-representational forms. Even if we invert the picture so that the forms lose their object reference, there will still be forms. A second result of the simultaneous perception of many colors is that any color in the aggregate or organization may be endowed for the spectator with completely new properties which it does not have when observed singly, outside a picture. Colors interact to produce, for example, the well-known contrast effect (Osgood, 1953, pp. 233–35). A gray card on a black background looks darker than on a white one, just as red and yellow in juxtaposition are modified perceptually into a bluish red, and a greenish yellow (Burnham, Hanes, & Bartleson, 1963, p. 63; Newhall, 1940). Finally, colors in the framework of a painting may greatly vary in saturation, brightness, and the extent of the area on which they appear. All these factors may affect the experiencing of colors, e.g., the same color appears to be more saturated and brighter in a bigger than in a smaller area, although when extended over a very big area, the saturation of the color decreases (Burnham, 1952). But they cannot be controlled or neutralized within the framework of a painting.

For these reasons, a picture is a poor device to use in the study of the tension-and-relief effects of colors. So are some of the other methods commonly applied in the investigation of sensation. Expanse colors—as they are seen, for instance, when one looks at a uniform surface through a tube or a smoked glass—do not suffer, to be sure, from the interaction between colors and from object reference, but they appear unnatural, partly because they lack the surface character of a color in a picture but mainly because they are separated from the ordinary level of illumination of the surrounding objects (Osgood, 1953, pp. 540, 607). The impression created by such colors is different from the one we get when looking at a picture, whose level of illumination stands in constant relation to that of the environment in which it and we are placed. The same is true for the method in which light of one color is used, either by active illumination of a room with certain light waves or by making the spectator look at objects through uniformly colored glasses. In both cases, the circumstances differ radically from those under which we ordinarily look at a picture; the white light, a basic standard condition of everyday observation of pictures, is missing.

In view of these difficulties, the experimental procedure we adopted was to study colors as they appear under normal illumination, in conditions so constructed as to keep to a minimum the role played by the form in which the colors are embedded—that is, by using colored matte cards all identical in shape and material, presented on a background of neutral light gray. In the first experiment five different sets of colors were used. Each of these sets included eight colors, drawn randomly from a certain section of the color solid.

The *first set* consisted of colors drawn from the circumference of the central circle of the color solid, i.e., from the region representing colors in maximum saturation at a medium level of brightness. The *second set* consisted of colors drawn from the circumference of a circle inside the central circle of the color solid, the region representing saturation of a middle value between the circumference and the central neutral gray. Thus in each of these two sets of colors, brightness and saturation were constant, while the hues changed. The difference between these two sets consisted only in saturation: the colors of the first set were more saturated than the colors of the second set. A *third set* of colors was drawn from along the central perpendicular axis of the color solid which runs from white down to black. The colors in this set manifested variations in brightness. In order to check also the effects of different values of saturations in the same set, a *fourth set* of colors was chosen from the level of the central horizontal circle of the color solid at mid-brightness. However, the sampling was done not from the circumference of the circle (as in the first set) but along two axes running inside the circle, combining opposite colors through the central neutral gray. Finally, in order to check the effects of different values of brightness in colors of the same set, a *fifth set* of colors was drawn from the circumferences of two separate circles in the color solid: four colors were chosen from the circumference of a circle at approximately the midpoint between the central circle and the whiteness pole, and four colors were chosen from a circle at the midpoint between the central circle and the blackness pole. Thus, the colors in this set varied in brightness as well as in hue.[3]

The task of the sixty people who served as subjects in this experiment, and who were adults of both sexes, from various social, cultural, and educational backgrounds, was to select from each set of colors, presented separately, one or more combinations of two colors which were most tension-laden or maximally stimulating. When this task was finished, the subjects were presented again with the five sets but were asked to select combinations of two colors which were least tension-laden or least stimulating. The subjects were asked to disregard as far as possible personal associations to the colors.

Of the 285 color combinations forwarded by our subjects as tension-laden in the first four sets, 83 percent consisted of colors maximally distant, i.e., mostly complementary or almost complementary colors, or if strict complementaries were not available, then colors as nearly opposing as possible; the minority, 12 percent, of the tension-laden combinations consisted of two hues very similar to each other, such as two shades of pink or a yellowish green and a bluish green. Essentially the same results were got for each of the four sets, regardless of the brightness and saturation of the colors in the set. Only 5 percent of the tension-laden combinations did not conform to the above two principles. These represented combinations explained by the subjects as including at least one color which for personal reasons, e.g., memories of past traumatic experiences, evoked tension in them. In the fifth set of colors the results were less clear-cut: 23 percent of the 62 tension-laden combinations consisted of colors opposite each other in the circle but equal in brightness, such as a bright blue and an equally bright yellowish hue. A further 15 percent consisted of complementaries, i.e., a bright green and a darkish red. The rest (59 percent), apart from 3 percent which represented combinations experienced as tense because of personal associations, consisted of juxtapositions of any bright and any dark color, with the emphasis on maximal differences in brightness.

No less sharply delineated were the results concerning the least tension-laden combinations. Of the 332 combinations forwarded from all five sets, the majority, 92 percent, consisted of two colors which were similar but not too similar to each other, at positions in between the complementaries and the very similar colors. In the third and fourth sets, which included grays, approximately 36 percent of the combinations of similar hues consisted of two similar but not oversimilar shades of gray. The rest (about 8 percent) consisted of combinations experienced as least tense because of personal reasons.

Further experiments were carried out in order to clarify various points left unanswered by the findings. In the second experiment, thirty subjects were presented each with ten color combinations which were tension-laden according to at least 80 percent of the subjects in the first experiment. These combinations, which varied in saturation, included seven juxtapositions of complementary or almost complementary colors, and three juxtapositions of very similar hues. The task of the subjects was to rate these combinations according to the degree of tension evoked by them. The major finding of this experiment is that combinations of more saturated colors are experienced as more tension-laden than combinations of less saturated colors.

A third experiment was conducted in order to clarify whether least tension-laden color combinations may act as relieving for tension-laden combinations. For this purpose eleven tense color combinations were used: the ten combinations viewed as tense by at least 80 percent of subjects in the first experiment (and which were used in the second experiment) and one which represented a sharp contrast in brightness (drawn from the findings of the fifth set in the first experiment). In addition five sets, each consisting of five colors, were prepared. These sets were selected according to the same principles that governed the choice of the sets in the first experiment, i.e., from the circumference of the central circle, from the circumference of an inner circle on the central circle of the color solid, from the perpendicular axis of the color solid, etc. Each tense color combination was coupled with each set of five colors, yielding 55 pairings. Each of thirty-five subjects was presented with ten randomly chosen pairings. The subjects were asked to add to each tense color combination one or more colors from the presented set so that the tense color combination plus the added colors would be experienced as balanced, harmonious, and non-tense. On the average, each subject added three or four colors to the tense color combination.

An examination of these added relieving colors revealed that a very clear principle underlay their choice. In 80 percent of the cases, these were colors which combined the complementaries or embedded the similar-hues combinations within a suggested scale of homogeneous transition in terms of hues, saturation, or brightness. Thus, for example, the tension of the equally saturated yellow-blue combination was relieved by the addition of similarly saturated green-blue and yellow-green or of less saturated yellow and blue, while the tension of the juxtaposition of two hues of red was relieved, for example, by adding other reds or shades of red available in the set of colors. In the case of the color combination which represented the contrast in brightness, the relieving added colors consisted mostly of colors intermediate in brightness. A closer examination of the relieving colors revealed first that in about 60 percent of the cases in which the grays were included in the presented set, subjects chose a scale which included gray and sometimes even restricted themselves to the choice of one gray hue only; and secondly, that less saturated colors figured more often than highly saturated colors in the colors selected as relieving.

The selection of colors—colors which were merely suggestive of the scales and not complete scales—may have depended in part on the availability of colors in the presented sets. However, about 20 percent of the subjects also mentioned that their choice of particular colors was determined by a relieving color atmosphere which seemed to them to characterize some colors more than others. Yet such personal principles did not contradict the principle stated above. Rather, they may have determined the choice of one scale over another when several transition scales were available.

By way of summary, these experiments show (i) that combinations consisting of strict or almost complementary colors or of colors contrasting in brightness, as well as combinations of colors similar in hue, are experienced as tension-laden; and (ii) that scales of colors representing relatively homogeneous transitions in hue or saturation or brightness as well as the grays are experienced as least tension-laden and as most relieving. More saturated colors are in general more tension-laden than less saturated colors. Thus factors which increase the perceived saturation of colors, such as moderate brightness, up to a certain degree the extent of the color area (Burnham, 1952), or the spatial contiguity of complementary hues (Burnham et al., 1963, p. 63; Tennant, 1929–30), may be expected to increase the experienced tension of the color combination.

Tension-Laden Color Combinations

Now, how can these results be understood? Let us concentrate first on the most tension-laden combination of complementary colors.[4] Although complementaries seem to be quite unrelated optically, from an organic viewpoint there must be something which connects them. For one of the most essential facts about complementaries, also used as a basis for their definition, is the known phenomenon that they serve as negative afterimages for each other. This means that if a person looks steadily at one of a pair of complementaries long enough and then looks away, particularly to a bright surface, he sees a color complementary to the original one, in hue as well as in brightness. He sees a patch of green instead red, yellow instead of blue, and even black instead of white. Again, the fact that the most frequent types of color-blindness (protanopia and deuteranopia) are manifested precisely in the inability or difficulty of discriminating between reds and greens also testifies to an intimate physiological relation between complementaries—in particular between the red and the green, for insensitivity to yellow-blue is very rare.

Changes in the sensitivity of color perception brought about by nonvisual stimulation also demonstrate the peculiar relations between complementaries. For example, auditory stimulation of moderate intensity (Kravkov, 1937a, 1937b, 1939a; Semenovskaia, 1946), stimuli of temperature, taste, and odors (Dobriakova, 1941; Kravkov, 1939b, 1942), toxins which stimulate the sympathetic nervous system (Kravkov, 1941), and contact of the eyes with weak anodal electric currents (Kravkov & Galochkina, 1947) have been found to increase sensitivity to blue-green colors and simultaneously to decrease sensitivity to the orange-red colors. Tilting the head backwards (Kravkov, 1947), the injection of toxins which stimulate the parasympathetic nervous system (Kravkov, 1941), and contact of the eyes with cathodal electric currents (Kravkov & Galochkina, 1947) have been found to decrease color sensitivity to green light and to increase sensitivity to the red colors.

Of course, the relation between complementaries is taken into account by all theories of color vision. There are a few dominant theories of color vision and many variations and developments of each, but none is fully satisfactory in accounting for all the facts of color perception. Most of the theories present a variant of either the Young-Helmholtz theory or of Hering's theory. The *Young-Helmholtz theory* (Osgood, 1953, pp. 169–73) postulates three types of cones—red, green, and blue—in the eye which react to all wavelengths of the visible spectrum, each type with a maximal response to wavelengths which correspond to the specific chemical in the type. The particular color seen depends on which cones are acted on by the light and how much they respond to it. A complementary afterimage arises when, after stimulation, the red cones, for example, are fatigued, so that white light affects maximally the green and blue cones that produce a greenish sensation.

According to a variant of this theory, suggested by Göthlin (1943), the retina represents a system of balances between excitatory and inhibitory effects. Thus, light which excites maximally the green receptors, simultaneously inhibits the red and blue receptors. When the green light is removed, the red and blue cones are released from inhibition and thus produce the red-purplish complementary afterimage.

Hering's (1920) *theory* forms the core of a second major group of color-vision theories (Adams, 1923; Graham, 1959; J. von Kris, 1905; Müller, 1930; Schrödinger, 1920). A recent quantified version of this theory by Hurvich and Jameson (1957) is considered as accounting successfully for more recorded facts of color vision than any other theory. According to this group of theories there are six basic unitary colors: red, green, yellow, blue, black, and white. One set of cones is responsible for the vision of red and green, another for the vision of yellow and blue, and a third for the vision of black and white. The processes in the cones stimulating the perception of red, for example, are antagonistic to the processes stimulating the perception of green, so that a particular color may look either reddish or greenish but never both at the same time, i.e., red cancels green and vice versa.

Our sketchy outline of the color-vision theories shows that in most of them complementaries are regarded in one way or another as contrasts, due to processes antagonistic to each other, mutually inhibiting or at least not simultaneous. The effects on color vision of nonvisual stimulation and drugs, mentioned before, also demonstrate that complementaries react as contrasts on the physiological level.

On the level of psychology there are many observations which show that people regard the colors of complementary pairs as maximally dissimilar or as contrasts. This has been demonstrated in particular with regard to the pairs of red-green and blue-yellow which figure in most experiments, since they are considered primaries and are easily labeled. Thus, Wicker (1966) found that when people are requested to judge the similarity of pairs of colors, red and green, blue and yellow turn out to be the poles of two distinct dimensions. As we shall see in the next chapter the complementaries appear as contrasts also on most measures of meaning and emotional reactions (e.g., Aaronson, 1967; Osgood, 1962).

Thus, on several levels complementaries seem to be related to each other as opposite poles, as the limiting points of the free-swinging movement of a pendulum in the color cone or solid. Their juxtaposition is therefore likely to create the experience of tension. The alternative conclusion would be based upon the assumption that complementaries, as opposed poles, act as relief the one for the other. However, this would be illogical for several reasons. First, it would lead us to conclude that red relieves the tension of green and conversely, that green relieves the tension of red. We would be forced then to accept each of the complementaries in both the function of tension-producer and that of relief-provider. Secondly, if the two complementaries relieve each other's tension, their juxtaposition would unavoidably represent a climax of relief. Why, then, were our subjects in the experiment so perverse as to find the juxtaposition most stimulating and tension-laden?

Moreover, and this is the most important point, the assumption of a mutual relief between opposite poles stands in flat contradiction to the basic striving of any organism for equilibrium. Indeed, it is commonly held that when one is depressed, one longs for gaiety, or that the experience of coldness calls forth the wish for heat, and generally that extremes attract each other. But here, everyday modes of speech and commonplace opinion are misleading. It is not the contrast which relieves tension, but the intermediate stability. Like coldness and heat, complementary colors are extremes which may perhaps sometimes arouse longing one for the other, although not in the function of relief, but in the sense of a possible striving for a still greater tension. This is understandable, as the greater the tension, the more intensely experienced is the pleasure of relief.[5]

It is by means of the homeostatic principle that we are also able to account for the experience of the minority of our subjects who felt the juxtaposition of two similar hues to be extremely stimulating. Indeed, any woman who pays attention to the colors of her dress will readily admit the truth of this claim. We get no direct clue for the explanation of this phenomenon from the color solid. However, it is a well-known psychological fact that the striving of the organism for equilibrium manifests itself in the perceptual field in the general tendency to organize, simplify, harmonize, and regularize visual phenomena as far as the controlling circumstances allow. Since we shall deal with this process at greater length in Chapter 4, it suffices to mention here that this is the driving force behind the tendency to see somewhat open figures as closed, or to disregard small irregularities in symmetry or completeness of perceived forms, and other such tendencies. Evidently, the sight of two very similar hues, almost but not quite identical, raises in the perceiver precisely this kind of tension and even creates a pressure to bridge or annihilate the narrow gap between them. Up to a certain limit, the less difference there is between the hues, the greater the tension that is felt.

It is only when the difference between the hues is neither small enough to be disregarded (so as to enable us to identify the two colors as the same) nor big enough for the hues to be simply accepted as disparate, autonomous entities, that there arises this tension-laden wish to "simplify" and "regularize" the situation by bringing the two hues as near to each other as possible. Still, the wish remains unsatisfied, and the colors do not intermingle, but are set by the perceiver in a field of tension so that they represent, as it were, a promise of relief and pleasure inhibited at the very last moment on the threshold of its fulfillment.

Finally, the results of the second experiment described above show that the saturation of the colors is a factor enhancing the tension of a tension-laden color combination, regardless of whether the clashing colors are complementaries or highly similar hues. If we accept the likely assumption that psychologically saturation may be equated with intensity of the color stimuli, this finding becomes highly meaningful. It has repeatedly been shown in the various sense modalities that the more intense the stimuli the greater the tension they evoke. High-pitched tones (R. C. Davis, Buchwald, & Frankmann, 1955), intense light (B. A. Campbell & Sheffield, 1953; Sokolov, 1963), and other strong stimuli (Schneirla, 1965) disrupt the homeostatic state and evoke arousal to a greater degree than weaker stimuli. Like intense stimuli, saturated colors have been shown to command more attention than less saturated colors or white light (Berlyne, 1960, p. 60; Razran, 1939). Moreover, it may be concluded that factors increasing the apparent saturation of colors increase the tension which these colors evoke. Thus, tension will be greater when two colored areas are separated by sharp rather than poorly defined contours, when they are of approximately equal brightness, when saturated complementaries are adjoining rather than separated, and when the brightness and area of the colors are intermediate (Burnham et al., 1963, pp. 63–64), etc.

Relieving Color Combinations

We have seen then that combinations of either complementary colors or of two very similar colors are experienced by spectators as very exciting—that is, as arousing tension which stands in need of an adequate relief or gratification. What is this "adequate relief"? It shows up in the further results of the cited experiments. As you may remember, our subjects claimed that a resolution of the tension between two clashing colors can be attained by the simple device of presenting a more or less complete and homogeneous scale of hues which joins the two poles. Our findings also show that the grays and the less saturated colors are regarded as relieving tension between clashing colors. If we think of our color solid again, it can be readily seen that in both cases it is the bridging of the two clashing colors which serves to relieve—either a direct bridging by the scale of the combining hues, or a less direct one through the grays in the center of the color solid.

Let us now take the problematic gray. What can be said for gray as a relieving color? In the color solid it lies at the very center; it forms the midpoint of the dimensions of brightness and of saturation in general, and in regard to each color specifically; it is the point at which the middle circle, if suspended on a needle, would hold itself in perfect balance; it is the locus at which an imaginary pendulum, swinging freely in the solid, would come to final rest. Could all this be accidental? Obviously, the arrangement itself proclaims the neutrality of gray, for as we have seen before, equilibrium never lies at an extreme, it is neither in heat nor in coldness, neither in depression nor in mania, but always in the middle. But there are also some further physiological and psychological observations which support this special position of the grays. One important fact concerning gray and specific to it only, among all the colors, is that its so-called negative afterimage is also gray (Woodworth, 1938, p. 557). This means that the stimulation by gray does not prompt a swinging movement to any other extreme, but leaves the pendulum undisturbed, as it were. The counterreaction of the visual apparatus to gray is identical with the reaction. The perception of gray, corresponds, then, analogically to a bodily posture of perfect balance, so that it is as inadequate to speak about relief of tension in the case of gray, as it is to talk of the need of balance in the case of a man who stands firmly on solid ground. Further, gray or a somewhat purplish gray is also the color seen by a person when he closes his eyes and allows free play to his relaxed visual apparatus.

From physiology we learn that the cones of the retina are less involved in the vision of gray than in the vision of any other hue or brightness. This fact may lead us to assume that the perception of gray proceeds with less expenditure of physiological energy, or with a more limited disruption of retinal equilibrium, than the perception of any other color. This also speaks for the comparatively relieving character of gray.

From physics, we get further support for this conclusion, but in connection with a different aspect of gray. Whenever the waves of any two complementary colors are mixed in proper proportions, the color seen is gray. Furthermore, the mixing of two or more gray-producing mixtures also produces gray. However, a mixture of any two colors which differ less in wavelength than the complementaries produces the intermediate hues, and the mixture of those that differ more than the complementaries results in the purples (Burnham et al., 1963, pp. 115–22). In order to avoid misunderstanding, it should be stressed that the mixture here mentioned consists in the superposition of various colored lights and has nothing to do with the mixing of pigments, with which the artist deals. Such a retinal mixture means the addition of lights of dissimilar wavelengths, extracted from the spectrum by means of color filters and thrown simultaneously on a white screen or directly upon one and the same part of the retina. What the artist does, with different results, is to bring about by the conjunction of two pigments, a double subtraction of the range of wavelengths in the spectrum, for each pigment singly absorbs all the waves except those which correspond to its specific color. The result is mostly an intermediate color—for instance, green when yellow and blue pigments are mixed.

The significant fact for us is that the appearance of gray, as a result of mixing light waves, serves as an unmistakable sign that the mixed waves correspond to complementary colors. Here again, the simultaneous presence of the two extremes creates, through a yet unknown process, their integration in the form of the relieving gray. Yet gray may under certain circumstances be experienced as rather heavily tension-laden—for example, when for certain individuals it comes to evoke the terror of death or loss of individuality. Such relations will be dealt with in Chapter 3.

Some may be wondering why gray and not black, which in physics denotes the absence of light waves, is the point of least tension. This is another case of noncorrespondence between physics on the one hand and physiology and psychology on the other. Not only the turning on of light but also the abrupt turning off of light, i.e., the appearance of darkness and the observation of darkened objects, produces an increase in the frequency of EEG waves from the brain (Sokolov, 1963, pp. 108, 112–13, 141–43), and an increase in the frequency of electrical impulses in the retina ("off-effect", R. Granit, 1947). To these findings may be added the fact that black has a distinct negative afterimage, which is white; that is, the perception of black stands physiologically in need of counterbalancing. From a psychological viewpoint, black, unlike gray, is far from being experienced as dull, monotonous or neutral. When asked to match expressions of mood with colors, subjects tend to defy the implicit assumption of experimenters that black is not a color. They choose precisely black, a so-called achromatic color, to stand for the so important unpleasant experiences and dejected states of mind (Kouwer, 1949, pp. 87–94). People in the qualms of depression or strong pains also "see black" or are in a "black mood," as the saying goes, and do not even dream of comparing the intensity of their suffering with the dull gray which commonly stands for monotony or simply boredom.

Many observations tend to support the distinction, emphasized by Gestalt psychologists (D. Katz, 1935; Koffka, 1936), between the dimension of blackness vs. whiteness and the dimension of darkness vs. brightness. Indeed, as Kouwer (1949, p. 87) remarks, "Black as a color becomes evident only in relation to light, in connection with and against the background of other colors. . . . The most intense black is not perceived in darkness but against a bright white background." However, brightness and whiteness are evidently in a reciprocal relation, for the same amount of radiation may produce a color of greater whiteness and smaller brightness or of smaller whiteness and greater brightness (Koffka, 1936). It is clear, then, that in spite of physics, the proposition that black as a color represents the point of greatest equilibrium or least tension must be rejected.

So much for gray. But what about the resolving power of a homogeneous bridge of hues between the clashing extremes? Here, the equilibration tendency in the perceptual field that we mentioned before should be invoked. If two people quarrel, one of the best ways of making peace between them is by enabling them to approach each other, for instance, by showing them that their mutual antagonism is more apparent than real and that the gulf between them can be bridged. The same method proves valid in reference to colors, although here there is no danger of bloodshed. A scale of intermediate graduated hues resolves the clash of complementaries, by bringing them nearer to each other over a bridge, and relieves the tension of two similar colors by setting them back into the complete continuum of hues from which they have been arbitrarily, even brutally singled out. A homogeneous scale of hues best accords with the generally intense wish on the part of perceivers to bring the visual field into a state of maximum regularity, simplicity, harmony, and coherent organization.

Hints for the assumption about the relieving power of intermediaries are already to be found in Goethe. In his *Theory of Colors* he mentions, in regard to complementaries, that "a single color stimulates in the eye, through a specific sensation, a striving for totality" (Goethe, 1917a, §805). He probably considers this drive to be primary, for in another place he writes: "Thus the need for totality, which inheres in this organ [the eye] leads us beyond the limitation" (§539) and also that "when the totality of colors is presented to the eye from the outside it experiences it as pleasurable . . ." (§812). But in Goethe, there are also more specific statements about the nature of the totality that gives pleasure—for instance: "There is a certain gap between the yellow and the blue which lies in nature itself, but though they can be connected through the green, the true intermediation of yellow and blue can occur only through the red" (§794).

Color Combinations in Paintings

Observation of the color solid reveals interesting possibilities for intermediary scales of colors. Any two colors on the solid can be bridged in any of several ways. Green and red, for instance, can be combined by the scale of the yellows and orange or by that of the blues and purples, as well as through any of the longer bridges along the dimensions of saturation or of brightness. Thus, red and green can also be bridged "horizontally" by a scale consisting of gradually less saturated greens, passing through the gray on to the gradually more saturated reds, or by an "oblique" scale consisting of gradually duller greens, black and gradually brighter reds, or again by an "inverse" scale passing through the white at the upper apex of the solid. Theoretically at least, any combination of intermediaries along any or all of the dimensions of hue, saturation, and brightness can be used. So far there is little support for Munsell's (1926, pp. 81–82) contention that while a bridging scale of intermediaries along the dimension of brightness is "tame," and a scale of intermediaries along the dimension of hue is less tame but monotonous in brightness and saturation, the bridging path which "connects opposite hues by a sequence of chroma balanced on middle gray . . . is more stimulating to the eye."

However, in practice—that is to say, in paintings—the possibility of using any of the available bridging paths is complicated by other circumstances. In most paintings there are many colors, some of which can be regarded as singled out from a scale that bridges any two colors in the picture which are experienced as clashing. But this is not necessarily so. Since the so-called intermediary hues may also be perceived as autonomous to the same degree as any of the other clashing or nonclashing colors in the picture, there must be some additional specific conditions which enhance the role of some colors as relieving intermediaries and facilitate our perception of them as such. Or else there must be some particular emphasis laid on the clashing colors by means of contents, location, form, etc., so that they are grasped as contrasting poles that stand in need of a bridge. Thus, the role of certain colors as possible tension-producers or tension-relievers depends to a certain degree on the entire constellation of the painting. In a picture which consists, for example, of a patch of saturated red below and a big circle of green in the center, a series of blues and purples, even if it is located in one of the upper corners and not between the complementaries, is more likely to be experienced as a tension-reducing bridge than as a focus of intense tension. On the other hand, if the contrasts are not emphasized, as for instance, in a picture with two delicate small centers of blue and yellow, a patch of gray in the middle, far from serving as a bridge, might even be experienced as extremely tension-producing.

There are, however, some further considerations affecting the choice of one of several possible bridges in a picture where the contrasts are sufficiently strong. In the first place, there is the problem of the accord of the intermediaries with the other colors in the picture. A bridge of blues between red and green will not perform its function as resolution if there is a lot of yellow in the picture with which the blues will create a further source of tension, competing for supremacy with the red-green focus of tension. Secondly, the length and complexity of the bridging scale have to be considered. While a simple scale, easily grasped, offers immediate relief, a longer, more complex series of intermediaries serves to intensify the tension by postponing the resolution and thus produces a more pleasurable balance. Of course, a similar effect can be attained by using a simpler scale of intermediaries out of which only a few signal points are actually presented, the rest being left for the spectator to figure out for himself.

We may now apply our conclusions concerning the tension and relief effects of color combinations to the observation of paintings. There are all sorts of combinations in a picture. Even a casual observer casting a superficial glance at the painting will note some. Though he may not choose to observe the picture carefully, certain juxtapositions will immediately exert their effects upon him, raise tension, or seem entirely devoid of stimulation. If the spectator continues to observe the painting, he may discover still other combinations. It might be assumed that the ultimate aftereffect of the picture, which stays with the spectator for a little while after he has moved away, will depend to a certain degree on the kinds of predominant color combinations in it. Probably, if the picture contains several color contrasts, closely bordering on one another, but is devoid of any grays or homogeneous intermediary hues, the spectator will carry along the memory of a slightly exciting experience, mildly tense, perhaps even disagreeable. Yet, tension-relieving combinations need not necessarily border directly on the clashing colors. They may be placed anywhere in the picture, their position being determined by the structure of the painting as a whole. Since a picture is a static, organized, and limited visual field, in most cases grasped as a totality, no strict placement of tension-arousing and tension-reducing combinations is required.

From a logical point of view tension and relief should be successive experiences, tension being followed by relief. But if the whole of the picture is grasped instantaneously, there seems to be no place for such a succession. However, studies in perception reveal that even in the course of a single-shot fixation of some percept, the eyes continuously move, and that "scanning"—motion of the eyeballs over the visual field—is indispensable if there is to be any sensation of vision at all (Ditchburn & Fender, 1955; Pritchard, Heron, & Hebb, 1960; Riggs, Ratliff, Cornsweet, & Cornsweet, 1953; Riggs, Armington, & Ratliff, 1954). Although these motions are too rapid and delicate to be detected by the observer, they become integrated in more marked movements characteristic of perception. There are usually several stages in the observation of a painting (Brighouse, 1939a; Buswell, 1935). The first stage is invariably an overall survey of the whole painting, which consists of a series of relatively short fixations of the main parts of the picture. If the spectator is interested enough he will continue to observe the painting, but his manner of observation changes. The second stage usually involves a concentration on particular parts of the painting and consists of relatively prolonged fixations on smaller areas and a more detailed examination of fine details. A third stage of observation may follow, but in contrast to the two preceding stages it seems to be more characteristic of observers with particular education in the arts and of paintings endowed with marked richness and complexity. This third stage consists essentially in a series of observations on relations between previously observed features, and attempts at understanding the particular constellations of colors, forms, and theme in an effort to integrate the various impressions. Thus, since the usual observer seems to survey a painting several times in different sequences and from changing points of view, the chances are high that he will relate perceptually the relieving combinations of colors to the tension-laden ones in a proper psychological ordering, even if he happens to inspect the former before the latter.

The same studies (Brighouse, 1939a; Buswell, 1935) also reveal that even the sequence of the primary sweep of observations of a painting is far from random. Indeed the findings do not support the common assumption that paintings are so constructed as to lead the attention in a "dynamic tension path" from left bottom inward and up in a spiral (Cheney, 1948, pp. 136–61). But the studies definitely demonstrate that observers follow perceptually the main structure of a painting, whatever it happens to be, concentrating usually first on the central and bigger and particularly dominant parts before they turn to the observation of peripheral and smaller and less dominant areas. Thus, it seems likely that the spectator's attention will be drawn first to the dominant clashing colors before he notices the first transitions and relieving intermediaries. (See, for example, Nolde's picture, Plate 6: the clashing of the yellow hues in the center and the quasi-complementaries orange and blue will probably be noticed before the lighter and darker shades of blue and violet and the green area under the central figure's head).

An interesting way to test the usefulness of our theory is to apply it to one of the most controversial problems in the domain of painting, that of the changes that have taken place in the use of colors in Western painting during the last few centuries. In paintings of the classical period it is invariably easy to locate both the locus or loci of tension created by clashing colors and the combinations designed to produce relief. However, on the one hand attempts are made to attenuate the tension, and on the other hand the afforded relief is very elaborate. The attenuation of tension is achieved, for example, by avoiding highly saturated colors, as is evident in the paintings of the medieval period and even in Da Vinci's and El Greco's pale almost transparent shades, by removing the clashing colors from each other spatially (see, for example, in Giorgione's painting, Plate 7, the spacing between the blue and yellow on the left and between the red and green on the right), or by sometimes avoiding clear-cut complementaries and by using graduated transitions instead of sharp contrasts. In classical paintings ample relief is afforded for the evoked tension usually by presenting more or less elaborate scales of hues designed to mediate between the opposing complementaries or embed the clashing similar colors in the context of fuller transitions. The intermediaries can often be found at the very locus of tension, thus attenuating the suggested clash. For example, in Giorgione's painting the clash between the red and the green on the right is amply relieved by the chain of brown and yellowish hues, all tinged by the outside sunlight and the expansive browns of the background. The paintings of Rembrandt often show striking use of intermediary colors to balance tension in the classical fashion.

Tension in his pictures is often elicited by the contrast between bright and illuminated colors and the darkened black, a contrast which appears all the sharper in his paintings that have been recently cleansed. However, the tension is relieved by an elaborate scale of rich browns, yellows, darkened golden and red shades which extend back from the illuminated areas to the dark background.

In the course of time these crystallized conventions concerning the means of evoking tension and affording relief through colors no longer produced the desired effects in an audience that had become immune to the recurring stimuli. The contrasts designed to elicit tension became too familiar, and although familiarity may not always breed contempt, it certainly blunts the sharpness of what previously seemed a clash. Thus, habituation attenuates the poignancy of tension and greatly reduces the consequent pleasure of relief. New, surprising, complex, interesting, or intense stimuli evoke tension, as we have seen in Chapter 1. But after being exposed to viewers many times or few, they lose their capacity to evoke tension. Active exploration and tension are then replaced by habituation, which is reflected experientially in boredom with these stimuli, and behaviorally in absence of exploration and attention. After a period of familiarization, whose length depends on the intensity and complexity of the stimuli as well as on the sophistication and background of the observers, stimuli which previously seemed to occasion too much tension have to be introduced in order to evoke interest and thus allow the elicitation of at least a moderate degree of tension.[6]

The gradual satiation of the public with the conventional means of arousing tension is usually reflected in the growing dissatisfaction of artists with the existing techniques. They are forced to devise new sources of tension in paintings in order to continue to achieve a real emotional impact on the audience and compel it to take part in the experience. But how can tension be intensified in paintings on the level of perceptual color effects? In the light of the preceding discussion, there seem to be essentially only two ways to enhance the tension elicited. One is to sharpen the clash in tension-provoking color combinations. But this procedure is limited in its scope, since the strongest available means for creating tension through colors is presented by the juxtaposition of highly saturated complementaries, and to a lesser degree by the juxtaposition of highly similar hues. The only other possibility for increasing the degree of tension is to cut down the stimuli which serve to relieve the tension. This would mean to reduce the scales of intermediaries, which anyhow were already familiar to the public, or as

Van Gogh trenchantly expressed it, "to exaggerate the essential and leave vague the obvious."

Thus, after Rembrandt we find a growing tendency on the part of painters to shorten the scale of intermediaries and to rely increasingly on implication rather than on explicit presentation. By the time of the Impressionists the renunciation of mediating hues had progressed so far that it drew forth a vehement protest from Cézanne. In a letter he wrote in 1904 (quoted by Read, 1955, p. 19) he blamed modern painters for not possessing enough self-control and mastery over their means when they proceed to relate two contrasts such as black and white. Instead of dwelling on "the half tones and quarter tones" of brightness, they impatiently skip too many intervening grades. Yet although he says that despair drives him to find "a solace and a support" in the old masters, his own paintings (e.g., Plate 10) already reveal a certain degree of reduced intermediary relieving colors. In spite of protests by Cézanne and others, the development, urged forward by tendencies conforming to psychological laws, could not be hindered. In Dérain, Lautrec, and Gauguin the style is already very pronounced: contrasting saturated colors are used, the one bordering on the other along sharply outlined contours, with few if any transitions between them. As Gauguin expressed it (quoted by Read, 1955, p. 165), they discovered that harmony is not confined to a restricted range of the color scale, but can be keyed up to a vibrant pitch of primary oppositions, reveling in the richness of saturation rather than in the finesse of transitions. In Miro, Dufy, Nolde (Plate 6), Kandinsky (Plate 11), and Mondrian the renunciation of intermediaries is often complete. In contemporary painters, such as the Chromatic Abstractionists (e.g., Barnett Newman or Mark Rothko), the Post-Painterly Abstractionists (e.g., Ellensworth Kelly and Helen Frankfurter) as well as the Pop artists, and in Hip productions, all these features have reached the stage of a convention. ·

The outcome of such a use of colors is the disappearance of plasticity from paintings. Since the effect of three dimensions—depth, space, and distance—is attained in painting mainly by gradual color scaling and fine transitions, which reflect the differential illumination of surfaces in various dimensions, to renounce intermediaries and to juxtapose contrasts is to produce flat surface-painting (e.g., Matisse, Plate 15). The technique also results in a growing distanciation from reality, for tridimensionality and presentation in perspective are the main tools of naturalistic painting and guarantees for it.

The Impressionists struggled with the problem, for they were still trying to make the best of both worlds: to produce sharp contrasts and yet to preserve somehow the illusion of deep space and traditional Renaissance perspective. The Pointillists tried by the dot-and-dash system of color application to accomplish both aims, giving up indeed more on the side of perspective than of tension, and even replacing the conventional definition of depth by the vague phrase "atmospheric perspective" (Hunter, 1956, pp. 76–77). But the compromise could not be maintained for long. As far back as 1890 the cry was heard: "Down with perspective! The wall must be kept as a surface, and must not be pierced by the representation of distant horizons. . . . There is only decoration!" (ibid., p. 91). Gradually, however, artists have learned to paint "on the surface" and still avoid pure decorativeness, which is devoid of meaning.

The theory presented above can be criticized as one-sided. It can be pointed out that the painters who brought about this revolution were largely unconscious of its strict conformity to psychological laws. This does not in the least disprove our theory. On the contrary, it can be argued that compelled as they were by a drive of whose basic lawfulness they were unaware, they could not but proceed with an unavoidable development, while devising a host of theories to explain the process to themselves and to the public. The theories they proposed can perhaps be regarded as rationalizations, in the Freudian sense of the term, or more simply, as desperate attempts to secure orientation amid phenomena that did not explain themselves. The wealth and diversity of the theories are also telling in this respect.

We cannot disregard the grain of truth inherent in many of the explanations offered by painters and critics for the phenomena, but these truths lie on another level than the psychological one and sometimes relate to the process not strictly as causes but rather as consequences. When, for instance, Kandinsky writes that by the new means "pure and eternal artistry" is created, when Malevich desires the saturated colors so that they may serve as screens for the projection of the deepest emotions, when Seurat renounces intermediaries with the aim of producing strong complementary afterimages of the colors so that they may blend with the neighboring colors, or when Van Gogh writes that he attempts to use only pure red and green in order "to express the terrible passions of humanity" (Hunter, 1956, pp. 53–101), these utterances are not completely mistaken. The new developments, once they had occurred, could be used to express motives or achieve aims other than the enhancement of tension.

We should, of course, be aware that there were additional forces at work here. The new style of painting reflects many other law-conditioned tendencies in form and content, as well as a multitude of processes that pervade the atmosphere of the twentieth century. Admitting the correctness of the objection against the one-sidedness of our theory only proves that there is a price to pay for any reduction to elements—indeed, for any abstraction.

The consideration of colors by themselves is an abstraction. Yet we have pushed the abstraction some steps further by ignoring the object references and connotations of colors. We have carried our study on this level far enough to realize its limitations as well as its advantages. The purpose of the abstraction was to find out whether under these stringent conditions colors could be shown to produce tension and relief in the spectator of paintings. Having answered the question in the positive, we are now under pressure to restrict the illusion of abstraction, which was necessary for the duration of this chapter, and to proceed in search of further effects of colors in a painting and their potentialities for creating tension and relief.

3. The Meaning of Color

The Meaningfulness of Color

In the context of all the meaningful qualities of things in the world around us, color seems to enjoy an honorable position. Poets have always spoken effusively about the "character," "soul," and deep-reaching symbolism of colors. In this they seem to make explicit an impression which many non-poets share. Colors appear to most people to be endowed with richer, more significant, more compelling meaning—although not always accessible to easy verbalization—than other meaningful qualities such as odors, tastes, shapes. In part, this impression may be due to the fact that language includes a great many metaphoric references to colors. Thus, a person may have a colorful personality or background, or look at the world through rose colored glasses; or failing that, he may have dark thoughts and suffer from the blues, and so on. However, since such conventionalized color words can be found in most cultures, the impact of colors must be sought in sources underlying the codification in language.

Two major observations permeate explicitly or implicitly the voluminous literature on this theme. The first is the general impression that the impact of color is particularly noticeable in childhood and in so-called primitive cultures, as well as in adults who undergo a loosening of conscious control due to autism, regression, or psychosis or to a poisonous delirium or a drug-induced intoxication. Thus it is frequently mentioned that young children when requested to classify or match objects attend primarily to color (G. G. Thompson, 1952, pp. 211–12; Werner, 1957, pp. 234–38), while consideration of form develops gradually with age. Even babies are reported to fixate colors more persistently than forms or achromatic patches (Staples, 1932; Valentine, 1914). And Huxley's (1959, pp. 24–25) ecstatic references to color experiences under the influence of mescaline ("Mescaline raises all colors to a higher power and makes the percipient aware of innumerable fine shades . . . colors are more important, better worth attending to than masses, position and dimensions") may stand for many reports about the perceptual and experimental enhancement of colors following ingestion of various psychedelic drugs.

The second major observation concerning colors refers to the intimate relation between colors and emotions. Such relations, for example, as that between red and anger or other ardent passions, or between yellow and jealousy, are not only expressed in metaphors and compendia of popular opinion (e.g., Luckiesh, 1918a, p. 138; Stevenson, 1934, p. 1650) but also underlie many philosophical views of man (e.g., Bachelard, 1943) and are prominent in the modern psychodiagnostic use of color for the detection of emotional and other mental disorders.[1] Rorschach, for example, who has accorded a great role to color in his inkblot test, started from the observations that "the gloomy person is one to whom everything looks 'black' . . . one cannot imagine a gay party without color . . . colors draw people into extratension . . . it was not without reason that the army clung to colored uniforms for so long a time" (Rorschach, 1951, p. 99). Thus, the reactions to colors in the inkblots are regarded as revealing the dynamics of emotional life and attitudes to oneself, others, and the world at large. It is, for example, assumed that a withdrawn individual will tend to disregard color, while the impulsive person will respond to color in a diffuse uncontrolled manner. Other personality tests are based on the further assumption that specific responses to particular colors reveal determinate personality types as well as conscious and unconscious tendencies. For example, a strong attraction to or revulsion from the blue colors is characteristic of introverted and emotionally highly controlled individuals, while a fascination with red suggests aggressive impulses (E. Stern, 1955).

Without entering into a discussion of these views, which admittedly are controversial, it is clear that the two approaches converge at one focal assertion: colors exert a strong experiential impact on human beings. Since at least in popular psychology, primitive or primitivized states of mind and emotionality are interrelated, indeed sometimes even identified, color seems to be regarded as a factor appealing to the deeper nonrational layers of personality.

Even on the level of cognitive functioning, some indications can be interpreted as due to the strong experiential impact of colors. Although colors are salient in the environment and serve in various cultures as signs for major classifications—e.g., types of people, directions of the compass, magical and ethical concepts, chemical elements—they appear to be among the last features of objects to be abstracted and become independent of concrete situations. Many experiments show that there is a steady increase up to the third decade of life, in the ability to perceive and to use color correctly, to match colors and name them, and to discriminate properly the saturation, hue, and brightness of colors. In other spheres of perception the discriminatory potentialities are developed far earlier (Thompson, 1952, pp. 213–15).

Also on the intercultural level "it is not unusual to find a confusion in the color sensations of primitive people, if the colors are not apprehended as the specific properties of some known objects" (Werner, 1957, p. 99). Even when we allow for the fact that the spectrum may be subdivided in different ways, it is evident that in some other cultures, languages do not include separate names for certain colors which appear distinct to us; for instance, there may be only one name for blue, green, and even black, or for white, yellow, and gray. Moreover, names for other colors are often identical to the names of objects to which they happen to be attached (Kouwer, 1949, pp. 11–32). A famous example of this is furnished by the language of the Brazilian Bakairi Indians, which includes only one word for the denotation of emerald green, cinnabar red, and ultramarine, the word being the name of a parrot which bears all these colors (Werner, 1957, pp. 225–26). Some investigators tried to prove that ancient peoples—the Greeks (Gladstone, 1858), the Hebrews, the Hindus, the ancient Chinese (L. Geiger, 1871; Magnus, 1877)—had color vocabularies that were deficient in comparison with modern vocabularies. Although the controversy whether these vocabulary gaps are related to actual deficiencies in vision has not been resolved (Segall, Campbell, & Herskovits, 1966, pp. 37–48), observations in this domain suggest that colors may be such a salient, vivid, and impressive quality of things that they tend to be grasped as an inseparable part of concrete events and consequently impede abstraction. This may be a reason both for the frequent use of colors as signals for whole objects or situations (*pars pro toto*) and for the meaning-charged atmosphere which hovers so frequently about colors. Even after colors have undergone abstraction from concrete objects, something of the original situations in which they were embedded may linger about them.

In the light of what has been said above, we may expect colors to evoke emotional and associational responses. The term associational responses refers to recollection of objects, of situations, or of scenes in which a color was involved, while the term emotional reactions refers to sensations, actual feelings, or expressive movements. Responses of both types form a part of the meaning of color and may be manifested on a variety of levels and in a wide range of reactions. Meaning, however, is a multidimensional concept and includes more than these examples suggest (S. Kreitler & Kreitler, 1968). Judgments of preference, evaluation of colors, abstractive analyses of color as a physical phenomenon, metaphoric and symbolic appraisal are just a few of the types of reactions subsumed under meaning. Each of these types could embrace a great variety of responses, more and less abstract or concrete, more and less personal or interpersonally shared or conventionalized, more and less contributive to an experience.

Although certain observers of colors in paintings may become engrossed in a physical analysis of pigments and the reflection of light by colored surfaces, most observers seem to respond personally. Our concern will therefore be with special aspects of the meaning of colors, those which we assume to be more commonly involved in the experience evoked by colors, and which contribute to the shaping, specification, and enhancement of the overall experiential impact of paintings. Such responses run the gamut of responses, from the personal to the almost universally shared. The purely personal and the strictly universal responses are only extremes, far outweighed by meaning elements shaped to varying degrees by personal, cultural, and possibly even physiological factors. In the following sections we shall analyze some of the major types of meaning which are evoked by colors in a painting, abstracting as far as possible from the forms with which the colors are bound up in the framework of a painting.

Personal Associations to Colors

Associations are obvious and common reactions to colors. They may involve images and memories of people, objects, situations, occurrences, even wishes and daydreams, in which the perceived color has been involved. It is not unusual to encounter a subject in an experiment on colors or an observer of a painting who expresses pleasure at seeing red because it reminds him, for example, of a former beloved (who preferred this color in clothes) or displeasure at perceiving yellow because that was the dominant color in a distasteful office in which he once worked. Some of these associations may be affectively neutral and evoke only a slight surprise on recognizing the color of a familiar object. More often the memories are emotion-toned, and at least part of the affect accompanying the memory may be expected to be evoked at the sight of the color.

Upon seeing a color a person may react affectively—i.e., feel attraction, repulsion, or merely a vague resonance of an emotion—without being aware of the origins of his experience. Such emotional reactions can doubtless often be traced back to events in the spectator's past life with which the color is associated. The only element of such an event which rises to his consciousness may be the emotion, while definite circumstances and the role of the color in that past context have been forgotten and are inaccessible to him.

The evoked emotion may even lend the color a more definite meaning, but it usually does not lead the person to the discovery of the origins of the experience. These, however, may be revealed in the course of psychotherapy.

Psychotherapeutic reports contain many examples of the origination of a specific attitude towards a color in a forgotten or repressed association of the color with a certain experience. In the records of psychotherapies performed by one of the authors of this book there is the case of a patient, a woman then thirty years old, suffering from accident-proneness and headaches, who had a complex emotional attitude toward a particular shade of violet. Although she preferred it in her own clothes, she always felt restless or excited when she wore it and strongly disliked seeing it on other people or in objects. She could not account for her intense attraction and rejection with regard to the color nor for her preoccupation with it, nor for the fact that she never wore it for the psychotherapeutic sessions. Her only associations to the color were on one occasion "freedom" and on another occasion the remark that violet was intimately related to "jealousy." It was only after a year of analysis, when for the first time she came wearing violet, that the mystery was solved. Upon entering, she made a significant slip of speech, saying: "Look, I am all violent today," substituting "violent" for "violet." It suddenly dawned on her that her younger sister was wearing a violet dress when, twenty years before, at the age of five she had been run over and killed by a car. By that time the patient was well aware of having been jealous of her sister, whom she thought the parents preferred, and of feeling guilty for the death, because of her former death wishes towards the girl. Yet it was only when the violet was inserted into the picture that the patient was freed from her symptoms. It then became clear that her feelings of guilt and jealousy toward the sister led to identification with her by wearing violet, and that her own accidents occurred only when she wore this color. She must have wished herself to undergo, though only in a symbolic manner, the death of her sister, so as to be liberated from her symptoms, just as previously she had been liberated from her sister by means of an accident in violet.

Of course, not all unconscious associations which people have with colors are equally dramatic. But even when a person has come to recall the particular situation which gave rise to the association, the color may retain at least some of its impact, particularly if the association was established at an early age. The relative ease with which colors may become associated with emotional attitudes has been demonstrated with children by Staples and Walton (1933) and with adults under hypnosis by Wolberg (1945). Staples and Walton first recorded the preferences of children for red, yellow, green, and blue. Then they presented to each child his least preferred color with a box containing a gift, once or twice a day, for 15–20 days. At the end of this period, preference for the initially rejected colors increased greatly. Even after five months some effect persisted. Wolberg on the other hand hypnotized his adult subjects and made them feel as if they were young children. By means of suggestion he then manipulated the association of colors with emotional experiences. Thus, in a single sitting he was able to condition one patient's reaction to red from half-conscious anxiety to a feeling of elation.

Associations of colors with experiences lying far back in one's life are probably more constant than associations with more recent or topical events, which are notoriously unsteady (e.g., Pressey, 1921, pp. 331–32; Valentine, 1962, p. 30). Writers on art tend to discount most associations of the types mentioned, as essentially nonaesthetic (e.g., Bullough, 1910; A. R. Chandler, 1934; Pepper, 1949; Valentine, 1962, pp. 30–32), presumably because they derive from nonaesthetic origins or motives and divert attention from the work of art. Although the latter may occasionally occur, we do not possess any criterion other than the experiential impact for branding some reactions as less aesthetic than others. Neither are we much helped by Valentine's (1962) attempt to distinguish between associations according to whether they are "fused" or not "fused" with the percept, in our case the color. For even if initially the association occurred on the basis of an arbitrary contiguity between the color and a certain experience, the very act of associating the two led to a fusion in a certain sense. The association may indeed become so strong that not only does the color evoke the experience or the concept but also mention of the experience invariably evokes the color (Dorcus, 1932). Yet, whether the associative reaction will become fused within the framework of the whole experience of a painting may depend at least as much on other features in the painting as on the observer. Moreover, doubts may be expressed concerning the absolute arbitrariness of the association between colors and situations, since even though colors are always present, they do not become associated with just anything under any or all conditions. Hence, it may be suggested that for an association to occur the color must be grasped as a significant part of the situation, as characteristic or even "symbolic" of it to a degree which makes of it a proper representative of the whole situation. A frequent recurrence of the color in a particular kind of situation, an intense emotional experience occasioned by a single occurrence of a situation, and perhaps primarily qualities of colors as carriers of mood and meaning may be major conditions facilitating the establishment of associations between colors and concepts, objects, emotions, or experiences.

Culturally Shared Meanings

Over and beyond personal conscious and unconscious associations, color may evoke associations of culturally shared meanings. These meanings are learned, and may be shared to varying degrees by members of specific groups, communities, religions, or cultures. In most cultures of all times colors have been used as signs with conventional meanings. Since the emotional impact of signs is relatively restricted, and since painting in general relies but little on formalized meanings, painters probably do not very often use colors as signs. Yet painters as well as spectators insofar as they are members of a culture, sharing in a specific network of meanings, can hardly rule out all suggestions of the role of colors as signals.

In modern Western culture most people are aware of the association of green with hope, yellow with hatred, white with purity, black with mourning, and red with love and revolution. Remarkably, this systematization parallels the meanings of colors in liturgy (*Catholic Encyclopedia*, 1908) and in the late medieval heraldic system (Hulme, 1908, pp. 16–29). Yet in the traditional Chinese culture (Groot, 1901) white stood for righteousness and yellow for trustworthiness, while in the classic Indian philosophy (Zimmer, 1956, p. 230) black denoted the dullness, bluntness, and stupidity of the complacent self-centered person, white an illuminated repose and understanding, and red ambition, desire, heroism, and the ruthless striving for pleasure and material goods or power. Such examples, multiplied across periods, ages, and different cultures, invariably show, on the one hand, an expected variability in the meanings of any color, but on the other hand also a striking similarity in at least a part of such meanings. Some of the origins of conventional meanings of colors, which may shed light also on their variability, are fairly obvious. An experiment on associations to colors performed in 1941 in Jerusalem (Kreitler, 1956) showed yellow to be an extremely unpleasant color for most subjects (86 percent), since it reminded them of the "yellow patch of the Jews." This association to yellow, the color which had been used for centuries in Europe as a discriminatory sign for the Jews, was revived by the Nazi persecutions, which reached their climax at that time. In contrast, blue, and not the traditional green, figured as an optimistic color of hope for 72 percent of the subjects, since the "blue shirt," the popular uniform in Palestine at that time, stood for generally shared hopes for a national revival of a socialist and brotherly society. A repetition of the same experiment with another generation of Israelis in 1960 (Kreitler & Elblinger, 1961) showed a great preference for yellow as the color of the reviving desert in the country (41 percent), but almost no (3 percent) association of blue with hope.

The conventional uses of colors in culturally determined contexts may also account for other cases of marked changes in meanings of colors across cultures or generations. Thus, for example, the frequent mentioning by European and American subjects during the last decades of red as expressing power, mastery, and revolution (Aaronson, 1967; Kreitler & Elblinger, 1961; D. C. Murray & Deabler, 1957; Wexner, 1954) may in part be traced to the red communist flag, while the dominant associations to red in Goethe's (1917a, §§ 792, 796–98, 916) time, i.e., sanctity and majesty, reflect the traditional red or purple robes of popes and emperors.

The above examples demonstrate how topical events and circumstances may effect an association of a color with a certain concept or group of concepts. The manner in which such an association may develop, regardless of its primary source, shows up in an experiment by Hofstätter (1957, pp. 63–68). He found that when people are asked to describe concepts such as love, lonesomeness, anxiety, and each of a series of colors in terms of bipolar continua of adjectives, such as hot-cold, good-bad, beautiful-ugly, high-low, soft-loud, empty-full, the resulting profiles for some of the concepts are strikingly similar to profiles for some of the colors. Thus, the profile of love is almost identical to the profile of red, but is antithetical to that of gray, while the profiles for lonesomeness and anxiety are highly similar to the profile of gray and are completely opposite to that of yellow. For German subjects however *Einsamkeit* (lonesomeness) is not only similar in profile to gray but also, though to a lesser degree, to blue and green and is not so sharply opposite to the profiles of yellow and red, as are the profiles of lonesomeness and anxiety for the American subjects.

These results, of which the subjects of the experiment were unaware, mean not only that love may be expected to be a primary association to red, just as lonesomeness and anxiety are to gray, but that the connotational spheres of meaning of the corresponding concepts and colors have converged so far as to become almost identical in certain cultural circles. Yet more important are the consequences of this phenomenon for the meaningfulness of the colors. Associations of colors with abstract concepts may be presumed to persist in cultures as well as in the minds of individuals, even after the actual situation which brought about the association has long been forgotten or has lost all significance. But concepts are known to undergo changes in the course of generations. Since the association with the color nevertheless persists, the change in the concept can be expected to contribute to a change in the meaning of the color. If, for instance, the concept of love acquires an overtone of aggression in the framework of a certain culture, the color red may also absorb this theme, so that spectators may unawares associate aggression with their perception of red in a picture. Similarly, if the concept of lonesomeness is endowed in the United States with a somewhat mysterious aura of mental illness, gray may also gradually come to stand for morbid withdrawal.

Mediation through a concept may also help to account for extensions in the meaning of a color. If yellow, for example, was wholly associated in the Middle Ages with treason—Judas was often depicted as wearing a yellow robe—it is to be expected that yellow would gradually generalize also to other groups of people who share with traitors a low standing or expulsion from society, e.g. prostitutes, Jews, and plague-ridden people (H. Ellis, 1906; Ewald, 1876).

Generalization may operate not only with related concepts but also with related colors. Dorcus (1932) has shown that if a color evokes associations of specific concepts or objects, these concepts or objects themselves, when presented as stimuli, may evoke associations not only of the color to which they were initially related but also of colors similar to it. This example demonstrates how meanings of colors may spread to similar colors, a phenomenon which is particularly likely to occur for colors whose names and distinctness are not sharply delimited.

In the examples above we have attempted to demonstrate the effects of the association of a color with an event or a concept, without probing into the causes which may have determined the initial use of the color as a representative or a sign of the event or concept. Although some of the roots of these conventionalized meanings of colors should doubtless be traced back to deeper and more generally shared levels of experience, with which we shall deal in later sections, other roots seem to be more culture-bound. Some element of arbitrariness is operative whenever a color is established as a sign within the context of a culture. Yet, the factors underlying the establishment of a color as a sign are not always as arbitrary as those resulting from the dictates of fashion, propagated by the modern mass media. If, for example, it is advertised that an orange-colored typewriter belongs in the office of the successful executive, there is a good chance that orange will turn into a sign of business success at least for a season.

Less arbitrary circumstances must be assumed to have contributed to the formation of more lasting associations to colors, particularly those we have inherited from past centuries. To this class of circumstances belong, for instance, the effects of climate. White will remind spectators more readily

of snow, coolness, winter, or purity of air and also analogically of the soul
in the cold, northern countries than in the warm, tropical ones. For people
who have grown up in a sun-flooded country, yellow may be less exciting
than for the inhabitants of a gray metropolis, who are, like Van Gogh, more
predisposed to become enthusiastic about the yellow of Provence and see in
it a color of wish fulfillments, relaxation, freedom, and joy. An etymological
comparison shows that in India too the association of red with aggression
and the pursuit of material goods arose indirectly from characteristics of the
climate. The word which connotes "red" stands also for "dust," that dust
which is continually stirred up by the wind over the soil which remains dry
during the long rainless season (Zimmer, 1956, p. 296). Analogically then,
just as the red-brownish dust whirling in the air dims the clarity of the sky
and of vision and soils all exposed objects, the strivings for power and pleasure were regarded as obscuring the view one may attain of oneself, as
soiling the character, and as dimming comprehension.

A specific association to a color on the basis of environmental phenomena
may also arise in a less direct manner, through the mediation of a concept
that was primarily tied up with the phenomenon and was later transferred
to the color involved in it. For example, the Indian Jainists considered the
lotus flower to be the symbol of compassion and nonviolence. Since the
dominant color of the flower is yellow, the significance of the symbol attached to the form was gradually bestowed on that color too. Similarly, the
Greek association of yellow with a choleric character may have been due to
a theory prevalent in the culture at a certain period which attributed the
choleric personality to the predominance of the yellow bile, *cholé*, in the
body; while the Chaldean convention of using the color of silver as a sign
for calmness and serenity is traceable to their cult of the silver moon as the
origin of wisdom and peace of mind (Chochod, 1949, pp. 92, 114–15).

The examples above show that studies of the history, traditions, social
structure, concepts, and language of various cultures may uncover some of
the lost origins of the conventionalized meanings of colors, just as individual
psychotherapy can be of help in tracing the sources of personal associations
to colors. Yet even without knowledge about these origins, both personal
and cultural associations may figure as factors in the determination of the
experience of art. They may modify, overshadow, or interact with the effects
of complementaries and of homogeneous intermediary colors. Thus, red and
green splashes in a picture may form a sharp contrast, but if a certain observer spends many hours of his working day in painting these colors on
bus-stop posts, it may be supposed that he becomes blunted to this contrast.
If, on the other hand, another observer happens to associate the lights of the

traffic signs with the red and green, the contrast may become endowed for him with a still greater meaning, since the perceptual effects and the signality of the colors will reinforce each other. Similarly, various levels of associations may mitigate or sharpen one another's effects, as well as interact with other dimensions of the meaning of colors. As we shall see in later sections, deeper levels of meaning may resonate in the conventionalized culturally shared meanings of colors.

Color Preferences

For many years color preferences have been a highly preferred theme for study by psychologists. In such studies people of various groups, ages, sexes, nationalities, etc., are asked to express their differential preferences for certain presented colors or color combinations by arranging them in the order of personal preference, by comparing them in sets of two, or by judging each separately in terms of a given scale of values.

Two questions seem to be of prime importance for evaluating the mass of findings on color preferences: (i) Does there exist a universally shared order of preferences for colors? and (ii) What is the nature of the preference response? The two questions are related, for if it turns out that there exists a universal preference ranking, color preferences may be assumed to reflect supracultural, perhaps even biological factors, while if the preference ordering is shown to be subject to great variability, color preferences will be regarded as dependent on learning, personal experiences, and other situational factors. Indeed, as far as the aesthetic experience is concerned, the importance of the answer to the first question lies mainly in the light it may shed on the nature of color preferences.

As may be expected, studies invariably report differences in color preferences among groups, as the surveys by Clarkson, Davies, & Vickerstaff (1950) and by Norman & Scott (1952) show. Young children have different preferences than older children or adults (Gale, 1933; Granger, 1955a; Staples & Walton, 1933), women seem to differ from men according to some studies (Guilford & Smith, 1959; Jastrow, 1897; Warner, 1949), but not much according to others (Mercer, 1925; St. George, 1938), and of course one individual, whoever he may be, differs from another individual in the same group. Yet while some investigators have concluded that color preference is subject to great individual and group differences (e.g. Allesch, 1925; A. R. Chandler, 1928, 1934), other investigators, notably Eysenck (1941c) and Guilford (1934, 1939, 1940), would have us believe that in spite of variability there is a universal order of preference, although even the findings of these two latter investigators do not match. Eysenck's widely quoted preference order (i.e., blue, red, green, violet, orange, yellow) is indeed not a finding but a hypothetical "true order" calculated on the basis of results of two experiments, in which the average correlations among the preferences of the subjects (12 in the first, 30 in the second) were nonsignificant ($r = .28$). Likewise, Eysenck's demonstration that the mean of average preferences of subjects in sixteen experiments of other investigators correlates with the "true order" seems to prove the power of statistical artifacts rather than the dependence of color preferences on "the functioning of the central nervous system" (Eysenck, 1947, p. 208).[2] Moreover, according to Guilford (1939, 1940), who bases his universal laws on forty subjects, saturation and brightness play a greater role than hue in determining color preferences, so that a light yellow should be preferred to a dark blue, in spite of Eysenck's claim that blue is the most and yellow the least preferred color. Since, however, both Eysenck and Guilford admit the involvement of factors other than the universal order in determining color preferences, the problem reduces essentially to the role which is to be attributed to the presumed general order. It is roughly estimated that the general order contributes about 30 percent to the variability in preferences. However, in view of the great individual differences in preferences, this probably represents an overestimation of the role played by the fictitious general order. Practically this means that when we get down to the individual observer of colors, we cannot expect to predict his preferences without asking him to express them, and that he may prefer or reject any of the colors with an almost equal probability.

Similarly, the attempts to detect laws with regard to color combinations, either in terms of the size of interval in hue, brightness, and saturations between the combined colors (Cohn, 1894; Eysenck, 1941d) or in terms of the preference for the single colors which make up the combination (Allen & Guilford, 1936; Geissler, 1917; Kido, 1926), or in terms of both factors (Granger, 1955b, 1955c), seem to turn up too many exceptions to the rules (Dashiell, 1917; Gordon, 1923; Lo, 1936; Tomada, 1934; Washburn, Haight & Regensburg, 1921; Woods, 1956). Some of the factors which affect color preference responses and thus contribute also to the variability in the findings have been uncovered in a long series of studies. These factors include, for example, the area of the color (Washburn, McLean, & Dodge, 1934), the spatial arrangement of the colors (Valentine, 1962, pp. 67–69), and the forms in which they are embedded (Gordon, 1923), the nature of the scale of judgment (Hunt, 1941; Hunt & Volkman, 1937), the degree of pleasantness of other colors in the set through affective contrast (Beebe-Center, 1929; Harris, 1929), the background on which the colors appear (Allesch, 1925;

Helson, 1964, pp. 353–60), the light in which the colors are seen (Helson & Grove, 1947), the duration of looking at colors (Crawford & Washburn, 1911), etc. Moreover, judgments of preference have been shown to be susceptible to changes by conditioning, mainly in children (Khozak, 1934; Kovshavora, 1934; Staples & Walton, 1933). In adults great changes in expressed likes and dislikes for colors may result from voluntarily controlled acts, such as imagining the color in combination with various objects, evoking pleasant or unpleasant associations with it, or imagining it as extending on larger or smaller surfaces (Washburn & Grose, 1921; Washburn, Mac-Donald, & Van Alstyne, 1922).

In the light of the above findings, what is the nature of the preference reaction? Many investigators share the explicit or implicit assumption that preferences express the pleasure or displeasure evoked by a color and thus reflect the affect or emotion attending the perception of colors. Yet, judgments of preference do not tend to be accompanied by any of the usual manifestations of emotions.[3] Even on a purely semantic level we would not expect a person who says he likes a certain color or he likes fine weather to be referring to an intense experience. On the other hand, preferences have all the earmarks of a meaning response: they are intimately related to associations, personal and culturally determined (Chou & Chen, 1935; H. N. Peters, 1943; Walton & Morrison, 1931), they change with the frame of reference of the color which is given or imagined (Washburn, Haight, & Regensburg, 1921), they shift in accordance with various sets (Philip, 1945; Sumner, 1932), and they are learned. Like other dimensions of meaning, preference as a type of response is shared by many people, but specific preferences actually vary among individuals. Preferences may indeed be based on emotion-laden past experiences, but they may equally well reflect nonemotional associations, conventions, personal evaluations, or predilections for specific uses of colors. Yet the stated preference as such tells us nothing about the why, when, and where of the preference. Thus, when no attempt is made to specify what the preference reflects, as is the case in too many of the studies, the utility of the results for an understanding of the aesthetic experience remains unduly restricted. An observer may prefer red dresses over blue dresses, and blue wallpaper over red wallpaper, yet he may like the red in a picture not because a picture is similar to a dress but because the red reminds him of a pleasant experience. These remarks lead to the commonplace conclusion that an answer depends on the content and context of the question. In studies on preference the experimenter usually poses too general a question, so that the subject is bound to rephrase it more specifically for himself. But since too little is known about the question the subject poses himself, it is often difficult to understand the answer he gives the experimenter.

Symbolic Meanings of Colors

While the proof for the existence of a universal color-preference system is shaky, there seems to be evidence for other meanings of colors which are more widely shared than are the culturally determined meanings, although they have not been formally conventionalized. These meanings, variously referred to as symbolic, physiognomic, mood associations, emotional reactions, aesthetic responses, or connotative meanings of colors, show up in a variety of forms in modern studies as well as in ancient mythologies, rituals, and traditions of various cultures, past and present. Sometimes they seem elusive and heavily laden emotionally; at other times they turn up more clearly conceptualized in definite formulations. Such appear to be the meaning levels suggested by Goethe (1917a, §918) when he referred to the "mystical" nature of colors as pointing to "primordial relations which belong both to nature and to human vision itself," by Gauguin, who felt that "colors are inherently enigmatic" (quoted in Read, 1955, p. 165), and by Bullough (1908), who emphasized the "character" aspect of a color as "the appearance in a color or the expression by a color of what, in the case of a human being, would be called his character, or mood, or temperament."

Some of these meanings have become conventionalized in the context of different cultures, a development which might account for the similarities in the meanings of colors found in such disparate cultures as Old Mexico, China, India, Chippewa, Zuni, and the east Mediterranean sphere including Babylonia, Egypt, Israel, and Greece (Chochod, 1949, p. 114; Cushing, 1896; Wallis, 1939, pp. 165–67; Werner, 1957, p. 88). Indeed, there are many examples of colors, forms, and other perceptual configurations, e.g., the image of a bridge or the Christian cross, which have turned from symbols into signs, and whose initially symbolic meanings show up as stereotyped verbal conventions. Yet in other cases the codification of the meaning has not completely voided the color or the form of its vitality as a symbol.

There is a striking similarity in the findings of a wide range of studies[4] on the meanings of colors, based on such disparate methods as the pairings of adjectives with colors, free introspection of reactions to colors, the checking of responses on the Semantic Differential, or the experiencing of the world as having a specific color, under the influence of hypnotic suggestion.

Red turns up in all studies as a most meaning-laden color. Subjects are almost unanimous in regarding it as most exciting and stimulating, a powerful, strong, vigorous, masterful, energetic, and impulsive color. Yet the fiery and outgoing warmth of the color is not only gay, exuberant, happy, and sociable but may also have a note of aggression, resentfulness, destruction, and danger. Another aspect of its vitality may take the form of affection, passion, and love. Anthropological data (H. Ellis, 1900; Wunderlich, 1925) about the meanings and uses of red in various cultures amply support the variety of meanings attributed to it nowadays by subjects in psychological experiments. The intimate relation of red with life is attested by the frequent use of red in the magic of healing the sick, in ceremonies intended to scare away demons or to assert the continued existence of the dead, and in various rituals to increase the fertility of the earth. Thus, agricultural fecundity necessitated in ancient Egypt the killing of red-haired people, in Rome the slaughtering of red puppies (Frazer, 1952, pp. 17–18, 439–41, 514, 551–52). Even in modern times we speak of red Easter eggs, which originally signified fertility, and of the "red-light district." The relation of red with power and aggression is glaringly evident in the use of red by rulers over most of the world, and in the ample application of red to face and clothing by warriors in such different cultures as the Greek, German, and Aborigine Australian.

A very different network of meanings hovers about blue. In modern studies blue emerges as a tender, soothing, cool and passive, secure and comfortable color which inspires calm, confidence, and harmony, a sense of control, and responsibility, but may also be slow and mildly depressing. It is an unobtrusive color which recedes into the distance and suggests whatever is far away in past or future, in space, in thoughts, in fantasy. There seems to be a quality of the unattainable suggested by the blue, which has been made famous through the bluebird in Maeterlinck's play and in hundreds of popular songs. Even before the blue flower had been sanctioned by the Romanticists as a sign for devotion to the mysterious and attraction to the depths of the world beyond, blue was always regarded all over the world as the color of the spirit, of the upper world of sublimity and mysticism (Bachelard, 1943; Jacobi, 1959, pp. 160–65), and of most heavenly gods. In Christianity, there is not only a Blue Monday of spiritualization for the faithful, but Christ is frequently represented in a blue mantle, and Mary, as Virgin Queen of Heaven, has gained so many blue attributes that she came to be called the Blue Lady. In India too, the primordial state of matter was considered to be blue light, which is the color of supreme wisdom, of the body of Buddha and of the heart of the creative universal principle. In other contexts, blue, as the representative of the spiritual and the world beyond, has been commonly used as a safeguard against demons or in magical rites designed to ward off evil ghosts.

Yet the quality of sublimity and spirituality of blue may also have a less attractive connotation of moralism and emotional repression, reflected in the "bluestocking" and in the "blue laws" of American puritans (Nogué, 1943). Similarly, the restraint and coolness of blue may not only be soothing but also hard, cold, and calmly hostile, while the distance implied by the blue may turn into withdrawal.

In contrast to blue, yellow is conceived as a cheerful, jovial, and joyful color. It may be dazzling and outgoing, but is sometimes felt to be shallow, treacherous, dominating, and even destructive. A double set of meanings attaches also to green: it expresses youthfulness, hope, and nature, but also poison and danger. Similarly, purple is sedate and dignified, but carries an aura of deceit, misery, and adversity. The meanings of black, which implies death, night, anxiety, defeat, and depression, with its contrast in the white of innocence, purity, and freedom, are too well known to require elaboration.

Although most investigators tend to lump all these meanings into one group, studies into symbolic-personal meanings of various percepts and concepts (S. Kreitler, 1965; S. Kreitler & Kreitler, 1968) show that the described meanings of colors include at least five types or dimensions of meaning. These are meaning in terms of bodily expression, e.g., blue constricts bodily movements; in terms of sensations and feelings, e.g., blue is a cold color; in terms of general abstract interpretations, e.g., blue denotes spirituality; in terms of metaphors based on resemblance in the characteristics of the color and the meaning, e.g., blue is like the world beyond; and finally, meaning expressed in terms of what could be called true symbols, whereby the color comes to represent a contrast and its solution, e.g., blue denotes the fusion of heavenly peace and the destructive fire of lightning.

How can we account for the fact that many of the described meanings are almost universally shared? This question is as much of a challenge to those who hold symbolic-personal responses to be a primitive, infantile, or regressed form of reaction, deriving from an intellectual or psychological inability to grasp reality objectively without distortion through projections and associations (Arieti, 1959; Piaget, 1959) as it is to those who proclaim symbolism to be an innate form of thinking and perceiving at least as valid as the scientific "geometrical-technical" (Werner & B. Kaplan, 1963), matter-of-fact perception (Arnheim, 1949, 1958; Eliade, 1952; Langer, 1948).

Synesthesia and the Organismic Approach

The phenomenon of synesthesia may provide a clue to the interpersonal sharedness of symbolic meanings of colors and other percepts. Synesthesia is traditionally defined as responding to a stimulus of one sense modality with sensations which belong to another sense modality. The synesthetic reactions are assumed to be involuntary sensations, merging with the regular sensations of the stimulated sense organ, to which they correspond in a predictable manner. Some familiar and well-established synesthetic experiences bound up with colors are specific sensations of temperature, weight, size, and distance evoked at the sight of colors. For example, the various hues of red, orange, and yellow are experienced as warm, while the blues, greens, and purples are cool. Dark colors, like black and brown, appear to be heavier than the bright colors, like white, yellow, or light blue. Surfaces with bright colors appear larger than surfaces with dark colors. Red surfaces seem to advance while blue surfaces seem to recede. Yet distance seems to depend mainly on the saturation and brightness of the colors relative to their background, so that the more the colors contrast with the background, the nearer they appear.[5] Colors have also been observed to appear as synesthetic responses to other perceptual and nonperceptual stimuli as tones, odors, tastes, and even numbers.

The invariability of synesthetic relations has tempted many to consider their origin to be in physiological connections between the various sensory brain centers (London, 1954; Werner, 1957, p. 98). These contentions have been based in large part on experiments which demonstrate the effects that stimulation in one sense modality may have on the threshold and other qualities of simultaneous perception through other senses.[6] However, the relations between the relevant brain centers have not yet been detected, and the same findings have served as a basis for other hypotheses about the origins of synesthesia. Major among these is the hypothesis—inspired by the organismic approach—that a person reacts to every stimulus with the whole organism and not just with one sense organ. In a series of experiments Goldstein (1939) showed that color affects not only the visual organ but also movements, sensations in other senses, and the overall attitude to the world. He concluded, for example, that red and yellow have a generally "expansive" effect on the organism, increasing the impact of the external world and producing the emotional background from which ideas and action will emerge, while green and blue have the reverse effect, causing "concentration" and "contraction" which are more suited for the execution of actions. Other investigators have extended Goldstein's findings and showed that colors may affect physiological, emotional, and perceptual functioning.[7]

Werner (1930, 1934) regards the state in which a stimulus affects the whole organism as a special mode of perception, i.e., "sensing" as contrasted with "perceiving." In "sensing" a person feels the stimuli and does not just see or hear them, and he responds synesthetically, just as children do in the stage before the differentiation of the senses from the "primordial matrix composed of affective, interoceptive, postural, imaginal elements, etc." (Werner & B. Kaplan, 1963, p. 18). Synesthesia is thus due to residues of the primary unity among the senses.

While Goldstein and Werner tend to attribute synesthesia as well as the other symbolic meanings of colors to an innate global reactivity of the organism, another group of writers with a nativistic approach maintains that the symbolic meanings of colors are qualities of colors, just as saturation or hue. To perceive colors at all entails automatically the perception of the expressive qualities of colors. The gaiety of yellow is thus part of the constitutive nature of yellow (Hartshorne, 1934, p. 123); it is given as a sense datum together with the sensation of yellow and is as characteristic of yellow as yellowness itself, if not more so (Arnheim, 1949, 1958; Köhler, 1938; Kouwer, 1949; E. Straus, 1963). According to the supporters of this view, the perception of expression is innate and most natural, while what needs explanation is the matter-of-fact perception, which is a late development and an artificial product of scientific civilization. Matter-of-fact perception certainly stands in need of explanation. Even more do synesthesia and symbolism, which are neither manifested by all human beings nor so natural that they do not depend on learning and maturation (Honkavaara, 1961). Relegating these phenomena to the realm of innate tendencies, on the one hand, and to the unspecified structure of color, on the other hand, does not seem to add much to understanding them, apart from endowing them with a somewhat metaphysical aura.

Less comprehensive hypotheses about synesthesia are offered by those who assume that it is mediated by certain qualities which are common to sensations of various modalities. Thus, Hornbostel (1931) showed brightness to be a feature common to tones, odors, and colors, and Stevens (1962) found that intensity is a quality which applies to practically all sense modalities. This hypothesis suggests the possibility that correspondences among sensations of various sense modalities may be inferred or learned. Indeed, Howells (1944) succeeded in developing a synesthetic response by presenting 5,000 times a low tone with red light and a high tone with green light. When later he showed his subjects a pale greenish-reddish color and sounded a high tone they saw the color as red, but when he sounded a low tone they saw the color as green.

Conditioning of sensory responses is a usual procedure in the laboratory (Brogden, 1947), and Ellson's (1941) finding—that after pairing of a light with a tone, the presentation of the light alone produces a faint hearing of the tone—is by no means exceptional. Moreover, the fact that many of those who react synesthetically do not actually have real synesthetic sensations but only a vague feeling, image, or mere verbal association of the synesthetically appropriate sensation (Karwoski, Odbert, & Osgood, 1942) suggests that synesthesia may be a product of learning. This conclusion would seem particularly plausible with regard to the synesthetic relations of colors with temperature, weight, and distance. The warmness of red, the receding quality of blue, and the heaviness of black have become almost proverbial in daily language. Moreover, these relations are exemplified frequently enough in the environment common to all people. Many heavy objects are also dark, owing possibly to the density of materials; not only is the sun red-yellow but so also are heated objects, which assume reddish hues more often than green-bluish ones; and nearer objects usually appear to be brighter than more distant objects. Knowledge and verbal habits may well be the cause of the synesthetic experiences of many individuals. This cause might also explain why meaning responses corresponding to synesthetic relations and other so-called expressive qualities of colors and other percepts do not appear, at least according to the studies of Honkavaara (1961), at the earliest ages as Werner and Köhler would have us assume, but only after matter-of-fact perception and some degree of mastery over language have been acquired. However, the assumption that synesthetic relations are learned does not mean that they are mere associations superimposed on sensations. In spite of the fact that, for example, the cues for depth are at least partly learned, we see depth directly and do not associate it.

In view of the regularity of synesthetic experiences and the evidence about various interactions between the senses in general, the hypothesis that synesthesia may be learned should not lead to rejection of the alternative hypothesis that it might depend on innate intersensory relations and organismic reactivity. Rather the two hypotheses should be regarded as complementing each other.

Regardless of their origin, synesthetic relations could serve as the core around which may be developed richer and more extensive meaning of colors, shared by various cultures. This hypothesis is based on the finding that terms like warmth and heaviness, and qualities of colors like saturation and brightness, form elements within larger clusters of meaning which are common to many cultures (Osgood, 1960, 1962; Suci, 1960). For example, the polarity heavy/light appears often in conjunction with the polarities big/little, deep/shallow and down/up, which form together a meaning cluster of potency. Similarly, the polarity hot/cold seems to be embedded in a meaning cluster of activity. Thus, if a color is viewed as warm, the other correlated meanings of the activity cluster will tend to be attached to it, e.g., it will be viewed metaphorically as young, intense, quick, impetuous, and the like. The fact that clusters of this type are shared by different cultures could thus account in part for the sharedness in meanings of colors across cultures.

Colors and Archetypes

Although synesthetic relations may lie at the core of interpersonally shared meanings of colors which extend beyond purely sensory qualities, they may be insufficient to account for the more complex symbolic meanings which hover about colors. This would apply in particular to multidimensional Janus-faced meanings, which are no less common than synesthetic and metaphoric meanings. A possible hypothesis to account for some of the universal meanings of colors would be that human beings have innate structures of meanings, called by Jung "archetypes" (Jung, 1953a, 1956a), which apply to various percepts and may represent the quintessence of many primordial associations of colors with various significant experiences in the history of man. It is characteristic of the manifestations of archetypes that although they may take different forms, all have a common core and seem to be loaded with a peculiarly fascinating significance. The various individual archetypal manifestations, called by Jung "symbols," represent in a sense culturally and personally determined variations of a basic, haunting theme shared by all people. Common to such symbols is, first, the fusion of the representing sign with the represented meaning, and second, the fusion of various contrasting meanings through the symbol. Thus, if red is grasped by a certain individual as an archetypal symbol, we may expect that for this individual the vitality of red would seem to fuse with the redness itself, and that a wealth of contrasting meanings would appear to inhere in the color and become harmonized through it.

Innate archetypal structures could fill in the domain of contents the role attributed by the philosopher Kant and the psychologist Bruner (1957) to innate categories in perception, or by the linguist Chomsky (1965) to universal structures in grammar and syntax. The innate structure provides in a sense only a framework within which more concrete and elaborate meanings can be developed.

If one is willing to accept the hypothesis of archetypal meanings, one could go a step further and speculate about their hypothetical origins. One clue is afforded by the involvement of colors in primordial phenomena highly significant for man. For example, the variety of meanings of red could be traced back to the association of red with blood and fire. Both blood and fire enjoy a long history of symbolic meanings, highly similar in contents and bipolarities to those inherent in red (Frazer, 1952). Indeed, the involvement of blood in rites of fertility, its uses for appeasement of the gods' anger, its frequent identification with life and with murder, are as well known as the sacredness of fire, the stolen gift of the gods, whose warmth and light were so fundamental for the security and comfort of the home, but which also spread destruction and death. Similarly, the evil of black and its intimate relation with death, the devil, and the cosmic *prima materia* may go back to prehistoric associations of black with the insecurity of night and hollow spaces, ranging from caves to the mouths of dangerous beasts. In spite of the finality of the association of black with night, blue with sky and ocean, green with the revival in spring, and so on, the intensity of the experience of night, ocean, or spring for prehistoric man should not be judged by the yardstick of man in the twentieth century. It remains for us only to suggest the possibility that these experiences have left residues in human nature which may resonate with a distant but significant note when modern man views colors.

A second clue to the origins of archetypal meanings of colors may lie in the role of colors in the world of animals. Various colors serve for animals as signal stimuli releasing instinctual behaviors. Both the signal stimuli and the instinctual behavior sequences are innate. Red, for example, has been found to be a signal stimulus for the release of courtship behavior in the female of the stickleback fish (Tinbergen, 1951, p. 38), while in the stickleback male, red releases the fighting instinct when a rival male appears in his "territory" (Tinbergen, 1956, p. 28). In newly hatched chicks of the herring gull the sight of red triggers the food-begging behavior (Tinbergen, 1956, pp. 29–30), and in the English robin red arouses the actions designed to impress and to overawe both allies and enemies (Tinbergen, 1951, pp. 28–29, 42). On the other hand, blue has been found to be the most effective color for evoking following and approach responses in young domestic chicks (Schaefer & Hess, 1959), but the least preferred for food pecking (Hess, 1959).

It is remarkable that red signals for at least some animals what may be viewed in the human world as aggression, sexuality, pride and authority, and that blue stands in the chicks' world for security, just as in the human world. Naturally, there are in the animal world color preferences which make less sense to humans—for example, the domestic chicks' innate pecking preference for light desaturated colors (Hess & Gogel, 1954) or the ducklings' preference for green and yellow-green (Hess, 1956). But the correspondences which do appear might provide a basis for speculating about residues of instinctual reactions which could have survived through evolution and form a kind of prespecies "memories" of times before human time began (Portmann, 1950).

Colors, Paintings, and Observers

The meeting ground of all the varied possible effects of colors is the individual observing the colors of a painting. Naturally, there is no reason to expect that every spectator when viewing any kind of painting under any circumstances whatsoever would respond with personal and general associations, with preferences, synesthesia, and all the variety of other symbolic meanings of colors. Rather there is much more reason to assume that the spectator's personality and mood and the nature of the painting would combine to elicit in each case a more or less restricted range of responses out of the whole reviewed spectrum, while other responses may just resonate weakly in the background or not be evoked at all.

Since the responses to color depend on both the spectator and the painting, and since these responses change from one painting to another and even in the course of observing any one painting (Brighouse, 1939a), it seems unwarranted to classify spectators into steady types according to their responses to colors. Nevertheless, such attempts are rather common and usually follow one of three courses. The first is based on the distinction between observers who react primarily to colors and prefer colorful pictures as against observers who react primarily to forms and content, and presumably prefer noncolorful pictures (Eysenck, 1941a; Lindberg, 1938; Valentine, 1962, pp. 188–90). A second group of typologies is based on classification according to preferred colors, e.g., warm vs. cold colors (Jaensch, 1936), saturated vs. unsaturated colors (Eysenck, 1940; Stephenson, 1935); or according to colors with particular emotional significance for the individual observer, in line with psychodiagnostic observations. Finally, the third and most common kind of typology is based on dominant color responses. The best-known of these is Bullough's (1908, 1910) classification into the "objective" type, who reacts to the formal relations among colors and their objective qualities, the "physiological" type, who reacts on the basis of mood and sensation, the "associative" type, who reacts with personal associations, and the "character" type, who is sensitive to symbolic meanings and the expressive qualities of colors. Sometimes the system reduces to a distinction only between the first type, who does not respond to meanings, and the three others lumped together into one group of responders to meaning (Feasey, 1921).

The best case which could be made for such typologies is that they are restricted to a particular encounter between a spectator and a painting within a limited section of the observation period, when one type of response to colors may dominate. A spectator viewing for example Nolde's painting (Plate 6) may indeed note first the red, since it appeals to his unconscious aggressive tendencies, but this preference reaction is bound soon to be replaced by another response to the red, or rather by reaction to the yellows in the painting, which are much more prominent than the reds. Similarly, it does not make much sense to speak of observers who are noncolor types when they are confronted with the dazzling colors of a stained window or with a painting in which colors predominate. On the other hand, when colors seem to play in a painting a subsidiary role to forms, most observers would concentrate first and more on forms and contents.

Hence it seems more plausible to assume that the nature of the painting and the kind and role of colors in it channelize and control to a great extent the manifestation of personal tendencies of responsiveness to colors and the manner in which they unfold. Since there are no research findings on this theme, we may only suggest some general hypotheses. One important factor which determines the range and intensity of responses to colors is the contents of the painting. For example, paintings depicting familiar scenes or objects in a conventional manner may be expected to restrict the responses to colors in line with the associations evoked by the perceived contents. In such paintings the contents may have an overriding impact which can hardly be ignored, so that responses to colors do not unfold as freely as when familiar contents are absent. On the other hand, contents suggestive of imaginative scenes, as in surrealist and fantasy paintings, produce an atmosphere which may facilitate the evocation of mood responses, synesthesias, metaphors, and even symbolic interpretations.

Color responses depend also on the role colors play in a painting. If colors appear principally as a decorative means, subsidiary to other means which carry the main load of experiential impact, color responses may be less intense than when colors figure prominently in a painting as in some nonrepresentational and monochromatic modern paintings. However, reduction of the role of forms and of representational contents in a painting is certainly not the only means of enhancing the experiential impact of the presented colors. Other means include for example, the use of colors in a manner which contradicts everyday experience, like the green profile in Chagall's painting (Plate 16) or the blue face in Nolde's painting (Plate 6). Another means is exemplified in the painting by Matisse (Plate 15). Here neither the depicted scene nor the hues defy realism unduly, yet one's attention is riveted to the colors through the sharp contrasts they form. There is very little in the nature of the colors to relieve the tension produced by the two sets of juxtaposed complementaries.

Another factor in paintings which codetermines the kind and intensity of color experiencing is the quality of the colors. For example, highly saturated colors are more likely to evoke synesthetic experiences than very pale desaturated colors which appear almost achromatic. A different aspect of quality is the particular hue used in a painting. Linguistic labels are as a rule very deceptive in the domain of colors. We use a word like blue to denote a whole range of blues, each of which may have a very particular experiential impact. An apposite example is provided by Chagall's (1962) famous Jerusalem windows. Three of the windows, those designed to represent the tribes of Reuben, Simeon, and Benjamin, are blue. Yet the blues are very different, and each was meant to evoke a particular set of symbolic reactions, duly facilitated also by the forms and contents of each window. The cerulean blue of Reuben, the eldest son of Jacob and Leah, is clear and airy, "evoking the limpidity of air, the transparent foaming of the sea, the amplitude and freshness of a newly created Biblical space" (Chagall, 1962, p. 29); the blue of the second window, of Simeon the violent but absolved son, is somber and "establishes a grave and nocturnal atmosphere" (pp. 41–42); while the blue of Benjamin, the last of Jacob's sons, is a sacred and spiritual blue, as befits a tribe whose territory included the Holy City of Jerusalem.

The perceived quality of colors changes also through their being embedded in the context of painting which is usually a field of many colors. The perceived saturation of colors depends on the neighboring colors and on the area filled by the color. Moreover, as Allesch (1925) demonstrated, adjoining colors determine which particular shade of a hue is perceived. A dark green bordering on blue may appear to be more bluish than when it borders on yellow, and light gray on a black background appears much brighter than on a white background.

However, responses to colors of the various types do not simply succeed each other in time. They interact in a variety of ways so that the significance and intensity of each are modified by the other responses which colors evoke.

A mood response to a color may change the significance of a previously evoked personal association, while a metaphoric interpretation may reveal to the observer the deeper meaning underlying a common use of the color as a signal. Color responses of the various kinds may, however, also produce tension-laden contrasts. A spectator may grasp the relieving function of a range of yellows in a painting as intermediating between clashing colors, yet on a symbolical level the yellows suggest to him perfidiousness and treacherous fickleness.

Responses to colors in a painting interact not only with each other but also with responses to the contents and forms, on which they are partly dependent, as suggested earlier. Owing to the interpersonal sharedness of at least a part of the meanings of colors, painters may use colors as a kind of language in order to communicate moods, impressions, and even contents. These may stand in a variety of relations with the moods, impressions, and contents conveyed through the other elements in the painting. The aggressiveness suggested by a painted arrow or by an authority figure depicted in a painting may be blunted by the calmness of a cool blue in the interior of the arrow or the garment of the figure. The gentleness of a soft profile may be contradicted by the saturated redness of the face. Contrasts of forms may be resolved through colors, as when two clashing elements of form or representational contents bear the same color or present a harmonious color combination. Similarly, colors may reveal the relatedness or affinity between apparently unrelated elements in the painting or may emphasize the disparity between what seems related on a certain level. Moreover, symbolic meanings of colors may be used to suggest a resolution of a contrast between colors on the perceptual level, as when the tension of a clash between juxtaposed blue and yellow is relieved through making both the part of one and the same face, thus suggesting that the irradiating extrovert quality of the yellow may be as necessary for the fullness of life as the withdrawing coolness of the blue, or that there is both a treacherous and a reliable aspect to every face.

The variety of possible color effects and the complex interrelations among them demonstrate the power of colors to evoke an experience which may be dynamic, intense, and multileveled even without the almost unavoidable interaction with forms and with representational contents if present. Undoubtedly, awareness of the impact of colors underlies the attempts of the Synchromist group of Expressionists to relegate to colors some of the functions of forms in painting, such as production of depth and movement effects (Cheney, 1948, pp. 243–64) or the attempts of modern Chromaticists, such as Ad Reinhardt and Franz Kline, to use color in painting to the utmost possible exclusion of forms and other contents. Yet the most daring and fascinating experiments with colors to date seem to have been undertaken by Thomas Wilfred, whose color organ (the Clavilux) produces an orchestral succession of colored lights which fill the whole visual scene, and more recently by Moholy Nagy, Dan Flavin, François Morellet, Takis, and others who create stable or moving colored-light paintings. By presenting color through the medium of light instead of pigments and by coupling it with movement rather than with forms, as in traditional painting, these artists seem to have created a new art form which promises a wide extension in the range and depth of effects produced by colors.

4. Forms as Gestalts

Studying Forms in Paintings

Kandinsky, who was not only a great painter but also a noted theoretician, wrote: "The contact between a pointed angle of a triangle and the contour of a circle has in fact no less effect than the contact between the finger of God and the finger of Adam in that picture by Michelangelo" (Kandinsky, 1955, p. 141). We will go a step beyond Kandinsky and claim that the meeting of a triangle and a circle could under certain circumstances be even more tension-laden than is the meeting of the fingers of God and of Adam. Indeed, even the tension evoked by the approaching fingers of God and man derives in great part from the forms of these fingers and from their location —in relation to both the overall space of the picture and each other, being as they are near but not contiguous.

Though forms arise from dishomogeneities in hue and brightness in the visual field, this does not mean that forms are a secondary element in paintings. Quite on the contrary, they appear to the perceiver as much primary as colors are, and sometimes as even more elementary, with colors playing the role of modifying planes and volumes formed or suggested by lines. Like colors, forms may be analyzed on a variety of levels, and the range of their potential effects is in no way more restricted than that of colors. Some of the major aspects under which forms may be studied are revealed through the various stages which the perception of forms undergoes when they are seen under gradually improving conditions of vision—increasing exposure times (Freeman, 1929; Wever, 1927), successive removal of colored filters (J. L. Brown, Duhns, & Adler, 1957), or shifts from the extreme periphery to the center of the visual field (Zigler et al., 1930). Characteristically, observers first note a vague area, an unorganized "something," a formless form, which is seen as near or far, right or left, up or down. When conditions improve a little, they see a form with clear contours, differentiated from its background, an unidentified "thing" which protrudes in the visual field. Only under optimal conditions does the "thing" turn into an object or a familiar form.

The sequence of perceptual development just described suggests at least three major aspects of forms: their structural characteristics, their role with regard to differentiation in space, and the meanings with which they are bound up. In the present chapter we shall deal mainly with the first two aspects of forms, and defer the third aspect for later discussion. This discussion requires from the reader an attempt to imagine forms as abstracted from the various meanings which attach to them as well as from colors. This procedure is didactically necessary so as to bring into focus characteristic structural and spatial features of forms. The required abstraction is naturally difficult to sustain, since forms are rarely if ever "abstract" or "non-representative," as technical and popular terminology designates forms which are not direct copies of familiar objects and the paintings in which they appear. The unfortunate terms "abstract" and "nonrepresentative" are based on the unwarranted distinction between form and content, and seem to reflect the remnants of expectations, nourished by materialist and objectivist ideologies, that the contents of paintings must be imitations of the observable rather than "exercises in perception" (Gibson, 1966, p. 225) or representations of the unobservable. The origin of these terms lies probably in the bewilderment and disappointment of spectators who, like Maritain (1955, p. 156), have expected to observe the conventional nudes, battles, and flowers, but found instead a transmutation of these "into volumes and surfaces," and concluded that these "unnatural" paintings do not represent anything except the failure of painters to find a compromise between the perception and expression of things. For those who share rather the opinion of Shahn (1957) that form is always the shape of content, we would suggest to replace the terms "abstract" and "nonrepresentative" art by the designation "paintings devoid of an explicit object reference." The emphasis is to be put on "explicitness," for nonexplicitly, forms in modern paintings may suggest to spectators various imaginary or actual objects and evoke a wealth of meanings. Possibly, after we have reviewed the multidimensional effects of forms in painting, many a reader may be tempted to call abstract painting "concrete art," as indeed several painters have suggested.

Laws of Gestalt

The first questions which we raise with regard to forms refer to their potentiality to evoke tension and relief when they are contemplated maximally stripped of meanings, object references, and color differences. The importance of the answers to these questions derives from one of our major hypotheses about the experience of art. According to this hypothesis, works of art evoke specific tensions which absorb more general tensions in the observer, and provide a specific relief which resolves summarily the specific as well as the general tensions. With regard to forms, this hypothesis leads us to ask such questions as these: Can a triangle be tension-laden or relieving? Can two intersecting lines evoke a feeling of discomfort? Can a square in a particular location be disturbing? Is it possible that an observer may actively search for a circle in a painting?

According to the Gestalt school of psychology, the answer to all of these questions is unequivocally positive (D. Katz, 1950; Köhler, 1929; Koffka, 1935). The major questions asked by Gestalt psychologists referred to phenomena which are also significant for us. For instance, they asked: Why is it that a triangle seems to us to be an independent entity and not merely an aggregate of three lines plus three angles? Why is it that we see an angle and not simply two converging lines? Or how is it that when we see a circle from an oblique angle, we nevertheless perceive it as a circle and not as an oval? Why does a triangle with its apex down seem to be in such precarious equilibrium? Or (to take a problem we have mentioned before) whence does the tension stem that we feel when looking at two very similar hues? Their answer to these and to a multitude of other puzzling questions of the same kind was that both the experience and its causes are determined by the laws of Gestalt.

According to the basic tenets of the Gestalt theory any form whatsoever is a gestalt. But what is a gestalt? According to the first of the two basic statements about gestalt, formulated by the theory's originator, Christian von Ehrenfels, a gestalt is more than the sum of its component parts. A gestalt is a whole, a new kind of organization with qualities and properties of its own which neither reside in the parts nor can be reduced to them. More concretely, such a gestalt as a triangle or an angle is an independent entity, different from the sum of a specific number of intersecting lines; and a circle is more than an aggregate of adjoining points. Similarly, a melody is not simply one tone plus another plus another, etc., nor is it the sum of the relations between the tones. Nor, for that matter, can the impression of strawberry ice cream be accounted for by adding coldness to redness, sweetness, softness, and so forth. However, this apparently simple, but most revolutionary statement about gestalts implies not only that a form may have such a high degree of organization that it appears as a self-contained whole, separated from its background and surroundings, but also that the whole and its parts mutually determine one another's characteristics, so that the qualities of the whole dominate the qualities of the parts. In Fig. 4.1, one and the same small square appears to have different qualities when it forms a part of the elongated figure on the left than when it is seen in the context of three identical squares arranged diagonally.

The second basic law states that gestalts are characterized by transpos-

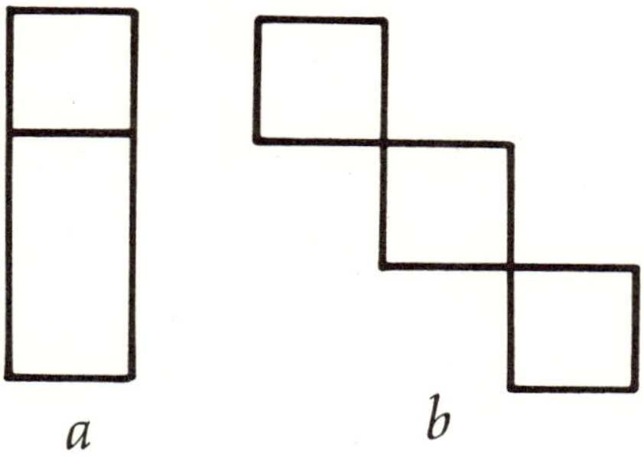

Fig. 4.1 The effect of the whole on the qualities of the parts. The top square seems different in the context of *a* than in the context of *b*.

a   *b*

ibility, which means the parts of a gestalt can all change in different senses, e.g., in size, position, or direction, while the gestalt nevertheless survives and remains recognizable. Thus, a square remains a square whether it is drawn or painted, red or black, large or small, constructed with sticks or carved in stone, just as a melody remains the same melody even if all its tones are changed when it is played in a different key. It is, of course, the first characteristic of gestalts which renders their second characteristic possible.

These two basic gestalt laws pertain not only to forms which consist of lines, but also to the lines themselves and even to points. In general, any whole which is grasped as a whole, for instance, a sentence, an idea, a melody, a painting, a play, an action, as well as colors, movement, tactile sensations and so forth, can be regarded as a gestalt. Thus, there can also be wholes which contain subgestalts, these being dominated in turn by the qualities of the whole itself.

The degree of organization varies from one gestalt to another. Gestalt psychologists coined the term "good" or "prägnant" gestalts for those gestalts which are the best organizations of the stimuli in the given circumstances. More specifically, good gestalts are usually characterized by regularity, symmetry, inclusiveness, unity, harmony, maximal simplicity, and conciseness.

Naturally, there are stimuli which do not allow organization into good gestalts. Yet, the organization of stimuli into forms is not random but follows certain rules. For example, the elements which are closest to each other (Fig. 4.2) or are similar in any respect (Fig. 4.3a, b) tend to be grasped as belonging to one unit. Lines which enclose a surface (Fig. 4.4), as well as lines which form a "good" and continuous contour, or have a common fate in that they seem to move together in the same direction (Fig. 4.5), are perceived as independent units or as autonomous subunits of a larger figure.[1]

When the existing stimuli do not admit of organization into clear-cut

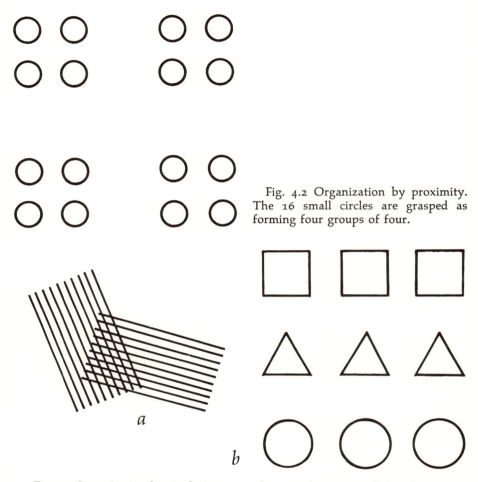

Fig. 4.2 Organization by proximity. The 16 small circles are grasped as forming four groups of four.

Fig. 4.3 Organization by similarity: *a*, similarity in direction underlies the perception of the two planes; *b*, similarity in form may lead to the perception of three rows with identical elements, or similarity in sequence of the same elements may lead to the perception of three columns.

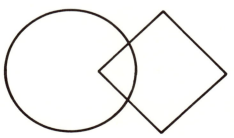

Fig. 4.4 The principle of closure. In spite of the intersection of lines, we perceive two unified forms, a circle and a square, each enclosing a surface.

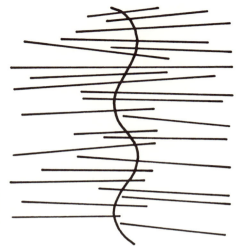

Fig. 4.5 The principle of good continuation and common fate. In spite of frequent intersections by horizontal lines, the vertical curved line is perceived as one form.

good gestalts, spectators nevertheless manifest a strong tendency to change, amplify, eliminate, or disregard the features which prevent the gestalt from being a good one. Thus, for example, a number of dots arranged in an approximately circular fashion are liable to be perceived as a circle; an angle of 85 or 95 degrees is grasped as a right angle; figures with gaps are "closed" or completed; and a somewhat non-symmetrical figure is experienced as symmetrical (Fig. 4.6). Even when the irregularities cannot be "corrected" in the act of perception itself, the figures may be regarded as deformations of something which evidently serves as a norm and is in fact the concept of the good gestalt of that form. Thus, a line with a gap somewhere in its mid-

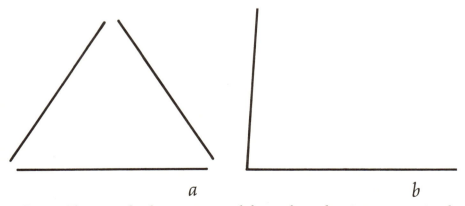

a   *b*

Fig. 4.6 The principle of pressure toward the good gestalt: *a* is seen as a triangle and *b* is seen as a right angle.

dle is still grasped as one line, though broken or incomplete, rather than as two lines; and lopsided shapes, as the term indicates, are perceived not as shapes in their own right, but rather as deviations from imagined symmetrical shapes. The same applies to inverted top-heavy forms, too big heads on thin necks, and leaning towers, all of which are disagreeable sights, arousing a desire to correct or somehow perfect them.

The tendencies to organize and "correct" given stimuli or figures into the best possible gestalts are manifested with particular clarity by children (Werner, 1957). When copying figures, children tend to make them more uniform and indivisible—for instance, by drawing a circle instead of copying a square, by closing the open figures, by making parts resemble each other in form and size, by emphasizing symmetry, or by turning most of the lines in the same direction, so that a starlike form appears as a leaf. These phenomena do not seem to be due to reduced or undeveloped perceptual or motor capacities, but rather to a dominance of the striving for good gestalts even if it leads to distorted representation.

Striking demonstrations of the operation of gestalt laws at the expense of realistic perception have been provided by studies which minimized the impact of the objectively presented stimuli. When forms differ in brightness only slightly from their background (Hempstead, 1900), are perceived only for very short time durations (A. R. Granit, 1921; Koffka, 1935, p. 143; Perkins, 1932), are recalled a day, a week, or more after original perception (Wulf, 1922), are viewed on a slowly rotating background (Karwoski & Warrener, 1942), or appear as afterimages (Rothschild, 1923), then the forms undergo clear deformations: they are seen as simpler, more symmetrical, with rounded instead of pointed corners, with filled-in gaps, and devoid of most irregularities.

Yet, the degree to which the various laws of organization become manifested seems to depend not only on the conditions of perception but also on the qualities of the stimulus array. For example, an uncomplete triangle with a markedly acute angle at the apex tends to be completed in perception more often than an incomplete triangle with a less acute apex angle (Bobbitt, 1942). When the stimulus array allows organization along similarities of subparts in various aspects, people tend to organize the stimuli according to similarity in colors or size of forms more than in terms of similarities in direction of the forms, or their contours (Otis, 1918). The observations mentioned about the organization of discrete stimuli into the best possible gestalts suggest the existence of a striving for organization which may take the form of a need. It arises whenever there is no gestalt or an impaired gestalt in the visual field, and is satisfied whenever the grasped gestalt is good or whenever certain perceptual processes, even modifications, have occurred, so that an adequate organization has been brought about.

Gestalt psychologists designate this need by the term "the pressure of the gestalt," referring thereby to the felt aspect of the experience undergone upon looking at a bad or an incomplete gestalt. This pressure to straighten out, to improve, or to perfect the perceived figures may be so potent that it can be neither disregarded nor withstood by the spectator and is accompanied by tension and discomfort until it is resolved by a proper perceptual act. As Woodworth (1948, p. 117) aptly writes: "With the gap [in a gestalt] there is a condition of unbalanced tension, but closing the gap brings equilibrium," namely, a decrease of tension both in the perceptual field and in the perceiver. The power of this need for gestalts with the greatest possible prägnanz may also be inferred from the great difficulty we have in liberating ourselves from a certain gestalt once we have grasped it, be it a perceptual form (Hochberg & Silverstein, 1956), an idea, or a certain way of thought. Thus, in the sphere of concepts, this clinging to gestalts may be responsible for social prejudice stereotypes with all their attendant dangers, and it may sometimes take a genius to destroy a given gestalt, so that the field is again open for new constructions of solutions.

The Nature of the Striving for Good Gestalts

Gestalt psychologists tend to view the striving for good gestalts through perceptual organization as a manifestation of the general principle of dynamic self-regulation of the organism, namely, of the overall homeostatic tendency to produce and maintain external and internal equilibrium to the degree that circumstances allow. Thus, they assume that both the phenomenal field of vision and the sensory projection areas in the brain are energy fields striving for equilibrium (Köhler, 1940). There are two sets of antagonistic vectors operating in these fields: the cohesive forces, which press towards the state of maximum stability and minimum energy flow, represented ideally by a complete fusion of all stimuli; and the restraining forces which counteract the cohesive forces by pressing for segregation and disintegration of the stimuli. The greater the discrepancy between the cohesive and restraining forces, the greater the energy in the visual field and the more numerous the perceptual changes. The perceived figure is always the product of a balance attained between the cohesive and restraining forces. The balance usually does not eliminate all tension in the field, but it reduces it. According to Gestalt psychologists, these same processes are paralleled by corresponding physiological processes in the brain.[2]

Both the vectorial and physiological explanations offered by Gestalt psychologists suggest that gestalt perception is innate. Yet, although the capacity for perceiving gestalts may be innate, there can be little doubt that learning and experience play an important role in determining which gestalts one perceives. The influence of learning is evident not only in the ability to identify gestalts like the letters of a particular alphabet in spite of missing contours (Fig. 4.7), but also in the more basic organizational tendencies of perception. While people of the Western culture tend to see in inkblot cards of the Rorschach test percepts different in size or inclusiveness, primitive desert Moroccans tend to concentrate on tiny, scarcely perceptible details (Bleuler & Bleuler, 1935), while Samoans (Cook, 1942) largely neglect the detail and consider the whole blot as representing one percept, e.g., an animal or a map. Even optical illusions depend on specific prior experience. Congenitally blind people upon first regaining vision after surgery do not seem to be subject to many of the illusions characteristic for normals (Gregory & Wallace, 1963); and people from different cultures are illusion-prone to different degrees (Segall et al., 1966). On the other hand, the tendency to organize discrete stimuli into unities (Hebb, 1949) and the operation of the basic Gestalt laws with regard to simple good gestalts seem to be uniform and to vary but little across cultures (Michael, 1953). It is primarily with regard to more complex organizations that the effects of prior learning come to dominate. The tendency to organize stimuli into structured percepts which are the best possible gestalts under given circumstances is of immense importance for both men and animals. Organization in terms of similarities, closure, good continuation, or common direction facilitates perception and recognition of stimuli constellations, makes possible an efficient and relatively effortless grasp of information from the external world, and thus provides the basis for orientation in the environment in which we live. As a means of orientation, the perception of gestalts may be assumed to be pleasurable by resolving the tensions of disorientation evoked by chaos. The striving for organization is more than the tendency to perceive formally stable patterns. It is an "effort after meaning" (Bartlett, 1932) which provides for the perception of the most meaningful forms that circumstances allow. These may, indeed, sometimes be the famed simple geometrical figures, but at other times they may be highly complex designs or merely familiar objects (Bartlett, 1916) whose prägnanz derives more clearly from meaning.

Another way of stating this conclusion is embodied in the more recent attempts to reformulate the gestalt laws in terms of information theory (Attneave, 1954; Fitts & Leonard, 1957; Hochberg & McAlister, 1953). Starting with the assumption that information processing is the essence of

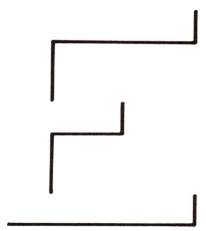

Fig. 4.7 Though a contour is missing, the capital letter E can be discerned by people who know the Latin alphabet.

perception, these investigators have demonstrated in various ways that good gestalts are visual patterns characterized by a high degree of redundancy or, conversely, by low degrees of uncertainty and randomness. For instance, if we know some part of a pattern which is a good gestalt, its other parts are predictable to a higher degree than the parts of a pattern which is not a good gestalt. Thus, organization in terms of gestalt laws makes for economy in the encoding of information, and allows us to grasp maximum information through a relative minimum of means and effort.

Simple and Complex Gestalts

What bearing do the principles of gestalt perception have upon the experiences of tension and relief evoked by forms in a painting? The intimate relevance of gestalt laws of organization to the experiencing of paintings is highlighted by an experiment which shows that people experience visual patterns as most pleasant when the level of illumination allows them to perceive the maximum possible degree of organization in the forms, while they reject as unpleasant glimpses of unorganized and unstructured forms (Wilcox & Morrison, 1933). This experiment confirms the conclusion that unorganized stimuli are experienced as much more tension-laden than stimuli organized into a relatively good gestalt. The striving for organization or the pressure towards the formation of gestalts constitutes the first moment of tension with regard to forms. The second major source of tension is bad gestalts, forms which deviate from the good gestalt, for they stimulate in the observer a striving for the good gestalt. Confronted with either unorganized stimuli or bad gestalts, the observer does his best under the given conditions to find a perceptual relief for the tension. As Koffka (1940) says, though "these conditions will not, as a rule, allow him to do a very good job (good, from the point of view of aesthetic harmony) . . . a work of art is made with that very idea." In other words, a painting is constructed, although not necessarily consciously, in such a way as to make possible the grasp of good gestalts and to dissolve through these the tensions aroused by worse ones.

Many investigators confirm that it is indeed the forms or structures with the qualities of good gestalts which are experienced as good figures, most pleasing, and least tension-laden. When subjects are asked, for instance, to draw a beautiful and pleasing line, they almost invariably present the line which is the best gestalt of its kind, i.e., they generally draw a smooth, continuous and straight line, and when they introduce change into it, they do so with repetition or rhythm, which again lends the line the character of prägnanz. On the other hand, when asked to present an ugly line, the subjects draw, as may be expected, an unorganized mass, lacking continuity, with mixed angles and curves, with intersections, and unrelated spaces—a figure, or rather a non-figure, which presents all the characteristics contrary to those which constitute prägnanz (Woodworth, 1938, p. 390).

In other studies subjects were asked to change visual patterns so as to make them good and pleasing forms. These studies show clearly that the simple good gestalts, such as the isosceles triangle, the circle, the hexagon, rectangle, and square are mostly left unaltered, which means that they arouse very little tension and are perceived as satisfactory, while open as well as asymmetrical designs are changed either into geometrically good gestalts or into familiar objects, mostly in accordance with the presented pattern (Lund & Anastasi, 1928; Mowatt, 1940). Further, people tend to evaluate simple and symmetrical patterns as beautiful and "strong," while they assess highly complex and asymmetrical forms as ugly and weak (Berlyne & Peckham, 1966; Eisenman, 1968). Moreover, it has been specifically demonstrated that the observation of visual patterns characterized by relatively high complexity, i.e., patterns which include a great number of different units arranged irregularly or asymmetrically, is accompanied by the usual indicators of heightened arousal, e.g., desynchronization of EEG (Berlyne & McDonnell, 1965) and increased incidence of the psychogalvanic skin response (Berlyne et al., 1963, 1964).

However, as may be expected, very simple and regular gestalts are considered by many people to be uninteresting, while more complex and less organized gestalts are evaluated as much more stimulating (Berlyne & Peckham, 1966; Day, 1965; Eisenman, 1966b). It is precisely the more complex as well as the worse gestalts which evoke more curiosity and a more intense and prolonged visual exploration than the more easily grasped simple and good gestalts. This is true of infants and children as well as of adults (Berlyne, 1958a; Berlyne et al., 1963; Smock & Holt, 1962). Evidently, the meaningful organization of more varied and larger sets of unfamiliar stimuli is a more difficult and tension-laden task than the identification of a simple form or a repetitive pattern. Yet, we may expect that people will sometimes prefer gestalts which are not maximally good and regular, precisely because they arouse tension which can later be resolved through a different and better organization of the same stimuli or of other present or imagined stimuli. In spite of the difficulties attendant upon defining complexity,[3] there seems to be evidence to support the conclusion that experience with art in general or with visual patterns in particular makes people prone to prefer the less regular and the more complex forms (Barron, 1953; McWhinnie, 1966; Munsinger & Kessen, 1964; Weber, 1931).

In line with our hypothesis about the crucial influence of habituation on developments in art (Chapter 2), it may be expected that the introduction of complex as well as bad gestalts into pictures must have occurred at a stage when the growing habituation of observers to simple and good gestalts necessitated the use of increasingly potent means for evoking tension. The history of art indeed provides support for this presumed sequence. The art of primitive peoples consists mainly of good gestalts, characterized by simplicity, closure, regularity, and symmetry. The rich material on primitive art accumulated by the anthropologist Boas testifies to "the general prevalence of the plane, the straight line, and regular curves such as the circle and the spiral" (Boas, 1955, p. 31), to the universal characteristics of symmetry (Boas, 1955, p. 32) and rhythmic repetition (Boas, 1955, p. 36), and to the widespread use of devices that accentuate the form, such as marginal patterns, thickening of rims or of contours, sharpening the crest, and overall arrangement of the forms in distinctly separated fields (Boas, 1955, p. 59). All of these features, according to Boas (1955, p. 32), may be "observed in the art of all times and all peoples" in its initial stages.

Boas seems to be genuinely astonished at this dominant concentration on simple and good gestalts, for they "are of rare occurrence in nature, so rare indeed, that they had hardly a chance to impress themselves upon the mind" (Boas, 1955, p. 31). However, it is precisely the contrast between the good gestalt and the relatively unorganized stimuli of everyday life which constituted the primal fascination of these artistic designs. The contrast must have been further reinforced by the fact that these works of art, far from being viewed on smooth canvases hung in harmoniously furnished museums, were presented against the background of crudely fashioned sur-

faces of pots, woven baskets, textiles, combs, dishes, weapons, boats, etc.—
that is, against a background of objects and instruments which neither in
surface nor in overall shape can be expected to exhibit the organization
and structure characteristics of prägnanz (Boas, 1955, pp. 17–62). Indeed,
it is this function of the visual arts—the presentation of good gestalts—
which lends meaning to the image of the artist as a god or a magician who
lures order out of chaos and vanquishes the formless by forms.

Even in so-called primitive art a significant development takes place in
the use of good gestalts, whose fascination undoubtedly decreased with
growing familiarity and habituation. The exclusive use of good gestalts is
by no means given up, but by greatly increasing their complexity an additional source of tension is introduced. The gestalt remains good, but
instead of being simple, it is now articulated and increasingly differentiated.
The simple and explicit structure of the good gestalt having become as
boring as a solution without a riddle or as the detailed explanation of a
joke, the design is now being made so elaborate that it obliges the observer
to study it carefully before he can grasp and enjoy its good organization.
A tension-laden interval is thus interposed before the relieving pleasure
of the grasp, which is consequently intensified. It is noteworthy that tension
is thus produced by a factor inherent in the work of art itself, and not by
the contrast between the work of art and its surroundings at large.

As the design grows more complex, another modification occurs. The
patterns now become much more confined to one or a few areas, instead
of spreading, as they did before, over most of the surface of an object
(Boas, 1955, pp. 57, 60, 62). Instead of a wide surface spotted or cluttered
with many separated fields, each consisting of a more or less simple design,
there are now only a very few concentration spaces of complex designs,
with empty areas or meager decorations between them. Thus, the spectator
is now required to penetrate rather than to follow, to understand rather
than simply to examine. The concentration of decorative designs within
limited spaces marks the origin of what painting was later to develop into,
namely, compositions of forms and colors, presented against a background,
from which they are separated and which serves to enhance their effects.

Through the progressive concentration of visual patterns in space and
in design, the picture emerged gradually as a whole endowed with gestalt
qualities. Yet, its parts, the forms and patterns in it, are of course also gestalts, albeit of a simpler kind. While in a simple gestalt, such as a square
or a circle, the parts have become more or less indistinct, in a complicated
gestalt such as a picture, the parts are distinguishable and exist in their
own right as subgestalts of the whole organization. Or more concretely,

although from the viewpoint of the whole gestalt it does not make much sense to consider the points of which the contour of a circle consists, it is still meaningful to talk about the circles and squares which constitute the picture gestalt.

The degree to which the various units in a painting are grasped as independent, interdependent, or dependent on the whole structure of the painting, is determined both by the organizational properties of the painting and by the perceiver's mode of perception (see note 3 to this chapter). A comparison of the responses of people to three types of visual patterns, i.e., simple good gestalts, complex good gestalts, and complex bad gestalts (Fig. 4.8), reveals that more than 90 percent of responses and associations to the first two groups of forms refer to the patterns as a whole, while only about 70 percent of the responses to the third group of forms are such "whole responses" (S. Kreitler, 1965, p. 179). Obviously, the latter forms evidenced a much lesser degree of organization and thus were grasped more often in terms of subgestalts.

By investigating the perception of differently constructed visual patterns, Otis (1918) elucidated some of the conditions which determine whether a perceiver will grasp a pattern as a unified whole or as a manifold of subwholes. The main conclusion of this ingenious series of studies is that the perception of the whole or of a manifold depends on the nature of the whole as well as of the parts. For example, when a pattern consists of a great number of dishomogeneous parts, varying in both form and color, an overall arrangement in the form of a rectangle is more conducive to the perception of a whole than an overall arrangement in the form of a circle or a triangle. This may possibly be the reason why most paintings actually are on rectangular canvases. If, however, the parts are fewer and if they differ only in form but not in color, triangular or circular arrangements facilitate grasping them as wholes better than rectangular arrangements. Moreover, Otis has shown that grouping by colors predominates most often, while grouping by forms, directions, or size occurs mainly under conditions when these factors are emphasized by the painter and rendered salient or central in the overall structure.

Paintings thus evidence various degrees of organizational schemes, which may be more or less suggestive for perceivers. For example, the clear mirror symmetry of so many medieval paintings can hardly be overlooked by observers and sets incomparably narrower limits to their freedom of organizing the units of these paintings than less evident organizations in paintings of later periods. The same holds for another feature of medieval paintings: construction in separate juxtaposed panels or clearly delineated spaces in

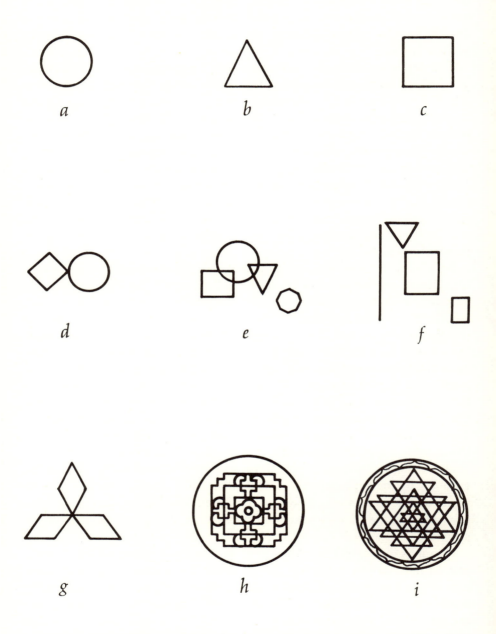

Fig. 4.8 In *a–c*, simple good gestalts; *d–f*, complex but not good gestalts; *g–i*, complex good gestalts (*h–i*, Indian mandalas in simplified form).

the framework of one panel. Such constructions encourage organization by several subwholes which may or may not be integrated by the perceiver. However, in accordance with the principle of habituation and the consequent demand for evoking increased tension within any tradition of painting the clearly spelled out directives for organization are gradually abandoned, and the divided panels are replaced by paintings with more intricate organizational schemes.

One course in which such a development may progress is highlighted in the following example from the history of painting: "In Andrea del Castagno's 'Last Supper,' each of the twelve apostles forms an isolated island, in Leonardo's 'Last Supper' they form groups of three, which again are inter-related by connecting gestures. In Rubens' 'Descent from the Cross' all the nine figures are intimately combined into one continuous flow of curves" (Koestler, 1949a, p. 403). What Koestler outlines here so succinctly and concretely, is in fact an extremely important development in painting. In the Del Castagno example, dating from the early fifteenth century, the subgestalts of the picture are clearly separated from each other and are self-subsistent in a way. In the late fifteenth century (Leonardo) some of the parts are already combined, while in the Rubens example from the second part of the sixteenth century the parts are almost merged into "one continuous flow of curves," as if the picture were no more articulated than is a unitary wavy line. This might at first glance be paradoxical, for fusion of parts is a characteristic of simple rather than of articulated gestalts. However, the fact that we find this very feature characterizing pictures at a certain level of historical development demonstrates that paintings may become so very compact and unified that, though articulated, they acquire as wholes the prägnanz properties of the simplest gestalts; which is only another way of saying that they are now truly good gestalts, in which "no line, no form, no color can anywhere be changed without detracting from the quality of the whole" (Koffka, 1940, pp. 247–48).

Tight organization may well be a characteristic of many masterpieces, but it may not evoke much tension in spectators who have grown used to discovering the hierarchization in the classical paintings. Indeed, the fact that modern paintings do not always evidence the compactness and clarity of structure achieved in many paintings of the thematic contents tradition may be due to the necessity of rediscovering these qualities whenever new means, new techniques, and new concepts are introduced into painting. Yet, the possibility that tight and clear organization in paintings has been abandoned in order to enhance tension cannot be ruled out. This is not to say that the modern paintings which are devoid of explicit object references lack organization. Rather, all too often they allow for a multiplicity of different organizations, each of which integrates the variety of presented forms into a meaningful whole. Thus an additional source of tension is created. There is not only the striving to integrate the various units of the painting into an encompassing whole but also the additional striving to integrate the various competing, equally valid wholes into a comprehensive experience.

Hence, there seems to be no unique meaning to the traditional maxim accepted by Vischer and Fechner that beauty consists of unity in variety. Discrete stimuli are organized into gestalts, the gestalts are organized into more or less extensive groupings, the latter in turn may be further organized, and the organizational principles themselves may again be organized into more and more encompassing unities. Yet, with every successive stage of development in painting, the units and the unity shift as observers become increasingly adept at uncovering the unity in the multiplicity. Possibly the best summary for this development is the interesting finding that when given the choice between Mondrian's painting *Composition with Lines* (1917) and a less organized pattern generated by a digital computer, 59 percent of the subjects liked the computer picture better. Moreover, since they expected modern paintings to be random designs, 82 percent even incorrectly guessed that the computer design was created by Mondrian (Noll, 1966).

The Use of Imperfection in Art

Some forms and relations between forms are notable for arousing more tension than others. An example of a tension-laden relation between figures is provided by *forms similar to each other* in size, shape, location, direction, or color (Chapter 2), but still perceptibly different. The tension evoked by such similar yet not identical forms is particularly strong when the forms are essentially simple gestalts and when they are placed near each other. Under these conditions the small dissimilarities between them are glaringly evident and are therefore experienced as much more disturbing than when the similarity is less remarkable. The reason for these phenomena, according to the laws of Gestalt psychology, is that the existence of almost identical figures in one and the same visual field evokes in the observer a strong striving for maximal prägnanz, i.e., for disregarding the small irregularities so that the almost similar forms would become fully identical and enter into a symmetrical and balanced overall gestalt. However, such deviations from identity can be disregarded only when they are small and trivial enough and are not accentuated through the contiguity of the forms. On the other hand, the deviations are readily accepted by the spectator if they are large and important enough. But, as they are small, though not small and trivial enough, or small but accentuated, the striving of the spectator cannot be fulfilled, and he remains both disturbed by the disharmony between the forms and attracted by the longing or hope for a possible solution. That is probably also the reason why faces in which there is a small asymmetry of this kind impress us as extremely stimulating and attractive. Many examples of this effect can be found in Mondrian's pictures, in which rectangles slightly differing in dimensions are placed side by side.

Another type of forms which are often experienced as highly tension-laden is the *incomplete figure*. Let us take first forms that are incomplete to a high degree, for instance, a "triangle" without an apex, an open "square," two parts of a curve which might be a circle. The striving for prägnanz is here at least as strong as for forms which are less incomplete, for the gap in the suggested but not presented gestalt is so great as to evoke an urgent demand for closure. Yet closure depends on a complex act of completion. It requires at the bare minimum a fusion between the principle of organization underlying the presented figure and an imagined schema of a form that would fit this organization. Both aspects of this process present interesting possibilities. The organizational principle may not be easy to determine. For example, in Kandinsky's picture (Plate 11) the set of lines on the right suggests a series of sharp-angled arrows, but also a network of intersecting lines. An observer may experience a figure as incomplete without immediately knowing exactly where the gap lies. Situations of this type are used in the well-known gestalt completion test by Street (1931). The schemas in accordance with which a figure can be completed are also by no means determinate. A triangle without an apex may as readily be completed into a trapezoid as into a triangle (Fig. 4.9). There is, however, no clear criterion of which completion is the best. Naturally, closure into a simple triangle conforms to expectation and is thus relieving, but closure into one figure consisting of two juxtaposed (Fig. 4.9d) or superimposed (Fig. 4.9g) triangles may be as good a solution and much more striking in the surprise it presents.

Painters make ample use of such creative solutions to closure problems. Some of the solutions may even be more tension-laden than the original incomplete figure. The triangle which is fitted into the central circle in

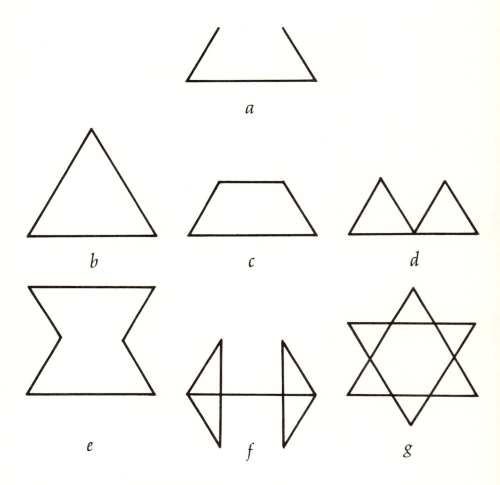

Fig. 4.9 In *b–g*, various closure possibilities for *a*.

Chagall's picture (Plate 16) is an example of such a tension-laden solution. Yet this solution does not exclude the expected completion into
a circle. It is also in line with other triangular elements in Chagall's
picture. When the outlines of the incomplete form are clear and suggestive
enough a painter may choose to omit altogether the expected solution and
rely on gestalt pressure for increasing the tension and on the perceiver for
identifying the missing parts. Such is the case in Matisse's picture (Plate
15). The three squares on the table clearly suggest what the missing part
is supposed to be. However, tension is further increased by contrasting
this implied solution of a square with the two presented circles. Car-

toonists also make ample use of this technique, which leaves the obvious untold and suggests the main point through implication. The effect of omission depends on the perceiver's ability to recognize the missing part. He may fail to do so when the gap in the figure is too big (Bobbitt, 1942), when the cues presented in the painting are not clear enough, or when he is not sufficiently trained in identifying incomplete forms, as may be the case with children (Gollin, 1960). Yet when he does identify the omission, the major moment of tension derives from the multiplicity of the possible closure solutions.

Similar determinants of tension are operative for figures which are complete formally, but are left *indeterminate* in that they do not present any clear-cut recognizable form and cannot be subsumed in any definite class of geometrical shapes. The problem posed by these figures is that they point, as it were, in too many directions at once, without suggesting any one direction in particular. For instance, an essentially circular form the curves of which are not smooth but somewhat angular may lead the observer first to round it out into an ellipse and then to realize the possibility of construing it also as an inflated or stretched-out rectangle.

Since all gestalts may be regarded as ultimately flowing into one another through a scale of changes (Fig. 4.10), forms which present transition points between good gestalts of several kinds are most likely to be experienced as foci of extreme tension. Such forms are perched, as it were, at the crossroads of paths leading to several possible completions. How tension-laden these forms may be is demonstrated by the fact that the necessity to pinpoint their identity may cause "experimental neurosis" in animals (Gantt, 1953), while the difficulty of tolerating their ambiguity may lead some people to prefer a clear-cut label at the price of distorted perception (Frenkel-Brunswik, 1949). For other people, such forms with an indeterminate identity offer the thrill of unsolved problems or undeciphered riddles whose resolution may involve the tension accompanying a creative act of perception or conceptualization. As in the case of incomplete figures, the solution suggested in the painting may clash with the solution expected by the observer and thus evoke both the tension of contrast and the pleasure of resolution.

Another example in this context is offered by *oblique and unbalanced forms*. A triangle with its apex down is experienced as less stable than a triangle with its apex up. An oblique line is grasped as a tipped vertical or a displaced horizontal (Radner & Gibson, 1935). Many forms when seen in unusual positions are not recognized (Gibson & Robinson, 1935). These findings illustrate the Gestaltist tenet that every form is a product

Fig. 4.10 Stepwise gradations from circle through triangle to square.

of forces and exists in a field of forces. Only in this sense can a form seem stable or precariously balanced. The orientation of a form in space and the position and directionality of lines are thus integral characteristics of the gestalt. The claim that the right or normal position in space is learned may be true with regard to familiar objects, but is hard to defend in the case of geometrical forms and particularly of random asymmetrical shapes. Even the latter are clearly perceived as having a dominant axis and a center of gravity (Michels & Zusne, 1965, p. 79), and thus they may be perceived as tipped or stable (Radner & Gibson, 1935). An oblique form which is perceived as tilted, either because it deviates from its normal expected position or because it is nonaligned with the major axes of the painting in which it appears (Kopfermann, 1930), arouses a striving to set it right. If the tilt is minor, there is a tendency to overlook it, but the tension is strongest and the tilt is overestimated when it is small enough to suggest the right position, yet not so small as to be overlooked (Radner & Gibson, 1935).

Almost all the types of tension-laden forms discussed above exemplify the tension which derives from the contrast between an implied or imagined good gestalt and a presented form which is not a good gestalt. But note that what a good gestalt may be in a particular instance depends on the context. A circle is universally considered a good gestalt. In comparison with it, the contour of a human face is undoubtedly a very bad gestalt: it is neither regular nor symmetric nor simple, concise, balanced. Nevertheless, it is precisely this bad gestalt which is the best one in the context of a human figure. In drawing a man, if we put on top of a well-proportioned body a perfect circle instead of the irregular form of a face, the otherwise good gestalt of the circle will strike us as a very bad gestalt. For the same reason we experience as so tension-laden the abnormally elongated human faces characteristic of El Greco's and Modigliani's pictures. To illustrate the effects of context it might suffice to imagine a single inverted lopsided cone, and a series of such cones. Being embedded in a repetitive pattern, the bad gestalt of the single cone becomes endowed with certain qualities of a good gestalt. Similarly, an ellipse in a context of circles or even a circle in a context of ellipses will be experienced as a bad gestalt.

Finally, tension may be created not only through contrasting various worse gestalts with good gestalts, or good gestalts with expected gestalts, but also through two or more dissimilar forms. A picture dominated by the forms of a circle and an arrow (e.g., Kandinsky's painting, Plate 11) or of a sharp angle and the curve (e.g., Chagall's painting, Plate 16) poses a problem which calls for a solution. One type of solution is represented by integration of the two forms in the framework of one good gestalt. Several notable examples of such resolutions, mostly fascinating in their perfection, can be found in well-known religious and magical symbols, such as the Indian mandalas, in which the circle is combined (Fig. 4.8i) with the triangle or the square (Fig. 4.8h). In a painting, however, a number of solutions are suggested, presented, variated, and sometimes combined with each other.

No less potent sources of tension may be created in painting through contrasts of lines or forms in direction, size, and position, or through contrasts of surfaces in texture, density, etc.[4] The principles of tension evocation and of relief production would in these cases be similar to those described above, with the ever-present possibilities of increasing tension through omitting the obvious and enhancing relief through surprising and original resolutions.

Variation, Symmetry, and Balance

In our discussion about creating tension and relief by means of forms, one principle was basic: a gestalt can be changed, in a greater or lesser number of its features, and still retain its identity. It is precisely this transposability of gestalts that is the essence of the artistic technique of variation. The technique, which can best be understood through Gestalt principles, is so basic that some art theoreticians have identified it with art itself or at least with the greater part of it.

Variation consists essentially in the introduction of changes in some elements of a form with the simultaneous conservation of unvarying elements. It is generally defined as the development of a theme or the unfolding of a motif through presenting it in successively different versions, all of which may be grasped as interrelated through their basic derivation from and exemplification of the original theme. This original theme, which in the context of painting may be a line in a certain direction, a point in a specific color, or a geometrical or random closed figure, is then grasped as a good gestalt. This means that there is a striving to retain it and a resistance to altering it. Changes in this gestalt through its variated restatements are thus grasped as worse gestalts in comparison with the original good gestalt, and consequently evoke tension. Nevertheless, the original gestalt is also the factor which remains responsible for the ultimate cohesion of the overall series of variations, since otherwise they would have been experienced as autonomous units, unrelated to each other.

The simplest case of variation is repetition. In a repetition the original gestalt is changed only in its location in space. Recognition of the gestalt is thus easy, the change is very small, the relation of the variation to the original is obvious, and the tension through comparison and the striving for integration are minimal.

In a picture, variations occur mostly through changes in size, form, direction, location, and color or some of these simultaneously. For instance, one may start with an angle, then present it inverted or tipped to any desirable degree, change one of its sides to a curve, diminish or increase the length of its sides or even the angle itself, cross or divide it by means of other lines or forms, and obviously also place some such angles in various contrasted positions so that a new figure such as a variety of a rectangle is produced. Kandinsky's picture (Plate 11) contains a wealth of variations on the themes of a sharp angle and of the curve. Matisse's picture (Plate 15) is dominated by variations on the inverted V, and to cite still another example, Cézanne's picture (Plate 10) illustrates a series of variations on the theme of a sharp-angled triangle, represented by the spacing between the trees.

If the theme in a painting is emphasized through centrality or salience in another respect, it is relatively easy to identify. Yet, in some pictures any of the variations may be grasped as a theme, and in other pictures no single pattern can be unequivocally identified as the theme. In them the theme is left for the observer to infer by abstraction as the denominator common to the variations presented.

By means of variation dramatic plots can be introduced into a picture. A gestalt can be endowed with new meanings, deepened, and enriched as one or another of its aspects or facets is made salient through modification of its components or through change of place and context. In the course of transformations, transfigurations, and transpositions a gestalt may undergo a complete metamorphosis, as it were; it may finally be completely destroyed by disruption, dissolution, or a sudden tension-laden break; it may be "born," integrated, or constructed, reborn or reconstructed; it may even be made to marry happily, that is, to merge with another gestalt that has undergone its own transmutations. All of these possibilities may also serve to enhance the symbolism of the picture as representing human ways and fates, on the level of reality as well as on those of wishes and wish fulfillments.

A variation can of course be unfolded step by step with steady continuity, as well as by means of sudden shifts. Some phases of the variation are, however, mostly forgone in art, others are expanded, and still others are only hinted at. Obviously, the more phases presented, the less thrilling or exciting the sequence. Overt patterns of variations quickly become boring. Therefore, as may be expected, the developmental trend in painting has been towards increasing implicitness in the variation of gestalts. The already familiar phases are forgone or skipped, and fewer steppingstones, as it were, are presented for the spectator to combine into a gestalt, namely, to grasp as a sequence of variations upon a single original theme. The spectator is called upon to fill in the gaps, to reproduce gestalts, and thus to become an accomplice of the artist.

Though any single variation represents a deviation from the presented or implied theme and is therefore a source of tension, yet the variations all share the invariable common element of the basic theme. If, thanks to this constant element, they are grasped as a series of variations, the tension deriving from the changes is reduced. Variation may also be applied in ways which greatly enhance relief. Most notable among these are presentation in a serial pattern or in a symmetrical form.

Although all too often serial patterns and symmetry are confused with each other, the distinction between them is rather clear. Symmetry consists of left-right or up-down mutual mirror reflections of a theme, juxtaposed to one another, while in a serial pattern the repetitions should neither be reflections nor be strictly juxtaposed. Naturally, the two means may be combined in a variety of ways, e.g., the theme of symmetry may be a serial pattern, and a serial pattern may consist of a series of symmetrical elements.

In its simplest form a serial pattern consists of a chain of repetitions of the same form such as may be found in many ornaments. Yet this example certainly falls short of demonstrating the immense possible variety of serial patterns. For in art the basic element of the series is usually variated, as in the triangle series in the upper right part of Chagall's (Plate 16) painting, or the series of inverted V's in Matisse's (Plate 15) painting. Vasarely's picture (Plate 1) illustrates how the serial pattern of variations of the same simple form not only creates the effects of depth and movement but even produces a wholly new form. Serial patterns may be further complicated by subjecting the variations to specific laws, for instance, sequential or consecutive progressions, which characterize many Op Art productions.

Since the time of the Greeks, and even more intensely in recent decades, mathematically oriented artists and art theoreticians have attempted to demonstrate not only that every work of art is based essentially on serial patterns of variations of basic forms but that art, especially in the technical era, should rest on such variations of basic good forms, sometimes called modules (e.g., Kepes, 1966; Schillinger, 1948). The major response to these arguments seems to be that such patterns indeed evoke tension by means of variation and by frustrating aroused expectations (e.g., see the church cupola as the last element in the triangle series and as a part of the background series of curves in Plate 16) and that they provide relief by means of their rather obvious unitary principle and rhythm; yet there are also many other means with very potent experiential effects at the disposal of the visual arts.

Symmetry in the arrangement of forms is certainly a most basic and straightforward means of relief. It endows a whole structure with the quality of balance characteristic of good gestalts and introduces redundancy to a degree which greatly facilitates perception and understanding. These conclusions seem more convincing than the other suggested explanations for the relief provided by symmetry as, for instance, that it is due to a presumed desire for equal muscular innervation in both parts of the spectator's body (Puffer, 1903) or to an assumed need for balancing attention and eye movements (Valentine, 1962).

Since symmetry is a quality of good gestalts, there should be little wonder that it dominates so many of the early art products and paintings of former cultures from Sumer to Latin America and from ancient Persia and Greece to the beginnings of the medieval period. There should also be little surprise that so few later products in art manifest strict symmetry (Puffer, 1903). Indeed, if the factors of habituation and the consequent necessity to increase tension play any role in the development of art, then it is to be expected that strict symmetry will gradually be loosened up and modified by some variation. In the beginning the departures from symmetry are slight, even hidden. Yet since "even in asymmetric designs one feels symmetry as the norm from which one deviates" (Weyl, 1952, p. 13), the new source of tension was bound to be pursued. The product of this development is variously called "substitutional symmetry" (Puffer, 1903), "symmetry" (Platt, 1961; Speiser, 1960; Weyl, 1952), or more accurately, balance. The principle of this development consists in the replacement of symmetry by experiential balancing.

Some basic manifestations of balancing were uncovered through experiments in which people were asked to place various forms in a pleasing manner, to complete partial arrangements of forms, or to judge the pleasingness of completed arrangements. These studies show, for example, that in order to produce a balanced impression, lines of greater length or narrowness, figures of greater area, and darker colors have to be placed nearer to the center of a square background than shorter or wider lines, smaller figures, and brighter colors, respectively (Legowski, 1908; Pierce, 1894, 1896). Puffer (1903) found a tendency to locate larger forms nearer the center than smaller forms, outline drawings nearer the center than blank rectangles, stamps that were changed for each trial than unchanged stamps, a picture favoring depth perception than a two-dimensional flat picture, and forms that suggested outward movement than forms that suggested inward movement (also Valentine, 1962, pp. 102–3). Further, Angier (1903) showed that a short expanse of densely placed vertical squiggles balanced a longer expanse of monotonous horizontal parallel lines, and Rowland (1907) demonstrated that bigger and heavier-seeming forms are placed in the lower part of an area to compensate for the relative instability of forms in the upper area.

Findings of this type lend support to some of the simpler practices long used by painters in most painting traditions. Yet it would be futile to expect most paintings to exhibit perfect geometrical or mechanical balance. One major conclusion suggested by the studies mentioned is that interest in and meaning of a form serve to increase its experiential "weight." But while in some pictures with explicit object references it is still possible to guess what may be the more meaningful elements, in paintings without such object references the determination of meaning, and hence of meaningfulness, rests more with the observer. Thus, the task of balancing the painting as part of the more comprehensive task of organizing meaningfully the stimuli presented in a painting devolves increasingly on the observer, who thus becomes a participant creator of the painting.

Foreground, Background, and Depth

The balance of a picture as it is experienced depends to a great extent on the process of centering in perception, i.e., the grasp of interrelations between the presented forms and planes. A common manifestation of centering consists in the articulation into nearer and farther surfaces. In every act of perception some of the forms spring into the foreground while others lie, as it were, in the background, which serves as a kind of screen upon which the inspected figures appear and from which they seem to be separated. Which forms are perceived in the foreground and which in the center of observation depend in part on the spectator, though the artist probably attempts to make his own centering predominate. The spectator's decision is based mainly on the salience of some figures, which may be brought about by means of enhanced colors, clarity of form, definiteness of contour, originality of outline, articulateness of the gestalt, its size, location, density, convexity, etc. (Rubin, 1921). Of course, the meaning of the forms also plays its part in the decision. In general there is no difficulty in deciding what is foreground and what is background. By means of centering, separated parts of the picture may be brought into experiential contiguity, and contiguous parts of the picture may be separated into foreground and background. The centering may also occur on different levels of inclusiveness, so that what may have served as a background to a figure in the lower corner of the picture may at another centering appear as foreground, together with forms from other parts of the picture.

In a few cases, the articulation into foreground and background may be more difficult, particularly when the background, if turned into foreground, may also be meaningful. Such figures, known in general psychology as "ambiguous figures" with a "reversible contour," exhibit the interesting phenomenon of frequent shifting of roles between foreground and background in the course of observation. The reversibility may be enhanced by such means as verticality of the decisive contour and sharp contrasts of brightness or color between figure and background (Woodworth, 1938, pp. 629–34). Shifting as well as the occasional simultaneous perception of both figure and background (Page, 1968) are unstable perceptual states accompanied by tension. However, this means of dynamization of the picture is rarely used in art. More frequent is the use of a contour common to two forms, whose ambiguous role may be tension-evoking but not to the same degree as a reversible contour (Hochberg, 1964).

In general, the background of any figure is more relieving than the form which serves as the figure. This is probably so, first, because anything which · is not particularly attended to cannot be as tension-laden as something which at the moment engages attention; and secondly, because the background usually serves to enhance tension precisely in what is then the figure. The last factor also operates for the picture as a whole on its own background, namely, the wall. The process may thus help to explain why forms outside a picture fail to arouse the intense experience that they are liable to stimulate when appearing within the framework of a picture.

Even though it is a function of the background to intensify or concentrate the tension in the figure, figure and background are so tightly interwoven that from a certain viewpoint they may be regarded as one gestalt. Any figure stands in need of a background, and a background can only be what it is in relation to a figure. In view of this intimate bond between the two, it may then be claimed that the relation between the figure and its ground is in itself tension-laden, for it poses for the spectator the problem of integrating them in one perceptual act. The same factor of tension is operative regardless of the level of inclusiveness of the particular figure and ground. Yet all of these tensions aroused by the partial figures and backgrounds in the picture are ultimately integrated in the overall gestalt of the picture as a whole. As an integrated gestalt it includes all of the less extensive possible foregrounds and backgrounds, and as a good gestalt it should lead to the dissolution of the tension thus aroused.

It should not be overlooked that foreground and background are mere abstractions of the more complicated situation which exists in many pictures with depth effects. In such pictures there are usually more than two planes, conjured up by means of a whole set of spatial cues (Abbot, 1950; A. Ames, 1925; Arnheim, 1954; Schlosberg, 1941) which are at the disposal of painters. The introduction of additional planes and depth directions introduces further possibilities of evoking tension. Some of these depend on the fact that the creation of depth effects through overlapping, foreshortening, etc., necessitates far-reaching departures from good gestalts in the depicting of the forms (Arnheim, 1954, chaps. 3 and 5). Yet, more important in the present context are the tension-laden effects produced by the simultaneous representation of spaces from various points of view. Relatively simple cases of such simultaneity include the examples of pictures in which the perspectival center of the depicted scene does not coincide with the center of the painting (e.g., Leonardo's *Last Supper*), or pictures in which the space of the scene as viewed by the spectator differs from the represented space which is depicted from the viewpoint of a figure in the painting (e.g., Tintoretto's *Finding of the Body of St. Mark*). Greatly complicated cases include examples of more recent pictures in which objects in the same space are depicted in terms of non-corresponding perspectival laws—e.g., surrealist paintings by Dali or Di Chirico; pictures which portray familiar objects from unusual observation angles or in a theoretical fantasy space—e.g., Abstract Expressionism (Donnell, 1964); or Cubist paintings in which views of an object from different hypothetical angles of vision and even its internal structure are superimposed one on another. The growing difficulty of integrating the differential spatial views corresponds to the developmental trend we have repeatedly observed in painting: the ever-present demand to devise new means for evoking tension by sharpening contrasts and omitting the obvious.

Although Gestalt psychology has enabled us to understand many of the effects exerted by forms, we nevertheless remain in "tension." We have seen how potent figures can be in evoking tension and affording relief and can now understand how a picture by Kandinsky composed of several angles and curves can arouse an even more intense experience than a crowded battle picture; but there is much more to be said about forms. Until now, in accordance with our self-imposed limitations, we have regarded forms as personally neutral to the spectator, merely exerting their pressure, evoking strivings for prägnanz, and standing in various interrelations with one another. We will now repeal this limitation and proceed with the aim of widening our view and deepening our understanding of the processes of experiencing forms in art.

5. *Meaning of Lines and Forms*

Associations and Preferences

In everyday language, compositions of points or lines are called forms and
not gestalts. We may therefore infer that form is a more inclusive term than
gestalt, and so, by the way, also a vaguer term. Although the concept of
gestalt refers to the basic organization of a form, it is only partly inclusive
in the domain of art, for spectators bring into the observation of forms in
a picture not only their capacity to perceive gestalts but also other modes of
perception and meaning determination by which they endow the perceived
gestalts with additional dimensions of experience.

One such dimension, obvious in process, frequent in occurrence, and
variable in its manifestations, consists of the associations which the observer
may have to the forms he sees. According to Rodin, a beautiful landscape
is interesting, not only because of the more and less agreeable impressions it
evokes, for instance, on the level of the forms as better and worse gestalts,
"but first and foremost through the representations which it arouses. . . . In
the silhouette of trees, in the shape of an horizon, the great landscapists
have recognized thoughts, light-hearted or serious . . . peaceful or anxiety-
laden, which correspond with their own mood" (Rodin, 1918, p. 216). The
same is true of any spectator of a picture. The figures may remind him of
personal events, objects, or emotions, and also of forms and shapes whose
meaning is rooted in more widely shared experiences. Thus on the personal
level of associations, a square may arouse the image of a certain visiting card,
a box, or the window in one's childhood bedroom, while a circle may stimulate the memory of a street sign, a disc, a cherished medal, or the crown of
a certain tree. On the level of more interpersonally shared associations a
pointed angle is apt to evoke the image of a knife, a spear, or any sharpened
object which may cause injury, in contrast to a curve, which is likelier to
evoke representations of calm waves of water, of gentle caressing movements, of the agreeable cool smoothness of rounded objects.

These more or less conscious associations stem, as we noted in reference
to colors (Chapter 3), from the involvement of the form in a situation which
carries personal or culturally shared meanings, so that this form has come
to represent that situation. Sometimes, although perhaps less frequently than
in the case of colors, the association may be to the form in its function as a

sign commonly used by a certain community. Thus, certain forms may remind spectators of the alphabetic letters of a language, of numerals, of old heraldic emblems, of the cross or other religious symbols, of professional signs in the fields of mathematics, botany, etc., of national emblems on flags, and the like.

In general, the sensations of tension or relief and other moods accompanying such associations are transferred by the spectator to the forms he actually sees in the picture. The intensity of the aroused feelings depends of course on a variety of factors, for instance, the intensity of the original experience which has given rise to the association, the range of meanings which in the course of time have come to be attached to the form by the spectator, the earliness of the association, and the vividness of the memory.

The associations may sometimes follow the perception of the gestalt, while at other times they may even direct perception, so that the gestalt springs into focus. It may also happen that associations lag behind the evoked feelings to which they are bound. For there are some associations which arise very readily together with the accompanying feelings, while others emerge only gradually into full consciousness from a state of vagueness or of concentration, as it were, at a nodal point of tension, as yet unidentified. In such cases of repressed associations it may happen that the spectator even intentionally calls up an association, though not necessarily the original one, in order to account for the emotion evoked by a form in a picture. In this event, the currently evoked association is apparently related more to the emotion and only indirectly to the form in the picture.

It may be expected that forms stripped of explicit object references may stimulate even more associations and of greater variety than forms suggestive of specific objects (Vanderplas & Garvin, 1959). Similarly, while the clear-cut form of a tree tends to restrict associations to the theme of trees or settings in which they have been seen, the form of a circle on top of a vertical line is potentially more likely to evoke associations to a great many things outside the realm of trees. Apart from resemblance to a specific object, there seem to be other factors that determine the amount of associations that forms evoke. Forms with many curves (Arnoult, 1960; Edelman, 1960) and symmetrical forms (Arnoult, 1960; Edelman, Karas, & Cohen, 1961; Munsinger & Kessen, 1964) seem to elicit more object associations than rectilinear and asymmetrical forms, respectively. Curvature and symmetry are also important factors in determining whether a form seems familiar to the observer (Arnoult, 1960; Zusne & Michels, 1962 a, b). With regard to random asymmetrical and rectilinear forms, it appears that forms with few or a moderate number of objectively distinct units (Chapter 4, note 3) elicit more associations than forms with a great number of such units (Eisenman, 1966a; A. G. Goldstein, 1961; Vanderplas & Garvin, 1959).

Associations seem to play a major role in determining the preferences of people for various forms. A person may reject a form when it reminds him of a human face, but may like it as a visiting card or a cigarette case (Barnhart, 1940; Haines & Davies, 1904; Legowski, 1908; Martin, 1906). Owing, however, to the ambiguity of the task of expressing preferences, the subjects may base their judgments on principles different from association, such as formal criteria, symbolic meaning, familiarity with the design, etc. (Barnhart, 1940; Haines & Davies, 1904; Wiley, 1940). The variability in responses is thus so great that the reported averages can hardly be taken to represent group preferences (Austin & Sleight, 1951; Valentine, 1962, pp. 73–75). For the same reasons the persistent attempts to prove the existence of universally shared preferences for specific visual forms have produced up to date evidence which is anything but convincing (Jahoda, 1956; M. Lawler, 1955; McElroy, 1954). The best-known attempts of this kind—and they are far from successful—are the attempts to demonstrate preferences for the venerable Golden Section or other figural proportions, such as Hambidge's (1920) "dynamic symmetry" of the irrational root rectangles, and the more recent attempts to anchor figural beauty in some version of Birkhoff's (1933) formula of complexity and order.[1]

Symbolic Meanings of Forms

When people are confronted with the task of expressing the personal meaning which various forms (e.g., Fig. 4.8a–i) have for them, responses vary along the whole range of symbolic meaning dimensions (S. Kreitler, 1965). These meanings include not only associations to objects and situations but also sensations, moods and feelings, abstract concepts, metaphors, and symbols. For example, a response such as, "the spiral is like life—a series of repetitions on consecutively higher levels" is metaphoric, while a response like "the wavy line is soft and happy" includes reference to sensations and feelings.

As in the case of colors, some of the meanings carried by lines and forms seem to be widely, possibly even cross-culturally, shared. Our language contains examples of some such meanings which seem almost self-evident (S. E. Asch, 1958), e.g., a person may have a *crooked* or *rigid* character, or may even be a *square* and yet move *up* in society; if he thinks *straight*, we might decide to include him in the *circle* of our friends even though he makes *sharp* remarks and may sometimes be *down*. A great number of studies show not only the readiness with which people express meanings through forms and grasp the meanings of forms but also the high consensus which characterizes these meanings.

Studies of expression usually apply the method of asking people to draw lines which may denote specific meanings. Concentrating on clusters of adjectives signifying various emotions and moods, Lundholm (1921), one of the early investigators in this domain, found that most of his subjects tended to represent the meaning of "sad," "melancholy," "doleful," and "sorrowful" by lines that were directed downward from left to right, while they represented gayness by lines that were either horizontal or directed up from left to right. In general, this and other studies show that people express agitated emotions like "raging" (Krauss, 1930), "angry," "furious" (Peters & Merrifield, 1958), "hate," and "wild pain" (Hippius, 1959) and situations like "massacre" (Scheerer & Lyons, 1957) by irregular, jagged, and sharp-angled lines, while they express the more quiescent states of mind, e.g., happiness, graveness, or idleness, through gently curving or relatively straight lines. However, as Werner & Kaplan (1963, chaps. 22–24) showed, abstract conceptions and conceptual or grammatical relations can also be represented through lines in a manner which communicates the meaning to others rather reliably. For example, the past tense is expressed by a down-sloping arrow, the future by an upward directed line, "and"-relations through contact and intersection of lines. These representations take as a rule the form of expression indicated by one or another of the meaning dimensions (S. Kreitler, 1965; S. Kreitler & Kreitler, 1968). Obviously, the meaning of the referent must first be determined in terms of "a situation," "a scene," "a metaphor," "consequences of the indicated action," etc., before it can be expressed through spatial relations, forms, and lines.

Other studies concentrated on investigating the consensus in grasping the meaning of various lines and figures. Using line drawings prepared by other subjects as representations for concepts such as iron, silver, and gold, Krauss (1930) found that up to 80 percent of his German subjects matched gold with regularly curved or wavy lines, and iron with regularly square forms. Besides confirming these findings with American subjects, Scheerer & Lyons (1957) found high consensus in matching a mood like "happy" with upwardly directed, open, curved, lightly drawn and repetitive patterns; a trait like "proud" with straight, heavy, regular, and upward lines; and a concept like "forever" with regular and simple patterns of horizontal straight and open lines. Concerning the matching of emotions with line drawings, Poffenberger & Barrows (1924) found the expected general trend for sadness to be coupled with slightly curved down-sloping

lines, serenity and tranquillity with horizontal lines, cheerfulness with undulating horizontal or ascending lines, and vivacity, agitation, and anger
with angular and curved lines. High unanimity was found also with regard
to abstract concepts (K. R. L. Hall, 1951; K. R. L. Hall & Oldfield, 1950).
"Philosophy," for example, is regarded as expressed more fittingly by a
regular spiral than by the intersection of lines, while "crisis" is better represented through a jagged outline than by a rounded square enclosing another square (McMurray, 1958).

Another line of investigation is suggested by the practice of graphology.
For a long time it has been known that various features of handwriting may
denote specific characteristics of the writer, and that drawing style may
be used for diagnostic purposes (e.g., Biedma & D'Alfonso, 1959; K. Koch,
1954). However, more important in our context are the repeated demonstrations that people untrained in graphology show much agreement in
identifying by handwriting traits such as anxiety and compulsivity (Castelnuovo-Tedesco, 1948), and even the sex of the writer (Eisenberg, 1938).

An interesting modification of the graphological method was applied by
Tagiuri (1960), who asked his subjects to imagine the character of people
likely to move according to the "paths" formed by various lines. In spite
of variability in expression, unanimity of responses was again the rule. The
straight horizontal line, for example, was seen as expressive of the rational,
goal-oriented, practical, determined, and persevering type of person; the
archlike line was interpreted as characteristic of people who are somewhat
unsure, undecided, thoughtful, unhurried, casual, and complacent; while
a very curved roundabout pattern was made to stand for the immature,
emotional, careless, disjointed, confused and happy-go-lucky person. The
interpretations varied somewhat, although not basically, when the goal of
the imaginary path was later specified as desirable or undesirable.

The findings just described testify to the generality of some meanings of
forms, mostly within the boundaries of one culture. Yet there is experimental evidence that meanings of forms are shared by people in various cultures. The most ambitious effort in this direction was made by Osgood
(1960) and his associates (Jakobovits, 1969), who used in their studies the
method of the Semantic Differential. Osgood (1960) found that Anglo-
Saxon Americans, Navajo Indians, and Japanese people all regard crooked
lines as denoting concepts like "bad" and "noisy," thin lines as denoting
concepts like "woman," "white," "fast," and "weak," and rounded forms
as denoting "calm." In the same vein, Jakobovits (1969) showed that
Americans, Hindis, Finns, Germans, and Japanese all tend to evaluate symmetrical in contrast to asymmetrical drawings as good, pleasant, sweet,

beautiful, and happy. Similarly, directions and regions in space—e.g., up and down, left and right—and differences in size—e.g., large and small—seem to share a range of common meanings.

When one considers that because of cultural differences similar meanings of forms may be couched in dissimilar terms, the unanimity in the meanings of forms becomes even more striking. Mythologies, religions, folklore, rituals, legends, and literary sources provide all too many examples of the universal significance of some forms, in spite of the differences in conceptualization. The *triangle*, for instance, was regarded in ancient Egypt as sacred and as a symbol for the godhead (Jung, 1958, p. 3), in Greece it represented wisdom, for Christianity it has served as a sign of the Holy Trinity, and in India, as the symbol of creativity and energy (Zimmer, 1962, pp. 147–48). All these meanings obviously share the common denominator of striving up and away from earthliness, dullness, and blunted routine. Similarly the *square* has often been regarded as having the special significance of setting limits, ordering chaos, and stabilizing permanent flux (Jacobi, 1959, p. 166). We can see this meaning recurring in China, where the square stood for the earth; in India, where it was identified with the mandala, the protected and sacred precinct; and in gnosticism, which viewed the square as the soul itself, the first mortal human being, as well as the matrix for the birth of the "immortal Adam" (Jung, 1958, §594).

Yet an inspection of time-honored figural symbols in various cultures reveals that most do not consist of a simple good gestalt like the square or the circle. The cross, the swastika, various mandalas (Fig. 4.8g, h), the yin-yang symbol, all present some kind of good gestalt combination of at least two simpler gestalts. Starting from this observation, S. Kreitler (1965, Part IV, Exp. I) showed that the combination of two simple gestalts is grasped as expressive of contrast or conflict. When confronted with the task of matching simple concepts or statements of conflicts with simple or complex gestalts, people tend overwhelmingly to couple simple concepts with simple gestalts and conflict statements with complex gestalts. However, further experiments (S. Kreitler, 1965, Part IV, Exp. II), in which people were asked to express freely the meaning of various forms, showed that complex good gestalts, formed through the combination of two simple gestalts, not only express a conflict but also and foremost suggest a resolution of the conflict. For example, if a simple circle represents, metaphorically, infinite freedom, and a simple square represents restriction and limitation, a mere juxtaposition of these two forms may be grasped as representing the conflict between these two concepts (Fig. 4.8a–d). A good gestalt combination of the two forms in a mandala (Fig. 4.8h) may reflect not only the conflict but also suggest solutions, such as that human freedom consists in awareness of limitations or their transcendence. Thus, complex good gestalts (Fig. 4.8g–i) are more likely to be grasped as true symbols, containing a problem and its solution, than simple gestalts (Fig. 4.8a–c)—as it were, a solution without a problem—and mere juxtapositions (Fig. 4.8g–i)—a problem but no figural solution. Simple forms which also lend themselves to symbolic interpretations, although to a smaller degree, include the *spiral*, with its double meaning of progression and withdrawal, repetition and change, extension and limitation; the *dot*, which is the modest conceptual origin and the end of all; or the pointed *Gothic arch*, which combines the soft roundness of the circle with the triangle's determined upward striving to the apex.

Accordingly it appears justified to conclude that forms in pictures may evoke a wide range of interpersonally shared meanings whose formulation may be colored by personal dispositions and cultural conceptualization, and whose nature depends on structural features of the forms themselves.

Archetypes, Synesthesia, and Dynamization

In the preceding section we have seen that some of the meanings of forms are shared by people in various cultures and historic periods. What may be the determinants of these meanings? One theory, greatly preferred by psychologically oriented art theoreticians, attempts to anchor these meanings in archetypes. The concept of archetype was, indeed, applied by Jung first to forms, and only later to all kinds of patterns and happenings in the biological, psychobiological, and general ideational domains.[2] According to Jung (1956b, 1958), an archetype is a kind of schema which is rooted in the collective unconscious and which becomes manifest through symbols.

Although Jung states merely that archetypes are genetically inherited, his theory points towards a possible connection of archetypes with basic and recurring human experiences of physical, social, and possibly cosmic nature. We could thus implement the Jungian conception by suggesting that the symbolic meaning of the vertical upward direction is grounded in a sort of racial "memory," reinforced for each human being by his experience of adopting the upright posture; or that the symbolic meaning of the circle is correlated with the age-old imprint of a round sun as the source of life and energy.

Another line of thought concerning the generally shared meanings of forms leads us back to the synesthetic mode of perception. Forms, like colors, enter into a variety of predominantly synesthetic relations. Some of these are direct, which means that in response to certain forms some spectators are likely to experience definite and constant sensations which are usually elicited by stimuli other than forms. Yet, spectators who do not actually experience these sensations can also imagine or otherwise evoke them as associations (Karwoski, Odbert, & Osgood, 1942). Many people have undoubtedly had the experience that angles may be sharp or prickly, that lines may be soft or rough, and that certain figures are light and bright while others are dark and heavy. Karwoski et al. (1942) have shown that many people regard large, thick, angular, upward directed, and distinct forms as corresponding to loudness in music, while they see small, thin, angular, and straight-lined forms as equivalent to fast music. Similar observations have been made with regard to sounds in language: small, light, and pointed forms are considered by people as characterized best by names with bright (i.e., *i*) vowels, but heavy, big, and round forms by names with blunted and hollow vowels (i.e., *a* or *o*) (Brown & Hildum, 1956; Sapir, 1920). Similarly, few people can overcome the urge to couple a round-curved form with the name "Maluma," and a sharp-angled line drawing with the name "Takete" (Köhler, 1933, p. 153; Scheerer & Lyons, 1957).

As in the case of colors, synesthetic experiences may be in part physiologically determined, and in part acquired through language usage and experience. Even on the cross-cultural level, there are interrelations, on the one hand, among various characteristics of forms, e.g., large and near, thick and dark (Osgood, 1960) or moving, up, distinct, and thin (Karwoski et al., 1942) and on the other hand, among various meanings, e.g., good, pleasant, inspiring, and happy (Karwoski et al., 1942), strong and man, or energetic, excitement, noisy, and joyful (Osgood, 1960). Thus, synesthetic experiences are likely to be generalized beyond the original bond between a feature of lines and a specific sensation. If, for example, bluntness represents slowness, while slowness is related to heaviness and weakness, then bluntness may gradually come to represent also heaviness and weakness.

There seems, however, to be an additional type of response specific to lines and forms which many of the described meanings may codetermine. This is the dynamic or dynamizing mode of response. When people are asked to explain why they chose a certain form for the expression of a certain feeling or other concept, they often refer to an hypothetical quality of motion along or by the lines. For example, a circle may represent infinity because movement along its circumference is endless and repetitive; a sharp angle may be experienced as thrilling because it involves a sudden change in direction of motion (S. Kreitler, 1965); and long curves stand for calmness and indolence because their motion is slow (Lundholm, 1921). The readiness with which forms are dynamized has been noted by many investigators

(Peters & Merrifield, 1960; Tagiuri, 1958; Werner & Kaplan, 1963) and is most remarkable in the writings of many art theoreticians and critics.

But how can we understand this "dynamization" of forms? Indeed, normal nonhallucinating people may sometimes perceive motion where objectively there is none, for example, when they themselves are moving or when static visual stimuli are projected in rapid succession. Yet forms in painting are not usually seen through the window of an express train or in rapid projections. Any attempt to account for dynamization could be based either on the assumption that dynamization depends on "objective" qualities of the stimuli, i.e, forms, and/or on the assumption that it constitutes a contribution of the perceiver.

The Gestalt theory of expression (Arnheim, 1949, 1958; Gibson, 1954; Köhler, 1938) represents the clearest elaboration of the first assumption. Its main tenet is that whatever is perceived, all expressive qualities included, has its objective basis in the stimuli. But it does not further specify the properties of stimuli which are responsible for the expressive qualities. Werner and Kaplan's (1963) theory of physiognomic perception and Lipps' (1903) theory of empathy are the two major examples of elaborations of the second assumption. According to Werner and Kaplan, dynamization is one of the main characteristics of the physiognomic mode of perception which reflects in the adult the residues of the infantile primary matrix of perception, in which the external and the internal, the motoric, affective, sensual, and imaginal elements are all intermingled prior to their differentiation. The empathy theory, however, concentrates mainly on the participation of motor elements in perception. According to it dynamization is due to the fact that observers imitate motorically or kinesthetically the major outlines or directional axes of the perceived forms.

Both physiognomics and empathy seem to be plausible theories with regard to dynamization in light of existing evidence. Many observations support the conclusions that perceptual sensitivity and attention to movement, response to external stimuli mainly by motor actions, motoric imitation, and perception of the world in terms of motions and dynamics predominate in earlier phylogenetic and ontogenetic stages of development.[3] Yet, even when these modes of perception and reaction subside, kinesthesia undoubtedly remains an integral part of perception (Witkin et al., 1954), the dynamic world-view and the early tendency to grasp all objects as things-of-action become compressed into one dimension of symbolic meaning (S. Kreitler, 1965; Osgood, 1962), and the earlier tendencies to actually imitate motorically survive mainly in the form of subdued kinesthetic imitation.

The dynamization response seems accordingly to be a joint product of enhanced kinesthetic reactivity, empathy, and the prominence of symbolic meaning dimensions. The processes on which dynamization depends are all enhanced in the confrontation with art. Yet dynamization itself may strengthen empathy and the elicitation of symbolic meanings. A dynamized form is grasped as more animate than a static immobile form and may thus facilitate empathy into it, identification with it, sensitivity to its tension and relief-evoking qualities, and attention to emotional and personal meanings which it may carry.

Forms and Colors in Interaction

In the last two chapters we have learned to know a variety of reactions to forms. We have studied forms as gestalts and forms as carriers of meanings, ranging from personal associations to interpersonally shared symbolization, possibly reflecting archetypes, synesthetic sensations, and dynamization tendencies. On this background forms undoubtedly emerge as an exceptionally potent means not only for the evocation of tension and provision of relief but also for the arousal and shaping of a meaningful experience. As we saw in Chapter 4, lines and forms may evoke tension by deviating from good gestalts in organization, figural qualities, and the role they fulfill in a certain figural or ideational context. Relief, in turn, may be provided by actual, implied, subjectively imagined, or conceptualized goodness of gestalt on the level of forms, of interrelations of forms, or of meanings. Meanings, however, widely extend the range of possibilities for experiencing tension and relief. Personal and more interpersonally shared meanings add further dimensions of tension-laden contrasts, e.g., the contrast between the sharp-pointed angle and the soft curve, between a big and a small form, between the left and right or the up and down directions, between heavy and light forms, the sad and the joyful, finite and infinite, the striving and the resigned ones. Moreover, meanings may also sharpen the contrasts between good and bad gestalts, for example, by adding to this confrontation the literal meanings of good and bad as evaluations. Yet meaning is also the major factor underlying the attainment of relief. By enabling us to recognize similarities, where previously only differences were perceived, or by allowing differentiation of what seemed a unity, meaning provides for integration and resolution of contrasts on progressively more comprehensive levels, up to the complex of the whole picture. It is thus essentially meaning which turns the multiple tensions and reliefs into an integrated experience.

Forms are obviously a kind of abstraction, albeit a very common and familiar one. So are colors, which are one set of the facets we have abstracted from forms. When by way of summary we consider some of their joint effects, the horizon of the experiential possibilities of pictures expands instantaneously in an unexpected manner. Even if we concentrate merely on effects of tension and relief, the range of factors which enter into an analysis of the experience becomes hardly visualizable. Tension may, for instance, be aroused by a distorted incomplete gestalt in the picture, and somewhat moderated by a pleasant association to a color; the intense clash between two complementaries may be relieved by soft dropping curves; the strong symbolic impact of a blue can be counterbalanced by a series of sharp-angled figures; and the tension evoked by the contrast of centrifugality and centripetality of a spiral may be relieved through a homogeneous scale of hues on the background. Some of these factors may mutually reinforce one another, so that a real nodal point of tension is produced in the picture, as for instance, when a pointed angle is painted red (Hevner, 1935a), when the inside of an open square with sharply outlined contours is filled with the juxtaposition of blue and yellow, or when upward directed sharp, black arrows emerge from a background of pure white. At other times, through the simultaneous occurrence of some of the processes, a certain aspect of a color or a form is particularly emphasized, as when a pale violet brings out the concentricity rather than the eccentricity of a circle, or when precisely the downward direction of a vertical is stressed, owing to a greenish background. By the same means several concentrated loci of tension may be produced in a picture. These would constitute a potent factor of tension, that stands in need of a forceful dissolution, if the picture is not to leave the spectator in a state of unsatisfied tension.

Obviously there is no reason to assume that all these processes occur in an observer during each confrontation with any painting, or that all of the factors are equally pronounced or utilized in every picture. Yet, the experience may expand in range or depth the more one returns to the observation of a picture. It is, however, quite as probable that on each encounter, or even during one and the same encounter with a picture, various factors come successively to the fore, so that the experience may be said to change its focus, level, or quality. For instance, a spectator who is initially arrested by the symbolism of the circles and the reds may only later respond to the contrasts between the colors and the variations of the forms, or to the clash between the rough, warm, and dynamic red and the softness of the delicately traced waves and arcs. Later on, or on another occasion, he may produce associations to the colors and the forms which did not occur to him before.

It may be assumed that the various possible reactions to colors and forms operate as if they were subject to the law of figure-background reversals, without however obeying a strict time limitation. Factors predominating now in perception and experience may later revert to the background, though they may still exert their influence, but in a comparatively subdued manner and without the specific attention of the spectator.

The review of major effects of colors and forms enables us to understand why modern painters who renounce the use of explicit object references can confidently rely on the colors and forms they display to stimulate in the spectators an experience as intense as any evoked in the past by depicting realistic objects and scenes. The experience of a battle can be aroused not only by the traditional means of representing horses, swords, and two hostile armies each headed by a general, but also through the drawing of a sharp angle touching the contour of a circle, both of which appear against a background of two saturated hues of red. Thus, our long stepwise investigation of the various modes of response lays the groundwork of a schematic model of processes which constitute the experience aroused by a picture. Yet the understanding of a specific experience in a specific observer in the here and now would require a reformulation of all the discussed processes in terms of the context of that particular experiencing subject, with his idiosyncrasies and uniqueness, in whom the processes ultimately intermingle to produce a unified experience and a meaningful encounter. However, on a more general level the outlined processes have enabled us so far to attain some insights into the dynamics of art development, in the course of which forms and colors have turned from tools for representation to independent means for creating experience, pictures have changed from pseudophotographic replicas to images of new realities which disclose to us unsuspected facets of familiar realities, and observers of pictures have learned to exchange the role of passive spectator for the most difficult and rewarding role of active participant in the act of creation (H. Kreitler, 1960).

6. Music: Harmony and Melody

Theories of Consonance and Dissonance

How is an experience evoked in the listener by sequences and structures of musical tones? In line with our already familiar hypotheses, we shall explore the means through which tension may be aroused and relieved by music, as well as the meaning processes through which tension and relief are integrated in the framework of a comprehensive experience.

At first glance it might seem that explorations in music may be attended by more difficulties than in painting, due to the need to use musicological technical terms which may be unfamiliar to some readers. However, our task is actually much easier. We will be spared the strenuous attempt to abstract literary contents; for music, the pre-eminently "non-representational" art, tells no story, refers to no object and depicts no scenes or situations—a feature which has evoked envy and admiration on the part of many an artist and philosopher. Formal means and communicated contents are essentially identical in this art, being fused as inseparable aspects in the sound-organizations and tonal structures of which music consists.

Our task is further facilitated by the fact that, unlike the visual arts, music is based on a clear and explicit theory. It is, moreover, a single theory and provides a code of rules and instructions whose validity can be verified by referring to any single piece of music from any age and culture, including our own. This theory is so basic and unconditionally binding that not only does it remain unimpaired through the abolition of one or another formal rule and through the addition of several new tones, but even revolutionary changes like turning away from tonality are directly derived from it. Kurth (1947, p. 62) was therefore right in claiming that "all the main anchorage-points for a Western psychology of music lie manifest in the theory" of music, which indeed provides the best starting point for investigating the experience aroused through music.

It is in harmony that the basic lawfulness of music is most strikingly revealed and therefore most easily grasped. The study of harmony constitutes a major part of the theory of music. Harmony deals with chords, which are a simultaneous sounding of tones. The theory of harmony includes the laws pertaining to the mutual influences between a chord and its constituent tones, as well as among the chords themselves, each regarded as a unity. Although the theory of harmony specifies many rules about the formation of and the connection between chords, it states very little about the dynamism of the chords themselves. In fact, all it tells us about this point is that there are only two kinds of chords: dissonant chords and consonant chords. The dissonant chords are described as those which stand in need of a resolution, while the consonant chords are described as the resolution itself. When heard, the dissonant chords arouse a feeling of "unrest [and] dissatisfaction, calling for further motion towards something satisfactory" (Schoen, 1940, p. 61) and are experienced as "harsh and unpleasant . . . incomplete and unfinal" (W. S. Pratt, 1944, p. 40), while the consonant chords are pleasant sounds of peace, completion, and relief (W. S. Pratt, 1944, p. 33). Accordingly, the theory of harmony is the code of rules regulating the creation of chordic tensions and the production of adequate reliefs.

Musicians will readily accept these descriptive definitions of consonant and dissonant chords. While in the other arts the use of the terms tension and relief is still rather unusual, in music references to tension-laden and relieving chords have become so naturalized that they have in fact attained the rank of technical terms. On the other hand, to those unversed in the theory of music the continuation of our study of music may appear indeed superfluous, since the principles we are looking for seem to be clearly stated by the formulations that tension is aroused through dissonant chords and that relief is offered through the consonant ones, i.e., the unison, the octave, the fifth, the fourth, and the major and minor thirds and sixths.

In spite of the clarity of the theoretical definitions of tension and relief in music, and even because of it, a psychologist is bound to raise the question: Why is it that some chords arouse tension while others are experienced as relieving? What is it about dissonances which makes them dissonant and why are consonants consonant?

The problem of consonance and dissonance has intrigued many minds in the course of centuries.[1] Theoreticians of ancient Greece are responsible for the first serious attempt to reduce the qualitative difference in the experience of dissonance and consonance to quantitative mathematical features. Their main claim was that the numerical ratios between the producers of the constituent tones are simpler in the case of consonant than of dissonant sounds. Thus, referring to the lengths of the strings producing the sounds, they found that chords for which the strings showed lengths with simple numerical ratios of 2 : 1 (the octave), 3 : 2 (the fifth), and 4 : 3 (the fourth) are consonant in contrast to the dissonant chords which result from plucking strings of lengths showing complicated or irreducible ratios like 5 : 4 (the major third, which for us is already consonant), 6 : 5 (the minor third), 9 : 8

(major second) and of course, 10 : 9 (the minor second). The lengths of the strings are correlated with frequencies of vibration and with the oscillations of rarefaction and condensation that constitute sound waves in air.

Since these statements render approximate descriptions of what is accepted as consonance and dissonance, mathematical reasoning dominated this field of thought for centuries, in spite of the insoluble problems against which it continuously stumbled. Even Leibniz in the seventeenth century still espoused essentially the same view, adding that the soul counts the oscillations without being aware of it. It is indeed fortunate that the counting is performed by the soul subperceptibly and thus remains unconscious, for otherwise the soul or its possessor might find it hard to make these calculations and simultaneously to enjoy the effects of harmony. Euler later modified this "unconscious arithmetics" theory by assuming that the less counting the soul has to do, the more consonant the chords are felt to be. Euler obviously equated the decreased effort demanded from the hearer with the experience of pleasantness, calm, and well-being.

Although simple as well as fascinating in the correspondence it highlights between experiential and mathematical properties, the theory is unacceptable, mainly because it makes on the listener a demand which he is unable to fulfill. So far, no conceivable psychophysical process, conscious or unconscious, is known by means of which a person could count, calculate, and compare such enormous numbers of oscillations within fractions of a second. The immediate range of attention and perception is extremely limited in comparison to what is demanded by mathematical harmony. While the upper limit of immediate grasp hovers around seven items only, the listener of music is expected to decide quickly, as Schönberg (1922) protested, whether 8/234 is greater or smaller than 23/680. For the theory to be acceptable, the person would have to be endowed with the potentialities of an elaborate computer; but then he would no longer be a human, capable of the enjoyment of consonance and dissonance. Moreover, the mathematical theory in general fails to account for historical changes in the determination of consonance and dissonance. For example, the major third was considered dissonant by the Greeks but is accepted as consonant in modern times. Thus, after having counted the vibrations and calculated the ratios, on what basis can the soul then decide whether a chord is consonant or dissonant?

We return to our starting point and take up the problem again, this time from the viewpoint of the physical theories which dominated the scene during the nineteenth century. Of these, the most significant was offered by Helmholtz (1912), although its basic ideas were clearly formulated by Rameau, D'Alembert, and Sauveur in the eighteenth century. Helmholtz' theory rests on the decisive phenomenon of beats, namely, those fluctuations in loudness which may be heard when two or more tones with an unequal number of vibrations are sounded simultaneously. Physically, the phenomenon stems from the interference between sound waves which differ in frequency. This interference occurs not only between the waves of the fundamental tones, but also, and this is even more important, among the waves of the series of overtones (partials) produced by each of the sounded tones. In general, the greater the difference in frequency between tones, the more beats there are. It has been observed that consonant chords produce no beats or fewer beats than dissonant ones, and that the beats which do occur in consonances are typically equal in intensity and identical in number in each second, while those of dissonant chords are not only more frequent but are also unequal and irregular. Helmholtz, therefore, concluded that consonance derives from a general mutual facilitation of sound waves with regularity of those beats which nevertheless do occur, while the source of dissonance is the interference of the waves and a resultant multiplication of beats which are of an irregular type.

This theory accommodates the fact that the highly consonant thirds and sixths have scarcely perceptible beats, while the strong dissonances have audible beats. In addition, it does not require the listener to engage in complicated calculations, for he may safely rely on an overall estimate of total quantities.

Then (1898) Stumpf remarked that the perceptibility of beats depends on the pitch of the tones. Thus, while there are in bass tones consonant intervals with clearly perceivable beats, in the higher tones there are dissonant chords whose sounding produces no audible beats at all. More important is Stumpf's rejection of the beats principle on the basis of his famous observation that tones produced by tuning forks so constructed as to avoid beats may also be perceived by listeners as consonant or as dissonant chords. Yet, this observation does not disprove Helmholtz' theory. In the course of time, listeners may have grown so habituated to accepting certain intervals as consonant and others as dissonant that when beats are missing, they may still judge and experience according to criteria which they associate to these phenomena. On the other hand, Révész (1954) noted that according to Helmholtz, the same dissonant interval must sound much more harmonious in a higher octave than in a lower one, a conclusion which stands in flat contradiction to the facts. Moreover, within the framework of tempered tuning, which aims at an equalization of beats, it is only the fifths which actually have equal beats, while the thirds produce irregular beats and are nevertheless experienced as consonant.[2] Indeed, in the U.S.A., piano tuners generally count the number of unequal beats of the thirds and the sixths in order to ascertain whether the right tempering has been achieved (Howe, 1941).

Stumpf (1883) offered one of the most prominent explanations for consonance and dissonance. His fusion theory is based on experimental findings which demonstrate that dissonant bitonal chords are identified as dissonances with greater ease than consonant bitonal chords are recognized as consonances. Stumpf's basic assumption was that the fusion of the fundamental tones, for instance, in the fourth or the fifth, is an irreducible phenomenon and depends on the vibration ratio of the tones. The stronger the impression of fusion of the two tones into a whole, the more consonant is the chord. Yet this theory ignores some facts, such as that the fusion character of a bitonal chord may be largely lost when the two tones differ in loudness although its consonance effects remain unimpaired, or that intervals beyond the octave have lower fusion than the corresponding equally consonant intervals within the octave (Faist, 1897). More important, however, is the argument that Stumpf uses fusion, henceforth one experiential characteristic of consonant chords,[3] in order to explain why such chords are consonant.

A very different and much more promising theory was offered by Arnold Schönberg (1922). Essentially this is an eclectic theory, which combines fruitfully a thesis suggested by Helmholtz and a theory developed by Lipps. The idea of Helmholtz is that tones in consonant chords have a greater number of common overtones than tones in dissonant chords—an observation which does not enable us to understand why intervals of tones produced by tuning forks, i.e., devoid of overtones, may nevertheless be grasped as dissonant or consonant. Lipps (1926), on the other hand, following the older mathematical theories, starts from the heterogeneity of the frequency of vibrations of each tone and concludes that this heterogeneity must necessarily lead to differences in the nerve reactions, these being the ultimate source of the experiences of consonance and dissonance.

Schönberg's basic assumption is that the consonance property of an interval depends on the distance of the tones from each other in the scale of the overtones. This scale consists of an infinite number of tones, arranged in order of pitch and all standing in a definite relation to the fundamental tone. Thus, the first overtone has a frequency of vibrations double that of the fundamental, so that it is the octave; the second overtone has a frequency three times higher, which means that it is the fifth; the third overtone is again the octave of the first partial; the next overtone is the third, and so on.

According to Schönberg, the nearer a tone is to the fundamental in the overtone scale, the more consonant it sounds when appearing with the fundamental in a chord. Accordingly, the most consonant of all is the first, namely, the octave chord, and next comes the fifth, then the third, etc. Conversely, the farther a tone lies from the fundamental in the scale of the overtones, the more dissonant it will sound in combination with or in relation to the fundamental as, for instance, in the case of the second C and D, which are actually far removed from each other in the overtone series.

The most important achievement of this theory is the emphasis which it lays on the differential grade of dissonance of a chord. No chord is absolutely consonant or dissonant. There are only more and less dissonant chords, the degree of dissonance being determined only through the "distance" in the overtone scale. Yet "distance" as a criterion of dissonance accords well with the other two criteria of dissonance which we have described, and which now appear as derivatives from the more encompassing principle stated by Schönberg. Thus, the tones which form consonant chords, are not only "near" to each other in the scale of overtones but also evidence a greater number of common overtones as well as simpler ratios of the frequencies of vibration than dissonant chords do.

Nevertheless, Schönberg's theory does not offer the conclusive solution to the problem of consonance and dissonance. It is descriptive rather than explanatory. For it still remains as puzzling as before why precisely the chords formed by means of the first overtones are more consonant than the others, or why the third, which was considered dissonant as recently as six hundred years ago, nowadays counts as completely consonant. Neither is it by any means clear why the boundary between the consonances and the dissonances lies today precisely at the sixths.

The Progressive Conquest of Tones

In spite of the inconclusiveness of his theory, Schönberg's emphasis on the significance of the overtones offers a hint which can ultimately lead us towards an explanation that will account plausibly for the perplexing phenomena of dissonance and consonance.

The explanation seems basically to stem from the whole structure of our tonal system, which is at once quite puzzling and extremely logical. The existing tone system consists of the subdivision of the large interval called octave into successive steps, with a tone at each determined degree. Different cultures may use different scales of tones; e.g., Chinese, Arabian, and Gypsy scales are different from the Western scales (Hamel & Hurliman, 1946). Thus it is obvious that at least some measure of arbitrariness must characterize the size of steps in the tonal system.

Far more basic is the problem why precisely twelve tones are used in our Western tonal system and why just these twelve and not others. To put it more concisely, the problem refers to the principles which have led to the choice of the tones that are used in music. The most significant phenomenon in this context is the fact that the tones of music correspond approximately to the first tones in the overtone scale. This correspondence, if taken as a starting point, may warrant the assumption that most tones now in use were found through overhearing of the easily perceptible overtones, which are of course the first overtones (Redfield, 1928). The rest of the scale was established through the addition of tones within the intervals, these in turn being divided according to the already existing and familiar intervals. More concretely, this hypothesis suggests that one of our primitive ancestors, far back at the dawn of history, may have once produced a tone, perhaps by touching a tense cord or string. He may have liked the sound and so he and others reproduced it, until eventually through close attention someone overheard and reproduced the first overtone. Thus a bitonal system consisting of the fundamental and its octave may have been established. A song consisting of three tones—fundamental tone, octave, and again the fundamental—could now be produced, with numerous repetitions of the basic motive. In a similar manner, the second overtone of the fundamental must have been overheard and reproduced to form the interval of the fifth, so that the scale soon consisted of three tones.

Moreover, it can be assumed that each new tone must have been experienced, at least in the beginning, as dissonant, if for no other reason than that it was new, strange, and exciting in its relation to the fundamental tone. This means that the intervals formed with this new tone were felt to be tension-laden and stood in need of relief. The relief must have lain in the already known tones or intervals, which were accepted as consonants. However, in the course of time, the new tone, like any new stimulus, lost its particularly exciting character, so that necessarily it became gradually less dissonant. Indeed, both Moore (1914) and C. C. Pratt (1928) have demonstrated experimentally that when chords which are initially grasped as dissonant are listened to frequently, they are gradually endowed with qualities of consonances. Accordingly, a need was felt for new sources of tension, which could be provided by adding new stimulating tones to the scale that form dissonances with the familiar fundamental ones. This development must have been repeated several times in the course of the history of music.

If these assumptions are valid, the earliest tone systems should be found to consist of very few tones, for instance, only of three: a fundamental tone, the octave, and the fifth. Only the first two overtones would have been primarily overheard and reproduced. The facts available from history and from surviving primitive traditions lend ample support to these conclusions. The oldest tone systems really consisted of very few tones. Even today, a five-tone system is in use in Java and in Siam, just as it was in the early period of ancient times in Europe (Blaukopf, pp. 37 ff.).

On the basis of the scarce available information from rudimentary surviving traces and some preserved traditions, it seems highly probable that this five-tone system developed from a still more ancient three-tone system. In the three-tone system, the octave was experienced as consonant, and the probably newer fifth interval played the role of dissonance. In the course of time the exciting property of the fifth must have been blunted, so that a new source of tension was necessary. It is hard to determine which was the next tone to be incorporated into the system. It could have been either the third, which is the next nearest overtone after the fifth, or the fourth, which does not appear in pure form as a near overtone, but could have been easily constructed as a step in the scale by means of simple inversion. It seems probable, however, that both the third and the fourth were inserted into the system at more or less the same time, the fourth somewhat earlier, since it is so naturally related to the discovery of the fifth. However that may be, both tones were used initially in the function of gliding tones, bridging over the already consonant-inclined fifth, and only later were incorporated into the tone-system as secondary steps, before they ultimately became independent tones. Indeed, in the five-tone systems the third and fourth tones seem to have been considered merely as secondary tones (Blaukopf, p. 43). More important, however, is the fact that as new tones the fourth and the third were used first as dissonances. Yet the fourth, as a tone discovered earlier, also became consonant before the third did. Thus, in the earliest known bivocal folk songs of the Middle Ages, it is the fourth which is already used as consonance in a manner similar to the use made nowadays of the third (Riemann, 1921, pp. 24 ff.).

A similar development to the one outlined here must have led later to the seven-tone system (including the octave), which was used in Europe during the Middle Ages and is still in use in China, Japan, and Siam (Blaukopf, p. 45). Historical traces suggest that before two new tones were added to the system, the last two tones incorporated into the five-tone system acquired the status of regular tones. For "the equalization of functions of the regular and auxiliary degrees is typical for a musical consciousness, which, upon reaching the final stage of development within a given tonal system, antic-ipates a scale of relatively higher order, and exerts every possible effort to utilize the latter" (Yasser, quoted by Blaukopf, pp. 52–53). Such may have been the case with the Javanese who made use of a pentatonic system in which the main and secondary steps of the scale were dealt with in the same manner.

In the seven-tone system, the two new tones were at first used primarily as auxiliary degrees and were experienced as dissonant. In the course of time, familiarization with these new tones has led to their incorporation into the system as regular tones, and habituation has turned them into con-sonances. The scene was again prepared for the addition of new tones. This is the process that eventually led to the establishment of the modern Western scale which splits the range of the octave into twelve equal steps.

This whole process of reproducing as tones the overheard overtones and of habituation which spurred repetition of the cycle on a subsequent level must have taken place first in melody, which in nonharmonic music produces the harmony, and after a few thousand years within the framework of harmony proper. The slowness with which the tonal system developed may have been due to the reluctance to upset the already existing frames of reference, as well as to the almost insoluble problems of tuning and temper-ing involved in any change of the tonal material. The whole development of music can be viewed as the expression of the conflict between the striving for clean tuning and the striving to incorporate new tones, affording new possibilities for arousing tension. Yet at least as important a role has always been played by convention, which in each successive stage clearly estab-lished what were dissonances and consonances and how they were to be interrelated. Regardless of whether these conventional rules were formally codified by an institution like the church, as in medieval Europe, or whether they persisted as an oral tradition, the rules were communicated and im-printed on the minds of musicians and listeners alike by means of the com-mon familiar melodies of the time. Thus, it is the intentional and even more the incidental learning underlying the process of "musical acculturation" (Francès, 1958) that explains how listeners of a certain period readily identify the dissonant and consonant chords without having personally undergone the previous developmental history of music.

The role played by learned cultural conventions in the perception of con-sonance and dissonance is amply demonstrated in the deficient judgments of consonance by children (Valentine, 1913) and by the general improvement in these judgments with specific and general musical training (Francès, 1958, Exp. XII). However, a most dramatic example for the effects of learned conventions is provided by the preferences of people for tempered over "natural" intervals (Esbroeck & Montfort, 1946). Indeed, the tones and intervals we hear deviate from what they should be according to mathematical and physical rules. This is due mainly to the practice of tempering, but also to styles of musical performance and idiosyncrasies of performers (Greene, 1937a, 1937b; Small, 1937). These deviations do not interfere with the perception of consonance. The listener seems to correct for the deviations from the norm which he assimilates within the fluctuation range of the heard tones (Francès, 1958, Exp. I) just as the observer of forms does with regard to small irregularities and gaps in the lines. Tones are then endowed with the qualities of gestalts no less than forms are.[4] Hence, the strong dissonant quality of chords composed of highly similar yet distinguishable tones, and the unimpairment of the good gestalt of consonance through deviations from the norm. Further, just as in the domain of painting, what is a good gestalt, i.e., consonance, depends also on the musical context in which the chord is sounded (Guernsey, 1928; Heinlein, 1925), and on accepted convention.

The major asset of the suggested theory of consonance is that it combines the acoustic explanation of dissonance in terms of "distance" between the tones in the overtone scale, and hence also in terms of vibration ratios and beats, with the psychological explanation that accounts for the historical evolution of dissonances and their intimate relation to the structure of the tonal system. Indeed, both elements of the theory, the acoustic and the psychological, are essential for understanding consonance and dissonance. In recent years there has been a growing tendency to explain these phenomena as purely or at least largely cultural products.[5] Yet the focal role played by the octave in the music of all cultures, the almost universal consonance of the fifth and the fourth, and the described regularity in musical development rule out such a one-sided approach. The suggested theory which reveals the relation of dissonance to the extensions of the tonal system serves to anchor these culturally modifiable phenomena in less arbitrary and more cross-culturally shared human processes.

Enhancement of Tension Within and Between Chords

As we have seen, dissonant chords serve in music as a source of tension, for which adequate relief is supplied by consonant chords. Obviously, there are in music additional means of producing new experiences within the framework of chords and their interrelations. Let us take up first the process of building up chords.

Chords in modern music mostly consist of the simultaneous sounding of four tones or often even more. Why is this so? How did this practice come about?

The first chords we know were composed of two tones only. In the beginning of chordic music, the major and the minor thirds were soon established, after brief experimentation with the fourth, as the basic harmonic building blocks. When boredom set in, a new element of tension in music had to be created. Thus, a second third was added to the customary third, so that a three-toned chord consisting of a root, its third, and its fifth came into being. This was the "almighty triad," which has dominated Western music for centuries. When the blunting forces of familiarity dulled the effects of this triad, a new third was added to form the four-toned seventh chord, and later still another third was added to form the ninth chord, so prominent in Debussy's music, and so on. Why it was precisely the third which served as a unit in chord building remains essentially unknown. A possible hypothesis would be that the third was preferred because a major and a minor third constitute the fifth, which is a highly consonant chord. However that may be, the third has been established as a convention, whose power became so binding that even Schönberg's attempt to base chords on the unit of the fourth has more or less failed. As simple and consonant chords, the triads do not demand any solution and thus can glide one into another following only the rules of different cadences. However, when one or two thirds are added to the triad, the resulting seventh or ninth chords are not only more complex; in contrast to the triad, they are also dissonant, and hence make it necessary to establish special rules which regulate their relations with the resolving consonances.

Here again, in the sphere of the mutual relations between chords, the principle of tension and relief proves fruitful in explaining characteristic developmental features. It can be expected that at the beginnings of chordic music, when a dissonant chord as such was still highly tension-laden, a dissonance was followed immediately by a consonance. This practice was actually followed by Haydn, for example, who leads almost every dissonance into immediate harmony, posing, as it were, a riddle and directly presenting its solution. But this procedure, which must have been extremely satisfying for those to whom the solutions were unfamiliar and the riddles still particularly fascinating, could not be expected to please even the audience of the following generation. For familiarity breeds not only contempt but also boredom. Tension had to be reinforced. Thus, Beethoven extended the distance between the tension-arousing chord and the relieving consonance by interposing two or three dissonant chords, though of varying tension levels. The presentation of the dissonant chord thus aroused an expectation of relief which was not immediately fulfilled (Meyer, 1956). Brahms and Wagner dared to widen the gap even more or to skip familiar solutions; and in some modern harmonic music the arc is already so very expansive, that there is some danger that listeners may fail to grasp the relation of tension and relief between the widely spaced chords they hear.

This development is of course strictly lawful. Delay in presentation of the resolutions, skipping intermediate links of already familiar solutions, and implicitness in the presentation itself are known means for the production of enhanced tension. We have seen the operation of these processes in painting and shall dwell on them again in relation to other arts. But the procedure is, of course, not quite as simple. The mere hinting at or the complete omission of not-yet-familiar solutions may impair the listener's enjoyment. Even when the solutions may safely be skipped, they should somehow be foreshadowed so that relief, when it arrives later, does not produce the disagreeable and absurd impression of a *deus ex machina*. Similarly, while reading a thriller it would indeed be very disappointing to learn the solution to the murder on the tenth page, but it would be no less disappointing not to find as early as the tenth page some hint of the riddle's solution, although it might be misleading or misunderstood at that point. Hence, foreshadowing fulfills the role of a signal on the way, of a promise of pleasure to come, which itself is forepleasure, and also of a link lending integration to the musical phrase. Its importance is particularly great in music, which as a time gestalt incurs the danger of disintegration into subgestalts.

The same principles of tension and relief may also shed some light on modulation, another important set of harmonic rules which regulate the complex interrelations between different keys. In the beginning, a musical composition had to stay within the framework of a specific key, that is, within the prefixed arrangement of tones which served as a frame of reference for the composer and was also familiar to the listener. When the possibilities of producing tension by these limited means had become too familiar to listeners, a new procedure had to be devised for the enhancement of tension. Tones outside the key began to be used, so that these formed a new dissonance. The resolution, however, followed immediately, by means of a return to the harmonic tones of the key. Thus, the key really formed the center of the composition; it was its fundamental gestalt, from which everything started and to which everything sooner or later returned.

In the course of time, new means of tension had again to be developed, and the practice of using several keys in the same composition set in. Modulation is the technique of passing from one key to another, so that shiftings of center take place in the course of one musical piece. In the Western music cultures twenty-four different main keys are used (orthographically there are more), each of which consists of seven out of the twelve tones in general use. The characteristic feature of a key resides in the specified, more or less arbitrarily established, intervals between the tones. However, there are only two basic modes of keys, namely, the major and the minor. All scales of the same mode are constructed identically and are generally experienced by listeners as more or less equal, except perhaps for some variations of brightness. Each is then as tension-laden or as tension-free as any other key of the same mode. The main differentiating feature between keys is the "distance" which separates one from another where "distance" is determined by the number of tones common to the two keys. Keys which are "near" to each other share a greater number of tones than those which are "farther" from each other. This being so, where does tension reside in modulation? The problem is particularly important nowadays, when a marked turning away from tonality makes modulation difficult.

The answer to this question may best be elucidated by investigating the classic procedure of modulation. Changes from one key to another were, of course, not performed capriciously. Initially, even the permitted shifts were strictly limited to near or related keys. The reason for this limitation resides in the definition of "distance" between keys. Since the shifting from one to another was performed through triad chords common to both keys, the shifting could occur only between near keys since only near keys have a number of chords in common. Upon hearing the chords which are to serve as steppingstones or as a springboard to the new key, the listener is still imprisoned within the framework of the former keys and has no presentiment of what awaits him. It is only when he suddenly realizes that he has been led to another key that tension sets in. This tension arises not because of any special properties of the new key as such, but simply because the new key is new, that is, in relation to the former one. It is as if the listener had been exiled from his own house to another one, which is identical with it but for the fact that it simply is not his home. The possible momentary feeling of disorientation within the framework of a newly presented "environment" as well as the surprise and the experience of "strangeness," are then the primary sources of tension through modulation. This tension can, naturally, be adequately relieved through getting acquainted with the new key, which in music is done by means of cadences, that is, sequences of chords within the framework of this new key.

When the fascination of modulation wore out, how could tension be further intensified within the framework of the passage from one key to another? The answer may be deduced from our foregoing principles. It may be expected that instead of passing to nearby keys over elaborate and lengthy bridges, modulation would tend to be performed with markedly trimmed-down bridges. That is precisely what took place. Gradually, the modulations took the form of ever shorter passages over the chords common to or almost common to the two keys, so that keys increasingly removed from each other were used consecutively with no bridge between them. The similarity of this development in music to the modern practice in painting of juxtaposing complementary colors, with no intermediary scales of hues between them, is really striking.

These potentialities of modulation were carried to such limits by Wagner, Franck, Debussy, and others, that a new development was bound to occur. It was initiated by Schönberg, whose introduction of relativity into music, through the abolition of absolute frames of reference for harmonic and melodic relations, turns him into a worthy contemporary of Einstein.

Contrary to the common view, there are not only chordic tensions in atonal music, i.e., twelve-tone music, but tonal ones too (A. Pike, 1963). The tension possibilities of modulation are even increased here, though it is often claimed that in atonal music no modulation can occur at all, for there are no keys in it. Schönberg indeed did away with the conventional keys, but the idea of tonal frames of reference has been preserved. These frames of reference are not the ones dictated by traditional and habitual use, but are created anew by every composer for each individual piece of music. It is, then, the artist who determines the scale as well as the adventures which this scale undergoes in the course of the musical piece, both as a frame of reference and as the motif of the whole composition.

Changes of frames of references can, then, occur in atonal music, but the listener has far more difficulty in becoming acquainted quickly enough with each scale, with which he is confronted for the first time through this particular composition (Francès, 1958, Exp. IV). The scales he hears are completely new, very different from any of the scales characteristic of the music that he has learned to know. Herein reside both the difficulty of listening to modern music and its great fascination, and the even greater vistas of possibility which open for and through it.

Intervals and Directionality in Melody

A melody is a succession of tones forming a chain of tonal intervals which is grasped as a sequence with distinct qualities of a whole, a gestalt. Most music in the Western world consists of both harmony and melody. The relations, however, between these two aspects of music are not exhausted by the fact that their co-occurrence in music implies intricate intermingling, mutual reinforcement and supplementation, as well as other complex forms of codetermination. Since the simultaneous sounding of the tones of a chord produces harmony while their successive sounding produces melody, melody could be viewed as a horizontal harmony. In general, the laws of harmony are also valid with regard to melody, to which they were, indeed, applied long before the advent of chordic music. Tones when sounded simultaneously constitute dissonant and consonant chords, but when sounded successively they form dissonant and consonant intervals. Tension resides primarily in the dissonant intervals, such as the major second and seventh, which are experienced as incomplete, relative to the consonant intervals, which provide completion and the adequate resolution. The "farther" the consonant intervals are from the dissonant ones and the more fragmentary the sounding of the consonances, the greater the tension.

The generality of the statement that consonant or dissonant intervals correspond to consonant or dissonant chords is limited through the actual or expected function of the tones in the melodic sequence. For example, a minor second when sounded as a chord is experienced as possibly the sharpest dissonance, but when sounded as an interval it may not at all be tension-laden, provided that it is grasped as a bridge to the consonance of the third. Thus, in melody the directionality of movement to a consonance is relieving even when the path from a moderate dissonance to consonance leads over a stronger dissonance.

The role of a tonal interval as a bridge to relief depends to a certain extent on the closeness of its tones to the ensuing tones and on the size of the interval itself. Thus, for example, in the gradually descending movement E D C in C major, E is more tension-laden than D, although from the viewpoint of harmony it is E which forms a consonant relation with the fundamental tone C and not D. Yet in this series D is the nearest tone to the fundamental tone C, and hence its relieving function. This illustrates one basic melodic rule: the greater the distance between successive tones, the greater the tension aroused in listeners, while small intervals are relieving. It is remarkable that a count of intervals used in 160 songs by Schubert, Schumann, Brahms, and R. Strauss showed that the order of frequency of the intervals corresponds to their size from smallest to largest, i.e., the unisons and seconds are overwhelmingly frequent and the tritones and sevenths very rare. Yet there were two major exceptions: the octaves are rather frequent and whole-tone steps are more frequent than semitone steps (Ortmann, 1937). However, the frequency of the octave is due to its familiarity and ease of reproduction, while the preference of whole-tone over semitone steps seems to be, as we shall see, a reflection of musical style. An inverse relation between the frequency of an interval and its size was also found in analyses of the solo line of Mozart's Bassoon Concerto in B-flat Major, in Chopin's Etude in F Minor, Op. 25 (Zipf, 1949), and other works (Hiller & Isaacson, 1959, Exp. 4).

The use of small intervals in melodies, particularly in the initial development of music, seems to contradict the hypothesis, described above, that the first tones acquired corresponded to the overheard partials and were thus the big-step intervals of the octave, the fifth and the fourth. Yet the development of melody seems to have been bound more intimately with singing. The first melodies were sung and not played, and the big intervals were more difficult for the voice than small intervals, which were initially bridged by glissandi. It was only gradually that fixed tones were articulated within these gliding notes. Since larger intervals, which are also judged less accurately (Maltzew, 1913), are generally more tension laden than smaller ones, the developmental trend in melody has taken the expected course of gradually maximizing intervals, as can readily be seen by comparing the small-step melodies of Schubert with some big-step ones of G. Mahler or Hindemith. When, however, the intervals become so large that successive tones can hardly be related, as can occur in modern serial and aleatory music, melody may turn into a series of "sound points," related through the series rather than through melodic rules (V. M. Ames, 1967; Lissa, 1965). There exists also an alternative course of intensifying tension by using intervals smaller than the semitone interval, as occurred, for example, in Arabic music.

However, the role of the size of the interval in producing tension or relief is restricted by the directionality of the whole melody, i.e., its contour of ascent and descent in terms of relative pitch. As a rule, ascending intervals are more tension-laden than descending intervals. Indeed, also high-pitched tones are more tension-arousing than low-pitched tones (Zagorul'ko & Sollertinkaia, 1958). Of the many theories proffered to account for this observation, for example, pure convention or the greater difficulty in counting the vibrations of high than of low tones, the more plausible theories suggest associative linking of the tones to body movements (Thurstone, 1920) or the persistence of musical habits from the times of *basso continuo*. Even more convincing appears the explanation which stresses the role of singing in the genesis of melody. The singing of high tones is accompanied by resonance in the head, by a rise in the larynx and by greater effort, while the singing of low tones is accompanied by resonance in the chest or possibly even in the abdomen, by a lowering of the larynx and less tension in the vocal chords and musculature. Modern listeners of music do not participate as their ancestors a few centuries ago did in singing, dancing, and acting, but the kinesthetic sensations involved in these acts may still exist subperceptibly and lend the ascent to higher pitches a stronger tension than descent into lower pitches.

The basic symmetric melodic model, which consists of ascent and descent, offers many possibilities of tension enhancement. For example, the ascent stage may be repeated, accentuated by intensity of the tones, or decelerated in speed: it may become longer and include several parts with minor descents and ascents; the climax before the descent may be lengthened and its tension increased through enlarged tonal intervals; while the descent stage may be accelerated and made steeper by gradual shortening and omissions. This development may be traced both in the history of music and in the melodies produced by children in our culture (Werner, 1917).

Because descent produces a relieving impression, chains of descending intervals are frequently used to introduce the approaching melodic end. In thousands of compositions from Gregorian chorals to Negro spirituals descent and ending are combined, so that even intermediate descending passages acquire the flavor of finality. Yet experiential finality, the striving towards the end, is more often produced by a purely harmonic means, which may either be combined with descending intervals or be used in juxtaposition with them as the overriding finality effect.

Melodies, even those by Schönberg, Webern, and Alban Berg, delineate a certain scale, and in tonal music, a certain mode and key. The lowest tone of the scale is perceived as its basis, or in tonal music, as its tonic. A melody need not start with its tonic, and a great many do not. Yet, as soon as the tonic appears or is assumed through recognition of the mode, it turns not only into a harmonic anchor (Schoen, 1940, p. 38) but into the final goal of the melodic movement (Francès, 1958, Exp. IV). Experientially it is as if the listener, carried by the melody, were drawn towards this tonic finality long before he arrives there. Yet, although this melodic orientation towards the ending implies a permanent *memento mori*, finality is rarely experienced as saddening, for one of the most impressive means of melodic music is turning ending after ending into a new beginning until satiation or exhaustion are reached. Yet, these norms of style or tonality should not be conceived of as absolutistic in any sense, for they may be altered by training (Farnsworth, 1926), knowledge, and expectations (Bingham, 1910), as well as by other standards of finality established purely within the melodic framework itself.

Causally related to the tonic-centered and the key-obeying structure of melodies is the habit of experiencing melodies as accompanied by harmonies. In Western music melodies usually appear against a background of a series of harmonies. When these are not actually presented, listeners perceive them implicitly, i.e., supply imaginatively the adequate harmonies (Francès, 1958, Exp. II). These automatically assumed harmonies were up to the twentieth century the simple major or minor triads, although in musical reality they often differed from these. Thus, a melody tone which deviated from the implied triad, i.e., a tone which was not the tonic, the third, the fifth, or the octave appeared as dissonant in relation to this harmony. Obviously, this deviating tone could be related to another triad in which it was consonant. Whether it actually would be consonant or not, depended on the accompanying harmonies and/or on expected harmonic sequences. If, for instance, a melodic movement follows the shape of the first chords of a customary cadence, there is a strong tendency to relate the next melody tones to the final harmonic sequence of this very cadence. It goes without saying that deviation from this expectation creates tension while its fulfillment is experienced as relief.

There are, however, more sophisticated means of using our harmonic habits. Until the chromaticism of Wagner's *Tristan* and Schönberg's twelve-tone revolution, it was customary to relate every melody to a certain mode and key. Tones alien to the key of the melody were perceived as dissonant. Yet, the resolution of such a dissonance need not be produced by returning to the key; it can also be attained by modulation, that is, by treating the dissonant tone as belonging to another key which from now on will be the key governing further melodic movement. Nevertheless, the surprisal value of such modulation may counteract the effect of this kind of resolution, and thus enable the composer to combine tension and relief in a highly exciting manner. This type of excitement gradually wears out in long chromatic passages, which are in fact a permanent modulation, and is unattainable when the use of habitual keys is totally abandoned.

In all the discussed series of effects produced by melody, expectations of the listener play a major role. Such expectations arise, for example, for the resolution of dissonant chords or intervals, for the course of the melody and its finality, for the size of the intervals, etc. The expectations derive from the listeners' general familiarity with the musical style and culture and are also built up through repetitions and emphases in the course of attending to the unfolding harmonies and melodies. When the expectations are fulfilled, the listener experiences relief which is particularly pleasurable if the form of the resolution is surprising; but when expectations are frustrated or delayed in fulfillment, tension is evoked (Meyer, 1956). The existence of expectations allows the composer to deviate from habitual norms, to introduce surprise effects and to increase tension by omitting the expected.

In recent years analysis of the structural features of music which may serve as basis for listeners' expectations has advanced beyond the level of intuitive examination. This progress has been due primarily to the use of information-theory terms and tools in analyzing musical structures. Major among the concepts relevant for the description of a musical tone sequence, or any other sequence, are the number of possible alternatives and their respective probabilities. These define the degree to which the sequence is regularly ordered, i.e., redundant, or the amount of information it communicates. Analysis of various musical pieces or groups of musical compositions in these terms allows us to specify the degree of redundancy in the music and to set up hypotheses about its structure which may be tested by generating musical compositions through computer programs (e.g., Hiller & Isaacson, 1959). However, in the present context, comparative studies of music may be of greater interest. Such studies show, for example, that the degree of redundancy in Gregorian chants is greater than in Romantic songs by Schubert, Mendelssohn, and Schumann (Youngblood, 1960) and even exceeds that of the highly redundant rock-and-roll songs (J. E. Cohen, 1962). This finding reflects a developmental trend which has been demonstrated also on the level of individual listeners: the greater the familiarity of people with a certain piece of music or the higher their musical training in general, the more they enjoy musical sequences of greater unexpectedness and complexity or of lesser redundancy[6] (Simon & Wohlwill, 1968; Skaife, 1967).

The computed average of redundancy in a musical piece, whose meaningfulness depends on the number of musical features considered in the computation, should not be interpreted as reflecting directly the listener's state of uncertainty about what is going to happen next, because the listener is familiar only with what he has heard of the composition up to a certain point (Kraehenbuehl & Coons, 1959), unless he has had a long previous experience with music of the type. Thus, the listener's state should rather be viewed as characterized by continuously shifting probability networks. Yet, these probability networks undoubtedly do not exhaust the description of the experience undergone by the listener who brings into the confrontation with music his ability to follow the tone sequences and interpret them in terms of musical and extramusical meanings (Moles, 1966).

All the basic structural features of melody and its experiential effects which we have discussed up to now apply not only to uni-level melodic movement, but also to polyphonic music, that is, music in which several melodies or different passages of the same melody are sounded or sung concomitantly. They are particularly clear in that special polyphonic type of melodic interplay known as counterpoint. In contradistinction to both the ancient or medieval music, which was predominently uni-melodic, and to the later developed harmonic music, which consisted primarily of a single melody with accompaniment, in contrapuntal polyphonic music, which thrived in the late Middle Ages and reached its climax with J. S. Bach, there appear one or more different melodies together with the given part (the *cantus firmus*). Each of the melodies in counterpoint has its independent direction of movement and autonomic melodic structure, yet as all of them move along, they preserve an ever-shifting harmonic interrelation and produce an overall impression of an organized whole. Voice is made to act against voice; they approach and then draw away again, pursue one another, and then hurry on in advance, are entangled in one another in a close interpenetration, only to be released from each other, so as to attain separately the unifying end-chord. Each voice exerts all the effects of tension and relief operative in any single melody, but the main fascination stems from the interrelations—harmonic and structural—among the voices, which are independent wholes in themselves and still only parts of a greater whole.

As could be predicted according to the described rules of harmony and melody, development in contrapuntal music has consisted, on the one hand in gradually increasing the number of voices, while sharpening the dissonances and progressively delaying their resolution; and, on the other hand, in the mastery of varied motions between the voice parts, and in the growing effect of coherence and organization of the composition as a whole. Indeed, it demands no elaborate discussion to demonstrate that the fundamental rule and attraction of this play of voices—be it in the form of the simple canon or the more complicated fugue, with its essential contrast between tonic and dominant in the presentation of the same theme—consist of a continuous production of tension and relief. A writer of thrillers who would like to devise a pursuit in which a high level of tension is continuously maintained could do worse than study the laws of the fugue.

Still, it should be emphasized that tension and relief among and between the voices are produced not only by means of consonance and dissonance but also through spatial or temporal removal and approach. It may be assumed that visual associations and representations play a part in facilitating as well as in enriching the acoustic articulation and integration of the many which are one and the one which is many.

Melody as a Gestalt

In all the aspects of melody discussed above, the gestalt quality of melody has been an indispensable presupposition. Indeed, since von Ehrenfels pointed out that a melody is a gestalt because it is more than the sum of its elements and can be transposed, most musicologists have concurred in the opinion that the nature of melody transcends the effects due to its tones and their interrelations. Moreover, it has been demonstrated that the perception of melody as a gestalt depends on factors similar to those operative in the case of forms, e.g., proximity, size of intervals, good continuation, continuity in pitch direction, similarities, repetitions, etc. (Ortmann, 1926). By analyzing characteristics of melody as a figure in music, Vernon (1934, 1935) found that the figure is usually higher in pitch and loudness than the ground, has a different timbre, moves differently, and also has more movement, different rhythm, and different crescendos and diminuendos. These features, as well as the devices of commencing the melody before the background harmony or after the hearer has got used to the harmony, reinforce the perception of melody as a relatively autonomous gestalt. Vernon rightly notes that melody as the figure often contains notes even discordant with the accompaniment, which nevertheless are not experienced as dissonant, since they are grasped as belonging to the figure. Yet, at any moment the listener's attention may shift, so that harmony turns into figure, only to be replaced sooner or later by the return of melody into the focus.

Like gestalts in general, the good gestalt in melody is determined partly by convention and context. It is the gestalt qualities of melody which both enhance the expectations of the listeners and allow for the tension-laden deviations from the good gestalt of melody and for variation. Variation in music, just as in painting, consists essentially in introducing changes while conserving a theme as an invariable. The primary and most primitive kinds of variation are the transposition of the melodic theme into another timbre, key, or context of harmonic accompaniment. When melodies grow in complexity and variations range along distant registers, listeners may encounter difficulties in identifying the theme (Francès, 1958, Exp. IX). However, the more common and elaborate forms of variation consist in more or less gradual changes of the theme itself. The tension produced by the variation arises from its comparison with the original gestalt, which attains, in fact, the status of a good gestalt through being viewed in relation to the consecutive variations. Correspondingly, these in turn are perceived as worse gestalts, which means that they arouse tension. The major relief-producing factor is represented by the abstracted invariant of the theme, the element common to all variations which binds them together.

In general, the laws and effects of variation which we discussed within the context of forms apply to variation of musical themes too. But there is also a marked difference between the variation of pictorial and of acoustic gestalts. In painting, which is a space art, theme and variations can continuously be compared because they are all there at any given moment; but in music, an art which depends on temporal extension, variation is only feasible if the theme can be retained in memory. Temporal primacy facilitates indeed the identification of the theme in music, but seems also to restrict the possibilities of variation, since these could readily lose their relation to the original theme and become autonomous gestalts. However, this limitation is amply counterbalanced by the fact that in music each of the elements can be freely varied, for music is not bound through any resemblance relations to any nonmusical reality. In practice, composing music always means variating.

Meaning in Music

Any attempt such as ours in the present context to dwell on the meaning of some elements in music and not on the meaning of whole musical compositions must necessarily be fragmentary and yield highly limited conclusions. For unlike the other arts, which use elements that are encountered also outside art, the tonal material of music is restricted to the domain of music. Even modern paintings devoid of explicit object references present colors and forms which are embedded in human environment and have thus become the carriers of the most varied meanings. Meanwhile, even if tones may sometimes be heard in the song of birds, such things as chords, melodies, and musical scales exist only as musical elements. This implies not only that extramusical associations to these elements might be more restricted than in the case of colors, forms, or dance movements, but mainly that the meanings of the musical elements are dominated by the meaning of the whole musical piece and can hardly be studied in isolation from it. When a person hears a tone, an interval, or a chord, he tends to embed these isolated stimuli in a musical context, so that the evoked meanings relate to the imagined context as much as to the actually sounded elements—all the more so when the elements are perceived within the actually sounded context of music. The musical meaning of the whole dominates the meaning of the parts, which can hardly be abstracted.

Attempts have been made to demonstrate the specific meanings of musical elements such as tones, intervals, keys, and modes. The clearest findings have been reported concerning the synesthetic effects of tones. Major among these are the correspondences between pitch of tones and brightness of colors (Ginsberg, 1923; Karwoski & Odbert, 1938; Karwoski, Odbert, & Osgood, 1942), color saturation (Myers, 1911; Zietz, 1931) and the hue of colors (Myers, 1914; Simpson, Quinn, & Ausubel, 1956), as well as other visual attributes like position, definiteness of a form, pointedness and size of objects (Karwoski, Odbert, & Osgood, 1942; Myers, 1911). More ambiguous is the synesthetic experience of loudness, which has been aligned with darkness (Riggs & Karwoski, 1934) as well as with brightness (Stevens & Galanter, 1957) and that of volume in tones, which, again, was found to correspond to both brightness (Moul, 1930) and darkness (English, 1923).

Synesthetic sensations seem to pervade also many of the experiential effects reported for timbre of tones and for musical intervals, but mood associations appear to be no less frequent (Huber, 1923; Sterzinger, 1916, 1917; Valentine, 1913). These usually take the form expressed poetically by Robert Browning when he writes about "those lesser thirds so plaintive, sixths diminished sigh on sigh . . . those commiserating sevenths—'Life might last! we can but try!' " Some of the effects seem to reflect also evaluation of the consonant intervals as good and the dissonances as bad (Van de Geer, Levelt, & Plomp, 1962). Some of the mood meanings attached to tones and intervals seem to be widely shared, e.g., loud and high-pitched music is apt to be regarded as happy, exciting, or triumphant, while dissonances and complexity in harmony suggest sadness (Rigg, 1964). But often the effects seem to be due to associations of these features with musical styles. This appears to be the case particularly for the connotations of keys. Even the traditionally famous though not so widely shared (Heinlein, 1928), associations of the major mode with strength, joyfulness, and brightness, and of the minor mode with gloomy sadness (Hevner, 1935b) probably derive from habitual uses of these modes in particular musical compositions (Meyer, 1956).

There can be no doubt that connotative meanings of musical elements exist, but their crucial role in the musical experience is disputable. They seem to be marginal and appear more often as background rather than as figure. The figure is the tonal movement, whose meaning may be so overriding that it leaves little room for content associations even when they do emerge (Schoen, 1940).

Within the context of tonal movement, even a single tone or a chord is experienced as a beginning, as a bridge, or as an ending and is thus related to movement. The greater part of musical movement abides by codified laws of harmonic relation and linear variation. The explicit and implicit effect of these laws is so overriding that a musical passage which does not conform to the customary laws constitutes experientially an outright defiance of laws or an endeavor to introduce new laws. Moreover, a dynamic structure like music, which is so lawful that every deviation appears as the breach of

a certain rule, induces in the open-eared and open-hearted listener a continuous cycle of expectation, disappointment, surprise, and fulfillment. It
is this phenomenon which makes the emotional impact of a musical experience so powerful and its verbal description so difficult. Beginning and ending, movement and final standstill, expectation, frustration and fulfillment,
law obedience, law defiance, and law creation—these are in fact the essence
of human life and fate. Great works in all domains of art exemplify this
essence by presenting some of its concrete manifestations which are more
familiar to the spectator, but by virtue of their everyday familiarity are connected to more obvious and less fundamental developments. Hence, nonmusical works of art may seem meaningful also on their surface as it were,
even when the spectator does not respond experientially or intellectually to
the deeper latent basic dynamics. But melodic and harmonic progressions,
stripped as they are of these surface layers, hardly present more than these
basic dynamics. The listener is bound to experience primarily the objectless
desire for solutions, the excitement of promising beginnings, the frustration
of expectations and the pleasure of foreseen endings, preexisting regularities,
the revolt against their absolute dictates, and the final compliance. He may
or may not connect these movement principles of life with some of their
daily manifestations; he may or may not conceive them intellectually; but
if he is at all capable of having a musical experience, these form the basic
framework of the experience and its meaning.

7. Rhythm

The Nature of Rhythm

Unlike harmony and melody, which are primarily musical elements, rhythm plays an important role also in other arts and seems to be a universal, perhaps even a cosmic phenomenon.

What is rhythm? There is no immediate or simple answer to this question. For the term is used indiscriminately in order to characterize such disparate phenomena as the movement of waves, the beat of our hearts, designs on Polynesian straw baskets, the undulations of a frieze on a Greek column, the beat of drums, the nervous drumming of bored fingers, the rocking of disconsolate children, the obsessive repetitiveness of certain neurotic or psychotic acts, the monotony of magic incantations, the temporal unfolding of music, the vicissitudes of evolution and history, and so on. This list implies that rhythm may be viewed as an aspect of most if not all processes and occurrences in the internal and external worlds. Indeed, this conclusion should evoke but little surprise, for rhythm is a phenomenon of time—the dimension which is inseparable from all processes and being. Strictly speaking, rhythm applies first and foremost to temporally unfolding phenomena. Applied to spatial events, the term must generally be regarded as figurative. Yet, where static percepts are "dynamized," especially in the framework of the visual arts (Chapter 5), "rhythm" may be regarded as literal rather than metaphorical.

The very range of phenomena to which the term is applied implies some important features of rhythm. First, rhythm seems to be of a general nature and is not bound to any particular process. Secondly, it appears to be a perceptible characteristic of various temporal sequences. Finally, in many cases it emerges as an organizational principle that we, as observers, impose on or discover in processes or materials. Indeed, our task of abstracting rhythm from its multiple concrete modes of manifestation is rendered easier by our tendency to perceive it, to impose it, and to express it through so many instances. This being so, it would appear that rhythm is an easily grasped principle, which may be further imposed on or discovered in other phenomena and may readily be made into an abstract logical frame of reference or preference.

These features of rhythm predominate in most definitions offered in the rich literature on rhythm. A common denominator of these definitions is that rhythm constitutes a certain ordering or patterning, usually of time, based on cycles of appearance of something and its recurrence after a certain temporal interval. Three elements are central in this suggested definition: periodicity of occurrence, temporal intervals, and patterning. Periodicity of occurrence obviously implies repetition. Nevertheless, when we designate a phenomenon as rhythmic, it need not be actually the whole phenomenon which repeats itself but only a certain aspect of it. If, for example, we deal with the rhythmic gait of two people, the aspect which is repeated may be certain bodily movements, while the speed of walking changes, or it may be the accentuation of certain footsteps within a given unit of time, while the distance between the two walkers varies. This means that rhythm relates to a certain aspect of a phenomenon which impressed us, or to which we pay attention for any reason whatsoever.

The second major feature of rhythm is the intervals between the occurrences. Since the intervals are defined by nonoccurrence, by silence or emptiness, one may be tempted to regard them as periods of nothingness intervening between successive appearances of something. Yet these intervals are as crucial for the perception and formation of rhythm as the recurring phenomena are. Intervals in music are music, claimed Beethoven. If intervals are too short, the recurrences fuse into a continuity, while if they are too long, the recurrences are grasped as independent nonrhythmic events (Fraisse, 1956). The indispensable role of intervals in rhythm is demonstrated by the observation that people who are asked to repeat a tapped rhythm reproduce not only the taps but also the intervals with astonishing accuracy and with minimal variability. But when a change in reproduction of the heard intervals is demanded, a marked change occurs instantaneously in the rhythm forms themselves (D. Katz, 1950, pp. 130–32). Thus, although intervals may remain unnoted, "without them there would be no rhythm set off in relief" (D. Katz, 1950, pp. 135–36). What intervals actually are may best be grasped if we view rhythm as a gestalt. The intervals would then play the role of background. As background they are not a part of the gestalt itself, but constitute an indispensable condition for its existence, for rhythm can be neither perceived nor conceptualized without them.

This brings us to patterning, the third major factor in the definition of rhythm. The claim that rhythm is a gestalt implies that it consists in an organization of stimuli into successive units in line with principles such as duration or intensity of certain sounds. In the case of an already formed rhythm, as in music, the perceiver's task is to grasp the organizational principles, which sometimes allow for varied competing groupings of the units.

In the case of spontaneous rhythmization of stimuli, the perceiver structures a sequence of sounds, such as the ticking of a clock, by providing subjective accentuation of some of the stimuli, so that the sounds fall into discrete units. Gestalt psychologists (Koffka, 1909) consider the perception of rhythm and the tendency to organize stimuli rhythmically as innate characteristics of the organism. Although the tendency may be innate, there is a lot of evidence that the ability to perceive varied and more complex rhythms develops in children with age (Christianson, 1938; Pflederer, 1964). On the adult level, however, the tendency to rhythmize a series of equal-sounding auditory stimuli is highly prominent. As a rule, any more or less regular series of identical sounds, taps, or clicks, i.e., a sequence which is not extremely irregular or in which the intervals are not too short, will immediately and spontaneously be heard by listeners in a rhythmical form, as a series of groups with recurring subjective accents. Moreover, the grouping is subject to specific rules. For instance, with increase in rate, the number of sounds grouped together in one rhythmical unit rises from two to six; in a group of two, the first sound is usually accented, while in groups of three or four the first sound is perceived as strongly accented and the third only slightly so (Stevens, 1951, pp. 1232–34). Further, when some of the presented sounds differ from others in intensity or pitch, the tendency is to organize the series so that these accented sounds are placed at the beginning of rhythmical units, which may then take the form of trochee (— ◡) or dactyl (— ◡ ◡), while if some of the sounds are longer than others, these longer sounds tend to be placed at the end of the units (Stetson, 1905).

The gestalt qualities of rhythm are apparent in a whole set of characteristic phenomena (Fraisse, 1967). For example, sounds following each other closely are more likely to be grouped together than sounds separated by longer intervals; and a rhythm imposed on a series of sounds resists change into another rhythm. As a gestalt, rhythm is naturally amenable also to transposition. A series may preserve its rhythmic character when tempo changes over the range from slow to fast, or when the acoustic stimuli are altered—for example, when taps are replaced by piano sounds, or drum beats by steps of dancing feet, which continue to move in rhythm even when the rhythm is no longer sounded by the drum.

By way of summary, rhythm is a structuring of time. It consists of a series of acoustic stimuli divided by spacing and/or accentuation into repetitive units, each of which includes two or more stimuli. At least one of the sounds in each unit is accented through duration, intensity, pitch or some other special quality. While the units manifest the qualities of a gestalt, the intervals between the stimuli and the units play the role of background.

The Experience of Rhythm

Why is rhythm so fascinating? Whence arises the pleasure it provides? How does it happen that rhythm forces itself on people, so that everything tends to be brought in accord with it? And why is rhythmization such a preferred and ubiquitous habit?

Rhythm should of course be differentiated from tempo, i.e., the speed characteristic of a tonal sequence. Tempo raises further questions concerning the experiential effects of rhythm. On the one hand, the notorious tendency of musicians to speed up the playing of the generally tension-laden ascending melodic movement suggests that acceleration of rhythm evokes tension. On the other hand, the difficulty musicians find in slowing down relative to the ease with which they speed up playing, and the tendency of orchestras to increase rather than decrease pace if they change the tempo at all, speak against the complementary conclusion that deceleration is relieving. Could it be that both acceleration and deceleration, beyond a certain range of speed, are tension-laden?

There is a lot of evidence that accelerated rhythms arouse tension. In various cultures, a gradual acceleration in the rhythm of songs, beat of drums, magical incantations, and movements is used to arouse the participants in a simultaneously performed activity, be it dance, work, or battle, to great excesses of enthusiasm and violent outbursts of energy. These may sometimes result in orgies, trances, or self-mutilations—that means, in peaks of tension which can be relieved only through vehement release acts (Wallis, 1939, p. 83). Yet it is not only acceleration of tempo but also fast speed as such that is experienced as tension-laden. In music it has repeatedly been observed that listeners describe fast-played music as very exciting, stirring, agitated, even unpleasant, or—depending on the other mood effects of the music—as joyful and triumphant! The continuation of fast rhythm, particularly when it is accompanied by sustained bodily movements, may produce a slight decrease in alertness, yet possibly not in arousal (Seashore, 1938, pp. 142–43). Concerning slow rhythms observations are less clear. On the one hand it is known that relatively slow rhythms may have the effect of disenergizing people. Monotonous, slowly repeated orders, clicks, and metronome beats may be used for hypnotizing (Weitzenhoffer, 1957), and rocking or slow tunes lull many infants to sleep each night. Moderately slow music is usually experienced as sad, calm or dignified. On the other hand, the playing of a dance tune too slowly is irritating, and slowed-down music may under certain circumstances be fairly tension-laden.[1]

These different observations allow some tentative conclusions. There seems to be an optimal range of tempo in rhythm which is relatively less tension-laden than much faster and much slower rhythms. Acceleration towards the fast rhythms as well as deceleration towards the markedly slow rhythms appears to be tension-provoking. Within the optimal range itself, slower tempi are more relieving than faster tempi, and the maintenance of a steady tempo seems to have the effect of decreasing alertness.

How can the effects of rhythm be accounted for? The number of theories and studies on rhythm[2] is so great that only a few relevant conceptions can be dealt with here. One well-known and intriguing explanation has been offered within the framework of the psychoanalytic theory. The clue to this theory lies in the observation that rhythm plays a paramount role in one basic activity of animals and men: sexuality. Freud (1961, p. 160) and his followers (L. Kaplan, 1930, chap. 14) suggested that the pleasure of rhythm and of rhythmical activities in general derives from the connection of any rhythm with the rhythms of sexuality. This connection is based either on an associative linking or on low-grade sublimation. In this manner, the pleasure accompanying sexual activities is transposed, though perhaps with less intensity, to any other rhythmical activity, while rhythm acts as a link between the two otherwise nonrelated spheres of action.

As might be expected, Freud's theory of rhythm aroused great resistance on the part of many musicians and other artists, although it was by no means new or revolutionary. About fifty years before Freud, Darwin (cited by L. Kaplan, 1930, p. 68) had already pointed out the primary function of rhythm in the process of natural selection. Darwin based this conclusion on the "dance of love"—a sequence of rhythmical movements unaccompanied by sound—performed by many kinds of birds, presumably in order to release in the partner the appropriate sexual responses. Similarly, Berg (1879) suggested that music had developed out of the howls of monkeys in heat, which hit trees rhythmically and perform other rhythmical movements in the foreplay of the sexual act.

The erotic theory of rhythm may account for a variety of rhythm phenomena. It might explain, for instance, why musicians tend unintentionally to accelerate the tempo of music, why accelerated or fast rhythms lead to orgies and ecstasies in various so-called primitive cultures, and why jazz and the varieties of rock music provoke excesses of excitement in the reportedly less primitive peoples of Western culture. The acceleration of tempo up to a climax followed closely by steep relief would be taken to reflect the dynamics of sexual intercourse. Similarly, the common tendency to impose rhythm on so many activities and perceptual phenomena would be interpreted as due to the desire to derive quasi-sexual pleasure from the neutral or the necessary.

Much less convincing would be the explanation provided by the theory for the tenseness of markedly slowed-down rhythms. These would be regarded as the result of repression of sexuality or reaction-formation against it, even though the slowed-down rhythms may be experienced as tense by the same people who experience fast rhythms as exciting.

A more crucial argument against the erotic theory of rhythm is that sexuality is not the only organic process characterized by rhythm. Indeed, if it were merely that some other activities such as breathing or walking were rhythmic, the Freudian theory would have been hardly set in doubt, for sexuality seems to be a more likely source for the pleasure of rhythm than these other activities which are emotionally neutral. But the facts go so much further, that they even suggest a different theory of rhythm.

Rhythmic periodicity lies, in fact, at the very core of all organic life. The pulsations of protoplasmic substance, the contractile movements of amoebae, infusoria, and worms, the ciliary movements of spermatozoa, the locomotion of quadrupeds and bipeds (Tinbergen, 1951), the motion of human fetuses (Stevens, 1951, pp. 294–95), the first impulsive movements of infants, and the primary voluntary motoric habits (Stern, 1923, pp. 44 ff.), electrical activity in the brain, neural transmission, respiration, heartbeat, circulation, and many other visceral activities, separately and in patterns, are all rhythmically structured (Stevens, 1951). Moreover, not only sexuality, but hunger, thirst, and other needs also follow a periodic pattern in their occurrence, and rhythm characterizes the actions designed to satisfy them, from the sucking reflexes of neonates to the chewing and swallowing activities of adults (Fraisse, 1967). Further, on the human level, many phenomena occurring during a relaxation of conscious control have also been observed to be rhythmical, for instance, various automatisms, stereotypes, and verbigerations. In view of this evidence, Piaget's (1960, p. 169) conclusion that "rhythm characterizes the functions that are at the junction between organic and mental life" seems hardly exaggerated. Freud too would have probably concurred in this opinion for he proclaimed repetitiveness, which lies at the core of rhythm, to be a basic organic principle (Freud, 1922).

What are the implications of these facts for the experience of rhythm? A possible hypothesis would be that perceived rhythm taps the permanently active conscious and unconscious rhythmical processes within the listener, focusing them, perhaps also reinforcing them, and centering the perceiver's attention on these processes, which lie at the very core of life. The increased awareness of basic life processes, brought about by rhythm, may enhance the perceiver's sensations of being alive. This sense of life pulsating and surging within him could be experienced as pleasurable. Hence the pleasure accompanying the perception of rhythm.

This hypothesis, congenial because of its emphasis on the familiar concept "Hi! We are alive!" could account for the fascination of rhythm in general, were it not for a serious difficulty against which it stumbles. Why should awareness of being alive be at all pleasurable? Is it that without this reminder we would not know that we are alive? The awareness of being alive can be accorded meaning, only if we assume that there exists a permanent danger or a sense of danger of death. In order to make the hypothesis plausible, it would be necessary to postulate that people live with the constant temptation to destroy themselves and to die; namely, that there exists a death drive, which Freud (1922) indeed suggested as a manifestation of the striving to return to the state of unorganic matter. Yet, the concept of the death instinct is too doubtful and controversial to buttress an hypothesis whose validity and explanatory power are in any case so restricted.

However, the facts mentioned about the commonness of rhythm in the sphere of biological processes suggest another, more comprehensive and satisfactory hypothesis. This hypothesis is based on the relation between the perception of external rhythm and the course of internal rhythmical life processes.[3] It is a well-known fact that the perception of rhythm is invariably accompanied by actual movements or kinesthetic motoric impulses in line with the rhythm (Fraisse et al., 1953; Mursell, 1937; Ruckmick, 1913). Motoric activities, however, affect the pace of internal processes. Hence, the speed of external rhythm may be expected to alter the rate of internal processes. This means that fast rhythm, for instance, will tend to cause a rise in the level of arousal, but not that the tempo and rhythm of heartbeat, respiration, etc., will correspond precisely to the external tempo and rhythm (Fraisse, 1967, pp. 32 ff.). However, any considerable changes in the rates of basic life processes are not likely to be experienced as pleasurable. Great increases of arousal level which occur, for instance, in states of extreme excitement, rage, or mania and in pathological conditions of hypertension, hyperthyroidism, etc., are very unpleasant, even painful. No less unpleasant is a marked slowing down of life processes as, for example, in deep depression. In extreme cases a very pronounced acceleration or deceleration of internal processes may even cause death.

These observations might explain why rhythms which deviate markedly in speed from the range of tempo characteristic of standard life processes evoke tension in the perceiver, and why relief attends the return of tempo to the standard range. The tempo of life processes is, in fact, the level of arousal. It differs within limits from one person to another, and in the same individual on various occasions (Berlyne, 1960, pp. 211–16). The level of arousal probably depends both on physiological determinants and on long- and short-term activities and environmental features. Yet when the level deviates too much from the customary range, there is a tendency to raise it or lower it back to the habitual (Fiske & Maddi, 1961).

Thus, although an acceleration of rhythm arouses tension, it may be wished for as a means intensifying the pleasure which will accompany the subsequent relief from this enhanced tension. Since acceleration of internal processes is more frequent in various emotional and motivational states in life than is deceleration, unconscious speeding up of tempo is in general more characteristic of musicians and orchestras than a pronounced slowing down in playing. Owing to the tension qualities of any changes in an established rhythm, shifts in rhythm may be expected to be generally preferred to a monotonous rhythm.

However, this hypothesis does not provide a satisfactory answer to the question, Why is rhythm pleasurable? For in many cases, rhythm is enjoyable even when no changes in speed or in other qualities take place. Many of the rhythms spontaneously imposed by people on sequences of phenomena are precisely of a slow or medium tempo, adapted to the rate of internal processes, without a wish being manifested by the perceivers for changes in the rhythm. Sometimes, for instance in the rhythmization of material for memorization or of phenomena such as windows or trees along a street, it seems that any changes of tempo may be even feared or resisted. Where, then, does the pleasure afforded by such rhythms derive from?

This further aspect of rhythm may best be considered within the framework of our former conception of rhythm as a gestalt. The perception of gestalts plays an important role in the life of organisms, for gestalts introduce order, organization, meaningfulness, economy, and simplicity into the external and internal environments (Chapter 4). The grasping of gestalts thus not only facilitates understanding and action, but as an aid in orientation it is an indispensable means for survival. Without orientation no security and no orderly activity is possible (Chapter 1). Even the experience of daily life demonstrates that things we do not understand, intruding stimuli we cannot control, and phenomena we cannot conceive may be sources of fear, which sometimes takes the despairing form of anxiety. On the other hand, the attainment of orientation is obviously a source of pleasure. For to conceive mentally means to control and thus to regain security. By satisfying orientation—a vitally important need of man on the biological and psychological levels—the appeal of rhythm is greatly enhanced.

Rhythm, as a simple, economical, and efficient means of imposing organization on disparate stimuli and sequential processes, must then be an outstanding source of enjoyment. This is so, even in situations where orientation is not urgently and vitally needed—i.e., even when we are supposed to be already largely oriented, as when traveling in a train or sitting in a concert hall. For it is the very act of organizing and conceiving, as such, which is pleasurable. The functions of rhythm as a means for organization and orientation help to explain such disparate phenomena as the use of rhythm in learning and memorization (Woodworth, 1938) and in uniting people for work and march. Moreover, without assuming that "the rhythmic sense of primitive people is much more highly developed than our own," which has presumably been dulled by "the simplification of the rhythm of modern folk song and of poetry intended to appeal to popular sense" (Boas, 1955, p. 310), it would not be too difficult to understand why children and so-called primitive peoples tend so markedly to rhythmization in most domains of life. Maturity and civilization provide us with further means of orientation in complex environment. However, both in the more and in the less primitive worlds, rhythm, whenever it is perceived, produced, or reproduced, serves the function of reducing, condensing, and mitigating the complexity of stimuli in constant flux, by ordering them into graspable and organized patterns which, while they do not solve the insoluble, at least satisfy through the illusion they give of controlling the uncontrollable.

If rhythm is viewed as a temporal gestalt providing orientation, it is clear that both the rhythm in an even tempo and the return of the tempo to an even rate may be experienced as pleasurable, for any change in the even rate, when grasped as a disruption of the basic framework, arouses tension. The continuation of a rhythmic pattern evokes in the perceiver the expectation that the pattern will persist. Richards (1926, pp. 134 ff.), who emphasized this aspect of rhythm to the exclusion of others, aptly remarked that "rhythm depends upon repetition and expectancy . . . all rhythmical effects spring from anticipation. . . . This texture of expectations, satisfactions, disappointments, surprises . . . is rhythm." But regardless of possible changes in rhythm, the actual gestalt of rhythm constantly provides tension and relief, deriving from the ever-nascent striving for the closure of the gestalt which is never wholly there but gradually materializes in time.

How is it that precisely rhythm came to be what Plato (1937b, 672) called "the present of the gods to men," whereby they can distinguish order from

disorder? In view of the ubiquity of rhythm in the world of natural phenomena, this should no longer be surprising. Rhythm, as a cosmic manifestation pervading life and nature with lawfulness, can indeed be seen as an
excellent means for introducing orientation into our small cosmoses, integrating these within the basic framework of the universe at large.

These last remarks also serve to suggest a conclusion: the three theoretical
accounts of the pleasurable effects of rhythm are by no means mutually
exclusive. The hypotheses that the pleasure in rhythm derives from its
associative linking with the rhythm of sexuality, from the degree of its correspondence to the basic rhythms of internal life processes, and from its
orientative function as a gestalt are supported by similar observations and
complementing theoretical frameworks. Sexuality is but one instance from
the overall complex of vital life processes, and orientation draws its importance from its functions in making possible the satisfaction of life-
supporting needs in general and of sexuality as a particular instance. Rhythm
is then pleasure-laden as a result of its multideterminative relations to many
and various functions of the human being, which lends it not only the power
to arouse tension and provide relief but also to fascinate, bind, and in certain
cases dominate the perceiver.

Rhythm in Music

In music there are two types of rhythm. First, there is the fundamental
rhythm, sometimes called "meter," which is the basic temporal articulation
of the musical flow into a series of regularly occurring equal beats or pulses.
These are differentiated and grouped into units called "measures" by means
of accents at equal intervals. Accordingly, each measure contains a definite
number of "beats" or counting-units which, combined with the differentiation of the beats into accented, less-accented, and unaccented ones, fall into
a series of definite and fixed patterns, such as the double (2/4), the triple
(3/4), the quadruple (4/4), etc. By means of further subdivisions or combinations of these primary forms, more compound rhythms may be produced
(W. S. Pratt, 1944, pp. 125–27).

The basic meter, with its implied scheme of accents, is presented explicitly
or implicitly at the beginning of the musical piece and in traditional music
usually persists throughout a whole composition, a movement, or its major
parts. Though it may hardly appear in the playing itself, or may only be
hinted at, it is nevertheless felt. It thus acts as a basic framework which
facilitates perception of the music and lends it unity on a certain level.
Though barely present, it is immediately and spontaneously grasped by the

listeners, for it is as a rule a part of their general cultural background. In dance-style music, the basic meter is naturally prominent and frequently or continuously presented.

The forms of basic meter are few and tend to vary with cultural areas and sometimes also with historical periods. Chinese, Negro, Arabic, Polynesian, and Western basic rhythms differ from each other, and it is probably no accident that a passion for certain rhythms prevails in certain times. The basic rhythms of a culture are as much created by and characteristic of the culture as they are expressive of it.

The fundamental meter serves mainly as a framework for the unfolding of melodic rhythm and other rhythmic figures, created, for instance, by percussion instruments. The rhythms that are superimposed on the basic meter or grow out of it are much less rigid, are less limited in form, and offer more scope for individual creativity than the basic rhythm.[4] The differentiation between the counting-units occurs here not only by means of accents, as in the fundamental meter, but also through longer and shorter durations of tones and of pauses. The interplay of accents and differential temporal duration lays the foundation for a series of various rhythmical forms, which may change in the course of a composition. While even in a small form, such as a hymn tune, each phrase may have a distinct rhythm, in part music the different voices may present the same phrase in different rhythms. Similarly, rhythmic patterns of increasing complexity may be used to build up a climax, and patterns gradually decreasing in complexity will serve in the preparation of relief. In modern music different rhythms may succeed each other and interpenetrate so irregularly that the composition may seem to have no rhythmical structure.

The two kinds of rhythm are by no means independent. On the contrary, they are tightly interwoven, and the matrix of complex interrelations between them offers many possibilities for the production of tension-and-relief effects. The melodic or higher-level rhythms do not unfold as a rule in a vacuum, but manifest a patterned relation to the basic meter from which they definitely differ. Longer or shorter tones or pauses of the melody may not coincide with the basic counting-units and often cut across them with little formal regularity. Particularly tension-laden are the cases when an accent in the higher-level rhythms is delayed relatively to the accents of the basic meter and when an apparent or sometimes an actual change of meter takes place.

Within the framework of the basic rhythm itself, the possibilities for arousing tension are rather limited, unless there is a temporary overall change in meter or an opposition of several different simultaneous meters, as frequently occurs in Beethoven's sonatas. This is so, because the measure is in general grasped as a necessary frame of reference for the composition as a whole; and for the modern listener in particular, it has already turned, as a result of long acquaintance, into an inherently good gestalt. It is mainly by reference to the fundamental meter that the potentialities of the higher-level rhythms are enhanced, for it is this basic rhythm which establishes for each musical piece what is slow, what is measured flow, and what is unbalanced progression.

The higher-level rhythms are also relatively good gestalts and form what is called rhythmical motifs. This means that any temporal deviation from such a pattern of rhythm may arouse tension, while the return to it is felt to be relieving. The rhythms of melodies or motifs can be submitted to variations, i.e., to changes of gestalt, so that each variation is experienced in reference to the original rhythmical theme as a worse gestalt and arouses the tension involved in the striving for a closure of the gestalt in the form of a final resolution.

Apart from these specific effects, the more general experiential impact of rhythm, discussed above, may be evident in music to a greater degree than in the other arts. First, music is the art of order par excellence. Not only is it ordered, but the organization, particularly of the rhythm, can be sensed at each instant, so that at almost every single point the direction of the whole is felt and could be determined. Within the framework of music proper, the orientative function of rhythm is often particularly evident in the basic meter. According to the hypothesis which relates the effects of rhythm to the pace of life processes, the fundamental meter can be viewed as corresponding to the average arousal level, so that deviations from it are felt to be tension-laden. Finally, the experiences accompanying acceleration and deceleration of tempo, the extreme tension involved in the insertion of small pauses just on the threshold of the climax, and the ecstatic responses to highly rhythmized music can also be interpreted from the viewpoint of the erotic theory of rhythm. As in the case of any complex phenomenon, the effects of musical rhythm may be as varied and multileveled as the cues in the music and the receptive elaboration of the listener allow for.

8. Dance

Deviation from the Familiar

Man has always danced—in ecstasy, for expression, in submission to nature, and as a means for controlling nature (Sachs, 1937). In the context of this book, however, we shall deal only with dance as an art performed before and for an audience as a single or major element of a spectacle. Although dancers appeared before audiences also in the Greek and Roman worlds, the art form of Western dance known to us today is the product of a relatively new development. It originated officially in 1581 with Le Ballet Comique de la Reyne, mounted before Catherine de Médicis, and made its first steps in the French and Italian courts, although its origins lay in medieval religious processions and tournaments, aristocratic banquet spectacles, and traditional folk dancing.

Ballet is usually viewed in a theatrical context which includes also drama, music, and stage decoration. In spite of recurrent attempts to strip the art of dance from its musical and theatrical accompaniments, even the modern nonballetic dance, which relies rather more often on expressionism than on an explicit dramatic plot, is rarely performed without music and stage design. Yet, only when we abstract these contextual elements can we come nearer to the basic medium of dance, which is movement and postures of the human body.

All people move and see others moving constantly. What, if any, are the differences between dance movements and movements in daily life? In what sense does a dance depiction of a boxing match differ from an actual match, a ballet scene of love from any love scene, or Martha Graham's "Dance of Work" from real work with machines? The answers to these questions form a focal point of our investigation, for on them depends the possibility of accounting for the special experiential effects of dance. All too often, however, attempts to pinpoint the special features of dance movements end up either in the admission that dance movements do not differ from other movements or in the reduction of their special nature to the content they portray. An example of the first approach is provided by Schertel (1926), who writes that "any kind of dance derives its style, its law of form, from those hidden internal bodily processes which cause and direct the movements of the single parts of the body." More common is the second approach, which consists in reducing the specifity of dance to its "inspired message" (Selden, 1935, p. 42). This message is conceived as universally valid human conceptions (Selden, 1935), as the abstract symbolization of "virtual force" (Langer, 1953), and most commonly as the expression of emotions (J. Martin, 1946). This approach may at best serve to identify dance movements as belonging to the special class of human expressive movements, which have traditionally been distinguished from functionally oriented movements (K. Bühler, 1933; Buytendijk, 1957). But it does not in any way help to recognize in what way the dance movements of joy, sorrow, despair, and elation differ from movements attending the spontaneous evocation of these emotions.

Attempts at delimiting the specificity of movements in dance are relatively rare. These usually emphasize that dance movements are characterized primarily by rhythm (Laban, 1966, p. 117; Selden, 1935, pp. 41–42; Sachs, 1937, p. 6) or a "unity of character or expression" (J. G. Sulzer, 1794, p. 507), which results in "organized movement" (Kandinsky, 1955, p. 71). When taken at face value, characterizations such as these are hardly informative and can readily be shown to be insufficient. Is not a marching row of soldiers an example for "organized movement"? Doesn't a callisthenics class perform with rhythm "and unity of character"? Yet, on a deeper level the enunciation of these and other similar features reveals an awareness on the part of spectators and analysts of dance that there is something special about the movements of dance. What is it?

In view of the complexity and multifacetedness of human movements it can be presumed that the specificity of dance movements will be found to consist not in one feature but rather in a set of characteristics, which to a certain extent complement and may even replace each other.

The search for specificity may start with an almost commonplace observation. If we ask an adult to perform a routine action, such as walking or taking a glass, in a dancing manner, not only will he find the task easy, but observers can instantly identify his movements as a mimicry of dance. When questioned about the criteria underlying this identification, people readily offer the answer: "These movements are different from those one regularly performs."[1] This simple criterion, which may variously be called "unfamiliarity," "remoteness from habitual movements," or "strangeness," proves to be a useful clue of wide applicability. Its exemplification is particularly straightforward for dance forms which have undergone codification, like the classical Western ballet.

Ballet[2] consists of a series of highly formalized bodily postures and movements which form in a way the "vocabulary" of ballet and are combined by choreographers and dancers, who thus provide the "grammatical rules" for any unfolding of a specific ballet. The major postural building blocks of the ballet include five positions of *feet* (Fig. 8.1), five positions of the *arms* (Fig. 8.2), five whole-body postures of the *arabesque* type (Fig. 8.3), in which the dancer stands on one leg, straight or slightly bent, while the other leg is extended in a straight line at right angles to it, and an indeterminate number of *attitudes* (Fig. 8.4), i.e., poses in which the body is supported on one leg, with the foot flat on the ground or the heel slightly raised, while the other leg is raised with the knee bent. Even a cursory view of these postures reveals that they are unlikely to be assumed in daily life and that a situation requiring their assumption outside dance is hardly conceivable.

No less remote from daily practice are the codified balletic movements. Formally they include seven types, e.g., to bend, to stretch, to rise, and to jump, which, however, indicate habitual motions only by name. Thus, while the usual way to take a step is to place the heel first, in ballet the placement of the toes always precedes that of the heel. Examples of the better-known balletic movements include the *pas de bourrée*, i.e., a progression on the tips of the toes by a series of very small and even steps; *entrechat*, i.e., a jump which starts with the feet in the fifth position and involves a reversal in their relative placement before the dancer comes down again in the fifth position; and the *fouetté*, i.e., a turn on one leg accompanied by a whipping

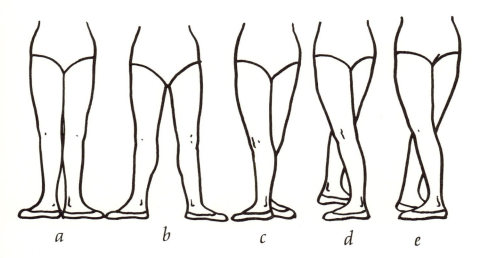

a   *b*   *c*   *d*   *e*

Fig. 8.1 The five basic positions of legs and feet in classical ballet: *a*, first position; *b*, second position; *c*, third position; *d*, fourth position; *e*, fifth position.

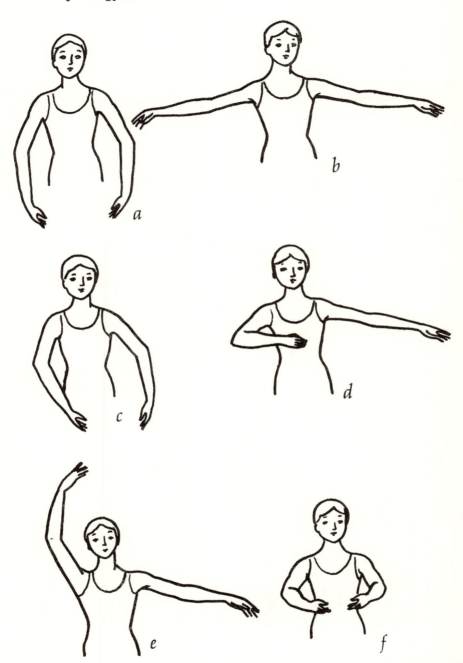

Fig. 8.2 Basic arm positions in classical ballet: *a*, first position; *b*, second position; *c*, third position; *d* and *e*, two versions of the fourth position; *f*, fifth position.

Fig. 8.3 The arabesque "line" in ballet.

motion of the other. Obviously, these movements are based on principles deviating sharply from those underlying nondance movements.

Although modern Free Dance has broken away from the stultifying balletic code and has striven instead towards a more natural dance, the characteristic poses and movements of modern dancers are in no way nearer to those of daily life. Commenting on the potentialities for dance of a theater in the round, Humphrey (1959, p. 90) aptly remarks: ". . . more intimacy does not help the dancer, because he does not seek to be more real and natural but more stylized and magical." Thus, remoteness remained, while the principles underlying it changed. In the expressionistic phase of modern dance, the motional repertory was extended through the inclusion of movements designed to correspond to the basic rhythms of the body and nature and to represent the primeval and direct expression of universal emotions. Thus, Isadora Duncan turned to idealizations of the ancient Greek dance in order to combat "the natural decadences of human movements" and to rediscover their instinctive forms as manifested by child and animal (quoted

Fig. 8.4 An "attitude" in ballet.

from Sorrell, 1966, pp. 31–32). Mary Wigman (1966) looked towards the expressive means in old pagan rituals, and Ruth St. Denis (1939) drew movement motifs from the Far Eastern traditions. Out of these attempts a whole new set of movements, different both from balletic and daily-life motion, was introduced into the vocabulary of dance: the heavy falling movements, the expansive "unfolding" (e.g., Fig. 8.5) and closing-in "folding" sequence, the "swinging," "swaying," and "shaking" motifs (Selden, 1930), or the shrapnel-like "percussive strokes" of Martha Graham. The principle underlying these movements is the origination of motion in the torso in contrast to ordinary movement, which may originate in any part of the body.

More recent generations of dancers and choreographers have utilized other principles for enriching the motional repertory of dance without trespassing into the realm of daily life (S. J. Cohen, 1966; Jackson, 1966). Some of the techniques are these: combining randomly different movements in various parts of the body, as has been done by Merce Cunningham and Katherine Litz; presenting improbable sequences of movements—for instance, a clearly outlined walk culminates in a burst of vague and shapeless arm movements (e.g., Taylor), or balletic steps, folk-dance jump, and Free Dance movements follow each other irregularly; performing common movements in unusual ways, e.g., much faster or slower than usual, or sideways if forwards is customary; or improbable juxtapositions of movements, e.g., one dancer jumps excitedly, while another is motionless and a third moves lyrically (e.g., James Waring's and Aileen Passloff's dances). In the context of these improbable, remote movements, contemporary dancers sometimes insert motion sequences out of daily life, such as combing one's hair or playing ball. These serve to highlight the strangeness of "normal" dance movements and are as tension-laden as a simple major triad within the context of twelve-tone music.

It is obvious that remoteness from habitual movements could under no circumstances serve as a distinguishing characteristic of dance movements. Although the unfamiliar gait of a Balinese or the bending of an African to lift an object may impress Westerners as graceful and dancelike, the no less strange clumsy movements of a clown, the uncontrolled gait of a drunk person, or the bizarre movements of physically maimed people hardly impress one as art. Nevertheless, remoteness from the habitual seems to play a more important role in dance than in the other arts as a means of arousing interest and laying the groundwork for an art experience. All arts have their specific kind of remoteness, which may derive from the nature of the medium, as in music, or from the combination of the elements, as in painting. Movements not only play a prominent and continuous role in daily life, but many of the less frequent movements and their combinations have become familiar through sports, athletics, and dramatic acting. Since, moreover, the possibilities of new movements and of combining familiar movements are restricted through the anatomic and physiologic structure of the human body, the playground left for dancing is relatively narrow—hence, the striving for remoteness in dance movements. In India, a country that has produced a magnificent tradition of dancing, this striving may have determined the restriction of the use of basic dance postures and movements only to gods, dancers, and priests (Frédéric, 1957). It is our task now to try to uncover in what this remoteness from the habitual consists.

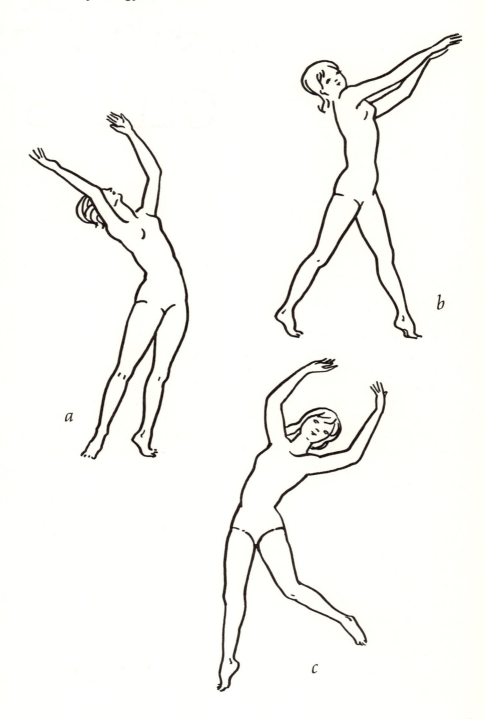

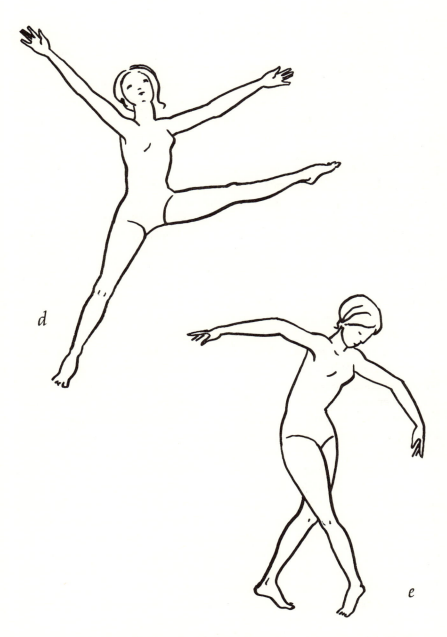

Fig. 8.5 Some characteristic postures of modern expressive dance: *a* and *c*, the "unfolding" motif.

Balanced Lability and Line

The human body of the dancer and the nondancer alike moves in a gravitational field and is subject to the laws of gravity. Unaided by machines and other special devices, the range of human motion spreads over a not too wide band of possibilities marked by the opposite poles of succumbing to gravity or overcoming it for seconds. Between the poles of a fall and a jump, human postures and movement may be characterized by varying degrees of stability. Nondancers in their routine activities naturally try to preserve maximum stability. Not so the dancers in dancing. The kind of stability they present is different: it is a stability which makes the impression of lability.

Dance lability is illustrated strikingly by the classical ballet. Lability seems, in fact, to be the common denominator of the five basic leg positions in ballet (Fig. 8.1). These positions are all characterized by shifting the toes 90 degrees to the right or the left from their normal frontal placement. Thus, in the first of these positions, the heels are juxtaposed, and the toes are turned outward, so that the feet form a straight line; in the second, the feet are in one line, separated by a distance of about a foot, and are both turned outward; in the third the heel of one foot rests against the instep of the other, both feet being firmly turned out; in the fourth, one foot rests about a foot in advance of the other, both feet being turned out; and in the fifth, the feet are turned out and pressed closely together, the heel of the right foot against the toe of the left. In these positions one of the dimensions of the base formed by the feet is greatly shortened through the device of turning the toes. Thus, the dancer seems to preserve a slender stability, balanced between the pull backward and the pull forward, so that the impression of a precarious vertical equilibrium is created. This impression is even stronger in the "attitudes" (Fig. 8.4) and arabesques (Fig. 8.3) in which the whole body is supported on one leg while the other is bent or stretched high above the ground.

When we watch ballet dancers in motion, it often appears as if they had succeeded in outwitting gravity. Often their only contact with the ground is through the tips of the toes. The airy, light, indeed weightless quality of balletic spinning, twirling, leaping, and gliding is the most overriding characteristic of ballet. Ballet dancers seem more often to float, to be on the verge of alighting on invisible wings and to fly through a milky insubstantial medium than to move as gravitationally bound mortals. The highpoints of this motion are reached in the *entrechat* jumps, in the course of which the legs are crossed and recrossed, and in the prolonged elevations (Fig. 8.6) from which the dancer lands back as lightly and gently as if he had taken only a small step on the ground.

Yet the fascination of ballet does not stem from the lightness and floating as such. This is demonstrated by the quick abandonment of attempts, introduced in the eighteenth century, to enhance the duration and extent of jumps by attaching dancers to invisible wires and pulleys (Haskell, 1945). The exciting quality of ballet derives from the victory over gravity attained by the unaided human body, performing within the bounds of expanded natural potentialities, with which the spectator can identify kinesthetically and ideationally.

Actual flying would imply extreme lability, of the kind cultivated for example in acrobatics. In contrast, the major attainment of the dance is a perfectly balanced lability. While in acrobatics even stability seems labile, in dance lability is made to appear perfectly and gracefully balanced.

There should be little surprise that the revolution of modern dance against ballet was centered so heavily on the problem of manipulating weight. The revolt took initially the form of an emphasis on heavy motions replete with stamping, pushing, pulling, and a whole range of impulse movements, falls, and floor dancing of the kind found later in Martha Graham's dances (Selden, 1935, pp. 111–16). Yet soon enough balance was restored by adding light and floating movements as the indispensable opposite pole to "weighted," heavy movements (Laban, 1950). Broadening the range of dance movements has implied also increased possibilities for balanced lability.

Modern dancers proclaim their goal to be "dance that loves gravity rather than fights gravity; dance that hangs and falls rather than fights" (E. Hawkins, 1966, p. 242), and so the means they have devised for attaining balanced lability differ from those of ballet. For example, regardless of whether the feet are placed flat on the ground or on tiptoe, juxtaposed or apart, lability is attained by outstretching or far-swinging movements which displace the body's center of gravity (Fig. 8.5). Similarly, the slow measured sinking in Doris Humphrey's "Water Study" or the final noiseless fall in Martha Graham's "Heretic," both of which have entered the treasured classics of modern dance, represent victories over gravity no less impressive than balletic elevations off the ground. The discoveries of the early group of modern dancers about braving gravity while apparently succumbing to it have greatly enriched the medium of movement and thus broadened the scope of dance.

A different type of labile stability has been cultivated in the Indian dance.[3] This glorious dancing tradition is comparable rather to ballet than to modern dance, mainly because it is based on a strict code of rules regulating all movements and postures. But it is a far more demanding and strict code

Fig. 8.6 An "elevation" in ballet.

than has ever been developed in Western culture. The basic code, which underlies the various dancing styles of India and is presented in the two ancient sources *Natya Sastra* (Science of Dramaturgy) and *Abhinaya Dharpana* (Gestures and Expression), includes 108 fixed positions (karanas). Each karana is based on specific placement of the body, arms, hands, legs, and feet (Fig. 8.7a–d). The code includes also 28 positions for single hands and 27 positions for the two hands combined (Fig. 8.8a–c) which serve as a kind of sign language, as well as instructions for 13 different movements of the head, 6 movements of the nose, 6 of the lower lip, 7 of the eyelashes, etc., which are designed to express a rich variety of moods. The dance consists essentially in the combination of the various karanas by specific movements.

It is the karanas (Fig. 8.7a–d) and particularly the characteristic leg and foot positions (Fig. 8.9a–d) which best demonstrate the labile stability. For example, in the posture of Fig. 8.7c the left foot is placed on the ground, its toes pointing outward, the right foot is raised back, its heel near the ear, the right arm is stretched to the left, and the left arm bent, the hands being in a special position. Posed thus, the dancer now performs the following movements: she raises the right leg up, and she touches the tip of her nose, before she passes to another posture whose leg placement is presented in

Fig. 8.9d. The lability characterizing these postures could hardly be sur-passed. Yet, just like the floating of ballet, or the outstretching and the fall of modern dance, it is perfectly balanced, so well that the postures are pre-served while movements are performed. Yet the source of the balancing seems to be even more covert than in ballet and modern dance, which often use arm postures to counterbalance the lability, at least on the visual level.

Arm positions as well as the overall shape of the body and its parts may be a major compensatory factor for the lability inherent in dance positions. In ballet this factor is called "line" and has been cultivated particularly by the Italian and Russian schools of ballet (Praagh & Brinson, 1963). The "line" in ballet follows in general the rules of symmetry and balance in static forms. For example, an arm or leg stretched in one direction is bal-anced by the stretching of the other arm or leg in the opposite direction, usually at the same angle of inclination. Thus, in the arabesque (Fig. 8.3), the leg outstretched backward is counterbalanced by the arm outstretched for-ward, and in the "attitude" (Fig. 8.4) the raised bent leg is counterbalanced by the raised bent arm. When one side of the body is lowered or recedes, the other side is correspondingly raised or brought nearer to the spectator (Beau-mont & Idzikowski, 1940, p. 28). For instance, "when the dancer faces the audience—and with one foot . . . describes on the ground a semi-circle from front to back, the head should be inclined to the side opposite to the foot that makes the movement" (ibid., p. 29).

Obviously, not all balletic postures and movements are symmetric, as is demonstrated, for instance, by arm positions (Fig. 8.2c, d, e), the elevation line (Fig. 8.6), and the contrast in the arabesque (Fig. 8.3) between the sharp angle formed by the legs and the graceful line along the back. Yet in modern dance and in the Indian dance symmetry occurs less frequently than in the classical ballet. Through the ample use of asymmetrical lines in the various extension planes of the body, modern dance and Indian dance have used to greater advantage the possibilities inherent in the spatial aspects of dance than ballet, which has greatly favored postures in the full frontal view with balanced movement extending in the vertical plane.

"Line" places dance within the realm of the visual and spatial arts. The body, as a tridimensional object in space, presents a complex gestalt with a variety of shapes extending in a multitude of directions. The postures as-sumed by the dancer momentarily or during more prolonged periods before or after dance phases can be viewed as "living sculpture," subject to the experiential rules of shapes (Kandinsky, 1955). Angles and curves formed by different parts of the body, extending in different planes and directions, molded by the contours of costumes, may be opposed as contrasts, accentu-

Fig. 8.7 Karanas (body postures) of the Indian dance: *a*, karana 25, called *urdhva janu*, "raised knees"; *b*, karana 87, called *kari hasta*, "elephant trunk"; *c*, karana 26, called *nikuncita*, "bent"; *d*, karana 78, called *sucividdha*, "needle probing." [After Bhavnani, 1965]

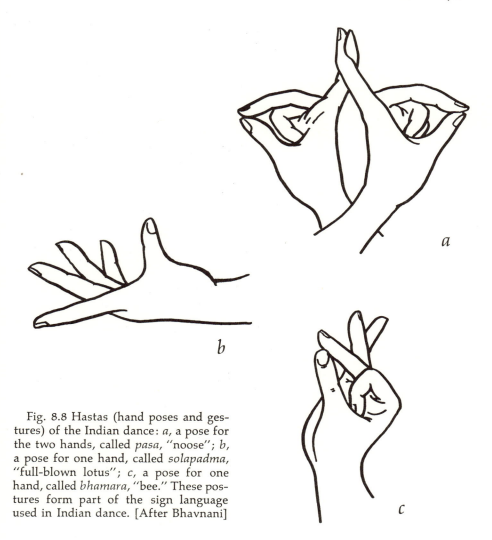

Fig. 8.8 Hastas (hand poses and gestures) of the Indian dance: *a*, a pose for the two hands, called *pasa*, "noose"; *b*, a pose for one hand, called *solapadma*, "full-blown lotus"; *c*, a pose for one hand, called *bhamara*, "bee." These postures form part of the sign language used in Indian dance. [After Bhavnani]

ated or combined, variated and balanced against each other, in many ways which evoke tension, provide relief, and contribute experientially to the unity of the whole design. Moreover, the shapes outlined by the body of one dancer may be complemented through those of other dancers, and the line created by a whole group of dancers is grasped in interaction with the line shaped by another group (Humphrey, 1959, pp. 49–59). The tridimensionality of the body allows for an incomparable enrichment of the experiential effects of shapes beyond those of the bidimensional forms in painting (Chapters 4 and 5). Formally, many of these effects can be analyzed in terms of Gestalt laws,

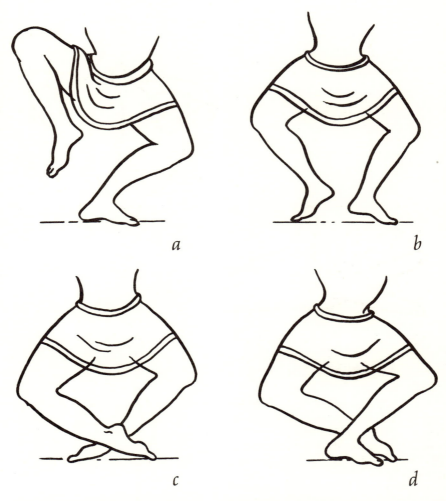

a   *b*

c   *d*

Fig. 8.9 Characteristic positions of legs and feet in the Indian dance: *a*, part of karana 18, called *alata*, "circling"; *b*, part of karana 21, called *viksipta*, "thrown over"; *c*, part of karana 85, called *nitamba*, "posteriors"; *d*, part of karana 77, called *ardha-suci*, "needle probing." [After Bhavnani, 1965]

but the elements are different, for volume and mass replace the painterly surfaces, real depth replaces the illusion of depth, and space—enclosed and enclosing—emerges instead of the background in painting. These aspects highlight the affinity of dance to sculpture (Chapters 9 and 10) rather than to painting. In spite of the inspiration that many dancers have found in sculpture (Selden, 1935, p. 39), the difference between the two arts should not be underrated. In dance, mass and space are shaped through movement of a living human body, while sculpture can create only the illusion of movement—for instance, through the portrayal of human bodies in moments of intense motion.

In dance it is a living human body which forms the "line" and the design of volumes and shapes, and this fact is crucial in the experiencing of these forms and shapes. Its importance becomes obvious when one considers that forms like the arabesque or some modern and some Indian postures may not impress us as particularly beautiful and balanced when portrayed in stone or metal or on a canvas. A shape created by a human body is spontaneously grasped in reference both to the habitual images of the body and the intimate experience we have of our own bodies. The habitual images, which come to play the role of good gestalts thanks to their familiarity, include the ordinary frontal posture of the erect body, and the forms of the body in accustomed actions or poses such as walking or sitting.

The dancer, however, usually acts within a range of postures which lie outside these habitual poses. Yet, the dance positions do not thereby become all bad gestalts. On the contrary, the dancer establishes a new norm of good gestalts, whose goodness depends on both balanced lability and figural gestalt principles. While he deviates, for instance, from the habitual frontal placement of the feet, he may spread his arms as in the second arm position (Fig. 8.2b) and thus present a bodily form which is not usual, but figurally is a good gestalt. The numerous possibilities of opposing and combining habitual images of the body, figural gestalt principles, and balanced lability are limited only by the principle that dance positions should not overstep the borderline set by the extension of natural potentialities of the human body.

Dynamic Line

The unique quality of shapes in dance derives from motion. Shapes changing one into another, forms-in-the-making, lines created through movement—these are major stimuli of the dance experience. The temporal dynamic unfolding of forms is such an overriding factor that it hardly allows for experiencing even static postures as if they were sculptures in space. "In a dance a pattern or line is justified, or not justified, by what has preceded it, by the way in which the dancer has come to it" (Selden, 1935, p. 142), as well as by what it foreshadows for the subsequent unfolding of the dance. This implies not only that a nonmobile "line" is perceived as a part within a sequence of movement, which prepares it and serves as its contextual background, but mainly that a posture represents a moment of repose in the flow of movement. Hence, the experiential effects of a posture cannot be divorced from its function in the dynamic unfolding of the dance. A posture at the beginning of a dance or of a dance phrase is much more tension-laden and pregnant with movement than the same posture at an intermediary or final ending, when it is grasped as the culmination of movements and the fulfillment of a motional sequence.

Perceptually, the difference between stationary and moving objects is considered to be relative. Motion is perceived when forms undergo translational and rotational transformations under specified temporal relations, regardless of whether the forms are actually static or moving (Gibson, 1957). Yet, experientially there seems to be a qualitative difference between the perception of stationary and that of moving objects, just as there is between the movement of an inanimate rigid object and the movement of a plastic organic body (Gibson, 1966, pp. 201–3). The observation that there are static postures which seem like frozen movements, or movements which are experienced as slow transformations in static postures, does not alter the essential difference between repose and movement. This factor is of major importance in dancing, since it allows for organizing the dancing flow into *phrases of movements* marked off through stationary postures, and underlies the *structuring of dynamics* in dancing.

A basic aspect of "phrasing" is the recurrence of some pattern, which in classical ballet was mostly postural and in modern dance is more often motional. In classical ballet a major contrast is formed through the opposition of stationary positions and movements either in the unfolding action of one dancer or through the counterpoising of a moving dancer and stationary dancers in the background. Ballet consists essentially in the stringing together of separate units of motion divided by positions or "attitudes." "Each motion . . . should begin and end in one of the five positions" (Selden, 1930, p. 59). The stationary positions thus feature as contrasts to the preceding and subsequent phrases of motions. More important, however, is the role of the stationary positions in setting a standard which establishes a frame of reference for the experience of both motion and the forms created through motions in the dance. As we have seen, the postures of dance are endowed with stimulating qualities when compared with the standard, balanced, and erect good-gestalt posture of the human body. Yet, the postures and movements which occur within the dance are experienced rather in reference to the standard established by the basic postures of the dance. Thus, the five positions represent in ballet the analogue to key determinants in music.

The standard established by the positions is twofold: they are stationary elements in contrast to movements, and they determine what is considered good-gestalt posture or "line" within the dance. Thus, the tension effects of the dance sequence are enhanced through deviations from the five positions in terms both of motion and of the forms traced by movements and other positions assumed in the course of dancing. Since the spectator is induced to accept the outward turned toes of the basic positions as the good gestalt of the ballet, a sudden frontal placement of the toes would represent a tension-laden deviation from expectation. Hence, the exciting quality of George Balanchine's ballets. Although he remains within the framework of the classic technique, he introduces into it unexpected changes. For example, routine ballet steps are performed with the knees turned in instead of out, a conventional pose is shattered by the flexing of a foot which should be pointed, or a dancer may not only lift his partner as in the conventional *pas de deux* but will actually place her limbs as if she were a puppet. Since the basic ballet positions are already familiar to spectators, the deviations can be performed without presenting the standard model from which they deviate.

Another developmental trend in modern dance is evident in the replacement of the balletic stationary positions by motional motifs. In line with Selden's (1930, pp. 115–17) classification, these motifs included during the first phases of modern dance the following major action-modes: folding/unfolding, rise/fall, press/pull, bending/reaching, rotating and twisting, undulating and leaning, swinging, swaying, and vibrating and shaking. This list serves merely the purpose of exemplification, for the categories are abstractions of an infinite variety of movements, and the range has been extended further by more recent generations of dancers. The emphasis on motional motifs corresponds to the general trend in modern dance toward minimizing stationary elements while cultivating motional rhythms. Since the perception of movement is essentially more interesting than the perception of immobility,[4] this development accords well with the striving to counteract habituation through the enhancement of tension. Yet, more important is another revolutionary step related to this development: the replacement of standard positions, common to all ballets, by motional motifs which are established uniquely for specific dances. This development is analogous to the technique of twelve-tone music, which has abandoned the familiar keys in favor of series of tones, determined anew for each musical composition.

However, by giving up the stationary positions, which in ballet denoted the natural beginning and ending of motional units, modern dance was forced to cultivate other means of dynamic structuring. These took characteristically the form of emphasizing the sequence of preparatory building up, crest, and descent path ending in relaxation (Selden, 1930, pp. 36–41; Laban, 1948). The introduction of the sequence was a departure from the balletic procedure of minimizing or omitting the first and last stages, and corresponded to the striving for naturalness. When presented in complete form with the climax in its middle, the sequence is experienced by spectators as a meaningfully integrated unit of movement. However, in practice, this simple model of tension-climax-relief is rarely presented. More often the tension-laden preparation is greatly prolonged or shortened, the climax is enhanced, and the relaxation only hinted at.

Motion and rest, beginning and ending, preparation and relaxation mark only the outlines of a framework for that factor on which the spectator's attention is most closely centered: the dancer's motion. In analyzing dance movements it is customary to distinguish three aspects: first, the form of the movement traced by the whole body as it moves in space (floor track), second, the paths in space described by movements of the dancer's arms and legs (space patterns), and third, qualities of the movement, major among which are the degrees of its effortfulness, expansiveness, and smoothness of flow.[5]

It is tempting to assume, as is mostly done, that the forms of the floor track and of space patterns affect the spectator as do forms in painting. Thus, a circle or a spiral shaped by a dancer's body or arm is regarded as more relieving than angles or other combinations of straight lines. On a certain level this may indeed be so. Yet, because of the temporal unfolding of the forms and the multitude of forms which emerge simultaneously in a dance, the identification of forms in movement may be less differentiated than in the static visual arts. Thus, the major effective forms in dance are probably reduced to large categories, such as wavy lines, circles, loops, or angles (Selden, 1930, pp. 136–37), and do not include finely discriminated forms within each class, unless the forms are delineated by groups of dancers who as a mass retain the outlines of the forms. The range of forms in space patterns is further restricted by the body's anatomy, which favors the production of wavy lines over angles.

It seems doubtful whether the experiencing of fully drawn forms on a canvas and of danced forms-in-the-making are similar in essential respects. In dance the forms are never actually presented. Perceptually they are always the contribution of the spectator, who participates in their emergence by following the dancer's motions. They are not a being, but a perpetual becoming. The forms have to be discovered through approximations, and as soon as one is identified, the dancer is already engaged in tracing another. Thus, a circle emerging from the dancer's body or arm movements may be incomparably more exciting than a circle on a canvas. The thrill attending perceptual participation in the forms' creation and their identification may compensate for the restriction in the range of different forms which can be identified in dance.

The dynamic quality of these motional forms enhances the experiential dimensions of some effects which in painting and sculpture can at best be merely suggested. Major among these are the effects of sequence, simultaneity, and directionality of the motional forms. Sequence not only allows a temporal unfolding of formal themes, variation, contrasts, and balancing but also lends to dynamic forms the special existential dimension of fluidity. No form traced by a moving dancer is an absolute discrete event like a form in stone or on canvas, for in dance, forms are momentary crystallizations of potentialities. Not only may an angle be the preparatory stage for a wave, but in the course of its very emergence it still bears the traces of a preceding wavy motion and is already being transformed into what might seem to be a circle, but upon completion turns out to be a loop. Thus, forms in dancing are not only becoming rather than being, but are a knot of various paths of becoming, momentarily integrated, before they burst out as concretizations.

Contrasts, variation, balanced resolution, and dynamic fluidity are further expanded through the possibilities provided by simultaneous motions. The Spanish dancer who combines a sinuous, sensuous movement of the arms with exciting heel beats, the ballet dancer who draws circular air-pictures while rotating fast on one leg—these are modest examples of the rich complexity of simultaneity whose effects are incommensurably expanded through the interplay within groups of dancers.

The unique character of dance as a spatiotemporal art is evident in the complementation of temporal sequence and simultaneity through the directionality of the movements. Directionality both depends on space and defines it. For it not only occurs in space but also recreates its major dimensions for the spectator. Classical ballet, which as a rule relied heavily on movements radiating sideways from the straight axis of the frontally placed body, has presented the spectator with richly elaborated but rather flat planimetric space (Selden, 1935, p. 40). This is what dancers usually call the vertical plane, which connects all the imaginary points lying across the body in the direction from hip to hip and shoulder to shoulder. By cultivating leg movements, ballet has placed a special emphasis also on the lower section of the horizontal plane which cuts across the center of the body parallel to the floor. The depth dimension, along the back-forward plane was much less exploited. However, the major axis of balletic movement, which was cultivated to dramatic peaks, is the up/down dimension. It is only to be expected that parably more exciting than a circle on a canvas. The thrill attending perceptual participation in the forms' creation and their identification may compensate for the restriction in the range of different forms which can be identified in dance.

The dynamic quality of these motional forms enhances the experiential dimensions of some effects which in painting and sculpture can at best be merely suggested. Major among these are the effects of sequence, simultaneity, and directionality of the motional forms. Sequence not only allows a temporal unfolding of formal themes, variation, contrasts, and balancing but also lends to dynamic forms the special existential dimension of fluidity. No form traced by a moving dancer is an absolute discrete event like a form in stone or on canvas, for in dance, forms are momentary crystallizations of potentialities. Not only may an angle be the preparatory stage for a wave, but in the course of its very emergence it still bears the traces of a preceding wavy motion and is already being transformed into what might seem to be a circle, but upon completion turns out to be a loop. Thus, forms in dancing are not only becoming rather than being, but are a knot of various paths of becoming, momentarily integrated, before they burst out as concretizations.

Contrasts, variation, balanced resolution, and dynamic fluidity are further expanded through the possibilities provided by simultaneous motions. The Spanish dancer who combines a sinuous, sensuous movement of the arms with exciting heel beats, the ballet dancer who draws circular air-pictures while rotating fast on one leg—these are modest examples of the rich complexity of simultaneity whose effects are incommensurably expanded through the interplay within groups of dancers.

The unique character of dance as a spatiotemporal art is evident in the complementation of temporal sequence and simultaneity through the directionality of the movements. Directionality both depends on space and defines it. For it not only occurs in space but also recreates its major dimensions for the spectator. Classical ballet, which as a rule relied heavily on movements radiating sideways from the straight axis of the frontally placed body, has presented the spectator with richly elaborated but rather flat planimetric space (Selden, 1935, p. 40). This is what dancers usually call the vertical plane, which connects all the imaginary points lying across the body in the direction from hip to hip and shoulder to shoulder. By cultivating leg movements, ballet has placed a special emphasis also on the lower section of the horizontal plane which cuts across the center of the body parallel to the floor. The depth dimension, along the back-forward plane was much less exploited. However, the major axis of balletic movement, which was cultivated to dramatic peaks, is the up/down dimension. It is only to be expected that modern dance greatly extended the use of various spatial planes and motional directions (Humphrey, 1959; Selden, 1930). Thus, it not only expanded the planimetric space of ballet into a multidimensional open space but also increased the complexity of the dynamic motional forms. It is customary to regard movement in oblique planes, which intersect with the vertical plane at sharp or obtuse angles, as more tension-laden than movement in the vertical and horizontal planes (Selden, 1935, pp. 121–22), and movement to the right as different from movement to the left (C. Sachs, 1937, pp. 170–71). The major determinant of these effects, insofar as they exist, seems to be the meaning of the various spatial regions and directions. However, the richer the spatial extension of the movement the more complex becomes the spectator's task of integrating experientially the various planes and axes of motion.

While directionality of movements shapes the dance space and defines its major dynamic axes, other qualities of movement lend texture to this space. If movements are made to seem heavy, effortful, piercing through with apparent difficulty, a resistant or obstructive space is conjured up, while if motion seems light and floating, the spectator experiences a fluid and yielding space (Sheets, 1966, pp. 126–27). The experience of space described by a dancer could well also be that of the spectator as he follows the dancer who sometimes forces his way through space, at other times seems to be driven by it. "The experience of my feet as they press against the weight of the floor can be transferred to my hands as they push against space. . . . The air around me seems to have the capacity to solidify or melt. It can be heavy, then rarefied, or agitated and then becalmed" (Marsicano, 1966, p. 240).

The qualities of movement, however, affect the spectator also directly and not only through their reflection on the sensation of space. "It is axiomatic," writes D. Humphrey, "that sharp dynamics plus speed is stimulating and that smooth dynamics plus moderate or slow is soothing." But what is sharp or smooth dynamics? Humphrey (1959, pp. 97–101) stresses the flow of the movement as a major factor. A movement segmented with accented thrusts, an abrupt, explosive, and ballistic movement like the percussive strokes introduced so brilliantly by Martha Graham, is obviously tension-laden and exciting. The contrasting pole is represented by the smooth-flowing continuous movement, the sustained waving legato which is caressing, relieving, and mostly lyrical in mood. Other striking contrasts are between contractive movements, folding as it were upon the inward curved body, and wide-swinging expansive movements reaching beyond the body into an infinitely expanding space; movements which are hardly noticeable, vibrations which transcribe minute paths in space, and wide-arched open movements; and finally, movements which manifest vigor and strength, and languid movements which may fail to attain their end point.

The experience of both the dynamic forms shaped by movements and of the qualities of the dance movement itself depends greatly on the tempo of the movement and on its rhythm. Graham's percussive movements performed in slow motion may lose their dynamic quality and become almost irritating, while a soft wavy motion if speeded up may turn exciting and thus change the effect of the motional form. Fast and slow tempo, acceleration and deceleration are an inseparable aspect of dance. More ambiguous are the roles of meter and rhythm in dance. Owing to the close alliance between dance and music, it has often been claimed that while the meter of the accompanying music sets the pace of the dance, higher-level rhythms of melody determine the rhythm of the dance. These conclusions are forced and fail to do justice to the complexity of relations between music and dance (Lloyd, 1966; Praagh & Brinson, 1963, pp. 151–61; C. Sachs, 1937, pp. 175–203). Indeed, there are examples of dances which move in line with the meter of music or translate the melodic rhythms into motional forms. Yet, Blasis' (1888, p. 9) classic injunction that "perfect analogous concord should subsist between what we see and what we hear" has usually been interpreted much more freely. Sometimes the concord between dance and music exists mainly in the mood, as in many Free Dance performances. At other times there is a close correspondence in the temporal structuring and phrasing of the dance and the accompanying music, as in most ballets. Interpretation of the music through movement and choreography is dominant, for example, in Balanchine's productions. But interpretation may take a form far from obvious, as in Tudor's "Jardin aux Lilas" when the whole cast stands still on the stage during the greatest musical climax, or as in the beginning of Martha Graham's solo "Frontier," when she very slowly raised her arm above her head to the sound of Louis Horst's active and excited music which reflected rather the emotion of viewing the opening vistas of the American plains. The interactive modes of dance with music thus range along the whole expanse marked on one pole by the Absolute Dance of Doris Humphrey or Noa Eshkol, which is unaccompanied by music, through the bizarre atmosphere effects of John Cage's few assorted sounds in Merce Cunningham's "Antic Meet," down to the servile subjugation to music of the dancer who accents in movement every beat in the music.

Hence, no generalization is possible concerning the correspondence of rhythm in dance and music. Most dances, however, do have rhythm, which may be no less complex and variable than the higher-level rhythms in music. "Rhythm orders the relation between the component parts of the dance, that is: movement, rest, force, feeling, intensity, line, besides establishing the measure . . . of the ever recurring pulsations within the larger whole" (Selden, 1930, p. 22). Its complexity is usually increased by introducing different rhythms for various simultaneous and sequential dance parts, and by slightly variating each as soon as the spectator forms an expectation based on familiarity. When music accompanies the dance, as it usually does, the interaction between the rhythms of dance and of the music affords rich experiential potentialities ranging from discordant opposition, syncopation, and figure-background effects to harmonious interlacing and even simple correspondence.

Meaning of Movements

Movements of the human body are carriers of meaning. They are often grasped as expressive of inner states even when not thus intended by their performer, and convey information to the perceiver even when he is unaware of the communication. In routine interpersonal interaction, movements may complement meaning conveyed through words, may replace words, and may be used for communicating meanings which are poorly or not at all expressible through words (Ruesch & Kees, 1961). Indeed, the role of movements in conveying meanings is so dominant and important that "to interpret movements and to use them for communicative purposes" may be regarded as basic human abilities (Dittmann, 1963, p. 155). Some investigators regard communication through movements to be a system no less structured than verbal communication and strive to establish the "kines," the "kinemorphs," and the "kinemorphic constructions" of movements which fulfill analogous functions to phonemes, morphemes, and syntactic sentences in language (Birdwhistell, 1952, 1963).

There can be little doubt that many of the meanings of movements and postures are learned. Learning is particularly conspicuous for movements which serve as signs, like the movements of saluting or greeting. Gestures and hand movements underlie a great variety of non-verbal sign language all over the world (Critchley, 1939). The Indian dance, for instance, uses a conventionally established system of hand gestures for communicating highly specific meanings and grammatical constructions (Bhavnani, 1965, pp. 82–143). The use of movements in the role of signs is relatively rare in Western dance traditions, although the possibility that spectators identify motional signs in dancers' movements, or that dancers use a stylized form of a signal movement like the handshake (D. Humphrey, 1959, pp. 119–23) cannot be ruled out.

Learning takes place also with regard to movements' meanings which are less conventionalized yet widely used within the framework of a certain culture or society. Such is the case with many movements expressing friendliness, hostility, displeasure, resignation, etc. Although many investigators insist that perceiving the expressiveness of movements is an innate capacity manifested already by infants, this cannot be unconditionally accepted, first because expressive movements are partly culture-specific, and secondly because comprehension of expressive movements has been shown to be subject to variability and to improvement with age.[6]

However, beyond these levels there seem to be some bodily movements with universally shared meanings. Approaching, flight and attack, jumping with joy, and drooping with sorrow are only the most obvious examples. No less universally shared is the symbolic movement of raising arms in prayer, supplication, and invocation of sublime forces, as is attested by the recurrence of this movement in prehistoric cave drawings, in Mexican and African clay figures, in the Egyptian protective *ka* symbol, Polynesian carvings, Greek relief, and ancient Hebrew documents (Neumann, 1955, pp. 115–16). Similarly, while the positive and negative meanings attached to a movement to the right or left respectively seem to be more culturally bound, the meanings of movements along the vertical axis are shared crossculturally (Osgood, 1960). Phenomenologists, such as Binswanger (1967) or Merleau-Ponty (1945, p. 329), advocate that the vertical axis is the basic axis of human existence to which our most vital experiences are related. Even though this view represents an imaginative overstatement, people across the world regard the upward direction as expressive of an energetic striving and elation, and the downward movements as expressive of heaviness, renunciation, dejection, and finality.

The wide sharedness of some motional meanings can be traced back partly to synesthetic tendencies (Osgood, 1960) and to abstractions from emotional and other human situations which transcend cultural boundaries. The abstraction may be grounded also in the tendency to imitate kinesthetically some of the perceived motional patterns. Various observations, however, demonstrate that man may share some of the symbolic meanings of movements even with animals. In most of the animal species movements designed to threaten and to impress a member lower in rank are characterized by increase of tonus and self-enlargement through inflating the body, blowing up the cheeks, setting oneself erect, spreading out the tail, or setting up the fins, the ears, etc. On the other hand, the self-humbling movements of an animal lower in the hierarchy are generally characterized by decrease of tonus leading to self-diminution by drawing together, stooping, drawing in the tail, laying down the ears, etc. (Heberer, Kurth, & Schwidetzky-Roesing, 1959, p. 103). The corresponding human movements are, on the one hand, standing erect and increasing the volume of the body, which may also be achieved by technical means—thrones, crowns, stilts—and on the other hand, bowing or bending the knee, taking off the hat, kneeling down, and throwing oneself on the floor. An hypothesis that at least some meanings of human postures and movements have instinctual roots reaching far back in evolution is hard to resist.

Similar conclusions may be suggested with regard to patterns of movement in space traced by one or more dancers or formed by a group of dancers. C. Sachs (1937, pp. 139–74) has shown that folk dances around the world and in very different cultures are characterized by a few motional patterns in space (floor tracks) or their variations, such as the circle, the serpentine, the straight line, and movement forward and backward. Some of these patterns, primarily the circular or elliptical paths and the forward-backward movement, have been observed even in the dancelike motions of chimpanzees (Köhler, 1922). Paths in space formed by a person's movement not only reflect certain characteristic emotional tendencies and personality traits but are readily grasped by observers as expressive of feelings and general attitudes. Tagiuri (1960) showed people drawings which represented paths of motion, or films of moving dots, and asked them to describe the kind of people which would move along such paths. The descriptions offered by the subjects were highly constant. A horizontal straight path suggests to most people features such as aggressiveness, determination, and purposefulness; a curved path stands for nonchalance, lack of stability, casualness, or complacency; and a highly indirect path represents untrustworthiness, vacillation, and dependence. These meanings seem to depend on specific cues in the paths, such as the angle of movement, and approach or withdrawal from the designated goal of the movement.

When more than one visual stimulus is seen moving, structural features of the kinetic situation give rise to definite impressions about emotions, intentions, and interrelations between the moving stimuli. By using two small colored rectangles which were moved independently along a horizontal slot, Michotte (1950, 1963) showed that people actually see a variety of interrelations between the rectangles, e.g., "A joins B and unites itself with it" or "A pushes B and follows him." These impressions depend on several factors—the initial spatial distance between the objects, the time they begin to move, the direction and speed of their motion, etc. For example, if A moves to B rather slowly and touches it without pausing, and then A and B move together quickly at the same speed and in the same direction, the impression is that A carries off B by brute force. But if there is a momentary stop after contact followed by a movement of A and B in the same direction, the impression is that they go together. The kinetic structure of situations created by the motion of geometrical objects is suggestive of human dynamics to such a degree that people often interpret them in terms of full-fledged dramatic plots (Heider & Simmel, 1944).[7]

These studies show that when inanimate objects are seen as moving along specified paths, various characteristics of their movement, which are subject to Gestalt laws of perception, give rise to perception of human actions and motives. This perception seems to be direct and depends on structural features which reflect basic human acts and emotions—friendly approach, attack, withdrawal, repulsion, etc. Yet the moving objects are not always seen as human. Definite structural features of motion are responsible for the impression of the animate or inanimate nature of the object. For example, the impression of organic, internally propelled locomotion may depend on dilation followed by contraction and on movement of the whole with its parts in the same direction (Michotte, 1963, chap. 12).

These findings are of great importance for understanding the spectator's experience of dance. The intimate relation of meaning to characteristics of motion greatly expands the experiential potentialities of dance movements. Meaning of the perceived dynamics may not only accentuate contrasts, such as that between fast and slow or circular and angular movement, but provides possibilities for the creation of new contrasts, such as that between animate and inanimate motions or pursuing and approaching. Since, however, meaning is so essentially interwoven in the dynamics of motion, it is the major factor which allows for integrating the different types of motional effects on the various movement levels, i.e., of limbs, of body, and of the whole group of dancers, into an experience which is both varied and unified enough to qualify as an artistic experience.

The Nature of Dance

Balanced stability is a characteristic of many dance postures. It implies the existence of several forces pulling in different directions, but counterbalanced through a particular structural organization. Such seems also to be the position of dance as an art. Its medium is movements, whose experiential effects depend largely on spatiotemporal characteristics. On the one hand, there is the temptation of bringing dance ever closer to sculpture. On the other hand lurks the danger of reducing dance to the status of a dimension of music, a dimension which is sometimes regarded as merely subservient to musical rhythm and melodic movements. Yet sculpture and music are by no means the only opposing forces in the dynamics of dance's equilibrium. If one concentrates mainly on the formal effects of dance movements, dance may seem at times suspiciously close to acrobatics. Even a ballet expert like Haskell (1945, p. 41) suggested that "the difference between dancing and acrobatics lies not so much in technique as in a state of mind," in the striving to depict a definite idea. But if we turn to the depicting of ideas through movements, we stumble against the art of pantomime. Doesn't the pantomime artist use bodily movements for depiction of ideas?

It would not be difficult to cite examples of dances or phrases in dances which lean too heavily towards acrobatics or pantomime, or which serve sculpture and music too servilely. Nor would it be difficult to cite examples of dances which avoid skillfully all these pitfalls, and many more, and are recognized as true masterpieces of the art. In times such as ours, when traditional artistic media shift in significance and context, it would be futile to argue about artistic borderlines, were it not for the possibility that its discussion may shed light on the nature of dance.

The affinity of dance to acrobatics is evident only with respect to stability and remoteness from the habitual. Both the dancer and the acrobat seem at times to renounce stability, but while the dancer's posture seems balanced in spite of lability, the acrobat's posture seems labile even when it is stable. The balance in a dance posture is between stability and lability; in acrobatics it is between lability and a fall, a crash. Hence, the remoteness from the habitual is in acrobatics mainly in the direction of apparent or real danger, while in dance it is in many and varied dimensions, shunning precisely that of danger.

The pantomimist also cultivates remoteness from habitual movement, but in a sense different from that of dance and acrobatics. He performs the customary movements, yet omits or changes selectively some of the elements of these movements and of the context in which they habitually occur. His art consists essentially in conjuring up the representation of the habitual in spite of these omissions and changes. Obviously dancers may choose to use the pantomime principle as a technique, and pantomimists may prefer to deviate from the habitual along dimensions which have traditionally been cultivated by dance. Moreover, dancers may strive to communicate certain meanings as much as the public expects pantomimists to do. Yet, even when the rapprochement is great in some cases, it seems possible roughly to draw the distinction in terms of the means used by these artists for the communication of meanings. The pantomimist tends to concentrate on descriptive movements, while the dancer's domain is expressive movement.

Meaning, however, is an aspect of movement. Thus, the expressive movement of the dancer can only be defined in terms of both the meaning and formal features of movements as they unfold on the levels of limbs, of the whole moving body, and of groups of dancers. The essence of this unfolding is the interaction between forms and forms-in-the-making, between "lines" and the dynamic line, between gestalt and rhythm, all of which present contrasts and resolutions expressing meaning and unified through meaning.

9. Sculpture and Space

The Medium of Sculpture

In the Indian story of a sage and a king, the king had a great desire to learn about the deep meaning and power of art. The sage told him that he should first learn the rules of one of the arts, dance. When the king returned after several years, he was told that he should now study literature. On his third visit, he was given the task of applying himself to music. He did not come back again. It would be in the best tradition of Indian tales to assume that the king, rather than give up, finally grasped that in order to know the rules of art, one must become acquainted with the concrete form which art takes in each of its domains.

Like the Indian king, we have been pursuing our goal by proceeding from one art domain to another, studying the specific effects of each art form on the spectators, as well as some of the general rules underlying these effects. Yet, the more ground we cover, the more do the general rules gain in definiteness and comprehensiveness, and the more clearly do the specific media of each art emerge as the overriding determinant in molding the art experience.

Sculpture has often been regarded as an art which represents both concretely and symbolically the magic-laden combination of spirit and matter, meaning and material, which lies at the base of all culture. Yet, before we can attempt to answer our standard question about the determinants of the experience evoked by sculpture, we should define what is the "matter," the "material," of this art, in which it embodies "spirit" and "meaning." What is the medium of sculpture?

A cursory view of sculptural objects reveals a wide range of materials, from ivory, wood, porcelain, terracotta, clay, and plaster to glass, plastics, leather, and all sorts of stones, hard as marble and granite or soft as alabaster, as well as the metals, from iron and bronze to steel, lead, brass, tin, and aluminum. The controversy that has raged for centuries about the materials proper for the sculptor to use, or about "truth to material," as well as the quarrel between the carvers, who appropriated for themselves alone the term "sculpture," and the somewhat less esteemed modelers, have finally been resolved in the last decades in favor of the free and full use of every material in the scale of solids.

In the course of centuries many and varied features of sculptural works have been suggested as the media specific for sculpture. However, most of these features, such as color, attachment to the ground, heaviness, or polish, prove to be characteristic only for some sculpture, but by no means for all. A closer look reveals that, besides visibility, which has entitled sculpture to be classed among the visual arts but is a much too general category, the only feature which is common to all sculptural works is that property of objects which is known variously as solidity, volume, multifacedness, or most precisely, three-dimensionality. Yet, particularly within the framework of sculpture, this one property should be regarded as manifesting itself in a twofold manner. On the one hand, there is the form, which, depending on the angle of vision, may be seen either as plane or as cubic, and on the other hand, there is space, which, though always present, is impellingly conjured up when the third dimension is added to a surface.

Three-dimensionality and space are far from being separate or conceptually distinguishable aspects. Wherever there is a three-dimensional form, there is space serving as its environment and background. The perception of form and space is simultaneous and is frequently based on cues which are not only common to the two but are also developmentally interdependent and mutually codetermining (Gibson, 1950). Consequently, in sculpture too, no space effects can be achieved without manipulation of the three-dimensional form, and no form effects can be created without the spectator's experience of space.

The intimate relationship between these two aspects is the source of the apparent incompatibilities that sometimes arise concerning sculpture. Rodin (quoted by Read, 1955, p. 222), for example, says, "I find the cubic form everywhere, so that plane and volume seem to me to be the laws of . . . all beauty," while Kandinsky (1955, p. 71) writes: "The elements of sculpture are the single spatial extensions with the positive and negative air-formations." The one designates volume, the other space as the primary medium of sculpture. Both are right and both are wrong, for the two aspects, like the sides of one and the same coin, are simultaneously manipulated and molded through and in sculpture.

Sculpture and Architecture

Our contention that space and tridimensional forms are the specific media of sculpture stumbles against the argument that architecture too shapes these very media while producing three-dimensional material objects. The major aspects of an architectural object are the effects produced by the exterior surface, the bidimensional form of the façade—its proportions, ornamentations, and interrelations of windows, doors, and stories; the effects of the tridimensional form of the building as a plastic unit placed in space, with its interrelations among shapes of block, roof, projections and recesses, cupolas, spirals, and angular projecting volumes; and the effects of space organization in the interior, such as the form, sequence, and interrelation of rooms, as well as the effects of its relation to external space and objects in it. This means that the architect, like the sculptor, actually works with surface, volume, and space. Since, however, sculpture and architecture are identified as two distinguishable arts, there must be some essential difference between them, whose elucidation may lead to a better delineation of the media of sculpture.

The features differentiating the two arts are not the size of the objects produced, nor yet the attachment or nonattachment of the objects to the ground nor the balance between aesthetic and functional considerations and purpose. Both sculptural and architectural products may evidence any degree of these often proposed features, and yet preserve each its own identity.

What sets sculpture and architecture apart is their inherently different approach to space. Both the architect and the sculptor deal with the organization of space. Yet the architect, following the essential definition of his profession, starts by *separating* the internal from the external space in order to create an exterior form and an enclosed interior space, while the sculptor, who is entirely free from the need to divide space, starts by *occupying* space so as to shape the outside form. Thus, the architect always deals with two spaces, the internal enclosed space and the external surrounding space, shaping each, while paying equal attention to both, with the aim of harmoniously integrating their mutually determined effects. The sculptor, however, is always concerned primarily with only one type of space, the external, enclosing space, which he shapes by elaborating the outside form of the statue. The architect has thus to determine a twofold relation—that of the internal and external spaces to each other (Zucker, 1966) and of both these types of space to the forms on the outside and the inside; while the sculptor concentrates only on the relation of the form to the outside space.

Structuring internal space is an art specific to the architect and differs in its goals, means, and effects from the art of shaping external space (Zevi, 1957). Shaping external space is a province common to sculptor and architect. Yet the sculptor seems to be freer in pursuing this goal than the architect. Statues do not necessarily have to be fitted into an already structured space like an urban environment, as architectural objects often do; and the sculptor has greater freedom in the formation of shapes, volumes, and their interrelations, without being restricted either by surrounding objects or by the structure and requirements of creating enclosed spaces.

From the basic criterion differentiating sculpture from architecture derive other more secondary peculiarities of each of these arts. Since the sculptor is not concerned with creating hollow inside space, he is, for instance, much freer than the architect in the use of materials. The degree of opacity and substantiality of the material is rarely a limitation for him as it may be for the architect.

The suggested criterion may also help to account for the impression we may get from works of art which seem to lie on the borderline between sculpture and architecture. A blurring of frontiers occurs, on the one hand, with regard to architectural-sculptural objects which lack internal space, like arches, fountains, or columns in urban plazas, or where the architectural construction is designed mainly as a closed volume whose outside is more important than the inside. A classical example of the latter is the Greek temple, about which Pevsner (1957, p. 27) writes: "Its interior mattered infinitely less than its exterior. The colonnade all around conceals where the entrance lies. The faithful did not enter it and spend hours of communication with the Divine in it as they do in a church." Indeed, the interior of the temple was not enclosed, but closed. On the other hand, in the last decades sculptors have been proceeding towards a convergence with architecture. This tendency appears, on the one hand, in sculptural works which suggest a separation between inside and outside space, as do some of Henry Moore's sculptures, which allow the spectator to view the interior, or John McCracken's works which consist of transparent cubes that allow viewing of the enclosed space; and on the other hand, in a more marked manner, in sculpto-architectural products which present a structuring of enclosed spaces. Examples of the latter are the "environments" produced by Yayoi Kusama and the Argentine artists around Marta Minujin, who use sculptural, tactual, olfactory, and acoustic means for creating a new kind of experience of enclosed roomlike spaces; or sculptures, such as those by Rüdiger-Utz Kampmann, which consist of a series of sculptural pieces placed around in one closed space, say a room, thus molding its atmosphere and structure (Kultermann, 1968).

The Dynamics of Space

Up to now we have used the concept of space in order to define one aspect of the sculptural medium and to differentiate sculpture from architecture.

What is this space we have been talking about? There are various philosophical, physical, or psychological possible approaches to the reality of space and to the objective basis of the perception of space. But, in our context it does not greatly matter whether space is an a priori Kantian form of perception or a product of more or less complex relations of succession in time, as the English empiricists claim; whether there is an original space transformed by internal forces (D. Katz, 1950, pp. 59–60) or space "goes out of existence as soon as a man's sensations cease" (Jeans, 1943, pp. 55–56). From the viewpoint of art we may start with Bergson's (1950, pp. 91–92) concluding statement: "In short, our senses perceive the qualities of bodies and space along with them." For our concern lies in that intimate perceptually given something of a void nature, in which we, along with all objects, are set and move about. This space, with its emptiness, sometimes with its airiness, heaviness, lightness or even palpability, is far removed from theoretical constructions like infinite uniform geometrical space, be it Euclidean or as multidimensional as desired, the physical astronomical space, the absolute space of Newton, or the relative space of modern physics. In the view of Cassirer (1953a, pp. 62–72), these constitute "a purely functional and not a substantial reality," so that any properties can be added to or subtracted from them, according to the demands of theory. Experientially judged, "I do not have perceptions, I do not pose this object at the side of this other object and I do not establish their objective relations, I have a flux of experiences, which imply and explain one another in simultaneity as well as in succession" (Merleau-Ponty, 1945, p. 325). This means that space is manifested to us simultaneously with the objects themselves, and that rather than being a logical construction (Gibson, 1950, chaps. 1 and 2), it is an intimate reality with its own properties and specific dynamics. It is with this kind of experiential space that the sculptor works, manipulating and re-creating it by means of his art.

Yet, in view of the close relation of space to forms, it may still be objected that what the sculptor does is create forms and not manipulate space, so that effects of space should not be investigated separately at all. This argument was answered succintly by Lao-tse: "Pots are created out of clay, but the void within produces the essence, the Being of the pot." But what is the source of the experiential effects produced by the space enveloping a sculptural object?

Imagine the visual experience of an observer placed in completely empty space. Experimental observations lead to the conclusion "that what an observer would perceive in a space of air would not be space, but the nearest thing to no perception at all" (Gibson, 1950, p. 5). He would see a kind of homogeneous luminosity, perhaps even colors, characterized by being neither near nor far, a space which would be neither flatly bidimensional nor three-dimensionally deep. His eyes would be unable to fixate or converge. There would be no horizontal or vertical axes, no up and down, no right and left. Suppose now, that an invisible power conjures up a real object in this empty sphere of air. A whole world will suddenly spring into being for the lonely, disoriented observer. He will instantly perceive not merely the object, but also a background. The space around will suddenly evidence continuity, depth, and directions. There will be a near and a far, gradients of verticality and horizontality, a center and a periphery—in short, a world of immanent structure and organization, capable of accepting or absorbing many new objects and intricately complex relations.

This is precisely the kind of "revolution" which a sculptural object brings about in our world, in the space in which we live. The dimensions of the object, its protrusions, major axes of directionality, suggested movement, and formal structure introduce a specific new organization into our habitual and familiar space.

But, it may be asked, is our ordinary space devoid of organization until we happen to see a statue? Do we need to observe sculpture in order to structure our space? Of course, if this were so, we would have perished through disorientation long ago. The crux of the matter is precisely that the ordinary space, which we continually see with our eyes and carry along in our minds, *is* organized, even on various levels. The fundamental space scheme, based on kinesthetic, motoric, and postural cues as well as on the overall body image, is implemented through further information on spatial structure gained through the distance receptors, mainly the eyes and the ears, and through the senses providing sensations of touch, temperature, pressure, etc. However, it may be assumed that this spatial scheme is also influenced by information and concepts about space prevalent in the cultural system.[1]

The main point is that not merely does the sculptural object introduce a new type of space organization, but this organization clashes with the other usual types of space structures. At first glance, the same claim could be made with regard to any nonsculptural object too; every object may potentially impose a structuring on the surrounding space. But under usual conditions of observation in daily life, we are unaware of this structuring, mainly because we are confronted with too many objects at once, with too many uncoordinated organizations, so that at best we may be able to grasp a blurred impression, based on the whole array rather than on the effects of any single object. This would also be in line with the general striving for maximum prägnanz and simplicity in the perceived visual field. But when an object happens to engage the whole of our attention, some of its specific effects upon space can nevertheless be salvaged, as it were. This would be likely to happen particularly in the case of a single object in an open space, as when a telegraph pole, a house, or a single person is perceived against the background of an empty field or a cloudless sky.

Hence, it can be concluded that in order to exert its effects upon space, a sculptural object should be placed alone, preferably in as free a space as possible, or if in a limited space, then removed from other objects. Only then has the structure of a statue a chance to permeate the enveloping space, to impose on it its own directions, its dimensionality and partitions. A sculpture forms the center of a dynamic field of forces. The freer the surrounding space, the stronger the contrast between the ordering of the space near the object and the rarefied voidness of the far-extending space which serves as a background. Structuring of space by the statue is an important condition for the spectator's experience, for its novelty not only enhances awareness of space but also reveals a usually overlooked aspect of its dynamics.

A piece of sculpture may shape space not only by structuring it but also by endowing it with various qualitative characteristics. When people leaving an exhibition were asked to describe the sculptures, they referred to experiences of space almost as often as to their impressions of the forms. The experiences most frequently mentioned were of dense or rarefied space, expanding or contracting space, and dynamic or quiescent space.[2]

All these qualitative experienced attributes of space seem to depend on the form of the sculpture as well as on the interrelations between it and the enveloping space. The experience of an expanding space is more likely in the case of a sculpture with many spiky protrusions in various directions than in the case of a rounded closed sculpture. Similarly, experienced spatial dynamism is an aspect of dynamic forms that interact with space along variously directed surfaces rather than along one major enclosing contour. These different experiences are reminiscent of the basic though simplified distinction drawn by Focillon (1948) between l'espace limite, which circumscribes the expansion of the form pressing against it, and l'espace milieu, which surrenders readily to the expanding volumes of the sculpture.

Of particular significance for the experiencing of sculpture are differential degrees in spatial denseness. These seem to depend on a series of factors highlighted by Gestalt psychologists (Chapter 4). Space that is surrounded or partly enclosed by the surfaces of a sculpture, or even merely by a linear contour, appears denser and therefore less bright than the space surrounding the contours. Similarly, two objects that are grasped as being related in any way seem to lie nearer to each other than objects which, although separated by the same distance, are not grasped as belonging to each other. If the objects are viewed as antagonistic in any way, space between them becomes, as it were, rarefied, so that the apparent distance increases. A perceptual increase in density of space occurs as well when missing contours are "filled in" under the pressure of the closure of gestalts. The subjectively "added" contours are then perceived as space which is differentiated from the surrounding space by its quality of greater concentration and density.

Thus it may be assumed that the observer of a statue experiences the space enclosed or "cupped" by the statue in various locations as denser or more concentrated than the surrounding space (Arnheim, 1948). The space lying, for instance, between the legs of a figure or within a concave surface may have a more vivid or "enlivened" quality about it than the surrounding space (Plates 3 and 4).

This contrast between the qualities of enclosed and free surrounding space acquires particular significance in view of the more fundamental contrast between the mass of the object and the void of the space. It may be assumed that the juxtaposition of fullness and emptiness, of heaviness and airiness, of the centrifugality of the mass and the centripetality of the space are experienced as tension-laden contrasts, each being reinforced by the other. The relatively denser space within more or less enclosed locations occupies then a somewhat intermediate position between the mass and the surrounding space. But since there is no actual substantiality about it, the denser space cannot be viewed as bridging the contrasts of mass and space. It is more probable that denser space itself contrasts with each extreme of the continuum of mass and space. A mediating role between the extremes could rather be accorded to lighted up surfaces which may appear almost transparent, or to actually transparent surfaces made of nylon threads or Plexiglas like those produced by Gabo (e.g., Plate 5) or Pevsner.

The history of sculpture provides support for the assumption that the relatively enclosed spaces are tension-laden. Since in each art there exists the need to counteract the bluntness arising from habituation by discovering new means for the arousal of tension, it may be expected that there has been an increasing tendency in sculpture to emphasize enclosed spaces so as to utilize the effects they produce. Up to the twentieth century, the greater part of European sculpture is of the one-block type, following Michelangelo's dictum (quoted by Hofmann, 1958, p. 89) that a good sculpture should be so densely closed that if it were rolled down a mountain slope it would not be damaged (Plate 8). But the newer developments clearly take the course of loosening the massed block of a sculpture—for instance, by enclosing completely or partially certain areas of the surrounding space (e.g., see re-productions of works by Arp, Gabo, and Giacometti in Plates 4, 5, and 3). This tendency, which is already very pronounced in the works of Boc-cioni, Laurens, Lipschitz, Gabo, Archipenko, and Moore, takes a more ex-treme form in the recent skeletal sculptures of Kenneth Snelson, Carmello Capello, Lassaw, and David Smith. In these works, opening up the volume has been carried to the point where sculpture turns into a drawing in space. While the mass is reduced to lines, the major contrast of mass and void is replaced by the contrast between enclosed and enclosing space. But since these structures are more often open than closed by a delimiting contour, the categories of internal and external space seem to collapse in the course of perception itself.

Opened-up and delineated sculptures have indeed lost some of the com-pactness and solidity of traditional sculptures and might in consequence be badly damaged if rolled down a slope, but they have undoubtedly gained in effects of tension. Since these developments are particularly pronounced in modern times, it seems unwarranted to distinguish, as Werner Hofmann (1958, p. 28) does, between "two fundamental tendencies of the plastic form —blockification (massification) and ramification, the simplification of form and its multiplication, the impenetrable cube and the transparent articulated scaffolding." Essentially there is only one tendency: to extend the use of space in sculpture in order to enhance the spectator's experience.

Changing Angles of Observation

The relations between statue, space, and observer also give rise to effects of a different order than those we have discussed so far. Our interest shifts now to the changed views which the observer gets when looking at a statue from various angles or directions. How different the images of an object actually are when seen from various angles, would be rather hard to judge on the basis of ordinary visual experience, since here the law of constancy rules the appearance of things. Moreover, the set of perceivers under the usual circumstances of daily life, which as a rule is functional and objective, reinforces shape constancy (Brunswik, 1933; Thouless, 1932). In everyday observation we are generally oriented towards keeping as stable an image of each object as possible, in spite of the radical changes in shape, size, brightness, etc., which sometimes take place in the appearance of the object, even when only the head is moved. It is different when we regard a statue. Here we are more likely to be attuned to note any changes in the view we get while walking around it. Upon first seeing a statue, we know of course that the view we get is only one of many possible views, but we do not yet know what these other views may be. We thus proceed to examine it from various positions so as to learn how it appears not only from here but also from over there.

Yet, a strange tension-laden feeling may arise in the spectator while he is gradually discovering the sculpture. He becomes suddenly aware of the fact that the more views he gets of the object, the less he really knows what it is like. This feeling is all the more puzzling, not only because the spectator has actually learned more about the object in the meantime, but also because each single view was in itself the image of the object as it appears in reality when viewed from that specific angle. The rear view of a statue may be as valid as the frontal and the various side views.

The problem confronting the spectator can be regarded as arising from the basic experiential discordance between knowing the parts and knowing the whole, though in this case each part is also a whole and constitutes one manifestation of the larger whole—the statue. What the spectator feels now, after having scanned the sculpture from various angles, is the need for integrating his impressions, for bringing the various views into a comprehensive stable image which can be preserved. The need arises both out of the multiplicity of the views he has got, as well as out of the tension-laden relations which may exist between the views when compared to one another.

The striving towards wholeness could act in either of two directions. The spectator may attempt to reduce the different views to one view and to persist in it, or he may try to synthesize his impressions in the simultaneity of one complete unifying grasp. As for reduction, no particular view is on a priori grounds better suited to be chosen by observers than another. Theoretically at least, any one of several views could represent the whole. A case could be made for that view which presents the best gestalt of a particular sculpture, as well as for the view which allows for the most complete grasp of the object, etc.

In order to learn whether any preferred positions exist in the observation of statues, we have made a survey of the habits of spectators in an exhibition of sculpture. The kind and duration of the positions that were taken by 80 randomly chosen spectators in regard to six statues were recorded.[3] Three of the statues were modern, and three were more classical in style. Each statue was placed in a fairly free space, so that it could be observed from various directions. Altogether there were 480 cases of confrontation of a spectator with a statue. Of these, 55 percent consisted in viewing the sculpture from only one angle, i.e., that which disclosed the frontal position. In the remaining 45 percent, the spectators walked around the statue, circling it wholly or in part, so that they got more than one view of it. Our interest centers on these 45 percent, i.e., the 216 cases in which the spectators had to deal with the problem of a multiplicity of views. What their probable solution was can be derived from the following findings. Out of the two minutes' average time spent by each spectator in observing one statue, approximately 50 seconds were spent by him in viewing the statue frontally. Further, in each confrontation between observer and statue, the position of facing the statue frontally was more frequent than any other position taken by the spectator; that is, each spectator returned in the course of his observation at least twice to the frontal position. Finally, in each case the last intentional view which the spectator got of the statue before leaving it was the frontal one. These findings apply equally, with no significant differences, to the observation of the modern and of the classical statues.

The results of our study show that observers of statues evidence a marked preference for the frontal view if they get only one view, and for the frontal view as the last view if they walk around the statue. Moreover, it seems probable that if a reduction of the multiplicity of views into one view takes place, then it is the frontal view which most likely serves this reduction and fulfills the summing-up role.

These findings accord well with the results of experiments carried out in other contexts of psychology. In the course of studying the general dynamics of visual space, D. Katz (1950, chap. 12) presented subjects with the task of reproducing with appropriate materials tridimensional shapes which they observed only while these were revolving continuously on a horizontal surface. Thus the person "was forced to decide upon a specific scene for his copy of the turning scene," while "no position of the model was distinguished from any other as far as the observer was concerned," since "perceptually all the positions of the revolving scene were equal." The results showed that the subjects "chose, with almost no exception a frontal-parallel position or one perpendicular to it" (D. Katz, 1950, p. 64). Again, as is the case in the observation of statues, the frontal view dominates. Similar findings are reported about children's habits of observation and reproduction (D. Katz, 1950, pp. 62–63). Osgood (1953, p. 284) mentions too that when a person is casually asked to compare the shapes of two objects, he invariably holds them with their surfaces in the frontal plane. Essentially, it is the frontal view which dominates also the phenomenon of shape constancy (Forgus, 1966, p. 91).

Why then is the frontal view preferred by observers of objects? It is doubtful whether this preference can be explained in terms of habit formation resulting from more opportunity in daily life to observe frontal views, and hence greater familiarity with them. On the contrary, the frontal view is a rather rare view, or at least less frequent than the various oblique ones to which we are continuously subjected, along with our own almost unremitting movement. D. Katz (1950, p. 63) concludes that "this departure from an oblique image of environmental structure, and towards a frontal parallel view, is an expression of prägnanz." Indeed, some supporting evidence for this assumption could be derived from the fact that out of the several possible frontal views, the subjects in Katz's experiments almost invariably chose to reproduce the simplest and most symmetrical image (D. Katz, 1950, p. 65).

However, the other alternative open to sculpture viewers, i.e., to synthesize the different views in one comprehensive grasp, may be no less prominent than the reduction to one view. The tendency to grasp simultaneously all of the views of a tridimensional object can be inferred from observations on the attempts of children at a certain developmental stage, and of primitive people, to reproduce cubic shapes (Werner, 1957, pp. 113–24). These attempts usually take the form of simply juxtaposing the various views by placing them side by side. Thus, a six-year-old child may represent a cylinder by drawing an oblique, somewhat curved oblong with an incomplete ellipse at each end, and a cube by drawing three adjoining squares (Werner, 1957, p. 119). Similarly, Solomon Islanders are reported to draw a cube by setting down five successive squares side by side, forgoing the sixth square since, as a bottom surface, it cannot be seen (Werner, 1957, p. 138). These practices, which result neither from a failing motor capacity nor from pathological vision, although they seem to reveal a fragmenting tendency, are in fact expressive of a striving to grasp or represent all views of an object simultaneously. This striving may be operative as a source of tension in the course of regarding a sculpture, though in this case its satisfaction is less likely to be achieved by the primitive juxtaposition of views than through a total integrative synthesis, as is evident also in the memory image we sometimes preserve of statues. There is no correlate in reality to such a total and simultaneous view. But on the perceptual level, the level where traces of actual stimuli and stored information fuse, such an image is conceivable. It is reminiscent, on the one hand, of what Bergson calls "intuition," and, on the other hand, of Bartlett's (1932) concept of "schemata" and Neisser's (1967) "figural synthesis."

Yet the "synthesizing activity" of the spectator should not be regarded as antithetical or exclusive in regard to the "reductive tendency." Both are not only expressive of the same overall striving towards prägnanz and constancy in perception, but may lead to similar experiences.

The interplays between partial and whole views of the same statue under observation are essentially dynamic in nature and occur in time. These processes may be regarded as drawing sculpture into the sphere of the temporal arts, since they clearly reveal the importance of the time dimension for the perception of a tridimensional spatial form. In a certain sense it could be concluded that in sculpture, time becomes in practice the fourth dimension of space, intimately integrated with the other three dimensions, whose holistic nature and effects can·be grasped perceptually and conceptually only in view of this particular space-time unity.

The Liberation of the Third Dimension

As we have seen, the interrelations between volume and space provide several possibilities for evoking experiential effects, tension, and relief, ranging from the organization of space through the statue to the different views of it from various directions. But since in art the creation of means for the arousal of tension depends on the ever-recurrent cycle of habituation and its counteraction through novelty, it can be assumed that the present free use in sculpture of the potentialities inherent in space is an outcome of a long and gradual development. Necessity must have been, in this case too, the mother of invention.

Let us, then, turn to the history of this art and study it from our own special viewpoint—that of the gradual conquest of space in the domain of sculpture. The history of sculpture presents a unique phenomenon in the framework of art: it illustrates not merely a lawful development in the use of a medium, but reveals the laborious discovery of the medium itself.

Let us start with the sculpture of India, a country where plastic art has undergone a very long and quite independent history. If one leafs through the photographs reproduced in the fairly representative book by Stella Kramrisch, *The Art of India Through the Ages* (1955), one finds first only various forms of reliefs. The author testifies that sculpture in India has "a long ancient history on . . . buildings of wood and brick, on the walls of sanctuaries cut out of the rock, and on structural monuments" (Kramrisch, 1955, p. 26), all of which had been in great part destroyed. The first extant sculptural objects date from the third millennium B.C., and these are panels and carvings on various pillars of temples, all set in the stone, so that there are absolutely no projections protruding from the surface of the round pillars. The carving itself is also shallow. It is remarkable that although sculpture started here as a nonspatial art, it was nevertheless intimately allied to another essentially spatial art—architecture. This early alliance between the two arts has been observed in so many different cultures that Read (1956, p. 5) assumes that both have emerged by "fission" from an original unity. Could this proneness of the early sculptors to work in the context of architecture be interpreted as a preconsciousness on their part of the importance which the medium of space was to assume in their art? However it may be, the alliance undoubtedly served well their aim. This seems to have been to create three-dimensional objects which make a flat impression and are well integrated in planes.

Up to the end of the first century of the Christian era sculpture in India continues to consist only of such low reliefs. During this long period, the carvings undergo changes in technique, enrichment in themes, and expansion of location, so that they now spread over façades, gates, beams, buttresses of walls, cross bars, ceilings, and other parts of buildings. Towards the end of the period, the minimal space in the form of hollows in the bas-reliefs practically disappears, for the panel is overcrowded with objects and figures which fill the whole of the surface. It is then that the frame bursts, and new types of sculpture start to appear side by side with the reliefs, which nevertheless continue for many centuries.

From the second century on we find sculptural objects which, though still attached to the building, protrude out of it into the free space—for instance, human heads, and other forms which stand out from pillars at the entrance or from balcony corners on the roof. Yet in some cases the sculptural nature of the form is blurred in favor of an architectural impression, as if the sculptors felt afraid of their own daring. From the end of the third century high reliefs set in (Plate 9). Thus starts the systematic removal of the figures from the wall, so that two of their dimensions are on a protruding surface—which they form, and not the wall—with a somewhat blurred third dimension that mingles with the background of the wall. It is only from the second half of the seventh century that we have figures wholly detached from the walls, but they are still connected with the building by a very wide base, which is attached to a pillar, a column, or even a wall. In a way, the expanded base itself serves as a kind of balancing factor compensating for the detachment of the whole figure from the wall, a reminder that the liberation is so far only an attempt, perhaps even an illusion.

It is not until the eighth century that we first find sculptural figures wholly detached from the background, though still placed very near the wall, so that their backs cannot be seen at all. It is remarkable that again an attempt is made to somewhat mitigate or even blur the effects of this daring step into space by placing the figure in a niche, so that the statue, like the low reliefs, does not much disturb the flat surface plane of the wall. But while the low reliefs left the wall actually intact, here it is only the outline of the wall which is made to appear continuous.

During the next century, the niches are given up in many sculptures, but the figures continue to enjoy an extremely wide base and are still protected by the background of the wall. At last, late in the tenth century, sculpture steps completely into the open, and makes a wonderful première with the bronze figure of Krishna dancing on a serpent (Plate 12). The god has indeed a base, but it is elaborated lengthwise rather than sideways, and the only direct contact of the god's figure with the ground, which for him is a shell, is through the foot of one leg.

In later centuries we still find many sculptures around columns and buttresses of walls and even cells of relief images, but the hard-won freedom of the liberated three-dimensional figure, which predominates from now on, leaves its marks on these too. There are, for instance, reliefs from the thirteenth century that stand completely in the open overlooking landscapes, and autonomous figures of the tenth century that embrace a pillar by moving round its axis, so that they overpower the impression of the architectural column. The sculpture no longer hides shyly in the pillar; it is the pillar that radically loses its character under the impact of the attached sculpture.

In the meantime, the free statues suffered a marked diminution of their bases, but never lost them completely. What can probably be viewed as the climax of this development is the interesting experiment made in the twelfth century to attach the figures to the ceiling instead of to the ground, so that they seem to have overcome the gravitational pull of the earth. But the experiment has no traceable continuation, possibly because of the high price of distorted perspectives for the observer which had to be paid for liberation from the ground, or because of archetypal fears and religious values involved in the detachment from the earth.

The same regular stages in the development of sculpture can be observed almost all over the world, from Sumer to Cambodia and from Assyria to the mysterious lands of the Maya, that is, even where destruction, insufficient information, or forced interruption of work has left us knowing only segments of the development. In miniature sculpture, too, a low-relief phase, evident in medals, seals, and coins, preceded the emergence into three-dimensionality, as is shown, for instance, in the history of Chinese miniature sculpture (Cheney, 1952, pp. 249–65).

The Egyptians, the great masters of sculptural creation, also started with low relief and shallow carvings, first on rocks and later on the walls of pyramids, palaces, and temples. Concern over preserving the flatness of the surface may even have been a factor underlying the Egyptian practice, so universal and so intriguing, of putting the trunk of the figures *en face*, but the head and feet in profile (Plate 13). It is only some centuries later, during the Middle Kingdom—side by side with the overcrowding of the reliefs and their frightening expansion on all surfaces, so that "architecture is in general sacrificed for a relief-decorators' holiday" (Cheney, 1952, p. 92)—that detached heads, already in the round, begin to appear. Even after the great artistic revolution of Ikhnaton, before the fully rounded statues could be made, the reliefs had, as it were, to complete their full cycle by culminating in the high-relief type of sculpture, in which "the figures often turn bulbous and exaggerated, escaping from the flat-relief idiom" (Cheney, 1952, p. 99). But even in the tridimensional statues, for which Egypt is renowned, every effort is made, as Worringer (1948, p. 102) has noted, "to conceal the depth-dimension through plane-formations, to make it forgotten. . . . The frontal parts often seem completely pressed flat . . . only the shoulders and head stand out," some of the body parts are turned into planes for hieroglyphs, a practice which helps to conceal the cubic dimension, and the depth impression is further subdued by a column rising in the background." Apparently, there was as yet no need to introduce the potent tension effects of fully evident tridimensionality; or possibly other factors inhibited this development.

In European sculpture, too, the whole developmental cycle was completed even more than once, which in itself is a very curious phenomenon. As for the Greeks, contrary to conventional opinion, they began to create truly three-dimensional statues, set in free space, mainly in the post-Periclean period (Cheney, 1952, pp. 171–74, 188–89, 192–203; Richter, 1930), namely, in the period which critics regard as that of decline and growing decadence in Greek sculpture. The great fifth century B.C. is still marked by the production of friezes (Plate 14), some of which are even in low relief, on parts of temples, and by the grand Parthenon sculptures, which were rather robbed of background space by being set between the triglyphs, and in the pediment.

Europe of the Middle Ages had to begin the whole process anew. More than once in the history of thought, science, and art, ingenious discoveries have been lost or put aside for many centuries, to be laboriously rediscovered when public opinion was again ready to welcome them. Thus, in the tenth, eleventh and twelfth centuries, European sculpture again consists of low-relief carvings and casts, which form parts of buildings. Probably when these had lost their stimulating power, about the thirteenth century, high relief began to make its appearance in the form of *statues colonnes*, as on the main portal of the San Marco Basilica in Venice. Confining ourselves to Italian sculpture, as it is presented chronologically, for instance, by Delogu

(1942), it appears that only in the fifteenth century do the overcrowded protruding reliefs reach their climax in the Florentine portals of Ghiberti, although statues in the round already exist from the preceding century, still
placed, of course, in niches and attached to the wall by a very wide base.
From the fifteenth century on, high reliefs start to disappear, and free statues
endowed with enormous bases, but keeping close to walls, like many of
Michelangelo's figures, dominate the scene.[4] When the protection of walls
is finally given up, statues are attached, as if by compromise, to water sources
or to fountains, which in the meantime have also suffered detachment from
walls and façades and have moved to the center of the piazza. On the other
hand, the freer the statues become in space, the greater and heavier grow
their bases, a tendency which is also evident during the eighteenth and
the nineteenth centuries in the sculptural gigantomanic figures of great men
that still populate the capitals of Europe.

These monuments mark the beginnings of a new era. The attachment to
the ground begins to shrink, stealthily as it were. Many of the statues not
only seem from a distance to be floating in mid-air without a base, but in
fact the horse on which the great man is seated often has two legs in the air.
But these germinating ideas come to ripeness only in the most modern sculptural developments. Passing through a short phase of sculptures which rest
merely on a pivotal point, like, for instance, Brancusi's *Le Commencement
du Monde* or Gabo's *Construction in Space X* (e.g., Plate 5), sculpture
has directly advanced to experimentation with statues devoid of any visible
connection with the ground, the ceiling, or the surroundings. This new phase
of exploiting the medium of space as fully as possible started in 1920 with
the Russian Constructivists, Tatlin and Rodschenko, who were the first to
hang sculptures from the ceiling by a thin invisible thread, so that they
seemed actually to be hovering in free space. Further floating-hanging compositions, like Barlach's war memorial at Guestrow, and works by Hans Arp
or Alexander Calder, followed.

There can be little doubt that the development just outlined of the use of
space in sculpture was brought about by a great many different factors.
Psychological determinants must have interacted with sociological, ecolog-
ical, technical, and materialistic conditions as well as with philosophical-
religious conceptions of world order and space in directing these sculptural
developments, setting their pace, and shaping their forms of manifestation
in different cultures. In line with our purpose, however, we emphasize one
major feature of regularity common to the development on an intercultural
level. This regularity consists in the progressive liberation of the third dimension in sculptural objects, or the gradual conquest of sculptural space.

The emphasized regularity is of course an abstraction. Not only are there some notable exceptions to the rule—mainly African wood sculpture (Fry, 1920), which seems to have enjoyed "complete plastic freedom" (Adam, 1940, p. 72)—but also sculptural forms which were suggested as examples of earlier developmental stages but have often been revived in later stages as art forms in their own right, e.g., the low and high reliefs produced by Archipenko and Zoltan Kemeny in the twentieth century. Thus, our generalization should not be interpreted as implying that the history of sculpture has been dominated by one overriding influence. The regularity noted is, however, clear enough to allow for the generalization. Even when sculpture in the round was cultivated from the earliest periods, as in Japanese wood carving, "a general frontal approach and flatness of planes dominate the whole" (Paine & Soper, 1960, p. 12).

In accordance with our theory we have emphasized the role of the ever-recurrent striving to enhance tension, and thus counteract the effects of habituation, as a major factor in the spatial development of sculpture. The simplicity of this explanation, as well as the fact that it derives from a principle whose validity has been demonstrated in the context of developments in the other arts, lends our theory a modicum of scientific utility and credibility. However, the principle of increasing potentialities of tension does not obviate other possibilities of explaining the developments, just as the very processes of tension and relief must be conceived within the framework of other processes, notably cognitive processes of meaning and orientation.

10. Surface, Material, and Motion in Sculpture

Mass, Texture, and the "Touching" Experience

Up to now we have discussed sculpture only from the viewpoint of those experiential effects of tension and relief which derive from the interrelations of the statue with space. Space is, however, only one aspect of three-dimensionality. Mass and surface are the other. Both facets are so intimately interrelated, that each can be postulated as basic for the derivation of the effects of the other. Thus, Rodin's famous secretary, the Austrian poet Rilke (1930, pp. 82–83) complements the spatial approach to sculpture by emphasizing: "To create beauty does not mean to descend into the depth of things, but to produce surface, closed in a very definite manner and at no place accidentally determined, a surface, which like those of natural things, is surrounded by the atmosphere, shaded and illuminated."

What are the experiential effects of surface and mass in sculpture? How do they arouse tension and how do they provide relief? What are the meanings they express and how do they affect the observer of sculpture?

An obvious aspect of surface is form, or what Rilke (ibid.) calls "a surface closed in a very definite manner and at no place accidentally determined." However, the "closed" surfaces obviously define three-dimensional shapes, which are not merely delineated forms but "masses in relation" (Gaudier-Brzeska, quoted by Cheney, 1924, p. 280). The major aspects of these masses are form, size of dimensions, and directional axis. When dealt with separately, each of these aspects lends itself to analysis in terms of Gestalt principles and other principles elucidated in the framework of painterly forms (see Chapters 4 and 5). Thus, the form of the mass can be described as a better or worse gestalt, as simple or complex, more and less ambiguous or determined, round or angular, convex or concave, etc. The dimensions may obviously vary in size in relation to each other and to those of other masses. Finally, the effects of the directional axis of the mass depend on the degree of its deviation from the vertical and horizontal planes, and on the interrelation between these planes when defined from the viewpoint of the observer's habitual spatial framework and from the viewpoint of the major gravitational axis of the sculpture.

Such an analysis hardly does justice to the wealth of producible effects, which depend simultaneously on all three of the aspects noted. The observer sees a mass of a certain form, size, and slant as a unit interrelated to other masses, again in terms of form, size, and slant. Owing to the depth dimension, the degree of overall balance in a statue acquires experientially a more complex meaning than in painting. What Moore says of the sculptor's relation to the solid shape is no less true of the spectator, i.e., "he identifies himself with its center of gravity, its mass, its weight; he realizes its volume, as the space that the shape displaces in the air" (H. Moore, 1946, p. xi.). Thus, in spite of the lack of empirical data on this point, one could expect balance as defined by form, size, and slant to be a major determinant of tension and relief experiences.

In line with Gestalt laws, a shape protruding into space far outside the main bulk of the sculpture can be assumed to be tension-laden even though its form at the tip may be a perfect sphere. Similarly, a regular conical or elliptical block balanced on a thin point of contact with the base implies more tension than a less regular form with a wide base or at least thinner in its upper region than below. Similar devices for producing tension have become popular in architectural constructions too, e.g., V-shaped columns, the offsetting of higher stories over lower ones so that a building has an inverted-pyramid shape; or placing a high oblong block of stories on very few thin supports linking it to a wide base (C. Siegel, 1962). These examples show that the disposition of mass relative to the vertical direction and the major gravitational axis may be a potent source of tension overriding the tension-and-relief effects of forms and slants.

In sculpture the experience of the three-dimensional shape can hardly be dissociated from the effects of texture, which is the most typical feature of surfaces. When asked about texture, people usually refer to the density of the material, the degree of its fineness and softness, its smoothness or roughness, hardness, elasticity, brittleness, etc. Texture is a quality apprehended primarily through touch. Although it may be evaluated also visually, through associations rooted in past experiences (Washburn, 1895), its specificity lies in the tactual domain. Indeed, the common adjectives describing texture either belong directly to the sphere of tactility—e.g., "softness," "smoothness"—or have correlative synonyms based upon tactility—e.g., "impenetrability" or "compactness" for "density," "grittiness" for "powderiness," "inflexibility" for "hardness."

The intimate relation between texture and tactility is manifested in the inclination of observers to touch surfaces of sculptures and thus to actually feel them. How forceful this tendency is may be gathered from the fact that in most indoor Western museums spectators are urged "not to touch the exhibits," a ban reiterated by the guards. Needless to say, when a certain act is strictly forbidden, there must exist a strong temptation to perform it; otherwise there would be no sense in banning it. In other cultural spheres, notably in certain regions of India, the desire to touch statues is even institutionalized in the form of a requirement to do so under certain circumstances, for "the rite of touching evokes the presence, at the spot touched, of the essence that informs the shape" (Kramrisch, 1955, p. 27).

A record of the touching of six different statues by 80 randomly selected observers of sculptures in an exhibition (see Chapter 9, note 3) showed that 46 of them (about 57 percent) managed to stroke the surfaces, particularly when they thought they were unobserved. A further record of the touching of four different statues by 50 random visitors to a garden exhibition of sculptures revealed that the abolition of the ban on touching greatly increases the number of people who stroke the surfaces. Out of the 50 observers, 42 (84 percent) engaged in touching in addition to viewing the statues. No significant differences were detected in the tendency to touch the various statues.

Without probing into conjectured origins of the tendency to touch,[1] we may ask, Why is this tendency so much stronger in regard to sculptural objects than in the usual circumstances of daily life? What is it about statues that is so tempting for a tactile experience?

The answer to these questions lies partly in the nature of sculptures and partly in the nature of the act of touching. It seems that the tactile fascination of the sculptural surfaces derives particularly from the contrast which they form with the surfaces we usually encounter. The surfaces of most statues are wholly or partly smooth. It has been shown that passing the hand over smooth surfaces is a pleasant experience (Gellhorn, 1961; Major, 1895, pp. 72–77). Most of the manufactured objects around us also have rather smooth surfaces; this fact does not weaken the validity of our assumption, but rather supports it. An informal survey by the authors showed that when people are asked which surfaces they most like to feel and stroke, they mention primarily the smooth surfaces of various stones, precious stones, ivory, amber, pearls, mother-of-pearl, velvety cloth, and furs; but they rarely mention glass, plastics, leather, wood, etc. Apparently, the materials preferred for touching are primarily those which we either do not frequently encounter in daily life, such as ivory and mother-of-pearl, or do not encounter in their smooth and polished form, as is the case with most stones. Now, most sculptures consist of stone, and it is especially for stone that the contrast between the roughness of its surface in natural surroundings and the smoothness in sculpture is particularly marked. This sharp contrast between what we find in nature and what we may feel in sculpture is probably a potent source both of the attraction which spectators feel for stroking the stone surfaces of a statue and of the relief which touching them provides.

The stimulating power of texture qualities may be enhanced by the introduction of textural contrasts. Major (1895), who studied the reactions of people to experiences of touching 51 cloth materials differing in smoothness, stiffness, fineness, and thickness, found that stiffness, roughness, and coarseness are unpleasant to touch, while softness and smoothness are pleasant. Since, moreover, smoothness and roughness are grasped as expressing contrasting meanings (Tanaka, Oyama, & Osgood, 1963), their simultaneous presentation in a sculpture may be a potent source of tension, the smoothness counterbalancing the unpleasantness of the roughness. It is notable that while classical post-Renaissance sculptors strove to produce maximally smooth surfaces, mostly in marble, modern sculptors use also mottled or striated stone and tend to contrast smooth planes with rough surfaces, less elaborated or showing the marks of chisel and hammer. Sharp textural contrasts may also be created by juxtaposing various conventional, unelaborated materials, as is often done by Pop artists and in relief collages.

Another source of the fascination with stroking statues lies in the nature of the act of touching. The unique feature of tactility, which sets it apart from the other senses, is the close reciprocity of subject and object upon which it is based. In contrast to acts of vision or hearing, every touching is simultaneously also a being touched. Indeed, the person himself may remain a passive agent only. For instance, the process may start with an involuntary being touched and end with the discontinuation of the stimulus, as frequently happens in daily life in regard to objects and other people. In such cases, the sensation is stripped of the fascination it might otherwise have. This may also happen when the person is an active agent, but the touching serves merely as a means of grasping, transposing, lifting, or dropping an object. The sensation of touch turns into an experience only if the person plays an active role in the process, and when, moreover, the act of touching is an end in itself. It is then, only under these specific circumstances, which rarely occur outside art but are characteristic of touching statues, that the full reciprocity of touching and being touched is achieved.

This reciprocity consists in a repeated cycle of interdependent motion and sensation (D. Katz, 1925), in which the awareness of the external surface and the subjective impression on the skin form experientially a unity

(Gibson, 1966, p. 99). In this cycle the motion of the spectator's hand, which is an active voluntary act, may be singled out as the moment of tension, both from the physiologic-motor viewpoint and from that of the experiential rhythm, while the sensation, as a complementary simultaneous counterpart, may be regarded as the relief. It is in this sense that an act of touching is transformed into an experience. Indeed, at least in English, French, and German the word for touch has these two meanings—the tactile and the emotional-experiential.

In this very reciprocity between subject and object in the act of touching lies not only the uniqueness of tactility but also the problematical role it fulfills in the overall experience of sculpture. Since every touching involves a being touched, tactility is obviously dependent upon the physical proximity of the spectator to the statue. Yet, the nearer the spectator is to the statue, the less he can see of it. Thus, the experience of touching a statue limits considerably the range of the possible visual experience.

We have here two sense-modalities, which depend on mutually exclusive conditions (Strauss, 1958). While the touching hand needs a physical contact with the object, the seeing eye requires distance. This basic difference between the two senses has several additional implications which highlight the divergence of the two resultant experiences. The optical distance makes for a comprehensive grasp, which is usually of a lower overall intensity, while tactile proximity affords only a sequential series of momentary contacts, each of which may be more intense and intimate than that offered by vision (Révész, 1938). Moreover, the space revealed by vision is much larger, its horizon lies further away, and objects located in it are changed in appearance when viewed from near or far. Touch space, in contrast, is greatly restricted, and distance in this space does not change the appearance of objects, but rather reveals a different aspect of their textural qualities (Lowenfeld, 1953, pp. 234–35, 240–41). While the optically perceived object always remains in a sense aloof, out there, beyond me, touching allows a closer, even intimate, though restricted contact. Thus, vision affords an acquaintance without complete encounter, while tactility provides for an encounter without complete acquaintance.

Even when touching is forgone, textural qualities may be apprehended visually, as an additional experiential dimension enriching directly and synesthetically the visual effects of surfaces and shapes. Even when not directly experienced, smoothness is evaluated as pleasanter, yet less exciting and "active" than roughness, by people in various cultures (Tanaka, Oyama, & Osgood, 1963). The jagged, spiky forms mostly characteristic of rough surfaces may be a contributing factor to the exciting visual effect of roughness. Since tactility and vision are developmentally closely interrelated (Piaget, 1952; Werner, 1957, pp. 104–42), and remain so also in adulthood (Gibson, 1966), the occurrence of tactual impressions in the course of a visual experience is only to be expected (Washburn, 1895). Thus, the mentioned effects of roughness and smoothness, coarseness and fineness, and perhaps even of differential thermal qualities of the materials (Weinstein, 1968) may be experienced not only tactually but also visually, though less intensely.

The quality and texture of materials produce a further effect of surfaces, which is mainly visual in nature: reflectance. In a certain sense, reflectance may be used as a defining criterion of texture (Gibson, 1966), for essentially surface is, in the poetic words of Rilke, (1930, p. 17), "an infinite number of encounters of light with the things, each encounter being different and marvelous." When light falls on a surface, it may be reflected in varying degrees, or even refracted. If polished, stones such as marble, limestone, and granite and metals such as lead, patinated bronze, and wrought iron reflect light which impinges on them, so that areas of high light and of deep shadow appear on the surface. Finer gradations of brightness may be produced by small bosses and hollows on the surface, which lend it a quality of shimmering lightness, so characteristic of many of Rodin's sculptures.

By variating the quality and texture of surfaces and the direction and amount of impinging light, not only may the whole scale of achromatic hues be reproduced, including the more tension-laden juxtapositions of contrasting lightness and darkness or highly similar grades of brightness, but also effects of form and volume may be enhanced or moderated. A small protrusion may be made to appear large when more brightly lighted than neighboring surfaces; a sunk-in form may appear set-off; and a convexity may seem to recede. Light effects may also transform the apparent quality of the statue's material, i.e., airy lightness may be imparted to the most heavy and intractable masses, an effect favored by many Renaissance sculptors, while transparent surfaces may appear to dissolve into space, an impression sometimes produced in Naum Gabo's Plexiglas sculptures (Plate 5). More recently, sculptors tend to use light effects for the creation of real or apparent motion in the statue. Changes in reflected light thus produce changes in the perceived forms on the surface, or within the sculptor's material, and activate the dead heavy mass. These effects are reinforced through the "activity" element in the meaning of light and brightness which contrasts with the "potency" (strength) element in the meaning of heavy and dark materials (Tanaka, Oyama, & Osgood, 1963).

Material, Movement, and Activation

Stone and metal, the traditional materials of sculpture, are hard, heavy, and intractable. Their qualities—stiffness, immobility, heaviness, and hardness—are evaluated as negative and potent (Osgood, 1960; Tanaka, Oyama, & Osgood, 1963). If there had been no strong factors counteracting these impressions, sculpture might have turned into a sad and depressive art, reminiscent of resignation and death. It may be the striving to neutralize such associations that has driven sculptors of all cultures and periods to animate the heavy materials by the most effective available means. These have traditionally been, first, the portrayal of the human body and to a lesser degree animal bodies, and secondly, the presentation of bodies and figures in instants of intense movement.

From the earliest prehistoric times down to the modern era the greatest part of sculpture consists of human figures portrayed in moments of movement. This theme is so prevalent that instead of evoking surprise in spectators, it is the portrayal of anything but the human body which provokes wonder, if not rejection. Indeed, the portrayal of living bodies has also been common in painting, but certainly not to the far-reaching exclusion of most other themes as in sculpture.

The first famous examples are represented by the prehistoric "Venus," found at Willendorf in Austria. This somewhat grotesque female figure is portrayed with her head inclined so deeply forward that her face remains invisible. The strain involved in this posture can be readily felt by anyone who assumes it for an instant. Indian sculpture has evidenced a great predilection for portraying god and human figures in the most difficult and strained postures of classical Indian dance (Chapter 8; Plate 12). Even figures which are not actually engaged in dance may have at least the legs or hands placed in awkward dance positions while performing more commonplace activities, like killing a buffalo or bearing a lamp. No less strained are the nondancing figures, sitting in the common Yogi lotus posture or standing in the posture of "dismissing the body," whose erectness "exhibits a characteristic puppet-like rigidity, that comes of—and denotes—inner absorption" (Zimmer, 1956, p. 214). Of the figures of Indian sculpture in general, Kramrisch writes that they are "movement translated into measured lines and masses" (Kramrisch, 1955, p. 34), since everywhere "breath seems to inflate and permeate the smooth shapes . . . which are kept tense by an inner movement" (ibid., p. 28), and there are always "actions . . . held in suspense by the gesture of a hand or the crook of a finger" (ibid., p. 34).

Human bodies involved in an instant of strained motion are a feature that looms large in the sculpture of other cultures too. It will suffice to mention the Egyptian figures with their frontally placed torsos and their feet in profile (Plate 13); the monarchs of Assyrian reliefs engaged in dramatic acts of hunting or in complicated positions of worship; the Greek statues of the Laocoon group, the Discus Thrower, or the Elgin marble reliefs (Plate 14); the seemingly immobile medieval statues of the Chartres style that are actually in positions of forceful motion, though it is upwardly directed; the many statues of Jesus which portray the figure in the various differently directed forms of the S or C (e.g., Plate 8); Michelangelo's sitting "Moses," who is ever on the verge of rising (Freud, 1955); Rodin's struggling and tortured figures; and last but not least the emaciated striding figures of Giacometti (Plate 3) and Richier (Trier, 1962, pp. 53–129).

Sculpture's combination of moving human and inanimate stiff material is unique in the domain of the arts. The organic and the inorganic, the warmth, sensitivity, vibration of life and the petrified stiff bluntness of death, the moving and the motionless, the changing and the lasting—all these produce a matrix of dilemmas, conflicts, and contrasts, symbolized through sculpture and formative for its development. The effort to animate the inanimate through motion-laden forms is so deeply rooted in sculpture, that it may have inspired the introduction of *actual motion* into sculpture. Possibly this latter development has enabled modern sculptors to turn to the portrayal of forms besides the human body, though this still predominates as a theme. The attempts to present in sculpture what Einstein has inaugurated in physics, i.e., "the dissolution of mass in the ecstasy of movement" (Boccioni, quoted by Hofmann, 1958, p. 14) were introduced in the early twenties by Gabo, Boccioni, Moholy-Nagy, Pevsner, and the Russian Constructivists, and have recently matured into a flourishing domain of kinetic sculpture. The motions depicted may be as violent as Tinguely's monster machines of junk that work themselves to the point of explosion, or as free and swinging as Andy Warhol's *Flying Vessels* and Christo's helicopter-conveyed bundles. However, the majority of kinetic sculptures seem to portray very tension-laden, subtle, sometimes slow-motion forms of movement, produced, for example, by slight currents of air, magnets, reflection of light, or merely through the motion of the spectator (e.g., works by Camargo, Soto, Julio Le Parc, and Gerhard von Graevenitz). Kinetic sculptures of this type produce an effect similar to that of the traditional sculptural "arrested movement." Movement has indeed been unshackled, but inhibiting forces seem to prevent it from running wild.

Of course, the symbol-loaded antithesis of living movement and dead material is rarely the overt thematic content of sculpture. If, however, it is interpreted as an archetypal manifestation of the life-vs.-death theme, art psychology could treat it as a background motif, highly potent in its experiential effects, yet as neither necessarily universal nor indispensable for sculpture. Materials like wood, gold, silver, precious stones, and light materials in general may obviate the use of dynamization in sculpture and may even render it ineffective. When, however, stone, granite, and bronze have dominated sculpture, the implied meanings of the materials had to be counterbalanced through a theme which eventually became so prevalent that its recurrent depiction may have turned into an end in itself.

The experiential impact of a sculpturally portrayed movement far transcends the effect of counterbalancing the inanimate nature of the material. Quite apart from this antithesis, the movement depicted is itself a potent source of tension, first, because a human figure engaged in motion is mostly in a labile posture, and second, because the portrayed movement is a frozen, arrested movement. It is this second characteristic which makes sculptural motion so fascinating. For the human movement portrayed is mostly arrested at a point which is, in Lessing's (1930) phrase, a "pregnant moment," an instant that reveals not only the present but also the past and the future of a course of action. It is a movement which is forever exciting, since it always remains at the point of flowing, continuing towards its implied goal, but never reaching it. Its consummation is left to the observer, who may carry it on kinesthetically or imaginatively, spurred as he is by the tension evoked through his feeling-into the posture and through the impression of interrupted action that this posture implies (Zeigarnik, 1927).

The arrested dynamism of the sculptural object may be responsible for the production of a structured field of forces through the statue, a field into which the observer may be drawn. One major manifestation of this field is the structuring of space through the sculpture. The depiction of movement in the sculpture may be a crucial factor in making the observer aware of the spatial and three-dimensional effects due to the close developmental association between movement and space conception (Piaget & Inhelder, 1956). Touching and handling is another factor, intimately related both to movement and to spatial structuring in earlier development (Piaget, 1952). The sculptural field of forces may thus be the matrix which revives these deep-rooted relations of space, three-dimensionality, touching, perceived motion, and experienced movement and elevates them to the level of intense experience.

Being drawn into this field of forces implies heightened activation of the observer. Touching and walking around the sculpture so as to get different views of it are only two of the forms which this activation may take. Another is the tendency of observers (see Chapter 13) to imitate the posture of the sculptural figure. The tendency is very pronounced, even when it is acted on surreptitiously so as to avoid the glances of others, possibly even unintentionally. At present there is no reason to assume that these three forms of activation result from the same cause. Rather, it would be more plausible to attribute their concomitant appearance to mutual strengthening through progressively reduced motoric inhibition. In other words, if the observer anyhow moves around in order to see the statue from different angles he may have more opportunities to touch it and less motoric restraint about adopting for an instant its predominant posture.

Sculpture is rich in tension-producing and relief-producing effects. Some of them have been mentioned in this and the preceding chapter; others may be deduced from elements which sculpture shares with painting or dance. There are, however, two factors unique to the experience evoked by sculptur. The first is the sharpness of the contrast between the connotative meaning of the materials and the created form, a contrast heavily reminiscent of the polarity between life and death, which may be resolved partly through the harmony of the whole work and partly through the contribution of the observer himself. The other factor is the active participation of the spectator, who is required not only to perceive, construe, and re-create, but actually to move around, to touch, to coordinate the views and determine what the summative or final image will be. It may therefore not be accidental that sculptors were among the first who took the lead in actively involving the spectator in the art of creation. Lygia Clark and Yaakov Agam merely require the observer to create for himself the sculpture by arranging the parts prepared by the sculptor. Others have gone much further by creating "environments" which enable the observers to produce through manipulation rich tactual, acoustic, visual, even olfactory stimulations that turn into an enveloping experience of the observer, by the observer, and for the observer.

11. Literature: Prose and Poetry

Literature and Language

"Poetry is communication in language for expression's sake," while prose is "expression in language for communication's sake" (Scott, 1904, p. 269). This controversial opinion highlights an important fact: the difference between poetry and prose is merely in emphasis. So is the difference between literary and nonliterary uses of language. Poetry, prose, newspapers, casual conversation—all use the same medium, manipulate the same elements, sometimes even for similar purposes. Yet these uses of language do not have equal experiential effects. Starting from the assumption that the experiential impact of literary texts depends both on the what and the how, i.e., on the content and the form in which it is presented, we shall try in this chapter to concentrate mainly on the how. The how, insofar as it can be abstracted from the narrative contents, is a matter of the manipulation of language.

Investigators of literature and language tend to designate as "poetic function" that aspect of language which is prominent in literature. Yet this function can neither exist nor be understood when abstracted from the other general functions of language which are operative in literature; and conversely, the poetic function is operative to a certain degree in all uses of language. Wellek and Warren (1956, p. 177) assert that "language is to poetry as stone is to sculpture," but this ignores the fact that the structure and functions of language as a major means of human communication restrict the artistic manipulation potentialities of language to an incomparably greater degree than the laws of metallurgy and petrology restrict the potentialities of sculpture.

Language, whether literary or nonliterary, is first and foremost a system of communication. This means that its major factors are an *addresser*, who transmits to an *addressee*, with whom *contact* has been established, *a message* which consists of signs, representative of a *referent* by means of a *code* (Bühler, 1934; Jakobson, 1960). Although all six factors are operative in any act of verbal communication, their relative significance varies. Emphasis on any of the factors reveals the specific functions of language. Thus, orientation towards the addresser, which is most prominent in interjections, highlights the emotive or expressive function. Vocative and imperative sentences, which emphasize the signal to the listener, reveal language's conative function.

Attempts to establish contact with the listener, which are much more prominent in spoken than in written language (Horowitz & Berkowitz, 1964), subserve the phatic function. The referential function is evident in the relation between the sounds and the thing spoken about. This relation is grounded in a code shared by the addresser and the addressee. It is this code which carries the meaning load of language and makes reliable communication possible. Language which is oriented mainly towards clarifying the code fulfills the metalingual function.

Within this multifaceted context, the poetic function is most prominent in language oriented towards the structure and form of the message itself, that is, the sounds, the words, their sequences, interactions, and effects. The other functions mentioned in our outline are, however, never absent. Their weight may vary, but they are always present implicitly if not explicitly.

Focus on the message implies manipulation of the elements constitutive of the message. These elements are a set of sounds combined into words, chained in sequences to form larger units—a phrase, a line, a sentence. Language itself is a system constructed by selection on a number of progressively more complex levels. Of the numerous distinct sounds that our articulatory system can produce (K. L. Pike, 1934), all known languages use no more than a few dozen (K. L. Pike, 1947), while English distinguishes at most fourteen or fifteen different vowel sounds and twenty-two to twenty-four different consonantal sounds (G. A. Miller, 1951, pp. 23–26). Of the wide range of possible pitches, English uses at most four levels (Trager & Smith, 1951). Selection is no less stringent on the next level, which includes the formation of words from sounds. Statistical studies show that the various possible sequences of sounds are characterized by highly different probabilities (Shannon & Weaver, 1949). In English, some sequences never occur, e.g., no syllables begin with /zr/ /sr/ or /rd/ (Whorf, 1956) and a word such as "Btfsplk" is an impossibility even when it appears in Al Capp's *Li'l Abner*, while other sequences are highly frequent, e.g., /th/ /gn/, so that words in which they are used sound like English even when they are not actual words (R. W. Brown & Hildum, 1956; L. Jones, 1954). When we move to the higher level on which words are combined into sentences we again find high selectivity in the sequences (Fries, 1952; Z. S. Harris, 1951). Random sequences produced by a computer, e.g., "The head and in frontal attack on an English writer that the character of this point" (Shannon & Weaver, 1949, pp. 13–14), belong to the category of the syntactically impossible, while a sentence like "The book is laughing" is syntactically correct in spite of violating expectancies with regard to subject-verb relations. Similarly, though subject, predicate, and object allow theoretically for six different arrangements, a study of thirty languages around the globe showed that only three of the arrangements appear in declarative sentences, i.e., verb-subject-object, subject-verb-object, and subject-object-verb (Greenberg 1962).

Just as language itself consists of selections from a large pool of possible sounds and combinations, so poetic language manipulates language further through selections within the framework of sounds, words, and their combinations established by linguistic tradition. Thus, if the subject of a sentence is "man," the writer may choose the word "person" because of sound, meaning, or other considerations. Likewise, he may opt for the order "bread and butter" instead of the less balanced "butter and bread," or "Joan and Margery" to replace the worse-sounding combination "Margery and Joan" (Jakobson, 1960, pp. 356–57). These are obviously simple examples of the principle of selection which allows the formation and structuring of literary products. In the following paragraphs we shall concentrate on some of the linguistic means whereby experiential effects may be produced on the successive levels of phonology, morphology, and syntax, i.e., sounds, words, and their combinations into progressively more complex units.

Sounds and Phonetic Symbolism

Sounds are the primary material of language, and hence of literature. When formed into words they are usually regarded as arbitrary signs of referents. Yet, as sounds they have qualities that have often been viewed as providing what Poe called an "undercurrent of meaning." What are these qualities?

The basic unit of linguistic sounds is the phoneme, i.e., a category of sounds which may differ phonetically but are identical in their informational function. Thus, an aspirated *t*, as in *t*one, and an unaspirated *t*, as in s*t*one, are assigned to the same phoneme, for the phonetic difference does not imply a difference in the informational content of the *t*'s. Phonemes are thus sounds which are perceived as identical by listeners, even when the actual frequencies underlying them, their duration, manner of articulation, etc. differ greatly, for example, in line with voice qualities and surrounding speech tones (O'Connor, 1957). Differences between phonemes may be analyzed from two points of view, the articulatory and the acoustic (Gleason, 1955). The articulatory or physiological approach is based on the assumption that the characteristics of speech sounds depend on their manner of production. The major factors used in an articulatory classification of speech sounds are the activity of the larynx, which determines whether a sound will be voiced or voiceless, the position of the vocal cords and of the articulators, e.g., the lips and the tongue, and finally the sound-modifying mechanisms in the mouth or pharynx. This system allows, for example, distinctions between vowels, which are modified only by the filtering action of the head cavities, and consonants, in which the tongue and lips also participate to impede the outgoing breath pulse.

The second phonetic approach is based on the assumption that an acoustic analysis of the articulationally produced waves of sound will yield the best characterization of speech sounds. An analysis of this type helps to classify sounds according to their tonal or noise qualities, e.g., vowels, which are relatively pure tones, and consonants, which resemble noise, the role of partials, the degree to which energy is concentrated in a certain region of the spectrum, etc.

A combination of articulatory and acoustic determinants has been attempted in the classificatory system suggested by Jakobson and his co-workers (Jakobson, Fant, & Halle, 1952; Jakobson & Halle, 1956). Their approach is based on the assumption that each phoneme can be uniquely characterized through a set of binary "distinctive features," defined acoustically and articulationally.

Some of the acoustic and articulational variables seem to suggest contrasting types of phonemes, e.g., vowels vs. consonants, nasals like /m/ and /n/ vs. laterals like /l/. Can these distinctions be assumed to underlie differences in the experiential effects of speech sounds? Some findings seem to suggest a positive answer. Thus, Folkins & Lenrow (1966) found that "tense" vowels (e.g., /ā/, /ē/, /ō/, /ōō/) are experienced as more active and potent than the "lax" ones (e.g., /ĕ/, /ŭ/). Similarly, they found that voiced consonants (e.g., /b/, /d/, /g/) are experienced as more potent than unvoiced consonants (e.g., /p/, /s/, /t/), while Miron (1961) found that anterior vowels and consonants (e.g., /p/, /b/, /m/) are experienced as more potent than posterior ones (e.g., /k/, /g/) by both American and Japanese subjects.

Other experiential effects of speech sounds do not seem to be related so closely to articulational and acoustic features, but rather reflect meaning qualities which are interwoven with physiological and physical characteristics in different degrees. Thus, for example, it has been found that frontal consonants (e.g., /m/, /p/, /f/) are experienced as more pleasant than back consonants (e.g., /k/, /h/) (Folkins & Lenrow, 1966; Miron, 1961; Roblee & Washburn, 1912), that nasals (e.g., /n/, /m/) and spirants are more pleasant than semivowels (e.g., /uw/, /aw/) and affricatives (e.g., /f/, /z/, /r/) (Forer, 1940), or that /a/ is more pleasant than /u/ or /oi/ (Roblee & Washburn, 1912). Observations of this type seem to be better explained through associations than through acoustic and articulational qualities (Forer, 1940; Garver, Gleason, & Washburn, 1915; Valentine, 1962, pp. 272–73).

Poets and linguists have long insisted that speech sounds have a soul of their own, and that there exists a mysterious correspondence between sound and sense, word and thought. Since Plato (1937c) argued in the dialogue *Cratylus* (383) that "there is a truth or correctness in names, which is the same for Hellenes as barbarians," many attempts have been made to demonstrate correspondences between types of meanings and specific sounds (Grammont, 1946; Macdermott, 1940). In former centuries these attempts took the form of abstracting sounds from words in various languages and correlating them intuitively with meanings. Thus, Humboldt (1836) claimed that the phonetic group /st/ is regularly used for the evocation of the impression of endurance and stability, and /l/ for the melting and fluid, while Grimm (1870–98, book 3, chap. 1) found that in the Indo-Germanic languages, /k/ "the fullest consonant of which the throat is capable" is used in questions, inquiring, and calling.

The main methods used by modern investigators are to ask subjects to choose the appropriate meanings for nonsense sounds, and to devise names for presented meanings and objects. Most of the findings support the conclusion that speech sounds may be expressive of rather definite meanings. One of the most consistent results points to the relation between vowels and the dimensions of size and brightness. Children and adults both in the United States and in Germany consider the sounds /a/ (as in "large"), /u/ (as in "book") and /o/ (as in "paw") appropriate to designate large objects; /e/ (as in "bed") and /oe/ smaller objects; and /i/ (as in "bid") the smallest objects (Czurda, 1953; Newman, 1933; Sapir, 1929; Wissemann, 1954). Correspondingly, the "larger" vowels were also found to be darker, and the "smaller" vowels brighter (Czurda, 1953; Newman, 1933; Wissemann, 1954). In consonants, alveolars like /d/ and /t/ are experienced as smaller than labials like /b/ and /p/, and these in turn as smaller than palatals like /g/ and /k/ (Newman, 1933). Brown (1958, p. 114) aptly remarks that the English word "God" and the Hebrew word "Jehova" illustrate the largeness deriving from these findings on phonetic symbolism.

Another line of evidence derives from studies which consist in letting subjects guess the meanings of unfamiliar words in foreign languages. The guesses have usually been correct above the level of chance, e.g., by Americans with regard to Japanese words (Maltzman, Morrisett, & Brooks, 1956; Rich, 1953; Tsuru, 1934), Hungarian words (Rich, 1953), Finno-Ugric words (G. W. Allport, 1935), Croatian words (Maltzman et al., 1956), Chinese, Czech, and Hindi words (R. W. Brown, Black, & Horowitz, 1955), and by German subjects with regard to African languages (Wittman, quoted by Rohracher, 1959, p. 160).

In view of the overwhelmingly positive evidence, the existence of phonetic symbolism can hardly be doubted. Controversial, however, remain both the extent and the origin of this phenomenon. While members of one linguistic culture manifest a fair degree of consistency in the meanings they attribute to phonemes and unfamiliar words, members of diverse linguistic cultures do not always evidence a comparable degree of agreement.[1] Thus, although few doubt the existence of phonetic symbolism, some doubt whether there is a universal phonetic symbolism (R. Brown, 1958; Taylor & Taylor, 1965).

As may be expected, the origins of the phenomenon seem at present to be multiple and diverse, though not mutually exclusive. Certain forms of phonetic symbolism may be attributed to onomatopoeia, i.e., the imitation in words of certain characteristics of natural sounds. These seem to be primarily movement and rhythm patterns (Wisseman, 1954), as is illustrated by words like "twittering," "butterfly," "rattle," "bottle," and by Tennyson's famous sound-painting lines, "The moan of doves in immemorial elms,/ And murmuring of innumerable bees." When the onomatopoeic phenomenon is extended to include imitation of stimuli other than sounds, it turns out to be a subdivision of the more general phenomenon of synesthesia (see Chapters 3 and 5). Synesthetic relations, such as those which exist between phonemes and forms (Czurda, 1953; Usnadze, 1924) probably underlie many of the uniformities in phonetic symbolism.[2] Synesthesia is essentially the principle underlying theories, such as those of Paget (1930) and Wundt (1900–1909), who assume that language has originated in the imitation of motion and contour in the external world by articulatory muscles. Such synesthetic relations could be learned on the basis of regularities in the external world, e.g., small objects usually emit high-pitched sounds.

Since, however, phonetic symbolism exists to a certain degree in language (Householder, 1946; Jespersen, 1922; Marchland, 1958–59), e.g., /i/ is used in many Indo-European words denoting smallness, the individual may also grasp it intuitively in the course of using the language (I. K. Taylor, 1963). He may then possibly extend its range through personal experiences as well as acoustic (Masson, 1952) and kinesthetic-articulational cues (C. Johnson, Suzecki, & Olds, 1964; Newman, 1933).

However that may be, phonetic symbolism and onomatopoeia do not play any important role in the ordinary usages of language (R. Brown, 1958, pp. 136–39). This is so because people do not expect correspondences between sound and sense, as well as because these phenomena are, in the words of K. Bühler (1934, p. 196), like grass springing up in the crevices between the paving stones in an old courtyard. It is only under special conditions that people become attuned to phonetic symbolism and other properties of speech sounds. These conditions constitute what Werner & Kaplan (1963) called physiognomic perception.

Can we assume that such a perception exists with regard to literature? The possibilities of creating experiential effects through qualities of speech sounds and their nonconventionalized connotations are greatly limited both through the overriding effect of conventional linguistic meaning and through the phonemic structure of language. The writer's freedom of selection among phonemes is restricted by the prominence of the various distinctive features and by the frequency distribution of phonemes in a particular language.[3] Yet, since "it is the business of the poet to give us the feeling that there does exist the closest possible unity between word [viz., sound] and sense" (Valéry, 1947, p. 101), poets and writers in general have a variety of means at their disposal for drawing readers' and listeners' attention to phoneme qualities. Major among these means are repetitions of sounds, for instance, alliterations and assonances, as well as of words and word groups (Yoshida, 1952). Repetition of particular sounds may make people aware of these sounds irrespective of their general frequency in language. Battig (1957, 1958) showed that in a task of forming words by guessing at letters, people tend to guess in accordance with the letters' general frequency in language. When however words with which they have been confronted in the experiment contain uncommon letters, they change their guessing in conformity with this recent experience. Thus, irrespective of whether certain sounds are highly frequent in language or not (Householder, 1960), their repetition in a literary text may accord them a new and special significance.

Repetition does not guarantee the reader's attention, it only makes it more likely. Both Lynch (1953) and Hymes (1960) attempted to demonstrate how poets like Keats and Wordsworth highlighted the nexus between meaning and sound by repeating certain phonemes more frequently than others. Yet both emphasize that the repetition gains weight when the sounds also appear in a "summative" word which has a culminating effect through its meaning and position in the poem. Even when sheer repetition is missing, as in some of Shakespeare's sonnets (Skinner, 1939), phonemes may nevertheless be accorded prominence through their use in words which fulfill particularly important roles in the literary text, for example, words which are crucial for rhyme or rhythm (Hřebiček, 1964; Levin, 1962; Masson, 1953) or key words which sum up the poem's theme (Hymes, 1960).

An extreme means of enhancing the effects of phonemes consists in reducing the role of conventional meaning. This meaning hardly existed in many primitive poems which are mere strings of vowels and consonants (Boas, 1955, p. 301). More recently, poets in the tradition of the French Symbolists and Surrealists—Rimbaud, Mallarmé, Hart Crane, Wallace Stevens, E. E. Cummings, and Dylan Thomas—attempted to place phonemic qualities in the foreground by reducing the effects of conventional meaning. Spurred partly by the mystic idea that "the perfumes, the colors, and the sounds correspond" (Baudelaire, 1918, p. 11), these poets strove to use linguistic sounds for the evocation of experiences of other senses and of a world beyond the senses (Michaud, 1947, pp. 77–81, 86–87). Their major techniques consisted in using words out of their context, in writing words as they are heard, adding nonsense syllables to familiar words, and even inventing new words (Lanson, 1952, p. 1125). The climax of this development was reached indeed not by Cummings, who presents phonemes that could be rearranged into words (e.g., the grasshopper poem), but by the Dadaists and their followers, who wrote pure sound poems in which vague associations to words replace conventional meanings. However, these attempts have never become more than a rivulet in the mainstream of modern poetry, for the stripping of words of conventional meanings maims language. It implies the sacrifice of the referential and conative functions of language for the sake of the poetic and emotive functions, whose impact is paradoxically reduced, even eliminated, when thus isolated.

In the framework of more conventional poetry, written by those who agree with T. S. Eliot (1953, p. 58) that poetry is "all the same one person talking to another," the effects of phonemes may indeed be more restricted than in "sound poems." However, the coexistence of sound and sense lays the groundwork for complex interactions between the phonemes and the meaning of a word. It is only because the French words *jour* (day) and *nuit* (night) have conventional meanings that Mallarmé (1935, p. 242) could complain of the contrast between the brightness of day and the murkiness suggested by *jour*, or between the darkness of night and the brightness of the phonemes of *nuit*. Thus, similarities in phonemes may highlight similarities in meanings, and contrasts in phonemes may reinforce contrasts in content. The interactions between sound and sense may also reveal unexpected resolutions between contrasting meanings and may suggest that "day" and "night" have more in common than the conventionalized lexical code reveals to the uninitiated.

The Impact of Words

"A man crossed the street." Consider the effects of replacing successively the noun "a man" by "a fellow," "a chap," "a guy," "a human being," "a male anthropoid," or even, following Dryden, "an unfeather'd two-legged thing." All these words or word combinations share a common nucleus of meaning, which can be summarized by any of them. Yet they are unmistakably different to a degree which reduces the common core meaning to little importance. Thus, while the words "man," "chap," and "guy" keep the sentence within normal conversational bounds and lend it a declarative sense, the phrase "a human being" evokes an atmosphere of dignity and importance. In contrast, "a male anthropoid" renders the meaning of the sentence ambiguous and sets it hovering between the domains of science and of humor, while the phrase "an unfeather'd two-legged thing" is not only slightly humorous and derogatory but through its incongruity disrupts the meaning of the whole sentence. The change of a single word may thus imply a change in the meaning of a sentence, as well as of larger units.

In daily life we often behave as if we were following Buffon's dictum, "The style is the man." A major manifestation of style is the words a person uses. They indicate not only attitudes, feelings, states of mind, security, etc., but also social and professional status (Pittenger & Smith, 1957). Many studies corroborate that the words indeed change with personality type, emotional state, attitudes, and mental health. For example, obsessive compulsives tend to use many qualifiers and words of improbability, while hysterics use many adjectives and few verbs (Balken & Masserman, 1940). Persons who are about to commit suicide use in their last notes more nouns and verbs than adjectives and adverbs, repeat often the same words, and express themselves through fewer different words than people writing ordinary letters (Osgood & Walker, 1959).[4]

Writers also vary greatly in their use of words.[5] Do differences in word use affect the readers of literature? The findings of some studies suggest a positive answer to this question and point to major variables in the use of words which affect the percipient's experience. Carroll (1960) studied the interrelations between subjects' ratings of 150 different prose passages on 29 bipolar adjectival scales, and 68 objective indices of these passages, most of which reflected characteristics in the use of words. He found that the subjects' general positive or negative evaluation of the passages was not related to any word qualities, but that other more specific aspects of the subjects' impression definitely were. Thus, the degree of "Personal affect" in the passage is rated high in ratings along scales such as personal/impersonal, intimate/remote, and emotional/rational, when the passages include many short words, cognitive verbs, nouns with natural genders, many pronouns—personal, possessive, and indefinite—and many references to people (Flesch, 1948), but only a few Latin-derived verbs, passive verbs, gerunds, common nouns, articles, and prepositions. The impression of ornamentation in style arises when the passage includes many common nouns preceded by adjectival or participial modifiers, nouns with Latin suffixes, long words, and descriptive adjectives, simultaneously with a low proportion of action verbs and other pronouns. Passages that impressed the subjects as abstract, elegant, complex, and somewhat hazy had many nouns with Latin suffixes, indefinite and demonstrative pronouns, but only a few participles, personal pronouns, common nouns, indefinite and quantitative determiners, and numerical expressions. Finally, the evaluation of a passage as "serious" seems to depend on the use of many nouns with Latin suffixes, many indefinite and quantitative determiners and demonstrative pronouns, and only a few action verbs, indefinite articles, and possessive pronouns.

Since characteristics in the use of words change from one period to another, and depend so much on the writer's theme that they are not constant even for one author (e.g., Boder, 1940; J. Miles, 1964), it is difficult to generalize. Nevertheless several variables in Carroll's study suggest features that are fairly characteristic of literary texts in general. For example, short, affixless, familiar words, which are highly frequent in daily use, are particularly characteristic of easy and readable prose of the "slick" and "pulp" fiction type (Dale & Tyler, 1934; Gray & Leary, 1935; Lorge, 1944). On the other hand, better fiction works rely much more on less familiar (Flesch, 1948) and longer words, which are often burdened with affixes and are not very current in daily conversation (Zipf, 1935). As might be expected, verbal diversification, i.e., the use of many different words and the avoidance of frequent repetitions of the same words (W. Johnson, 1946) is greater in literary texts than in casual conversation and newspaper English. While in a count of 80,000 words of telephone conversations there were only about 5000 different words (G. A. Miller, 1951, p. 121), good fiction uses roughly 10,000 different words, a peak being attained by James Joyce's 29,899 different words in *Ulysses* (Hanley, 1937).

The tendencies to use in literature less familiar words and a richer vocabulary than in nonliterary contexts suggest that authors may sometimes strive to emphasize remoteness from the habitual. The fulfillment of this striving is possible, since in most languages layers of archaic forms are usually preserved, and even the dominant layer contains competing forms from different social strata or regional areas (Stankiewicz, 1960). Thus authors may draw elements from more antique contexts, as does Agnon from the old Mishna Hebrew, or as many British authors did, preferring words of Anglo-Saxon origin over Latinisms. Writers may also call on strange, exotic, and foreign words, as the Romantic poets did, or scientific terms, as many modern poets are wont to do. The cultivation of remoteness may, however, spur the development of specific styles for different literary genres—e.g., in classical Greek poetry the epic, lyric, and dramatic works were written in different dialects—and can also lead to innovations in language through the creation of new words from old roots.

Remoteness from the habitual may be a means for drawing attention to peculiarities of language or content and may thus facilitate experience. Yet, it is not a necessary condition, as is attested by many literary texts which show a large proportion of commonplace words, striking in their familiarity and simplicity. As may be expected, the effect of current or quaint words depends greatly on the content communicated. The description of extraordinary experiences in simple words, as in Camus' novels, or of commonplace events in archaic or strange language is a potent means for introducing tension-laden contrasts. The effect of these may be extended by juxtaposing different linguistic styles within the same text in accordance with shifting themes, characters, or described environments.

What is the source of the impact of words? Why, for example, does the use of many action verbs reduce the seriousness of a style but add to its concreteness (J. B. Carroll, 1960), vividness, and personal tone (R. Wells, 1960)? The various strings of answers to this question hinge upon the central fact that a word is a nucleus of meaning. Meaning is the primary difference not only between verbs and nouns or active and passive verbs but also between more and less familiar or frequent words. For example, frequent words have more different meanings attached to them (Koen, 1962; Zipf, 1945) and are evaluated more positively in an affective sense than infrequent words are (R. C. Johnson, Thomson, & Frincke, 1960). Similarly, the substitution of "thou" for "you" implies not merely the use of an older word but carries with it the aura of a different social world where power and relations of authority predominate over those of solidarity and intimacy (R. Brown & Gilman, 1960). However, we are rarely aware of the wealth of meanings crystallized in a word, for when reading nonliterary texts we are mostly intent on securing information in a speedy and efficient way, disregarding as far as possible the *means* of communication. Yet it is precisely the unique character of a poetic message that it is so constructed as to call attention to its elements, reveal their usually neglected aspects, and thus—paradoxically—"dislocate language into meaning" (Eliot, quoted by Brooks, 1947, p. 192).

When one concentrates on words, each word emerges as a microcosmos embedded in a multifaceted, multilayered, multidirectional space of meaning. What are these meanings? There are several theoretical and methodological approaches to the word's meaning, which complement each other and reveal the nucleus under different aspects and emphases. According to every approach a word would be the convergence point of specific values of general attributes. But the approaches differ in the identification of these general attributes. One approach is exemplified by J. J. Katz and Fodor's (1963) suggestion to view the meaning of words as a bundle of features expressed in syntactic and semantic markers—nouns/non-nouns, human/animal, and male/female—which are by definition the semantic atoms that enable successively finer disambiguations of meaning. A similar approach which does not assume a hierarchical relation between the markers is exemplified by Osgood's (1970) attempt to represent the meaning of one class of words, i.e., interpersonal verbs, through values on polar semantic markers like active/passive, initiating/reacting, and deliberate/impulsive. In both cases the markers have not been empirically derived and refer only to lexical conventional meaning.

The second approach to a word's meaning is represented by a theory of Osgood and his colleagues (1957), the theory and technique of the *Semantic Differential*. This approach consists in measuring three dimensions of connotative or emotional meaning, i.e., evaluation, potency, and activity, through scales defined by bipolar adjectives representing the dimensions. The technique of measurement is based on the assumptions that synesthetic tendencies are general enough to make possible the expression of other meanings, and that meaning is encodable in terms of bipolarities. The generality of the three dimensions across people and languages, and their applicability to words and other stimuli of different types, have been demonstrated reliably and frequently enough (Osgood, 1962; Tanaka, Oyama, & Osgood, 1963) to support Osgood's (1962) suggestion that evaluation, potency, and activity reflect major factors of emotional reactions and hence of emotional meaning.

When we turn to studies of meanings of words we find that many aspects of subjects' responses are left unaccounted for, even overlooked, by the two systems. J. E. Downey (1927) asked his subjects to report on their introspective reactions to various words. These reactions included many visual images (e.g., "Lily—tall, white lilies in a garden," ibid., p. 329) auditory images ("Rustling— . . . soft leaves moving," ibid., p. 330), memories ("Dusk

—Visualization of our ranch at dusk. General memory," ibid., p. 330), as well as organic, olfactory, and gustatory experiences ("Quinine—lump in throat," ibid., p. 331). Some of these connotative responses reflect indeed a variety of synesthetic reactions to the meaning and even to the visual form and sound of the words. These may underlie Osgood's three dimensions of evaluation, potency, and activity. But other responses reveal meaning components expressed for example in images, metaphors, or abstract terms that may not be tapped by scales of bipolar adjectives and lie outside the domain of synesthesia.

A more comprehensive set of meaning dimensions, reflecting both connotative and denotative meaning of the lexical and personal-symbolic types, was suggested by S. Kreitler (1965) and S. Kreitler and Kreitler (1968), on the basis of their studies. The experimental situation consisted in requesting subjects to communicate to an hypothetical "other," supposedly ignorant of the meaning, the lexical-conventional meaning, or the innermost personal-symbolic meaning of words—more and less abstract—and of the other stimuli. A categorization of the responses which were expressed in words, in drawing, or through acting and pantomime yielded a series of dimensions, each of which reflects a certain aspect of the meaning, i.e., answers in part the question, What is the "thing" referred to by the word? Thus, the thirteen lexical meaning dimensions include indication of the function, purpose, or role of the "thing" referred to, the causes for its existence or the manner of its origination, consequences of its existence, its manner of occurrence, what it includes or consists of, its sensory qualities, e.g., shape, color, and size, its potentialities for action, etc. The ten symbolic-meaning dimensions include the demonstration of meaning aspects through an exemplifying instance, a situation, an activity, or an unfolding scene, through bodily, postural, and gestural expression, sensations, and feelings evoked by the denoted "thing," through abstract interpretations, metaphors, etc.

The actual meaning responses constitute values along one or more of these dimensions. The "values" may be expressed in words, images, bodily postures, or gestures and may reflect informations, memories, sensations, synesthesias, etc. They may be abstract or concrete and interpersonally shared to any degree. Some meaning values may be highly personal and idiosyncratic, others may reflect conventions, and still others may be widely understood without being actually codified. Such is the case, for example, with sensory qualities which are used as metaphors in spheres other than sensory (Asch, 1955).

The dimensions mentioned define a complexly structured semantic space in the framework of which the diverse components of the meaning of any word may be arrayed. The system is comprehensive enough to include conventional lexical and personal-symbolic meanings, as well as semantic markers and Osgood's three factors as more specific and more abstract dimensions.

The semantic space of a word is not constant. It undergoes changes on both interpersonal and personal levels. In the course of historical, cultural, and social developments, new values and even new dimensions may be added to a word's meaning, old values are reinterpreted, the hierarchic arrangement of the dimensions and values may be restructured (Osgood & Sebeok, 1967, pp. 158–63).

Again on the level of the single individual, the semantic space of a word is an open system which undergoes changes not only developmentally but also from one occasion to another. The degree of expansion or contraction of a word's semantic space depends on situational factors, on the individual's set, and on the context in which the word is used. For example, a continuous and frequent verbal repetition of a word results in an extreme contraction of the meaning (Lambert & Jakobovits, 1960; Messer et al., 1964). A less extreme contraction takes place under conditions of routine linguistic communication, which is usually oriented towards speedy and efficient transmission of information. The individual may then be assumed to be aware only of the bare minimum of the "core potentialities" of a word's meaning (Rommetveit, 1968, pp. 170–82).

In contrast, a physiognomic perception of words represents an extreme expansion of semantic space. It involves a rich unfolding of meaning along many dimensions and over those twilight regions of meaning which mostly remain suppressed. Physiognomic perception consists in embedding the word in a dynamically loaded "atmospheric context of feeling and action" (Werner, 1955, p. 12), in a far-reaching breakdown of the differentiation between the word and what it represents, and in responding to the word with the whole organism (Werner, 1955; Werner & Kaplan, 1963). For example, the dynamic atmosphere of words is manifested in perceiving such words as "rising" and "climbing" as if they were localized spatially higher than such words as "falling" and "plunging," even when all the words are actually presented at eye level (Kaden, Wapner, & Werner, 1955). The identification of the visual and acoustic properties of the word with its meaning brings sound symbolism to the fore, while the organismic involvement in the response is most apparent in the wealth of synesthetic reactions and in the actual reflection in experience of abstract meaning elements (Solarz, 1963).

Physiognomic perception of words may occur under the influence of special experimental instructions (J. E. Downey, 1927; S. Kreitler & Kreitler,

1968), when a person is thinking or "conversing" with himself (E. Kaplan, 1952), and to a certain degree also with regard to words in literary contexts, particularly in poetry. Comparing reactions to the same words in a poem and in prose, Raeff (1955) found that personal-symbolic responses predominate over lexical responses to words in a poem. When, for example, the word was "velvet," in the context of prose the response "soft" was not only relatively unimportant but constituted a value along the lexical meaning dimension of sensory qualities. In contrast, "soft" in response to "velvet" in a poem was linked up with the softness of the *elv* sound of the word "velvet." Thus, the meaning responses to a word in a poem depend also on other elements in the word than meaning responses to the same word in the context of prose. This may underlie also the richer unfolding of meaning in such contexts.

One implication of the expansion of semantic space is the evocation of a wide band of associations to the word. Studies of word associations (e.g., Karwoski & Schachter, 1948; Palermo & Jenkins, 1964) show that many of the evoked associations are responses which form part of the stimulus word's meaning. Such is the case for responses or words whose relation to the stimulus word is superordination, subordination, similarity or contrast, part to whole or whole to part, etc. But many other word associations, particularly the less immediate ones (De Burger & Donahoe, 1965), reveal an amazing variety of ways in which words are related. The associative link may be formed, for example, through a similarity in sound (e.g., rite—right, might—bright), in kinesthetic articulatory cues (Masson, 1953), in context (e.g., cottage—cottage cheese, black—blackboard), or merely in "atmosphere," which may be one of the sources for metaphoric expressions. In addition, many associations arise from partial intersections in the semantic spaces of words or involve literary and etymological elaborations (Richards, 1960, pp. 14–15) as well as personal memories of circumstances in which the word was used (J. E. Downey, 1927).

Neither meaning nor associations to a word are independent of the context in which the word appears. As we have seen, the general context of a word, the milieu of prose, poetry, or nonliterature in which a word is embedded determines the range of the unfolding meaning as well as the direction—lexical or symbolic—in which it unfolds. A more specific influence on meaning and associations is exerted by the narrower context of a word, i.e., by words immediately preceding and following it, or the sentence in which it appears. The fact that a great number of word associations given by adults are paradigmatic, i.e., similar to the stimulus word in their grammatical function, so that they are substitutable in the identical phrase or sentence (Ervin-Tripp, 1961; McNeil, 1963), reveals that even when words are presented in isolation, they are conceived by the listener in the framework of a verbal context. But when a context is presented, the relation of the word to the other words in the context determines to a large extent the basic outlines of the word's meaning. Hence, the larger the number of random words presented as context, the smaller the number becomes of words which can fit into the context (Shepard, 1963). A context functions not only as a restrictive framework, but may bring to the fore certain aspects of a word's meaning. When subjects are asked to associate only to the last word in a list of four unconnected words, the associations evoked depend not only on the stimulus words but also on those which precede it (Howes & Osgood, 1954). The word "dark" in the sequence "devil—fearful—sinister—dark" evokes the association of "hell" much more often than in the sequence" 439—124—73—dark."

The determination of meaning through context becomes more pronounced when the context is a sentence in which the word fulfills a certain grammatical role. By studying words supplied by subjects to fill vacant positions in incomplete sentences, Clark (1965) found that animate nouns formed 81.5 percent of the words suggested for the subject position in active sentences but only 26.7 percent of the words suggested for the active object position. In passive sentences, 68.3 percent animate nouns were used in the subject position, and 45.8 percent in the object position. Connotative meaning is also shaped to a certain degree by the word's position in a sentence. Nonsense syllables placed in the subject position are rated on the Semantic Differential as more active and potent than those in the object position (M. G. Johnson, 1967). Grammatical function and surrounding words may even lead to the creation of new meanings for artificially concocted words (Werner & Kaplan, 1952).

The influence of context on meaning may be used in art to facilitate unfolding of richer meaning. Poetry has at its disposal many devices for alerting the reader or listener to a particular word. Some of these are identical with the means used for lending prominence to phonemic qualities—repetitions and use of words in strategic, regular, or deviating positions for rhythm and rhyme, or in a "summative role" (Hymes, 1960). Other devices are shared by poetry and prose to a greater degree. Major among these are the elaboration of ambiguity and of unpredictability.

Of the many effects of ambiguity, which Empson (1953) identifies as "among the very roots of poetry," the enrichment of a word's meaning is undoubtedly among the most remarkable. Note, for example, the unexpected enrichment of the words "haven" and "heaven" created through

ambiguity in Wallace Stevens' poem "An Ordinary Evening in New Haven":
"The instinct for heaven had its counterpart:/ The instinct for earth, for
New Haven, for his room . . ." No less striking is the suggestiveness of
the ambiguous exclamation by the dying Caesar, "Et tu, Brute!", in which
"Brutus" and "brute" intermingle.

However, relations like those between "New Haven" and "new heaven,"
"Brutus" and "brutish," when laid bare through ambiguous uses of words
strike readers partly because they are new and unexpected. Relative unpredictability, which enhances tension and thus facilitates experience, may
be produced also by the mere use of unusual words. Another and most
effective means for producing surprise is by exploiting the relations between a word and its context. Placement of usual words in unusual contexts
or unusual words in usual contexts can hardly fail to alert the reader. A
prime example is Cummings' (1953, p. 12) famous sentence ". . . although
[my mother's] health eventually failed her, she kept her sense of humor to
the beginning." By one stroke, the meaning of the word "end" which is
inevitably supplied by the reader is expanded to unexpected horizons.
Essentially, unpredictability consists in violating the expectations that users
of a language have about the words, their roles and sequences. When words
at predetermined random positions are deleted from a text, the reader's
guesses at the missing words reveal that expected sequences depend partly
on the words themselves but mainly on the whole structure of the sentence
or word series from which the word was deleted (Selfridge, 1949).[6] As in
the other arts, it is a medium degree of unpredictability—the degree which
avoids both the incomprehension attending high unpredictability and the
boredom of total predictability—which appeals most to readers (Kammann,
1966). Thus, unexpected words introduced by a writer should preserve a
certain plausibility in the context in order to be both sufficiently novel to
evoke interest and sufficiently familiar to facilitate an expansion of their
meaning and hence of their impact.

Sentences

The primary object of our inquiry on the syntactical level is the sentence.
Although a sentence consists of words, its impact cannot be described as a
sum of the effects of the single words. For the major feature which turns a
sentence into a unit is its structure. The simplest way to show this is by
comparing two arrangements of the same set of words: "Sentences consist of words," vs. "Words consist of sentences." Here the transmission of
meaning depends mainly on the sequence of the words. Different arrange-

ments of the same set of words may change meaning to varying degrees. When we alter the sequence "The girl walked home" to "Home walked the girl," the general meaning is preserved in spite of the shift in emphasis. But when we alter the sequence "The girl walked home" into "The walked home girl," meaning is disrupted. On the other hand, similar meanings may be conveyed through several different sequences, if one allows for certain changes in words, e.g., "This section deals with sentences," vs. "Sentences are dealt with in this section," or "It is with sentences that this section deals."

The sequence of words is not the only factor responsible for the meaning transmitted, as is demonstrated by the following examples: "The boy said, 'the girl' " vs. " 'The boy,' said the girl"; or "Jack, the plumber, came" vs. "Jack, the plumber came." Thus, differences in pitch, stress, emphasis, breaks, and overall intonation are no less important than the arrangement of the words for the specification and transmission of meaning. Can such structural features account for different experiential effects of sentences?

A simple sentence may be regarded as a hierarchical structure whose "constituents" are phrases: a noun phrase (e.g., Paul) and a verb phrase (e.g., sleeps). This basic structure may be made more complex in various respects. One direction would be exemplified by adding modifiers to the single noun of the noun phrase, e.g., "The wise Paul," or by including a noun phrase in the verb phrase, e.g., "sleeps on a bed." The permissible combinations which indicate the ways in which the sentence can be decomposed into its constituents on the various levels down to that of the single words describe the sentence's characteristic phrase-structure. Such a surface analysis of a sentence's structure is, however, not purely theoretical. The grammatically constituent units seem to correspond to the perceptual units into which sentences are articulated by the listeners. When a different segmentation of a sentence is suggested by a series of clicks which do not fall at the points of syntactically relevant breaks, listeners tend to preserve the integrity of the syntactically meaningful units by displacing these clicks and perceiving them subjectively as occurring at the boundaries of the syntactical units (Fodor & Bever, 1965; Garrett, Bever, & Fodor, 1966).

Even the framework of an essentially simple sentence with an uncomplicated phrase-structure allows for elaborations which have a not too restricted range of experiential effects. Major among the possibilities provided by simple sentences are word inversions (e.g., "Cold was the night"), deletions, and chaining of the single-sentence units. Consider Camus' (1959, p. 1) opening of *The Stranger*: "Mother died today. Or, maybe, yesterday, I can't be sure. The telegram from the Home says: Your mother passed away. Funeral tomorrow. Deep sympathy. Which leaves the matter doubtful; it could have been yesterday." Many of these sentences lack one or more phrases, which are indeed supplied by the reader but when missing lend the passage an urgent insistence and an almost breathless speed.

The hallmark of Camus' style is simplicity, which is due in no small part to the shortness of his sentences. Longer sentences are not necessarily more complex. A sentence like "I saw in the zoo a lion, a tiger, a crocodile, an elephant, a horse . . ." could be extended indefinitely without becoming more complex. Therefore, it is difficult to interpret such a finding as the one that more popular magazines tend to use shorter sentences than less popular magazines (Gray & Leary, 1935) or that authors tend to use sentences of constant length (Gerwig, 1894; Sherman, 1892; Williams, 1940) or of varying length (Buch, 1952; Moritz, 1903). More crucial is the manner through which sentence length is attained.

A better measure of complexity and its characteristics is provided by the application of Chomsky's (1957, 1964) transformational grammar. Essentially, this method allows for an analysis of the surface phrase-structure of sentences into underlying kernel sentences. It specifies which grammatical operations have been performed upon the kernel sentences to produce the particular original sentence, which is in fact one among several alternative constructions of the same underlying kernel sentences. Thus, a sentence like "I expected the man who quit work to be fired" has three kernel sentences:

(a) I expected it;
(b) Someone fired the man;
(c) The man quit work.

These kernel sentences, subjected successively to six transformations, can account together for the generation of the original sentence (Chomsky, 1966, pp. 53–54). The transformations are these:

The relative transformation; i.e., (c) "The man quit work" turns into "who quit work."

The generalized embedding transformation; i.e., "who quit work"+(b) "someone fired the man" turn into "someone fired the man who quit work."

The passive transformation; i.e., "someone fired the man who quit work" turns into "the man who quit work was fired by someone."

The deletion transformation; i.e., "the man who quit work was fired by someone" turns into "the man who quit work was fired."

The generalized embedding transformation; i.e., "the man who quit work was fired"+(a) "I expected it" turn into "I expected the man who quit work was fired."

The singulary transformation; i.e., "I expected the man who quit work
was fired" turns into "I expected the man who quit work to be fired."

It may in general be expected that the more transformations necessary
to generate the textual sentences, the more complex the style. Thus, C. W.
Hayes' (1968) finding that Samuel Johnson's textual sentences are based on
an average of 5.2 and Gibbon's on an average of only 4.3 transformations per
sentence gains significance through the following psychological findings:
the more numerous the transformations that underlie a sentence's structure,
the longer the time required for understanding the sentence (Gough, 1965;
G. A. Miller, 1962) and the more difficult it is to memorize (Mehler, 1963;
Savin & Perchonock, 1965). Characteristically the errors made by subjects
in comprehension and memorization manifest a shift towards the kernel
sentences, i.e., to the simpler underlying deep structures (Mehler, 1963).

The type of transformation is a no less crucial factor in determining complexity than the sheer number of transformations performed. Some transformations yield much more complex sentences than others, as is illustrated
by G. A. Miller's (1962) examples: "The race that the car that the people
whom the obviously not very well dressed man called sold won was held
last summer" vs. "The obviously not very well dressed man called the people
who sold the car that won the race that was held last summer." Centering
upon the kind of transformations required, Ohmann (1964) showed how
the intricacy of Faulkner's style depends greatly on the use of the relative-
clause transformation, the conjunction transformation, and the comparative
transformation, while Hemingway's intimate reporting is attained through
the transformations of quotation, indirect discourse, and deletion.

Thus, the underlying structure of a sentence reflects various specific features of the style, including stylistic complexity, which play a role in centering the reader's attention on the sentence's structure and in heightening
tension in general. The underlying structure is important also from another
viewpoint. It determines to a certain degree the particular form of the melody
of a sentence—a factor which is most crucial in shaping the art experience
of literature.

Melody is a quality of all sentences. Essentially the sentence's melody
consists of a contour of changing pitch or intonation, modified by varying
duration of the different parts of words, and sometimes by additional stresses
attained through intensity or other means. For example, the basic melody
of a simple declarative sentence is an intonational contour that rises from
a medium pitch to a higher pitch at the stress peak and falls at the end of
the sentence. In contrast to this contour, which is referred to as the "archetypal normal breath group" (Lieberman, 1967, p. 27), the contour of a

question sentence typically rises at the end of the utterance. These contours of intonation, which are superimposed on the pitch differences between various phonemes and syllables (ibid., p. 102), emerge clearly for the listener in spite of "pitch perturbations" which characterize natural speech (ibid., p. 36) and in spite of variations among speakers in the range of fundamental frequency and in some of the underlying articulatory mechanisms (ibid., chap. 4).[7]

The intimate relation of intonation contours to the syntactic structure and meaning of sentences is evident already in the first stages of the acquisition of language. Children seem to respond to intonation of phrases before they are able to respond to words (Lewis, 1936). The basic intonations of a language are acquired before the words (Jakobson, 1941) and appear to be the first and most important means by which words are integrated into sentences (Werner & Kaplan, 1963, pp. 150–54).

In normal adult conversation, intonational contours may serve as one important cue to the sentence's syntactic structure, e.g., in case of possible ambiguity in meaning the division into breath groups may indicate separate phrases, and a nonfalling contour at the end of a phrase may signal that the sentence is not yet over (Lieberman, 1967, chaps. 5 and 8). However, these cues are not absolute, nor do they function in isolation from the listener's knowledge about a sentence's syntactic structure (Chomsky & Miller, 1963). If a sentence is not understood and its various syntactic parts are not correctly identified, its adequate intonation cannot be reproduced even after the sentence has been heard (G. A. Miller, 1962).

The intonation contour of a sentence is in many respects similar to a melody. It is "transposable" and depends on relative differences between pitch points, not on differences in absolute number of vibrations per second. Yet there are also major differences between a sentence melody and a musical melody. First, while in Western music the intervals between the tones are determined by the tonal system and hence are absolute and constant, the intervals in the sentence melody are relative and variable, do not represent any scale, and can be compressed or expanded along the pitch dimension without losing the contour's identity. Secondly, while a musical melody is characterized by a fixed relative duration of its tones irrespective of tempo, a sentence melody can be expanded or compressed temporally to fit sentences of varying duration (Abercrombie, 1967, chap. 6; Daneš, 1960).

Side by side with these differences, there are similarities in the experiential effects of musical melodies and melodies of sentences. Major among these is the tension-laden effect of a rise in pitch and the relief provided through return to a pitch of the initial level (Armstrong & Ward, 1926). The relation between heightened tension and higher tone level is strengthened by the fact that questions and incomplete phrases are usually marked by a higher pitch at the end. Since reading is seen developmentally as a kind of internalized speech, it may be assumed that sentence melodies exert these and other effects even when merely read.

As mentioned, sentence melodies characterize also nonliterary prose. What, if any, could be the differences between sentence melodies of literary and nonliterary prose? Although empirical findings are missing in this domain, we may set up a few hypotheses based on the assumption that melodies of literary sentences are often planned and constructed rather than abandoned to the random fluctuations of nonliterary language. A major characteristic of literary prose sentences is balance. Its clearest form is a symmetrical rise and fall of pitch, e.g., in shorter sentences, "For whatever a man soweth, that shall he also reap," or in longer ones, "He brought himself into so composed a gravity, that I never saw him laugh, and but seldom smile" (quoted by Baum, 1952, p. 47). This basic symmetrical contour may be elaborated in a variety of forms which contribute to the enhancement of the tension evoked. The principle underlying the various elaborations is the postponement of relief through extending one or another part of the symmetrical rise-peak-fall model. Compare what Saintsbury (1912) called "gradation," e.g., "Laodemeia died; Helen died; Leda, beloved of Jupiter, went before" (from Landor's "Aesop and Rhodopé") and the various forms of cumulative series. The latter involve expansions of any part of the sentence, and may reach excesses as in a sentence from Burke's "Appeal from the New to the Old Whigs" whose subject is subdivided into no fewer than fourteen clauses, which become gradually more elaborate.

More complex examples include sentences whose intonational contour consists of a series of secondary contours, parts of a complex melody whose various strings are resolved in a final relief. The secondary contours are characterized by minor ups and downs in pitch, and their melodies may be repetitions or variations of a theme. They are, however, integrated within the major intonational contour to which they are subservient. A prime example is the opening sentence of Sterne's *Tristram Shandy*: "I wish either my father or my mother, or indeed both of them, as they were in duty both equally bound to it, had minded what they were about when they begot me; had they duly considered how much depended upon what they were then doing;—that not only the production of a rational Being was concerned in it, but that possibly the happy formation and temperature of his body, perhaps his genius and the very cast of his mind;—and, for aught they knew to the contrary, even the fortunes of his whole house might take their turn

from the humours and dispositions which were then uppermost;—Had they
duly weighed and considered all this, and proceeded accordingly,—I am
verily persuaded I should have made a quite different figure in the world,
from that in which the reader is likely to see me" (Sterne, 1950, book I,
chap. 1, p. 3). Baum (1952, p. 137) has justifiably compared the suspense
created by such sentences to the tension evoked by "a pyramid held aloft
as though poised on its apex."

Sentences of this type, which represent a wide-swinging elaborate extension of the intonational contour far beyond the habitual range, are characteristic of writers like Faulkner, Thomas Mann, Proust, Agnon, Tolstoi,
and Flaubert. A very different type of sentence has been cultivated by authors
like Dos Passos, Feuchtwanger, Hemingway, and Camus. In their prose,
sentences are mostly short, often chopped off, with a melody which resembles a convulsive burst rather than a flow. Since a sentence is often too short
to allow for a terminal lowering of the tone, relief sometimes comes only
at the end of a paragraph.

Obviously, the two types of sentences described may also be used to-
gether in one text, even in one paragraph. Thus, while G. K. Chesterton and
G. B. Shaw use about the same average number of words per sentence,
Chesterton's sentences are regular, while Shaw's vary greatly in length
(Williams, 1940). Such contrasts in form may reflect or contrast with the
content conveyed through the long and short sentences.

Since a sentence is primarily a unit of content, the major effects of its melody arise through the interaction between melody and content. Parallelism
or equivalence characterizes prose passages in which a nonexciting content
is conveyed through sentences with wide-swinging arcs, or an exciting content in spiky, breathless sentences. Yet at least as strong an effect is created
by sentences in which melody and content are sharply contrasted, mutually
enhancing each other's effects. A similar enhancement of tension is created
when a foreshadowed melody of a sentence is unexpectedly changed through
a stress on a certain word required by the content.

In music a melody without rhythm is hardly conceivable. Is the melody
of prose sentences also rhythmized? Opinions vary greatly on this point.
Some are ardent supporters of the idea that prose is essentially rhythmic (e.g.,
Lipsky, 1907; Marbe, 1904; Thomson, 1923; Saintsbury, 1912), while others
contest the idea with varying degrees of vehemence (e.g., Baum, 1952; J. M.
Murray, 1922; Wimsatt, 1941). The problem is complicated mainly through
inconsistencies in the definitions of rhythm and its elements, as well as
through differences in sampling from prose. There can be little doubt that
characteristic prose is not structured in line with a strict meter, i.e., a sub-

division into units of equal duration marked off by regularly recurring stresses on phonemes or syllables. Although a sentence may be easily subdivided into parts, such as phrases or clauses, the divisions seem to follow grammatical rules more closely than metrical rules, and the distribution of emphases in these subgroups is more often irregular than regular.

Classe (1939) found that in sentences of strict prose read aloud by subjects, the subgroups vary to different degrees in number of syllables and of emphases. But he also found that regularity in the length of subgroups and the number of their accents depends to a great extent on phonetic and grammatical similarities between the sequential groups. Since these conditions are rarely met with in ordinary speech and regular prose, the perception of rhythm is impeded. Nevertheless, owing to the presence of stresses in speech and to the perceiver's tendency to group acoustic stimuli rhythmically, various parts of a prose passage may seem rhythmic to varying degrees. These degrees depend to a certain extent on structural features of the prose. The chances that rhythm will be perceived are, for example, high when the sentences lend themselves to divisions into short clauses which are similar in grammatical structure and meaning, as they do, e.g., in the biblical Song of Songs.

In spite of these findings, which correspond on the whole to the findings of Scott (1908), Thomson (1923), and others, it is possible to point to clear cases of meter in prose. Yet these metrical patterns are irregular in the sense that they do not appear in sufficiently long sequences or with anything like sufficient predictability to impress the reader as meter (Baum, 1952, chap. 4). Hence, when they do occasionally appear, their effect resides mainly in the surprise they evoke as patterns which deviate from the otherwise nonmetric context. All too often, however, the occasional metric patterns may even remain unnoticed by the reader, first, because he does not expect meter in regular prose, and secondly, because the normal speed with which prose is read is usually faster than that of poetry (Wallin, 1911–12) and thus leads to the overlooking of minor or secondary stresses that contribute to the meter of poetry (Baum, 1952, p. 222; Lipsky, 1907).

Apart from regular prose, which is essentially nonmetric, there are other forms of prose in which metric patterns are much more frequent and consistent. Such is the case with "polyphonic" and "spaced" prose, for example, Rilke's "Die Weise von Liebe und Tod des Cornets Christoph Rilke" (1906), biblical prose, and earlier English prose. Thus, characteristic prose and regular verse seem to form the poles of a continuum along which are placed various literary forms intermediate between the two extremes.

While regular prose is devoid of meter, it certainly is not devoid of rhythm in the sense of "the ebb and flow of sounds, the alternation and balance of ideas or feelings or syntactical arrangements" (Baum, 1952, p. 214). This type of prose rhythm hinges largely on rhetorical emphases and is manifested in the grammatical and meaning-conditioned grouping through pauses into phrases, clauses, sentences, and paragraphs.

Voice recordings of readings of prose (Griffith, 1929) and blank verse (Snell, 1918) show that modern literary prose is much more flexible in the structuring of its flow than the "spaced prose" of Malory, Bacon, Donne, or Burke. While the latter resembles blank verse in the length of its groups and the intervening pauses, modern fluid prose is characterized by fewer pauses, longer groups, and an overall greater variety and flexibility in the length of the groups and in the placement and duration of the pauses. However, while in newspaper prose the sequences of shorter and longer groups or pauses are highly irregular, and there is no detectable relation between the length of a pause and that of a preceding group, modern literary prose is characterized by clear patterns of movement, evident in the sequences of the groups—their length, their duration, and the tempo at which they are spoken. Fast and slow phrases alternate with a certain regularity, but the tempo and the duration of the phrases are determined mainly by the meaning and syntax rather than by the absolute number of syllables in the groups or their phonetic duration. Moreover, number of syllables in groups, duration of syllables, and the sequences of stressed and unstressed syllables play a role subservient to the major rhythmic flow of the sentence.

This ordered flow of prose sentences whose balance is determined more by meaning than by phonetic and syllabic regularities seems to have a marked experiential effect characterized by the building up of tension up to a peak and its resolution either in the framework of the same sentence or in the following ones. The effects of this "thought rhythm" (Baum, 1952, p. 214) are closely interwoven with the effects of the intonational contour. In relatively simple cases we may expect the fast groups to be characterized by a rising pitch, the slow groups to lie at the declining part of the intonational contour, and the peak of tempo to coincide with the highest intonational pitch (Griffith, 1929; Lieberman, 1967). However, a study of more complex exemplary cases (Baum, 1952; Patterson, 1916) reveals that sentences and, even more, paragraphs may have competing peaks of tension, one dependent on intonation, another on syntax and the flow of rhythm. Similarly, the grammatical grouping may not coincide with the units of meaning, pauses dictated by rhythm may not always be those dictated by intonation, or as Read (1931) put it, the logical, syntactical, and rhythmic punctuation systems may slightly deviate from one another. Since the overriding factor in prose is meaning, which governs both the intonational contour and the rhythmic flow, prose seems to have at its disposal the means for integrating the contrasting effects either in the form of a variegated sequence, or in terms of the content conveyed by a whole paragraph. Yet the possibility of an unpleasant, tense experience cannot be ruled out when the effects remain unintegrated or do not adequately correspond to the content.

Meter, Rhythm, and Rhyme

"While prose has everything but regularity, verse has everything including regularity" (Baum, 1952, p. 32). Regularity is such a notable feature of poetry that in spite of the evident continuity between prose and poetry, it enhances the poetic function of poetry to a degree which sets it in a domain of its own, defined by a perfect intertwining of acoustic, visual, and meaning effects.

The most obvious manifestation of regularity in poetry is meter (De Groot, 1957; Lotz, 1960). Meter is essentially a norm. Though seldom presented actually, it is communicated to the reader with sufficient clarity to enable him to perceive deviations from it in the actualized rhythm. At the bare minimum a metric system consists in the specification of the number of syllables within a syntactic unit like a phrase, a line, or a sentence. A pure syllabic meter of this kind can be found in Japanese or modern French verse. However, the more common metric systems, i.e., the syllabic-prosodic meters, consist of a specification of both the number of syllables in a syntactic unit and of the distribution of the more and the less emphasized syllables within such units. Emphasis on some syllables relative to others may be attained by using long vs. short syllables, as in the quantitative meter of classical Greek, Latin, and Sanskrit verse, by using high-pitched vs. low-pitched syllables, as in the tonal Chinese verse, or by using stressed vs. unstressed syllables as in the accentual meter characteristic of English,[8] German, Italian, and Russian poetry.

The metric specification of the distribution of emphasized syllables may involve a strict regulation of the number of unemphasized syllables preceding or following each emphasized syllable within a metric unit, or it may entail merely the regulation that a line should include a certain number of emphasized syllables without specification of the number of unemphasized syllables preceding or following each.

The first system, i.e., the syllable-stress meter is characteristic of the main bulk of traditional English poetry. A verse from Collins' "Ode" exemplifies it in a regular form:

> When Spríng with déwy Fíngers cóld
> Retúrns to déck their hállow'd Móld, . . .

The number of syllables in the line is constant, i.e., eight, and each stressed syllable is preceded by one unstressed syllable. It is customary, although by no means necessary (Chatman, 1960, p. 161), to express the periodic recurrence of stressed syllables by dividing the line into small groups, i.e., feet, each of which consists in the verse above of one unstressed syllable followed by one stressed syllable. Thus, each line may be described as consisting of four iambs.

The second system, i.e., the strong-stress meter, is characteristic of Old English poetry and of some modern poetry, e.g., Pound's, Auden's and Eliot's. It is exemplified by the following lines from Yeats's "Purgatory":

> Hálf-dóor, háll dóor,
> Híther and thíther dáy and níght,
> Híll or hóllow, shoúldering this páck
> All cóld, swéet, glístening líght . . .

Although the number of syllables in these lines differs along the range of four to nine, the number of stresses in each line is four.

Meter is obviously a means of ordering the flow of sounds. The ordering is accomplished by embedding the sounds in the framework of an acoustic gestalt. The effects of meter in language resemble thus the effects of meter in music (see Chapter 7), and the pleasure to which it gives rise is due to its general orientative function no less than to its correspondence to the basic rhythms of life processes. However, there is a difference between rhythmization in music and in language. While the tones of music can be ordered according to almost any kind of rhythm, rhythmization in language is restricted by the fact that speech sounds are ordered through convention by systems of stress, juncture, and pitch which cannot be ignored. Yet these systems do not give rise to any regular organization similar to that of meter. Hence, the surprising novelty with which almost any metric system is endowed. On the other hand, the coexistence of these different and noncorresponding patterns—the metric pattern and the patterns of stresses and syntax in habitual language—sets the scene for a constant and challenging interplay which lies at the core of the most thrilling effect of poetic rhythm: variation or modulation.

Modulation consists essentially in a deviation from the basic meter. The simpler cases of such deviation result from a contrast between the requirements of meter and of normal word stress, as in the following examples—the first from Tennyson's "Morte d'Arthur" and the second from Bridges' "The Christian Captives":

For whát/are mén/bétter/than shéep/or goáts . . .

The flásh/of árms/and dúst/of troóps/móving . . .

In the first example meter would demand reading "bétter" as "bettér," and in the second—"móving" as "movíng." Normal English pronunciation leads thus to a deviation from the meter by replacing the iambs in these lines with trochees.

More complex examples of deviation result from noncorrespondence between meter and meaning. This is the factor modulating the iambs in Coleridge's verse from *The Ancient Mariner*:

Alóne, alóne, all, all alóne,

Alóne on a wíde wíde séa!

or in Pope's line:

Thús much I've sáid, I trúst withoút offénce.

Another frequent type of modulation of the base meter concerns the phenomena of pause and overflow. A perfectly regular line, such as Milton's (from *Paradise Lost*):

And swíms,/or sínks,/or wádes,/or creéps,/or flýes

in which stresses and pauses of meter and regular speech coincide perfectly, is extremely rare. Much more frequent are cases in which the meter cuts across words, as in Collins' verse:

When Spring/with dew/y Fing/ers cold . . .

Similarly, while meter often requires a break in the rhythmic flow at the end of every line, the sense may require a pause within the line or a combining of two lines, as in Hopkins' verse from "The Handsome Heart":

"But tell me, child, your choice; what shall I buy

You?"—"Father, what you buy me I like best."

Some of the deviations from the base meter are so common that they are regarded as departures within the limits of the law; they are "not an opposition to its majesty the meter but an opposition of its majesty" (Jakobson, 1960, p. 364). Such is for example the case with the shift of stress in polysyllabic words from the downbeat to the upbeat, or the use of an attention-arousing trochee for the first foot in a line of iambs (Hamer, 1951, pp. 10–11), as in the following line from Stevenson's "Requiem":

Únder/the wíde/and stár/ry skÿ

Thus, there is a constant tension between the abstract and potential metrical system, which is the product of historically coded convention, and the ordinary systems of stress, pitch, and juncture in spoken English, determined by the requirement of meaning and emphasis (Chatman, 1956).[9] The tension arises from two major sources: the first is the frustration of built-up expectations to which the basic meter gives rise (Richards, 1926, p. 134); while the second is the challenge of integrating two essentially different rhythmical systems, two gestalts, each of which is "good" in its own right though for different reasons. Naturally, in a poem these two rhythms are not simply superimposed on each other. Rather, they intertwine, continuously diverging and converging, suggesting solutions which are sometimes ambiguous, at other times enticing before they prove untenable. Attempts at integrating the two disparate rhythms which lie at the core of poetry are the main hallmark of the art of poetic recitation (Jakobson, 1952; Levin, 1962).

Meter, however, interacts not only with the system of stresses and syntax in habitual language but also with meaning and content of the poem. The metric system of stresses may highlight overlooked relations between words or bring a word to the fore, particularly when the metric stress is neutralized or shifted through the requirements of meaning. Moreover, "rhythmic structures are expressive forms . . . communicating those experiences which rhythmic consciousness can alone communicate" writes Gross (1964, p. 12). This assumption is common enough with investigators of meter, who often comment about the "light tripping motion" (Hamer, 1951, p. 40) of a trochaic heptasyllabic meter, about the note of sorrow struck by a pyrrhic (i.e., foot of two unstressed syllables), or the weariness and despair expressed by a spondee (i.e., a foot of two stressed syllables) at the end of the line (Hamer, 1951, p. 11).

The hypothesis that meters are expressive forms has been verified by Hevner (1937b), who experimented with nonsense syllables recited in various meters. She found that predominantly anapestic meters were experienced by most subjects as jovial, joyous, humorous, merry, playful, etc., while predominantly iambic meters were described as solemn, sober, ponderous, majestic, or dignified. There is, however, too little empirical material to support hypotheses about the origin of the expressive qualities of meter. The effect may possibly be attributed in part to structural qualities of the meter, such as the intervals between the stresses, the suggested tempo, and the implied size of the metric units. Yet associations between meters and specific contents in traditional poetry, as between blank verse and a specific type of drama in English literature, cannot be ruled out as a possible source for the suggestive expressiveness of meter.

Hevner's (1937b) findings also showed that when explicit meaning and narrative content are absent, meter is the most strongly and clearly experienced factor in a nonsense-syllable poem. Its effectiveness is greater than that of speech sounds and of voice inflections. This finding is particularly relevant in the case of poems devoid of narrative content. Such poems, frequent in various so-called primitive cultures around the world, consist in singing or reciting nonsense syllables and/or vowels, as in the Kwakiutl poem quoted by Boas (1955, p. 314):

> Aw, ha ya ha ya hä
> ha ya he ya ä
> he ya ha ya ä
> A, ha ya ha ya hä, *etc.*

Strings of nonsense syllables designed to carry a meter or to emphasize some of its characteristics are also frequent in poems which do have a narrative content or at least an explicitly communicated meaning (Boas, 1955, pp. 312–20). In poems of this type the expressive function of meter is so pronounced that content may sometimes seem to be subordinate to it. When a poem does have a narrative level, as most poems do, the expressive undercurrent of meter may be expected to interact with the content. Such interaction may take not only the form of parallelism between the mood suggested by the meter and the atmosphere communicated through the content, but also that of tension-laden contrasts such as might arise from a galloping light meter juxtaposed intentionally with a solemn content. A masterly example is Auden's "The Unknown Citizen," in which metric features—light anapests, a too clumsy meter—serve as a sneering commentary on the glib complacency conveyed by the content.

The range of interactions of meter with content and with the rhythms of language and meaning has been greatly expanded in modern poetry through the abandonment of strict metrical structures (Gross, 1964; Hrushovski, 1960). Although the rebellion of modern poets against conventional meter often took the form of renouncing continuous regular meter in favor of rhythms akin to prose rhythm, "free rhythms" are neither a new phenomenon in literature nor should they be identified with lack of meter. Modern "free rhythm" implies quite as often the application of a wealth of different metric procedures: the combination of various prosodic modes, such as Auden's mixing of strong-stress meter and iambic meter; the use of very different meters in the same poetic text, as in T. S. Eliot's *Four Quartets* (Gross, 1964, p. 207); the replacement of the accented meter by a quantitative one, as in Pound's poems; the use of meters hovering between the regular and complete irregularity; the elaboration of new meters unique to a certain poem; the revival of archaic and no longer familiar meters. Through these devices modern poetry has gained the means of greatly enhancing evoked tensions. Although sometimes the metric complexity may prevent the grasp of the gestalt, more often the contrasts between various meters, the ambiguity of the overall meter and the difficulty of identifying it clearly, the swinging variations of novel metrical themes, and the counterpointing of the shifting meters with contents and sentence flow are potent experiential factors.

As mentioned, meter is a major manifestation of regularity in poetry. Another is the schemes of sound repetition, which have been closely related to meter and rhythm in the earlier developmental stages of poetry. Just as some poetic texts are more metric than others, so some poetic traditions, like the old Germanic and the Welsh, have used sound-repetition schemes, e.g., alliteration, more than others. But a certain measure of sound repetition is as characteristic of poetry as meter or metric allusions are, for both are manifestations of the parallelism which is an important poetic device (Hopkins, 1937).

Sound repetition schemes may be classified according to two main principles. The one is the placement of the recurring sounds in the word, i.e., at the beginning of the word, as in initial consonant repetition (e.g., "furrow follows free"); at the end of the word, as in the varieties of rhyme; or in the middle of the word (Chatman, 1960). The second relevant principle is the type of repetition, i.e., repetition of the sounds in the same sequence without variation (e.g., "A smoke-*stained stars* and *stripes*") or with variation (e.g., "That *slid* into my sou*l*"), repetition of the sounds in an inverted order (e.g., "*virgin river*"), and repetition of merely similar sounds, as is frequent in the poems of Heine and Goethe (Masson, 1953, 1961). The scheme becomes more complex when one considers the patterns of sound repetition, as in the following lines by Dylan Thomas:

> *W*oke to my *h*earing from *h*arbour and neighbour *w*ood . . .

or

> Above the lilting *h*ouse and *h*appy as the *g*rass was *g*reen . . .
> And *g*reen and *g*olden I was *h*untsman and *h*erdsman . . .

Sound repetitions are a well-known phenomenon outside poetry too. They seem to be bound up with the early stages of the acquisition or use of language. They are remarkably frequent in the speech of children and in primitive rituals and songs, as well as under conditions of impaired conscious control, as in dreams or in manic attacks. Although the functions and effects of sound repetition in these various contexts undoubtedly differ, it may be suggested that sound repetition in poetry shares some general effects with sound repetition outside poetry. For example, sound repetition in poetry may have a slight hypnoidal effect (Snyder, 1930; Yeats, 1924) similar to that of magic incantations and primitive songs. Likewise, the regularity of the repetition may have an organizing, orientative function in poetry as in other contexts. However, the effect of sound repetition more specific to poetry seems to be primarily the highlighting of relations between words. Sound repetition is thus not only a means for counteracting the habituation to words and their neutralization through constant use in daily life, but also suggests implicitly meaningful relations that may cut across and implement the explicit communication on the narrative level.

These and other effects of sound repetition are most clearly manifested in rhyme. Because of its specific technical aspects and the code which governs its use, rhyme is often regarded as a special poetic technique. Aside from the classical rhyme which consists in the repetition of final stressed vowels and the following consonants (e.g., hill/mill, morrow/sorrow), most languages admit of further rhyming procedures which may be used in specific poetic texts. While the feminine rhyme, which consists of the classical rhyme plus the repetition of additional unstressed identical syllables (e.g., taker/maker), is much used in English for humorous effect, in Italian, Polish, and medieval Latin it fulfills a completely serious role (Wellek & Warren, 1956). In addition, there are also variations on rhyme, which are often identified as imperfect rhymes, e.g., the eye rhyme, which is a kind of assonance in which the vowels are similar but differ in pronunciation, as in home/come.

Is rhyme tension-laden or relief providing? If rhyme is considered a rare phenomenon or a surprising or even shocking occurrence (Wimsatt, 1944), then it has to be presumed that it is a source of tension. The unrhymed words preceding and following it would then serve as relief. But if one considers the fact that the overwhelming majority of rhymes are placed at the ending of lines or phrases, namely, at structural points which are expected to provide relief, it seems more likely that rhyme is relief. Does it then follow that unrhymed language is tension-laden? The paradox may be resolved through an analogy. Ordinary buildings do not seem particularly unsatisfying until one happens to see an exceptionally beautiful architectural structure; and regular food comes to be experienced as unsatisfactory after an exceptionally good meal. Thus, the occurrence of a rhyme brings relief which is more complete than that provided by the ordinary imperfect sound sequences which through habituation have come to represent the norm. Upon its occurrence, rhyme creates a kind of a gravitational point, it sounds a basic keynote, in reference to which unrhymed words and, even more, unrhymed lines are experienced as imperfect and tension-laden. Essentially, the contrast consists of an acoustic gestalt which is inherently good and acoustic gestalts that are accepted as good by force of habituation and familiarity.

Why is a rhyme an inherently good gestalt? "There are two elements in the beauty rhyme has to the mind," writes Hopkins (quoted by Jakobson, 1960, p. 368), "the likeness or sameness of sound and the unlikeness or difference of meaning." Yet, that is only a first approximation of rhyme's effect. A closer approximation was stated most succinctly by Karl Kraus (1961, pp. 257–58): "It is the shore of their landing, / As two ideas reach understanding."[10] Thus, the special thrill of a good rhyme consists in revealing unexpected equivalences in meaning between words or ideas which seemed very different to begin with. What is the relation between "law" and "flaw" in Pope's verse:

> Whether the nymph shall break Diana's law
> Or some frail China jar receive a flaw . . .?

Wimsatt (1944) who elaborated this example noted convincingly that the rhyme reveals the affinity in meaning between losing one's virginity and scratching a precious vase: in a certain social atmosphere both are regarded as signs of diminished value. Yet parallelism between sound and sense need not necessarily reveal the convergence of apparently unrelated or contrasting ideas. The rhyme may also reflect the sense, and thus reinforce it, while in less remarkable cases it may serve a merely decorative function.

A rhyme, however, has also a structural role which may strengthen or sometimes weaken its relief-providing quality. The function of rhyme has conventionally been to mark breaks in metrical units as line endings and to emphasize the integrity and separateness of the stanza, as well as of sections within complex poetic forms like the sonnet. In this role, too, rhyme proves to be a means with unique potentialities. It may serve to separate that which apparently belongs together or combine that which seems unrelated. The first aspect is exemplified in the famous German verse:

> Hans Sachs was a shoe-
> maker and a poet too,

while the second aspect is best illustrated through the effects of internal rhymes, as in the following lines from "Hassan":

> We are they who come faster than *fate*: we are they who
> ride early or *late*:
> We storm at your ivory *gate*: Pale Kings of the Sunset
> beware.

In this case the rhyme serves mainly to create unexpected breaks within a line. In Dylan Thomas's "The Conversation of Prayers," the intriguing crisscross pattern of the rhymes foreshadows the central theme of the poem:

> The conversation of *prayers* about to be *said*
> By the child going to *bed* and the man on the *stairs* . . .

Just as the rhymes cross, so do the prayers: the child praying for quiet rest will "drown in a grief," and the man who fears the worst for his beloved will find her "alive and warm."

As any reader of poetry knows, meter, rhythm, and rhyme are powerful means for evoking an aesthetic experience. The readers' expectation of these means only serves to enhance their effectiveness. By using meter and rhyme the poet announces as it were that the text is a poem. The announcement carries an invitation to the readers or listeners to participate in the "game" of poetry (G. A. Miller, 1960, p. 390), and hence sets them in a particularly receptive mood.

The effective use of these means forms but a small part of the wide range of means for evoking experience which are at the disposal of language, in poetry and prose alike. The undercurrent of sound symbolism, the magic of words, the tension-arousing and relief-providing effects of grammatical structures, the often puzzling interactions between kernel sentences and transformations, the melody of sentences and their rhythm—these are the pillars on which all good literature rests. Yet, these pillars turn into hardly more than ornamentation if they do not carry the weight of the narrative, the representational contents. The colors and forms of paintings, the tones of music, the shapes and surfaces of sculpture, the movements of dance are exciting and experientially loaded even without such contents. But the means inherent in language remain an empty hulk when there is no narrative, no interpersonally meaningful message.

Part II

12. Beyond the Tension Principle

The first part of our book has been devoted to the problem how colors, forms, tones, movements, and other elements in works of art may generate tension and relief in the spectator. The hypothesis guiding this analysis is that works of art are capable of producing tensions which have two main characteristics: they are sufficiently variegated and multidimensional to absorb diffuse residual tensions in the spectator; yet they are specific enough to be resolved through other aspects of the work of art. Thus the resolution of these specific tensions, amplified by the more diffuse tensions, affords a summative relief to the diffuse as well as the specific tensions.

Up to this point we have concentrated on testing and demonstrating this hypothesis for the formal elements of art, first, because the operation of tension-and-relief processes on this level of art is far from obvious; second, because this level offers the best means for demonstrating the essentials of the processes discussed and their importance for the experiencing of art; and third, because analyzing the stimuli for tension-and-relief processes from the viewpoint of the formal elements lets us point up the features of the various arts which distinguish them from one another on the background of the many characteristics which they share.

A restrictive assumption underlying the discussion up to now has been that the processes of tension and relief and the elaborations of meaning on which they depend do not suffice for describing the domain of the art experience. Since the hypothesis has so far been tested and demonstrated only for the formal elements of the arts, the impression might arise that tension-and-relief processes do little to explain effects in the representational-narrative contents of the arts. This impression is mistaken. Indeed, the role played by tension-and-relief processes on the level of the contents of art is even more obvious, was identified earlier, and is more widely recognized than their role with regard to the formal elements. The limitations of the tension-and-relief hypothesis also apply equally to both these levels of art, as we will see.

Tension and Relief in Narrative-Representational Contents

Of all the arts, literature is oftenest associated with the principle of tension and relief. Most readers will admit that the tension evoked by the plot of a novel or story, i.e., the desire to know what happens next and at the

end, is what drives them to go on reading the text. Even so-called good literature, particularly novels and dramas, generally follow the principle of
thrillers, which consists in introducing a puzzle at the beginning and presenting a more or less unexpected resolution at the end. While most thrillers
center upon enigmas of murder and on hide-and-seek games between de-
tectives and criminals, the bulk of literature is devoted to conflicts of a different type—conflicts within a person, among people, between a human
being and nature, reality, society, time, death. Though these conflicts differ
from the puzzles of thrillers in content, range of significance, setting, and
manner of elaboration, they are no less tension-laden than acts of pursuit,
dangerous adventures, and surprise developments in the usual detective
story. The same is true of other common literary themes which may not be
viewable as explicit conflicts but are nevertheless nuclei of dramatic suggestion and development. Such are descriptions of situations or images which
include contradictions or incompatible viewpoints, and unconventional
treatment of common events—a comic presentation of the usually serious,
or a revelation of the familiar as strange and shocking (Ehrlich, 1965,
pp. 150–51).

Consider some common devices for creating and maintaining suspense:
(1) suggestion of alternative courses of development and resolution which
do not always mature into events or solutions; (2) gradual build-up towards
a climax over a series of crises; (3) foreshadowing and unchronological presentation of a story, with recurrent flashbacks or revelations; (4) use of
ambiguities (Empson, 1953); (5) resort to possible and explicable though
unexpected resolutions (e.g., Lubbock, 1957; Forster, 1927).

Tension and relief undeniably play a role in the experiencing of literary
plots. The role seems to be greater in novels of former centuries than in modern fiction, and it is as a rule more prominent in thrillers, in mystery tales,
and in detective and adventure stories than in poetry and in so-called "great"
or classical literature. But regardless of the specific literary techniques used
to evoke tension and to resolve it, tension and relief are an integral element
of the dramatic nucleus of every literary plot.

An additional source of tension, different from the unfolding of the plot,
becomes evident in literary works which depend on shocking and puzzling
the audience. In the Theater of the Absurd, for example, there may indeed
be a plot or a quasi-plot, but since it usually does not conform in its premises
and underlying structure to the expectations of the common reader or observer, there is no firm basis for suspense concerning what will happen next
or how the problem posed will be solved. Thus, in view of the strange, contradictory, bewildering, and ambiguous situations which continue to pile up

as the story proceeds, the readers "are in suspense about what the next event to take place will add to their understanding of *what is happening*" (Esslin, 1967, p. 398). The tension is epitomized by the question, What does all this mean? The problem provoking the tension is posed by the reader and not by the author, just as the relieving answer is provided by the reader himself, mostly after he has finished reading the literary work. In contrast to suspense evoked through the plot, which has some affinities with curiosity and is satisfied through further information provided largely in the context of the literary work, the suspense created through failing understanding derives from disorientation or impaired orientation and can be relieved only by an active search for meaning on the part of the percipient.

The two types of tension and relief just discussed can be identified also in other arts in which narrative content takes the form of an unfolding plot or of a gradually emergent representation of an idea. This is notably the case in film and in some types of dance, particularly ballet, and in most theatrical dancing.

The situation is different for music and the visual arts, which do not present plots in the usual sense of the word. Indeed, with regard to music there arises first the problem of the existence and nature of narrative-representational contents. However, to the extent that melody and musical motifs and themes can be regarded as the musical analogues of narrative contents—a thesis which will be discussed in the next chapter—there is little doubt that following the adventures, history, and fate of these motifs and attending to their interactions, variations, and unexpected transformations evoke tension and relief in the listener. As in literature, the intensity of these effects varies with the work of art. Tension and relief may be assumed to be stronger in music heavily dependent on the development of themes—melodic, harmonic, or rhythmical—than in music which has hardly any identifiable themes, like some recent compositions of serial music. Of course, the effects are greatly diminished, if not eliminated, for listeners who fail to identify the themes and to follow their development.

Many works of art in painting and sculpture are similar to music in that they have no explicit narrative-representational content. Yet when such content does exist, its presentation is different than in the other arts. Since sculpture and painting consist of objectively static images, the portrayal of a temporally unfolding plot in a picture or a piece of sculpture must be highly concentrated and reduced to one representative instant, rarely more. Lessing (1930) applied the term "dramatic moments" to such instants portrayed in sculpture and noted that as a rule they represent either the climax of an implied plot or a situation at its very threshold. Both are highly tension-laden junctures of an underlying plot or sequence of actions. Some preceding and succeeding phases of an event are, however, often suggested through cues. For example, the main figure is portrayed in motion, but some folds of its robe may indicate a previous state of motion, while other folds or the posture of one bodily part may portray a future state of motion. Similarly, in a painting, past and future events may be suggested by side themes or secondary figures on the canvas. Thus, tension is evoked through the presentation of dramatic climax moments as well as through the fragmented portrayal of the merely implied plot. The intensity of the tension evoked depends not only on the dramatic nature of the represented scene, figure, or plot but also on the force with which the images suggest to the spectator the questions, How will the scene end? and What happened before?, and on the strength of the tendency of closure for the gestalt of the plot.

These conclusions are valid only for paintings and sculptures suggestive of plots and dramatic developments. The possible stimuli for tension and relief would be different for visual art products which represent images or scenes with no underlying dramatic connotations or without explicit object references. Art works of these types can be assumed to evoke tension and relief only indirectly, in the form of reaction to the perceived contents. Thus, a spectator may react with tension-laden indignation to a depicted image of misery, or with pleasantly relieving associations to a pastoral scene. The reactions are, however, different to paintings and sculptures of the more modern type which constitute a revolt against the traditional themes by presenting poles of a new scale of contents for the visual arts. These include, on the one hand, art objects characterized by notable deviations from common reality or by lack of explicit object references, and, on the other hand, works of art of the Dadaist and Pop schools, which are much more "common" and "real" than works sanctioned by the traditional conventions of the arts. As in the case of symbolic and "absurd" literature, the source of tension here is failing orientation, enhanced through frustrated expectations and a reduction of cues for unequivocal answers. The quest for meaning is evoked no less by the objects too near to reality than by quasi-representational surrealist and other images which remind only vaguely of reality and by compositions of forms and colors which can hardly be embedded in any conventional frame of reference. In less intense forms, disorientation can also be produced by more classical works of art. But while with regard to the latter a spectator may ask specifically, What does the Mona Lisa's smile signify?, with regard to many modern works he starts with a much more inclusive question, such as, What is portrayed on the canvas?

By way of summary, it is apparent that tension and relief are involved in the experience evoked by the narrative contents of the arts. A major role in the evocation of tension and relief on this level is played by suspense, which is a characteristic factor in the experiencing of a temporally unfolding plot, and by orientation, which remains incomplete until the whole story or the main theme is exposed or comprehended. The different arts dispose of a variety of devices for enhancing the tension evoked through contents.

So far there is no way of comparing the degree and quality of the tension and relief evoked through narrative-representational contents with that evoked through the formal means of the various arts. Too little is known about the relation between stimuli and experiencing to allow even a clear-cut hypothesis. On the one hand, it appears that tension and relief from various sources are experientially different. The rationale for this conclusion is that tension and relief are a product of both physiological and cognitive reactions, so that even if physiologically there may be no detectable differences between tension evoked through a clash of colors and that evoked by failing orientation, cognitive elaboration may provide differential cues for experiencing. On the other hand, since tensions due to stimuli as different as hunger and heat (Braun, Wedekind, & Smudski, 1957) or as hunger, thirst, and curiosity (Glickman & Jensen, 1961) interact, there is reason to believe that tension and relief produced by stimuli on the levels of narrative contents and of the formal means of the arts also combine in a variety of counterbalancing, facilitative, and inhibiting ways in the unitary experience.

Limitations of the Tension Principle

Although tension and relief processes play a role in the experiencing of the narrative contents of art, the tension-and-relief hypothesis is too limited to account for crucial aspects of experiencing these contents. To the extent that tension and relief are assumed to derive from the dynamics of the unfolding literary plot or the developments of a musical theme or melody, one may justifiably wonder why people are willing to expose themselves to the same literary or musical works more than once. Why do they listen repeatedly to *Romeo and Juliet*, with whose story they are familiar, or why do they read Thomas Mann's *Joseph and his Brothers* at all, whose plot they have known since childhood? Wherein resides the fascination of the universal duels between God and Satan, Don Quixote and Sancho Panza, Faust and Mephisto, which does not wear off with familiarity? Would the appreciation of a listener be appreciably reduced if he were told beforehand about what precisely will be done with the motifs in the course of the musical composition he is about to hear? If so, why do so many music lovers study the score before they go to a concert? Or how can we explain the observation that listening to the same detective story three times successively is accompanied each time by a progressive increase in arousal, viz., muscle tension, up to the end of the story, although the overall level of tension declines with each repetition (Wallerstein, 1954)? Or for incompletely presented plots, one may ask what drives the observer to look at a painting or sculpture after he has once reconstructed the plot or has learned it from another observer. Although the tension derived from disorientation in view of puzzling surrealist, symbolic, and "absurd" contents may be assumed to be fully resolved only after several confrontations with the work of art, one may wonder about the persistent fascination of such works even after they have been studied to a degree which would satisfy curiosity in the case of more difficult intellectual tasks.

Observations of this kind strongly suggest that there are more things in heaven and earth than are dreamt of in the tension-and-relief philosophy. Human responses to the contents of the arts are much more complex than is indicated by the tension principle epitomized in the implied question, What will happen next? There seem to be potent factors which render the very confrontation with great works of art fascinating in spite of previous familiarity. The next chapters will be devoted to the elaboration of hypotheses about some of the major factors and processes which account for further essential aspects of the art experience. These hypotheses will be elaborated mainly with regard to the narrative-representational contents of the arts, since this level seems to be best suited for their analysis and exemplification. However, it should be emphasized that just as the processes of tension and relief apply equally to the contents and to the formal means of the arts, the processes we are about to discuss are not only relevant for the level of the formal elements but even depend on this level no less than on the level of the narrative-representational contents.

13. Emotional Involvement

Set

Artistic experience is a joint product of the stimuli presented in a work of art and of the spectators' responses to these stimuli. In general, the more responsive the spectator is, the more intense is his experience and the more emotionally involved he may become. The responsiveness of the spectator is due in no small part to his expectations with regard to art in general and the art experience in particular. Expectations of this kind form a part of what is known as the observer's "set."

Set is the concept most often invoked to explain why people are more likely to undergo an art experience when they are confronted with art stimuli in the framework of a work of art than in another context; or why they tend to become more emotionally involved in a work of art when it is presented under conditions generally regarded as proper for the appreciation of art than under the ordinary circumstances of daily life.

We all notice how very differently we can be affected by stimuli which may be much alike—e.g., scaffolding of buildings and geometrically patterned paintings, stories people tell each other and themes of great literary works, color constellations in nature and in man-made pictures. Again, most of us are aware of a special sense of expectation and preparedness before we expose ourselves intentionally and voluntarily to works of art. "We feel different in ourselves before listening to a symphony or to the reading of a poem than before the performance of our professional activities" (Segal, 1906, p. 91). Could expectations and special readiness of the spectator explain differences in response to stimuli within art and nonart contexts? What is the nature of the expectations and readiness of which the art-receptive set consists?

In order to answer these questions, the concept of set should be examined more closely. Far from being an exclusively aesthetic phenomenon, set is generally considered "a universal aspect of behavior . . . that shows itself within the time during which the behavioral aggregate is undergoing its structuring" (F. H. Allport, 1955, p. 217). Although not all psychologists would agree with Uznadze's (1966) extreme claim that set is indispensable for all conscious and unconscious behavioral acts of human adults, enough evidence has accumulated since the early experimental studies in Wundt's laboratory and the Würzburg school to support the conclusion that set is a crucial factor which codetermines speed, accuracy, intensity, maintenance, course, and completion of behaviors ranging from perception, learning, and thinking to motor activity and satisfaction of needs (F. H. Allport, 1955, pp. 208–41; Gibson, 1941; Sanders, 1966). There is hardly any domain of psychology in which the importance of set has not been recognized, as can be gathered from the plethora of terms by which it was designated as early as 1941: "mental set, motor set, neural set, voluntary set, unconscious set, postural set, organic set, preparatory set, task-set (Aufgabe), situation-set, goal-set, temporary set, permanent set, set to react, set to perceive, expectation (expectancy), hypothesis, anticipation, foresight, intention (aim, end, purpose, determination), attitude, directing tendency, determining tendency, tension, vector, need, attention, perseveration, preoccupation" (Gibson, 1941, pp. 781–82). In spite of several decades of research, the nature, causes, and dynamics of the phenomenon of set are still poorly understood, but *expectation* and *intention* emerge as aspects common to various manifestations of set (Gibson, 1941, p. 784). These two aspects may sometimes seem to have relatively autonomous functions within the context of set (Hilgard & Humphreys, 1938; Lindner, 1938; Woodworth, 1938), but usually they are closely interrelated.

Expectation may be conceptualized both in psychological and physiological terms. On the psychological level, expectation appears as an hypothesis about future events which may vary in definiteness, concreteness, veridicality, subjective probability, etc. (Bruner, 1951) in line with situational circumstances and the specific domain of behavior. Such a set is a crucial factor in attending to stimuli, identifying them, and remembering them (Haber, 1966). Motivational factors, including needs, attitudes, or values as well as past experiences and learning, contribute in varying degrees to the shaping of expectancies (F. H. Allport, 1955, chaps. 13–14). Thus, a specific expectancy is most often a product of more general expectancies formed in the past and is adapted to the present situation on the basis of cues and other demand characteristics of that situation. The physiological manifestations of expectancy have been convincingly demonstrated by Sutton et al. (1965). Their experiment consisted in presenting sequences of a single and double acoustic stimuli to the subjects, who had to guess the nature of the next stimulus in the series. The records of the electric brain waves (EEG) of the subjects showed definite distinguishable traces not only of the perceived stimuli but also of stimuli which were merely expected yet not actually perceived at the time. These findings suggest that a facsimile of an expected event is constructed in the brain at the expected time of occurrence (John, 1967, p. 406).

The aspect of intention in set has usually been associated with sets which precede motor actions (F. H. Allport, 1955, p. 216). Since, however, behaviors which are less visibly motoric in nature, e.g., perception or learning, also involve activity on the part of the individual, there is no justification for restricting intention to motor sets only. The psychological manifestations of intention seem to differ with the particular domain of behavior. Thus, in thinking and problem solving it may assume the form of a directional, goal-oriented determining tendency (Gibson, 1941, pp. 798–99), while in motor actions it may be manifested as a need responsible for maintenance of the behavior until its completion (Lewin, 1951) and for subjective disturbances when completion is prevented (Mandler & Watson, 1966). On the physiological level it seems plausible to assume with Freeman (1948a, 1948b) that intention consists of tensions in muscle groups involved in the specific action for which the organism is set, and that these tensions form a focal tension-pattern on the background of the ever-present diffuse muscular tensions in the organism, which help to maintain a general state of vigilance and alertness. However, in line with more modern findings about arousal, it should be remembered that muscular tension is only one of the manifestations of the general alertness which forms the background arousal, and of the specific readiness which is set. Moreover, it may be assumed that intention is represented in the cortex not merely through backlash from the muscles to the central nervous system (Freeman, 1948b, pp. 226–27), but is, like expectation, a cognitive, centrally determined phenomenon.

Thus, set emerges as a complex state which involves both central and peripheral changes in the organism and facilitates, first, attention and meaningful elaboration of stimuli, and second, the elicitation and completion of a behavioral act when it is called for. However, since perception and identification of stimuli are themselves behavioral acts in which intention is involved, and since behavioral acts depend both on perception of stimuli and on expectancies, e.g., of outcomes and of sequences, expectancy and intention can hardly be dissociated within set. They are both involved, although in different degrees, in the various phases of the behavioral sequence, increasing the probability of certain modes of perception and of response relative to the other alternative modes which may be available or at least possible.

The paramount importance of set for art can be demonstrated by a great variety of experiments which show the role that different sets play in the elicitation of art experiences of many types and intensities. As a first example, consider an experiment performed by Lazarus and his associates on reactions to stress. In this experiment (Lazarus, Opton, Nomikos, & Rankin, 1965) three groups of people were shown a short documentary film on work accidents which featured some bloody incidents. Different information was given to each group before the film was shown. The first group received only a short synopsis of the film and thus was not influenced to adopt a set against excitement; the second group was told that the film was poorly performed and presented merely a fictitious demonstration of the dangers occasioned by lack of caution; finally, the third group got some hints about the contents of the film and was led to assume an analytic attitude in order to make socio-psychological observations on working conditions. Measurements of heart rate and skin conductance as indices of the subjects' emotional excitement while viewing the film revealed that the first group manifested the highest level and the third group the lowest level of arousal, with the second group occupying a mid-position.

The importance of these findings in our context is not merely that they show the dependence of emotional arousal on set. Equally significant is the demonstration that emotional arousal was not reduced so much by the set of the second group as by the set of the third group. Otherwise expressed, awareness of the artificial features of a filmed event and knowledge about the fictitious character of a story, even if enhanced, do not prevent emotional involvement to the same degree as an analytic attitude, similar to the one often adopted by art critics and professional reviewers. Moreover, further experiments in the same series show, first, that the effect of set is greatest when it is formed before the film is viewed and not in the course of it, and second, that set functions mainly through influencing the spectators' interpretation of the film events (Lazarus & Alfert, 1964; Lazarus et al., 1962).

Related points about emotional involvement are highlighted in a second example (Stotland, 1969). Three groups of subjects were requested to observe a person, i.e., a confederate of the experimenter, undergoing an emotionally neutral, an obviously joyful, or a convincingly painful experience. While the subjects of the one group were instructed merely to watch, those of the second group were asked to imagine the feelings of the observed person, and those of the third group were told to imagine themselves in the place of the observed person. Measurements of sweating and vasoconstriction as well as verbal reports of subjective impressions showed that the spectators who were instructed merely to watch the person undergoing an experience reacted in the same way to the neutral and to the emotionally laden situations, while the other groups reacted differently to these two types of situations. Yet, the reactions of the subjects whose task was to imagine the feelings of the observed person were weaker than of those who were instructed to place themselves in that person's role. These findings show that empathy, i.e., feeling into the emotional state of an observed person, can be elicited even in the sterile atmosphere of a psychological laboratory when the proper cognitive set is formed.

Our third and last example concerns the dependence of general aesthetic evaluation of a work of art on the prestige of the artist who produced that work. Farnsworth and Misumi (1931) asked observers to judge the quality of eight paintings, four of which were presumably painted by well-known painters, i.e., Da Vinci, Rembrandt, Raphael, and Rubens, and four of which were attributed to unknown painters, i.e., Doughty, Kensett, Dewings, and Smibert. As may be expected, the subjects showed a tendency to rate more favorably the paintings to which were attached the names of prestigious painters. A similar effect with regard to paintings was found by Bernberg (1953) and others, and with regard to prose passages by Sherif (1935). Moreover, it seems that the influence of prestige may be secured not only by citing an artist's name but also by mentioning the opinion of a well-known critic or other prestigious figures. Naturally, the effect of prestige is subject to restriction or enhancement under specific circumstances. For instance, it decreases when the opinion of a prestigious figure on a work of art is not backed up by logical arguments (Cole, 1954) or when the observer makes a special effort to dissociate the work of art from the reported artist's name (Sherif, 1935).

Studies of this type support the impression gained from unsystematic observations in daily life about the widespread effects of publicity, fashions, and general social standards on the consumption, appreciation, and even enjoyment of art by the public. The prestige and popularity of an artist or of a supporting critic reflect more often than not a set shared by many members of wider or narrower circles of society. In recent decades such sets are promulgated, even created, by the mass media and often take the form of a star cult. Yet, at least in Europe, even before the artist was honored as an individual, and long before Beethoven could successfully refuse to play for a dining audience, information about the arts and a presumed ability to enjoy them were regarded as marks of status, privileges of the well-educated elite. When at the end of the eighteenth century the royal revolutionary Kaiser Josef of Austria sponsored public concerts without admission fees, the prestige of music was not at all harmed. Rather, the Viennese learned to love what they anyhow had to admire and thus turned into an ideal musical audience which produced and attracted an increasing number of great musicians.

Even nowadays the social pressure to admire music is still so strong in Austria that many unmusical people who have never visited the recently rebuilt opera house possess detailed information about opera programs and opera scandals or mishaps in some of the performances. However, the relative prestige of the arts varies with the cultural setting. In Germany one may still succeed socially without being able to speak about sports, the stock market, and politics, but one is certainly expected to be able to drop in a conversation some expertlike sentences about a new book, a new play, or a recent painting exhibition. In London the expertise must not only be serious, but should also be clever; in Paris it should, in addition, be witty. Only in Italy, where opera is still a living, popular art, it may suffice to whistle an aria, which is simply known or may be picked up on every street corner in the smallest town some time before the opera starts at the stadium. In the United States the heroes of many best sellers of the fifties used to demonstrate their intellectual acceptability by saying something "remarkable" about Kafka, Joyce, or Picasso. In the sixties, the subject of the remarkable sentence seemed to be Hesse. In Moscow of the late sixties one said nothing, yet everybody seemed to understand at once this allusion to a circulated typewritten copy of a suppressed novel or play.

Social standards and habits of this kind are important not only for the social history of the arts; they also determine the set of observers of art, i.e., their expectations and readiness to experience in a certain manner. S. Asch (1948) showed that when the same quotation is attributed to different authors, more and less esteemed, the change in the readers' attitude, which seems to depend on the authors' prestige, reflects in fact differences in the grasped meaning of the quotation. Similarly, when a Western observer hears the name Picasso in conjunction with a certain painting, we may assume that a specific set is elicited in him: he expects a nonrepresentational painting, with symbolic and other latent meanings, which he may not instantly grasp, but for which he might be inclined to look because of the painter's reputation. More specific cues, such as the painting's name, may serve to shape further the spectator's set. Thus, when the same picture is seen once with the caption, "At the Station: Reunion," and at another time with the caption, "At the Station: Parting," its meaning and consequently the mood it evokes change greatly; with the first caption it appears a much happier picture than with the second caption (Osgood et al., 1957, pp. 313–14).

Social standards and habits contribute to the elicitation of aesthetic sets by shaping not only expectations about meanings and probable experiences but also the specific settings in which art is experienced. The importance of these external trappings is evident to anyone who has compared his experience of a piece of music played by an orchestra in a big concert hall and the same piece heard on records at home. Maslow & Mintz (1956) demonstrated that drawings which when observed in a beautifully furnished room are experienced by people as expressing "energy" and "well-being," are, when viewed in a run-down, ugly room, experienced as expressing "fatigue" and "displeasure." The traditionally ostentatious decorations of opera and theater halls, the solemn atmosphere of museums, the formal dress of orchestra musicians, the elaborate frames of pictures, and formerly the cover and binding of books bear witness to age-old endeavors to produce in the audience of art a special and festive mood. Remarkably, the audience seems to cooperate in these endeavors. An unpublished survey carried out by students of the Theater Department at Tel Aviv University in the year 1962 showed that the majority of theater visitors make special preparations before going to see a play. The subjects interviewed—randomly chosen 50 men and 50 women—were asked before entering any one of three different theaters: "Have you prepared yourself in any way for this specific performance?" The responses were that 88 percent of the women and 62 percent of the Tel Avivian males, traditionally sloppy dressers, changed their clothes, 43 percent read reviews about the play and/or asked their friends about its contents and quality, 28 percent rested or slept, 11 percent read either the play or poetry, and an odd 4 percent took an especially extended bath. Another survey carried out with 60 people, audiences of three chamber-music concerts in Haifa, yielded similar results, with the addition that 33 percent said that one to five days before the concert they had listened to records of at least a part of the expected program, and 9 percent had read the score or looked at it.

Although there seem to be so far no reliable empirical findings about the suitability of particular sets for particular kinds of works of art, general psychological knowledge about set combined with the great amount of available information about measures designed to create artistic sets in different cultures warrant some conclusions. Major among these are, first, that the creators, observers, sponsors, and organizers of art favor and promote the creation of specific sets as a necessary or at least beneficial condition for the elicitation of an aesthetic experience, and second, that they are psychologically justified in their belief that set may strongly enhance aesthetic perception and emotional participation.

However, this does not mean that specific preparatory sets are a necessary condition for every experience of art. An aesthetic experience—like almost any other behavioral act—could take place without an adequate preparatory set. Thus, a great many people are capable of intensely enjoying a work of art even when they are confronted with it unexpectedly. Yet, since all cultures induce in some form aesthetic attitudes which may function as permanent sets in the observers, it is difficult, if not impossible, to determine whether people could experience the extraordinary or at least unique impact of works of art without any previously established set. This problem is, however, largely academic and of little relevance in our present context. The abundance of factors which function as general agents of set, for instance, socially conditioned value judgments, or as specific agents of set, for instance, overtures, prologues, and the like, provides a satisfactory answer to the major question posed at the beginning of this section: established psychological knowledge about sets warrants the conclusion that stimuli which without a suitable set may go unobserved may, owing to a suitable set, function as the source of an aesthetic experience, if and only if they have the other qualities necessary for the fulfillment of this function. In other words, a set neither prevents us from seeing that Hans Christian Andersen's emperor has no clothes on nor forces us to see him dressed; it only proves helpful in both cases.

Empathy and the Theory of Feeling-Into

Emotional involvement is undoubtedly a key problem in art psychology. Regardless of the various qualitative and restrictive epithets often attached to the description of emotions evoked through art, it can hardly be disputed that emotions are frequently a dominant element in the experience of art. The problem may be reduced to a series of intriguing questions: Why does the audience in a theater feel the gradual resurgence of anxiety upon hearing the ominous prophecy of Macbeth's three witches? Why are the autonomic reactions of film spectators increased when they observe dangerous, cruel, or erotic scenes (Dysinger & Ruckmick, 1933; Lazarus et al., 1962)? Why do the readers of a novel feel sad, even cry occasionally, upon the death of a hero? How does it come about that observers of a painting may actually sense the pain in the back of a toiling woman portrayed? Or why do the observers of a dance representing the movement of flowers experience the lightness of the moving petals? In short, what are the processes mediating this occasionally very intense emotional involvement in events and destinies which are not only fictional but also have in fact no bearing on our own well-being?

Unlike most other processes basic for the psychology of art, emotional involvement through observation is a process which was first studied in the context of art and only later in other contexts. However, like most other processes basic for the psychology of art, it is a process of crucial importance also in other domains of psychology, notably interpersonal communication and interaction.

Empathy is the usual term used to designate that type of the spectator's emotional involvement which consists in a reflection of the emotions represented or implied in the work of art rather than in an emotional reaction to the work of art or any part of it. The word empathy was coined by Titchener as an English rendering of the original term *Einfühlung,* whose literal meaning is "feeling into," the translation suggested by Aldous Huxley. Through wide application in several psychological domains, notably psychotherapy, group dynamics, education, and social psychology, the meaning of empathy has undergone various extensions which have contributed to a blurring of its original usage. Thus, in recent years it is commonly used to denote an ability to apprehend the state of mind of another person (English & English, 1958, p. 178) and consequently to perceive him accurately (Cronbach, 1955), to predict his behavior adequately (Kerr, 1960), or to accept him tolerantly and nonpunitively (Sulzer & Burglass, 1968). A sharp differentiation should however be drawn between these meanings of empathy and the cluster of meanings which emphasize the "feeling-into" element in empathy, the element so crucial for the experiencing of art. In this latter sense, empathy is defined as "an observer's reacting emotionally because he perceives that another is experiencing or is about to experience an emotion" (Stotland, 1969, p. 272). Another definition which better highlights the fact that the observer's reaction is similar to the experience of the observed person is suggested by R. L. Katz (1963, p. 3): "When we experience empathy we feel as if we were experiencing someone else's feelings as our own. Our involvement becomes physical"; yet "to empathize does not mean that the individual must experience physical sensation; empathy can be physical, imaginative, or both" (R. L. Katz, 1963, p. 4).

Contact with and observation of other people undergoing emotional experiences have long been identified as a stimulus for emotions, no less potent than any other direct stimulation. Thus, fear manifested by a few people in a crowd rapidly spreads to most others present who have had no direct contact with the fear-arousing stimulus; children often acquire phobias (Bandura & Menlove, 1968) and possibly even negative emotional attitudes towards various minority groups (F. H. Allport, 1924), not through actual injurious experiences, but rather from observing the expressed emotions of others. There is evidence that an emotion evoked through the threat of actual injury to the self and an emotion evoked through viewing a film showing injury to another person are highly similar experientially and physiologically (Alfert, 1966). Empathic communication between the baby and a rejecting or anxious mother was even postulated as a basis for the formation of schizophrenic or neurotic disturbances in adulthood (Sullivan, 1953). In support of this claim Escalona (1945) showed that babies who stayed with their imprisoned mothers were especially nervous when handled by their mothers on days on which they expected to appear before the parole board.

More direct evidence for empathy derives from studies about conditioning through vicarious emotional instigation. In the typical experiment of this kind the subject observes a person who is exposed to an apparently painful stimulus, say an electric shock, and acts as if he were being hurt. Delivery of the shock is preceded by the occurrence of a neutral stimulus, such as a light or the ringing of a bell. After a few repetitions of this sequence, the observer reacts emotionally, e.g., with increased psychogalvanic responses, to the light or bell, the conditioned stimulus. Since the observer is assured that he himself will neither be subjected to the conditioning procedure nor be shocked, his emotional response to the conditioned stimulus without having directly experienced any aversive stimulation suggests that he has had an empathic experience. Empathic conditioning was demonstrated not only in humans (Berger, 1962; Craig & Weinstein, 1965; Haner & Whitney, 1960) but also in animals, e.g., rats (Church, 1959) and monkeys (R. E. Miller et al., 1959, 1962, 1963). Some of the major conditions which bring about or enhance such empathic experiences are observation of bodily emotional reactions (Berger, 1962), acquaintance from prior learning with the meaning of these reactions (R. E. Miller, Caul, & Mirsky, 1967), concentration on the model's responses rather than attempts to disregard them and think of something else (Bandura & Rosenthal, 1966), the observer's awareness of similarity between him and the model, and an active effort by the observer to imagine how he would feel if he were subjected to the treatment given to the model (Stotland, 1969).

In view of the above remarks it seems probable that the emotional involvement of spectators of art in the contents and form of works of art is a manifestation of the basic human tendency and capacity to empathize. How does empathy occur, and why do we empathize? There are two basic psychological theories which attempt to answer these questions. They also form nuclei around which similar or less comprehensive hypotheses may be grouped. The first is the theory of representation, while the second is Lipps's theory of feeling-into. These two theories have traditionally been regarded as contrasting. Yet, as we shall see, they not only share various theoretical components but necessarily complement each other in crucial points.

The account of the processes underlying empathy provided by the traditional proponents of *the theory of representation* (e.g., Geiger, 1911; Winterstein, 1932; Witasek, 1901) runs as follows. The spectator who perceives a situation has first to understand it intellectually. He then reconstructs it imaginatively as a quasi-perceptual representation, adding some details if necessary, relying in part on associations and general relevant information he may have. This representation evokes in the spectator several chains of associations, one of which may result in the memory of some experience or event from the spectator's past which resembles the presently perceived situation. It is the traces of this retrieved memory which may revive the emotional experience similar to the one the spectator had in his past.

Two major points should be noted concerning this theory. The first is that it considers empathy to be dependent upon an accurate cognitive understanding of the perceived situation and on processes of imagining. If a spectator construes a certain tragic scene comically or represents to himself a sequence of nontragic events, his evoked memories and revived emotions will be more joyful than is warranted by the actual situation and will consequently prevent empathy in the strict sense of the word. The second major point is that the theory does not fully underscore the actuality of the emotional experience. While empathy refers to an actual emotion induced in the observer, the proponents of the representation theory tend to emphasize the attenuated or derived form of the observer's emotion, e.g., "the sorrow of the other is objective, while I myself am not sad" (Winterstein, 1932, p. 4), or associations "may arouse deposits of a disposition towards real feelings" (ibid., p. 9).

This theory is evidently open to criticism from many and varied viewpoints. One of the commonest objections raised against it is that the theory cannot account for feeling-into emotions one has not previously experienced, while spectators of art seem often to empathize novel emotions, some of which they had perhaps experienced in fantasy but have undoubtedly repressed. Further, in the case of temporal arts, notably film, theater, and dance, the theory predicts an intermittent emotional involvement, first, because only some scenes, even trivial in the plot, could be reminiscent of personal experiences, and second, because the process of remembering and reviving emotions may require attention and time. Finally, the paradox inherent in the theory is that if empathy takes place, the observer is preoccupied with an "anamnestic" experience which diverts his attention from the present situation, while if he concentrates on the latter he could not empathize.

The identification of empathy with an anamnestic emotion, and the observation that revived emotions are not real, actual emotions—these seem the most serious weakness of the theory. Indeed, it would hardly deserve to be considered a theory of empathy if it were not for its emphasis on the relation between empathy and cognitive processes, i.e., understanding of the perceived situation, and its representation in imagination. The crucial importance of these factors for empathy is attested by many modern studies. Thus, S. Schachter (1964) and others (Valins & Ray, 1967) showed that the specific emotion which is felt depends on how a person interprets his physiological state by means of the information available to him from past experience and present perceptions. However, even without any prior changes in physiological state, the mere imagining of a situation or event may cause a full-fledged actual emotion with the corresponding physiological changes (Barber & Hahn, 1964; Folkins et al., 1968; Grossberg & Wilson, 1968; L. W. Rowland, 1936). The import of these findings is clarified particularly through Stotland's (1969) study, which showed that empathic responses are stronger when observers are asked to imagine how they would feel in the observed situation rather than how the observed person feels.

In contrast to the representation theory, Lipps's (1903–6; 1907)[2] *theory of feeling-into* emphasizes much more the actual emotional experience in empathy. Lipps's main argument is based on two major sets of observations. The one refers to the primary tendency to imitate externally perceived movements or dynamic postures of people and objects (Lipps, 1903–6, vol. 1, p. 117). The imitation is assumed to be external and full-fledged only in children. Owing to cultural conventions, in adults it usually takes the form of greatly reduced, incipient movements in the muscles, which are experienced kinesthetically (ibid., pp. 109, 124). The second set of observations refers to the relation between emotions and motoric movements. Motor expression is highly characteristic of emotional experience. Thus, not only may it serve as a visible cue that an observed person is subject to such an experience, but emotions also become associated subjectively with kinesthetic sensations. This association depends upon prior experience. Binding together these two sets of observations, Lipps arrived at the conclusion which forms the core of his theory of feeling-into. When undergoing an emotional experience, a person performs certain movements. If an observer notices these movements, he tends spontaneously to imitate them. The imitation leads to specific kinesthetic sensations. These, however, have previously become so intimately associated with emotional experiences that their occurrence evokes the experience of the emotion itself. Thus, the observer comes to feel an emotion which is at least similar to the one that the observed person was undergoing (Lipps, 1907, pp. 718–19).

The main emphasis in Lipps's theory is not merely on our understanding the other's movements and emotion through imitation, but on actually experiencing that emotion as if it were our own and directly evoked in us. Although improved understanding may result from feeling-into and partly depends on former experiences of feeling-into (Lipps, 1903–6, vol. 1, p. 125), there is a major difference between understanding and feeling-into. In understanding an emotion we always distinguish between our own ego and the other's ego, while in feeling-into, this distinction is effaced, i.e., the other's emotion becomes actually our own (Lipps, 1962). However, although feeling-into depends on imitation, so that the emotion we consequently feel is due to an activity of our own, the emotion is apprehended as deriving from the observed person or object and is imputed to it. Yet in spite of the fact that imitation is an involuntary process, the full unfolding of feeling-into requires in a certain sense the active participation of the observer, i.e., he must be ready to experience. Without the appropriate set, the clash between inner resistance and imitation would result in the unpleasant state of "negative feeling into" (Lipps, 1903–6, vol. 1, pp. 21 ff.).

Since Lipps's theory was formulated at the turn of the century, it cannot be expected to have been based on more modern findings. But does it conform to these? The question could be answered by examining recent research on the three major points on which Lipps's theory rests. These are the tendency to imitate, the expression of emotion through movements, and the evocation of emotion through the performance of movements.

The bulk of research on imitation, or as it is also called, observational learning, modeling, copying, vicarious learning, behavioral contagion, etc., has provided, particularly in recent years, such rich and compelling evidence that hardly any doubts can be raised concerning the existence of a tendency to imitate. It is manifested by children and adults with regard to almost any behavioral act, ranging from linguistic, conceptual, and moral behaviors to emotional and motional ones, regardless of whether the model is real or fictional, live or pictorial (Bandura, 1969). Further, Lipps's observation that overt imitative movements are reduced in adults to covert kinesthetic processes is well in line with the general developmental course (Werner, 1957), while his assumption about the importance of kinesthetic sensations is confirmed by a wealth of findings about the role played by these sensations in most human activities, including perception (Werner & Wapner, 1952), imagining (Hebb, 1968; Jacobson, 1930–31; Max, 1935), set (Freeman, 1948b), etc. However, Lipps's assumption that the process of kinesthetic imitation is automatic and direct fails to be confirmed. It was indeed shared by some later researchers (e.g., F. H. Allport, 1924; Holt, 1931), but more recent evidence seems to point to the mediation of imitation through other processes, notably cognitive, such as representation of the observed situation in images or words (Bandura, 1969, pp. 133–35; Flanders, 1968; Stotland, 1969).

Similarly, Lipps's second major point is so amply supported by evidence about the "strong bond between emotion and muscular action" (Sherrington, 1947, p. 266) that some have considered movements to be not merely an essential expressive aspect of emotions (Kennard, 1947), but an integral part of emotion itself (Jacobson, 1929; Washburn, 1928). However, motor patterns and expressive gestures do not seem to suffice for the unique characterization of emotions, e.g., a body can be bowed in grief, in humility, in laughter, in devotion, in longing, or in preparation for attack. Thus, the accurate identification of emotions requires further cues, notably knowledge of the situation and of the whole behavior pattern in which the other's emotions are embedded (Hunt, Cole, & Reis, 1958).

These remarks apply also to Lipps's third point, that the performance of certain movements may evoke a corresponding emotion. Indeed, there is some observational evidence from practices of psychotherapy and meditation (Hillman, 1960, pp. 126–34) and experimental support for this assumption, which formed the cornerstone also of the much debated James-Lange theory of emotions. Bull (1951) found that when hypnotized subjects get the instruction to assume a certain posture or perform movements which in other studies were found to be characteristic of a certain emotion (Bull, 1951, chap. 4), they tend to report a subjective feeling which corresponds to those movements (Bull, 1951, chap. 5). For example, the instruction, "Your hands are getting tense and your arms are getting tense. You feel your jaw tightening" (Bull, 1951, p. 76) usually corresponds to anger and may even prevent the subject from feeling an emotion such as joy which corresponds to another motoric pattern. However, since it has repeatedly been shown that the correspondence between physiological patterns, which include motoric indices, and specific emotions is far from perfect (Ax, 1953; J. Schachter, 1957), and that the mere induction of physiological changes does not suffice for the evocation of emotional experience (Marañon, 1924), we are led to assume that the partial success of Bull's studies depended on the participation of further factors. The nature of these factors has been clarified by the studies of S. Schachter (1964) and his co-workers, which show that "cognitions arising from the immediate situation as interpreted by past experience provide the framework within which one understands and labels his feelings" (S. Schachter, 1964, p. 51).

The above discussion of the two major theories of empathy leads to the conclusion that a combination of the two is necessary in order to account for the salient features of empathy in general and of aesthetic empathy in particular. As we have seen, the common denominator of the criticisms raised against Lipps's theory on the basis of experimental findings is that it overlooks the crucial role of cognitive processes in imitation, in identification of emotional expressions, and in the evocation of emotions through kinesthetic sensations, while the major failing of the representation theory is that it underrates the role of physiological arousal in emotion. Empathy, however, consists in an actual emotional experience evoked through observation of emotional expression. Consequently it is, like any other emotion, a product of interaction between physiological and cognitive processes. While the former element is emphasized by Lipps's theory, the latter is highlighted by the representation theory. Accordingly, a combination of the major principles of these two theories in light of experimental findings suggests that *empathy arises through imitation of motional-dynamic features in the observed situation, which produces a state of physiological arousal identified by the observer as a specific emotion in line with his interpretation of the inner state and the externally perceived situation.* The observer's interpretation reflects, first, learned and perhaps also physiognomic associations about the relations between specific emotions and certain inner sensations, and second, the cognitive elaboration of meanings involved in the observed situation. Further, it may be expected that physiological arousal due to imitation interacts with cognitive interpretation in various forms. For example, a certain cognitive interpretation of the situation may enhance imitation by directing the attention to expressive features of the model (Bandura, 1969, pp. 136–37) or may even facilitate an imaginary representation of the situation which affects arousal in a manner similar to imitation proper. Finally, both imitation and cognitive elaboration are determined by a host of situational factors, and personality dispositions of the observer (Bandura, 1969), which are too many and complex to be even mentioned in this context.

Feeling-Into and the Experiencing of Art

How is empathy manifested in the context of experiencing art? What determines imitation and cognitive elaboration in the confrontation with each of the arts?

The empathic impact of *literature* is almost as generally appreciated as that of film and theater, with which it shares many aspects of contents. Indeed, the power of literature to evoke feeling-into is often regarded as the feature distinguishing literature from other forms of linguistic reporting. There can be little doubt that in literature the stimuli for empathy reside mainly in the representational contents, i.e., the story, the described events, situations, or processes, and predominantly in the characters presented. Since the presentation of characters and situations relies necessarily on descriptions of gestures, movements, and more general dynamic patterns of change and transformation, literature provides a wealth of stimuli for imitation-mediated empathy. As far as the emotions and inner dynamics of the characters themselves are concerned, the stimuli for empathy are similar to those which mediate empathy in real-life situations. For, in line with the truism that "it does no good for the author to state bluntly, 'He was sad,' nor is it ever convincing to rely entirely on intensifying modifiers—'He suffered a great sorrow' " (Bacon & Breen, 1959, p. 40), writers usually use descriptions of gestures, movements, and actions in order to convey emotional experiences. These descriptions usually refer to bodily and facial expressive movements or to more comprehensive action patterns which may range from displacing objects to a protracted behavioral sequence signaled through a few prominent motions. However, the impact of these stimuli may be assumed to be weaker than in real life situations, first, because verbally described movements are not as compelling as visual stimuli, and second, because verbal report must rely on a sequential and lengthened description of movements which actually occur simultaneously and instantaneously.

On the other hand, literature disposes of various devices for the enhancement of empathic stimuli. Major among these are a selective description, with emphasis on the particularly expressive movements which in nonliterary contexts may even escape attention (Bacon & Breen, 1959, pp. 24–25), suggestion of nonverbal action through verbal phrases which are conventionally accompanied by specific gestures (ibid., pp. 295–96), and amplifying descriptions of movements through word sounds and sentence melodies evocative of an emotional tone similar to the one conveyed through the report itself (ibid., pp. 296–97). These devices may be supplemented by description of motions of nonhuman agents, such as the swaying of daffodils in the wind, or a clash of objects, and by description of physiognomic traits of scenes and things (Arnheim, 1949) which provide further stimuli for empathic imitation.

Motional stimuli of this type elicit kinesthetic imitation which forms in the reader a physiological background of arousal. Since the process is involuntary, it may occur and recur on repeated reading or hearing of the same plot without being impaired through foreknowledge of the plot and its expected resolution. Essentially the act of empathic imitation is reductive and consists of merely incipient movements or bodily postures. It may be assumed that with increased experience the reader or listener of literature learns to select from among the depicted motions and to control the degree of the induced imitation, so that he imitates only those movements which are, at least for him, maximally effective in evoking an emotion in the minimally required degree of intensity that will allow for the attainment of empathy. This selective process, which underlies what Bacon and Breen (1959, p. 35) call "style in reading," is particularly important for the sequential changes in experiencing which take place while reading literature or listening to it.

However, an emotional experience is evoked only when the physiological changes induced through imitation are subjected to and coupled with cognitive elaboration. The cognitive interpretations of the physiological cues are obviously shaped by previous experience, but to no less a degree also by the scenes and events described in the literary text. Since too little is known factually about empathy in literature, we may only hypothesize that at least two processes play a crucial role in transforming excitement into experience. The first of these consists in going beyond the given information, i.e., in elaborating and amplifying the facts described in the text. The second major process could be called identification with the author; it helps to maintain continuous experiencing.

Since the author cannot present all details, he must rely on a suggestive reporting of significant facts which may prompt the reader or listener to fill in missing details, so as to complete a gestalt. This activation of the closure tendency is all the more probable since it corresponds to our usual habit of understanding people in daily-life contexts by interpreting their overt acts and by inferring from these further facts as well as the underlying dynamics and motives. Indeed, Koestler's (1949b, p. 31) conclusion that "the images of *real people* in our memory are not as different from our images of *fictional characters* as we generally believe" is confirmed by the findings of a study (Kreitler & Kreitler, 1971a) which show that the concepts and techniques used to describe people in general and literary figures in particular do not differ in any major respect. But while in nonliterary contexts one rarely indulges in fantasied and reconstructed images about others, the reader of literature can better afford this luxury. These reconstructions, in which personal recollections and even projections probably play a role, may enhance empathic responses and may even trigger empathy into feelings previously unknown to the reader or listener. Moreover, when they are elaborated and developed, particularly during pauses in reading or after its completion, these imaginative representations may form the nucleus of more lasting identifications with literary figures of the kind frequent in adolescence (Havighurst, Robinson, & Dorr, 1946) and occasionally observed in adulthood. However, when such fantasized reconstructions are indulged in to excess in the course of reading, they may impede empathy by distracting attention from the plot. In such cases, when the reader or listener is over-whelmed by his own experiences and loses contact with the literary text (i.e., he commits the "affective fallacy," Wimsatt, 1954, pp. 21–39), empathy is replaced by an emotion which may have been triggered by the text but is no longer subject to the selective inhibitions, partly controlled through literary conventions, which make empathy possible.

While fantasized reconstructions are essentially an intermittent process which may even endanger empathy, so-called identification with the author is a process which contributes to the continuity of contact with the literary reality even when the descriptions refer to inanimate objects, landscapes, and other nondynamic features. Like empathy itself, it is largely an involuntary process. It consists in assuming the literary conventions and tolerating the fiction of the literary reality by adopting temporarily the standpoint of the writer, who may occasionally appear in the role of narrator or speaker while at other times his existence is merely inferred (Dobrée, 1934, p. 13). Although the writer may play a role even in drama, for example, in the guise of a Greek-like chorus or of commentators who step out of the scene to speak directly to the audience, the personality of the writer is more prominent in fiction, owing to the re-presentation nature of narration, and in poetry, owing to its explicit or implicit confessional nature. Indeed, major landmarks in the historical development of the Western novel lend support to Lipps's (1903–6, vol. 1, p. 503) claim that "my feeling into this world [of literary fiction] occurs through the writer."

The origins of the novel seem to lie in epic tales, which were orally communicated to an audience by living bards who were aptly called *histriones*, "actors," for they dramatized the stories by appropriating them to themselves and by acting them with voice, gesture, and mimicry. The use of these devices must have greatly facilitated and reinforced empathy in the listeners. The actual novel came into being when telling was superseded by written communication. In the beginning, however, the novel was written in the first person, the author appearing as a narrator playing, first, the role of an active participant in the plot, and later the role of a spectator who tells the story as a witness, so that feeling-into could be mediated through identification with the writer. It was only much later that the more modern form of direct description was introduced. Regardless of the factors which have determined this development, from the viewpoint of technique it illustrates a gradual dispensing with the means facilitatory of feeling-into. Thus it implies that the public must have been trained through experience to feel into several different figures and sequentially changing situations without the explicit mediation of the narrator. For example, a modern reader of a novel seems to be able to "live" in the course of reading in the time of the author who wrote the story, in the time in which the story occurred, in the several times of the hero and the minor figures, etc., without losing cognizance of his own time of reading, which may be 5 P.M. on 28 February 1972, and without being in the least disturbed by this complicated state of affairs.

The various factors discussed—imitation of depicted movements, interpretation of physiological cues, fantasized reconstruction and amplification of described events, and identification with the author—play a role in the experiencing of every type of literature, but prominence may vary with type. It may be assumed that in viewing enacted drama, imitation of observed movements and their direct interpretation are greatly facilitated, while identification with the author and fantasized reconstructions are stronger in the case of prose and poetry. The quality of the empathic experience may depend on the weight of the different factors which contribute to it.

Which factors facilitating empathy are prominent in confronting *sculpture*? There is one feature important for empathy which sculpture shares with literature, i.e., preoccupation with human beings. Since the major bulk of sculpture consists of the representation of bodies—human and sometimes animal—and since sculptural figures are usually presented in strained and labile positions which stimulate tendencies of dynamic closure (Chapter 10), one might expect observers to imitate sculptural postures, although these are essentially immobile. This expectation was tested by the authors in a set of systematic recordings of the movements of 90 randomly selected observers in an exhibition, 15 in front of each of six sculptures. The sculptures were the *Dancer* and *Mother with Child* (Plate 17) by Lipschitz, *Woman with Clasped Hands* by Moore, a cast of *A Man* by Rodin, and *A Woman*, as well as *Bust of a Man* by Daumier. The unaware observers were watched unobtrusively by two experimenters, placed in two corners of the exhibition hall. The recordings were made in terms of the Eshkol and Wachmann (1958) "notation system" and included all the overt body movements of the observers during the time they directly confronted the statue or watched it from further away. The postures of the statues as viewed from the eight major angles of observation were photographed, so that two independent judges could determine which of the movements of observers were imitatory of the motions depicted in the statues.[3]

The results show that 84 percent of the observed spectators displayed overt imitatory movements during their inspection of the statues, while an additional 3 percent displayed them after having left the statue when casting their eyes back on it. The remaining 13 percent did not reveal any overt imitation, but in the case of 3 percent there were records of movements of straightening the head or stretching the limbs in a manner suggestive perhaps of covert kinesthetic imitation. The percentage of "imitators" did not vary significantly across five of the statues, but it was reduced to 62 percent in the exceptional case of Daumier's *Bust of a Man*, which represents only a facial expression with no body posture for copying.

No less remarkable than these results, are the findings concerning the amount and type of the displayed imitation. Most of the "imitators," i.e., 65 percent, performed only one imitatory movement, while 35 percent of the "imitators" copied more than one movement, usually two to five, apart from one spectator, a child about five years old (the only child in our sample), who engaged in a series of eight fully imitatory motions. Concerning the nature of the imitation, it should be noted that most of them (92 percent) did not involve more than one body part. Thus, a person may move his head in the same way and direction as portrayed by Lipschitz's *Dancer*, or stretch one leg forward as Daumier's *Woman* does, but he would rarely copy the posture of both legs and head. "Imitators" who imitated more than one position did so in all cases sequentially, i.e., they threw the head back in imitation of the figure, and only after returning the head to its normal position proceeded to copy the position of the arms, the torso, or the legs. The conclusion that the spectators tried to hide their imitatory activity is further confirmed by the following impression. Most of the postures copied by the spectators seem to have been those whose adoption by an observer at an exhibition would hardly attract attention. For example, in the case of Lipschitz's *Mother with Child* (Plate 17), 90 percent of the "imitators" copied the somewhat curved posture of the torso as it appears in profile, while only 10 percent imitated the posture *en face*, which, objectively judged, involves a much greater deviation from the normal behavior of a museum visitor.

Thus, our findings suggest that overt imitation of sculptures might represent a compromise between the imitatory and the inhibitory tendencies. However, inhibition, which in this case is due largely to cultural conventions and the general trend towards suppression of overt expression, does not restrict empathy. Rather, if it does not actually raise imitation to the level of consciousness (Bacon & Breen, 1959, p. 303), it may enhance the kinesthetic effects.

As with literature, an empathic experience may be assumed to arise when the sensations elicited through overt and kinesthetic imitation are coupled with a cognitive elaboration of the internal and external cues. A major role is undoubtedly played in the process by the interpretation of the posture depicted in the statue, which depends, as we have seen (Chapter 10), not only on physiognomic perception and cultural conventions but also on a reconstruction of the dynamic sequence of which the statue depicts only a particularly "dramatic instant" (Lessing, 1930). However, the fantasized reconstructions in sculpture are predominantly dynamic in nature and consist mainly in completion of the movement one of whose stages is indicated in the statue. Thus, the role of reconstruction in sculpture is more primary and crucial than in literature, for without it we would perceive a figure with outspread wings instead of a flying woman, or a bent form instead of a man in agony.

In general these same principles of empathy remain valid for *paintings* in which human figures are depicted, although here the tendency to imitate posture is probably weaker, while the reconstruction of the suggested scene is more complete, since a greater number of cues is usually available. Indeed, the record of the movements of eight observers in front of three projected paintings, i.e., Cézanne's *Chestnut Alley* (Plate 10), Picasso's *Ironing Woman*, and Cahanowitsch's *Cossack Pogrom*, in an experiment similar to the one conducted with sculptures (H. Kreitler, 1956, pp. 108–15), showed that in 10 out of the 24 confrontations between a spectator and a painting (41 percent), there were explicit imitatory movements. This percentage is significantly lower than for sculpture. Even when Cézanne's picture, which does not include a human figure, is removed from the computation, the percentage does not rise appreciably.

Similarity to sculpture seems to be more pronounced in the *dance*. While imitation is elicited through the viewing of movements performed by the dancers and is reinforced by rhythm and music, cognitive elaboration is supported by the interpretation of the movements, and often also by the unfolding plot and the contextual background of the performance. However, regardless of the contents of the danced plot, there is always in dance as in drama at least one central figure with which the spectator may empathize.

In contrast, many *paintings* and some *sculptures* do not depict any human figures. When the theme is an object, a plant, a landscape, or forms without explicit object references, with what does the observer empathize? Remarkably, Lipps's theory was suggested primarily in order to account for empathy with forms and inanimate objects. His major claim was that since the world and each event or phenomenon in it are systems of dynamic forces and counterforces and are perceived as such, we imitate kinesthetically the interplay of forces in forms and shapes, e.g., the push of a circular line to move straight forward and the curbing inhibition (Lipps, 1903–6, vol. 2, p. 295), or the conflict between the upward movement and the gravitational pull in a vertical column (ibid., vol. 1, p. 258). Thus, when the sensations in one's body are fused with the perception of the object and imputed to it, empathy arises (Lipps, 1962).

When discussing forms (Chapter 5), we saw that Lipps's assumption is supported by many observations about the tendency to grasp forms as dynamic structures and about the intimate relations between perception of forms and the evocation and distribution of muscular tensions. Moreover, there is fairly specific evidence about imitatory movements in response to forms. Werner and Wapner (1952) found that viewing a line or form tilted in a certain direction may cause the observer to change the position of his body towards that direction.

Can we conclude on the basis of these findings that observers empathize with inanimate objects and forms? Such a conclusion would require the assumption that inanimate objects are subject to emotional experiences and that the latter are the stimulus for the emotional responses of observers. Since there is no basis for this animistic assumption, the observations that people may grasp objects in dynamic terms, perceive them as expressive of moods and emotions, and respond to them emotionally warrant rather the conclusion that expressiveness is a dimension of the meaning which inanimate objects may have. The same conclusion is valid with regard to colors, the other major element of painting. Since the perception of expressive qualities should not be confused with empathy proper, there seems to be no basis for the assumption of empathy in the case of paintings and sculptures which do not depict human figures.

A similar problem confronts us in the realm of *music*. What could be the object of feeling-into in music? Apart from the truism that music as such is dynamic in nature, a theoretical analysis shows that each of the major elements of music could elicit kinesthetic responses. The fact that rhythm stimulates active movements, motor impulses, or at the very least, motoric imagery is too well known to deserve any further elaboration at this point (Chapter 7). Yet this obvious fact should not obscure the possibility that harmony may also have dynamic effects arising from the relations between dissonant chords as bad gestalts and consonant chords as good gestalts; or that melody as a movement of tones, or a system of passages between more and less prägnant tone gestalts, could evoke motoric impulses (Chapter 6). The dynamizing effects of music have been demonstrated in many studies (e.g., Fraisse, Oléron, & Paillard, 1953; Vernon, 1930, 1933), but due to the fact that the greater part of music includes all three elements, though with different degrees of emphasis, it is difficult, if not impossible, to point to one of the elements as the object of feeling-into.

Nor are studies of other physiological effects of music, such as changes in brain waves, psychogalvanic reactions (Francès, 1958, pp. 157–77), electrocardiograms and blood pressure (Hyde, 1927), or heart rate and respiration (Weld, 1912), of much help here. These usually show that physiological changes are subject to pronounced individual differences and possibly accompany fluctuations in attention rather than experiential changes.

Thus, although it is tempting to assume that the listener could not empathize into the whole of the composition at once and that he concentrates on one aspect or the other in the interests of emotional orientation, even studies designed specifically to elucidate the role of each of the factors for the musical experience are not conclusive. Washburn and Dickinson (1927) asked listeners of music to indicate which of the major factors of music contributed most to their enjoyment of instrumental music selections. The results show that melody predominated as the most noticeable source of pleasure, with rhythm coming next, followed by harmony, design, and tone color in the last place. These findings correspond to the commonly heard view that melody is the main object of feeling-into in music. This claim is further supported by an experiment performed by H. Kreitler (1956, pp. 127–32) which was based on the reasoning that if there is a more pronounced feeling-into with regard to any one of the elements of music, then a sudden, nonorganic change in this element would be spontaneously experienced by listeners as more disturbing than such a change in any other element. The piece of music selected for this experiment was Beethoven's *Sixteen Small Variations on an Original Theme*, since it makes a comparison possible between the effects of organic and nonorganic changes in the elements of music. Thus, while the theme and the first variation of the composition were left unchanged, the second variation was played with the original melody and rhythm but with changed harmonies, the third variation had the original harmonies and rhythm but a new melody, and the fourth variation was Beethoven's first variation with a new rhythm. Finally, the original theme was again presented. All the experimentally introduced changes were not only alien to Beethoven's style but were also intentionally crude; melodic jumps in the modern style, harmonies of the type used by Debussy, and rhythms reminiscent of jazz were used freely.

Only after having listened "as if they were in a concert hall" to the whole selection, played on a piano, were the thirty subjects requested to point out which part of the composition, if any, they felt as most disturbing, inadequate, or even disagreeable. The results show that while 44 percent of the listeners experienced a sharp disturbance in the third variation, namely, the one with a changed melody, only 16 percent felt a disturbance in the second variation with the changed harmonies, and a mere 10 percent rejected the fourth variation with the foreign rhythm. Finally, 4 percent felt a disturbance in the first unchanged variation, and 26 percent remained undecided.

However, the results of the two experiments mentioned could not be interpreted as pointing unequivocally to the special role of melody from the viewpoint of feeling-into. An equally valid interpretation would be that, owing to psychological, cultural, or educational factors, melody attracts more attention than the other elements do, or that it is easier to grasp melody as a gestalt and hence also easier to identify changes in it. If these latter interpretations hold, it must be assumed that attention may be concentrated also on other musical elements, depending on their prominence in the musical piece and on the musical sensitivity and training of the listener.

Even if in certain cases a theme, melodic or rhythmic, could be identified as the object of special attention, its effects, emotional or other, could not be regarded as empathic. For even when the experience is viewed as deriving from certain features of music, it is a response to these features but is not similar to an experience we could attribute to any musical feature. Regardless of how intense our experience is, we never feel as if we were the melody, the rhythm, the harmony, or the tone. At most, we may be carried by each of these as by a current or a mighty wave, but we do not identify with them in the same sense as we temporarily do with Othello or with a sculptural figure.

These conclusions, however, do not mean that music evokes no emotional effects or responses due to cognitive elaboration. In spite of the insistence of various theoreticians (Gurney, 1880; Hanslick, 1891) that the genuine and proper response to music should not carry the listener beyond the music itself, empirical studies have repeatedly shown that emotional, associational, imaginal, and ideational elements recur consistently in the responses of listeners to music. The weakest and possibly least relevant to the enjoyment of music seem to be the imaginal responses which relate to its so-called representational contents (Gatewood, 1927; Weld, 1912). Several studies failed to uncover any common elements in the imaginal contents suggested to subjects by various musical selections or any similarity between these and the declared intention of the composer, even when the music contains clear imitative sounds, such as the rending of the temple curtain in Bach's *Passion According to St. Matthew*, or sounds of thunder, hoofbeats, bells, or the obvious cuckoo (Downey, 1897; Gilman, 1892, 1893; Weld, 1912). Emotional and mood effects seem to be more intimately related with the enjoyment of music (Gatewood, 1927; Washburn & Dickinson, 1927) and manifest more consistency across subjects (Gatewood, 1927; Hevner, 1935c,

1936; Pratt, 1968; Watson, 1942) although general moods, such as restfulness, longing, reverence, and devotion, seem to be more characteristic of the
responses elicited than definite emotions like anger, fear, or jealousy (Schoen,
1940, p. 91). Yet, mood effects may induce the listener to remember certain
events from his past. Such responses are necessarily highly personal, but
may condition the receptivity towards certain types of music, musical preferences, enjoyment of music, and even deeper-reaching emotional processes.

All these factors which may contribute to the experiencing of music, and
whose relative prominence was used as a basis for classifying listeners into
types (e.g., Myers, 1927; Ortmann, 1927), seem to be less crucial than effects
which derive from the inherent structure of music and depend on expected
and unexpected developments in melody, harmony, rhythm, and general
design (Chapter 6; Meyer, 1956). In musically trained listeners and real
music-lovers these effects seem to be more pronounced than effects due to
moods, associations, and other cognitive and emotional responses to music.
The experience thus evoked seems to be equally intense and no less emotionally toned and cognitively shaped than empathic experiences elicited in
the context of other arts. Yet, their unique quality depends precisely on the
feature which prevents the occurrence of empathy proper in music, i.e., the
nonresemblance of the musical structure and material to anything which is
not part of the intrinsic musical reality.

Aesthetic Distance

Preceding sections of this chapter are devoted to the emotional experiencing of art, i.e., to empathy and other processes which contribute differentially to the evocation of an actual, occasionally intense experience upon
confrontation with works of art. There is, however, one feature which is
characteristic of most art experiences, regardless of the particular factors
which shape and mold them. This feature, which has been identified by
many philosophers (Kant, Schopenhauer, Croce, Bergson, etc.) as crucial
for the experiencing of art (Stolnitz, 1961), is a specific type of inhibition,
usually called "disinterestedness" (Kant, 1931, p. 55) or "distance" (Bullough, 1957). While there has been relative agreement that this inhibitory
process generally leads to refraining from action that might correspond to
or be called for by the evoked emotional experience, there has been but little
agreement about the nature of the process itself.

The variety of views on this latter point can be reduced to two basic approaches. According to the first view, among whose proponents one can
list Shaftesbury, Schopenhauer, Kant, and Bullough, distance "is obtained

by separating the object and its appeal from one's own self, by putting it out of gear with practical needs and ends" (Bullough, 1957, p. 95), by filtering our personal relation to the object (ibid., p. 97) of factors irrelevant to it, such as "questions of origin, of influence, of purposes . . . of marketable value, of pleasure, even of moral importance" (ibid., p. 129). The complementary positive effect of distance is claimed to be an intensification of the internal experience and an enhanced concentration on the work of art, which turns into an "end in itself." According to the second major viewpoint, the apparent detachment and inhibition of action are due to the richness and complexity which characterize the experience evoked when a person concentrates fully on a work of art. Since the spectator identifies with several different figures and becomes aware of various incompatible viewpoints expressed in the work of art, no single impulse of action can predominate and no canalization of interest in any specific direction can take place (Münsterberg, 1905; Ogden, Richards, & Wood, 1922; Schiller, 1964). Apparent detachment is thus a side effect of an intense, multileveled personal involvement in the work of art.

Far from being mutually exclusive, these two approaches differ in one major respect. According to the first, distance is a factor external to experiencing and limits its boundaries in some respects without reducing its intensity and the degree of personal involvement; while according to the second approach, distance is a factor inherent in the very act of experiencing art fully and uninhibitedly. Modern findings in support of both of these viewpoints could be cited. If the relatively detached behavior of the art observer is regarded as similar to that of a person who stands by idly when his fellow men are victims of crime or suffering, then one may hypothesize that the factors identified as inhibiting the impulses to help and to get actively involved are operative also in the case of the art observer. Such factors are, for instance, the presence of other, inactive bystanders, particularly strangers (Darley & Latané, 1968; Latané & Rodin, 1969), and the observer's belief that the victim himself is to blame for his fate (Lerner & Matthew, 1967). However, there is reason to doubt that the model of the bystander in the presence of crime and suffering represents characteristic features of the art spectator's situation. The main difference between the observer of crime and of art is that the former is expected to act and be immediately helpful in some specific way, while the latter is expected to refrain from action or at least from immediate action in the context of art. Thus, not helping a victim of violence is as inappropriate for the observer of crime as helping King Lear or attacking a statue of Ivan the Terrible in a museum would be for the observer of art.

It seems, therefore, that a certain kind and amount of inhibition is built into the very act of experiencing art. Bullough (1957) elaborated particularly determinants of distance which depend on the work of art—temporal remoteness and spatial distance of the art products and the presented contents, fanciful and improbable themes, framing of pictures, placement of sculptures on pedestals, staging techniques of drama, etc. But there are also conditions bound more closely to the experience which favor distancing on the part of the observer. Major among these is the structuring of the experience, i.e., its chainlike and multileveled nature.

When discussing experiencing in art we have concentrated on the dynamics of empathy with regard to single figures. Yet it is evident that experiencing art is a more complex process, first, because the observer empathizes simultaneously and sequentially with more than one figure, and secondly, because the observer not only empathizes but also *responds* emotionally to his own experiences and to the presented contents. Thus, a spectator feels into the emotions of the murdered *and* of the murderer (Bacon & Breen, 1959, p. 36). He identifies experientially with the various stages of a sculpturally suggested action, and he also reacts to what he experiences and perceives with anger, amusement, or awe (Butcher, 1951, pp. 261–63). Thus, the inhibition embedded in the complexity of experiencing functions not only through the multiple counterbalancing of emotional responses but also through the counterbalancing of cognitive meanings. For, when we move away from programmatic, propagandistic art, it is the rare case that an observer emerges from experiencing with a clear notion of a specific course of action required here and now. And even when his experience has been unidirectionally channeled, experience unattached to a clear-cut set of action instructions rarely leads to action (Leventhal, Singer, & Jones, 1965). The conditions under which art is viewed further preclude submission to any action impulses, not merely because of the code which regulates audience behavior at concerts, in museums, or at the theater, but mainly because there would not be much sense in actions performed in these contexts. Even when the viewing of aggressive figures in a film evoked strong imitatory movements, it was only when the observers were subsequently angered and rewarded for aggressive responses that the full impact of their imitation of the aggression was revealed (Bandura, 1965).

The impact of the various factors favoring inhibition may be enhanced or restricted through the social role, and hence the set, of the observer of art. This role and the expectations bound up with it seem to vary across cultures and centuries no less than the role of the artist. In its beginnings art seems to have been much more closely bound up with action and participation on the part of the spectators than in later periods, which gave rise to prohibitions forbidding observers to touch the exhibits in museums, for example, or to sing and dance during a concert. Similarly, the expectations of the medieval observer of religious drama and the awareness of the action demanded from him seem to have favored a much smaller distance than is nowadays achieved even by the most ardent supporters of the "living theater," who attempt to break through the barriers between the stage and the audience.

Thus, although a certain measure of inhibition is probably as necessary for the experiencing of art as empathy is, i.e., overdistancing is no less injurious for experiencing than underdistancing (Bullough, 1957), the optimal degree of inhibition can hardly be determined in isolation from the accepted social role of the observer. Consequently, Bullough's famous generalization that the goal should be "the utmost decrease of Distance without its disappearance" (Bullough, 1957, p. 100) has as little validity as the attempts of others to classify art according to whether it evokes empathy or distance (Worringer, 1948) or to sing the praises of the one type as against the other (Brecht, 1958; Ortega y Gasset, 1948). Inhibition seems to be as integral an aspect of experiencing art as of experiencing in non-art contexts, while its enhancement or reduction depends in art no less than in life on the complex system of interactions between observer, object, and situation.

14. Sublimation, Multileveledness, Abstraction, and Symbolization

Fusion of Personal Uniqueness and Interpersonal Generality

Art is humanly relevant. This truism, which has been expressed and elaborated on a variety of levels and from a diversity of viewpoints by aesthetical philosophers of all generations, contains in disguise the nucleus of a problem which the psychology of art can only begin to expand and to answer. In simplified terms, the claim about the human relevance of art suggests that art may signify, denote, mean, express, or reveal something of vital and intimate importance for human beings. Three major trends recur often enough in the variety of analyses of art to deserve special attention on the part of psychologists and to serve as a starting point for the analysis of the effects produced by the contents of art. These are the claims that art may provide satisfaction of wishes, solution to human problems of a personal nature, and insights into significant aspects of existence and the world. There are obviously a great number of specific psychological questions which arise with regard to each of these claims. Yet, underlying all three is the important assumption that the gratification, the solution, and the insight are uniquely relevant for each individual spectator of art. In other words, the same work of art may satisfy the specific wishes of a great number of people, may provide solutions to their individual problems, and may give rise to insights that are meaningful and significant in an intimate manner to many people. Such an accomplishment on the part of art is all the more intriguing when we consider, on the one hand, the specificity of contents in each work of art, and on the other hand, the conviction of each individual that his wishes and problems are unique, at the utmost similar but never identical to those of others.

It seems that there is more than one means at the disposal of art to accomplish this extraordinary feat of fusion between the uniquely personal and the interpersonally general. Each of these means may be characterized through certain features shared by a greater or smaller range of works of art and through certain potentialities of reaction in the human spectator. Major among these means are sublimation, multileveled structuring and perception, abstraction complemented through concretization, and symbolization.

Sublimation

The portrayal of an actual act of violence—say of a man hitting or slaying another person, the description of a competitive relation between two people, or the account of a desperate attempt to solve a scientific riddle—can be viewed as a presentation of the theme of aggression on successively higher levels of sublimation. Each of these descriptions could also serve to convey meanings other than aggression, depending both on the presentation of the theme and on the recipients of the communication. But when aggression is grasped as the salient theme of the description, then the difference between murder, competition, and the struggle for knowledge could be reduced psychologically to a difference in degrees of sublimation. In spite of its one-sidedness a reduction of this type is in art not only meaningful but also helpful in highlighting an important aspect of the effects of contents.

Sublimation consists in the satisfaction of needs on a level higher than the original—i.e., on a culturally accepted level—which is attained through changes introduced in the object and goal of the drive as well as in the manner of gratification. The replacement of an original sexual curiosity by scientific curiosity and pursuits, the channeling of aggression into competitive sports, and securing gratification by means of art—these are classical examples of sublimation. Thus in its original sense, sublimation refers to a cluster of processes involved in a certain form of indirect satisfaction of needs, drives, and wishes. The necessity for this and other indirect mechanisms of gratification is explained by psychoanalysis through a structural analysis of the human being and the world in which he lives. Because of internalized moral demands, represented by the superego, and because of cultural or social constraints and of obstacles inherent in reality, a great part of our needs and wishes remain unsatisfied. The psychoanalytic theory concentrated mainly on the wishes whose gratification is obstructed by the superego. This obstruction may reach the degree of rejecting the unsatisfied needs from consciousness, i.e., subjecting them to repression. However, since repressed wishes continue to press for fulfillment in reality, recourse has often to be taken to indirect ways of satisfaction. These are called defense mechanisms and involve various degrees of distortion in the wish or even in the perception of reality, so as to make gratification possible in spite of internal and external obstacles. Sublimation represents one of the most common and least pathogenic defense mechanisms.

That the artist engages in sublimatory activities by expressing his repressed wishes in an artistic form, which may be so successful that he may then even secure actual satisfaction of his wishes, viz., honor, power, and the love of women (Freud, 1963), is a fairly common claim. But how do the artist's sublimated wishes afford sublimated satisfaction to the spectator of art? How is it that a described act of murder or love or sacrifice may constitute wish fulfillment for the reader or observer? Concentrating on the gratification of repressed or at least severely censured and condemned wishes, psychoanalytic writers have emphasized that sublimated satisfaction through art is made possible by the application of two major means. The first is disguise and concealment of the original wish, while the second is the enticement of the observers through formal beauty which serves as an "incentive bonus" in the sense of forepleasure (Freud, 1955, pp. 187 ff.; 1959b, pp. 64 ff.). Both means are designed to allow for satisfaction in spite of the superego's watchful eye and without the evocation of anxiety, guilt, and remorse which would attend the gratification in actual life or even in daydreams (Lesser, 1962; Waelder, 1965). Consequently, by preventing "open conflict with the forces of repression" (Freud, 1959b, p. 64), these means make possible the attainment of satisfaction at minimum price and effort, but also contribute to the shaping of the sublimatory character of the gratification so that it is both less real and less intense than satisfactions in real-life situations (Freud, 1948a). However, a detailed analysis of the various devices of so-called disguise and enticement reveals unique features of artistic sublimatory satisfaction which set it apart from sublimatory gratification in nonartistic contexts. Indeed, this is demonstrated by the very fact that at least in works of art which have a clearly identifiable level of narrative-representational contents we often find realistic and detailed descriptions of acts and events sharply censured by culture and society and rarely if ever pursued in personal daydreams. How does art attain the privilege and authorization to represent in a clear, even intensified form various sexual and aggressive wishes which we hardly dare to imagine in fantasy?

Part of the answer to this question lies in the comprehensiveness of artistic representation. A description of murder in a novel like Dostoyevsky's *Crime and Punishment* includes indeed all the details of the violent act and also its bloody and sadistic aspects, but it does not conceal all the other facts related to the act: the realistic difficulties, the internal inhibitions, the suffering preceding and succeeding the murder, as well as the punishment, the guilt, the confession, and expiation on a variety of levels. Thus, while affording full satisfaction to aggressive desires and possibly even to the more specific wishes to murder one's mother and to reassert the right of the young in the struggle against the old and their greedy establishment, the described scenes provide no less satisfaction to other complementary wishes. Major among these are the superego-conditioned craving for punishment and the ego-induced demand for continuous control, which are gratified through the confrontation with all the psychological and realistic outcomes of the murder.

Comprehensiveness in presentation may be manifested in a variety of forms, for instance, by splitting wish fulfillments between two or more figures like Dr. Jekyll and Mr. Hyde or Lear and his Fool, or through a multileveled elaboration of a problem. Essentially it implies that satisfaction accrues not only to the wishes of the id but also to those of the superego and ego; that homage is done not only to the pleasure principle but also to the reality principle; and that gratification is extended to incompatible combinations of desires and counterdesires, i.e., to the craving to be Don Quixote and Sancho Panza, to the Othello and the Iago parts in us, to the saintly and the devilish tendencies which continue to coexist and refuse to compromise.[1]

Comprehensiveness in presentation, which varies in degree from one work of art to another, is supplemented by other means which help to sanction sublimatory wish fulfillment through art—for example, metaphorical and allegorical description, symbolizations, displacements, and other devices characteristic of secondary elaboration of id-related material (Freud, 1953). Most important among these means is the attribution of the wishes and their fulfillment to fictitious characters whose illusory existence renders their impulses and actions morally and socially harmless and hence tolerable. This device, which could be regarded as an integral part of artistic representation, enables the observer to hide behind the identity of some non-self figure while pursuing forbidden pleasures. Moreover, it contributes to the enhancement of pleasure by affording the observer a means of attenuating his suffering while attending the less enjoyable parts of the hero's adventures "through the certainty that in the first place it is another than himself who acts and suffers upon the stage and that in the second place it is only a play, whence no threat to his personal security can ever arise" (Freud, 1942). When it is thus formulated, this artistic means is reminiscent of similar devices recurring in daydreams and night dreams where unconscious forces become liberated to a certain extent from conscious control. However, in dreams the attainment of satisfaction depends largely on unconscious processes. Not so in art. Here conscious processes are involved no less than the unconscious ones. Although on a certain level the observer uses the art figures as a cover and excuse for his experiences, on another level his involvement may imply a narrowing down of the distance and even a diminution of the differentiation between him and these figures. Indeed, it is the reduction of differentiation between observer and art figures that necessitates special emphasis on the fictitious nature of these figures and their experiences. For it is largely because of the fictitious atmosphere that the evocation and satisfaction of repressed wishes appears permissible.

The bridging of the gap between the observer and the art figures takes place mainly through projection of the observer's needs and wishes onto depicted characters and through his identification with them. The commonest types of projection in the context of art may be assumed to be "attributive projection," i.e., the perception in others of feelings and characteristics perceived in oneself, as when a person who hates feels that others hate him (Freud, 1938; Freud, 1956b, p. 449), and "complementary projection," which consists in perceiving in others traits different from those identified in oneself but complementing and explaining them, e.g., when a person feels fear, he may see the other as frightening (Freud, 1956b, p. 452). Projections of both types are activated mainly when a person feels threatened owing to the evocation of prohibited impulses and because of the difficulty of integrating what he perceives in himself with the demands of his superego, his self-image, and his beliefs in general (Holmes, 1968; Murstein & Pryer, 1959). Since empathic experiences which contain elements of gratifying prohibited wishes may evoke anxiety, fear, and embarrassment, the observer of art is induced to attribute these forbidden wishes and feelings to the art figures and thus unburden himself partly of guilt and even of responsibility.

It may be hypothesized that the contents of works of art also provide objects and situations adequate for projection. Shakespeare's observation in *Antony and Cleopatra* that "Sometimes we see a cloud that's dragonish; A vapor sometime like a bear or lion" should not be taken to imply that any cloud or vapor may equally well serve as a screen for projections. Several studies show that some pictures elicit more projections than others (Weisskopf, 1950), that some include more cues for projection of the achievement motive than of other motives (Jacobs, 1958), and that in general projections tend to be made with regard to figures which may plausibly be assumed to possess the projected characteristics. For instance, threatening features are projected more onto males than females (Hornberger, 1960), and one's negative traits are projected preferably onto people similar rather than dissimilar to oneself (Bramel, 1963; Edlow & Kiesler, 1966). Since projections are common in the course of experiencing art, art figures are probably so constructed as to facilitate projections relevant to the contents.

Apart from anxiety elicited by gratification of forbidden wishes and the nature of the art stimuli, there seem to be at least two other interrelated factors which greatly facilitate projections within the framework of experiencing art. Both depend on the characteristic structuring of a work of art and the manner in which its narrative-representational content is presented. Since many works of art are multileveled (see Multileveledness, below), the spectator is provided a certain degree of freedom in defining the theme and organizing the presented material around it. This largely creative activity may allow for the evocation of personal evaluations, subjectively appealing interpretations, and perceptions in terms of one's habitual attitudes or temporary feelings, as is usual when the stimuli allow for multiple interpretations (Jenkins, 1957; Leuba & Lucas, 1945). Such subjectively controlled perception, which could itself be regarded as projection in the wider sense (Freud, 1938, pp. 857, 879), may also facilitate projections in the more restricted sense of a defense mechanism. The second factor which facilitates projections in art was identified by Freud (1948d, p. 323) as dependent upon "a subtle economy of art in the poet not to permit his hero to give complete expression to all his secret springs of actions. By this means he obliges us to supplement, he engages our intellectual activity, diverts it from critical reflections, and keeps us closely identified with his hero." The activity of supplementing the presented information is essentially an integral part of a spectator's response to art, through which he becomes an accomplice of the artist in a variety of senses. However, insofar as the observer is called upon to supplement the motivations of the depicted heroes, he is driven to make use of his personal experience, often to an extent which favors projecting his own needs and motives onto the fictitious characters. Evidence for this conclusion derives also from the activity of "analogizing" which often follows the confrontation with a work of art and consists in assuming imaginatively the role of the hero and acting out his experiences as if they were one's own (Bettelheim, 1949; Lesser, 1962, pp. 203–4, 244–47).

"Analogizing" rests to a great extent on identification with art figures, which is the second major means—besides projection—of bridging the gap between the observer and the contents of a work of art. Although identification in art is usually much shorter and less intense than identification in real-life situations, the major motives for identification in these different contexts seem to be highly similar. Just as a child may attempt to emulate a person whom he envies for possessing "more efficient control over resources than he has" (Whiting, 1960, p. 118), such as "sex, . . . rest, information, freedom from restriction, freedom from pain . . . love and praise" (ibid.,

p. 113) in order to enjoy this person's power and mastery over the environment (Kagan, 1958), the observer of art may be induced to assume affectively and cognitively the role of an art figure in order to attain, at least in fantasy, the goals this figure has attained. Prominent among these goals are wish fulfillments which have been denied to the observer but are enacted by the character. This conclusion is supported, for example, by the evidence that violence programs on television are watched more by insecure and frustrated children than by children enjoying harmonious relations with their parents (Maccoby, 1954; Schramm et al., 1961). Mere imitation is also enhanced when the model is a celebrity (Hovland, Janis, & Kelley, 1953), highly competent (Mauser & Bloch, 1957; Rosenbaum & Tucker, 1962), or of high social status (Lefkovitz, Blake, & Mouton, 1955). Thus, qualities which are held in high esteem in a culture may act as cues for imitation and identification, even if not all of them are goals of a specific individual. Art figures are often endowed with qualities, e.g., extraordinary power, prowess, courage, wisdom, etc., which render them highly tempting objects for identification. Yet, as mentioned in the preceding chapter, identification with a character requires a more extensive process of cognitive elaboration than is usually possible in the course of confrontation with the work of art. Hence, it is more likely to unfold fully only later and is characterized by a more or less extended series of daydreams in which projections play an increasing role, while the differentiation between the I of the art observer and the art figure becomes gradually more and more blurred (Lesser, 1962, chap. 10; Wolfenstein & Leites, 1950).

Thus, the attainment of wish fulfillments through art presupposes a set of complex processes molded and triggered by the images and descriptions provided in a work of art. Two major factors seem to play the crucial role in determining the occurrence of wish fulfillments through art: the relevance of the art contents to the unfulfilled wishes or needs and the fantasy activity of the observer which makes projections and identifications possible. Relevance of the contents to the need greatly depends on the nature of the need. For culturally rejected wishes, which are consequently repressed in most individuals in the culture, the presentation of the wish and its fulfillment in art may be disguised and distorted so as to pass the general censorship of the public and the specific superego censor of the individual spectators without evoking revulsion and anxiety. Greater explicitness may be expected to characterize the presentation of wishes which are in general approved by the culture, yet are rarely fulfilled to the desired degree in reality or even in fantasy, through missing opportunities, restricted potentialities, or even lack of imagination. To this class belong, for example, wishes for great wealth, power, wisdom, and fame, the craving for security, freedom from fear, full acceptance, and unlimited love, and longings for purity, perfection, or devotion to some great idea. However, relative explicitness of presentation should not be regarded as a criterion for approval of the wish by the culture, while relative disguise in presentation should not be taken to imply that the latent content is morally objectionable. Wishes may be presented in a symbolic manner, and insights may be offered through multileveled images and metaphors, not because of repressions, but because direct expression is not yet possible, or rather, the symbolic, apparently disguised manner of presentation is the clearest and most adequate for that type of content (Jung, 1956, p. 290). Similarly, a specific content may be presented on a highly abstract level, without many of the cues suggesting the original wish and its fulfillment, not for the sake of disguising its significance but rather in order to increase the content's generality of appeal.

It is, however, through the fantasy activity of the art observer, in which projective and identificatory processes predominate, that the more or less manifest or latent contents of a work of art turn into wish fulfillments and insights for the individual observer. Yet unlike common daydreams, which are directed mainly by the individual's wishes and his limited experience (Singer, 1966), fantasies stimulated through art are greatly dependent also on the material presented in the work of art. This material, which undergoes personalization through the process of "analogizing" (Bettelheim, 1949, 1941; Wolfenstein & Leites, 1950) not only provides stimuli and objects adequate for specific projections and identifications, but may also lead to an extension of the wishes in scope and depth, may suggest new psychological and realistic alternatives for gratification, and by encouraging concomitant satisfaction of antagonistic tendencies may facilitate more daring fantasies than the individual would ordinarily undertake.

The hypothesis that the narrative contents of art may provide sublimated wish fulfillments raises the problem of whether such gratifications lead to cathartic relief, or possibly enhance or even stimulate wishes in the observers of art. Empirical studies concerning this problem usually take the form of showing subjects a filmed model who engages in violent and aggressive acts, and comparing their level of aggression before and after exposure to such contents. The overwhelming majority of these studies shows that the viewing of aggressive models under usual conditions evokes aggression and enhances its manifestations in children (Bandura, Ross, & Ross, 1963), adolescents, and adults (Walters & Thomas, 1963). Only under specific restraining conditions, mainly fear of consequences or absence of opportunities and reinforcements, does it fail to lead to enhanced expression of aggression, but it does not lead to a reduction of aggressiveness (Bandura, 1969, pp. 127–29, 194–96). These findings have led major investigators to doubt whether there is at all any cathartic effect following exposure to aggression (Bandura, 1969, chap. 3; Berkowitz, 1962, chap. 9). Indeed, in view of the strong imitative tendencies which underlie empathic experiences (Chapter 13) and the clear cues for aggression provided amply in films of violence (Berkowitz, 1962, chap. 8), there is no reason to doubt that observation of aggression instigates aggression. However, there are good reasons to doubt whether the cited experiments provide conclusive proof against the hypothesis of catharsis. The major reasons are that aggressive models and violence films depict pure and naked aggression, hardly contaminated by any sublimatory elements, that they appeal mainly to id impulses while failing to activate concurrently or subsequently the restraining forces of the superego and ego, and, finally, that they are provided with very few "distance"-securing means. These considerations on the one hand raise doubts whether studies using filmed violence are relevant to the problem of catharsis, but on the other hand, they also imply several hypothetical interrelated conditions under which catharsis could be expected to occur. These are, first, the presentation of the wishes and their fulfillment in a sublimatory manner, that is, on a socially acceptable level and in a context which also gratifies the superego and allows the exercise of control and reality testing; second, providing possibilities for an adequate degree of aesthetic distance on the part of the spectators, who will thus be able to preserve the borderline between the permissible in art and the tolerable in reality; and third, stimulating cognitive elaboration of the presented contents in a manner which will make the observer aware of new aspects and levels of reality and thus engage cognitive orientation in the service of controlling impulses. It remains, however, for further studies to show whether catharsis would actually take place under these conditions.

Multileveledness

At the conclusion of his famous interpretation of *Hamlet* in terms of the oedipal conflict, Freud (1953, vol. 4, p. 266) states: "Just as all neurotic symptoms, like dreams themselves, are capable of hyper-interpretation, and even require such hyper-interpretation before they become perfectly intelligible, so every genuine poetical creation must have proceeded from more than one motive . . . and must admit of more than one interpretation. I have here attempted to interpret only the deepest stratum." The analogy Freud draws here between works of art, symptoms, and dreams highlights a basic feature of art which is not only responsible for its extraordinary potential richness and wide appeal but also represents a unique solution to the problem of fusion between the general and the specific.

Interpreting and paraphrasing the contents of art has always been a tricky and ungrateful undertaking. Regardless of how convincing, comprehensive, and original a specific interpretation is, nothing seems to be easier than to refute it by suggesting another interpretation which may share very little with the rejected one. The difficulty of interpretation is particularly obvious for works of art esteemed great. What is the story of Captain Ahab and the whale Moby-Dick about? Undoubtedly it is a drama of whaling in the Pacific, of hunting and adventure. But who would not be impressed by Murray's (1941) suggestion that Captain Ahab is an embodiment of the fallen angel, the demigod identified by Christendom as Lucifer, the Adversary, Satan or Anti-Christ, and that he together with his devilish supporters, on a ship named after an aggressive Indian tribe exterminated by the Puritans, is on a crusade against the stern Hebraic-Christian ethics? If so, how should the depicted struggle be conceptualized? Does it represent the revolt of an individual against the restrictions imposed by the images of his stern and zealous parents, or the perennial clash between the forces of the id and the superego, or rather the antagonism between anarchistic nihilism and the upper-middle-class philosophies of materialism, commercialism, and shallow rationalism?

Similar problems of interpretation arise wherever attempts are made to paraphrase the meaning, the import, or the message of works of art in any domain. The volumes, indeed libraries, of art criticism and interpretation that have piled up in the course of centuries testify that the task is endless, possibly insoluble. Essentially the problem resides neither in the necessity to select *the* one interpretation rendering adequately the import of the *Guernica, Oedipus Rex,* or Moore's sculptures, nor in devising a method for integrating the various statements of meaning which are already fused in the work of art. Rather, it resides in clarifying what it is in the contents and structure of works of art which makes it the carrier of such a multiplicity of meanings and significations whose wholeness persists in the face of a variety of multileveled integrations. No less crucial are the complementary questions concerning the observer of art. How does he grasp the multileveled structuring, and what is the experiential effect of this polysignification?

Multileveledness is the capacity of a work of art to be grasped, elaborated, and experienced in several systems of connected potential meanings, each of which allows a meaningful, clear, comprehensive, and sometimes even autonomous organization of all the major constituents of the work of art. Each such system of meanings is called a level. The term multileveledness could be a misleading designation, first, because it refers only to a quality of the work of art while neglecting completely processes in the perceiver, and second, because it suggests an ordering of levels in terms of importance or primacy. But other terms which have been used to designate similar features seem to us even less adequate. Thus, the term "overdetermination," used by Lesser (1962, pp. 113–59) for the description of literary works, is a psychoanalytic concept which suggests that a work of art is produced by many factors and thus satisfies a variety of needs (Freud, 1953, vol. 5, p. 569). Complexity in structure and contents is not necessarily dependent on the nature of the preceding causal chains. Yet, terms such as "potential" (Kris & Kaplan, 1952), used to denote the power of an image or story to evoke more than one meaning, center indeed on the work of art but suggest nothing about the unique nature of this multisignification. Finally, "ambiguity" (Empson, 1953) or "equivocation" (Langer, 1967, p. 103) would be inappropriate, for each misleadingly suggests unclarity in the evoked meanings.

The inadequacies characteristic of the various terms suggested may serve to highlight the features of the phenomenon dealt with. Levels are not due to a selective abstraction from the wealth of items provided in the work of art, but to differences in organizing and meaningfully relating the very same items. A prime example of the process is provided by Kafka's (1947, pp. 268–78) elaborations on his famous parable "Before the Law." The parable, reported to K. by a priest, tells of a man who comes to ask admittance to the Law, but is denied entry by the doorkeeper, who remains immutable for years and only when the man is dying reveals that the door was intended solely for that man and is to be closed upon his death. When K. jumps to the conclusion that the doorkeeper deluded the man by giving him the message of salvation when it could no longer help him, the priest insists that there are at least two other interpretations of the parable which fit *all* the facts equally well, i.e., that the doorkeeper only fulfilled his duty and even behaved more compassionately than he strictly should have, or that the doorkeeper himself was deluded. The remarkable point about these three elaborations is that although they are very different, each is based on uncovering unique interrelations among the same reported facts, without distorting or forcing them in any way, and without adding any new information. Yet, as K. himself reluctantly admits, these different views are not merely possible but highly convincing, although they may even lead to contradictory conclusions and thus are to some extent incompatible.

The example from Kafka illustrates multileveledness in narrative contents.

A more comprehensive example of levels each of which encompasses both narrative-representational and formal elements is offered by Neumann's (1959) analysis of Moore's sculptures on the theme of the reclining feminine figure. On one level such a reclining figure looks like a woman, representative in its abstractness of the feminine in general, so that the holes in it are suggestive of the female genitals, as psychoanalytically minded viewers would stress (ibid., p. 39). From a different viewpoint the figure can be grasped as the mother, and the holes acquire the connotation of the womb. On another level the abstractly stylized formations of the body appear to suggest landscape features—mountain peaks and precipices—the holes assuming the role of caves in hillsides and cliffs, irradiating the fascination of caverns (ibid., p. 39). The bizarre fusion of feminine and terrestrial connotations would then represent from one viewpoint the symbolic image of Earth Mother, woman and earth at once (ibid., p. 53). But from another viewpoint it would indicate the emergence of a new level on which the reclining figure appears as a living organic body changing into the inorganic, or the human merging into the object. On this level the holes appear to be the external revelation of the inward, as "the emptiness that invites investigation" (ibid., p. 51), as the threshold of "the secret path of initiation that everywhere leads human beings into the darkness, . . . the darkness of the unconscious [which] promises them the discovery of a hidden treasure, the unveiling of the secret" (ibid., p. 50).

The examples from Kafka and Neumann demonstrate that in spite of the comprehensiveness and distinctness of each level within a work of art, the levels may interact in different ways. The examples illustrate two forms of interrelation between the multiple levels. In the case of the parable "Before the Law" each level seems to reveal the whole to a degree which might apparently even obviate the others. The different levels are thus not only autonomous but also largely unrelated to each other, so that one level may sometimes even contradict one or more of the others. In that latter sense some of the various emergent meanings may be viewed as disjunctive, i.e., "as alternatives, excluding and inhibiting each other" (Kris & Kaplan, 1952, p. 245).

Interrelations are much more characteristic of the various levels in the case of Moore's sculptures. Some of the levels seem to differ mainly in degree of specificity, while others, although distinct, merge naturally and complement each other in revealing a richer core of one meaning. All of the levels, however, may seem from one viewpoint (Neumann 1959, p. 110) to be different paths to one core meaning, whose revelation requires the unfolding of each level for the purpose of their integration. The two types of interrelations between levels could be expressed in terms of a metaphor used by De Tocqueville in comparing the American Union with Great Britain (cited by McLuhan, 1967, pp. 421–22): America is like "a forest pierced by a multitude of straight roads all converging on the same point" so that "one has only to find the center and everything is revealed at a glance," but "in England the paths run crisscross, and it is only by travelling down each one of them that one can build up a picture of the whole." Kafka's parable would then be like America, while Moore's sculptures would rather resemble England.

There are undoubtedly several additional ways in which the multiple levels of a work of art could be related to each other. However, regardless of whether the different levels complement one another, represent hierarchically more comprehensive meanings, remain autonomous, or tend to fuse within the framework of a more general conception, each level affords a view of the whole, without impairing the wholeness quality of the work of art, produced by many or all of the levels together. This wholeness quality experienced through any of the levels of a work of art highlights an important characteristic of communication through art in contrast to communication of meaning and information through science, philosophy, and other media of discourse. Communication through these latter media is essentially sequential; they afford a gradual build-up of meaning on the basis of successively presented discrete units of information and ideas. But insight into the meaning of a work of art is often instantaneous and comprehensive. The grasp of the whole in art depends on the parts, but may also precede the understanding of the parts and determines to a certain extent their meaning and function without the whole. The whole, however, consists in a specific organization of the parts—in a multileveled work of art, one of several plausible organizations. But art also makes use of sequential communication, while scientific and discursive presentations are not devoid of qualities which favor the grasp of the whole. Thus the sharp distinction drawn by Langer (1948, chap. 4) between artistic "presentational" logic and "discursive" logic is not fully justified.

In the light of the above remarks multileveledness appears to be a joint product of characteristics in the work of art and of certain modes of perception and elaboration on the part of the observer. A basic precondition for multileveledness is the use of stimuli which may evoke many different meanings. As was shown in Part I, the building blocks of the various arts, namely, colors, forms, shapes, movements, and words, are stimuli which through continuous and extensive use in many different contexts have become foci of associations, emotional connotations, and diverse symbolic significations. This quality renders them potentially capable of being integrated within different systems of meanings.

Another characteristic of works of art which facilitates multileveledness is the presence of cues suggesting possibilities for several equally valid organizations of the same set of stimuli. Such cues are provided through the conventionally identified aspects of a work of art. For example, in painting, forms clearly suggest a possibility for organization which is different from that indicated by colors or by the depicted scene; while in music melody, harmony, and rhythm may readily inspire distinct structurings of the musical material. Cues of this kind provide particularly strong anchorage points for multileveled organizations when the different structures suggest contrasting meanings. For example, in *The Lesson* by Ionesco, on the level of verbal interchange a professor and his pupil are engaged in a routine repetition of conventional schoolbook phrases while on the level of action we witness how the professor is gradually draining the vitality from the student until he finally plunges a knife into her body.

Two of the most notable means for enhancing the multileveledness of a work of art are symbols and motifs that have become foci for different meanings. Symbols (see Theory and Experiments in Symbolization, below) are representations of meanings through images, scenes, movements, etc. that also stand for other specific denotations. There are various symbolic categories and they differ both in the stimuli which serve to express the meaning and in the relation of these stimuli to the represented meaning. For example, the concept "life" may be represented through an image of a bustling street which may serve as an exemplifying instance for "life," or through an image of a whirlpool which may serve as a metaphor for "life." Yet in both cases the images have a double set of meanings: the original conventional meaning and a symbolic meaning which is suggested by the image. The symbolic meaning, however, is usually a wide range of meanings, none of which can be singled out as the proper one. A stormy musical passage in Bruckner's Seventh Symphony may be felt as reflecting a specific feeling or emotional outbursts in general, while a cubist painting may be taken as a metaphor for the disintegration of fixed values or for the multileveledness of reality. Thus, every symbolic expression is essentially multileveled. Moreover, multileveledness is built into the symbol in the sense that the symbolic meaning is not only suggested by the image but mostly embodied through it and fused into it.

The second means for enhancing multileveledness is the use of meaning-laden situations and plots. The main impact of such situations or plots derives from their potentiality for evoking a variety of meanings. This potentiality may usually be traced back to the commonness of the situations and to their recurrent elaboration in the art of a certain culture or society. Examples of such motifs, at least in Western art, are the chase after the source or perpetrator of evil, the conquest of love over difficulties, the Cinderella story, and the overpowering of the strong by the weak, i.e., the David and Goliath theme. Motifs of this type are amenable to treatment in any of the arts, with the possible exception of music, and on any level of abstractness and complexity. The chase theme can take, for instance, the form of a detective thriller which centers on tracing down the murderer, of a crime story, such as *Rashomon*, which suggests that the chase is in fact an abortive search for truth, or of a drama like *Oedipus Rex*, where the convergence between the searcher, the searched, and the crime raises the plot to the level of a veritable symbol. The chase motif is always laden with personal and social connotations, yet the extent to which it will also evoke deep symbolical overtones of the search for a hidden treasure like the Holy Grail, absolute truth, the panacea for happiness, etc., depends largely on its elaboration in the context of art. The theme of waiting may thus serve in a best-seller type of fiction as an element in a popular love story, or, equally well, it may be richly elaborated as in Beckett's *Waiting for Godot*, when it turns into a symbol of mankind waiting for God, for salvation, for a better personal and social tomorrow, or just for someone to come or something to happen.

Complementary to the various features of the work of art which make multileveledness possible, there is the capacity of the observer of art to grasp multileveledness perceptually, conceptually, and experientially. This capacity rests mainly on the ability to shift points of view, to exchange one frame of reference for another, and to replace one organization of the perceived stimuli by another organization. In the psychological laboratory the ability to shift is usually studied with reference to perceptual stimuli which admit of different organizations, e.g., figure and background which tend to exchange roles (Rubin, 1921), or a tridimensional view which competes with a bidimensional perception (Koffka, 1930, pp. 163–67), and with reference to conceptual tasks which require from the subject a reorientation due to changes in the problem (Kendler & Kendler, 1962) or for the sake of better solutions (Luchins, 1942). However, shifting in the context of experiencing a work of art differs from the shifting in such perceptual and problem-solving tasks. In contrast to shifting in perceptual tasks, which involves viewing the stimuli in terms of either one gestalt or another but not in terms of both simultaneously, shifting from one level of a work of art to another does not require the spectator to forgo the first organization in favor of the second. He may view the work of art in terms of two or more levels simultaneously and may even attempt their integration. Moreover, in contrast to shifting with regard to conceptual problems, which usually involves replacing a wrong or worse solution by a better one, proceeding from one level to another in art does not necessarily imply the superiority of a second level over a first. The various levels of a work of art may differ in the comprehensiveness or depth of the insight they afford, but may just as often all be equally meaningful and allow for comparable views of the whole.

In other respects there are similarities between shifting in works of art and shifting in perceptual and conceptual problems. To a certain extent shifting in these different contexts consists in discovering new relations among the perceived elements and thus combining the elements in new ways. This is the major characteristic which highlights the affinity between shifting and productive thinking in general (Koestler, 1964, p. 45; Mednick, 1962, p. 221). The occurrence of shifting in the different contexts is due at least partly to similar motivational factors. Major among these are satiation and the psychological as well as practical utility of the various viewpoints or solutions. Thus, although subjects prefer at first to grasp visual stimuli through the simplest and best possible gestalts, they tend to shift after a time to another, sometimes even worse organization (Sakurabayashi, 1953) for the sake of combatting satiation. Accordingly, shifting is less frequent when the perceived stimuli are more complex and articulated, contain movement, or are interesting in any other sense (Dember, 1960, pp. 160–61). In conceptual problems, however, shifting to another solution or hypothesis is facilitated when a previously adopted attempt at solution has not been constantly successful or practiced much and has not acquired the meaning of protecting the subjects against frustration and feelings of incompetence (Gardner & Runquist, 1958; Van de Geer, 1957).

The analogous motivational factors which could be hypothesized as affecting shifting in art would accordingly be, first, the tendency to overcome satiation by replacing an already familiar organization by a new one, and second, the expectation that further aspects and levels of the work of art may tap problems which were not dealt with on previously experienced levels. These factors are not mutually exclusive. Thus, the multiplicity of organizations and meanings which a multileveled work of art admits of plays a crucial role in determining whether it will preserve its appeal and hence its interest for the same observer on repeated occasions and for many different observers even in different cultural spheres and periods. In this sense multileveledness is undoubtedly one of the major features which enables a work of art to pass Longinus' test of aesthetic merit, i.e., "that is truly great which bears repeated examination." Thus, since the wide popularity of artistic products of the best-seller type can usually be traced back to their treatment of a problem with which for a time many members of a society are preoc- cupied consciously or preconsciously, their appeal fades when the problem loses its topicality. Such works of art may enjoy revival if they contain levels that may have been overlooked by former generations but are discovered by later ones. While such revivals of interest are somewhat rare, a progressive change in the meaning attributed to a work of art across generations is more frequent, although both phenomena depend on the multileveledness inherent in the work of art.

While shifting from one level to another is a sequential process, in the work of art the various levels coexist, sometimes like facets of a crystal, at other times rather like irradiations of a light source. Accordingly, although each level reveals the whole, an observer may not infrequently grasp a work of art on more than one level simultaneously, or integrate in a single insight several levels experienced by him sequentially. The processes underlying these more comprehensive experiences involve not merely shifting but the transcendence of shifting. This transcendence rests however on the same processes that enable us to understand another person simultaneously on the basis of what he literally says and of what he expresses indirectly through gestures, mimicry, and the choice of particular words. Moreover, these are also the processes which underlie complex orientations and thus enable a person to locate himself concomitantly on the temporal, spatial, psycholog- ical, and social levels of reality, to play multiple roles, yet to remain himself, and to apprehend the people with whom he interacts as partners, competitors, relatives, and friends all at once. The comprehensive grasp of the multiplicity of levels may take at least one of two forms. If it is an integrative grasp, then it may involve some of the processes most characteristic of perception and conception at the highest developmental levels, i.e., flexibility, hierarchical and centralized structuring, consideration of several factors simultaneously, awareness of viewpoints other than the egocentrical one, and integration of diversity into unity without divesting the parts of their heterogeneity and functional distinctness (Lewin, 1936; Inhelder & Piaget, 1958; Werner, 1957, chap. 1). Yet the comprehensive grasp could also assume a reductive form and consist in centralizing the experience on one level.[2] This one preferred level may be perceptually or conceptually the best possible gestalt, i.e., the simplest or conversely the most comprehensive one. But it may equally well be a level which lends prominence to a problem most meaningful to an individual spectator, a level that provides him with significant and personal insights and suggests new answers to old questions and new questions to old answers. The more multileveled a work of art is, the more needs it satisfies, the more disparate problems it unites, the more doubts it removes, the more questions it raises—the greater the chance is that the insights it suggests to an individual spectator are experienced as personally significant not only by that single spectator but by many individuals who seem to live in many different realities and to be haunted by problems whose specificity is more apparent than real.

Abstraction

Like sublimation and multileveledness, abstraction can be viewed as a quality of works of art, as a process which plays a crucial role in the spectator's experiencing of art, and as a major medium for the attainment of the unique artistic fusion between the general and the specific. But unlike the role of sublimation and multileveledness in art, which seems obvious even at a first glance, the function of abstraction in art and for its experiencing might appear doubtful. Thanks to habitual terminology, many would agree that a great part of modern Western art, as well as Egyptian, African, American Indian, and Pre-Columbian art, is abstract, yet few would be willing to go along with the implication that abstraction is built into the very essence of all art products and is essential for experiencing them no less than tension and relief or feeling-into. The difficulty of accepting these hypotheses arises mainly from the usual connotations of abstraction, which place it as a contrast to concreteness, perceptibility, and individuality as well as to emotional experiencing. In line with a long philosophical tradition (Cassirer, 1953b, chap. 1), which has been largely preserved in psychology (Arnheim, 1969, chap. 9; Pikas, 1966), abstraction is generally viewed as a high-level cognitive process which consists in the removal of features that characterize only the individual or particular phenomenon. Its product is a concept that includes those features which are common to a class of particular objects or events.

When these aspects of abstraction are emphasized, one may well wonder how abstraction relates to art products, which, regardless of their type or period, always remain highly individualized presentations. The paradox disappears when one remembers that the ignoring of some features in the course of abstraction always results in an increased emphasis on the remaining features and that these remaining features form a concept which invokes both the particular case and the whole class. Even though concepts are abstract and general, they need not necessarily be presented or expressed in an abstract or general form. Images, colors, musical tones, and bodily movements may be media just as adequate for the expression of concepts as words, which are usually considered the major means for the communication of concepts.

Thus, highly realistic art can present and communicate abstract concepts just as much as so-called abstract art. This statement implies that the evocative power of works of art can transcend the boundaries of the specific meanings they suggest. Accordingly, the painted figure of a man may represent many different human beings; a pointed form may stand for swords, aggression, or ambition; the tragic story of a hero may invoke a memory of personal misfortune; and the tumultuous unfolding of a musical sequence may represent a variety of stormy events, internal or external. Thus, though the work of art itself presents individual instances and specific features characteristic of particular objects, phenomena, or events, it may fulfill the function of "a smaller quantity containing the virtue or power of a greater," as Dr. Johnson defined abstraction. The extent to which the abstract is concretized in a work of art may vary greatly. The idea of man may be invoked through a circle and a few strokes or through a detailed presentation of a particular person with all his idiosyncrasies. Similarly, the implied concept may vary in generality along the whole range from the specific to the highly abstract and general. Yet, in the last count what determines the degree of concreteness in presentation is the interrelation between what is actually depicted and what is conveyed through the presentation. If the painting of a sword on a red background suggests to the spectator merely various sorts of weapons then the painting appears much more concrete than when it evokes the ideas of human aggression in general, cruelty, or determined and willful destruction. Thus, the concreteness of a work of art is a joint product of specificity in expression and the generality of the expressed. This conclusion implies that the general import communicated depends both on the work of art and on the spectator; the abstraction performed by the spectator is channeled by the abstractions which resonate through the work of art. Now, what is there about a work of art that turns it so often into a "concrete universal" (Wimsatt, 1954, pp. 69–83)? How does the expression of the uniquely individual suggest an abstract concept?

When the problem is approached as a task confronting the spectator of art, at least a partial answer to the question can be suggested, based on findings on "concept attainment" in experimental situations. The spectator of art who is bent on uncovering the general import of the work of art with which he is confronted resembles the subject in an experiment who gets the task of finding out the nature of the concept held by the experimenter on the basis of a presented series of positive and negative instances of the concept (Bruner, Goodnow, & Austin, 1956, p. 233). Thus, although studies on "concept attainment" are usually performed with stimulus materials like geometric figures or lists of words which are hardly reminiscent of art, some of the recurrent findings in the laboratory seem to be relevant for art. In particular, these studies show that concept attainment is easier when the subject is shown positive rather than negative instances of a concept (Hovland & Weiss, 1953); when the relevant information which has to be taken account of is restricted (Walker & Bourne, 1961) and is presented repeatedly (Bourne & Haygood, 1959, 1961) and in a concentrated manner (Bourne & Jennings, 1963), while the amount of irrelevant information which has to be overlooked is small (Bruner, Wallach, & Galanter, 1959) and is not repeated too often (Bourne & Haygood, 1959, 1961).

When these findings are applied to art, the conditions facilitating concept attainment in the laboratory are reminiscent of qualities of works of art that have been highlighted by many aestheticians, sometimes even as conducive to abstraction. The emphasis on the presentation of positive instances of the concept turns out to be a general characteristic of art in contrast to science or philosophy. Essentially it implies that the concept should be stated, demonstrated, and elaborated by means of concrete examples, through forms, colors, tones, movements, objects, situations, or events that will illustrate its meaning, scope, and depth. However, this does not mean that art is restricted to concrete expression and may not resort—as it often does—to the direct verbal presentation of generalities which might help to draw the spectator's attention to the intended import. More specific implications may be drawn from the second and third sets of conditions which concern the amount and form of relevant and irrelevant information. That unity, order, and fullness of development are basic standards for the excellence of art has been known at least from the time of Aristotle. In view of the empirical findings on concept attainment these standards may be rephrased as requirements to concentrate the work of art on clearly conceived themes and to present them by a maximum of pertinent and suggestive demonstrations and a minimum of distracting irrelevant material.

Two implications of major significance emerge out of this rephrasing. The first is the principle of variation. Variation consists in repeating a theme while introducing changes in some of the elements and conserving others as invariable (see Chapter 4 above). This prime artistic means allows repetition of positive instances of a concept and its gradual unfolding through a variety of demonstrations without evoking boredom and consequently inattention or habituation on the part of the spectator. Although variation is usually discussed with regard to forms (Chapter 4) and in the context of music (Chapter 6), it may be used not only on the level of the formal means but with equal impact also on the level of the narrative contents. If the theme of *Macbeth* is "the apocalypse of evil" (Knight, 1957, p. 158), then the various figures, i.e., not only Macbeth and his lady but also Banquo, the murderers, the traitors, Cawdor and Macdonald, and even the guilt-ridden Malcolm, as well as most of the actions and events reported in the play readily emerge as variation on the motif of evil. The madness, abnormality, fear, terror, cruelty, confused disorder, and uncertainty of evil are elaborated not only through the actual personages, but by other means as well. Notably, most of the scenes take place in darkness, the atmosphere is heavy with fierce and ugly animals, there is a ghastly tempest with "screams of death," and even "the language is tense, nervous, insubstantial" (Knight, 1957, p. 147).

The second analytic principle suggested by the findings on concept attainment demands presentation of the essential coupled with renunciation of the nonessential. The manner of presentation determines to a certain extent what would be deemed to be essential. In a realistic painting the spectator expects the theme of a city to be communicated through the detailed depiction of many houses and vehicles, while in an abstract painting a few small asymmetrical, different-colored rectangles would carry the message, as in Mondrian's pictures of Broadway. However, not even a highly realistic work of art presents an accurate photographic replica of a reality, but rather an image which is distorted, elaborated, amplified, and interpreted so as to convey the sense of a reality which may not only be truer than reality (Bacon & Breen, 1959, p. 100) but also more compellingly realistic than a photograph (Arnheim, 1969, p. 140). Each work of art which functions as a representation of a reality is in fact only a structural equivalent of that reality, i.e., of an object, phenomenon, or event (Arnheim, 1947, p. 72). Accordingly, the production of such a representation necessitates the use of special techniques and conventions to support the created illusion, as has been known to artists and aestheticians for centuries (Gombrich, 1969; Huss & Silverstein, 1968, pp. 151–56). Yet in a representation which conveys a concept there is more than the production of a structural equivalent or of an illusion. There is first and foremost a conceptual interpretation which consists in a selective presentation and organization of themes and of features essential for conveying concepts. Among the various available means for communication of general conceptions through art three are most conspicuous. These are the presentation of *schemata* or of features which evoke familiar schemata, the use of *generic images* in which general features are emphasized and particular attributes de-emphasized or omitted, and the elaboration of features which admit of *multiple interpretive organizations*.

A *schema* is a set of interrelated features which functions as a model. It is not a replica of any specific phenomenon but rather a prototype. Accordingly, the specific phenomena can merely be closer or freer approximations of the schema which they embody in varying degrees of clarity (Arnheim, 1969, p. 176). The relations between the schema and its manifestations in reality can, however, be expressed best in terms of overall similarity (Neisser, 1967, p. 50) and not by means of the number of present and absent features, as in the case of a superordinate concept and subordinate elements. The line drawings of humans in many of Klee's paintings are as true examples of schemata as are the idealized images of men and women in classical Greek sculpture. Although Klee's drawings are models stripped to their bare essentials, while the Greek statues are elaborate images endowed with all the marks of realistic replicas, both are representations of types that do not exist in reality in their pure forms. The main difference between the two examples is that the schema presented in Klee's paintings resembles innate models like the schema of a circle with two dots for eyes and a line for the mouth which elicits smiling in babies (Spitz & Wolfe, 1946), while the Greek statues are constructed models which reflect cultural ideals. Thus the two examples may be viewed as marking the poles of a continuum along which may be placed various kinds of types presented in the arts. These include the more universally significant types which sometimes reflect archetypal structures, like most of the mythological heroes and their later variations; types which represent social realities and problems, like the figures of the slave, the clown, or the king, which appear in so many novels and dramas; and finally the stereotypes of the "bad guys" and the "good guys" in westerns or the lover and the innocent girl in popular art, which resemble simplified formulas rather than real people or ideals (Kaplan, 1967). However, by presenting types, art not only reflects universally significant, possibly even inborn schemata or culturally molded ideals and realities; it also creates new types, which start their existence as artistic fictions and often end up by becoming culturally sanctioned models, admired and later imitated in narrower or wider circles.

The presentation of types in art has several affinities with another artistic means for the communication of concepts—the use of *generic images* which, though specific, suggest a concept or a class of phenomena. The generic function of such images is often attributed to the fact that they emphasize or include mainly generic features of the concept denoted. A frequently mentioned example of such images is the composite photographs invented by Galton (1907). Composite portraits are produced by photographing successively on the same region of a film the faces of a series of people seated at the same distance from the camera. The resulting portrait does not show the features of any of the single faces that entered into its making; but any one of the original constituent portraits, when compared with the composite photograph, looks like it. Moreover, the composite portrait seems to observers familiar in some general and vague sense, and even reminiscent of the faces of friends or casual acquaintances (Brunswick, 1937). In a certain sense a composite portrait represents the average face, i.e., a face in which the eyes, the nose, the mouth, the distances between them, etc., assume the average or the most common values in a certain sample of individuals. Like types or schemata, such images do not represent any specific phenomenon in reality but may evoke references to a whole range of individual phenomena. Yet in contrast to types which reflect ideal or idealized models, composite images present merely hypothetical "averages." The main point about the composite portrait is that it serves as an example for images which are generic in their function, i.e., in spite of being specific they stand for a whole class of references.

Although it is doubtful whether "composite" or "average" images exist at all in the stream of human consciousness, it is highly probable that there are generic images at least for certain kinds of meanings (G. Humphrey, 1963, pp. 278–81). As a result of their function and frequent evocation, such images may undergo a process of schematization in the course of which some of their specific features disappear while the essential and central ones become salient and distinct. Sometimes the images remain highly specific, but the particular features in them which represent accidental variations are treated as inconsequential. This is, for example, the manner in which we perceive illustrations in a dictionary. If the image is designed to represent a class of animals, we attend to the bodily contour, to the presence of legs, arms, and wings, and to the distribution of hair and feathers. But we disregard whether the eyes are open or closed, and whether the animal is seated or standing (R. Brown, 1958, pp. 88–89). Obviously some familiarity with the concept implied by the image is necessary in order to distinguish between essential and nonessential features. Yet the familiarity need not in all cases be specific to the concept. Even if we do not know the kind of mammal depicted in the dictionary illustration, we still know what features are generally considered important for defining any kind of mammal and that they do not as a rule include the position of the eyelids or bodily posture.[3] Identification of the insignificant features may also be favored when they are presented in a conspicuously careless and sketchy way, as often in successful cartoons.

These examples suggest some of the means available to art for highlighting the generic function of images, i.e., for evoking general conceptions and multiple references through specific images depicting individual people, objects, situations, and occurrences. Major among these means is focusing attention on features which are more central in the meaning structure of a concept or common in the class of phenomena referred to and suggestive of them, while de-emphasizing features which denote individual or accidental variations. Emphasis on the essential features is usually attained through repeated reference to these features and their variations, placing them in central locations or junctures in the work of art, and highlighting their interrelations with the major elements of the presented themes and plot. Nonessential features may be not only de-emphasized but actually omitted. In narrative-representational contents the omission of features which are expected by spectators to characterize individual figures or events and which are necessary for their identification is a most potent means for turning an apparently realistic image into a generic image. The omission of such features may take the form of presenting figures out of the usual context associated with them, or of failing altogether to mention any details suggestive of individual background and context, as in many modern novels. Alternatively, the generic function of what is depicted may be brought to the fore through the direct presentation of concepts in a personalized form (as in allegorical dramas whose characters are Wisdom, Charity, or Man) and by suggesting implicitly or even explicitly the multiple references of the contents presented.

A further step in the same direction leads to the third major means of communicating general concepts, which consists in presenting stimuli devoid of explicit conventional references. Such stimuli may be expected to allow *multiple organizations* through the evocation of many different references to specific objects and phenomena. A circle on top of a vertical line can stand for a tree, a flower, a lamp, a balloon, or a human being, just as Godot's identity is so vaguely circumscribed that he could equally well represent God or Satan. Music undoubtedly provides the most compelling examples of the presentation of abstract conceptions through stimuli which are fully concrete and specific, yet point towards the general. "Through the immateriality and meaninglessness of its building stuff, it [music] is forced to dwell technically on a very high level of sublimation and abstraction" (Hindemith, 1952, p. 48). Since apart from some minor elements of "sound painting," musical structures and sequences neither exist in extramusical reality nor represent anything specific in it, they are the purest manifestation of dynamized time (Langer, 1953, p. 109). Hence, they may evoke in the listener the resonance of any external or internal pattern of tensions, rhythmized movement, or dynamic development on any level of reality. As the highest conceivable form of concrete abstraction, music is in its very essence the fusion of the unique with the general and can thus easily dispense with the use of narrative contents and the various artistic means for elevating the particular to the level of universal appeal and significance.

When the abstraction has been performed, can we then assume that the process is at its end, that the conceptual grasp of a generality provides the conditions necessary for experiencing the communicated message? Is it not rather that grasping the abstract conception is merely one side of the complex processes through which the contents and form of art turn into a personally relevant communication for the spectator? Just as Pygmalion, spurred by his abhorrence of women, first created a statue more beautiful than anything in nature, and then turned it gradually—through his love and projections—into a woman of flesh and blood, the spectator of art performs the abstraction often as a prelude to the complementary process of concretization. Yet the cues and even the materials for concretization are largely provided in the work of art, as are those for abstraction. Pygmalion's statue was not only a prototype of beauty and purity but was endowed with all the features of life, except life itself.

Concretization consists essentially in endowing the abstracted conception with personal meaning by organizing the contents and form of the work of art around the core of the abstracted message, and by further elaborating it personally in line with projections, recollections, and other subjectively meaningful adaptations. This process is facilitated by the multileveledness of the work of art, which admits not only of multiple abstractions but also of multiple concretizations.

Abstraction and concretization are intimately related. They often occur together, complementing each other as steps of one sequentially structured process. In experiencing art, concretization and abstraction are both subservient to the function of rendering the content and form into a personally significant communication for each individual spectator. Sometimes abstraction is more prominent for a work of art, sometimes concretization. A work in the tradition of realistic and naturalistic art, which presents a wealth of particular details, may be expected to stimulate in the spectator more abstraction than concretization. Yet if the work of art provides few cues for conventional references, the observer is challenged to engage much more in concretization, sometimes at the expense of abstracting, at other times as a means for grasping the underlying abstraction. An analogue of this quite common process is provided by the transformations undergone by a stylized figure prevalent in the art of the Great Plains tribes of North America (Boas, 1955, pp. 121–22). The figure consists of an isosceles triangle with an enclosed rectangle, sometimes with spurs at the base. This figure in itself is not bound to any particular object reference. The Pueblo Indians, for example, who suffer from the aridity of their land, see in it a raining cloud; the tribes of the Western Plateau interpret it as a mountain pass with a fort protected by palisades, and therefore draw the triangle as more obtuse; while further to the north, where the bear abounds, the enclosed rectangle is omitted because the pattern is seen as a bear's paw, with the triangle as sole and the spurs as claws. In these examples concretization clearly assumed the form of subjecting the pattern to conceptual and perceptual adaptations reflecting the personal needs and beliefs of the perceivers.

As far as the relative roles of abstracting and concretizing are concerned, most works of art fall between the two extremes exemplified by realistic art and decorative designs. Moreover, the organization of the work of art and the cues provided through its form and contents largely determine the nature of the evoked processes of abstraction and concretization. When a work of art presents, for example, clearly outlined types or highly suggestive schemata, the abstraction which the observer is called upon to perform consists mainly in identifying the underlying conception, while concretization develops rather along the lines of amplifying this general conception in accordance with personal experiences. When the narrative content is strange and intriguing, as in Ionesco's *Amédée*, in which a corpse hidden in the next room begins to grow to monstrous dimensions until a giant foot crashes through the door onto the stage, or when initially diffuse and vague stimuli have to be organized into patterns as in "drip paintings" (H. Kreitler, 1960), concretization assumes the major role of rendering the contents meaningful and relevant to the individual spectator. But when the content is grasped as meaningful and relevant to basic needs and their satisfaction, concretization tends to involve more projections and identifications, which provide the material and the stimuli for further imaginative elaboration of the suggested insights and the sublimated wish fulfillments.

Both abstraction and concretization do something more than engage the perceptual, conceptual, and imaginative abilities of the spectator. They also afford him the opportunity to collaborate with the artist in a creative manner so as to realize the potentialities of the work of art. However, abstracting and concretizing may be assumed to afford further, more specific forms of gratification. While projections and the related processes of identification and "analogizing" (see Sublimation, above) may enable the spectator to secure sublimated gratification of wishes and insights into personal and general problems, abstracting and restructuring may be pleasurable in a functional and not necessarily instrumental sense. Indeed, when one considers the importance of abstracting for orientation, behavior, and even bare survival, it appears highly probable that its very activation has become endowed with pleasure. However critical one may be of Worringer's (1948) fantastic speculations about the origins of abstraction, there remains his essentially justified emphasis on abstraction as a means to introduce lawfulness into the chaotic, to control the uncontrollable, to foresee the unpredictable, and to become master of oneself and the world, even if only in a temporary and illusory sense. However, as an artistic means for bridging the gap between the general and the particular, abstraction makes possible not only a conceptual access to reality but also an experiential response to it.

Theory and Experiments in Symbolization

Among means for fusing the specific and the general, the symbol, whose very name derives from the Greek verb *symballein*, "put together," occupies a most extraordinary position. This is due no less to its structural qualities and the strata of meaning expressed through it than to its particular interrelation with art. Like sublimation, multiveledness, and abstraction, symbols occur and are formed and perceived also outside art and form a subject of major interest to many and varied disciplines, ranging from philosophy, religion, mysticism, psychology, anthropology, and sociology to linguistics and semantics. However, this variegated interest in the symbol seems to have contributed less to clarification of the processes it involves than to an extension of the uses and meaning of the term. Thus, words and numbers are designated "symbolic" no less often than images in dreams, the paintings of Chagall, idiosyncratic expressions of schizophrenics, mythological cycles, religious emblems, road signals, literary metaphors, language, and rituals, to mention just a few examples. The definitional confusion underlying this plethora of usages extends also to theories and hypotheses about the genesis of symbols, their meaning, their functions, and their effects (S. Kreitler, 1965, pp. 11–63). Our studies on the perception and formation of symbols (S. Kreitler, 1965; S. Kreitler & Kreitler, 1968, 1971) enable us, however, to introduce into this complex domain a classificatory ordering, which does not rest on the conventional device of choosing one or a few out of the many definitions while neglecting all the others.

Our studies are based on two assumptions which reflect major trends in the theorizing on symbols in the various disciplines. It is assumed that symbols constitute a particular form of expressing or representing meaning, and that the represented meaning is not completely fixed through convention. Together these assumptions imply that symbols may differ from signs in the characteristics of the significate or the "vehicle" of meaning as well as in the relations between the significate and the meaning(s) for which it stands. These broad differences between what we here call symbols and signs have been pointed out by many investigators, who have however preferred to designate these phenomena by different terms. Thus, Piaget (1951) distinguishes between egocentric and socialized meaning, Goldstein and Scheerer (1941) discuss differences between concrete and abstract thinking, Werner and B. Kaplan (1963) differentiate between sense and lexicalized meaning, Ogden and Richards (1949) set up the distinction between emotive and referential terms, and Bruner (1964) suggests a classification of iconic and symbolic modes of representation versus the enactive one. All these and many others seem to share the opinion that signs stand for relatively specified references on the basis of a rather arbitrary convention, while symbols evoke less specified and more personal or subjective meanings on the basis of relations other than strict convention between the significate and the signified.

Accordingly, our studies on the formation and perception of symbols were designed to clarify the relations between significate and signified which hold for symbols, and the processes on which these relations depend. Two major experimental tasks were used. In the first, intended mainly to tap processes of symbol formation (S. Kreitler, 1965, pp. 70–105), subjects were asked to find, for the most truly personal meaning of each of a series of verbally stated concepts, the most adequate, clearest, and deepest expression which would make the meaning immediately evident to a person who did not know it. The subjects were encouraged to use any medium of expression they thought fit—words, gestures, bodily movements, drawings, descriptions of drawings or gestures, etc. The verbal signs which served as stimuli were terms with abstract referents of various types and included terms indicating states, such as death, fatigue, and loneliness, generalized traits like wisdom, independence, and eternity, and feelings ranging from love and happiness to despair or sorrow. In the second experimental task, designed to tap mainly processes involved in symbol perception (S. Kreitler, 1965, pp. 106–21) subjects were asked to communicate to an hypothetical other, by any medium of expression they thought adequate, the most truly personal meaning of each of a series of verbal concepts. The verbal stimuli referred to concrete phenomena—objects of nature, parts of the body, and geometrical forms. In a further study (S. Kreitler, 1965, pp. 122–34) the stimuli presented were visual—drawings of geometrical figures, simple and more complex. In order to get a most comprehensive view of symbolic processes and forms of expression, not only were the stimuli varied, but the subjects in the three studies were chosen from many and different levels of education, social strata, and cultural settings. Moreover, besides normals they included schizophrenics and artists, i.e., representatives of groups commonly considered particularly capable of symbolic expression and perception.

The major findings of these studies which are relevant for our context are the categories of symbolic expression and perception defined on the basis of the subjects' responses. When these responses are analyzed for their content and the means used for communicating the meaning, while abstracting from the specific media of expression, i.e., words, drawings, etc., the results reveal a set of ten symbolic categories which form a continuum-like series in several respects.

In the first category the meaning is conveyed through *an exemplifying instance*, i.e., an object, a phenomenon, an animal, or a person which is related to the concept as a specimen of its connotation or as a part of its denotation. Beauty represented by the Madonna, aggression by the image of a tiger, and the technological age by a machine are examples of this category.

The second category makes use of *an activity* which may be performed with the referent, e.g., the representation of water through the act of drinking.

The third category utilizes for the presentation of meaning an *exemplifying situation*, an image which is richer in details or even in dynamism than an exemplifying instance, although it is essentially static and lacking in development, e.g., an image of a man wandering alone as representing loneliness or Picasso's rendering of the concept Life through a painting which shows in the foreground a woman holding a sleeping infant, and a young nude couple seeking each other's protection, and in the background a squatting nude lost in reverie, and a seated couple similar in attitude to the other couple.

In the fourth category *a scene* communicates the concept through a dynamic situation or a developing story, structured in a sceno-dramatic manner. Films, drama, and literature abound in examples of this category to a degree which renders other examples almost superfluous. For the sake of mere illustration it suffices to quote one of the subjects in the experiments responding to the concept of "despair": "A man wanders in the desert, looking for water. Suddenly it seems to him that the desert ends behind the near hill . . . he hears a human voice, he feels a cool hand . . . he falls down on a shrub of thorns, he is wounded, he is too thirsty to cry" (S. Kreitler & Kreitler, 1968, p. 1317). Notably, the scene expresses despair without using the word "despair." In the fifth category meaning is represented through *bodily expression and movement,* visible or kinesthetic. For example, pain is communicated through a contorted face, aggression through a clenched fist, and subordination through bowed body and knees.

A different element is emphasized in the sixth category, which uses depiction of *consequences,* mostly psychological or humanly relevant, as when the meaning of love is expressed through a scene of parting between the lovers, aggression through corpses, or crime through detention in prison.

Sensation and feeling predominate in the seventh category as the major means of communicating meaning. Here the emphasis is on emotions and sensations which are presented either as evoked through, by, or towards the referent, or as characteristic of it. Synesthetic elements often recur in responses of this type. The expression of motherhood through warmth, of truth through bright light, of rejection through coldness, or of loneliness through internal muteness are some of the tritest examples institutionalized in common discourse as well as in art.

A special position in the series is characteristic of the eighth category, in which meaning is expressed through an *interpretation,* stated mostly in abstract terms and not in the form of an image. The unique contribution of this category is that it allows a statement of the meaning by highlighting one or more of its usually covert aspects, so that new conceptual relations come to the fore. Interpretation is the major element in the following responses given by our subjects: "Love—a walk with yourself from one loneliness to another"; "Birth—emergence from the chaos into yourself, which is the world"; "Happiness—the not-to-be-found in that which is found" (S. Kreitler, 1965, p. 84).

The interpretative factor plays a crucial role also in the ninth and tenth symbolic categories, although it is not manifested directly. In the ninth, *the metaphor* proper, the concept is expressed through an image of some concrete phenomenon which does not belong strictly to the term's conventional spheres of connotation or denotation, but illustrates at least one aspect of its meaning to which it is related by means of an interpretation. The interpretative component is manifest even when the expressed concept is concrete, as in the case of most Freudian symbols, but it becomes particularly prominent when the concept is relatively abstract. When Elizabeth Browning writes, "I think of thee!—my thoughts do twine and bud/ About thee, as wild vines about a tree" (Sonnet XXIX), or when Elia Kazan in directing *A Streetcar Named Desire* juxtaposes the rape scene of Blanche Dubois by Stanley Kowalski and a scene of street washing by means of a hose spouting water at full blast before dribbling to a halt, the intimate conceptual relations between the image and its implied meaning are compellingly evident. A metaphoric image is thus always bilevel, for in it are interwoven the conventional reference of the image and the non-conventional reference highlighted through the image's function as a metaphor. Accordingly, the image is neither an interpretation nor a concept, but embodies the concept by means of an interpretation. Thus, metaphors may range all the way from trite, even meaningless comparisons to images which are hardly distinguishable from expressions ranged within the next category.

The tenth and last category is that of *the symbol* proper. Symbols are metaphoric images which embody a contrast and its resolution, a problem and its answer. This means that among the several aspects of the concept which a symbol reflects there is at least one pair of contrasting aspects whose reconciliation is suggested through the structuring of the symbolic image. An example which clearly illustrates the processes involved was offered by one of the subjects in response to the concept "wisdom." While drawing an eye he remarked that it represents that aspect of wisdom which consists in noting, remembering, and absorbing information; yet later he added rays to the iris, so that it turned into a sun, representing the other aspect of wisdom —irradiating the accumulated and elaborated knowledge (S. Kreitler, 1965, p. 85). The symbol however consisted of one unitary image which was simultaneously a sunny eye and an eyelike sun, implying much more than its creator could state in words.

This series of ten categories represents the modes of expression used by subjects engaged either in the formation of symbolic responses or in symbolic perception. From the viewpoint of experiencing art the perception of symbols seems more relevant than the formation of symbols, which has conventionally been considered the artist's domain. However, from the viewpoint of the symbolic categories the differences between these two tasks, the one whose starting point is a general concept and the other whose starting point is a concrete image, are neither major nor crucial (S. Kreitler, 1965, pp. 119–21, 147–49). Apart from the facts that the category of "activity" was not used in symbol formation, while the category of "bodily expression and movement" did not appear in symbol perception, the categories remain the same, though the frequency of their use is different. Common also to both tasks is the ordering of the categories along a continuum. This ordering is evident not only in the fact that each category serves as a conceptual bridge between the preceding and succeeding categories. It is also substantiated by the finding that chains of responses ending in any category consist mostly of responses in categories preceding that of the final response in the chain. Further, it is remarkable that for both symbol formation and symbol perception the subjects' chains of responses to the stimuli end more often in categories placed nearer to the end of the continuum than to its beginning (S. Kreitler, 1965, pp. 99–103, 117–19, 166, 176). Hence, responses in categories appearing later in the continuum may be assumed to be experienced as more satisfying in the comprehensiveness and depth of expression which they make possible. The last category may accordingly be viewed as the point at which the various symbolization processes represented in the continuum converge and culminate. However, the processes leading up to it differ for symbol formation and symbol perception. While the chains of responses leading to the formation of the tenth category include most often the categories of "scene" and "metaphor" or "interpretation" and "metaphor" (S. Kreitler, 1965, pp. 86–99), the categories prominent in the response chains preceding perception in terms of the tenth category tend to be "sensation and feeling" and secondarily "interpretation" (S. Kreitler, 1965, pp. 112–17). Accordingly, the dynamics of forming a "symbolic" response involve a more explicit effort to fuse imaginal and conceptual elements into one unique and adequate expression, while perceiving any stimulus as "symbolic" involves to a greater extent opening oneself up to its potentialities, mainly by responding to it in terms of sensations and feelings.

If we leaf through the literature of aesthetics looking for treatment of the ten symbolic categories and the unique features of each, we will find that most of them have been mentioned, discussed, or studied; but the investigators often prefer to single out this or that category as the only or the major manifestation of symbolism.[4] This observation supports the view that our findings are fairly comprehensive. Not only has each of these forms of expression been identified as symbolic, but all were also produced by one or another subject in the course of communicating personal meanings. This fact suggests that there are common features which the categories share—some more, some less. The significate may be communicated in words, through a drawing, or with gestures and movements, but the way it is expressed is sure to be concrete and mostly imagelike apart from "interpretation." Some of the categories admit also of expressions which are on the abstract side, but even for these an imaginal concrete expression is more characteristic of their uniqueness and more frequent. Conversely, the expressed meaning is likely to be more general and more abstract than that evoked directly through the image which serves as the means of expression. A metaphor, for example, may posit a relation between two equally concrete phenomena, e.g., a rose is like a melody, or between equally abstract concepts, e.g., love is like perfection; but a metaphor is more expressive and, paradoxically, even more metaphorical in which the implied relation is between a concrete phenomenon and an abstract concept: "O my luve is like a red, red rose/ That's newly sprung in June," or "Perfection is like a melody in which the separate tones preserve their identity while serving a function beyond themselves."

How do symbolic expressions differ from the expressions we call words? At first glance there is a strong resemblance. In language, also, something specific and concrete, usually a set of phonemes, stands for a more general concept. But there are notable differences between linguistic and symbolic expression. First, phonemes do not usually denote anything beyond the concept to which they refer, while symbolic expressions do; and second, the relation between phonemes and concept depends completely on convention, while in symbolism image and concept are related also through processes other than convention. Both of the differences mentioned are relative; symbolic expressions could utilize, for instance, geometrical forms that have little or no signification beyond their symbolic connotation, like the Taoist symbol *t'ai-chi tu*, or could rely much or little on convention (Gombrich, 1965), even before they become fully conventionalized. Yet for general characterization we can say that a genuine symbolic expression shows an interplay between at least two meanings: a direct meaning evoked by the significate and an additional meaning conveyed through it in its function as a vehicle for symbolic expression. Moreover, in a genuine symbol the relation of the significate to the meaning conveyed is based on some kind of structural resemblance (Berlyne, 1965b, pp. 126–30) or isomorphism (Arnheim, 1961) between them. When a symbolic expression is genuine in these two senses, then usually it is also endowed with the following further qualities by which symbols are usually defined. First, a symbolic expression is primarily multileveled and multisignificant. Then, there is close interrelation between the significate and the symbolic meaning; the significate is felt as particularly adequate to express the meaning and embodies it clearly without stating it explicitly. Again, the symbolic communication is widely comprehended even when it does not rest on learned conventions. Finally, it is difficult or impossible to state the symbolic meaning in non-symbolic terms and independently of the expression which conveys it.

The clarity, intensity, and effectiveness with which these characteristics are manifested depend greatly on the unique features of each symbolic category. These features are essentially structural and define the relations between the direct reference of the image used as vehicle of expression and the more general meaning conveyed through it. This relation is, for example, highlighted more emphatically through the "metaphor," in which one or more characteristics of the object or phenomenon are made salient by force of the implied comparison, than through "an exemplifying instance" or "an exemplifying situation," which consists in presenting an object or a situation without any further elaboration. On the other hand, in "an activity" and still more in "a scene" it is the dynamism of the depicted processes which carries the main load of the symbolic meaning. Of particular interest, however, are the structural characteristics of the tenth category, the "symbol" proper, which has fascinated so many artists and investigators in the course of centuries. From the viewpoint of content, it embodies a problem inherent in a concept of general import and its solution. Could any stimulus constellation be grasped in terms of the tenth category when the proper set has been induced in the spectators, or is there anything particular about the structure of certain stimuli which renders them adequate to fulfill the role of "symbol" proper?

The assumption that symbolic expression relies on an inherent resemblance between the expressive vehicle and the embodied meaning leads to the already mentioned hypothesis that stimuli eliciting "symbolic" responses are characterized by a particular structure, and that this structure includes some contrast and its resolution. This hypothesis was tested in two experiments (S. Kreitler, 1965, pp. 122–34) described earlier (see Chapter 5, Symbolic Meanings of Forms). These experiments showed that complex gestalts are experienced as adequate for expressing conflicts while simple good gestalts are adequate for expressing non-conflictual abstract concepts. Further, complex good gestalts (like the Greek pentagram, the Chinese *tai-chi tu*, and Fig. 4.8g,h,i), i.e., figures which include a contrast and its resolution, elicit the greatest number of responses in the tenth category, many more than complex bad gestalts, i.e., figures which include only a contrast, and simple good gestalts, i.e., figures which include as it were only a solution. The described experiment also showed that geometrical drawings with structural features different from those underlying "symbols" proper tend to elicit symbolic responses in categories other than the tenth (S. Kreitler, 1965, pp. 179–88). For example, simple good gestalts evoke more "interpretation" responses than the other types of drawings, possibly because their sharply outlined perfect forms suggest conceptual structures, while complex bad gestalts elicit more responses in the categories of "scene" and "exemplifying situation," perhaps because the tension-laden contrasts of the unintegrated forms in these gestalts correspond best to scenic dynamism or to the heterogeneity of elements in a situation.

Symbols in Art

Owing to their multileveledness and the relatively wide spectra of meanings which they convey, images, themes, and plots corresponding to the symbolic categories may be integrated into the fabric of a work of art in different ways. Some of these we have discussed while dealing with the symbolic functions of forms, colors, movements, etc., in Part I. Such elements, as well as analogous symbolic motifs on the level of the explicit narrative representational contents, communicate meanings which supplement, enhance, or underscore in a variety of ways the major themes and atmosphere of the work of art. However, as means for the presentation and communication of the artistic message, the symbolic categories depend on the context of the work of art in which they are embedded no less than they contribute to its shaping. The impact of the categories may be largely determined by the set induced in the spectators through the context. It may be assumed that works of art devoid of explicit object references, or with narrative contents suggestive of fantasy and of mythical or surrealist themes, sensitize the spectator to symbolic meanings and enhance his set to respond to the deeper connotations of the various symbolic categories. In contrast, the context of realistic and naturalistic art may even decrease the spectator's awareness of the rich symbolic aura over some of the formal or narrative motifs. Moreover, the interrelations between a symbolic motif and the other elements in a work of art may serve to emphasize certain aspects of the symbolic connotations and de-emphasize others. Thus, the context may facilitate a sharper delineation of the symbolic meanings embodied through any of the categories.

However, the role of the context and of the set it induces in the spectator is probably more pronounced for symbolizations corresponding to the first categories in the symbolic continuum than for those nearer its end. The impact of "symbols" proper and highly elaborate metaphors may be so intense and unique that they sometimes emerge as quasi-autonomous structures on the background of a work of art, dominating their context like a particularly strong source of light. Since in "symbols" and rich "metaphors" the prominent symbolic qualities of multileveledness, perfect correspondence between structure and meaning, and great concentration of effect often reach their climax, symbolic expressions of this type tend to be characterized by an autonomy and closure which separate them from their context. A "symbol" or a "metaphor" thus resembles a self-contained cosmos or a highly concentrated nucleus of meaning which may not merge easily with the other elements in a work of art. Two major solutions adopted in literature for integrating "symbols" and rich "metaphors" within the matrix of the narrative may serve to highlight both the particular impact as well as the limitations of such elaborate symbolizations. The first solution consists in presenting essentially non-symbolic figures passing through a series of "symbolic" or "metaphoric" actions, events, and situations, while the second solution consists in depicting "symbolic" figures embedded within an essentially non-symbolic plot. Through conjunction with non-symbolic characters or plot, the symbolic dimension is thus toned down to a degree which allows the full unfolding of the experience and lends it a depth and meaning beyond the limitations of a narrative restricted to the here and now.

The fairy tale is the model illustrating best the first solution. Little Claus, Prince Charming, Snow White, the Sleeping Beauty, and the host of bad stepmothers are not symbols, but rather familiar figures who represent us or parts of us with a transparency hardly to be equaled and difficult to overlook. "The hero" of a fairy tale, writes Langer (1948, p. 143), "is strictly individual and human, for although he may have magic powers, he is never regarded as divine. . . . he is not a savior or helper of mankind. If he is good, his goodness is a personal asset, for which he is richly rewarded." But the actions of these figures, what happens to them, and the twilight world in which they move are made of the stuff of which symbols are made. Obviously not all the adventures of the heroes should be symbolic. In the biblical story of Joseph and his brothers the central events—the throwing of Joseph into the well and his rescue—are indeed symbolic. On the other hand, in *La dolce vita* Fellini has made continuous use of one ancient symbol—water— in order to underscore and unify the various symbolic and nonsymbolic stages of his hero's adventures. While relying on the archetypal connotations of water, Fellini transcends these deep layers of symbolism by highlighting through them the futility and irony of Marcello's search for happiness in love, sex, family, alcohol, work, or religion. Thus, in a city whose ancient ruined aqueducts suggest its discontinuity with the past, Marcello makes love to the aristocratic Maddalena in the flooded apartment of a whore, is trying to kiss the angelic Sylvia under the romantic Fountain of Trevi when the water is suddenly turned off at the very moment she enacts for him the baptismal ritual, and is greeted by the critical eye of a sea monster when he goes to the sea for purification.

In contrast to the fairy tale, which, in combining human figures and a symbolic plot, illustrates the first mode of solution, the myth may serve as the model for the second solution, which integrates symbolic figures with human action and fate. The hero of myth, from the Iliad to the Kalevala and from the Ramayana to the Niebelungen cycle, is characteristically greater, richer, and deeper than any individual human being. Though he has a name and a biography, he is a personification rather than a person, cast on a scale which draws him nearer to gods than to men. Accordingly, heroes have always manifested a notorious tendency to blend with each other across cultural boundaries, as befits figures who are in fact revelations of one archetype with "a thousand faces" (J. Campbell, 1956), a hero of a "mono-myth" (Joyce, 1939, p. 581). Yet, these figures act and move in definite places—Mount Olympus, the sea, the sky, England, France, Israel—and are engaged in very natural acts. Rather than turning pumpkins into carriages, slaying "seven at a stroke," climbing to heaven on a beanstalk, and flying on eagle's wings in the best tradition of fairy-tale figures, they travel horse-back or on foot, slay one creature at a time, suffer, hesitate, love, and court girls. Their world is our world, so that one can identify with what they do, but not completely with what they are. Therefore, it is only logical that figures like Faust and Job, who are molded along similar lines, should not lose much of their symbolic aura when the settings in which they are em-bedded, their actions, adventures, and even achievements are modified in the course of their wanderings through world literature. Rather, such changes may serve to draw them nearer to ever-changing generations of readers.

The problem of integrating symbols within the framework of works of art is intimately related to the crucial questions concerning the function of symbols in art and the effect of symbols on the spectators of art. Although the meaning of symbols in the various categories could be fairly well pre-sented in simple verbal terms, we all feel that the effect of a symbolic expres-sion transcends in some sense that of the verbal statement. To see rhinoc-eroses on the stage seems to be more meaningful than to follow the actions of brutal and morally thick-skinned people. An Indian mandala appears to express in some mysterious manner more than elaborate treatises on cosmic and individual processes of creation and dissolution. A part of this unique effect of symbols can be attributed to the greater impact of sensory stimuli than of verbal terms. Yet why should an image be more expressive than a logically formulated message? Possibly because the relations between an image and its symbolic meaning are less sharply defined, so that an image leaves much larger margins for subjective elaboration than verbal statements do, and possibly because an image taps large reservoirs of prelogical, prim-itive or personal, sensed, felt, and imagined meanings which have never been quite integrated into formal language.

The incompleteness of this answer becomes all the more evident when one considers the categories nearer the end of the symbolic continuum. Symbolic expressions corresponding to these categories often illustrate so compellingly the major features of symbolic expressions—mainly multi-leveledness, perfect match between expressing form and expressed contents, and nontranslatability of the wide realms of meaning resonating through them—that they force even the sceptic to consider more specific hypotheses about the function and effects of symbols. These hypotheses reflect three major trends of thinking (S. Kreitler, 1965, pp. 52–60). According to the first hypothesis, the function of symbols is *unification*. Opinions and formulations differ, however, about what the symbols are supposed to unify. At one pole we find those who attribute to symbols the power to unite discrete entities, such as man with man, with nature, with society, with God (Inge, 1956, p. 263; Joyce, cited by Tindall, 1955, p. 50), or with the world of objects (Allemann et al., 1953, pp. 13, 47), while at the other pole we find those who regard symbols as unifying different levels of reality, experiencing, or psychical functioning. Thus, mystically oriented thinkers and poets view the symbol as blending the infinite with the finite (Carlyle, quoted by Tindall, 1955, p. 40), reason and understanding with the realm of the senses (Creuzer, 1810, pp. 63–64), that which is above with that which is below (Michaud, 1947, pp. 19–42), the spiritual and the material, the real and the apparent (Inge, 1956, p. 263). Psychologically oriented thinkers add that the symbol unites the particular with the general (Goethe, 1917b, pp. 555, 648, 675), grounds the specific in the overall organizing and harmonizing principle of the universe (Koestler, 1949a, pp. 321–31), or—in terms of Jung's comprehensive theory—is the great "conjunction of opposites" which, as the manifestation of archetypes, reconciles the major psychic opposites of the unconscious and conscious and hence also all the antithetical qualities they represent, e.g., constraint and freedom, internal and external realities, past and future, raw creativity and formative cognition, obscurity and clarity, femininity and masculinity (Jung, 1953a, 1953b, 1956a).

The second major function attributed to symbols is *revelation*. Most of the supporters of this view agree that symbols reveal reality, mostly the "true" reality, but they naturally disagree about the nature of the reality revealed. For some, who obviously include mystically oriented thinkers, the reality revealed is the deeper layer of Being which lies beyond logic and the senses and holds the key to the mysteries of life and the cosmos (Bachofen, 1954, p. 52; Creuzer, 1810, pp. 63–64; Otto, 1932, chaps. 4–5; Zimmer, 1962). For the followers of Cassirer (1953–57) and Langer (1948), who regard art, science, religion, mythology, etc., as symbolic systems, symbols represent different conceptualizations of reality which render its various aspects accessible to reason and experience. Finally, for depth psychologists the reality revealed and expressed through symbols is either the personal, repressed unconscious (Freud, 1953) or the collective unconscious, the archetypal, phylogenetically inherited layers of forces and meanings (Jung, 1956a).

The third and last hypothesis attributes to symbols the role of facilitating *adaptation* to reality. In line with the definition of symbol preferred by the specific investigator, this suggestion asserts either that symbols are cognitively primitive means of adaptation that may help adjustment where the higher mental processes fail (Lévy-Bruhl, 1910; Rank & Sachs, 1913, p. 17; Silberer, 1912, p. 692); or that symbols share with signs and all other media of representation and conceptualization the function of enabling man "to understand and interpret, to articulate and organize, to synthesize and universalize his human experience" (Cassirer, 1953a, p. 278), i.e., to be oriented and expand his orientation.

These three major views about the functions of symbols—unification, revelation, and adaptation—are far from being mutually exclusive. When combined, however, they suggest two hypotheses about the possible effects of symbolic expressions: the relieving effect and the orientative effect. The relieving effect is related more closely to the unification function of symbols, while the orientative effect derives rather from the two other functions, i.e., revelation and adaptation.

The manner in which unification may provide for relief could be conceptualized in different ways. On the one hand, there is Jung's assumption that the symbol, bipolar by definition, is a great "transformer of energy." As the visible expression of an archetype, it releases the energy accumulated in the repositories of the collective unconscious and by opening new paths for action contributes to a redistribution of psychic energy (Jung, 1953b, pp. 225–26, 325). On another level, confrontation with symbols rescues the individual from the tyranny of the unconscious, which means schizophrenia, and from the tyranny of the collective mass, which means loss of individuality, and thus it enables a person to become truly himself in the human and social senses of the word (Jung, 1956a). On the other hand, we find Koestler's suggestion that the unification of the specific with the general effectuated by symbols relieves the tensions evoked by the single event through its reduction to the universal, just as the grounding of a wireless receiver or any electrically charged body dissipates the vibrations through "contact with the earth and its infinitely greater absorptive capacity" (Koestler, 1949a, p. 331). For, "the only effective consolation in the face of death is that 'we must all die'—that is, that this particular experience is part of a general law" (Koestler, 1949a, p. 329).

In spite of the differences in the assumptions underlying Jung's and Koestler's suggestions, which need not concern us here, the two conceptualizations about the relation between unification and relief are highly similar. Both point towards the conclusion that confrontation with symbolic expressions may give rise to insights which enable the individual to transcend the suffering, embarrassment, and dangers of specific situations. The experiential and cognitive effects of the insight obviously depend on the importance and generality of the problem. However, the impression, even conclusion, of so many investigators (S. Kreitler, 1965, pp. 60–62) that at least "symbols" proper deal with problems of universal human significance, ranging from life and love to suffering and the fear of death, could hardly be accidental. When, moreover, the concrete expression of the problem and the solution takes the form of a perfectly good gestalt, whose structure alone is tension-reducing, the relieving effect of the symbolic expression is all the more salient.

These remarks also suggest the affinity between the relieving effect of symbols and their orientative impact. The implied solutions of conflicts, the insights into basic problems, and the new conceptual relations suggested through symbols in their unificatory function may act as relieving mainly because they affect cognitively and experientially the observer's orientation towards the presented problems. This orientative impact of symbols, which is even more pronounced when symbols are considered from the viewpoint of their revelatory and adaptive functions, consists in expanding the observer's awareness of meanings, implications, and even potentialities for action.

The interrelation between the relieving effect and the orientative impact is in fact as characteristic of symbolic expressions as of the other media discussed in this chapter: sublimation, multileveledness, and abstraction. The relieving and orientative effects, whose attainment and relative prominence vary across the media, may be regarded as the experiential manifestations of the basic quality which these media share within the framework of art: revealing the general in the specific, highlighting the particular in the abstract conceptualization, and thus providing the bridge between the single and the many, the individual manifestation and the universal law. Yet, "To see a world in a grain of sand/ And a Heaven in a wild flower" will always remain unique experiences even if their general significance reduces to what Blake expresses at the end of the same verse: "Hold Infinity in the palm of your hand/ And Eternity in an hour."

15. Cognitive Orientation and Art

The "More" in Art

"Poetry is indispensable—if I only knew what for." In this equivocal
epigram the late Jean Cocteau expressed both the persistent belief that works
of art can and therefore must do more than merely stimulate emotional and
intellectual experiences, and the uneasiness that sometimes accompanies the
proclamation of this belief. The thesis that art is or should be deeply involved
in promoting the religious, political, ethical, and intellectual goals of the
society in which it thrives is as ancient as the roots of aesthetics and as
deeply ingrained as our notorious tendency to equate the beautiful with the
good, the true, and the desirable. Yet, as might be expected, the specific
views about the nature of this "more" in art are about as many and as different as are the individual theorists, whether philosophers, artists, or critics,
who suggest them. Whoever has browsed through textbooks of aesthetics
is likely to remember the many, mutually inconsistent postulates about the
direct or ultimate functions of art, most of which have been subjected in the
course of centuries to elaborate interpretations and ideological adaptations.
Functions often attributed to art include revelation of immanent truth, concretization of the metaphysical "beyond," presentation of naked reality,
creation of a blissful fantasy world, confrontation with the gaping abysses
within the individual, revival of lost time and repressed childhood, promotion of self-knowledge, delineation of ethical norms and religious modes of
acting, presentation of values, enunciation of social rules, revelation of
eternal laws of beauty and of other basic principles ranging from the inevitable cycle of death and resurrection or the unreality of the here and now
to the eternal strife between good and evil and the eventual triumph of
good . . . or evil. No less familiar sound the following proclamations: art
should rouse patriotism, and enthusiasm for internationalism; it should
stimulate faithful family life and the courage for free love; it should make
people long for individualism and for collectivism; it should make them
strive for the equality of men, and for the privileges of an elite; it should
spur them to fight the establishment and to struggle for the reinstatement
of old mores; and it should ingrain and strengthen the desires for personal
happiness and for unlimited altruism, for fame and for humility, for bravery
in struggling against destiny and in acquiescence in what fate brings.

Even this small selection of proclamations on the functions of art, when condensed into slogans presented successively, sounds like satire. Yet the slogans stand for elaborated and logically consistent theories, reflecting ethical values and rooted in ideologically significant movements. Indeed, each of the theories has inspired artists, aroused expectations in audiences, provided guidelines for art criticism, and served as a focus for heated controversies, which in turn have led to its refutation, abandonment, and possible revival in a similar or different guise. The astonishing diversity and glaring incompatibility of these theories may have played a role in promoting the movement of Art for Art's Sake (Beardsley, 1966, pp. 284–90), which turned against the "more" in art in whatever form it was stated. The initiators and supporters of this doctrine, who included such illustrious men as Théophile Gautier, Flaubert, Walter Pater, Oscar Wilde, and Baudelaire, raised their voices against any approach to art which attributes to it goals beyond pure aesthetic enjoyment. Through the stress it placed on experiencing art as an end in itself, the movement of Art for Art's Sake initiated and influenced important developments in the art of the nineteenth and twentieth centuries. On the one hand, it made artists and audiences more aware of the power inherent in artistic means and thus paved the way for objective realism as well as for paintings and statues without explicit object references; on the other hand, it led to renewed attempts to solve the riddle of beauty through concentration on sensation and experiencing. However, none of the proponents of the doctrine succeeded in proving convincingly that his postulates of objective depiction of reality or cultivation of emotion and unhampered sensualism are more akin to art than are traditional requirements, such as revelation of immanent truth or promotion of social justice. Moreover, since many representatives of the movement tended to justify their demand for the autonomy of art by stressing that the free artist gives to society something of greater value than society requires him to give, the movement succeeded in replacing one "more" of art by another, but not in eliminating altogether the claims for "more" in art. In a certain sense, this failure reflects an immanent justice. Had the audience not been educated to believe that art consumption is not merely pleasant but also elevating or at least status-enhancing, the proponents of Art for Art's Sake could hardly hope to sell their productions and propagate their ideas.

A scientifically harmful heritage left behind by the doctrine of Art for Art's Sake is the still widespread conviction that art aspects and non-art aspects can or even should be distinguished in any work of art and in the experience it evokes. Accordingly, the features in the work of art which are designed to persuade the audience to accept a certain philosophical or political idea or to adopt a specific ethical attitude and mode of behavior are often classified as non-art, even when the social desirability of the advocated ideas, attitudes, and behaviors is not disputed. This standpoint is sometimes further supported by the argument that from the viewpoint of art there could hardly be a difference between persuading people to fight against social injustice and inducing them to buy a certain detergent. Similarly, the expectations of art spectators of gaining new information and new insights, of being elevated, purified, even cured through an art experience are often regarded as elements extrinsic to art itself. The major implication of this view is that just as the audience should ignore non-art aspects by assuming the attitude which Coleridge called "a willing suspension of disbelief," the investigator of art should concentrate on the nature and effects of stimuli which belong to art proper and leave the study and practical exploitation of the other aspects to educators, psychotherapists, and propagandists. Thus, the distinction between art aspects and non-art aspects of art may have been one of the factors responsible for the paucity of research about the "more" in art.

However, neither this distinction nor its implications are justified. There is no reason to assume or to conclude that responses to ideas, values, information, and meanings communicated through a work of art are in any way less "artistic" or less relevant to the experience of art than responses to colors, tones, movements, melodies of sentences, and the reflectance of sculptural surfaces. Responses to both types of stimuli are dependent on cognitive processes, and contribute jointly to the overall experience. Further, since so many works of art suggest this elusive "more" of art, and since artists keep referring to it while audiences have never stopped expecting it, the "more" of art must be assumed to fulfill some basic psychological function.

What kind of psychological function could be fulfilled by such a variety of ideological postulates and value-toned pronouncements as we have collated above? To what psychological need does the "more" of art appeal? An indirect answer to these questions is offered by psychoanalysis. Since, according to this theory, the art experience is assumed to provide satisfaction to primitive, mostly repressed, sexual and aggressive impulses, it could be argued that sublimation, symbolization, and other devices used by artists for the concealment of the "true" contents may not suffice to appease the superego and dissipate the spectators' guilt feelings. Hence, further apparent goals have to be appended to the work of art in order to mislead society and its internal representative—the superego. The subservience of art to accepted moral, religious, or political goals is ideally suited to fulfill this role.

The diversity of the attributed ends and the frequent contradictions between them are merely indices which reveal the true intent of these appendages, i.e., to serve in the best case as rationalization, and in the worst as thinly disguised pretext.

This hypothesis is far from plausible. Without delving into the serious and many-sided criticism leveled against the psychoanalytic theory, it may suffice to mention three major points concerning the hypothesis of rationalization. (i) There is little or nothing in psychology, anthropology, or sociology to support the idea that the main purpose of a cognitive effort carried on through many generations and in varied civilizations is none other than to disguise the already distorted presentation of some tabooed sexual and aggressive wishes and of their illusory fulfillment. (ii) The hypothesis does not specify limiting conditions and thus does not admit of a decision as to which cognitive elements in art are not mere rationalizations. (iii) Finally, the hypothesis is directly contradicted by the observation that relatively uninhibited social groups, such as the hippies, who openly strive for and indulge in tabooed wish fulfillments, also look for the socially relevant and intellectually stimulating aspects of art and apparently enjoy them. To be sure, society is almost as wasteful as nature, but not so wasteful as to devote persistent intellectual efforts through the centuries merely to justifying the relatively harmless activity that art is.

A better-founded and more satisfactory approach to the problem is provided by the theory of cognitive orientation (Kreitler & Kreitler, 1965, 1967, 1969, 1970a, 1970b, 1971b, 1971c, 1972a, 1972b). The theory says that meanings and complex structures of beliefs—i.e., cognitive orientation—determine, shape, and direct behavior. Even rather simple reactions, such as the orienting reflex and conditioned responses, are determined by a rudimentary form of cognitive orientation, i.e., by denotative meanings or labels attributed to the stimulus object specifically and to the whole stimulus situation in general. Examples of such simple denotative meanings which allow clear-cut responses are "Red light denotes: Stop!" or "An alarm means: Run for shelter." Yet in cases when no denotative meaning can be established or when the invoked meanings do not readily admit of an appropriate course of action, more complex forms of cognitive elaboration are required. In order to gain more knowledge the connotative meaning of the stimulus is established by checking the representation of the stimulus against the complex structures of beliefs in the extensive network of cognitive orientation. Even decisions about relatively common behaviors—say, whether to eat a piece of cake now—are determined by a vast array of implicit and explicit knowledge—about how many calories there are in cake, about the impact of

calories, about our past experience with cakes of this kind, about our incompatible goals to eat as much as possible and to remain as slim as fashion
requires, and about the various kinds of should and should-not that affect
eating between meals, etc. Since all this "knowledge" is highly subjective
and often false, unverified, or illogical, we prefer to call these various items
"beliefs" rather than informations.

Empirical studies show that at least four kinds of beliefs are necessary
for the understanding and prediction of molar behaviors. These are *general
beliefs*, which include beliefs about the world and anything in it, ranging
from people and objects to various interrelations and causal effects; *beliefs
about the self* which include beliefs referring to one's more constant or more
temporary traits, feelings, abilities, past events and present engagements,
etc.; *beliefs about one's wishes and goals* for the future, the long-term and
short-term ones, regardless of whether their attainment is planned, plausible, possible or not; and finally, *beliefs about rules and norms*, which reflect
the various shoulds and should-nots with regard to any act of behavior,
irrespective of whether they are widely accepted, socially enforced, or personally conceived. Interaction among these four types of beliefs, which are
evoked with regard to the relevant stimulus, produces a clustering of beliefs
that in turn gives rise to a behavioral intention. This intention, however,
has to be implemented through an appropriate plan of action before behavior
can be elicited. The retrieval of such a plan and its adjustment to the immediate situational requirements are determined both by the behavioral
intention and by the availability of plans and possible behavior alternatives.

Almost all the denotative meanings and labels involved in the evocation
of simple reactions, and all the beliefs involved in the determination of molar
behavior are acquired through any of the available forms of learning, including behavioral experience. But in spite of the fact that learning and
behavioral experience are the main contributors to the formation and extension of cognitive orientation, they themselves are influenced by the already
established cognitive orientation. Cognitive orientation, however, not only
precedes behavior, serves behavior, and is served by behavior; to a certain
extent it also transcends the immediate needs of behavior and is pursued
independently of it. Empirical findings leave little doubt that humans and
higher animals learn much more than is immediately useful or might be
needed in a foreseeable future. This does not mean that the recurrently
confirmed utility of acquiring orientation and the rewards attendant upon
its expansion do not play a role in strengthening the tendency to establish
and enrich cognitive orientation. But it does imply that the tendency itself
is primary and functions also autonomously from immediate requirements

and obvious utilities. Like the sexual impulse, which subserves the survival of the species, the cognitive feedback from exploration and learning subserves the survival of the individual. Yet just as sexuality is pursued also or even predominantly for the sake of the intrinsic pleasures it affords, cognitive orientation is being constantly elaborated, expanded, and renewed regardless of its possible short-term or long-term utility. Even in the face of death human beings do not completely give up their striving to comprehend and remember (Kreitler & Kreitler, 1970a).

There are thus two viewpoints from which the tendency toward orientation may be considered. The first viewpoint emphasizes the tension-reducing effects of establishing orientation when novel stimuli are encountered, uncertainty is experienced, or disorientation poses a threat. The second viewpoint stresses the autonomy of the tendency for orientation from present needs and the perusal of cognitive orientation independently of its value in the service of directing behavior.

It is mainly this second viewpoint which gives rise to implications relevant for the questions raised in this chapter. The diverse claims and suggestions about the spiritual, intellectual, social, ethical, and political functions of art, which we have summarily called the "more" in art, seem to be merely different aspects of the basic expectation that art should make a *direct* contribution to the expansion of cognitive orientation. While all experiences, including that of art, involve orientative feedbacks that may eventuate in new beliefs or changes in old ones, the artist is expected to create conditions designed to influence orientation in a direct and explicit manner. These conditions include confrontation of the audience with a well-defined set of new beliefs, presented in an intellectually persuasive manner and supported by a corresponding emotional impact. Brecht (1967), for instance, regarded the emotional impact as of secondary importance and tried to reduce it in order to intensify the intellectual confrontation of the spectators with the left-wing ideas presented in his "didactic" or "epic" theater. Although Brecht has undoubtedly remained an exception, many if not most artists would subscribe to the view that the mission of art is to attain lasting changes in the spectators' values and ideas. They would obviously differ in their views about the nature of the desired changes and about the means most adequate for their attainment. Yet even the most avant-garde among them would hardly reject the spectators' implicit demand to get instructed, to be provided with insights, or to learn and see something new through art.

A necessary condition for expanding cognitive orientation is confrontation with new ideas. Admittedly, such a confrontation may not always be a pleasant experience. The contradiction between the new ideas and one's cherished opinions may evoke a conflict, which—as many spectators have learned—is not likely to be resolved in the course of the art experience. The tension-laden nature of such conflicts is stressed particularly by the theory of cognitive dissonance, which assumes maintenance of cognitive consistency to be a motive of prime importance (Brehm & Cohen, 1962). This theory leads to the prediction that people will go to any lengths to avoid exposure to information and opinions which are at variance with their own views and attitudes. Thus, the evident eagerness with which people seek in art the challenge of ideas dissonant with their own habitual modes of thinking poses a problem for the supporters of this theory. They can solve this problem by recourse to two assumptions. They can either assume that art does not as a rule challenge accepted views, or they can suggest that spectators expose themselves to art mainly in order to apply and thus strengthen their various defense mechanisms while sticking to their time-proven ideas (McGuire, 1968, p. 799). Both explanations are implausible. So also is the underlying idea that people shun at all costs dissonant information. Even intuitively it seems unlikely that the human race could have succeeded in surviving and even make some progress if the preference for familiar information had been the rule in cognitive functioning. Fortunately, the overwhelming majory of empirical studies refutes the hypothesis of selective exposure to information and opinions (Abelson, Aronson, et al., 1968, pp. 769–800; Freedman & Sears, 1965; Kreitler & Kreitler, 1968b).

The domain of art, however, provides a lot of observational evidence that people care at least as much, if not more, for ideas dissonant with their own as for opinions and informations supporting their previous views. In pre-Hitler Germany it was the bourgeoisie that filled the theaters where the anti-bourgeois plays of Brecht and Toller were performed. Dada and the Dada-inspired Pop art, which have tried to shatter so many conventional values and beliefs about life and art, find their audience in those circles that ardently support the establishment and its values (H. Kreitler, 1957). Similarly, the anti-hippies are no less enthusiastic consumers of hippy art than the hippies themselves.

To our mind, the major motive underlying the tendency toward voluntary exposure to dissonant views and information in art and elsewhere is the motive to expand, elaborate, and deepen cognitive orientation and to test its range and various implications. It is not that people merely crave for the novelty, variety, and complexity of such information, as some investigators have claimed (Berlyne, 1965a, 1967; Maddi, 1968). Rather, novelty, variety, and optimal complexity seem to subserve the motive of expanding cognitive orientation by stimulating orientative tendencies. Possibly, the major relevant characteristic of dissonant ideas may not be dissonance as such but novelty. This assumption could explain both the great variety of theories and suggestions about the "more" in art as well as the frequent changes which occur in the popularity of these theories. The nineteenth century witnessed not only the controversies over Art for Art's Sake but also an enthusiasm for realism and an uncompromising scientific objectivism in art, the cult of ugliness, and the devotion of artists to the social improvement of people's lives. Whenever any of the theories gains salience for a time and becomes widely accepted, the works of art shaped exclusively along the lines suggested by this theory seem to lose much of their attractiveness. Habituation to a certain set of ideas evokes the craving for works of art presenting other ideas and providing another sort of information, sometimes even at the risk of personal danger which exposure to new ideas may entail in dictatorships with totalitarian ideologies.

These conclusions should not be taken to imply that the tendency to expand and elaborate cognitive orientation is the single motive on the cognitive level or that people will always prefer novelty, variety, and dissonance over familiar information supportive of their ideas. The dependence of responsiveness to novelty on personality factors and situational circumstance (Berlyne, 1967; McGuire, 1966; Maddi, 1968), and the difficulties attendant upon changing people's attitudes in experiments and natural settings (Hovland, 1959), clearly demonstrate the operation of other, even opposing tendencies on the cognitive level. Yet the context of art seems to provide particularly favorable conditions for the evocation and satisfaction of the motive to expand and elaborate cognitive orientation. In works of art the stimulating aspect of novelty is usually brought to the fore while the prominence of the shocking aspect is greatly reduced or canceled. This is accomplished by intermingling novel stimuli with familiar ones, by resolving unexpected developments, by embedding surprising events within logical sequences, etc. The expectation which spectators have that they will be confronted with some measure of novelty within the framework of art further increases their receptivity to the unfamiliar and unusual.

While novelty mainly stimulates the tendency toward orientation, the content and form of the work of art provide the material for the elaboration of cognitive orientation itself. This elaboration is greatly promoted through "aesthetic distance" and the particular set it involves. Aesthetic distance exempts the spectator of art from the requirement to act upon the insights he gains, to be committed in any way, or even to take a clear-cut stand with regard to the cognitive contents presented. He is thus free from the explicit or implicit necessity to choose between incompatible alternatives, to disregard the rejected alternatives for the sake of smooth action, to match his attitudes with his behavior, or to appear particularly logical and consistent. These freedoms enable the spectator to consider the various new ideas in a work of art and to check their implications at leisure, first in a playful manner and later as possible elements in his steady cognitive orientation.

In view of the conclusion that art contributes to the expansion of cognitive orientation, our major question is this: Which aspects of the art stimuli or what characteristics of form and narrative-representational contents may fulfill the function of enabling us to elaborate a cognitive orientation? In an attempt to answer this question it is important to emphasize that the four described components of cognitive orientation reflect four types of internal and external realities. When conceived in this manner, the resemblance between these four types of reality and the realities presented through art becomes evident. Thus, the major constituents of cognitive orientation— beliefs about the world, about one's own person, about rules and norms, and about goals and wishes—provide major avenues of approach to four main aspects of reality depicted in art and often discussed by aestheticians and artists. These are common reality, archeological reality, normative reality, and prophetic reality.

The use of the term "reality" in this context may raise the familiar question about the relation between the reality of life and the reality of art representation. Since Aristotle developed the thesis of art as imitation of life, the delineation of the differences and similarities between art and life has become a steady theme of Western aesthetic theory. This problem is however of less importance for psychology than for philosophy, which is concerned with the ontological status of the reality depicted through art and with the epistemological value of art communications in general. The questions of more imminent concern to psychology are, first, whether the spectators of art distinguish as a rule between the reality of life and reality in art, and second, whether these two kinds of reality are experienced differently.

Concerning the first question, there is little doubt that normal adults under normal conditions have no difficulty distinguishing between actual and imaginary realities, that is, between an actual conversation and a conversation in one of their daydreams, or between percepts they have in the course of driving and the images evoked while reading about the percepts of a driving person. Yet in spite of the fact that people can identify the two realities as different, there seems to be no crucial qualitative difference between experiencing percepts due to external stimulation and experiencing images evoked by internal stimuli, including cognitive events (Hebb, 1968). Stimuli representations of the two types may be equally vivid and impressive, though they can be distinguished by knowing their source. Consequently, we may enjoy a sexual act in a dream as we enjoy it in life; the happiness attendant upon a daydream may well compete with the happiness aroused by a real event; and the peculiar colloquial expressions of a character in a Damon Runyon story may be remembered even more accurately and vividly than an actual conversation with a hustler in New York. Nevertheless, we are not tempted in the morning to pay the debts we made in last night's dream, nor do we call the police to arrest the escaping Goldfinger. On the other hand, Charlie Chaplin's Monsieur Verdoux may teach us more about real and symbolic killing of women than the confessions of a person who has actually committed seven acts of murder. Similarly, a cubist painting or a walk through a sculptural "environment" may make us comprehend in a flash more about the nature of space than many years of moving around in the actual space of everyday life. The processes underlying learning through art sometimes differ from those operative in many situations of so-called formal learning. But in both cases the products may be viewed as fruitful contributions to cognitive orientation.

In an attempt to define by means of cognitive indices the kind of reality that is presented through art, the philosopher Walsh suggests that art mirrors neither objective reality nor the artist's subjective perceptions, but represents "the delineation of the possible" (Walsh, 1968, p. 288). In the light of her distinction between the actually possible, which relates to a causally determined existential context, and the ideally possible, which relates to a logically determined conceptual context, she concludes that art deals with ideal possibilities. So do mathematics and science. But while mathematics deals with the formally possible, and science with the hypothetically possible, art presents the alternative to the actual (Walsh, 1968, p. 289). This suggestion, which has been raised before by Dewey (1958, p. 346), reflects many and varied conceptions about the nature of art, all of which derive from one basic insight. This insight is that art confronts us with self-contained kinds of reality which are autonomous with regard to so-called actual reality and yet are related to it as different conceptualizations of its nature, or as different reflections of its various aspects. However, the suggestion that art reality is an alternative reality is useful only if the term "alternative" is conceived as expressing both the compelling actuality of art reality and the implied knowledge that its ontological status is that of an "as if" reality. Accordingly, art reality is an "alternative" mainly in the sense that it is distinguishable from other experienced realities, and confrontation with it may be initiated or stopped at will. But the experiencing of art reality is as actual as experiencing in real-life situations. The events depicted in art, at least in great works of art, are grasped and conceived as real and as necessary, and not as merely possible. When, owing to a too great aesthetic distance or because of shortcomings in idea and presentation, the content is experienced as merely possible, the work of art loses much of its power to induce empathy and turns at best into an entertaining intellectual game, and at worst into a boring speculation in words, tones, or colored forms. Since the events and situations in an art narrative are usually more logical than occurrences in life, and since even the most absurd scene in the Theater of the Absurd is, as a rule, far less absurd than our subconscious impulses or the proclamations and acts of politicians in hot and cold wars, there is no difficulty in conceiving and experiencing art reality as if it were actually real. Yet, since art reality is not meant to replace any other reality, and certainly not that of life, it is no alternative for but an addition to non-art reality. It is the integration of the actual and the "as if" which endows art reality with both its unique fascination and the capacity to impart insights that are meaningful for orientation in the non-art reality.

The Common Reality

In life as in art, common reality is far less common than common sense tends to assume. Its commonness, in the sense of "ordinary" as well as in the sense of "being shared," is more conventional than real and is due to communality of labels rather than to similarity in percepts and concepts. When two people see the same car, both may identify it as a Volkswagen with the plate number NHY-965. But one may observe its comfortable size while the other may note its small rear window; one may remember it by its leaf-green color, and the other by a bump on its left door. Of course, when they talk about it, the similarity in their perceptions concerning the model of the car and its plate number will be more prominent than the differences in their observations, which they will conveniently ignore. Yet the similarity reflects common semantics more than common images. Differences in angles and conditions of observation appear as the most obvious reason for these divergencies among different people concerning identically labeled percepts. Such differences undoubtedly determine the amount of identical perceptual information which is available to the observers. Yet even under controlled laboratory conditions, or sometimes in a natural setting when people perceive the same object under the same conditions of observation, their percepts remain far from identical. The reason for this is that perception is a highly selective process of categorization, guided by attention, and narrowed down through physiological "gating" and perceptual defense (Bruner, 1957; Neisser, 1967). Coding into categories, attention, and defense are greatly influenced by the scope of personal meanings, past experiences, wishes, goals, and fears, to mention just a few of the factors. Hence, what a person sees depends on what he expects and wants to see, on what he considers important, on his preferred modes of interpretation, and on his presence at or absence from a certain place in a specific moment of time.

Nevertheless, neither the special gift of certain individuals of always being present where the action is, nor the ability of some people to observe what others usually overlook or to grasp the ordinary in a unique manner, obviates the use of the concept "common reality" or renders it meaningless. Thanks to common conditions in human development and milieu of existence and to unifying factors such as common language and culture, there is a sufficiently large and sharply outlined core of shared meanings to justify the concept of "common reality." If we strip it down to its essentials and disregard epistemological and ontological considerations, common reality emerges as the sum total of the many widely shared features in people's observations. Alternatively, common reality could be defined as the set of objects or events which would be perceived in largely the same manner by anyone who is at the right place at the right time in the proper set of mind and who knows what to look at. It is mainly in this latter sense that common reality has served as a facet of art contents.

Common reality is a theme which runs through most of Western art. Obvious examples include the detailed battle reports in the Iliad, the super-realistic scenes in German naturalistic plays or in modern war novels, classical sculptures of great generals on horses, and Dada or Pop Art productions which present real objects embedded in an art framework. The depiction of common reality and its various aspects is a favored theme in representational art and is particularly stressed in realistic and naturalistic productions. But it is implied also in fantastic art and could be detected even in cubist paintings and in works of art without explicit object references. Although a complex set of art conventions and techniques underlies the representation of common reality in art (Gombrich, 1969), art spectators easily identify it as such and have come to expect it as a matter of course. From a psychological viewpoint, however, the major question is this: What is the reason for depicting in art that which anyone could see and experience for himself if he looked around at common reality?

The various answers to this question highlight the possible contribution of common reality in art to cognitive orientation. One often-mentioned approach to the problem emphasizes the role of art in combatting habituation to the familiar. In daily life we gradually come to regard the objects in our room, the houses in our street, and the small talk of our friends as a kind of neutral background devoid of any stimulating power. In the words of an artist (Shklovskij, quoted by Ehrlich, 1965, pp. 150–51): "We look at each other, but we do not see each other any more. Our perception of the world has withered away; what has remained is mere recognition." The isolation of ordinary and familiar objects or scenes from their habitual context in everyday life, and their presentation within the context of art which induces aesthetic distance, compel us to take the famous "new look" at the habitual and to note those "aspects of things that are . . . hidden because of their simplicity and familiarity" (Wittgenstein, 1953, §129). Consequently, the beauty and puritan strength of the squares in a Mondrian painting could lead us to rediscover the often overlooked square element in our customary surroundings, while reading in a novel about our social habits may make us realize that they imply some unwarranted assumption about interpersonal relations. By reducing habituation to the familiar, confrontation with common reality in the context of art reactivates our awareness with regard to habitual settings and thus re-infuses these settings with a new stimulatory impact.

The familiar object can hardly be expected to become an appealing theme in art merely through being presented in isolation from the habitual context. More is needed if its hidden potentialities are to be revealed. Since common reality depends largely on the constancy of objects and on their conventional labeling, there remain wide enough margins for the relatively uncommon within the boundaries of the common. The artist may present the ordinary object from an unusual angle of observation; he may emphasize its overlooked aspects and interrelations or suggest unexpected interpretations of common objects and events. These and similar devices which reflect the degrees of freedom allowed for by common reality make it possible to represent common reality in a manner which de-familiarizes the familiar without distorting it. Thus, a common story may be used in an uncommon way as a plot for a novel and nevertheless appear as a part of common reality. The reader may still know that it could happen to him, may feel as if it did, and may wonder that it did not. Such a blending of the familiar with the unfamiliar is particularly well suited to evoking orientative tendencies. The thoroughly familiar leads to boredom, while the highly unfamiliar may give rise to fear and withdrawal (see Chapter 1, notes 12 and 14). But when the unfamiliar is integrated within a familiar pattern of stimulation, when the new is made to appear as an aspect of the known, boredom and fear are replaced by interest, curiosity, and active exploration.

The depiction of common reality may also provide new information and thus contribute directly to cognitive orientation. Although common reality is by definition accessible to everybody, many of its aspects and experiential possibilities remain unknown to people who lack the means and miss the opportunities to explore it. Art can bridge this gap between possibility and accessibility by presenting common reality in a manner which does not necessarily emphasize its novel aspects, but renders it familiar or even likable. Gauguin's paintings of the scenes in the South Seas, Forster's *Passage to India*, as well as many pronouncedly naturalistic novels and dramas, illustrate how art experience is intensified through imparting information about parts of a common reality remote in space or time.

The fact that information may be communicated through art does not imply that this is the major function of art or that information is not communicated through other channels. Thus, the attempts of some aestheticians to prove that art content has no epistemological value (Richards, 1926) are as little justified as the alternative attempts of others to reduce art content to one factor, such as symbolization of human feelings (Langer, 1953) or communication of the import in human existence (Weiss, 1961). It could hardly be contested that scientific discourse is a more adequate, specialized, and economic means for imparting knowledge than art. But the use of this argument as a proof against the validity and utility of communicating information through art is as absurd as the claim that the greater clarity and distinctness of colors in a color atlas render doubtful and inappropriate the use of colors in painting. Moreover, there are several arguments in favor of communicating knowledge about common reality through art. For instance, since the "emotive force of the vehicle by which the message is conveyed" (A. Kaplan, 1954, p. 459) is greater in art than in science, the communicated information turns through empathy into "intimate" and "participatory" knowledge (Morgan, 1967). The very evocation of curiosity and its satisfaction are attended by pleasure, and the acquisition of information per se is experienced as a reward. By raising questions and by providing knowledge, even of the type which could be got from non-art sources, art disposes of an important means to evoke the spectator's interest and responsiveness.

Regardless of whether the common reality depicted is de-familiarized or even largely unknown to the spectators, it is endowed with an overall plausibility. This impression and the related tendency to regard the familiar as a better gestalt than the hitherto unknown are due to the fact that elements of common reality lend themselves to easy coding and labeling. They are quickly perceived and conceptualized. The persuasiveness of the common may fulfill in art the role of bridging the gap between common sense and visionary imagination. Long before surrealists like Dali and Kafka rendered hallucinatory fantasies plausible by framing them with a great many details of common and even trivial reality, the Greeks drew their gods and mythical heroes nearer to the human sphere by attributing to them habits and behavior characteristic of the most ordinary mortals. Similarly, the biblical report of Moses' doubts of the power of God to produce water from a rock strengthens the plausibility of the claim that Moses talked face to face with God. To cite another example, realistic details in medieval icon paintings compensate for the clumsy distortions of space in these pictures.

The presentation of the uncommon seems to be hardly possible without the framework and anchorage provided through the depiction or at least suggestion of common reality. In the words of Joyce Cary (1967, p. 247), the ghost, i.e., the products of creative imagination, needs the machine "which is at once its material form, its servant, its limitation, its perfection, and its traitor." Yet the alliance of the uncommon with the common is important not just from the viewpoint of technique, but mainly from the viewpoint of the processes of cognitive orientation. Since orientation consists essentially in relating the hitherto unknown to the known, the presentation of common reality in art enables art both to communicate orientatively new messages and to suggest the ways adequate for their integration into cognitive orientation.

The Archeological Reality

Below or beyond common reality there is a reality which eludes straightforward observation and defies rational consensus. It is the reality of the repressed and the forgotten which we often involuntarily avoid while being voluntarily engaged in pursuing it. The methods and strategies devised by Freud and his followers for the exploration of this reality have often been compared to those of archeology. Both the psychoanalyst and the archeologist are engaged in the unearthing of hidden traces, in the reconstruction of events from broken and dispersed fragments, and in extrapolating from meager evidence about missing parts and plausible contexts. But while the archeologist looks for the historical past, the depth psychologist digs his way into the various layers of the unconscious. His findings rarely show the earmarks of common reality. The realm of the unconscious defies the laws of Aristotelian logic which—we often like to assume—govern common reality. On the unconscious level an object may simultaneously be itself and its opposite; events appear as timeless and occur in two or more different places at the very same time; space relations are distorted; ideas and feelings may be personified; there is no negation; and the habitual identity and dis-

tinctness of people are replaced by bizarre interrelations, fusions, fragmentations, and contaminations which result, for instance, in splitting one person
into several figures or combining different people into one character (Freud,
1948e; 1957, pp. 186–89).

Nevertheless, the existential mode of the unconscious constitutes a reality
known to us from night dreams and sometimes from other temporary states
of reduced consciousness. In psychoanalysis it is treated as the inner, primordial reality which is covered up through secondary elaborations and
kept unconscious by powerful defense mechanisms, though it continues to
influence manifest behavior in common reality. On a still deeper level there
may be the more universally shared primordial stratum which the Jungians
call the collective unconscious.

A great many works of art deal with the presentation of what we suggest
calling the "archeological reality" of art. It includes mainly themes and
other manifestations of the unconscious, as well as additional aspects of
inner dynamics which may not be strictly unconscious, yet are rarely noticed
either because they are covered up by other internal representations or because their contents do not fit into the dominant life-style and the general
conception of the world. The depiction of archeological reality in art is
often mentioned as evidence for the special gift that artists have of gaining
direct access to the unconscious and immediate insight into the depths of
psychodynamics without the use of the laborious techniques devised by
depth psychology (Freud, 1956a, p. 27; Jung, 1933, pp. 167–72).

Concerning the spectators of art, the depiction of archeological reality
raises a serious problem. Why is the audience not repelled or frightened
through confrontation with archeological reality? The Freudian theory assumes that repressed contents represent anxiety-laden experiences, feelings,
or ideas which do not conform to the norms incorporated in the superego.
Repression, however, involves not merely expulsion from consciousness but
also avoidance of any information and withdrawal from any situation which
might resemble or evoke memories of the repressed. Hence, as a possible
source of anxiety, archeological reality should be avoided rather than enjoyed. Although Jung adopts a more positive view of the unconscious and
assumes that it might be endowed with fascination, he too concludes that
the themes of the "night world" (Jung, 1933, p. 163) are frightening and
"if ever they become conscious, they are intentionally kept back and con-
cealed," with the help of "the shield of science and the armour of reason"
(ibid., p. 162).

Three hypotheses may be suggested for explaining the attractiveness of
archeological reality to art spectators. The first, rooted in psychoanalysis, is

based on the assumption that repression is a kind of deal that consists in trading forbidden pleasures for the pleasure of being a "good boy." Although this may be a necessary and useful deal, a much better deal would be to remain a "good boy" and still enjoy the forbidden pleasures, without risking social disapproval and internal guilt. The striving for a better deal of this type, sometimes strengthened by a repetition compulsion, occasionally leads to the rather poor deal of a neurosis, characterized by the return of the repressed (Freud, 1922, 1959a, 1964b). Yet in the framework of an art experience the return of the repressed is camouflaged through projections and made morally palatable through the various art devices which promote sublimation (see Chapter 14, Sublimation). Thus, the experiencing of archeological reality in art is not merely free from anxiety and guilt but may actually be pleasurable.

The second hypothesis for explaining the attractiveness of archeological reality is based on the Jungian theory and thus is more speculative and lays greater stress on the cognitive function of unconscious themes. It assumes that archeological contents are terrifying only when they burst into consciousness in their bare, quasi-primordial state. Since in art they appear in a "translated form," elaborated into symbols which fit the conscious values and experiential needs and potentialities of a specific society (Jung, 1928, p. 248), they often appear fascinating and may exert in full measure their beneficial impact. This essentially psychotherapeutic impact consists in restoring relations between consciousness and unconsciousness. Consequently, the sphere of the conscious is expanded and amplified through the addition of new cognitive and experiential domains that are important for the development of the individual and of culture (Jung, 1928, 1933). In this manner Visionary Art, i.e., art which presents archeological reality (Jung, 1933), contributes to "mental self-regulation in the life of nations and epochs" (Jung, 1928, p. 248).

Less presumptuous is the third explanatory hypothesis, which derives from the observation that normal adults have a strong sense of self-identity and personal continuity (G. W. Allport, 1955; Rogers, 1951). This belief is sometimes shaken, even endangered, through sudden confrontation with alien forces operating within oneself. A slip of the tongue, the strange forgetting of a name known to us a minute ago, an unexpected attack of anxiety, a haunting childhood memory, the resurgence of a rejected yet irresistible impulse, or the overpowering sense of the uncanny which can hardly be pinpointed as something concrete produce a vague awareness of disorientation and a resulting weakening of self-identity. The ancient yet still popular slogan, "Know thyself," the superstitious fears of being "possessed" or bewitched, and the modern rush into all forms of psychotherapy bear witness to the persistent attempts of man to gain mastery through knowledge over the abysmal forces within him and to reassert his individuality in face of internal powers threatening his sense of self-identity. Art provides one of the most appealing media for attaining these strongly desired yet vaguely conceived goals.

Specific themes of archeological reality can be adequately described in ordinary and scientific language. But because they are orderly, compartmentalized, and sequential, these means fail to evoke the authentic atmosphere of the unconscious realm. Habitual modes of thinking and speaking are so different from unconscious processes that they may be partly responsible for the frequent forgetting of night dreams and early childhood experiences. In contrast, art disposes of means ideally suited for the reproduction and evocation of archeological reality. These means allow the simultaneous presentation of opposites without suggesting a logical compromise, the expression of polyvalent ambiguities, or the depiction of a-logical and a-causal sequences of events, bizarre time and space relations, multileveled condensations or fragmentations, etc. Symbols and metaphors are some of the better known means for reflecting unconscious material. Multileveled structuring, images, and the interweaving of different themes are examples of the less known, yet not less adequate means. Notably, it has often been claimed that many of these means are designed to disguise unconscious material so as to smuggle it through the strict censorship of the superego (Lesser, 1962). It may, however, be one of the paradoxical features of the unconscious that it is best expressed precisely through means which simultaneously also disguise it enough to elude the superego.

Archeological reality is such a common theme in art that many spectators have come to expect it as a matter of course. There is hardly a reader of theater reviews in the daily newspapers of the Western world who has failed to learn that not only Sophocles' *Oedipus Rex* but also *Hamlet* and Schiller's *Don Carlos* depict the oedipal situation. Similarly, in view of the repeated assertions about the goals of surrealism, it has almost become difficult to regard surrealist paintings and sculptures as reflecting something else than unconscious material. It may not be accidental that archeological reality is so prominent and so easily noticeable in the various branches of literature and in the visual arts. The narrative structure of literature is well suited to reflecting unconscious material. Some of the major devices are presenting plots which defy temporal and causal relations, as dreams do; describing directly inner processes, thoughts, and feelings in line with the principles of free association, as in Joyce's *Ulysses*; juxtaposing the depiction of manifest behavior and underlying dynamics, as is frequently done in drama; or using condensation and fragmentation as structural principles in the elaboration of the literary figures, so that different forces within the personality of one individual are presented as distinct people. Famous examples for the last-mentioned procedure are the triad of Dorian Gray, Lord Henry, and the painter Basil, who may be viewed as complementing aspects of one person; or Mephistopheles and Faust, who together reflect the frequent coexistence in a single individual of cynicism and ruthlessness with excessive idealism.

Painting and sculpture allow for the attainment of different and possibly even closer approximations of the unconscious world than literature. The reason for this is that visual images seem to be the most characteristic expressive medium of the unconscious. Accordingly, manifestations of the unconscious are not restricted merely to surrealism, which has provided us with almost programmatic demonstrations of dreamlike and hallucinatory images, or to Action Painting, which is devoted to reflecting unconscious processes through the semiautomatic, minimally guided manner in which the pictures are produced. A closer view reveals that paintings and sculptures of all traditions and periods present numerous examples of distorted space relations, juxtapositions of internal and external images of objects, bizarre constructions, and symbolic themes which could originate only in the twilight world of fantasy and the depths within us.

Since, however, the visual arts deal also with non-human phenomena, archeological reality in painting and sculpture includes not only manifestations of the unconscious but also presentations of the underlying structure of objects and events. Just as the specifically human archeological reality is explored by depth psychology, so the archeological reality of objects and events is studied by physics and the other natural sciences. Modern trends in the visual arts seem to reflect many of the basic scientific findings about the underlying structure of the physical world. For example, while cubist paintings show us mainly images of objects observed from various angles as well as from within, abstract sculptures often illustrate the hidden structure which makes the manifest form possible, and kinetic art presents concretely the close interrelations between mass and movement, the intimate intertwining of space and time, and the dynamism which underlies the apparent stability of the world of objects.

Film, which has at its disposal both the narrative medium of literature and the imaginal means of the visual arts, and dance, which combines the motional means with visual images, could be expected to attain particularly revealing reflections of the unconscious world. However, archeological reality is represented also in music, which lacks the narrative and the imaginal elements that are usually considered indispensable for reflecting the unconscious. Wagner's operas provide many illustrations of archeological reality expressed through leitmotifs and other purely musical means. A famous example is the beginning of the third scene of the third act in *Die Meistersinger von Nürnberg*. Beckmesser enters the workshop of Hans Sachs, limps silently around, looking here and there while tending his aching body. At the same time the orchestra music conveys very clearly the context and sequence of his thoughts by repeating, combining, and elaborating well-remembered characteristic musical themes from former scenes. A different aspect of archeological reality is represented in the music Stravinsky composed to the archetypal plot of *Le Sacre du Printemps*. This music reveals the depths and scope of orgiastic sexuality that in most individuals in the Western world has been reduced to a mere potentiality, well repressed and hidden in the darkest recesses of the unconscious.

Although there are very few reputed works of art which do not deal with archeological reality, there seem to be even fewer which do not deal also with realities beyond the archeological. Thus, while in some works of art archeological reality assumes a dominant role as the major aspect of existence, in most works of art it appears commingled with other realities, and most closely intertwined with elements of common reality. Indeed, part of the fascination exerted by Kafka's novels, by Pinter's plays, by Moore's sculptures, and by Picasso's paintings may be attributed to this strange blending of the common and the archeological realities which is so characteristic of human existence.

The Normative Reality

Since Plato proclaimed that art is too serious to be left to artists and should instead be submitted to the moral censorship of the state (Beardsley, 1966, p. 50), few aestheticians, critics, and artists have been able to avoid the issue of art's relation to morality (Wimsatt, 1948; Zink, 1950). Most of those who deal with art, including the spectators, seem to share the assumption that art should or does contribute towards the attainment of a better state of affairs. Regardless of whether this better state of affairs is defined in line with the prevalent standards of morality or in opposition to them, the expected contribution of art is conceived as dependent upon the expression and elaboration of norms through the content of a work of art. Normative reality is the aspect of content which is devoted to the direct or indirect presentation of rules that express how the individual and society should behave or be, or how they should not behave or be. Although normative reality always reflects some value judgments, it may or may not correspond to any specific set of moral laws or elaborate conception of the world. More often than not, it expresses ethical norms considered, at least by the artist, to be of general significance for society and the individual and valid beyond the boundaries of a restricted culture.

Normative reality is usually accorded such great importance that its presence or absence and its moral implications are often used even as a criterion for artistic quality. Shakespeare, for instance, was reproved for having described precisely those aspects of common reality which reveal the crude, arrogant, and foolish behavior of the poor in contrast to the generosity and nobility of the lords and sirs (Hauser, 1951, p. 403 ff.). Characteristically, even those who theoretically reject the relation of art to morality seem to find it difficult to appreciate works of art without reference to the normative reality they reflect. T. S. Eliot, for example, clearly stated that artists like Shakespeare or Dante did no thinking nor was it their job to think, and that their expression of "the thoughts current at their time . . . is of no importance" (Eliot, 1953, p. 54). Nevertheless, in another context Eliot emphasized that Wordsworth's greatness is not independent of his opinions on social affairs, his nature philosophy, and his religious sentiments (ibid., p. 173), and that Blake would have been a greater poet if his poems had been controlled by "a respect for impersonal reason, . . . for the objectivity of science . . . and . . . a framework of accepted and traditional ideas" (ibid., p. 171).

There are a number of reasons for the great importance accorded to normative reality in art. One reason is the general preoccupation with norms. A most difficult task facing every child and most adults is to learn and to obey the incredible number of shoulds and should-nots that are accepted as the yardstick for overt and often for covert behavior in all domains of life, work and leisure alike. Societies of every kind, from the Jesuits to typical hippies, and from the army to a scientific community, are more or less consciously preoccupied with safeguarding adherence to certain rules of conduct and thinking, with invalidating or rejecting other rules, and sometimes with the production of new rules. Just as teaching norms and supervising compliance with them are not the exclusive domain of formal education and official systems of reward and punishment, so the production of new norms is not the privilege solely of dictators, parliaments, political parties, sanctioned academies, or registered clubs. As a matter of fact, every individual participates actively in these endeavors, but the results attained do not seem very satisfactory to anyone. As members of society who have traditionally acquired the role of worrying over the fate of humanity, artists seem to have applied themselves assiduously to the problem of norms, either within the existing system or by envisioning and presenting new and "better" systems. In this they have been helped and more often hampered by the widely shared belief in the efficacy of art as a means for instructing the public. Although this belief has never been conclusively proved, it has persisted, possibly because of the desire and hope that art might succeed where other means of instruction have more or less failed.

The social and economic status of the artist in former periods may be another source for the special emphasis on normative reality in art. Long before the artist became free to express his personal biases about ethics, politics, and the social order, he had to express the biases of institutions, kings, and other patrons who were his only employers (Scharfstein, 1970). The alternatives to serving these patrons were at best to remain an unknown amateur and at worst to suffer starvation and excommunication without gaining any posthumous fame. The price that artists had to pay for making a living through art involved supporting the special interests of their employers, which often meant promulgating norms favorable to the masters. A prime example is provided by the music of the early medieval church, whose function, as defined by the Catholic church, was "to transport the believers into a state of abject contrition and utter humility, to crush every trace of individuality and weld them into a submissive collective" (Fischer, 1963, p. 187). Accordingly, the normative reality reflected by this music was "You are a worthless, helpless, sinful creature; identify yourself with the suffering of Christ, and you will be saved" (ibid., pp. 187–88). Since this music expresses the norm of collectivization, there should be small wonder that from the viewpoint of Marxism Fischer regards it as superior to later bourgeois compositions, which are devoted to the expression of personal feelings. It seems, however, that even after the artists became free of their traditional servitude to patrons, they did not completely overthrow their allegiance to normative reality. It is a telling fact that even Gautier, the ardent supporter of Art for Art's Sake, who fought for the total independence of artists, felt it necessary to justify this independence through statements such as the following: "The verses of Homer, the statues of Phidias, the paintings of Raphael, have done more to lift up the soul than all the treatises of the moralists" (cited by Beardsley, 1966, pp. 289–90).

Besides the ideological and educational concern of the artist, and the demands of patrons, institutions, and later the art critics, there may be a further motive for a special emphasis on normative reality in Western art. This motive is rooted in the ambivalent attitude of the Christian world to pleasure. Whatever else art may be, it undoubtedly is pleasurable. Yet for

centuries Christianity has rejected pleasure for the sake of pleasure. Moreover, many works of art depict wish fulfillments, offer possibilities for sublimated gratification of forbidden impulses, and provide insights into
archeological reality. These aspects of art must have appeared particularly
suspect to institutionalized or superego-conditioned censorship. The presentation of normative reality in the very same works of art which on another
level provide pleasure or appeal to tabooed wishes could help to appease
the external and internal representatives of morality. This device would
be particularly effective when the elaborated elements of normative reality
lent themselves readily to integration with the accepted moral standards.
Compromises of this type may often seem too transparent to be effective. But
the same argument could be raised with regard to no less transparent devices
used on the level of individual psychodynamics without detriment to their
efficacy. In commercial art and in the art produced in countries governed
by strict totalitarian regimes allusions to the official normative reality frequently serve to satisfy censorship and are probably also understood as such
by the audience. More often, however, normative reality fulfills a role
similar to that of rationalization on the level of the individual. Accordingly,
the depiction of aggression or sexuality, and even the identification with
characters who perform suspect acts, may pass superego control when presented as necessary for the learning of a moral lesson or as means mediating
the expected catharsis.

The many roots and long history of normative reality in art have contributed to the development of varied and subtle means for its presentation
and communication. The various types of literature and the visual arts
seem to provide the most direct and explicit means for the elaboration of
normative reality. The vivid depiction of good and evil and the penetrating
analysis of character, which Zink (1950) mentions as the major tools for
producing moral effects through art, seem to belong to the less subtle means.
The more subtle and less direct means, which are greatly preferred in the art
products of the twentieth century, usually consist in the presentation of
elements from the common, archeological, and prophetic realities in a manner which suggests to the spectators an underlying should or should-not.
This is clearly the feature common to such different works of art as Chaplin's grotesque parodies of man's struggle with the machine, Picasso's
communication of the horrors of war and fascism in the *Guernica*, Orwell's
prophetic *1984*, and anti-establishment Pop Art productions which show
a pile of canned food, a row of detergent boxes, or a big car that obstructs
most of the background landscape. With a striking clarity, which is more
akin to straightforward admonition than to symbolization, these works of

art express norms that may seem almost too commonplace when presented verbally: "Don't let the machine master the human being; don't kill; beware of totalitarian regimentation and dictatorships; get rid of commercially induced preoccupation with cleanliness, efficient cooking, mechanized vacationing, and the other trash 'pleasures' of this 'repressive society.'"

The presentation of normative reality through music may seem to be more difficult, particularly when the music is not accompanied by words or by expressive dance movements. Because of the abstractness of purely musical means and the nonspecificity of musically induced emotional moods, it is impossible to communicate through music clearly defined cognitive messages. Nevertheless, Bach's emotional *espressivo*, restrained through strictly observed contrapuntal rules, is regarded by many as a normative statement of a Weltanschauung. Similarly, it is to be expected that after listening for several hours to Wagner's *Tristan*, with its chromatically gliding, unresolved seventh and ninth chords, the audience will experience the obvious invitation to spend a lifetime in emotional longings, renewed and intensified through each fulfillment. However, even the revolutionary appeals that have so often been attributed to Beethoven's music hardly attain that degree of specificity and definiteness which could characterize similar messages conveyed through literature or the visual arts. Hence, fascists, communists, and fighting liberals alike could grasp and cite Beethoven's *Eroica* as a revolutionary call to arms for their specific cause. Accordingly, there is more than a grain of truth in Serebrini's famous statement in Thomas Mann's *Zauberberg* that music is politically suspicious.

What is true of music is true to a certain extent also of the other arts. An artist may try to convey very explicitly a certain view of normative reality, yet the spectators may grasp a very different view of the same reality. A pacifist mother urged her son to read Remarque's *All Quiet on the Western Front* in order to inspire him with horror of war. But when he finished reading the novel he remarked enthusiastically: "It's great! Too bad I missed out. When is the next one going to start?"

Because of the multileveledness of works of art and the selectivity of human perception, the same remarks apply to any aspect of art. But they are particularly important with regard to the normative elements in art contents, since there is a tendency to overrate the significance of normative reality in art. This tendency is evident even in modern aesthetic theories shaped along Morris's (1939) famous definition of art as "the language for the communication of values." However, overestimation of the function of normative reality is not restricted to art. It may be detected also in general psychological theories that deal with the impact of norms on the planning and shaping of behavior. The roots of this tendency may lie partly in the overlearned habit of associating compliance and violation of norms with reward and punishment, and partly in the wish to attain closer correspondence between the conduct of life and regulating norms. However, empirical studies (Kreitler & Kreitler, 1970b, 1972a) show that the orientative weight of rules and norms, and thus also their impact on overt behavior, are not greater than the orientative weight of the other cognitive components. Good artists seem to have known this intuitively long before science provided the proof. Thus, they introduced normative reality into art, but have mostly embedded its shoulds and should-nots within the context appropriate for them, i.e., a context which consists of the other realities—the common, the archeological, and the prophetic.

The Prophetic Reality

"Man ultimately seeks to anticipate real events. . . . Always he reaches out to the future through the window of the present" (Kelly, 1955, p. 49). This statement, which was suggested as a postulate rather than as an empirically based conclusion, reflects the change that has recently occurred in psychology with regard to the image of man and the factors determining human behavior. In spite of slowly accumulating evidence that future events are anticipated and exert an impact on present behavior, for a long time psychological research was devoted to elucidating particularly the role of present and past factors on behavior. It was mainly after the revival of cognitive psychology and under the influence of the almost concomitant concern with information theory that a new look was taken at the impact of future events on behavior in the present. Naturally, awareness of this impact does not involve adoption of a teleological view, for the future becomes a potent force codetermining behavior only insofar as it is anticipated and mirrored in the present expectations of humans and even animals.

The first major breakthrough is probably to be attributed to Tolman (1932), who showed that the learning of animals consists in building up cognitive expectations about the interrelations between stimuli and about the probable consequences of various response sequences. These expectations about the environment are gradually integrated into a "cognitive map" which is a major factor in determining behavior. Another major factor according to Tolman is "purpose," i.e., the striving to get or to avoid some expected object or event. Subsequent developments in psychology have led investigators to conclude that expectation is a crucial determinant of human behavior on the most elementary as well as the most complex levels (Sanders, 1966).

Not only learning (Rotter, 1954) but all cognitive activities—perception, memory, and thinking—alike depend largely on previously acquired and presently elaborated expectations (Bruner, 1951). For example, the identification of perceptual phenomena, vigilance, habituation (Mackworth, 1969), etc., are determined by expectations. Moreover, perception itself is a process which consists in setting up expectancies, testing them, and rejecting the disconfirmed ones (Bruner, 1957; Neisser, 1967), so that "it is not possible to separate perceiving from expecting by any line of demarcation" (Gibson, 1966, p. 279).

A no less crucial role is played by expectation in the domain of motivation. Numerous experiments have shown how expectations determine the striving for goals, the level of aspiration (Lewin et al., 1944), the attractiveness of goals, and the amount of effort we invest in trying to attain or to avoid this or that outcome (Atkinson, 1964, chap. 4). Furthermore, it seems likely that positive and negative deviations from expectancies often account also for feelings of pleasure and pain (McClelland et al., 1953). More generally, it appears warranted to conclude that we human beings are continuously engaged in anticipating future events, and that these anticipations, regardless of whether they are valid and realistic or improbable and fantastic, are a major factor in our overall orientation in the world as well as in the orientation which guides specific actions.

Anticipations of the future may range from a hardly noticed perceptual guess to a fully elaborate prophetic vision of a future world. Yet from a psychological viewpoint these different anticipations seem to fulfill a similar orientative function. "Anticipation is not merely carried on for its own sake," writes Kelly (1955, p. 49), "it is carried on so that future reality may be better represented." It seems that the clearer our representation of the future, the more oriented and secure we feel in the world of the present which is continuously replaced by the world of the future. Orientation with regard to the future reduces anxiety, first, because it turns the wholly unknown into something partly known, and second, because it makes planning possible and so furnishes some measure of control over the future. Most people seem to be endowed with imagination, abstraction, and the other basic abilities necessary for the formation of expectations. Moreover, the majority of the many predictions one makes in the course of a normal day do come true. We turn on the electric switch expecting light, and it appears. We press the brakes in our car, and the car—fortunately—slows down. We expect our neighbors to respond to our friendly "Hi," and they do. Life experience, general and specific learning, and the training most of us have in drawing logical conclusions help us to figure out the probable course of some future events.

Nevertheless, since anxiety with regard to the future remains so intense and widespread, our representation of the future may be assumed to be insufficient and incomplete. In particular, it lacks vividness and does not extend far enough into the more distant future. Since one cannot plan in view of unconnected, abstract generalities about the future, the image of the future, for which many of us seem to long, needs to be more concrete, scenelike, and dynamic. It should enable us not simply to know which things will occur, but actually to see, to hear, to smell, and to feel them. Moreover, the desired image of the future should be sufficiently similar to the known to remain comprehensible, and sufficiently novel and intriguing to be credible and plausible as a representation of the future.

It seems to be one of the major functions of art to provide us with concrete and vivid images of the future which may bridge the gap between the now and the later. These images form the aspect of art that we call "prophetic reality." It is only natural to expect that prophetic reality should appear in art under an almost explicit label, such as "This is the future!" A label of this kind is indeed often attached to works of art which clearly deal with the future. Plato's *Republic*, Bacon's *New Atlantis*, Thomas More's *Utopia*, Werfel's *Stern der Ungeborenen*, Orwell's *1984*, and innumerable science-fiction stories are all-too obvious examples of this type of art. Yet, just as archeological reality is not restricted to works of art devoted programmatically to revealing and expressing the unconscious, prophetic reality is not restricted to utopias and science fiction. More often than not, prophetic reality in art is formally hardly distinguishable from the variety of common realities and sometimes even archeological realities, with which it is intimately interwoven.

This form of presentation should indeed be expected, since the future is in large part an outgrowth of the present and the past. Even if one does not assume strict determinism, it is difficult both logically and psychologically to disregard the dependence of future developments on forces which already exist in some detectable form in the present. Human wishes and fears represent one form in which these forces are manifested, or at least reflected, in the psychological sphere. The detailed depiction of wished and feared events is often used in art for the reduction or induction of tension. But it may also be used to increase the spectators' awareness of what their wishes and fears actually imply. Confrontation with situations vividly reflecting our wishes and fears is not only a potent means for coming to grips with future-in-the-making; it also puts us in a far better position to decide what we really desire or want to avoid, and may give rise to the feeling that we have some measure of control over future developments. Moreover, since "it has always been one of the most important functions of art to create a demand for the complete satisfaction of which the hour has not yet struck" (Benjamin, quoted by Fischer, 1963, p. 205), confrontation with possible desirable and terrifying situations may help to shape a more precise, elaborate, and complex image of the future than that allowed for within the boundaries of individual wishes and fears.

The presentation of wished and feared events is so very common that at least in literature, painting, and sculpture there is hardly a work of art in which this theme cannot be detected. Of the innumerable available examples it might suffice to mention the literary theme of Dr. Faustus, as elaborated by Marlowe, Goethe, and Thomas Mann, which presents in a highly concentrated form a wide range of fulfilled wishes; the frequent depiction of abduction and rape in the visual arts; and the musical motif of celestial transfiguration which is elaborated in a great many compositions, from the last part of Bach's *St. Matthew Passion*, through Mozart's *Requiem* and Strauss's *Tod und Verklärung*, to the last song of Mahler's *Lied von der Erde*. Just as these examples reflect the fulfillment of widely shared wishes significant on the individual level, works of art which present utopias usually reflect wishes and fears significant particularly for society at large, or even for humanity as a whole.

A different conception of the future underlies another common artistic procedure for presenting prophetic reality. This conception reflects the probabilistic philosophy adopted in modern science. The major implication of a probabilistic view of nature is that no demonstrated relation between cause and outcome is absolute, while no alternative outcome is so improbable as to be completely discountable. Hence, any state of affairs may conceivably be followed by any other state of affairs, although some sequences or events are more probable than others. In the words of Jeans (quoted by Stebbing, 1937, p. 16), "If the universe goes on for long enough, every conceivable accident is likely to happen in time." Art often confronts us with images of eventualities which are conceivable yet highly improbable. Many intriguing examples are provided by modern paintings and sculptures. They reveal what the world would look like if people were reduced to wiry skeletons à la Giacometti; if the familiar spatial structure were replaced by a bizarre curved space or a space in which near objects look small and far objects immense; if the latent dynamism of shapes were to burst forth and envelop us in an infinite kinetic flow; or if ambient light consisted of colorful iridescent waves spreading simultaneously both centripetally and centrifugally.

Less playful and more terrifying examples of possible occurrences may be found in Kafka's short stories. One morning a modest clerk finds his body metamorphosed into the body of a gigantic insect, but goes on living through the trivialities of everyday life with this insect body and his own human consciousness. Another story tells of a village doctor who one night is summoned to visit a patient but can never return from the fantastic inferno of human suffering. There are of course many possible metaphoric and symbolic interpretations of these stories. Yet, Max Brod (personal communication), who was Kafka's closest friend and rescued his writings for posterity, was deeply convinced that these stories were conceived by Kafka himself as realistic reports of unlikely but always possible eventualities. Kafka's unparalleled clarity in description and his remarkable avoidance of the habitual cues for symbolization lend support to Brod's conception. Moreover, there is the astonishing fact that Kafka in his novel *The Trial* (written in 1914–18) gave a detailed account of judicial procedures and methods of prosecution which at the time were highly improbable but were later carried out with horrifying authenticity in the courtrooms of Stalin and Hitler. Was Kafka's prophecy a real vision of the future or did history by some strange accident catch up with the most terrifying nightmares of a tortured individual?

Kafka's stories contain no clue for a possible answer to this haunting question. This is rather rare in art. When artists choose the future as the background or the theme of their work, they usually provide us at least with some suggestion whether the depicted image of the future is a prediction or a prophecy. Although both prediction and prophecy ostensibly refer to the future, prediction concentrates on showing the future while prophecy includes also an evaluation of the future. The element of objective necessity that accompanies a prediction is replaced in prophecy by the implication that something could or should be done for the promotion or avoidance of the future presented. Consequently, the major difference between these two forms of dealing with the future consists in their relation to the present. Prediction uses the present in order to explain the future, while prophecy uses the future in order to change the present. In line with this criterion, the greater part of artistic and religious preoccupation with prophetic reality is more akin to prophecy than to prediction. Hence, in art the accuracy of the anticipation is usually less important than the implied exhortation. In other words, prophetic reality in art is as a rule neither an exact image of the future nor a revelation of the present. Rather, it remains hovering between the present and the future as a possibility which could become the actual future if we do not deal properly in the present and with the present. In the words of Orwell (quoted by I. Howe, 1957, p. 240), speaking of his prophetic novel *1984*, "I do not believe that the kind of society I describe necessarily *will* arrive, but I believe . . . that something resembling it *could* arrive."

Depiction of desired and feared events, description of improbable eventualities, and the presentation of predictions or prophecies are some of the methods used in art for representing the future and what it portends. These various methods neither reveal different kinds of prophetic reality nor define different levels of the future. Rather, they represent a variety of possible conceptions of the future which could lead to the apprehension of different aspects of prophetic reality. Common to all these methods and their underlying conceptions is the orientative function they fulfill. Regardless of how the future is apprehended and presented, the experiencing of the future in the framework of art strengthens the representation of the future as a major force in the orientative matrix of the present and for the sake of the present.

The Impact of Art Reality

The four types of reality discussed above are presented together as aspects of one multidimensional phenomenon within the framework of a work of art. Thus, they are grasped by the spectators of art as convergent manifestations of one reality which may best be called "art reality." By this term we would like to suggest that the narrative-representational content of art is experienced as a reality which is differentiable both from actual reality and from fantasized reality, familiar from day and night dreams. As a separate type of reality, which spectators have to learn to identify and experience as such, art reality may share quite a few features with the other familiar kinds of reality, but is also endowed with qualities which are more characteristic of it than of the other realities. The former features have misled many to assume that art reality is an imitation of other kinds of reality. These features are, for example, the compelling persuasiveness of art reality and its frequent resemblance in structure and contents to everyday reality. The features characteristic particularly of art reality are the enhanced plenitude, richness, and meaningfulness of art reality as well as the self-sufficiency, self-enclosure, and autonomy of the reality in each work of art relatively to art realities in other works of art and to other kinds of reality.

As aspects of art reality, the four discussed types of reality—common, archeological, normative, and prophetic—contribute to the satisfaction of the tendency to establish and expand cognitive orientation. As mentioned earlier, this tendency is as basic as the tendencies to react to stimuli, to maintain a certain level of homeostasis, etc. This does not, however, imply that every conceivable experience should satisfy orientative strivings. Yet, in contradistinction to many other types of stimuli constellations, art has been traditionally expected to make a contribution to cognitive orientation. Hence, if for some reason this contribution is missing or greatly reduced, or is unbalanced through overemphasis on one aspect and neglect of another, it may be presumed that art spectators will note the deficiency. Possibly they will feel that the art experience is in some sense incomplete and unsatisfactory, or they will raise the notorious question, What does all this mean?

So far there exists neither a theoretical formula nor a practical recipe which could help in stating how the blending of the four realities into art reality is attained, what determines the possibly different weights of the four realities within one work of art, or what the consequences are of overemphasis or underemphasis on this or that reality. By way of pure assumption, one can only suggest that the blending of the four realities and their differential weights as aspects of art reality depend to a certain extent on the media of the various arts and on the characteristics of the specific theme dealt with. For instance, musical means do not allow of an adequate featuring of common reality; an overemphasis on sound-painting may even impair constructive melodic and harmonic developments. On the other hand, literature certainly makes the depiction of common reality possible. But if this reality is overelaborated, the literary product borders too closely on an artistically written newspaper report and, in the best case, turns into an analogue of what is known in film as the documentary. Similarly, an overemphasis on normative reality would turn a literary work into a poeticized version of a moral treatise or a political manifesto, while stripping a Dali picture of its prophetic and normative aspects would make it on the level of contents hardly more than an illustration in art form of psychoanalytic theory. However, specific themes almost naturally predispose towards an overemphasis of one or another of the realities. Just as a novel dealing with the future utilizes many elements of prophetic reality, a medieval painting of inferno could hardly avoid being highly suggestive of normative reality.

Yet there is no reason to presume that any one aspect of art reality fulfills only one function within a specific work of art. By virtue of their role, the judges in Kafka's *The Trial* appear as personifications of superego forces, and as such represent archeological reality. Yet, since they are judges operating in a courtroom which is depicted with all the marks of the familiar

bureaucratic scenery, they suggest common reality. Through their pronouncements and proclamations they also reflect normative reality, while
their unusual judicial procedures and their overall behavior suggest that they
may be a part of prophetic reality. This example demonstrates that any aspect
of art reality can be as multileveled as any other element in a work of art.
Hence, which of the four aspects of art reality will come to the fore depends
also on how the whole work of art is grasped and organized by the spectator.
On the other hand, an artist may intentionally omit one or another of the
aspects of art reality, either because he feels that he can rely on his audience
to supply it, or precisely in order to stimulate the audience to note its absence
and add it if necessary. For example, a feature common to many of Andersen's fairy tales and Brecht's plays is the remarkable omission of normative
reality, which the readers or viewers are called upon to supply. Another example is provided by Hemingway. Even when his heroes engage in extraordinary actions, they remain such inordinately ordinary types that the reader
who identifies with them can hardly avoid providing them with some underlying psychodynamics, which are not even hinted at by the author. Just
as artists enhance tension by omitting some of the expected means for its
relief, they tend to stimulate the spectator cognitively by omitting one or
more aspects of art reality. Presumably, the spectator's tendency to be
cognitively oriented can be relied upon no less than the need to relieve residual tensions.

The assumption underlying our discussion up to now is that art reality
contributes to the audience's cognitive orientation. This contribution may
take any of a variety of forms. For example, confrontation with a work of
art may lead a spectator to form new beliefs and thus add new elements to
his cognitive orientation. Or it may induce him to modify his opinions,
judgments, and informations, sometimes to the extent of merely revising
his beliefs, at other times, to the extent of even renouncing them. Alternatively, the orientative change may be manifested in a modification of the
relations between beliefs, so that beliefs formerly interrelated are discon-
nected or new relations are discovered between previously unrelated beliefs.
Changes of this type should not, however, be expected always to occur immediately following the art experience. In view of the rigidity of parts of
cognitive orientation, the wealth of implications of any change introduced
into its extensive system, and the reluctance or even fear of many people
to face novelty, changes in cognitive orientation are slow to take place.
Accordingly, the orientative impact of a work of art may become evident
only after a period of "incubation" and slow elaboration. Moreover, when
it does occur, it may not be attributed even by the spectator to an art ex-

perience. Or a work of art may not have a sufficiently strong orientative impact to induce actual changes in the spectator's cognitive orientation, but the impact it exerts may combine with influences from other sources inducing change in the same direction, so that by a slow cumulative process an orientative revision comes about.

An orientative impact by no means implies a corresponding change in behavior. According to the theory of cognitive orientation and the experiments in this **domain**, molar behavior is not determined by any single item of orientation, i.e., by one belief or another, and not even by any of the four components of orientation. It is only an elaborate clustering of elements from all four components which may give rise to a behavioral intention, i.e., a willingness to act in a certain manner. Moreover, there is a large gap between the evocation of a behavioral intention and actual behavior. The intention has to be implemented through a plan of action. The plan may either be retrieved from memory and adapted to the actual behavioral situation, or if it is not available, it has to be produced for the sake of the particular act and in line with the specific intention. Sometimes there is a conflict between two available plans, or even between two behavioral intentions. Before an action can take place, the conflict has to be resolved. All these are only some of the many conditions which have to be met if an act of behavior is to be elicited.

Accordingly, there is almost no reason to expect that the orientative impact of a work of art will produce behavioral changes in the spectators. As mentioned, the orientative impact rarely extends beyond changes introduced in a few beliefs or their interrelations. These changed beliefs are integrated within the extensive framework of cognitive orientation and can thus hardly bring about radical and immediate changes in behavior. Further, behavior is a product of many and varied conditions which cannot be created or modified through art. One of the reasons for this is that the orientative impact of a work of art is merely one aspect of the whole art experience. Another major characteristic of this experience is "aesthetic distance," i.e., that type of detached involvement, which depends on a particular set as well as on a multifaceted range of counterbalancing responses. Thus, aesthetic distance is essentially inimical to the evocation of a behavioral intention, which is, however, a necessary condition for behavior.

Hence, a direct impact of art on the behavior of spectators will be rather the exception than the rule. If its occurrence can be demonstrated at all, it will still be plausible to assume that the observed behavioral change is due to the operation of forces external to art, with which the art impact must have combined. Such is the case when a spectator of art is already preparing some action and utilizes the art experience consciously or unconsciously as the excuse for its performance. On the other hand, our conclusion about the relations between the orientative impact of art and behavioral changes invalidates the frequent complaints that art does not contribute sufficiently to the moral improvement of humanity. There should be nothing surprising about the art-loving tendencies of monstrous figures such as Nero, Cesare Borgia, and Adolf Hitler. Their example proves nothing about art, but the use of this example as a proof against the moral impact of art reflects a number of deep-rooted misconceptions about the art experience. One is that the orientative impact of a work of art on spectators corresponds to the impact intended by the artist. The other is that the intended orientative impact corresponds to standard morality. And still another is that an orientative impact corresponds to a direct impact on behavior.

Misconceptions of this type derive from a basic misunderstanding of the function fulfilled by art reality in art. It is not a means of reforming humanity, and thus it should not be expected to function as a subtle method of brainwashing. Its importance derives rather from the satisfaction it provides to the spectators' craving for widening, deepening, and developing their cognitive orientation, regardless of imminent demands for action or required behavioral decisions. Thus, confrontation with new aspects of different layers of reality not only satisfies orientative tendencies but also widens the scope of cognitive possibilities and serves as a source for the unique kind of knowledge which is not merely known but also experienced.

16. Epilogue

Section after section in this book starts with an unsolved problem, presents some of the empirical material and theoretical assumptions necessary for its solution, and suggests directly or implicitly some new question for further research. Yet beyond questions of this type, which are limited to this or that domain of art and to some specific hypothesized process, there are problems more basic in nature and more general in scope, questions which can be meaningfully formulated only on the basis of a more general view of the processes assumed to be involved in the experiencing of art.

The first problem concerns the interrelations among the various processes. How does aesthetic distance promote the orientative impact of a theme, or intensify feeling-into? Could a special emphasis on feeling-into weaken the effects of the fusion between the general and the particular attained through multileveledness, abstractness, or symbolization? Under what circumstances, if at all, could a strong symbolic impact compensate for meager sublimatory possibilities? What are the relations between the sublimated gratification of wishes and the resolution of specific tensions provided mainly through the formal means of the arts? These questions mention some important forms of interrelation among the various processes. The interrelations may be conceived in terms of mutual facilitation or inhibition, compensation, additive or interactive combination, and modification of the impact of one process through the co-evocation of another.

When several processes are evoked in a person through a pattern of stimuli, the processes interact, and the impact of one will modify the impact of another; this, at any rate, is our usual assumption. What we know about experiencing art supports this assumption and even enables us to formulate several hypotheses, some of which have been suggested in preceding chapters. For example, by promoting detachment from immediate action, aesthetic distance may be assumed to enhance the range and depth of the orientative implications of art reality and responsiveness to symbolic meanings. In turn, aesthetic distance depends in no small degree on the counterbalancing effects of multiple identifications and feeling-into with regard to several characters, while feeling-into is facilitated through an adequate set. As a matter of fact, set interacts with all the processes and functions partly as a catalyst and partly as a background influence which enhances the effects of any of the processes.

The analysis of the interrelations may give rise to hypotheses about the determinants underlying the processes to various degrees. For example, meaning elaboration is involved in all the processes described, and factors such as expectations, changes in arousal, and relief of tensions are involved in many of them, but factors such as imitation or projection underlie only a few. Thus, some processes may be characterized by the sharing of a greater number of underlying determinants than others. When processes of this kind are supported by a selective emphasis on adequate aspects of the stimuli in a work of art, they may form prominent substructures which lend a particular coloring to the art experience. One example for such a substructure might include symbolization, abstractness, increased emphasis on orientative effects, and an enhanced aesthetic distance. This substructure is characterized by a variety of interrelations. While aesthetic distance provides conditions favorable for responsiveness to symbolic abstractness and orientative implications, these latter processes promote each other and together reinforce aesthetic distance. A more emotionally toned substructure may include increased feeling-into and personal involvement, ample opportunities for sublimatory gratification, and enhanced changes in arousal effected through pronounced specific tensions and their summative resolution. Here again the interrelations among pairs of processes are supplemented through more complex interactions which may contribute to the shaping of a substructure.

The problem of interrelations among the processes is related in several respects to a second problem of major concern for the psychology of the arts. Are all of the processes discussed necessary for the production of an art experience? This formulation actually serves only as a label for a series of more specific questions which reveal the import of the problem. Basic among these are the following. (i) Are all of the processes evoked whenever a spectator undergoes an experience which by general consensus qualifies as an art experience? (ii) Are the processes of equal importance or weight for the production of the experience or do they contribute to it differentially? And (iii) is the relative weakness or absence of one or more processes in the evoked experience correlated with judgments about the artistic qualities or aesthetic value of the pattern of stimuli? All three questions can be answered only on the basis of extensive studies which would involve many different works of art and various samples of spectators. The suggestions which could be formulated before these data are available reflect mainly general theoretical considerations.

We assume that all the processes discussed are involved in the production of a full-fledged art experience. This assumption is based, first, on an analysis of the stimuli provided in most works of art, second, on a pooling of analyses and assertions about art made by many investigators of art from a variety of theoretical points of view and by means of different methodologies, and third, on the conventional explicit and implicit expectations from art on the part of the spectators, i.e., the audience on whom the temporal survival of works of art eventually depends. The theoretical implications which are supported by each of these sources are not identical. They vary greatly in import, relative emphases, and terminology. Moreover, the sources are not independent. But when the determinants common to these sources are integrated with psychological findings about experiencing in general and about responses to specific art stimuli, it seems warranted to assume that all of the discussed processes are essential for the production of an art experience. When these processes are regarded as operating jointly, and when they are conceived in terms of the specific means through which they are implemented in the various domains of art, they provide a comprehensive framework for understanding and analyzing art experiences.

The assumption that all of the processes are essential for the production of an art experience does not imply that they are all of equal importance in shaping this experience. It remains for future research to ascertain what processes are of greater and what of lesser weight and centrality in the production of the experience and in determining its temporal unfolding. On an a priori basis, the answer to this question may be expected to depend on the structure and style of the work of art and, on the other hand, the personality of the spectator and his past experience with art. The existence of different schools and styles within each domain of art suggests that art experiences may be produced through different distributions of weight among the various processes. Such differential weight distributions may arise from a selective emphasis on specific stimuli within the work of art as well as from the expectations aroused in spectators by works of art classified traditionally within one or another school. Thus, the prominence of the effects of archeological reality in surrealist paintings is due no more to the special emphasis placed on this reality in the painting itself than to the heightened susceptibility of the spectator to this aspect of art reality when he is confronted with a surrealist work of art. On the other hand, the commonplace observation that the same work of art evokes different experiences in different people suggests that spectators vary in their responsiveness to art stimuli and may be more sensitive to some than to others. Hence, if one spectator has a greater need and capacity for sublimation than another, sublimation may figure more prominently in his art experiences than the other processes.

Whatever the source of the possible differential weighting of the processes may be, it seems plausible to assume that different distributions of weights produce differently colored art experiences. Yet only empirical studies can produce guidelines for the characterization and understanding of these different art experiences.

The assumption of differential weighting of the various processes could be tested and applied in different forms. On the phenomenological level it could be used to detect and describe the relative experiential prominence of the various processes. From an analytical viewpoint it could serve for the testing of hypotheses and description of findings about the relative contribution of the different processes to the shaping of various art experiences. Finally, the results of such studies could be used in order to determine the optimal weights which have to be attributed to the processes in order to allow prediction whether an art experience will occur and possibly even what type of art experience will be stimulated.

Studies of this kind necessarily involve the use of aesthetic evaluations as a basic criterion for differentiation among works of art. In spite of the well-known discrepancies among art judgments, there is enough agreement in this domain (Child, 1969, pp. 879–89) to justify the cautious use of aesthetic evaluations as a criterion. Thus, one may ask: How are aesthetic evaluations related to our set of processes in general and to the differential weighting and strength of the single processes in particular?

On the basis of an a priori analysis and in the most general terms the answer could be that low-evaluated works of art differ from the high-evaluated ones either in the absence of some art stimuli eliciting one or more of the processes, or in the relative weakness of such stimuli which does not allow for the evocation of one or more processes in a sufficient strength. On purely theoretical grounds the suggestion could be made that the first possibility refers to patterns of stimuli which are usually not regarded as art, while the second possibility would hold in the case of patterns of stimuli that qualify as low-evaluated works of art or as borderline cases of art.

If one were to compare patterns of stimuli which as a rule have not been included within the traditional domain of the arts with patterns of stimuli which, regardless of evaluation, qualify as art, it would not be too difficult to detect the absence of several of the processes in the experience evoked by the non-art patterns. For example, circus performances and boxing or baseball matches provide for feeling-into and for the evocation and resolution of specific tensions, even though the means may differ from those used in dancing. But they fail to provide stimuli for symbolization, sublimation, adequate set, aesthetic distance, etc. The situation seems, however, to be complex in the case of patterns of stimuli which can formally qualify as art and are much like what comes under the label of art, but which raise serious doubts of their aesthetic value and nature. Examples of such patterns of stimuli are detective stories and thrillers, cheap novels, low-grade films, and sometimes even popular entertainment music and folk dancing. The experiences evoked by productions of this kind seem to differ from the experiences evoked by productions generally acknowledged as works of art in the relative weakness of some of the processes. By way of pure conjecture, cheap novels and films appear to fall short of so-called artistic literary and filmic productions at the very least in their meager use of multileveledness, abstraction, and symbolization, in the restricted possibilities for sublimation which they offer, and in their limited orientative import.

These remarks raise a great many questions which could serve as hypotheses for extensive experimentation. However, at the present stage of knowledge, or rather non-knowledge, it would be futile even to speculate about basic problems such as the following: If all the above-mentioned processes are evoked, the weakness of which processes makes the pattern of stimuli appear a borderline case to art? Under what conditions does such a pattern evoke experiences more similar to authentic art experiences and under what conditions are the evoked experiences more similar to those evoked by non-art patterns of stimuli? Within the range of art productions, does the weakness of one or more specific processes correlate with a low art evaluation? Could a particular emphasis on some of the processes compensate for the weakness of some other processes, so that an otherwise poor work of art is judged to be of a higher aesthetic value?

The first two problems we have raised focus on characteristics of the experience and on the role of the different processes in determining its evocation, course, and quality. The third problem highlights aspects which supplement both theoretically and methodologically the two preceding problems. These aspects are bound up with the basic fact that the art experience is always the experience of an individual person. Accordingly, the problem is this. Given the information about what processes enter into the making of an art experience and about their optimal differential weighting, can we predict whether a certain work of art will evoke an art experience in a certain individual? In general terms the answer to this problem is both positive and negative. It is positive because if the various questions posed within the framework of the first two problems were answered satisfactorily, such a prediction would in principle be possible. However, only in principle.

Practically, the prediction would be impossible in the absence of information about the spectator's ability to respond in a manner which would make an art experience possible.

It is this problem of predicting a spectator's response to a work of art which lends relevance to the study of individual differences within the psychology of the arts. The study of individual differences would eventually enable us to answer questions such as these: Why does the same work of art evoke an aesthetic experience in one individual but not in another? Why does one spectator enjoy a certain work of art more than another? Why is it that the same novel has afforded one individual an unforgettable experience while it hardly impressed another reader? These and similar questions may be asked about not only individuals but also random or selected groups of spectators, and even larger samples—of generations, classes, nationalities, or cultures.

Although our theory of art experience may not apply to this or that individual case in the absence of the relevant information about the case, it provides a theoretical and methodological framework for studies which would eventually make it possible to predict and understand the individual's response to a work of art. These are several levels on which such studies could proceed. If interest is focused on predicting the occurrence of an art experience, its intensity or—in line with the assumption of differential weighting of the processes—its quality, two types of information are essential: first, information about the individual's general capacity or tendency to respond in line with each of the various processes, and second, information about the individual's susceptibility to the specific stimuli in the work of art which might evoke the various processes. These two types of information reflect two assumptions about differences in the responsiveness of various people to art. The first is that since the processes essential for an art experience define the basic dimensions relevant for analyzing individuals' responses to art, variations along these dimensions may account for differences in individuals' responses to work of art. The difference in the spectators' responsiveness need not always reflect differences in all processes. Possibly, differences in some processes or differences of particular magnitude may prove to be of greater weight in determining responsiveness or enjoyment of art in general or of specific works of art in particular than differences in other processes or of a different magnitude. The second assumption, however, serves to qualify the first, to which it is related. The qualification consists in highlighting the possibility that though two individuals may prove to be equally endowed with the tendencies to respond in line with the specified processes, they may still differ in their responsiveness to a certain work of art because they are not equally sensitive to the stimuli it presents. This assumption reflects the basic conception that an individual's response is determined no less by his disposition than by the eliciting stimuli, which in turn cannot be defined in isolation from the individual's ability and tendency to perceive them and to elaborate their meaning in line with the requirements of the situation.

If the investigator's interest not only includes establishing and predicting differences in responsiveness to art but also centers on understanding the sources or determinants of these differences, his studies will focus on tracing the correlates of differences in the processes and in susceptibility to the stimuli evoking them. These correlates might — theoretically at least — extend over an immeasurably large range of variables which would include not only perceptual, cognitive, emotional, and other personality characteristics but also biographical data, specific personal experiences, past encounters with art, individual memories and associations, etc. In a certain sense such information could be called "molecular," when it is designed to account for variations in more "molar" variables, such as need and capacity for sublimation, for feeling-into, or for elaborating cognitive orientation. Yet the "molecular" variables are themselves also "molar" in the sense that they could be traced to still more basic factors, about whose nature psychology leaves us still largely in the dark.

In everyday life good answers are those which satisfy the person who asked the questions. In science, however, the best answers are those which enable us to reformulate our former questions in a more precise manner and possibly to pose some new questions which would lead to further empirical research. Therefore we view the questions discussed in the above sections as an important and beneficial result of our inquiry into the psychology of the arts. We could not have asked them without having first determined the basic components of the art experience. In our explorations into art we used already existing knowledge about the art experience in order to learn more about the stimuli which elicit it, and then we used the attained information in order to learn more about the experiential impact of these stimuli. Thus, we have been led back and forth between the spectator and the work of art, testing each hypothesis in different domains of art and combining different hypotheses into an initial theory about the art experience and about its stimuli, namely, the work of art. We may now present our findings about the common denominators of art experiences in a short, definition-like review:

A static or a temporally changing pattern of stimuli may evoke an art experience if—because of its special structural and meaning qualities, e.g., its gestalt characteristics, novelty, complexity, narrative-representational contents, etc.—it

(a) arouses in the spectator specific tensions which are sufficiently variegated to combine with diffuse residual tensions in the spectator, and provides for these tensions a summative and adequate relief attended by pleasure;

(b) is preceded by and/or produces a set which through specific expectations and intentions enhances attention to the special structural and meaning qualities of the stimuli, and increases the readiness to be emotionally involved;

(c) makes possible the intensification and personalization of the elicited tensions by providing material adequate for the evocation of feeling-into;

(d) limits to a certain extent the degree of personal involvement and inhibits direct action by promoting aesthetic distance;

(e) activates repressed and ungratified wishes and provides for their imaginary fulfillment through sublimation, projections, and identifications;

(f) provides for the activation of various personality levels and appeals to many different personality types and people by means of multilev-eledness, abstractness, and different kinds of symbolization;

(g) contributes directly to the elaboration and expansion of cognitive orientation through the presentation and development of four major aspects of art reality.

Accordingly, static and/or dynamic patterns of stimuli which meet the above-stated conditions constitute a work of art.

In many respects our theory about the experiencing of art plays the role of a map illustrating major landmarks and pathways of a largely uncharted continent. How the map is used depends on the goals of the user. If he is a researcher, the map may provide him with a psychologically founded, stable, and comprehensive framework for posing meaningful questions to be answered through empirical studies which will contribute to improvements in the map, or eventually—as is usual in science—to its replacement by a better map. If the user is a teacher of art appreciation, he may apply the landmarks highlighted by the map as guidelines for developing in his students attention, sensitivity, and awareness for the aspects of art which might increase their understanding of it and responsiveness to it. If he is an art teacher, he may use the map to strengthen competence in the creative aspect of art through awareness of the effects of the artist's techniques on the consuming audience. If the user is an art critic, he may extract from the map objective, psychologically oriented criteria for the evaluation of works of art, for their analysis, and for an appreciation of their probable impact on the spectators of art. If, however, the user of the map is none of the above but an occasional visitor and enjoyer of the continent of art, i.e., if he prefers the role of spectator, the map may provide him with the means of better understanding why he enjoys a certain work of art, why he fails to enjoy another work of art, and how he can decrease the gap between his daily life and art so as to enjoy art more intensely and learn through it to cultivate that highest art of all—the art of living.

Notes

Chapter 1

1. Freud's major contributions to the psychology of the creative artist can be found in the following sources: Freud (1924, 1930, 1948a, 1948b, 1948c). Other major elaborations of the psychoanalytic ideas in this domain are presented, for example, by Alexander (1948), Bergler (1947), Bychowski (1951), Ehrenzweig (1953), Kris (1952), H. Lowenfeld (1941), Rank & Sachs (1916), H. Sachs (1951), Schneider (1950). Some random examples of psychoanalytically oriented analyses of works of art include E. Jones's (1955) study of *Hamlet*, H. A. Murray's (1941) study of *Moby-Dick*, Reitman's (1946) essay on Edward Lear, Schilder's (1938) analysis of *Alice in Wonderland* (a theme highly favored by psychoanalysts!) and Wight's (1946) study of Goya's paintings. Further examples can be found in the bibliographical sources presented by Hoffman (1957) and Kiell (1965a, 1965b). Major psychoanalytic studies which deal with the spectator's experience of art are by Brill (1931), Freud (1930), Kohut (1957), Kohut & Levarie (1950), H. B. Lee (1947, 1950), Margolis (1954), Rank & Sachs (1916), and H. Sachs (1951).

2. Indeed in limited and circumscribed domains the principle of summation seems to be a contributing factor. Thus, with regard to color preferences it seems that the degree of preference for a combination of two colors is predictable from the degrees of preference for each of the colors in the combination judged singly (e.g., Allen & Guilford, 1936; Eysenck, 1941b), although the prediction is far from perfect. But when broader aspects of works of art are considered or aspects other than preference, the response to the whole does not seem to be the sum of the responses to fragmentary, isolated parts. See also Leijonhielm's (1967) study and his survey of the relevant literature.

3. The idea that reinforcement acts by an expectancy mechanism was elaborated originally by Tolman (1932) and later, in one form or another, by others (Crespi, 1944; Mowrer, 1960; Seward, 1950; Sheffield, Roby, & Campbell, 1954; Spence, 1956). Stein (1964) may be credited with a precise physiological theory of anticipated reinforcement and the manner in which expectations can make contact with operant behavior.

4. For example, Yoshii and Tsukiyama (1952) found that EEG waves increase in frequency and decrease in amplitude as the rats in a maze approach the goal box which contains food. Di Lollo & Walker (1964) report that basal skin resistance drops as a rat enters the final segment, containing food, of a straight runway. Soltysik (1960) found that in an instrumental conditioning situation a dog's heart rate rises when food appears. According to Hess & Polt (1964) pupillary diameter reaches a maximum just before human subjects verbalize their solutions to a multiplication problem, and Blatt (1961) found that in a problem-solving situation, the heart rate of subjects who perform the task efficiently rises steeply just before the solution is reached.

5. At first glance it might appear as if McClelland et al.'s (1953) theory contradicted the importance attributed by us to the meaning attached to the evoked ten-

sion and to the interpretation of its causes. Yet meaning seems to be a crucial factor in accounting for the results of studies supporting or disconfirming this theory. McClelland et al. suggested that small discrepancies from adaptation level, regardless of direction, give rise to pleasant affect, while large discrepancies in either direction are unpleasant. Tests of the theory with regard to sensory events deviating from short-range adaptation levels, determined by a few minutes acquaintance with stimuli, have usually supported the theory (Beebe-Center et al., 1948; Engel, 1928; Conners, 1964; Haber, 1958). But tests of the theory in more complex situations, for example, with regard to self-image, life goals, or achievements— e.g., Block (1964); Harvey and Clapp (1965); Reimanis (1964); Verinis, Brandsma, & Cofer (1968); and Zeaman's (1949) study with animals—have usually failed to confirm the theory and have been interpreted as showing that affect depends on the direction of the discrepancy and not on its size. Now, it seems to us plausible to assume that with regard to short-range sensory events of the type used in the studies there are no significant differences in meaning between a small deviation in one or the other direction. Moreover, the meanings attached to immersing one's hands in somewhat colder or warmer water or in tasting moderate solutions of sugar or salt are so slight that they can even be ignored. Thus, the return to balance amply compensates with pleasure the slight inconvenience caused by the disturbance, which itself is regarded as pleasant. On the other hand, in contexts where elaborate meanings are involved, the evoked affect depends on the meaning of the event. If the event as such is evaluated as good, even if it disconfirms a previously stated expectation determined by situational factors, it does not constitute a large deviation from the more basic expectations of most people, since most people probably expect in general the best or at least not the worst. While if the event is evaluated as bad or noxious, in most cases and for most people it represents a deviation from their inherent optimistic expectations, and a prior specific expectation of it may only slightly mitigate the disappointment.

6. The conception of an optimal activation level is based mainly on the extensive findings which show that when people are put in conditions of reduced external stimulation or reduced variation in stimulation they may manifest after a time a wide range of disturbances in perceptual, sensory, cognitive, and motor functions (Solomon, Kubzansky, Leiderman, Mendelson, Trumbull & Wexler, 1961; Schultz, 1965).—The importance of arousal for proper functioning is supported by many studies which show, for example, that enhanced arousal facilitates learning and performance (e.g., Amsel & Maltzman, 1950; Amsel & Roussel, 1952; Kleinsmith & Kaplan, 1964; Maltzman, Kantor, & Langdon, 1967; Kreindler, 1960; P. S. Siegel & Brantley, 1951; E. L. Walker & Tarte, 1963). Yet, there seems to be an optimal level of arousal for the performance of each type of task, which tends to be lower the more difficult the task is (e.g., Hebb, 1955). The relation between behavioral efficiency and degree of activation seems to fit an inverted-U function, i.e., behavioral efficiency increases to a maximum as tension rises from a minimum to an intermediate level, optimal for the task, and then declines as tension rises still further (e.g., Freeman, 1948b; Lindsley, 1957; Malmo, 1959; Schönpflug, 1966).

7. Although Berlyne (1960, 1963, 1967) also accepts the notion that there is a striving to maintain an optimal stimulation level, his conception deviates from the one discussed in the text in that he assumes that insufficient stimulation, i.e., boredom, consists in a high and not low arousal level. Accordingly, Berlyne concludes that people would expose themselves to the stimuli of art so as to terminate

the aversive state of boredom. Although the view that increased stimulation may lead to arousal reduction is unconventional, Berlyne (1967) has quite convincingly justified this approach. The main difficulty of this conception is, however, that while describing the essence of art in terms of collative stimuli, Berlyne (1967, pp. 71–79) himself shows persuasively that in states of increased arousal there is a tendency to minimize or avoid exposure to collative stimuli. Hence, boredom should lead to the avoidance of art, unless the increased arousal due to boredom differs from other kinds of increased arousal—an unlikely possibility unmentioned by Berlyne.

8. The same principle seems to be exemplified by studies which show that arousal due to extraneous stimuli, such as shock, or stimulation of the brain, may combine with the tension of a concomitant activity and thus invigorate its performance (e.g., Dewes & Morse, 1961; Kish & Antonitis, 1956; Marx, Henderson, & Roberts, 1955; Moon & Lodahl, 1956). Another phenomenon which may demonstrate this principle is the perceptual displacement of the vertical to the right caused by a slight tension evoked through a simultaneous tickling in the left ear (Wapner, Werner, & Chandler, 1951). See also note 6 above on the effects of enhanced arousal on learning.

9. The problem of tension reduction through tension induction exists also with regard to the reduction of specific tensions. As mentioned earlier (see note 4 above) tension seems to reach a climax just before the state of gratification or completion. Some investigators have expressed the opinion that every state of reward consists in conditions conducive to increased tension. For example, Sheffield and his collaborators (1950, 1951, 1954, 1966) view the performance of consummatory responses rather than their completion of drive-reduction as the critical factor in reinforcement, while the ethologists (Tinbergen, 1951) interpret animal behavior as a matter of seeking opportunities for consummatory actions. Also some notable physiological experimentators (Grastyàn et al., 1965; 1966; Olds & Olds, 1965) have noted that escape from aversive conditions as well as drive reduction function physiologically through mechanisms of increasing activation in some brain center rather than through mechanisms of ceasing or declining arousal. Yet these observations do not afford an explanation to our problem.

10. Concerning the role of sensory cues in determining action see Bindra (1959, chap. 7). This role is exemplified by Beach's (1942) studies which show that after rats were made blind and anosmic and were deprived of tactual cues, they could not copulate. Evidence that stimuli that are not relevant to the source of the reinforcing effects can also serve as cues is provided for example by Amsel (1949) and Levine (1953). In these experiments the reinforcer was the termination of a noxious stimulus, but the interoceptive stimuli which controlled the actual behaviors were provided by hunger and thirst.

A well-known study by Spragg (1940) exemplifies the state of tension without directionality. Spragg established in chimpanzees a need for morphine by giving them injections of the drug. When morphine was withheld from the addicted chimpanzees for a day or more, they showed, in addition to the physiological withdrawal symptoms, signs of undirected general tension: they paced in their cages, cried, screamed, etc. They could not reduce the tension, since they did not yet relate the tension to the proper cue. A few weeks later when morphine was withheld, the animals showed directed tension, i.e., a need for morphine, which was manifested by trying to pull the experimenter into the injection room, handling themselves the injection tools, assuming the habitual posture for the injection, etc.

11. The orienting response is the name of a complex set of reactions evoked whenever a new stimulus appears. The orienting response includes a number of changes, among them reactions in the sense organs, e.g., lowering the threshold of perception in the senses, dilation of the eye pupil; changes in the skeletal muscles, e.g., arrest of all ongoing activities and a rise in general muscle tonus; EEG changes toward increased arousal; vegetative changes—slowing of heart rate and in respiration a delay followed by increase in the amplitude and decrease in frequency, occurrence of the galvanic skin reaction, etc. (Berlyne, 1960, chap. 4; Lynn, 1966; Sokolov, 1963). The function of these responses seems to be the facilitation of obtaining information about the occurrence or object.

12. When six-month-old children are exposed to strange sound stimuli, during the first and second exposures they react to these stimuli with fear and displeasure indicative of "disturbance of equilibrium." When the stimuli become more familiar, pleasure reactions gradually replace the displeasure (C. Bühler, 1928; C. Bühler, Hetzer, & Mabel, 1928). The frequency of negative reactions to novel stimuli declines with an increase in the babies' age (B. Löwenfeld, 1927), probably owing to increased familiarization with such stimuli. In animals fear reactions to novel stimuli have been observed, for example, in chimpanzees (Hebb, 1946; Hebb & Riesen, 1943; Riesen & Kinder, 1952; Welker, 1956a), chaffinches (Hinde, 1954), and dogs (Melzack, 1952) in response to highly novel stimuli—masks, stuffed animals, a moving toy snake, etc.—introduced into a familiar environment. Concerning reactions of fear, even "freezing" and immobilization, in animals to novel and strange stimuli, see also the studies by Andrew (1956), Bernstein & Mason (1960), Bindra & Spinner (1958), Denniston (1959), Haslerud (1938), Hebb (1958), and Patrick (1931).—These studies show not only that high degrees of novelty are tension arousing and that the tension decreases with familiarization, but also that the perception of novelty depends on a prior familiarization with the environment into which novelty is introduced.

While initially high degrees of novelty evoke fear, after some familiarization they may evoke exploration, just as mild degrees of novelty do (see note 11 above). Thus, a conflict between fear and exploration may sometimes be observed (Dolin, Zborovskaia, & Zamakhover, 1958; Harlow & Zimmermann, 1958; Hayes, 1960; Lorenz, 1956).

13. For example, A. K. Myers & Miller (1954) found that rats satiated with food and water would learn to press a bar in a shuttle box in order to gain entry into a black compartment from a white one, or vice versa. Chapman & Levy (1957) observed that visual changes in the goal box of a straight alley would reinforce rats' running speeds. Female rats would learn to go to that arm of a Y maze that provided the opportunity to explore a Dashiell or checkerboard maze, and would learn a reversal when the incentive is switched to the other arm (Montgomery, 1954). Monkeys would learn a position discrimination when the reward is an opportunity for visual exploration (Butler, 1953) or hearing sounds from a monkey colony (Butler, 1957). Monkeys would also learn the solution of complex mechanical puzzles with no other reward than the possibility of manipulating the puzzles themselves (Harlow, 1950). See also Butler (1954), Butler & Harlow (1954), Harlow & McClearn (1954), R. C. Miles (1958), Montgomery & Segall (1955), Symmes (1959), Thackray & Michels (1958), and Wenzel (1959).

14. There is extensive evidence that animals will approach and actively explore

situations and stimuli of mild novelty (Bindra & Spinner, 1958; Haslerud, 1938; Hudson, 1950; Welker, 1956a, 1956b, 1956c; Menzel, Davenport, & Rogers, 1961), and that within this range of novelty they would prefer the more novel and complex stimuli (Berlyne & Slater, 1957; Montgomery, 1954).

About human preference for moderate degrees of novelty or uncertainty in the performance of tasks see Eckblad (1963, 1964), Maddi (1961), and Mendel (1965). Many studies show that when presented with stimuli varying in complexity from simple to highly complex, people state their preference for stimuli which are intermediate in complexity. This has been demonstrated for example with regard to stimuli such as polygons (e.g., R. C. Davis, 1936; Munsinger, Kessen, & Kessen, 1964) and tone sequences (Skaife, 1967). These preferences will be discussed in greater detail in the context of the formal means of the arts in later chapters.

Chapter 2

1. Gibson (1966, chaps. 10–11) has shown that while the structure of an optical array or of ambient light from an illuminated environment depends on three mutually dependent factors—degree of slant, degree of whiteness or surface color, and degree of illumination or shadowiness of the surfaces—the structure of an optical array from a painted display, viz., a painting, depends primarily on the pigment structure of the surface. The latter factor is experienced as colors.

2. Many systems have been devised for the representation of colors (Judd, 1952). Since, however, they are inevitably inaccurate in detail, do not represent all the complex relations among hue, saturation, and brightness, and tell us very little about the underlying processes, their main use is restricted to exemplification. Most of the systems take account of the three dimensions of hue, saturation, and brightness. The same is true with regard to the variety of systems of object-color samples which are organized in terms of systematic mixture of pigments (or dyes), in terms of systematic combination of light in varied proportions, or in terms of the systematic judgment of color intervals.—The color samples used in the experiments reported in this chapter were drawn from the *Munsell Book of Color* (1966). This system of object-color samples was developed from judgments of equal hue, brightness, and saturation.

3. In terms of the notation of the *Munsell Book of Color* (1966), the colors of the *first set* had the brightness value of 5, and saturation values ranging approximately from 8 to 12, with the greens and blues tending to be less saturated than the reds, purples, and yellows. The colors of the *second set* had the brightness value of 5, and saturation values ranging from 4 to 6. The colors of the *third set*, from the central vertical axis, had a saturation value of 0, and varied in brightness from 0–1 for the black to 9½–10 for the white. The colors of the *fourth set* had the value of 5 in brightness and varied in saturation from 0 to 14. The two horizontal axes along which the colors were sampled are the axes defined by the two following pairs of colors: 5 R to 5 BG, and 5 Y to 5 PB. The *fifth set* of colors included four colors with the value 7 in brightness, and four colors with the value of 3 in brightness. The saturation value of all eight colors was approximately 3. The colors were: 5B 7/6, 5YR 7/6, 7.5GY 7/6, 7.5P 7/6, 5B 3/6, 5YR 3/6, 7.5GY 3/6, 7.5P 3/6.

4. It has, of course, to be remembered that complementary colors are not what are usually called red and green, yellow and blue, etc., but actually red and blue-green, yellow and purple-blue, yellow-red and blue etc. (Munsell, 1926, pp. 37, 49–50). In terms of wavelengths corresponding to the hues, it has been demonstrated (Pickford, 1951, pp. 4, 7) that complementaries are characterized by a ratio of wavelengths (expressed in angstroms) which is in the neighborhood of the range 1–1.2. For example, the wavelength of red is 6562, and of blue-green 4921. Thus, the ratio is 1.334 : 1. However, since it is a range of wavelengths and not an exact point of wavelength which corresponds to the perception of a hue, the diagram of complementaries prepared by Pickford (1951, p. 4) shows that the ratio depends on the part of the range of wavelength selected. For example, for gold-yellow (5853) and blue (4854) the ratio is 1.206 : 1, while for gold-yellow (5739) and blue (4821) the ratio is 1.190 : 1. Usually, under standard conditions, the light mixture which produces any given hue varies with the observer. The variations are much greater when intensity of the color stimuli, background illumination, etc., also vary (Burnham, et al., 1963, chap. 3).

5. Some authorities in the domain of colors or aesthetics have expressed views which support our findings on the tension characterizing the juxtaposition of complementaries; for example, Munsell (1926, p. 37) says that "the eye is stimulated by their [the complementaries'] difference" and that they require balancing, and Valentine (1962, p. 63) refers to complementaries as contrasts. But many other writers seem to support an opposing view. Thus, Arnheim (1954, p. 298) asserts that there is a tendency to perceive the complementaries as belonging to one unit owing to the similarity betwen them, and that together they create balance and "completeness." Likewise, D. Ross (1917) suggests that the complementaries represent harmony which is due to the resemblance of the colors in the pair on the dimensions of brightness and/or saturation. A similar view is held by Ostwald (1931). Hartshorne (1934, pp. 40–49, 159–66, 209–25) also maintains that complementaries produce harmony owing to their resemblance, but he attributes the resemblance not to sharedness in the usual dimensions of color (hue, saturation, and brightness) but to sharedness in expressive dimensions of colors, which he assumes to be warmth-activity (scarlet) vs. cold-passivity (sea green), and brightness-joyousness (yellow) vs. dullness-sorrowfulness (violet).

These and other authors who share in the opinion (Judd, 1955) seem driven to strained and unconvincing explanations of the similarity between complementaries because they stick to two conventional half-truths. First, they assume that complementaries represent harmony. This assumption, which is contradicted by our findings, seems to derive from a literal interpretation of the term complementary, as if one color supplements a part missing in the other color. Cold and heat may be complementary in this sense, yet it is obvious that balance lies not in their juxtaposition but in their merging. Secondly, the authors mentioned assume that harmony consists in similarity or identity of the parts constituent of the harmonious whole. If similarity were the guiding principle in the harmony of colors, then very simple hues like two shades of red should represent perfect harmony, which they certainly do not, in spite of Gotschalk's (1947, pp. 109–10) unbased statement that "ever so slight differences" in hue are harmonious. Moreover, since so many colors are similar either in hue or in saturation or in brightness or in connotation, and all of them share the quality of being colors, all colors should be harmonious, and the term harmony of colors loses then all meaning. Thus the principle of similarity between complementaries seems to lead to too many contradictions with facts and with its own implications.

The principle of similarity is, however, one version of the well-known aesthetic conventional truth that beauty is "unity in diversity." This principle is so vague that it easily allows for discovering or explaining beauty in no matter what, and flexibly accommodates very divergent views on beauty. It should therefore not be surprising that it has survived unmolested from Plato's days to the post-lunar-landing era. The underlying concept will, however, be discussed in later chapters.

6. Habituation to stimuli seems to be as characteristic of humans as of animals. For example, in the first few presentations intense tones raise arousal (e.g., heightened muscular tone, blocking of waves in the brain, GSR, etc.) but the repetition of a tone of a specified intensity gradually reduces the evoked physiological responses until they completely disappear in both men (R. C. Davis, 1948; R. C. Davis, Buchwald, & Frankmann, 1955) and cats (Sharpless & Jasper, 1956). The same is true, for example, of repeated flashes of light (Wilson & Wilson, 1959), electric shocks (Seward & Seward, 1934), responses to words with emotional significance (Woodworth, 1938), and responses to novel stimuli.

In animals, exploration of novel stimuli which is initially high, gradually decreases when the stimuli are presented repeatedly and thus become more familiar (Berlyne, 1950; Glanzer, 1953a, 1953b; J. D. Harris, 1943; Hinde, 1954). Stimuli which in the beginning were too unfamiliar, so that they evoked fear and withdrawal, are gradually approached when exposure to them continues (Haslerud, 1938; Hudson, 1950; Montgomery, 1955; Thompson & Solomon, 1954; Welker, 1956a, 1957; Williams & Kuchta, 1957); but as exposure continues, the interest they evoke and the involved tension gradually disappear (Montgomery, 1953; Welker, 1956b). The decrease of interest is quicker the shorter the interval between successive exposures to the stimuli (Heathers, 1940; Zeaman & House, 1951). A resurgence of interest, attention, and exploration may occur in such cases if the animals find new ways of using the familiar objects (Inhelder, 1955) or when changes are introduced into the situation, for example, intensity of illumination is increased (Darchen, 1952), the environment is made more colorful (Darchen, 1957), or surprising stimuli appear (Desai, 1939).

Of particular importance for the domain of art are the following two phenomena. (i) Habituation is slowed down when the stimuli are complex (Welker, 1954, 1956c), and (ii) with continued exposure to various stimuli, organisms approach more easily and even tend to prefer increasingly complex patterns of stimulation. The latter has been shown by Dember, Earl, & Paradise (1957) by Earl (1957) and by Williams & Kuchta (1957) for rats and for children in play situations. In the domain of preference by people for various art stimuli, it has been demonstrated that in choosing, for example, rectangles, the subjects preferred in their second choice, after two weeks, less stable and thus more tension-evoking rectangles than in their first choice (Weber, 1931) (Brighouse, 1939b did not find the same tendency). Moreover, Barron (1953), Barron & Welsh (1952), and Munsinger & Kessen (1964) showed that people with training in the arts, i.e., people who are more familiar with art stimuli than non-trained observers, prefer more complex geometrical designs and forms than non-trained observers.

Chapter 3

1. Colors are used as a diagnostic tool mainly in the Rorschach test (Rorschach, 1951), in the color-pyramid test of Pfister (Schaie, 1963; E. Stern, 1955), in the Lüscher test (Furrer, 1955), in the mosaic test, (M. Lowenfield, 1949), and in various more structured (Obonai & Matsuoka, 1952, 1956) and less structured personality tests, such as, finger painting (Alschuler & Hattwick, 1947; Napoli, 1947) or projections through play (Wolff, 1946). Reviews of studies relevant to the psycho-diagnostic use of colors have been prepared, for example, by Cerbus & Nichols (1963), Fortier (1953), Kouwer (1949, pp. 143–58), and Norman & Scott (1952, pp. 205–13). Concerning the use of colors in the Rorschach test see also Beck (1950), Rieckers-Ovsiankina (1943), and Schachtel (1943).

By way of summary, the assumption that reactivity to colors in general reflects emotional characteristics has received experimental support, while the more specific hypotheses, i.e., that reactions to certain colors reflect the dominance of particular emotions and affective attitudes, are supported by some studies but disconfirmed by others.

2. It can easily be shown statistically that if two people's rankings are only slightly similar and correlate to the degree of $r = .10–.30$, averaging the reactions of a few people and correlating them with the averaged reactions of another group will produce the impression of considerable consensus. This is the main principle underlying Eysenck's "proofs" (1941c; also Eysenck, 1941b, 1941d) for the existence of a universal color preference ordering. Thus, when Eysenck further shows that the averaged color rankings from 16 separate experiments, performed by different investigations, are highly correlated with each other as well as with the fictitious calculated rank-ordering, this finding does not mean that the 21.600 subjects, who participated in the 16 experiments, agree in their rankings of the colors. Rather, it means that averaging the results of 16 experiments involves disregarding individual differences in a manner which produces the illusion of a high consensus.

Another important argument in this context is that the great extent of individual differences in color preference makes it statistically difficult, sometimes even impossible, to demonstrate significant differences in color preferences between groups of subjects (Valentine, 1962, pp. 33–46). Eysenck tends to interpret these observations as suggesting the overriding impact of a universal color-ordering over group orderings.

3. In the twenties and thirties many attempts were made to clarify the nature of preference responses stated in terms of the degree of pleasantness or unpleasantness evoked by presented stimuli. Most of these studies rely on the introspective reports of the subjects. The findings of these early studies (e.g., Corwin, 1921; Young, 1921; see summary and review by Beebe-Center, 1932) usually point to the existence of actual or felt movements of approach or avoidance accompanying judgments of "Pleasant" or "Unpleasant." However, as Beebe-Center (1932, pp. 339–49) concludes, the experimental evidence does not show action tendencies to be a *sine qua non* of pleasantness/unpleasantness judgments. The same conclusion applies to other organic sensations which were found by some investigators to accompany pleasantness/unpleasantness judgments. Some of

these investigators concluded explicitly that pleasantness/unpleasantness judgments are meanings which do not depend on affective or sensorial processes even if originally they may have been bound up with such processes (Kellog, 1915; Yokoyama, 1921).

Out of the various physiological indices of emotion, the GSR reaction has been most frequently studied in relation to pleasantness/unpleasantness judgments. Using stimuli such as rectangles, geometric forms, and words, Dysinger (1931) and Feasey (1921) found no relation between degree of preference judgments and the extent of mean GSR deflection. A large GSR reaction was observed to occur only in solated instances of extreme pleasantness/unpleasantness judgments. Shock & Coombs (1937), using odors as stimuli, found that judgments of "very unpleasant" were accompanied by a higher mean GSR deflection than the other four categories of judgment, which did not greatly differ from one another. However, the studies by Lanier (1941) and H. M. Wells (1927) show fairly conclusively that GSR reactions are not associated with pleasantness/unpleasantness judgments but with conditions of conflict or indecision.

4. Reference in the text to interpersonally shared meaning responses of modern subjects to various colors is based on the studies of Aaronson (1964, 1967, 1968), Block (1957), Bullough (1908, 1910), Birren (1961), Collins (1924), Hevner (1935a), Hofstätter (1957), Karwoski & Odbert (1938), Kouwer (1949, pp. 78–136). C. O. Lawler & Lawler (1965), Lewinski (1938), Luckiesh (1923, 1938), D.C. Murray & Deabler (1957), Odbert, Karwoski, & Eckerson (1942), Osgood (1960), Osgood, Suci, & Tannenbaum (1957, pp. 299–302), Oyama, Tanaka, & Chiba (1962), R. T. Ross (1938), Schaie (1961), Stamm (1955), Tatibana (1937), Washburn (1911), N. A. Wells (1910), Wexner (1954), Wicker (1966), Wright & Rainwater (1962).

Most of these studies deal with the relation between specific hues and specific meanings. The studies of Osgood (1960) and Wright & Rainwater (1962) are exceptions in that they represent attempts to relate meanings with the various *qualities* of colors. For example, Osgood found that the brightness of colors corresponds to the meaning dimensions of evaluation (i.e., "white" is evaluated as favorable, and "black" as unfavorable); saturation of colors corresponds to the potency dimension (i.e., saturated colors are more potent); and the hue aspect is related to the activity dimension (i.e., "red" is judged as the most active color, and "blue-purple" as the most passive color). Wright & Rainwater dealt partly with much more restricted meaning clusters. They found, for example, that "happiness" is related to the lighter and more saturated colors, or that "elegance" depends primarily on the saturation and less on the blueness of the colors.

5. About the relations between colors and temperature sensations see the studies by Berry (1961), Collins (1924), Kimura (1950), Lewinski (1938), Mogensen & English (1926), Newhall (1941), Osgood (1960), Tinker (1938), and Wright (1962). Mogensen & English (1926), who studied the tactual sensation of warmth of differently colored objects, found that purple objects are perceived as cooler than green and blue objects, but red, orange, and yellow objects fall between the two extremes so that green and blue turned out unexpectedly to be the warmest colors.

Studies which demonstrate that darker colors seem heavier than brighter colors were done by Bullough (1907), DeCamp (1917), Kimura (1950), Koch (1928), Monroe (1925), Osgood (1960), Payne (1958), Taylor (1930), Wright (1962), and

Warden & Flynn (1926). The relation between darkness and heaviness turned up also in studies in which it was not the central object of the experiment, e.g., Karwoski, Odbert, & Osgood (1942) and Wheeler & Cutsforth (1928).

The relation between colors and brightness, on the one hand, and apparent size, on the other hand, are dealt with in the studies by Gundlach & Macoubrey (1931) and Oyama & Nanri (1960).

The relations of colors and brightness to apparent distance were studied by A. Ames (1925), Einthoven (1885), Johns & Sumner (1948), Loewenstein & Donald (1941), Luckiesh (1918b), Mount, Case, Sanderson & Brenner (1956), Oyama & Yamamura (1960), Pillsbury & Schaefer (1937), I. L. Taylor & Sumner (1945), and Verhoeff (1928, 1941).

6. Studies in intersensory interactions, reviewed, for example, by London (1954) and by Ryan (1940), include mainly experiments of three types. The *first type* centers on the demonstration that stimulation of one sense modality influences the sensitivity or acuity of perception in another sense modality. For example, H. M. Johnson (1920) showed that a brightly illuminated visual field may facilitate tactile discrimination in card sorting; Hartmann (1934), I. L. Child & Wendt (1938), and R. F. Thompson, Voss, & Brogden (1958) showed that visual stimulation affects auditory acuity; Kravkov (1934, 1937a, 1937b, 1939a, 1947) and Serrat & Karwoski (1936) showed the effects of auditory stimulation on visual and chromatic sensitivity; Freund (1929) showed the influence of light stimulation on color discrimination; and Maier, Bevan, & Behar (1961) demonstrated the combined effect of loudness of tones and color lights upon the critical flicker fusion frequency in vision.

Studies of the *second type* center on the demonstration that qualities perceived by one sensory system are influenced in a definite manner by stimuli in other sense organs. For example, Hornbostel (1931, 1938) found that when color X was matched in brightness with color Y, and was next matched in brightness with tone Z, then color Y turned out to match tone Z, i.e., brightness is a transitive quality of various sensations (not confirmed by N. E. Cohen, 1934); Zietz (1931) found that when subjects saw filmy, low-saturated colors, the simultaneous sounding of low tones made the colors appear darker, warmer, "dirtier," and reddish-blue, while the sounding of high tones made them appear brighter, colder, greenish-yellowish, more surfacy and more sharply contoured (not confirmed by C. C. Pratt, 1936). P. v. Schiller (1935) showed a corresponding effect of colors on tones. Filling the whole optical field with a color made low-intensity, blurred tones seem more sharply contoured and localized. Similarly v. Schiller (1932) demonstrated that the dimension of roughness/smoothness mediates effects of optical stimuli on auditory and tactile perception, and of auditory stimuli on tactile perception.

Experiments of a *third type* deal with the effects of stimulation in various senses on spatial localization within the framework of one sense modality. For example, K. Goldstein (1925, 1926), and K. Goldstein & Rosenthal-Veit (1926) showed that patients with cerebellar and cortical lesions, who could not keep their arms straight frontally, tended to localize tones in space in the direction to which their arms tended. Yet when a normal subject rolled his closed eyes to the left or fixated an object on the left, he also tended to hear a tone as if it also came from the left. Allers & Schmiedek (1925) showed that having an afterimage in one part of the visual field tended to cause localization of tones in the same section of the space. Compensatory effects, i.e., localization of stimuli in a space sector symmetrical to the one from which other sense stimuli seem to come, were demonstrated by Klemm (1909), K. A. Chandler (1961), and particularly by Werner's school within the framework of the sensori-tonic theory of perception (Wapner, Werner, & Krus, 1957; Werner & Wapner, 1949, 1952; Werner, Wapner, & Bruell, 1953). Finally, the interaction of kinesthetic with visual cues in the perception of distance and depth is too well known to require elaboration.

7. K. Goldstein (1939, 1942), K. Goldstein & Jablonski (1933), and Goldstein & Rosenthal (1930) found a great variety of mental and motor reactions produced by red and green colors. For example, their brain-damaged patients wrote more accurately with green ink than with red ink, and estimated lengths better under green light than under red light. In some patients red light increased loss of equilibrium, abnormal deviation of arms when held out frontally, errors in cutaneous localization, and myopic refraction, while green light had the reverse effects. Likewise, Ehrenwald (1932) found in 100 blindfolded subjects, irradiated successively with red, yellow, blue, and green lights, a tendency to move the arms in the direction of the red and yellow lights, but away from the blue and green lights. Other evidence corroborating Goldstein's conclusions comes from studies by Féré (1900), who found that in hysterics red light increases muscular power, breathing, and circulation; by Stefanescu-Goanga (1911), who found that red, yellow, orange, and purple produced various physiological tension effects, while green, blue, indigo, and violet produced relaxation effects; by Ovio (1932), who found that when a factory of photographic plates was equipped with red windows the workers grew excited and noisy, moved too much, and tired quickly, while green windows had a soothing effect on the workers, who felt much less tired at night; by Gerard (1958), who found that red light produces a greater increase in arousal (i.e., in systolic blood pressure, palmar conductance, respiratory rate, and frequency of blinking, as well as in subjective feelings of tenseness) than white light, and white light a greater increase than blue light; and by G. D. Wilson (1966), who found that red light evokes larger GSR responses than green light.

There are also contrary findings. Pressey (1921) found no differential effects of red, green, and blue illumination upon any of a series of mental and motor activities, e.g., finger tapping, estimates of pressure, multiplying, memory for nonsense syllables; nor could he find any evidence for differential effects on breathing and circulation. Possibly, the short durations of exposure to the lights may account for these negative findings. Yet in some tasks he found that brightness had a stimulating effect, while dim light produced a slowing-down. Similarly, Pierce & Weinland (1934) found that the output of men working at factory machines was neither stimulated by red light nor slowed down by blue light; but that white light produced the most satisfactory work efficiency, while colored lights tended to cause "nervous excitation."

Chapter 4

1. Techniques developed in more recent years have made it possible to demonstrate in a compelling way the organization of perception by units. One technique is based on stabilizing the image of the retina by means of a contact lens and an

optical projection. These keep the image on the same retinal spot despite normal nystagmus and voluntary eye movements of the subject (Pritchard, Heron, & Hebb, 1960; Riggs, Armington, & Ratliff, 1954; Riggs, Ratliff, Cornsweet, & Cornsweet, 1953). The second technique consists in using luminous drawings presented at reduced illumination (McKinney, 1963).

Under these conditions, parts of fixated visual patterns fade and disappear temporarily. Yet the disappearance does not occur randomly, but in perceptual units, so that the remaining parts are often meaningful figures. For example, simple good gestalts, straight lines, or parallel lines tend to be seen together or to disappear as units.

2. According to Köhler (1940) there exists in stimulated sense-organs and in the brain the possibility of the formation of energy fields with a specific structure, just as in the case of magnetic and electromagnetic forces. Both the creation and the structure of these fields depend upon chemical and electric processes. When the nerve impulses, activated by a perceived figure, reach the brain, the discharged ions form an area with a higher level of chemical activity than the surrounding areas of the brain. Thus, there arises presumably a difference in electrical charge between the area corresponding to the perceived figure and the neighboring regions, so that ions diffuse from the former to the latter area, establishing an electromotive force which drives a current about the contours of the figure. This current flow is hypothesized to be independent of anatomical conduction pathways, and depends instead upon functional relations between the figure and its background, which are represented in an isomorphic manner in the medium of the brain tissue. This hypothesis affords a physiological explanation not only of the spontaneous articulation of separate stimuli into gestalts and the involved influence at a distance, but also of the differential tension-grade between the stimulated and nonstimulated parts, that is, of the experienced differential density between the figure and its background.

An attempt was made by Köhler & Wallach (1944) to test the theory through the phenomenon of figural aftereffects, which they attribute to satiation of brain tissue. Yet the state of the theory is still far from clear.

3. A great number of attempts have been made to describe complexity of visual patterns in terms of objective properties of the patterns or forms. The most widely used measures reflect in one way or another Birkhoff's original definition of complexity of polygons as "the number of indefinitely extended straight lines which contain all the sides of the polygon" (Birkhoff, 1933, p. 34). More recent measures are usually couched in terms of information theory and derive from the demonstration by Attneave (1954) and Attneave & Arnoult (1956) that in plane figures information is concentrated at the vertices, i.e., at the points in the contour in which the change in gradient is steepest. Thus, the usual measure of complexity has become the number of sides or points of polygons, or the log transformation of these (e.g., Battig, 1962; A. G. Goldstein, 1961; Munsinger & Kessen, 1964; Vanderplas & Garvin, 1959). Other measures of complexity based on the same rationale include, for example, the number of line segments, angles, and points of intersection of line figures (e.g., Hochberg & McAllister, 1953; Vitz, 1966), number of log_2 transformations (i.e., bits of information) of the number of elements in dot patterns or metric figures (Attneave, 1955; Dorfman & McKenna, 1966), or the number of different parts of a figure which differ in form and location (Terwilliger, 1963).

A wider definition used by Berlyne and workers in his tradition (e.g., Eisenman, 1966b; Smock & Holt, 1962) identifies complexity with the collative variables, i.e., irregularity of arrangement, irregularity of shape, heterogeneity of elements, number of independent units, random distribution of elements, and incongruity.

Other workers in the field of aesthetics of forms have used still different measures of complexity; e.g., Wohlwill (1968) used ratings of paintings by judges who were instructed to rely in their judgments on variation of the stimuli along the attributes of color, shape, direction of dominant lines, texture, and natural vs. artificial, while Fritzky (1963) used the rating of complexity by uninstructed subjects.

In spite of the differences in the measures described, they all seem to share at least one element, which is particularly dominant in the definitions inspired by information theory: number of units. However, even intuitively it is unconvincing that increase in the number of units increases complexity. Why should a pattern of 10 equal parallel lines be considered more complex than a pattern of 5 lines which are unorganized or organized in a not immediately evident manner?

Using ratings of complexity of random shapes, Attneave (1957) found that three factors were needed in order to account for 90 percent of the variance of the ratings (i.e., number of independent terms in the contour, symmetry, and the arithmetic mean of algebraic differences in degrees between successive turns in the contour), and Arnoult (1960) found that even a fourth factor is necessary (i.e., perimeter^2/area). Berlyne, Ogilvie, & Parham (1968) found two major factors to be responsible for ratings of complexity: number of component elements or "information contents" and the degree to which the pattern can be articulated into easily recognizable parts. These two factors seem to be related by a U-shaped curve.

The factor of "information content" has been severely criticized on various grounds, e.g., Garner (1962, chaps. 5–6) demonstrated that redundancy, as a measure of amount of stimulus uncertainty, can apply only to sets of stimuli and not to single stimuli, and that the amount of redundancy has to be differentiated from the form of redundancy; and Michels & Zusne (1965) pointed out, first, that the application of the *bit* measure of information to forms assumes unjustifiably that the probabilities of perceiving all the vertices are equal or known, and secondly, that in the best case this measure specifies the amount of the conveyed information but tells nothing about the manner of the organization of the form. Moreover, Green & Courtis (1966) demonstrated in a series of highly challenging experiments that Attneave's (1954) proof of the concentration of information on the contours of forms may very well depend on artifacts of his methods, i.e., linear and not randomized scanning of forms, or letting subjects use a fixed number of points for specifying particular shapes. Further, by analyzing cartoons they showed that conveying information depends on selecting and omitting contours in accordance with principles which have to do more with meaning than with points of maximum curvature.

These criticisms lead to the main point of this discussion. Complexity seems to depend mainly on the clarity and firmness of organization of the pattern and on the meaning it conveys. This implies that a pattern which allows for the organization of a wealth of meaning and of forms, in one encompassing structure, that determines the role of each part, is essentially simpler than a pattern with fewer elements which are left unintegrated or are not organized into a whole in terms of form or meaning. Since, however, organization depends both on the qualities of the pattern and on the meanings determined by the perceiver, there is not much sense in the attempt to define complexity only in terms of the pattern properties. G. A. Miller (1956) showed how by organizing the stimulus input into "chunks" the load of transmitted information can be greatly reduced by the perceiver, and a visual array that would objectively be judged as complex turns into a relatively simple pattern. More specifically, S. Kreitler (1965) found that not only objectively complex forms may be grasped as simple, but objectively simple forms may become highly complex when grasped as expressive of complex meanings.

Since most of the studies that demonstrate preference for forms of intermediate complexity rely on the described "objective" definitions of complexity, it is difficult to assess the findings. It is to be noted, however, that a common denominator of most of the studies supporting the conclusion that subjects prefer stimuli of intermediate complexity (e.g., Dorfman, 1965; Dorfman & McKenna, 1966; Munsinger & Kessen, 1964; Munsinger, Kessen, & Kessen, 1964; Vitz, 1966; Wohlwill, 1968) is the fact that no gestalts that were good by conventional criteria were included. When they are included, preference seems to shift to them (e.g., Berlyne & Peckham, 1966; Day, 1965; Eisenman, 1967, 1968; Eisenman & Gellens, 1968; Eisenman & Rappaport, 1967). Since organization of stimuli which do not form conventionally simple and good gestalts depends greatly on the perceiver, it is possible that in the studies which demonstrate preference for intermediate complexity, subjects merely preferred the patterns which were easiest to organize meaningfully. Support for this conclusion derives from studies which show that in random shapes, the greatest number of associations (i.e., meaning responses) are evoked either by forms which are highly simple gestalts or by forms which are "objectively" of intermediate complexity (Eisenman, 1966a; A. G. Goldstein, 1961; Vanderplas & Garwin, 1959). (Findings dissonant with this conclusion are reported by Munsinger & Kessen, 1964. But they did not check the actual amount of evoked associations and relied only on the "meaningfulness" ratings by the subjects themselves.)

The above conclusion may be amplified by reference to studies which show that various people may prefer various degrees of complexity ("objectively" defined) in visual patterns (Dorfman & McKenna, 1966; Fritzky, 1963; Vitz, 1966). This is to be expected in view of the demonstrated individual differences in the capacity to process information and organize stimuli (Schroder, Driver, & Streufert, 1967). Moreover, the attempt to reduce the distribution of individual differences to a tight classification into those subjects who prefer complexity and those who prefer simplicity (Barron, 1953; Barron & Welsh, 1952; Eysenck, 1941d) does not seem to do justice to the data (Moyles, Tuddenham, & Block, 1965).

4. Elaboration of these and other instructive examples of tension-laden contrasts created through forms may be found in the books by Arnheim (1954), Garrett (1967), and Kepes (1944).

Chapter 5

1. Concerning the problem of preferences for the Golden Section and other proportions in forms see, for example, studies by Angier (1903), Austin & Sleight (1951), Fechner (1876), Haines & Davies (1904), Schiffman (1966), G. S. Thompson

(1946), Thorndike (1917), Weber (1931), Witmer (1893); and more general reviews and comprehensive bibliographies by Arnheim (1955), Graf (1958), Panofsky (1955, pp. 55–107), and Wittkower (1960).

Birkhoff's (1933) original formula for measuring the aesthetic quality of polygons, vases, poetry, and music is based on two variables: order, o, and complexity c (concerning the definition of complexity see Chapter 4, note 3 above), related as follows: M (aesthetic measure) $= o/c$. The formula has been extensively tested with regard to polygons. Some studies seem to support it, e.g., Beebe-Center & Pratt (1937) and Harsh & Beebe-Center (1939), while more studies contradict it, e.g., Barnhart (1940), Davis (1936), Eysenck (1941d), and Wilson (1939). Eysenck (1941d, 1942) suggested a revision of Birkhoff's formula, and Rashevski (1938) offered a doubtful, physiologically anchored version, which is reported to be related to Birkhoff's M curvilinearly.

2. A more detailed discussion concerning the nature of synesthetic experiences and of archetypes is to be found in Chapter 3, where responses of the same type are analyzed with regard to colors.

3. Concerning the importance of movement in earlier phylogenetic stages see the review by Werner (1957). For example, large groups of animals, such as the amphibians, react primarily only to moving optical stimuli. Others attack only moving objects, and dogs are reported to be unable to discriminate forms unless they are free to move around (Buytendijk, quoted from Werner, 1957, p. 66). This early attentiveness to motion possibly reflects the biologically significant fact that moving objects are potentially more dangerous than static ones. Developmentally viewed, the perception of form as a static phenomenon is a later achievement, following the primary discrimination of and attention to movement. An example of the transitional stages in this course of development is provided by the well-founded assumption that many insects, when flying over an object, perceive a static form as being transformed into a sort of rhythmic pattern of successive elements (Herz, quoted by Werner, 1957, pp. 67–68). We may then assume that one of the developmental phases before form is perceived as completely static would be the perception of form as if it were a frozen movement, or a product of an intensely concentrated movement held at rest. On the human level it has been demonstrated that babies are highly sensitive to motion and react primarily only to moving objects (Beasley, 1933; Morgan & Morgan, 1944; Shirley, 1931), and that children have a lower threshold for movement than adults (Wohlwill, 1960).

A lot of evidence has been adduced to show that the visual fields and world conceptions of children and primitive peoples are loaded with dynamism to a much greater extent than those of normal adults in the Western world. The object-naming, free talk, play, and artistic activities of children reveal that their orientation is primarily motion-directed. A dog is to them a barking-thing or a biting-thing, a bed is conceived as the lying-down-place, and in general, everything is moving, just about to move, has moved, or is at rest after a movement. For primitive people too, the things they see are far from being static and passive objects, but rather represent foci of dynamic powers or mutable things-of-action for ever in a flow of change (Werner, 1957, pp. 140 ff).

This sensitivity to motion is also reflected in the language of more primitive cultures. Objects in movement are often designated by names different from those that refer to the same objects at rest. Some languages may even lack a general abstract term for motions, such as "come" or "go", and highlight instead the movement itself in a grammatical form which may best be described as "eventuating." Likewise, they would speak not of an event as an object (noun) but rather as a verb, "eventing" (Whorf, 1950). According to some early language theorists (Grimm, 1879, and Humboldt 1836) the first words in all languages must have been verbs, that is, terms of motion.

A possible factor increasing the sensitivity to movement at earlier developmental stages is the characteristic primitive tendency to respond to the environment mainly in terms of motor activities. According to Uexküll, who refers primarily to animals, "movement in response to an optical impression is an integrating factor in the melody of the environment, by means of which the forms of objects are brought into inner realization" (quoted by Werner, 1957, p. 67). It has been repeatedly demonstrated that in young children too awareness of objects depends essentially on the extent to which these objects can be grasped, gripped, manipulated, or otherwise motorically handled (Werner, 1957, p. 66). Moreover, it is probable that by means of motor activities—reactive as well as imitative—the basic features of the environment first come to be understood by the small child. His intelligence is initially sensorimotor. It may then be that the inherent self-motional or motoric approach to things in the environment is projected outside, so that the static is endowed with the dynamism felt inside and is thus brought nearer to the individual, and consequently is better understood.

Chapter 6

1. Introductory reviews of various theories about the nature of consonance and dissonance are presented by Bugg (1933), Malmberg (1918), Révész (1954), and Schoen (1940).

2. This observation was pointed out by Wilhelm Kreitler in a course for piano tuners in Vienna, 1924.

3. Fusion has, indeed, been shown to be a characteristic of consonance, but there seem to be further features which define the experiential qualities of consonant chords and intervals. Already Wundt (1902) set forth the hypothesis that consonance is characterized by three criteria: unity of fusion, distinctness of tonal fusion, and dominating tonal element. On the basis of studies, Malmberg (1918) reached the conclusion that the perception of consonance rests on the factors of blending, smoothness, and purity. Kemp (1913) used in his studies the criteria of fusion, agreeableness, harmonic conformity, and sensory conformity. Pratt (1921) found fusion, smoothness, roughness, complexity or separateness of the components, pleasantness, volume and horrisonorousness (vibrant qualitative roughness). Bugg (1933) used the criteria of fusion, blending, smoothness, and purity. Yet, assessment of consonance according to several different criteria does not yield uniform findings. The phenomenon of consonance seems thus to be experientially highly complex, and its perception depends on a multitude of factors, of which loudness is only one of the most noticeable ones (Ortmann, 1928).

4. Köhler's attempt to account for gestalt perception by means of the field theory could be transposed to the domain of acoustics. If, as Helmholtz claims, the fibers of the basilar membrane in the inner ear actually resonate to external frequencies in a manner similar to the wires of a piano, each region being particularly attuned to a specific frequency, then it may readily be assumed that the vibrations activated

by a tone in a certain part of the membrane spread out with decreasing intensity to other parts of the membrane. This spread of the vibrations in the membrane means that a field, in Köhler's sense, is created by each perceived tone. Also within the framework of the resonance theory of hearing, there exists the theoretical possibility of accounting for the formation of a field in the perceiving ear.

5. Major supporters of this cultural approach are, for example, Cazden (1945), Guernsey (1928), Lundin (1947), Moore (1914), and Ogden (1924).

6. Concerning tone sequences it should be emphasized that the degree of complexity or uncertainty should not be estimated by the number of different tones only, as is suggested by Birkhoff (1933, p. 153). Such a definition ignores completely the fact that 10 different tones sounded as a scale present a simple acoustic phenomenon. Complexity can reside only in the relations between the tones. Similarly, there is no sense in attempting to reduce the complexity of a chord to the number of component frequencies or their nearness to equality of amplitude, as is also shown by the inconclusive findings of Berlyne, McDonnell, Nicki, & Parham (1967) who used this measure.

Chapter 7

1. The mood effects of fast tempo and relatively slow tempo rhythms seem to be consistent in the various studies which dealt with the problem. Gatewood (1927) asked her subjects to listen to 10 musical compositions and then to report both the most prominent element (i.e., rhythm, melody, harmony, or timbre) in each piece of music and the dominant mood it evoked. The results indicated that marked rhythm was the chief factor in arousing feelings of happiness, excitement, and stir, while sadness, restfulness, seriousness, and the like were rarely if ever attributed to it. Rigg (1940) played each of five phrases having different mood effects at six different metronome speeds. He found that when played fast, the mood of each piece changed towards the joyful pole, but that the mood of music with sorrowful effects tended to change towards "agitation." Watson (1942) found that fast music is "very exciting," and Gundlach (1935) found that it was characterized by "uneasy." In contrast, slow music is experienced as calm, sad, or dignified depending on other musical features (Gundlach, 1935; Hevner, 1937a; Rigg, 1940; Shimp, 1940).

2. Bibliographies on early studies of rhythm were prepared by Ruckmick (1913, 1915, 1918) and Weld (1912).

3. It has been suggested that the perception of rhythm depends on organic internal processes. McDougall (1902), for example, hypothesized that rhythm is experienced because it corresponds to the periodic facilitation and inhibition of nervous discharge, while Jaques-Dalcroze (1921), the main proponent of the school of eurhythmics, believed that rhythm is perceived on the basis of bodily experience, particularly heartbeat and breathing. The hypothesis suggested in the text is unrelated to these theories. It merely states that periodic life processes may provide criteria for assessing optimal, fast, and slow tempo, although the perception of rhythm may depend on different processes.

4. The recently spreading habit of characterizing musical rhythms in terms of prosodic units, such as iamb, anapest, or dactyl, seems to us inappropriate. The main reason is that a great many rhythmical groups in music do not lend them-

selves to this kind of classification, so that adherence to the prosodic terms does injustice either to music or to the meaning of the prosodic measure. The latter point is demonstrated in one of Meyer's examples which was meant to support the prosodic classification (Meyer, 1956, p. 105, Example 16: see first, third, fifth, and seventh bar). Incidentally, there has been a growing tendency to discard this prosodic terminology even in strictly prosodic investigations.

Chapter 8

1. The conclusions cited in the text are based on the findings of an unpublished experiment by the authors. The experiment was conducted with 30 subjects, all of Western parentage, living in Israel, in the year 1964. The age of the subjects ranged from 20 to 45 years. Fifteen of the subjects were assigned the role of performers, while the other 15 acted as audience. Each of the "performing" subjects got written instructions to portray two routine actions—walking, lifting an imaginary object, etc.—before the group, in a dancing or non-dancing manner. The actions as well as the instructions to portray them dancingly or non-dancingly were randomized among the "performers," so that 15 of the performed actions were designed to be acted dancingly and 15 non-dancingly. The audience was unaware of the performers' instructions. The audience's task was to identify each of the 30 portrayed actions as "dancing" or "non-dancing." These terms were not defined either for the performers or for the audience.

Of the 450 audience responses, 442 represented correct identifications, where "correct" was defined as corresponding to the instructions of the performer. Interviews with the audience and "performers" revealed that the term "dancing" was identified by 93 percent as denoting "different from the habitual." Other recurring features in the proffered definitions were: "expressive and not only functional" (59 percent), "elegant" (31 percent), and "light, floating" (24 percent).

2. The major literary sources on which the discussion of ballet in the text is based are Amberg (1949, 1953), Beaumont & Idzikowski (1940), Chujoy & Manchester (1966), Fokine (1961), Haskell (1945), and Noverre (1951). Comprehensive bibliographies may be found in Beaumont & Idzikowski (1940) and in Praagh & Brinson (1963).

3. The major literary sources on which the discussion of the Indian dance in the text is based are Bhavnani (1965), Bowers (1953), Chatterji (1951), and Frédéric (1957).

4. Habituation has been shown to be much slower with regard to moving stimuli than with regard to static stimuli (Berlyne, 1951; Carr & Brown, 1959; Welker, 1956b). Welker (1956b) showed that a stimulus which changes in position or intensity preserves its novelty quality for a longer period than a non-changing stimulus, unless its movement is rhythmical or otherwise regular.

5. The aspects of dance movements discussed in the text reflect the common denominators of classifications offered by various investigators of dance. Sheets (1966, chap. 4), for example, points out the following aspects of dance movements: tensional quality (amount of apparent effort, i.e., strong, moderate, or weak), linear quality (i.e., the linear design of the body as it moves and the linear pattern traced by the moving body), areal quality (the shape of the body, i.e., contractive vs. expansive, and space delineation, i.e., intensive or extensive, contained or diffused),

and projectional quality (i.e., abrupt, sustained, or ballistic). In contrast to Sheets, who classifies together figural features of body and motion and experiential qualities of movement, Selden (1930, pp. 131–41) emphasizes more the figural aspects, major among which are the floor pattern, the space pattern, and the spatial composition. More comprehensive classifications underlie the notational systems of dance movements. Major among these are the systems developed by Laban (Hutchinson, 1954), by Rudolf and Joan Benesh (F. Hall, 1966), and by Eshkol & Wachmann (1958). Although they differ in flexibility and accuracy, all three systems analyze movement in terms of part of the body that moves, spatial direction of movement, timing (tempo), dynamics (strong or light), and smoothness of flow.

6. The major proponents of the view that understanding of expressive movements is innate are Katz (1951, p. 82), Koffka (1952, pp. 148–49), Köhler (1922, pp. 27–28), and Lorenz (1943, p. 277). Yet this hypothesis seems doubtful in view of the following facts: first, a great part of expressive movements and gestures are culture-specific, i.e., differ across cultures (Bailey, 1942; Belo, 1935; Efron, 1941; LaBarre, 1947; Klineberg, 1940), so that their recognition implies learning; secondly, recognition of expressive connotations of movements increases with age (e.g., Bühler & Hetzer, 1928; Gates, 1923; about learning to recognize facial expressions see the bibliography in Honkavara, 1961, pp. 18–24). On the other hand, even though movements expressive of specific emotional states differ in details across cultures and individuals, they may share at least some general characteristics, such as degree of activation, as has been found by Osgood (1966) with regard to facial expressions. These general characteristics may facilitate the communicative value of movements across cultures.

7. Various aspects of movements, such as postures (Deutsch, 1947; Klein & Thomas, 1931), expansiveness or constriction (King, 1954), design of floor track (Kreitler & Kreitler, 1964; 1968a), etc. (Allport & Vernon, 1933; Enke, 1930; Estes, 1938; Franklin, Feldman, & Odbert, 1948; Wolff, 1945) were shown to be characteristic of people and to be readily apprehended as expressive of their emotional state and personality traits.

Chapter 9

1. Various cultural conceptions of space as they are reflected in the arts and in language are described and discussed by Dorner (1958), Giedion (1963), Hall (1966), Matoré (1961), Whorf (1956).

2. Forty-four observers of sculptures were interviewed upon their exit from a sculptural exhibition in Tel Aviv, Israel. The only question they were asked was: "Would you please describe in short any one of the sculptures you have just seen and liked?"

The results were as follows: 39 (~89 percent) observers described the form of the sculpture; 36 (~82 percent) observers described spatial experiences, 42 (~95 percent) observers mentioned the sculptor's and/or the sculpture's name.

3. The study was performed by the authors in 1964 in Tel Aviv, Israel. It involved recording observers' behavior on five different occasions, predetermined randomly. The subjects included 54 women and 26 men. The experimenters did not make any contact with the subjects, and made their recording unobtrusively so as to be unnoticed by the subjects or anybody else. The recording was made at

a distance from the subject, while the experimenter feigned making notes about a sculpture he seemed to be observing. In the case of 10 subjects, two different experimenters made recordings for the purposes of checking the reliability of the observations. The correspondence between the two recorders was full in 100 percent of the cases.

The four recorded angles of observation were: (a) frontal view, (b) side view (right), (c) rear view, (d) side view (left). The time spent by the observer in viewing the statue in any of the mentioned spatial sections was recorded. In addition, a recording was made of another item in the observers' behavior: touching or stroking the statue's surface. The findings are reported in Chapter 10.

4. The first free-standing Italian sculptures, such as Donatello's *David* of 1408–9 were still designed to be seen only from one side, i.e., frontally (Maclagan, 1935). This was the case even with regard to Michelangelo's *David* (1501–4). The committee set up for deciding the placement of this statue in Florence was unanimous that it required a wall surface and must not be placed in open space, as its bronze cast finally was (Wölfflin, 1952, p. 48). In general, as Rodin (1912, pp. 192–93, 202) pointed out, Michelangelo's figures were conceived as variants of the console, i.e., as a projecting mass that implies the support of the wall behind it. The difficulties encountered by Renaissance sculptors who attempted to create free-standing statues which look right from at least eight sides are admirably described by Benvenuto Cellini (quoted in Read, 1956, pp. 62–63).

Chapter 10

1. Extremes of theories about the origin of the tendency to touch are represented, on the one hand, by Gibson (1966, chap. 6), who regards the haptic system as a channel of information about the environment and the body, and, on the other hand, by Kaplan (1930, chap. 12), who assumes that a "drive to touch" satisfies in a displaced manner certain components of the sexual need.

Chapter 11

1. Positive findings about the existence of phonetic symbolism are to be found also in the studies by Dagiri (1958), Iritani (reported by Werner & Kaplan, 1963, pp. 219–26), Köhler (1910, 1911, 1913, 1915), Miron (1960), Stumpf (1926), Taylor & Taylor (1962).

Concerning the methodological problems which cast doubt on studies of guessing meanings in foreign languages, see Brown (1958, pp. 119–31), and Taylor & Taylor (1965).

Concerning the problem of the uniformity of meanings attributed to the same phonemes by members of different linguistic cultures: positive results were got by Davis (1961), who studied English- and Swahili-speaking children, and by Miron (1961), who studied American and Japanese students. A comparison of findings by Newman (1933) and Sapir (1929), who worked with American subjects, and Czurda (1953), who worked with German subjects, also points to cross-cultural correspondences, at least with regard to size and brightness of vowels. Absolute negative findings about uniformity of connotations were reported by Taylor &

Taylor (1962) with regard to Tamil and Korean, Japanese and Tamil, Japanese and Korean; and largely negative results were reported by Black & Brown (Brown, 1958, pp. 127–28) with regard to Chinese and English.

2. A famous instance of synesthetic relations between phonemes and colors is given by Rimbaud (1943, p. 141): "I have invented the color of the vowels!—A black, E white, I red, O blue, U green—I have ordered the form and the movement of each consonant, and with instinctive rhythms I have flattered myself that I have invented a poetic verb, accessible one day or another to every sense." For further references about synesthesias in literature see also Engstrom (1946), Erhardt-Siebold (1932), and Ullman (1945).

3. Concerning the role of the distinctive features in a phonemic analysis of literature, note that not all languages allow the use of all the features to an equal degree. Herzog (1946) found that in the languages of some American Indian peoples the features voiced/voiceless and nasal/oral are disregarded, particularly in poetry, while the features grave/acute and compact/diffuse are rigorously maintained.

Similarly, the manipulation of phonemes by writers and poets is restricted by the relative frequencies of the phonemes, and the probabilities which govern their sequences in the language. Thus, in English, voiceless plosives like /k/, /t/, and /p/ are more frequent than voiced plosives like /b/, /d/, and /g/ (Zipf, 1935); consonants are more frequent than vowels and diphthongs (i.e., vowels constitute 62 percent, consonants only 38 percent of all speech sounds); /n/ and /t/ are much more frequent than /g/ and /j/ (Dewey, 1923); some consonants, like /w/, /j/, /h/, and /b/ appear mainly in the beginning of words while others, like /z/, /v/, and /r/ appear principally at the end (Bagley, 1900), etc.

The importance of these observations for the role of phonemes in literature is attested by the finding that people are aware of the differential frequencies of sounds in their language. Attneave (1953) asked his subjects to indicate how many times, out of a thousand letters, each of the letters of the alphabet would occur. The correlation between these judgments and actual counts of printed English was .79, i.e., the subjects' estimates were fairly accurate.

No less restrictive are the sequential frequencies of phonemes. By studying the frequency with which each phoneme in English was followed by every other phoneme, Carroll (Osgood & Sebeok, 1965, pp. 102–3) found, for instance, a tendency to avoid clusters whose phonemes are highly similar or highly dissimilar in terms of distinctive features.

4. For other examples of individual differences in use of words see Mahl (1963) and Sanford (1942).

5. On different uses of words by various authors see the extensive bibliographies prepared by Bailey & Burton (1968, "Diction," pp. 76–80), and by Bailey & Doležel (1968, section 3, pp. 13–48, section 4, pp. 61–74, section 5, pp. 75–79).

6. The "Cloze procedure" of guessing deleted words was suggested by Taylor (1953). For other techniques of studying expectations about word sequences see Coupling (1948) and Miller & Selfridge (1950).

7. At the articulatory level the production of a breath group involves a coordinated pattern of activity by the subglottal, laryngeal, and supraglottal muscles (Liebermann, 1967). The unmarked breath group, i.e., the intonational contour of the simple declarative sentence, has been shown to result from the physiological fact that the tension of the laryngeal muscles remains constant during the articula-

tion of the phrase or sentence, so that there is a decline in the subglottal air pressure at the end. This effect can be counteracted by increasing the tension of the laryngeal muscles towards the end. The result is a marked breath group, i.e., an intonation contour that characterizes the typical question sentence that ends with a rise in pitch.

The major aspects of an intonation contour are (a) pitch, i.e., the fundamental frequency of the tone (in cps), which can be described, for example, in terms of the average fundamental frequency, its peak, its minimum, or in a successive manner; (b) stress, i.e., differences in loudness, which are usually described in terms of four levels (Trager & Smith, 1951); (c) emphasis, i.e., extra prominence on a vowel or vowels of a word and its consonants attained through an increase in fundamental frequency, amplitude, or duration, and which is to be differentiated from the stress that the vowels would have received in accordance with the phonologic stress rules governing (c) (Chomsky & Halle, 1966); and (d) junctures, i.e., pauses of various duration within a sentence and between sentences. For further qualities of the intonational contour, and about differences in contours in different languages, see, for example, Abercrombie (1967, chap. 6), Pike (1945), and the bibliographical sources summarized by Lieberman (1967, chap. 9).

It is obvious that emotion and particular attitudes of the speaker can modify the intonational contour of an utterance in various ways—raise or lower the average fundamental frequency, extend or narrow down its range, change the number and extent of pauses, etc. Intonational contours help listeners to identify a great variety of the speakers' emotional states (Lieberman & Michaels, 1962), but the emotions associated with a particular contour depend greatly on the sentences' words (Denes, 1959; Hadding-Koch, 1961; Uldall, 1960). The full impact of intonation contours as expressive of emotions may be expected to depend on qualities of the speaker's voice no less than on the sentence's meaning. Yet voice qualities, which provide highly potent cues for the identification of emotions (Davitz, 1964), exist only when there is an actual performer who reads the text aloud, and cannot be replaced through other cues in the course of silent reading by the usual reader of literature.

8. The view that English meter is an accentual meter, based on the periodicity of stresses, is contested by other approaches, major among which is the temporal view. According to the supporters of "temporal" prosody (Abercrombie, 1964; Baker, 1960; Lanier, 1880; Stewart, 1930) all verse has isochronic rhythm, and is based on a scale of duration of syllables similar to that of notes in music. The main arguments leveled against the "temporal" approach are, first, that syllables in English do not differ in duration in any consistent manner (De Groot, 1957) and, second, that the "temporal" approach gives free reign to subjective individual readings of a poem (Wellek & Warren, 1956, pp. 167–68). The first argument reflects the position that analysis of English meter in terms of durational differences between syllables is an attempt to impose the Greek or Latin quantitative meter on English; while the second argument is based on the view that a sharp distinction should be made between the structure of the poem and its rendering in different individual performances (Wimsatt & Beardsley, 1959). Concerning this whole issue see Fussell (1965) and Scripture (1921) as well as the discussion between Wimsatt & Beardsley (1959, 1961) and Hendren (1961).

9. About ways in which deviations from meter arise from interactions between meter and the rhythms of language (i.e., sequences of stress, pitch, and juncture)

and idea, as well as about the experiential effects of these deviations see also Chatman (1960, pp. 157–61), Halle & Keyser (1966), Levin (1965), McAuley (1966), Schramm (1935), and Wimsatt & Beardsley (1959).

10. The full quotation in the German original (Kraus, 1961, pp. 257–58) is as follows:

Nicht Würze ist er, sondern Nahrung,
er ist nicht Reiz, er ist die Paarung.

Er ist das Ufer, wo sie landen,
sind zwei Gedanken einverstanden.

The translation in the text is by the authors.

Chapter 13

1. The view represented in the text is that set is a centrally shaped phenomenon. The issue of the central vs. peripheral locus of set played an important role in the experimental study of set (Gibson, 1941, pp. 786–87) as it did with regard to thinking. Recent findings (Sanders, 1966; Sutton et al., 1965) render the issue antiquated, and highlight set as a phenomenon directed centrally and manifested also peripherally. See also Ryan (1970).

2. English translations of some of Lipps's articles may be found in Lipps (1926; 1962; 1965). A similar theory was suggested, apparently independently, by Lee (1913), while some of the major theoretical principles of the theory may be traced back to earlier philosophers, notably Lord Kames, Herder, and Vischer.

The fact that Lipps's theory has been largely ignored in American psychology may be due in part to the criticism raised against it by Langfeld (1920). This criticism, which seems to have become in some circles more famous than Lipps's theory itself, is grounded in a partial and biased account of Lipps's claims given by Langfeld. According to Langfeld, "Lipps has insisted that there is not in us the actual sensation of muscular effort. He believes in a purely mental process without any sensational basis, an idea which is entirely free of bodily processes, a mystical mind substance" (Langfeld, 1920, p. 116). Further, Langfeld asserts that the "mental process" stressed by Lipps refers to the manner in which a perceived form has presumably been constructed or drawn. However, it has been precisely Lipps's great contribution to the problem of empathy that he laid a particular emphasis on motoric imitation tendencies and on kinesthetic sensations as the major determinants of empathy. Citations in the chapter's text amply support this point.

Yet more astonishing is the fact that the theory of empathy suggested by Langfeld himself resembles so closely Lipps's theory. The major points Langfeld emphasizes, presumably in contradistinction to Lipps, are first, that the perception of a form touches off movements corresponding to the drawing of the form (Langfeld, 1920, p. 122); second, that "the impulse may be so far in an initial stage that there is no movement produced and frequently not even a consciousness of strain or of other similar sensations" (ibid., p. 126); and third, that "these sensations of movement or tendencies of movement are projected into the lines and shapes. They are not felt as movements of our body but fuse with the object . . . giving character and meaning to the object" (ibid., p. 122). All these points have been very clearly elaborated by Lipps, as the chapter's text shows.

3. The study was performed by the authors in the year 1964, in Tel Aviv, Israel. The observed subjects included 38 men and 52 women. The subjects were selected according to the following principle. After six sculptures were chosen by the experimenters for the purposes of the study, it was determined randomly on which days of the week and during which hours spectators of each sculpture will be observed. The observations continued until the movements of fifteen subjects observing each of the sculptures were recorded. The records were made independently by two trained experimenters. These experimenters never contacted the subjects and made their records in a manner which did not attract the subjects' attention. The reliability of the records was checked by comparing both the number of movement units noted by the two experimenters as well as the nature of the recorded movements or postures. The correlation between the two observers with regard to the number of movement units per observed subject was .91. The correspondence in the nature of the recorded movements was complete in 78 percent of the cases.

The task of the judges, who were well trained in the Eshkol-Wachmann notation system, was to match, if possible, each of the movements or postures of the 15 subjects observing any of the sculptures with 1 out of the 8 photographed views of that sculpture. The correspondence between the judgments of the two judges was complete in 76 percent of the cases. The findings mentioned in the text represent means computed on the basis of the results of the two judges.

Chapter 14

1. Concerning multiple identifications with various figures in the same work of art, see, for example, Buxbaum (1941), Wolf & Fiske (1949), and Wolfenstein & Leites (1950).

2. The problem of combining various organizations of the same work of art into a comprehensive grasp by concentrating on one of the organizations is dealt with extensively in Chapter 9, in the section Changing Angles of Observation. However, the discussion in Chapter 9 is devoted only to integrating the different views of a sculpture as seen from various angles of observation.

3. Bruner, Goodnow, & Austin (1956, pp. 30–33) refer to the essential features as criterial in the sense that they greatly facilitate the identification of what is perceptually presented, and point out some of the factors which determine the criteriality of attributes (Bruner et al., pp. 33–41). Major among these are the objective validity of the attribute, its location in innate and acquired cue-preference hierarchies, its utility for systematic classification of phenomena, and its linguistic codability. A similar conception but from a different viewpoint is offered by Arnheim (1969). He calls attributes of high criteriality "generative features," since he views their main function as enabling the perceiver to go beyond the given information and develop a more complete image than is strictly warranted by the presented stimuli. In an attempt to define their nature, Arnheim suggests that generative features reflect the structural dynamics of a phenomenon (Arnheim, 1969, pp. 144–48) and that they are features which affect many aspects of the represented object or event (ibid., p. 174).

These attempts to pinpoint the nature of criterial features seem to be as unsatisfactory as are similar attempts to regard the features essential for the identification of visual forms as turns and points of maximum curvature at the contours (Attneave, 1954). Approaches of both types fail to take account of the fact that the features criterial for identifying percepts or concepts must be central in the meaning structure of the corresponding percept or concept, and hence cannot be specified as identical for all percepts and concepts. While points of maximum curvature may be essential for identifying visual designs of the purely decorative type, they may turn out to be irrelevant for grasping human types depicted by skilled cartoonists, who often omit the presentation of changes in contours (Green & Curtis, 1966). Similarly, the criterial features for identifying a man in general may be a certain disposition of the head, trunk, and limbs, but for identifying a particular person they may include the specific tilt of the head and certain movements. Thus, the attempt to specify criterial features may in the best case prove fruitful for only limited classes of percepts or concepts.

4. In view of the extraordinary wealth of literature on symbols and the great diversity in the proposed definitions of symbols (S. Kreitler, 1965, pp. 12–45) only a few examples can be cited of correspondences between our symbolic categories and definitions suggested by other workers in this domain. Thus, "an exemplifying instance" seems to be the category to which Arieti (1959) and Von Domarus (1964) refer when they describe the symbolic thinking of schizophrenics; "bodily movement and expression" predominates in the definitions of "symbol" offered by the expression theorists (Bühler, 1933), by the psychosomaticists (Ferenczi, 1926), and even by Freud in some of his writings (Freud, 1953, vol. 4, pp. 218–19; 1964, pp. 98–99); "sensation and feeling" is emphasized, for example, by Fromm (1951, pp. 12, 17–18), Smith (1922), and Spiegel (1959) and is used by Osgood et al. (1957); "metaphor" was analyzed as the representative of symbolism by Freud (1953), Piaget (1951), and Werner & Kaplan (1963), each from a different viewpoint; and finally, the "symbol" has been defined, analyzed, and even extolled by Jung (1953a; 1953b) and by representatives of disciplines as different as philosophy (Buber, 1952), the study of religion (Eliade, 1955; 1959), and literary criticism (Bodkin, 1934), to mention just a few.

References

Aaronson, B. S. Hypnotic induction of colored environments. *Perceptual and Motor Skills*, 1964, *8*, 30.

Aaronson, B. S. Some affective stereotypes of color. Paper presented at the meetings of the EPA, Boston, Mass., 1967.

Aaronson, B. S. Color perception and affect. Paper presented at meetings of the Society of Clinical and Experimental Hypnosis, Chicago, 1968.

Abbot, W. *The Theory and Practice of Perspective.* London: Blackie & Son, 1950.

Abell, W. *Representation and Form.* New York: Scribner's, 1936.

Abelson, R. P., Aronson, E., McGuire, W. J., Newcomb, T. M., Rosenberg, M. J., & Tannenbaum, P. H., eds. *Theories of Cognitive Consistency: A Source Book.* Chicago: Rand McNally, 1968.

Abercrombie, D. A phonetician's view of verse structure. *Linguistics*, 1964, *6*, 5–13.

Abercrombie, D. *Elements of General Phonetics.* Chicago: Aldine, 1967.

Adam, L. *Primitive Art.* Harmondsworth: Penguin Books, 1940.

Adams, E. Q. A theory of color vision. *Psychological Review*, 1923, *30*, 56–76.

Alexander, F. *Fundamentals of Psychoanalysis.* New York: Norton, 1948.

Alfert, E. Comparison of responses to a vicarious and a direct threat. *Journal of Experimental Research in Personality*, 1966, *1*, 179–86.

Allemann, B., Caruso, I.-A., Davy, M.-M., Millet, L., Morel, G., Ruyer, R., & Trouillard, J. *Le Symbole.* Paris: Librairie Arthème Fayard, 1959.

Allen, E. L., & Guilford, J. P. Factors determining the affective values of color combinations. *American Journal of Psychology*, 1936, *48*, 643–48.

Allers, R., & Schmiedek, O. Über die Wahrnehmung der Schallrichtung. *Psychologische Forschung*, 1925 *6*, 92–112.

Allesch, G. J. von. Die ästhetische Erscheinungsweise der Farben. *Psychologische Forschung*, 1925, *6*, 1–91, 215–81.

Allport, F. H. *Social Psychology.* New York: Houghton Mifflin, 1924.

Allport, F. H. *Theories of Perception and the Concept of Structure.* New York: Wiley, 1955.

Allport, G. W. Phonetic symbolism in Hungarian words. Unpublished manuscript, Harvard University, 1935.

Allport, G. W. *Becoming.* New Haven, Conn.: Yale University Press, 1955.

Allport, G. W., & Vernon, P. E. *Studies in Expressive Movements.* New York: Macmillan, 1933.

Alschuler, R., & Hattwick, L. *Painting and Personality; A Study of Young Children.* Chicago: University of Chicago Press, 1947.

Amberg, G. *Ballet in America.* New York: Duell, 1949.

Amberg, G. *Ballet.* Mentor Book, M 42. New York: New American Library, 1953.

Ames, A. Depth in pictorial art. *Art Bulletin*, 1925, *8*, 5–24.

Ames, V. M. What is music? *Journal of Aesthetics and Art Criticism*, 1967, *26*, 241–49.

Amsel, A. Selective association and the anticipatory goal response mechanism as explanatory concepts in learning theory. *Journal of Experimental Psychology,* 1949, *39,* 785–99.

Amsel, A., & Maltzman, I. The effect upon generalized drive strength of emotionality as inferred from the level of consummatory response. *Journal of Experimental Psychology,* 1950, *40,* 563–69.

Amsel, A., & Roussel, J. Motivational properties of frustration: I. Effects on a running response of the addition of frustration to the motivational complex. *Journal of Experimental Psychology,* 1952, *43,* 363–68.

Andrew, R. J. Fear responses in *Emberiza. British Journal of Animal Behavior, Supplement,* 1956, *4,* 125–32.

Angier, R. P. The aesthetics of unequal division. *Psychological Review, Monograph Supplements,* 1903, *4,* 541–61.

Arieti, S. Schizophrenia: the manifest symptomatology, the psychodynamic and formal mechanisms. In S. Arieti, ed., *American Handbook of Psychiatry.* Vol. I. New York: Basic Books, 1959. Pp. 455–84.

Armstrong, L. E., & Ward, I. C. *Handbook of English Intonation.* Leipzig: Teubner, 1926.

Arnheim, R. Perceptual abstraction and art. *Psychological Review,* 1947, *54,* 66–82.

Arnheim, R. The holes of Henry Moore: on the function of space in sculpture. *Journal of Aesthetics and Art Criticism,* 1948, *7,* 29–38.

Arnheim, R. The gestalt theory of expression. *Psychological Review,* 1949, *56,* 156–71.

Arnheim, R. *Art and Visual Perception: A Psychology of the Creative Eye.* Berkeley: University of California Press, 1954.

Arnheim, R. A review of proportion. *Journal of Aesthetics and Art Criticism,* 1955, *14,* 44–57.

Arnheim, R. Emotion and feeling in psychology and art. *Confinia Psychiatrica,* 1958, *1,* 69–88.

Arnheim, R. Perceptual analysis of a cosmological symbol. *Journal of Aesthetics and Art Criticism,* 1961, *19,* 389–99.

Arnheim, R. *Visual Thinking.* Berkeley: University of California Press, 1969.

Arnold, M. B., & Gasson, J. A., S.J. Feelings and emotions as dynamic factors in personality integration. In M. B. Arnold & J. A. Gasson, S.J., eds., *The Human Person.* New York: Ronald, 1954. Chap. 10, pp. 294–313.

Arnoult, M. D. Prediction of perceptual responses from structured characteristics of the stimulus. *Perceptual and Motor Skills,* 1960, *11,* 261–68.

Asch, S. The doctrine of suggestion, prestige and imitation in social psychology. *Psychological Review,* 1948, *55,* 250–76.

Asch, S. E. On the use of metaphor in the description of persons. In H. Werner, ed., *On Expressive Language.* Worcester, Mass: Clark University Press, 1955. Pp. 29–38.

Asch, S. E. The metaphor: a psychological inquiry. In R. Tagiuri & L. Petrullo, eds., *Person Perception and Interpersonal Behavior.* Stanford, Calif.: Stanford University Press, 1958. Pp. 86–94.

Astrup, C. Pavlovian concepts of abnormal behavior in man and animal. In M. W. Fox, ed., *Abnormal Behavior in Animals.* Philadelphia: Saunders, 1968. Pp. 117–28.

Atkinson, J. W. *An Introduction to Motivation.* Princeton, N.J.: Van Nostrand, 1964.

Attneave, F. Psychological probability as a function of experienced frequency. *Journal of Experimental Psychology*, 1953, 46, 81–86.

Attneave, F. Some informational aspects of visual perception. *Psychological Review*, 1954, 61, 183–93.

Attneave, F. Symmetry, information and memory for patterns. *American Journal of Psychology*, 1955, 68, 209–22.

Attneave, F. Physical determinants of the judged complexity of shapes. *Journal of Experimental Psychology*, 1957, 53, 221–27.

Attneave, F., & Arnoult, M. D. The quantitative study of shape and pattern perception. *Psychological Bulletin*, 1956, 53, 452–71.

Austin, T. R., & Sleight, R. B. Aesthetic preference for isosceles triangles. *Journal of Applied Psychology*, 1951, 35, 430–31.

Ax, A. F. Physiological differentiation of emotional states. *Psychosomatic Medicine*, 1953, 15, 433–42.

Bachelard, G. *L'Air et les songes*. Paris: Corti, 1943.

Bachofen, J. J. Versuch über die Gräbersymbolik der Alten. In J. J. Bachofen, *Mutterrecht und Urreligion*. Stuttgart: Kröner Verlag, 1954. Pp. 1–62.

Bacon, W. A., & Breen, R. S. *Literature as Experience*. New York: McGraw-Hill, 1959.

Bagley, W. C. The apperception of the spoken sentence: a study in the psychology of language. *American Journal of Psychology*, 1900, 12, 80–130.

Bailey, F. Navaho motor habits. *American Anthropologist*, 1942, 44, 210–34.

Bailey, R. W., & Burton, D. M., S.N.D. *English Stylistics: A Bibliography*. Cambridge, Mass.: M.I.T. Press, 1968.

Bailey, R. W., & Dolezel, L. *An Annotated Bibliography of Statistical Stylistics*. Ann Arbor, Mich.: Michigan Slavic Materials, 1968.

Baker, S. English meter *is* quantitative. *College English*, 1960, 21, 309–15.

Balken, E. R., & Masserman, J. H. The language of phantasy: III. The language of the phantasies of patients with conversion hysteria, anxiety state, and obsessive-compulsive neuroses. *Journal of Psychology*, 1940, 10, 75–86.

Bandura, A. Influence of models' reinforcement contingencies on the acquisition of imitative responses. *Journal of Personality and Social Psychology*, 1965, 1, 589–95.

Bandura, A. *Principles of Behavior Modification*. New York: Holt, Rinehart, and Winston, 1969.

Bandura A., & Menlove, F. L. Factors determining vicarious extinction of avoidance behavior through symbolic modeling. *Journal of Personality and Social Psychology*, 1968, 8, 99–108.

Bandura, A., & Rosenthal, T. L. Vicarious classical conditioning as a function of arousal level. *Journal of Personality and Social Psychology*, 1966, 3, 54–62.

Bandura, A., Ross, D., & Ross, S. A. Imitation of film-mediated aggressive models. *Journal of Abnormal and Social Psychology*, 1963, 66, 3–11.

Barber, T. X., & Hahn, K. W. Experimental studies in "hypnotic" behavior: physiologic and subjective effects of imagined pain. *Journal of Nervous and Mental Disease*, 1964, 139, 416–25.

Barker, R., Dembo, T., & Lewin, K. Frustration and regression: an experiment with young children. *University of Iowa Studies in Child Welfare*, 1941, 18, no. 1.

Barnhart, E. The criteria used in preferential judgments of geometrical forms. *American Journal of Psychology*, 1940, 53, 354–70.

Barron, F. Complexity-simplicity as a personality dimension. *Journal of Abnormal and Social Psychology*, 1953, 48, 163–72.

Barron, F., & Welsh, G. S. Artistic perception as a possible factor in personality style: its measurement by a figure preference test. *Journal of Psychology*, 1952, 33, 199–203.

Bartlett, F. C. An experimental study of some problems of perceiving and imagining. *British Journal of Psychology*, 1916, 8, 222–66.

Bartlett, F. C. *Remembering*. London: Cambridge University Press, 1932.

Bastock, M., Morris, D., & Moynihan, M. Some comments on conflict and thwarting in animals. *Behavior*, 1954, 6, 66–84.

Battig, W. F. Some factors affecting performance on a word-formation problem. *Journal of Experimental Psychology*, 1957, 54, 96–104.

Battig, W. F. Effects of previous experience and information on performance on a word-formation problem. *Journal of Experimental Psychology*, 1958, 56, 282–87.

Battig, W. F. Interrelationships between measures of association and structural characteristics of nonsense shapes. *Perceptual and Motor Skills*, 1962, 14, 3–6.

Baudelaire, C. Correspondances. In C. Baudelaire, *Œuvres*. Bruxelles: Editions La Boétie, 1918. P. 11.

Baum, P. F. . . . *The Other Harmony of Prose . . .: An Essay in English Prose Rhythm*. Durham, N.C.: Duke University Press, 1952.

Beach, F. A. Analysis of the stimuli adequate to elicit mating behavior in the sexually inexperienced male rat. *Journal of Comparative Psychology*, 1942, 33, 163–207.

Beardsley, M. C. *Aesthetics from Classical Greece to the Present: A Short History*. New York: Macmillan, 1966.

Beasley, W. C. Visual pursuit in 109 white and 142 Negro newborn infants. *Child Development*, 1933, 4, 106–20.

Beaumont, C. W., & Idzikowski, S. *A Manual of the Theory and Practice of Classical Theatrical Dancing (Classical Ballet; Cecchetti Method)*. London: Beaumont, 1940.

Beck, S. J. Emotional experience as a necessary constituent in knowing. In M. L. Reymert, ed., *Feelings and Emotions, The Mooseheart Symposium*. New York: McGraw-Hill, 1950. Pp. 95–108.

Beebe-Center, J. G. The law of affective equilibrium. *American Journal of Psychology*, 1929, 41, 54–69.

Beebe-Center, J. G. *The Psychology of Pleasantness and Unpleasantness*. New York: Van Nostrand, 1932.

Beebe-Center, J. G., Black, P., Hoffman, A. C., & Wade, M. Relative per diem consumption as a measure of preference in the rat. *Journal of Comparative and Physiological Psychology*, 1948, 41, 239–51.

Beebe-Center, J. G., & Pratt, C. C. A test of Birkhoff's aesthetic measure. *Journal of General Psychology*, 1937, 17, 339–53.

Bell, C. *Art*. London: Chatto & Windus, 1914.

Belo, J. The Balinese temper. *Character and Personality*, 1935, 4, 120–246.

Berg, H. *Die Lust an der Musik erklärt nebst einem Anhang: Die Lust an den Farben, den Formen und der körperlichen Schönheit*. Berlin: Behr, 1879.

Berger, S. M. Conditioning through vicarious instigation. *Psychological Review*, 1962, 69, 450–66.

Bergler, E. Psychoanalysis of writers and of literary productivity. In G. Roheim, ed., *Psychoanalysis and the Social Sciences*. Vol. I. New York: International Universities Press, 1947.

Bergson, H. *Time and Free Will*. 6th impression. London: George Allen & Unwin, 1950.

Berkowitz, L. *Aggression: A Social Psychological Analysis*. New York: McGraw-Hill, 1962.

Berlyne, D. E. Novelty and curiosity as determinants of exploratory behavior. *British Journal of Psychology*, 1950, *41*, 68–80.

Berlyne, D. E. Attention to change. *British Journal of Psychology*, 1951, *42*, 269–78.

Berlyne, D. E. The influence of complexity and novelty in visual figures on orienting responses. *Journal of Experimental Psychology*, 1958, *55*, 289–96. (a)

Berlyne, D. E. The influence of the albedo and complexity of stimuli on visual fixation in the human infant. *British Journal of Psychology*, 1958, *49*, 315–18. (b)

Berlyne, D. E. *Conflict, Arousal and Curiosity*. New York: McGraw-Hill, 1960.

Berlyne, D. E. Motivational problems raised by exploratory and epistemic behavior. In S. Koch, ed., *Psychology: A Study of a Science*. Vol. 5. New York: McGraw-Hill, 1963. (a)

Berlyne D. E. Complexity and incongruity variables as determinants of exploratory choice and evaluative ratings. *Canadian Journal of Psychology*, 1963, *17*, 274–90. (b)

Berlyne, D. E. Measures of aesthetic preference. *Sciences de l'Art* (special number), 1965, *3*, 9–23. (a)

Berlyne, D. E. *Structure and Direction in Thinking*. New York: Wiley, 1965. (b)

Berlyne, D. E. Arousal and information. In D. Levine, ed., *Nebraska Symposium on Motivation*. Lincoln: University of Nebraska Press, 1967. Pp. 1–110.

Berlyne, D. E., Craw, M. A., Salapatek, P. H., & Lewis, J. L. Novelty, complexity, incongruity, extrinsic motivation and the GSR. *Journal of Experimental Psychology*, 1963, *66*, 560–67.

Berlyne, D. E., & Lawrence, G. H. Effects of complexity and incongruity variables on GSR, investigatory behavior and verbally expressed preference. *Journal of General Psychology*, 1964, *71*, 21–45.

Berlyne, D. E., & McDonnell, P. Effects of stimulus complexity and incongruity on duration of EEG desynchronization. *Electroencephalography and Clinical Neurophysiology*, 1965, *18*, 156–61.

Berlyne, D. E., McDonnell, P., Nicki, R. M., & Parham, L. C. C. Effects of auditory pitch and complexity on EEG desynchronization and on verbally expressed judgments. *Canadian Journal of Psychology*, 1967, *21*, 346–67.

Berlyne, D. E., Ogilvie, J. C., & Parham, L. C. C. The dimensionality of visual complexity, interestingness and pleasingness. *Canadian Journal of Psychology*, 1968, *22*, 376–87.

Berlyne, D. E., & Peckham, S. The Semantic Differential and other measures of reaction to visual complexity. *Canadian Journal of Psychology*, 1966, *20*, 125–35.

Berlyne, D. E., & Slater, J. Perceptual curiosity, exploratory behavior and maze learning. *Journal of Comparative and Physiological Psychology*, 1957, *50*, 228–32.

Bernard, C. *Leçons sur les propriétés physiologiques et les altérations pathologiques des liquides de l'organisme.* Paris: Ballière, 1859. 2 vols.

Bernberg, R. E. Prestige suggestion in art as communication. *Journal of Social Psychology,* 1953, *38,* 23–30.

Bernstein, S., & Mason, W. A. The role of age and stimulus characteristics in the emotional responses of young rhesus monkeys. Unpublished report, University of Wisconsin, 1960.

Berry, P. C. Effect of colored illumination upon perceived temperature. *Journal of Applied Psychology,* 1961, *45,* 248–50.

Bettelheim, B. Harry—a study in rehabilitation. *Journal of Abnormal Psychology,* 1949, *44,* 231–65.

Bhavnani, E. *The Dance in India: The Origin and History, Foundations, the Art and Science of the Dance in India—Classical, Folk and Tribal.* Bombay: D. B. Taraporevala Sons & Co., 1965.

Biedma, C. J., & D'Alfonso, P. G. *Die Sprache der Zeichnung.* Bern: Huber, 1959.

Bindra, D. *Motivation: A Systematic Reinterpretation.* New York: Ronald, 1959.

Bindra, D., & Spinner, N. Response to different degrees of novelty: the incidence of various activities. *Journal of Experimental Analysis of Behavior,* 1958, *1,* 341–50.

Bingham, W. V. D. Studies in melody. *Psychological Monographs,* 1910, *12,* whole no. 50.

Binswanger, L. *Being-in-the-World: Selected Papers of L. Binswanger.* New York: Harper & Row, 1967.

Birdwhistell, R. L. Body motion research and interviewing. *Human Organization,* 1952, *11,* 37–38.

Birdwhistell, R. L. The kinetic level in the investigation of the emotions. In P. H. Knapp, ed., *Expression of the Emotions in Man.* New York: International Universities Press, 1963. Pp. 123–39.

Birkhoff, G. D. *Aesthetic Measure.* Cambridge, Mass.: Harvard University Press. 1933.

Birren, F. *Color Psychology and Color Therapy.* Rev. ed. New Hyde Park, N.Y.: University Books, 1961.

Black, M. Metaphor. In F. J. Coleman, ed., *Contemporary Studies in Aesthetics.* New York: McGraw-Hill, 1968. Pp. 216–32.

Blasis, C. *The Theory of Theatrical Dancing; with a Chapter on Pantomime, Edited from the Code of Terpsichore,* ed. S. D. Headlam. London: Verinder, 1888.

Blatt, S. Patterns of cardiac arousal during complex neural activity. *Journal of Abnormal and Social Psychology,* 1961, *63,* 272–82.

Blaukopf, K. *Musiksoziologie.* St. Gallen, Switzerland: Verlag Zollikofer, n.d.

Bleuler, M., & Bleuler, R. Rorschach's ink-blot tests and racial psychology. *Character and Personality,* 1935, *4,* 97–114.

Block, J. Studies in the phenomenology of emotion. *Journal of Abnormal and Social Psychology,* 1957, *54,* 358–63.

Block, W. E. A preliminary study of achievement motive theory as a basis of patient expectations in psychotherapy. *Journal of Clinical Psychology,* 1964, *20,* 268–71.

Boas, F. *Primitive Art.* New York: Dover, 1955.

Bobbitt, J. M. An experimental study of the phenomenon of closure as a threshold function. *Journal of Experimental Psychology,* 1942, *30,* 273–94.

Boder, D. P. The adjective-verb quotient; a contribution to the psychology of language. *Psychological Record,* 1940, *3,* 309–43.

Bodkin, M. *Archetypal Patterns in Poetry.* London: Oxford University Press, 1934.

Bourne, L. E., Jr., & Haygood, R. C. The role of stimulus redundancy in the identification of concepts. *Journal of Experimental Psychology,* 1959, *58,* 232–38.

Bourne, L. E., Jr., & Haygood, R. C. Supplementary report: effect of redundant relevant information upon the identification of concepts. *Journal of Experimental Psychology,* 1961, *61,* 259–60.

Bourne, L. E., Jr., & Jennings, P. C. The relationship between contiguity and classification learning. *Journal of General Psychology,* 1963, *69,* 335–38.

Bowers, F. *The Dance in India.* New York: Columbia University Press, 1953.

Bradley, A. C. *Oxford Lectures on Poetry.* New York: Macmillan, 1909.

Bramel, D. Selection of a target for defensive projection. *Journal of Abnormal and Social Psychology,* 1963, *66,* 318–24.

Braun, H. W., Wedekind, C. E., & Smudski, J. F. The effect of an irrelevant drive on maze learning in the rat. *Journal of Experimental Psychology,* 1957, *54,* 148–52.

Brecht, B. Theatre for pleasure or theatre for learning? *Mainstream,* 1958, *11,* 1–9.

Brehm, J. W., & Cohen, A. R. *Explorations in Cognitive Dissonance.* New York: Wiley, 1962.

Brighouse, G. A study of aesthetic apperception. *Psychological Monographs,* 1939, *51,* 1–22. (a)

Brighouse, G. Variability in preferences for simple forms. *Psychological Monographs,* 1939, *51,* (no. 5), 68–74. (b)

Brill, A. A. Poetry as an oral outlet. *Psychoanalytic Review,* 1931, *18,* 357–78.

Brogden, W. J. Sensory preconditioning of human subjects. *Journal of Experimental Psychology,* 1947, *37,* 527–40.

Brooks, C. *The Well-Wrought Urn.* New York: Reynal & Hitchcock, 1947.

Brown, J. L., Duhns, M. P., & Adler, H. Relation of threshold criterion to the functional receptors of the eye. *Journal of the Optical Society of America,* 1957, *47,* 198–204.

Brown, R. W. *Words and Things.* Glencoe, Ill.: Free Press, 1958.

Brown, R. W., Black, A. H., & Horowitz, A. E. Phonetic symbolism in natural languages. *Journal of Abnormal and Social Psychology,* 1955, *50,* 388–93.

Brown, R. W. & Gilman, A. The pronouns of power and solidarity. In T. A. Sebeok, ed., *Style in Language.* Cambridge, Mass.: M.I.T. Press, 1960. Pp. 253–76.

Brown, R. W., & Hildum, D. C. Expectancy and the identification of syllables. *Language,* 1956, *32,* 411–19.

Bruner, J. S. One kind of perception: a reply to Professor Luchins. *Psychological Review,* 1951, *58,* 306–12.

Bruner, J. S. On perceptual readiness. *Psychological Review,* 1957, *64,* 123–52.

Bruner, J. S. The course of cognitive growth. *American Psychologist,* 1964, *19,* 1–15.

Bruner, J. S., Goodnow, J. J., & Austin, G. A. *A Study of Thinking.* New York: Wiley, 1956.

Bruner, J. S., Wallach, M. A., & Galanter, E. H. The identification of recurrent regularity. *American Journal of Psychology,* 1959, *72,* 200–209.

Brunswik, E., ed., et al. Untersuchungen über Wahrnehmung der Gegenstände. *Archiv der gesammten Psychologie*, 1933, *88*, 377–628.

Brunswik, E. The characteristics of the "average face." Unpublished experiment performed in the framework of the pro-seminar on experimental psychology, Psychological Institute of the University of Vienna, Winter, 1937.

Buber, M. *Images of Good and Evil*. London: Routledge & Kegan Paul, 1952.

Buch, K. R. A note on sentence-length as random variable. In *Den 11te Skandinaviske Matematikerkongress*, Oslo, 1952. Pp. 272–75.

Bugg, G. An experimental study of factors influencing consonance judgments. *Psychological Monographs*, 1933, *45*, no. 201, 1–100.

Bühler, C. Zwei Grundtypen von Lebensprozessen. *Zeitschrift für Psychologie*, 1928, *108*, 228–39.

Bühler, C., & Hetzer, H. Das erste Verständnis für Ausdruck im ersten Lebensjahr. *Zeitschrift für Psychologie*, 1928, *107*, 50–61.

Bühler, C., Hetzer, H., & Mabel, F. Die Affektwirksamkeit von Fremdheitseindrücken im ersten Lebensjahr. *Zeitschrift für Psychologie*, 1928, *107*, 30–49.

Bühler, K. *Ausdruckstheorie*. Jena: Fischer, 1933.

Bühler, K. *Sprachtheorie*. Jena: Fischer, 1934.

Bull, N. *The Attitude Theory of Emotion*. New York: Nervous and Mental Disease Monographs, no. 81, 1951.

Bulley, M. H. An enquiry as to the aesthetic judgments of children. *British Journal of Educational Psychology*, 1934, *4*, 162–82.

Bullough, E. On the apparent heaviness of colours: a contribution to the aesthetics of colour. *British Journal of Psychology*, 1907, *2*, 111–52.

Bullough, E. The "perceptive problem" in the aesthetic appreciation of single colours. *British Journal of Psychology*, 1908, *2*, 406–63.

Bullough, E. The "perceptive problem" in the aesthetic appreciation of simple colour combinations. *British Journal of Psychology*, 1910, *3*, 406–47.

Bullough, E. *Aesthetics; Lectures and Essays*. Ed., E. M. Wilkinson. London: Bowes & Bowes, 1957. Pp. 91–130. "Psychical Distance" as a factor in art and an aesthetic principle.

Burnham, R. W. Comparative effects of area and luminance on color. *American Journal of Psychology*, 1952, *65*, 27–38.

Burnham, R. W., Hanes, R. M., & Bartleson, C. J. *Color: A Guide to Basic Facts and Concepts*. New York: Wiley, 1963.

Buswell, G. T. *How People Look at Pictures*. Chicago: University of Chicago Press, 1935.

Butcher, S. H. *Aristotle's Theory of Poetry and Fine Art*. New York: Dover, 1951.

Butler, R. A. Discrimination learning by rhesus monkeys to visual-exploration motivation. *Journal of Comparative and Physiological Psychology*, 1953, *46*, 95–98.

Butler, R. A. Incentive conditions which influence visual exploration. *Journal of Experimental Psychology*, 1954, *48*, 19–23.

Butler, R. A. Discrimination learning by rhesus monkeys to auditory incentives. *Journal of Comparative and Physiological Psychology*, 1957, *50*, 239–41.

Butler, R. A., & Harlow, H. F. Persistence of visual exploration in monkeys. *Journal of Comparative and Physiological Psychology*, 1954, *47*, 258–63.

Buxbaum, E. The role of detective stories in a child analysis. *Psychoanalytic Quarterly*, 1941, *10*, 373–81.

Buytendijk, F. J. J. *Attitudes et mouvements: étude fonctionelle du mouvement humain.* Paris: Desclée de Brouwer, 1957.

Bychowski, G. Metapsychology of artistic creation. *Psychoanalytic Quarterly,* 1951, 20, 592–602.

Cage, J. To describe the process of composition used in "Music for Piano" 21–52. *Die Reihe* no. 3: *Musical Craftsmanship,* 1959, 41–43.

Campbell, B. A., & Sheffield, F. D. Relation of random activity to food deprivation. *Journal of Comparative and Physiological Psychology,* 1953, 46, 320–22.

Campbell, J. *The Hero with a Thousand Faces.* New York: Meridian Books, 1956.

Camus, A. *The Stranger.* New York: Vintage Books, 1959.

Cannon, W. B. *The Wisdom of the Body.* New York: Norton, 1932.

Carr, R. M., & Brown, W. L. The effect of the introduction of novel stimuli upon manipulation in rhesus monkeys. *Journal of Genetic Psychology,* 1959, 94, 107–11.

Carritt, E. F. *The Theory of Beauty.* 2d ed., London: Methuen, 1923.

Carroll, J. B. Vectors of prose style. In T. A. Sebeok, ed., *Style in Language.* Cambridge, Mass.: M.I.T. Press, 1960. Pp. 283–92.

Cary, J. The artist and the world. In J. B. Hall & B. Ulanov, eds., *Modern Culture and the Arts.* New York: McGraw-Hill, 1967. Pp. 243–47.

Cassirer, E. *An Essay on Man.* Garden City, N. Y.: Doubleday Anchor Books, 1953. (a)

Cassirer, E. *Substance and Function and Einstein's Theory of Relativity.* Chicago: Dover, 1953. (b)

Cassirer, E. *The Philosophy of Symbolic Forms.* New Haven, Conn.: Yale University Press, 1953–57. 3 vols.

Castelnuovo-Tedesco, P. A study of the relationship between handwriting and personality variables. *Genetic Psychology Monographs,* 1948, 37, 167–220.

Catholic Encyclopedia. Vol. IV, s.v. Colors, Liturgical. New York: Appleton, 1908.

Cazden, N. Musical consonance and dissonance: a cultural criterion. *Journal of Aesthetics and Art Criticism,* 1945, 4, 3–11.

Cerbus, G., & Nichols, R. C. Personality correlates of picture preferences. *Journal of Abnormal and Social Psychology,* 1962, 64, 75–78.

Cerbus, G., & Nichols, R. C. Personality variables and response to color. *Psychological Bulletin,* 1963, 60, 566–75.

Chagall, M. *The Jerusalem Windows.* Text and notes by J. Leymarie. New York: Braziller, 1962.

Champion, R. A. Studies of experimentally induced disturbance. *Australian Journal of Psychology,* 1950, 2, 90–99.

Chandler, A. R. Recent experiments on visual aesthetics. *Psychological Bulletin,* 1928, 25, 720–32.

Chandler, A. R. *Beauty and Human Nature.* New York: Appleton-Century, 1934.

Chandler, K. A. The effect of monaural and binaural tones of different intensities on the visual perception of verticality. *American Journal of Psychology,* 1961, 74, 260–65.

Chapman, R. M., & Levy, N. Hunger drive and reinforcing effect of novel stimuli. *Journal of Comparative and Physiological Psychology,* 1957, 50, 233–38.

Chatman, S. Robert Frost's "Mowing": an inquiry into prosodic structure. *Kenyon Review,* 1956, 28, 421–38.

Chatman, S. Comparing metrical styles. In T. A. Sebeok, ed., *Style in Language*. Cambridge, Mass.: M.I.T. Press, 1960. Pp. 149–72.

Chatterji, U. *La Danse hindoue*. Paris: Editions Véga, 1951.

Cheney, S. *A Primer of Modern Art*. New York: Boni & Liveright, 1924.

Cheney, S. *Expressionism in Art*. Rev. ed. New York: Tudor, 1948.

Cheney, S. *A World History of Art*. New York: Viking, 1952.

Cherry, C. *On Human Communication*. New York: Wiley, 1961.

Child, C. M. *Physiological Foundations of Behavior*. New York: Holt, 1924.

Child, I. L. Personal preferences as an expression of aesthetic sensitivity. *Journal of Personality*, 1962, *30*, 496–512.

Child, I. L. Esthetics. In G. Lindzey & E. Aronson, eds., *Handbook of Social Psychology*, 2d ed. Vol. 3. Reading, Mass.: Addison-Wesley, 1969. Chap. 28, pp. 853–916.

Child, I. L., & Wendt, G. R. The temporal course of the influence of visual stimulation upon the auditory threshold. *Journal of Experimental Psychology*, 1938, *23*, 108–27.

Chochod, L. *Histoire de la magie et de ses dogmes*. Paris: Payot, 1949.

Chomsky, N. *Syntactic Structures*. The Hague: Mouton, 1957.

Chomsky, N. *Current Issues in Linguistic Theory*. The Hague: Mouton, 1964.

Chomsky, N. *Aspects of the Theory of Syntax*. Cambridge, Mass.: M.I.T. Press, 1965.

Chomsky, N. *Topics in the Theory of Generative Grammar*. The Hague: Mouton, 1966.

Chomsky, N. *Language and Mind*. New York: Harcourt, Brace & World, 1968.

Chomsky, N., & Halle, M. *The Sound Pattern of English*. New York: Harper and Row, 1966.

Chomsky, N., & Miller, G. Introduction to the formal analysis of natural languages. In R. Luce, R. Bush, & E. Galanter, eds., *Handbook of Mathematical Psychology*. Vol. 2. New York: Wiley, 1963. Pp. 269–323.

Chou, S. K., & Chen, H. P. General versus specific color preferences of Chinese students. *Journal of Social Psychology*, 1935, *6*, 290–314.

Christianson, H. *Bodily Rhythmic Movements of Young Children in Relation to Rhythm in Music*. New York: Bureau of Publications, Teachers College, Columbia University, 1938.

Chujoy, A., & Manchester, P. W. *Dance Encyclopedia*. New ed. New York: Simon & Schuster, 1966.

Church, R. M. Emotional reactions of rats to the pain of others. *Journal of Comparative and Physiological Psychology*, 1959, *52*, 132–34.

Clark, H. H. Some structural properties of simple active and passive sentences. *Journal of Verbal Learning and Verbal Behavior*, 1965, *4*, 365–70.

Clarkson, M. E., Davies, O. L., & Vickerstaff, T. Color harmony. In *Color*. Great Britain: Imperial Chemical Industries, Ltd., 1950.

Classe, A. *The Rhythm of English Prose*. Oxford: Blackwell, 1939.

Claudel, P. Vitraux des cathédrales de France. In R. Mallet, ed., *Morceaux choisis*. 3d ed. Paris: Gallimard, 1956.

Cohen, J. Color adaptation of the human eye. *American Journal of Psychology*, 1946, *59*, 84–110.

Cohen, J. E. Information theory and music. *Behavioral Science*, 1962, *7*, 137–63.

Cohen, N. E. Equivalence of brightness across modalities. *American Journal of Psychology*, 1934, 46, 117–19.

Cohen, S. J. Avant-Garde choreography. In W. Sorell, ed., *The Dance Has Many Faces*. 2d ed. New York: Columbia University Press, 1966. Pp. 211–24.

Cohn, J. Experimentelle Untersuchungen über die Gefühlsbetonung der Farben, Helligkeit und ihre Combinationen. *Philosophische Studien*, 1894, 10, 562–602.

Cole, D. "Rational argument" and "prestige suggestion" as factors influencing judgment. *Sociometry*, 1954, 17, 350–54.

Collingwood, R. G. *The Principles of Art*. Oxford: Clarendon Press, 1938.

Collins, N. The appropriateness of certain color combinations in advertising. Unpublished M.A. thesis, Columbia University, 1924. Summarized in Poffenberger, A. T., *Psychology in Advertising* (New York: McGraw-Hill, 1932), pp. 450–59.

Conners, C. K. Visual and verbal approach motive as a function of discrepancy from expectation level. *Perceptual and Motor Skills*, 1964, 18, 457–64.

Cook, T. H. The application of the Rorschach test to a Samoan group. *Rorschach Research Exchange*, 1942, 6, 51–60.

Corwin, G. H. The involuntary response to pleasantness. *American Journal of Psychology*, 1921, 32, 563–70.

Coupling, J. J. Chance remarks. *Astounding Science Fiction*, 1948, 44, 104–11.

Craig, K. D., & Weinstein, M. S. Conditioning vicarious affective arousal. *Psychological Reports*, 1965, 17, 955–63.

Crawford, D., & Washburn, M. F. Fluctuations in the affective value of colors during fixation for one minute. *American Journal of Psychology*, 1911, 22, 579–82.

Crespi, L. P. Amount of reinforcement and level of performance. *Psychological Review*, 1944, 70, 19, 341–57.

Creuzer, F. *Symbolik und Mythologie der alten Völker*. Vol. 1. Leipzig, 1810.

Critchley, M. *The Language of Gesture*. London: Arnold, 1939.

Cronbach, L. J. Processes affecting scores on "understanding of others" and "assumed similarity." *Psychological Bulletin*, 1955, 52, 177–93.

Cummings, E. E. *I; Six Nonlectures*. Cambridge, Mass.: Harvard University Press, 1953.

Cushing, F. H. Outlines of Zuni creation myths. *13th Report, Bur. American Ethnology*, 1896.

Czurda, M. Beziehungen zwischen Lautcharakter und Sinneseindrücken. *Wiener Archiv für Psychologie, Psychiatrie, und Neurologie*, 1953, 3, 73–84.

Dagiri, O. On phonetic symbolism. In Y. Endo, K. Hatano, et al., eds., *Science of Language*. Vol. 3. Tokyo: Nakajima Shoten, 1958. In Japanese.

Dale, E., & Tyler, R. W. A study of the factors influencing the difficulty of reading materials for adults of limited reading ability. *Library Quarterly*, 1934, 4, 384–412.

Daneš, F. Sentence intonation from a functional point of view. *Word*, 1960, 16, 34–54.

Darchen, R. Sur l'activité exploratrice de *Blatella germanica*. *Zeitschrift der Tierpsychologie*, 1952, 9, 362–72.

Darchen, R. Sur le comportement d'exploration de *Blatella germanica*: exploration d'un plan. *Journal de Psychologie Normale et Pathologique*, 1957, 54, 190–205.

Darley, J. M., & Latané, B. Bystander intervention in emergencies: diffusion of responsibility. *Journal of Personality and Social Psychology*, 1968, 8, 377–83.

Dashiell, J. F. Children's sense of harmonies in colors and tones. *Journal of Experimental Psychology*, 1917, 2, 466–75.

Davis, F. C. Aesthetic proportion. *American Journal of Psychology*, 1933, 45, 298–302.

Davis, R. The fitness of names to drawings: cross cultural study in Tanganyika. *British Journal of Psychology*, 1961, 52, 259–68.

Davis, R. C. An evaluation and test of Birkhoff's aesthetic measure and formula. *Journal of General Psychology*, 1936, 15, 231–40.

Davis, R. C. Motor effects of strong auditory stimuli. *Journal of Experimental Psychology*, 1948, 38, 257–75.

Davis, R. C., Buchwald, A. M., & Frankmann, R. W. Autonomic and muscular responses and their relation to simple stimuli. *Psychological Monographs*, 1955, no. 405.

Davitz, J. R., et al. *The Communication of Emotional Meaning*. New York: Mc-Graw-Hill, 1964.

Day, H. Exploratory behavior as a function of individual differences and level of arousal. Unpublished doctoral dissertation, University of Toronto, 1965.

De Burger, R. A., & Donahoe, J. W. Relationships between the meanings of verbal stimuli and their associative responses. *Journal of Verbal Learning and Verbal Behavior*, 1965, 4, 25–31.

DeCamp, J. E. The influence of color on apparent weight: a preliminary study. *Journal of Experimental Psychology*, 1917, 2, 347–70.

De Groot, A. W. Phonetics in its relation to aesthetics. In L. Kaiser, ed., *Manual of Phonetics*. Amsterdam: North-Holland Publishing Co., 1957. Chap. 25, pp. 385–400.

Delacroix, H. *Psychologie de l'art*. Paris: Alcan, 1927.

Delogu, G. *Italienische Bildhauerei*. Zurich: Fretz v. Wasmuth, 1942.

Dember, W. N. *The Psychology of Perception*. New York: Holt, Rinehart, & Winston, 1960.

Dember, W. N., & Earl, R. W. Analysis of exploratory, manipulatory, and curiosity behaviors. *Psychological Review*, 1957, 64, 91–96.

Dember, W. N., Earl, W., & Paradise, N. Response by rats to differential stimulus complexity. *Journal of Comparative and Physiological Psychology*, 1957, 50, 514–18.

Denes, P. A preliminary investigation of certain aspects of intonation. *Language and Speech*, 1959, 2, 106–22.

Denniston, R. H. II. Escape and avoidance learning as a function of emotionality level in the Wyoming ground squirrel *Citellus richardsonii elegans*. *Animal Behavior*, 1959, 7, 241–43.

Desai, M. M. Surprise. *British Journal of Psychology, Monograph Supplements*, no. 22, 1939.

Deutsch, F. Analysis of postural behavior. *Psychoanalytic Quarterly*, 1947, 16, 195–213.

Dewes, P. B., & Morse, W. N. Behavioral pharmacology. *Annual Review of Pharmacology*, 1961, 1, 145–74.

Dewey, G. *Relative Frequency of English Speech Sounds*. Cambridge, Mass.: Harvard University Press, 1923.

Dewey, J. *Art as Experience.* New York: Milton, Balch, 1934; reprint ed., New York: Capricorn Books, 1958.

Dibner, A. S. Ambiguity and anxiety. *Journal of Abnormal and Social Psychology,* 1958, *56,* 165–74.

Di Lollo, V., & Walker, E. L. Speed and basal resistance level (BRL) in a segmented straight alley. *Psychological Record,* 1964, *14,* 499–505.

Ditchburn, R. W., & Fender, D. H. The stabilized retinal image. *Optica Acta,* 1955, *2,* 128–33.

Dittmann, A. T. Kinesic research and therapeutic processes: further discussion. In P. H. Knapp, ed., *Expression of the Emotions in Man.* New York: International Universities Press, 1963. Pp. 140–60.

Dobrée, B. *Modern Prose Style.* New York: Oxford University Press, 1934.

Dobriakova, O. A. On the influence of gustatory and thermal stimuli on color vision. In *Transactions of the First Session of the Moscow Society of Physiologists, Biochemists, and Pharmacologists.* Moscow: Medgiz, 1941. Pp. 80–82. In Russian.

Dolin, A. O., Zborovskaia, I. I., & Zamakhover, S. K. On the characteristics of the role of the orienting-investigatory reflex in conditioned-reflex activity. In L. G. Voronin et al., eds., *The Orienting Reflex and Exploratory Behavior.* Moscow: Academy of Pedagogical Sciences, 1958. In Russian.

Dollard, J., Miller, N. E., Doob, L. W., Mowrer, O. H., & Sears, R. R. *Frustration and Aggression.* New Haven: Yale University Press, 1939.

Donnell, R. Z. Space in abstract expressionism. *Journal of Aesthetics and Art Criticism,* 1964, *23,* 239–49.

Dorcus, R. M. Color preferences and color associations. *Journal of Genetic Psychology,* 1926, *33,* 399–434.

Dorcus, R. M. Habitual word associations to colors as a possible factor in advertising. *Journal of Applied Psychology,* 1932, *16,* 277–87.

Dorfman, D. D. Esthetic preference as a function of pattern information. *Psychonomic Science,* 1965, *3,* 85–86.

Dorfman, D. D., & McKenna, H. Pattern preference as a function of pattern uncertainty. *Canadian Journal of Psychology,* 1966, *20,* 143–53.

Dorner, A. *The Way Beyond Art.* New York: New York University Press, 1958.

Downey, J. A musical experiment. *American Journal of Psychology,* 1897, *9,* 63–69.

Downey, J. E. Individual differences in reaction to the word-in-itself. *American Journal of Psychology,* 1927, *39,* 323–42.

Dreher, R. E. The relation between verbal reports and galvanic skin responses to music. *American Psychologist,* 1948, *3,* 275–76. Abstract.

Dykman, R. A. Toward a theory of classical conditioning: cognitive, emotional, and motor components of the conditioned reflex. In B. A. Maher, ed., *Progress in Experimental Personality Research.* Vol. 2. New York: Academic Press, 1965. Pp. 229–317.

Dysinger, D. W. The comparative study of affective responses by means of the impressive and expressive methods. *Psychological Monographs,* 1931, *41,* no. 4, 14–31.

Dysinger, W. S., & Ruckmick, C. A. *The Emotional Responses of Children to the Motion-Picture Situation.* New York: Macmillan, 1933.

Earl, R. W. Problem solving and motor skill behaviors under conditions of free choice. Unpublished doctoral dissertation, University of Michigan, Ann Arbor, 1957.

Eckblad, G. The attractiveness of uncertainty. *Scandinavian Journal of Psychology,* 1963, *4,* 1–13.

Eckblad, G. The attractiveness of uncertainty: II. Effect of different rates of reduction in the level of subjective uncertainty. *Scandinavian Journal of Psychology,* 1964, *5,* 33–49.

Edelman, S. K. Analysis of some stimulus factors involved in the associative response. Unpublished doctoral dissertation, Purdue University, 1960.

Edelman, S. K., Karas, G. G., & Cohen, B. J. The relative contributions of complexity and symmetry to the perception of form. Paper presented at Midwestern Psychological Association, Chicago, 1961.

Edlow, D., & Kiesler, C. Ease of denial and defensive projection. *Journal of Experimental Social Psychology,* 1966, *2,* 56–69.

Efron, D. *Gesture and Environment.* New York: King's Crown Press, 1941.

Ehrenwald, H. Über einen photo-dermatischen Tonusreflex auf Bestrahlung mit farbigen Lichtern beim Menschen. *Klinische Wochenschrift,* 1932, *11,* 2142–43.

Ehrenzweig, A. *The Psychoanalysis of Artistic Vision and Hearing: An Introduction to a Theory of Unconscious Perception.* New York: Julian Press, 1953.

Ehrlich, V. *Russian Formalism.* 2d rev. ed. New York: Humanities, 1965.

Einthoven, W. Stereoscopie durch Farbendifferenz. *Arch. J. Opthalmologie,* 1885, *31,* 211–38.

Eisenberg, P. Judging expressive movement: I. Judgments of sex and dominance feeling from handwriting samples of dominant and non-dominant men and women. *Journal of Applied Psychology,* 1938, *22,* 480–86.

Eisenman, R. The association value of random shapes revisited. *Psychonomic Science,* 1966, *6,* 397–98. (a)

Eisenman, R. Pleasing and interesting visual complexity: support for Berlyne. *Perceptual and Motor Skills,* 1966, *23,* 1167–70. (b)

Eisenman, R. Complexity-simplicity: I. Preference for symmetry and rejection of complexity. *Psychonomic Science,* 1967, *8,* 169–70.

Eisenman, R. Semantic Differential ratings of polygons varying in complexity-simplicity and symmetry-asymmetry. *Perceptual and Motor Skills,* 1968, *26,* 1243–48.

Eisenman, R., & Gellens, H. K. Preference for complexity-simplicity and symmetry-asymmetry. *Perceptual and Motor Skills,* 1968, *26,* 888–90.

Eisenman, R., & Rappaport, J. Complexity preference and semantic differential ratings of complexity-simplicity and symmetry-asymmetry. *Psychonomic Science,* 1967, *7,* 147–48.

Eliade, M. *Images et symboles: essais sur le symbolisme magico-religieux.* 5th ed. Paris: Gallimard, 1952.

Eliade, M. *The Myth of the Eternal Return.* Bollingen Series, XLVI. Princeton, N.J.: Princeton University Press, 1955.

Eliade, M. *Traité d'histoire des religions.* Paris: Payot, 1959.

Eliot, T. S. *The Sacred Wood.* London: Methuen, 1928.

Eliot, T. S. *Selected Prose.* Ed. J. Hayward. Harmondsworth: Penguin Books, 1953.

Ellis, D. S., & Brighouse, G. Effects of music on respiration and heart rate. *American Journal of Psychology*, 1952, *65*, 39–47.

Ellis, H. The psychology of red. *Popular Science Monthly*, 1900, *57*, 365–75.

Ellis, H. The psychology of yellow. *Popular Science Monthly*, 1906, *68*, 456–63.

Ellson, D. Hallucinations produced by sensory conditioning. *Journal of Experimental Psychology*, 1941, *28*, 1–20.

Empson, W. *Seven Types of Ambiguity.* 3d ed. Norfolk, Conn.: New Directions, 1953.

Engel, R. Experimentelle Untersuchungen über die Anhängigkeit der Lust und Unlust von der Reizstärke beim Geschmacksinn. *Archiv der Gesammten Psychologie*, 1928, *64*, 1–36.

English, H. B. Colored hearing. *Science*, 1923, *57*, 444.

English, H. B., & English, A. C. *A Comprehensive Dictionary of Psychological and Psychoanalytical Terms.* New York: Longmans, 1958.

Engstrom, A. G. In defence of synaesthesia in literature. *Philosophical Quarterly*, 1946, *25*, 1–19.

Enke, W. Die Psychomotorik der Konstitutionstypen. *Zeitschrift für Psychologie*, 1930, *36*, 237–87.

Erhardt-Siebold, E. v. Harmony of the senses in English, German, and French Romanticism. *Publications of the Modern Language Association of America*, 1932, *47*, 577–92.

Ervin-Tripp, S. M. Changes with age in the verbal determinants of word-associations. *American Journal of Psychology*, 1961, *74*, 361–72.

Esbroeck, J. van, & Montfort, F. *Qu'est-ce que jouer juste?* Bruxelles: Lumière, 1946.

Escalona, S. K. Feeding disturbances in very young children. *American Journal of Orthopsychiatry*, 1945, *15*, 76–80.

Eshkol, N., & Wachmann, A. *Movement Notation.* London: Weidenfeld & Nicolson, 1958.

Esslin, M. The theatre of the absurd. In J. B. Hall & B. Ulanov, eds., *Modern Culture and the Arts.* New York: McGraw-Hill, 1967. Pp. 384–400.

Estes, S. G. Judging personality from expressive behavior. *Journal of Abnormal and Social Psychology*, 1938, *33*, 217–36.

Ewald, A. *Die Farbenbewegung.* Berlin: Weidmann, 1876.

Eysenck, H. J. The general factor in aesthetic judgments. *British Journal of Psychology*, 1940, *31*, 94–102.

Eysenck, H. J. "Type"-factors in aesthetic judgments. *British Journal of Psychology*, 1941, *31*, 262–70. (a)

Eysenck, H. J. Psychological aspects of color measurement. *Nature*, 1941, *147*, 682–83. (b)

Eysenck, H. J. A critical and experimental study of color preferences. *American Journal of Psychology*, 1941, *54*, 385–94. (c)

Eysenck, H. J. The empirical determination of an aesthetic formula. *Psychological Review*, 1941, *48*, 83–92. (d)

Eysenck, H. J. The experimental study of the "good gestalt"—a new approach. *Psychological Review*, 1942, *49*, 344–64.

Eysenck, H. J. *Dimensions of Personality.* London: Kegan Paul, 1947.

Faist, A. Versuche über Tonverschmelzung. *Zeitschrift für Psychologie*, 1897, *15*, 189–205.

Farnsworth, P. The effect of repetition on ending preferences in melodies. *American Journal of Psychology*, 1926, *37*, 116–22.

Farnsworth, P. Musical eminence. *American Psychologist*, 1946, *1*, 205. Abstract.

Farnsworth, P., & Beaumont, H. Suggestion in pictures. *Journal of General Psychology*, 1929, *2*, 362–66.

Farnsworth, P., & Misumi, I. Further data on suggestion in pictures. *Journal of Abnormal and Social Psychology*, 1931, *43*, 632.

Feasey, L. Some experiments on aesthetics. *British Journal of Psychology*, 1921, *12*, 253–72.

Fechner, G. T. *Einige Ideen zur Schöpfungs- und Entwicklungsgeschichte der Organismen.* Leipzig: Breitkopf und Härtel, 1873.

Fechner, G. T. *Vorschule der Ästhetik.* Leipzig: Breitkopf und Härtel, 1876.

Féré, C. *Sensation et mouvement.* Paris: Alcan, 1900.

Ferenczi, S. Disease—or patho-neuroses. In S. Ferenczi, *Further Contributions to the Theory and Technique of Psycho-analysis.* London: Hogarth Press & The Institute of Psycho-Analysis, 1926. Pp. 78–89.

Festinger, L. *A Theory of Cognitive Dissonance.* Stanford: Stanford University Press, 1957.

Finley, K. H. Emotional physiology and its influence on thought content. *Journal of Nervous and Mental Disease*, 1953, *118*, 442–46.

Fischer, E. *The Necessity of Art: A Marxist Approach.* Baltimore: Penguin Books, 1963.

Fiske, D. W., & Maddi, S. R. A conceptual framework. In D. W. Fiske and S. R. Maddi, eds., *Functions of Varied Experience.* Homewood, Ill.: Dorsey, 1961. Pp. 11–56.

Fitts, P. M., & Leonard, J. A. *Stimulus Correlates of Visual Pattern Recognition: A Probability Approach.* Columbus: Ohio State University Press, 1957.

Flanders, J. P. A review of research on imitative behavior. *Psychological Bulletin*, 1968, *69*, 316–37.

Flesch, R. A new readability yardstick. *Journal of Applied Psychology*, 1948, *32*, 221–33.

Focillon, H. *The Life of Forms in Art.* New York: Wittenborn, 1948.

Fodor, J. A., & Bever, T. G. The psychological reality of linguistic segments. *Journal of Verbal Learning and Verbal Behavior*, 1965, *4*, 414–20.

Fokine, V. *Fokine: Memoirs of a Ballet Master.* Boston: Little, Brown, 1961.

Folkins, C. H., Lawson, K. D., Opton, E. M., & Lazarus, R. S. Desensitization and the experimental reduction of threat. *Journal of Abnormal Psychology*, 1968, *73*, 100–113.

Folkins, C. H., & Lenrow, P. B. An investigation of the expressive values of graphemes. *Psychological Record*, 1966, *16*, 193–200.

Forer, B. R. A study of consonant preferences. *Psychological Bulletin*, 1940, *37*, 589. Abstract.

Forgus, R. H. *Perception: The Basic Process in Cognitive Development.* New York: McGraw-Hill, 1966.

Forster, E. M. *Aspects of the Novel.* New York: Harcourt, Brace, 1927.

Fortier, R. H. The response to color and ego functions. *Psychological Bulletin*, 1953, *50*, 41–63.

Fraisse, P. *Les Structures rhythmiques.* Paris: Erasme, 1956.

Fraisse, P. *Psychologie du temps*. 2d rev. ed. Paris: Presses Universitaires de France, 1967.

Fraisse, P., Oléron, G. Les effets dynamogéniques de la musique; étude experimentale. *L'Année Psychologique*, 1953, 53e année, 1–34.

Francès, R. *La Perception de la musique*. Paris: J. Vrin, 1958.

Franke, H. W. *Phänomen Kunst*. Munich: Heinz Moos Verlag, 1967.

Frankenhauser, M., & Post, B. Time relations of objective and subjective relations to d-amphetamine and pentobarbitone. *Scandinavian Journal of Psychology*, 1964, 5, 99–107.

Franklin, G. H., Feldman, S., & Odbert, H. S. Relationship of total bodily movements to some emotional components of personality. *Journal of Psychology*, 1948, 26, 499–506.

Frazer, J. G. *The Golden Bough*. New York: Macmillan, 1952.

Frédéric, L. *La Danse sacrée de l'Inde*. Paris: Arts et Métiers Graphiques, 1957.

Freedman, J. L., & Sears, D. O. Selective exposure. In L. Berkowitz, ed., *Advances in experimental social psychology*. Vol. 2. New York: Academic Press, 1965.

Freeman, G. L. An experimental study of the perception of objects. *Journal of Experimental Psychology*, 1929, 12, 241–58.

Freeman, G. L. *Physiological Psychology*. New York: Van Nostrand, 1948. (a)

Freeman, G. L. *The Energetics of Human Behavior*. Ithaca, N.Y.: Cornell University Press, 1948. (b)

Frenkel-Brunswik, E. Intolerance of ambiguity as an emotional and perceptual personality variable. *Journal of Personality*, 1949, 18, 108–43.

Freud, S. *Beyond the Pleasure Principle*. New York: International Psychoanalytic Press, 1922.

Freud, S. "Civilized" sexual morality and modern nervousness. In S. Freud, *Collected Papers*, Vol. 2. London: Hogarth Press and The Institute of Psycho-Analysis, 1924. Pp. 76–99.

Freud, S. *Civilization and Its Discontents*. New York: J. Cope & H. Smith, 1930.

Freud, S. Totem and taboo. In A. A. Brill, ed., *Basic Writings of Sigmund Freud*. New York: Modern Library, 1938. Pp. 805–930.

Freud, S. Psychopathic characters on the stage. *Psychoanalytic Quarterly*, 1942, 11, 459–64.

Freud, S. The relation of the poet to day-dreaming. In S. Freud, *Collected Papers*, Vol. 4. London: Hogarth Press and The Institute of Psycho-Analysis, 1948. Pp. 173–83. (a)

Freud, S. On narcissism: An introduction. In S. Freud, *Collected Papers*, Vol. 4. London: Hogarth Press and The Institute of Psycho-Analysis, 1948. Pp. 30–59. (b)

Freud, S. *Leonardo da Vinci*. London: Routledge and Kegan Paul, 1948. (c)

Freud, S. Some character-types met with in psycho-analytic work. In S. Freud, *Collected Papers*, Vol. 4. London: Hogarth Press and The Institute of Psycho-Analysis, 1948. Pp. 318–44. (d)

Freud, S. The antithetical sense of primary words. In S. Freud *Collected Papers*, Vol. 4. London: Hogarth Press and The Institute of Psycho-Analysis, 1948. Pp. 184–91. (e)

Freud, S. The interpretation of dreams. In *Standard Edition of the Complete Psychological Works of Sigmund Freud*, Vols. 4–5. London: Hogarth Press and The Institute of Psycho-Analysis, 1953.

Freud, S. The Moses of Michelangelo. In *Standard Edition of the Complete Psychological Works of Sigmund Freud*, Vol. 13, London: Hogarth Press and The Institute of Psycho-Analysis, 1955. Pp. 211–38.

Freud, S. Delusion and dream. In S. Freud, ed., P. Rieff. *Delusion and Dream and Other Essays*. Boston: Beacon Press, 1956. Pp. 25–121. (a)

Freud, S. Psychoanalytic notes upon an autobiographical account of a case of paranoia. In S. Freud, *Collected Papers*, Vol. 3. London: Hogarth Press and The Institute of Psycho-Analysis, 1956. Pp. 387–470. (b)

Freud, S. The unconscious. In *Standard Edition of the Complete Psychological Works of Sigmund Freud*, Vol. 14. London: Hogarth Press and The Institute of Psycho-Analysis, 1957. Pp. 161–215.

Freud, S. Inhibitions, symptoms, and anxiety. In *Standard Edition of the Complete Psychological Works of Sigmund Freud*, Vol. 20. London: Hogarth Press and The Institute of Psycho-Analysis, 1959. Pp. 77–175. (a)

Freud, S. An autobiographical study. In *Standard Edition of the Complete Psychological Works of Sigmund Freud*, Vol. 20. London: Hogarth Press and The Institute of Psycho-Analysis, 1959. Pp. 3–74. (b)

Freud, S. The economic problem of masochism. In *Standard Edition of the Complete Psychological Works of Sigmund Freud*, Vol. 19. London: Hogarth Press and The Institute of Psycho-Analysis, 1961. Pp. 157–70.

Freud, S. Introductory lectures on psycho-analysis. In *Standard Edition of the Complete Psychological Works of Sigmund Freud*, Vol. 15. London: Hogarth Press and The Institute of Psycho-Analysis, 1963.

Freud, S. Moses and monotheism: three essays. In *Standard Edition of the Complete Psychological Works of Sigmund Freud*, Vol. 23. London: Hogarth Press and The Institute of Psycho-Analysis, 1964. Pp. 3–137. (a)

Freud, S. New introductory lectures on psycho-analysis. In *Standard Edition of the Complete Psychological Works of Sigmund Freud*, London: Hogarth Press and The Institute of Psycho-Analysis, 1964. Pp. 3–182. (b)

Freund, L. Über den Einfluss des Lichtes auf die Funktionen des Gehör- und Geruchsorgans. *Strahlentherapie*, 1929, *34*, 110–16.

Fries, C. C. *The Structure of English: An Introduction to the Construction of English Sentences*. New York: Harcourt, Brace, 1952.

Fritzky, F. J. Aesthetic preference for abstract designs as a function of their perceived complexity. Research Bulletin 63–27. Princeton, N. J.: Educational Testing Service, 1963.

Fromm, E. *The Forgotten Language*. New York: Grove Press, 1951.

Fry, R. Negro sculpture. In R. Fry, *Vision and Design*. Harmondsworth: Penguin Books, 1920. Pp. 87–91. (a)

Fry, R. Art and life. In R. Fry, *Vision and Design*. Harmondsworth: Penguin Books, 1920. Pp. 11–22. (b)

Furrer, W. Der Lüscher Test. In E. Stern, ed., *Die Tests in der klinischen Psychologie*. Zürich: Rascher Verlag, 1955. Pp. 432–62.

Fussell, P., Jr. Meter. In A. Preminger et al., eds., *Encyclopedia of Poetry and Poetics*. Princeton, N.J.: Princeton University Press, 1965. Pp. 496–99.

Gale, A. V. *Children's Preferences for Colors, Color Combinations, and Color Arrangements*. Chicago: University of Chicago Press, 1933.

Galton, F. *Inquiries into Human Faculty and Its Development*. London: Dent, 1907.

Gantt, W. H. Principles of nervous breakdown: schizokinesis and autokinesis. *Annals of the New York Academy of Sciences,* 1953, 56, 143–64.

Gardner, R. A., & Runquist, W. N. Acquisition and extinction of problem-solving set. *Journal of Experimental Psychology,* 1958, 55, 274–77.

Garner, W. R. *Uncertainty and Structure as Psychological Concepts.* New York: Wiley, 1962.

Garrett, L. *Visual Design: A Problem-Solving Approach.* New York: Reinhold, 1967.

Garrett, M., Bever, T., & Fodor, J. The active use of grammar in speech perception. *Perception and Psychophysics,* 1966, 1, 30–32.

Garver, L. N., Gleason, J. M., & Washburn, M. F. The source of affective reactions to articulate sounds. *American Journal of Psychology,* 1915, 26, 292–95.

Gates, G. S. An experimental study of the growth of social perception. *Journal of Educational Psychology,* 1923, 14, no. 8, 449–61.

Gatewood, E. L. An experimental study of the nature of musical enjoyment. In M. Schoen, ed., *The Effects of Music.* New York: Harcourt, Brace, 1927, Chaps. 4 and 5.

Geiger, L. *Zur Entwicklungsgeschichte der Menschheit.* Stuttgart: Cotta, 1871.

Geiger, M. Über das Wesen und die Bedeutung der Einfühlung. Bericht über den IV. Kongress für experimentelle Psychologie, Leipzig, 1911.

Geissler, L. R. The affective tone of color combinations. In *Studies in Psychology Contributed by Colleagues and Former Students of E. B. Titchener.* Worcester: L. N. Wilson, 1917. Pp. 150–74.

Gellhorn, E. Prolegomena to a theory of the emotions. *Perspectives in Biology and Medicine,* 1961, 4, 403–36.

Gerard, R. M. Differential effects of colored lights on psychophysiological functions. Unpublished doctoral dissertation, University of California, Los Angeles, 1958.

Gerwig, G. W. On the decrease of predication and of sentence weight in English prose. *University of Nebraska Studies,* 1894, 2 (10), 17–28.

Gibson, J. J. A critical review of the concept of set in contemporary experimental psychology. *Psychological Bulletin,* 1941, 38, 781–817.

Gibson, J. J. *The Perception of the Visual World.* Cambridge, Mass.: Houghton Mifflin, 1950.

Gibson, J. J. A theory of pictorial perception. *Audiovisual Communication Review,* 1954, 1, 3–23.

Gibson, J. J. Optimal motions and transformations as stimuli for visual perception. *Psychological Review,* 1957, 64, 288–95.

Gibson, J. J. *The Senses Considered as Perceptual Systems.* Boston: Houghton Mifflin, 1966.

Gibson, J. J. & Robinson, D. Orientation in visual perception; the recognition of familiar plane forms in differing orientations. *Psychological Monographs,* 1935, 46, 39–47.

Giedion, S. *Space, Time and Architecture.* 4th ed., enlarged. Cambridge, Mass.: Harvard University Press, 1963.

Gilbert, K. E., & Kuhn, H. *A History of Esthetics.* New York: Macmillan, 1939.

Gilman, B. J. Report on an experimental test of musical expressiveness. *American Journal of Psychology,* 1892, 4, 42–73; 1893, 5, 558–76.

Ginsberg, L. A case of synesthesia. *American Journal of Psychology*, 1923, *34*, 582–89.

Gladstone, W. E. *Studies on Homer and the Homeric Age*. Vol. 3. Oxford, 1858. Pp. 457–99.

Glanzer, M. Stimulus satiation: an explanation of spontaneous alternation and related phenomena. *Psychological Review*, 1953, *60*, 257–68. (a)

Glanzer, M. The role of stimulus satiation in spontaneous alternation. *Journal of Experimental Psychology*, 1953, *45*, 387–93. (b)

Glanzer, M. Curiosity, exploratory drive and stimulus satiation. *Psychological Bulletin*, 1958, *55*, 302–15.

Gleason, H. A. *An Introduction to Descriptive Linguistics*. New York: Holt, 1955.

Glickman, S. E., & Jensen, G. D. The effects of hunger and thirst on Y-maze exploration. *Journal of Comparative and Physiological Psychology*, 1961, *54*, 83–85.

Goethe, J. W. Zur Farbenlehre. In *Goethes naturwissenschaftliche Schriften in Auswahl*. In Grossherzog Wilhelm Ernst Ausgabe, Vol. 16. Leipzig: Inselverlag, 1917. Pp. 423–647. (a)

Goethe, J. W. *Maximen und Reflexionen*. In Grossherzog Wilhelm Ernst Ausgabe, Vol. 13. Leipzig: Inselverlag, 1917. Pp. 527–676. (b)

Goldstein, A. G. Spatial orientation as a factor in eliciting associative response to random shapes. *Perceptual and Motor Skills*, 1961, *12*, 15–25.

Goldstein, K. Über induzierte Tonusveränderungen beim Menschen (sog. Halsreflexe, Labyrinthreflexe, usw.): VII. Über den Einfluss unbewusster Bewegungen resp. Tendenzen zu Bewegungen auf die taktile und optische Raumwahrnehmung. *Klinische Wissenschaftsschriften*, 1925, *4*, 294–99.

Goldstein, K. Über induzierte Veränderungen des "Tonus." *Schweizerisches Archiv für Neurologie und Psychiatrie*, 1926, *17*, 203–28.

Goldstein, K. *The Organism*. New York: American Book, 1939.

Goldstein, K. Some experimental observations concerning the influence of colors on the function of the organism. *Occupational Therapy*, 1942, *21*, 147–51.

Goldstein, K., & Jablonski, A. Über den Einfluss des Tonus auf Refraktionen und Sehleistungen. *Graefes Archiv für Ophthalmologie*, 1933, *130*, 395–410.

Goldstein, K., & Rosenthal-Veit, O. Über akustische Lokalisation und deren Beeinflussbarkeit durch andere Sinnesreize. *Psychologische Forschung*, 1926, *8*, 318–35.

Goldstein, K., & Rosenthal, O. Zum Problem der Wirkung der Farben auf den Organismus. *Schweizerisches Archiv für Neurologie und Psychiatrie*, 1930, *26*, 3–26.

Goldstein, K., & Scheerer, M. Abstract and concrete behavior: an experimental study with special tests. *Psychological Monographs*, 1941, *53*, no. 2.

Gollin, E. S. Developmental studies of visual recognition of incomplete objects. *Perceptual and Motor Skills*, 1960, *11*, 289–98.

Gombrich, E. H. On physiognomic perception. *Daedalus* (special issue: The visual arts today), Winter, 1960, 228–41.

Gombrich, E. H. The use of art for the study of symbols. *American Psychologist*, 1965, *20*, 34–50.

Gombrich, E. H. *Art and Illusion: A Study in the Psychology of Pictorial Representation*. Bollingen Series XXXV. 2d rev. ed. Princeton, N.J.: Princeton University Press, 1969.

Gordon, D. A. Artistic excellence of oil paintings as judged by experts and laymen. *Journal of Educational Research*, 1955, *48*, 579–88.

Gordon, K. A study of esthetic judgments. *Journal of Experimental Psychology*, 1923, *6*, 36–43.

Göthlin, G. F. Inhibitory processes underlying color vision and their bearing on three-component theories. *American Journal of Psychology*, 1943, *56*, 537–50.

Gotschalk, D. W. *Art and the Social Order*. Chicago: Chicago University Press, 1947.

Gough, P. B. Grammatical transformations and speed of understanding. *Journal of Verbal Learning and Verbal Behavior*, 1965, *4*, 107–11.

Graf, H. *Bibliographie zum Problem der Proportionen*. Speyer: Landesbibliothek, 1958.

Graham, C. H. Color theory. In S. Koch, ed., *Psychology: A Study of a Science*, Vol. 1. New York: McGraw-Hill, 1959. Pp. 145–287.

Grammont, M. *Traité de phonétique*. 3d ed. Paris: Delagrave, 1946.

Granger, G. W. An experimental study of color preferences. *Journal of General Psychology*, 1955, *52*, 3–20. (a)

Granger, G. W. An experimental study of color harmony. *Journal of General Psychology*, 1955, *52*, 21–35. (b)

Granger, G. W. The prediction of preference for color combinations. *Journal of General Psychology*, 1955, *52*, 213–22. (c)

Granit, A. R. A study on the perception of form. *British Journal of Psychology*, 1921, *12*, 223–47.

Granit, R. *Sensory Mechanisms of the Retina*. London: Oxford University Press, 1947.

Grastyàn, E., Karmos, G., Vereczkey, L., Martin, J., & Kellényi, L. Hypothalamic motivational processes as reflected by their hippocampal electrical correlates. *Science*, 1965, *149*, 91–93.

Grastyàn, E., Karmos, G., Vereczkey, L., & Kellényi, L. The hippocampal electrical correlates of the homeostatic regulation of motivation. *Electroencephalographia Clinica et Neurophysiologica*, 1966, *21*, 34–53.

Gray, W. S., & Leary, B. E. *What Makes a Book Readable*. Chicago: University of Chicago Press, 1935.

Green, R. T., & Courtis, M. C. Information theory and figure perception: the metaphor that failed. *Acta Psychologica*, 1966, *25*, 12–36.

Greenberg, H. J. Some universals of grammar with particular reference to the order of meaningful elements. In H. J. Greenberg, ed., *Universals of Language*. Cambridge, Mass.: M.I.T. Press, 1962. Pp. 58–90.

Greene, P. C. Violin performance with reference to tempered, natural and pythagorean intonation. *University of Iowa Studies in the Psychology of Music*, 1937, *4*, 232–51. (a)

Greene, P. C. Violin intonation. *Journal of the Acoustic Society of America*, 1937, *9*, 43–44. (b)

Gregory, R. L., & Wallace, J. G. Recovery from early blindness. *Experimental Psychology Science Monographs*, no. 2, 1963.

Griffith, H. Time patterns in prose: a study in prose rhythm based upon voice records. *Psychological Monographs*, 1929, *39*, 1–82 (Whole no. 179).

Grimm, J. *Deutsche Grammatik*. 2d rev. ed. Berlin, 1870–98.

Grimm, J. *Über den Ursprung der Sprache*. 7th ed. Berlin, 1879.

Groot, J. J. M. de. *The Religious System of China.* Vol. 4. Leyden: Brill, 1901.

Gross, H. *Sound and Form in Modern Poetry: A Study of Prosody from Thomas Hardy to Robert Lowell.* Ann Arbor: University of Michigan Press, 1964.

Grossberg, J. M., & Wilson, H. K. Physiological changes accompanying the visualization of fearful and neutral situations. *Journal of Personality and Social Psychology,* 1968, *10,* 124–33.

Grunewald, M. A physiological aspect of experiencing music. *American Journal of Psychotherapy,* 1953, *7,* 59–67.

Guernsey, M. The role of consonance and dissonance in music. *American Journal of Psychology,* 1928, *40,* 173–204.

Guilford, J. P. The affective value of color as a function of hue, tint and chroma. *Journal of Experimental Psychology,* 1934, *17,* 342–70.

Guilford, J. P. A study in psychodynamics. *Psychometrika,* 1939, *4,* 1–23.

Guilford, J. P. There is system in color preferences. *Journal of the Optical Society of America,* 1940, *30,* 455–59.

Guilford, J. P., & Smith, P. C. A system of color preferences. *American Journal of Psychology,* 1959, *32,* 487–502.

Gundlach, C., & Macoubrey, C. The effect of color on apparent size. *American Journal of Psychology,* 1931, *43,* 109–11.

Gundlach, R. H. Factors determining the characterization of musical phrases. *American Journal of Psychology,* 1935, *47,* 624–43.

Gunzenhäuser, R. *Ästhetisches Mass und ästhetische Information.* Quickborn: Schnelle, 1962.

Gurney, E. *The Power of Sound.* London, 1880.

Haber, R. N. Discrepancy from adaptation level as a source of affect. *Journal of Experimental Psychology,* 1958, *56,* 370–75.

Haber, R. N. Nature of the effect of set on perception. *Psychological Review,* 1966, *73,* 335–51.

Hadding-Koch, K. *Acoustico-Phonetic Studies in the Intonation of Southern Swedish.* Lund, Sweden: C. W. K. Gleerup, 1961.

Haines, T. H., & Davies, A. E. The psychology of aesthetic reaction to rectangular forms. *Psychological Review,* 1904, *11,* 249–81.

Hall, E. T. *The Hidden Dimension.* Anchor Books. Garden City, N. Y.: Doubleday, 1966.

Hall, F. Benesh notation and choreology. *Dance Scope,* 1966, *3,* 30–36.

Hall, K. R. L. The fitness of signs to words. *British Journal of Psychology,* 1951, *42,* 21–33.

Hall, K. R. L., & Oldfield, R. G. An experimental study on the fitness of signs to words. *Quarterly Journal of Experimental Psychology,* 1950, *2,* 60–70.

Halle, M., & Keyser, S. J. Chaucer and the study of prosody. *College English,* 1966, *28,* 187–219.

Hambidge, J. *Dynamic Symmetry: The Greek Vase.* New Haven, Conn.: Yale University Press, 1920.

Hamel, F., & Hürliman, M., eds., *Das Atlantisbuch der Musik.* 5th ed. Zürich: Atlantis Verlag, 1946.

Hamer, E. *The Metres of English Poetry.* 4th ed. London: Methuen, 1951.

Hampton, P. J. The emotional element in music. *Journal of General Psychology,* 1945, *33,* 237–50.

Haner, C. F., & Whitney, E. R. Empathic conditioning and its relation to anxiety level. *American Psychologist*, 1960, *15*, 493. Abstract.

Hanley, M. L. *Word Index to James Joyce's Ulysses*. Madison: University of Wisconsin Press, 1937. Statistical tabulation by M. Joos.

Hanslick, E. *The Beautiful in Music*. London, 1891; reprinted, New York: Liberal Arts Press, 1957.

Harlow, H. F. Learning and satiation of response in intrinsically motivated complex puzzle performance by monkeys. *Journal of Comparative and Physiological Psychology*, 1950, *43*, 289–94.

Harlow, H. F., & McClearn, G. E. Object discrimination learned by monkeys on the basis of manipulation motives. *Journal of Comparative and Physiological Psychology*, 1954, *47*, 73–76.

Harlow, H. F., & Zimmermann, R. R. The development of affectional responses in infant monkeys. *Proceedings of the American Philosophical Society*, 1958, *102*, 501–9.

Harrington, G. M., & Linder, W. K. A positive reinforcing effect of electrical stimulation. *Journal of Comparative and Physiological Psychology*, 1962, *55*, 1014–15.

Harris, A. J. An experiment of affective contrast. *American Journal of Psychology*, 1929, *41*, 617–24.

Harris, J. D. Habituary response decrement in the intact organism. *Psychological Bulletin*, 1943, *40*, 385–422.

Harris, Z. S. *Methods in Structural Linguistics*. Chicago: University of Chicago Press, 1951.

Harsh, C. M., & Beebe-Center, J. G. Further evidence regarding preferential judgment of polygonal forms. *Journal of Psychology*, 1939, *7*, 343–50.

Hartmann, G. W. The facilitating effect of strong general illumination upon the discrimination of pitch and intensity differences. *Journal of Experimental Psychology*, 1934, *17*, 813–22.

Hartshorne, C. *The Philosophy and Psychology of Sensation*. Chicago: University of Chicago Press, 1934.

Harvey, O. J., & Clapp, W. F. Hope, expectancy and reactions to the unexpected. *Journal of Personality and Social Psychology*, 1956, *2*, 45–52.

Haskell, A. L. *Ballet: A Complete Guide to Appreciation: History, Aesthetics, Ballets, Dancers*. Harmondsworth: Penguin Books, 1945.

Haslerud, G. M. The effect of movement of stimulus objects upon avoidance reactions in chimpanzees. *Journal of Comparative Psychology*, 1938, *25*, 507–28.

Hauser, A. *The Social History of Art*. 2 vols. London: Routledge & Kegan Paul, 1951.

Havelka, J. Problem-seeking behavior in rats. *Canadian Journal of Psychology*, 1956, *10*, 91–97.

Havighurst, R. J., Robinson, M. Z., & Dorr, M. The development of the ideal self in childhood and adolescence. *Journal of Educational Research*, 1946, *40*, 241–57.

Hawkins, D. R., Pace, R., Pasternack, B., & Sandifer, M. G., Jr. A multivariate psychopharmacologic study in normals. *Psychosomatic Medicine*, 1961, *23*, 1–17.

Hawkins, E. What is the most beautiful dance? In W. Sorell, ed., *The Dance Has Many Faces*, 2d ed. New York: Columbia University Press, 1966. Pp. 242–43.

Hayes, C. W. A transformational-generative approach to style: Samuel Johnson and Edward Gibbon. *Language and Style*, 1968, *1*, 39–48.

Hayes, K. J. Exploration and fear. *Psychological Reports*, 1960, *6*, 91–93.

Heathers, G. L. The avoidance of repetition of a maze reaction as a function of the time between trials. *Journal of Psychology*, 1940, *10*, 359–80.

Hebb, D. O. On the nature of fear. *Psychological Review*, 1946, *53*, 259–76.

Hebb, D. O. *The Organization of Behavior*. New York: Wiley, 1949.

Hebb, D. O. Drive and the C.N.S. (conceptual nervous system). *Psychological Review*, 1955, *62*, 243–54.

Hebb, D. O. *A Textbook of Psychology*. Philadelphia: Saunders, 1958.

Hebb, D. O. Concerning imagery. *Psychological Review*, 1968, *75*, 466–77.

Hebb, D. O., & Mahut, H. Motivation et recherche du changement perceptif chez le rat et chez l'homme. *Journal de Psychologie Normale et Pathologique*, 1955, *48*, 209–21.

Hebb, D. O., & Riesen, A. H. The genesis of irrational fears. *Bulletin of the Canadian Psychological Association*, 1943, *3*, 49–50.

Heberer, G., Kurth, G., & Schwidetzky-Roesing, I. *Anthropologie*. Fischer Lexikon. Frankfurt am Main: Fischer Bücherei, 1959.

Heider, F. *The Psychology of Interpersonal Relations*. New York: Wiley, 1958.

Heider, F., & Simmel, M. L. An experimental study of apparent behavior. *American Journal of Psychology*, 1944, *57*, 243–49.

Heinlein, C. F. An experimental study of the Seashore consonance test. *Journal of Experimental Psychology*, 1925, *8*, 408–33.

Heinlein, C. F. The affective character of the major and minor modes in music. *Journal of Comparative Psychology*, 1928, *8*, 101–42.

Helmholtz, H. *Sensations of Tone*. New York: Longmans, Green & Co., 1912. Translated from the 4th German ed.

Helson, H. *Adaptation-Level Theory: An Experimental and Systematic Approach to Behavior*. New York: Harper & Row, 1964.

Helson, H., & Grove, J. Changes in hue, lightness and saturation of surface colors in passing from daylight to incandescent-lamp light. *Journal of the Optical Society of America*, 1947, *37*, 385–95.

Hempstead, L. The perception of visual form. *American Journal of Psychology*, 1900, *12*, 185.

Hendren, J. W. A word for rhythm and a word for meter. *Publications of the Modern Language Association of America*, 1961, *76*, 300–305.

Henle, M. An experimental investigation of dynamic and structural determinants of substitution. *Contributions to Psychological Theory*, 1942, *2*, no. 3.

Hering, E. *Grundzüge der Lehre vom Lichtsinn*. Berlin: Springer Verlag, 1920.

Herzog, G. Some linguistic features of American Indian poetry. *Word*, 1946, *2*, 82.

Hess, E. H. Natural preferences of chicks and ducklings for objects of different colours. *Psychological Reports*, 1956, *2*, 477–83.

Hess, E. H. The relationship between imprinting and motivation. In M. R. Jones, ed., *Nebraska Symposium on Motivation*. Lincoln: University of Nebraska Press, 1959.

Hess, E. H., & Gogel, W. C. Natural preferences of the chick for objects of different colors. *Journal of Psychology*, 1954, *38*, 483–93.

Hess, E. H., & Polt, J. M. Pupil size in relation to mental activity during simple problem solving. *Science*, 1964, *143*, 1190–92.

Hevner, K. Experimental studies of the affective value of colors and lines. *Journal of Applied Psychology*, 1935, *19*, 385–98. (a)

Hevner, K. The affective character of the major and minor modes in music. *American Journal of Psychology*, 1935, *47*, 103–18. (b)

Hevner, K. Expression in music: a discussion of experimental studies and theories. *Psychological Review*, 1935, *42*, 186–204. (c)

Hevner, K. Experimental studies of the elements of expression in music. *American Journal of Psychology*, 1936, *48*, 246–68.

Hevner K. The affective value of pitch and tempo in music. *American Journal of Psychology*, 1937, *49*, 621–30. (a)

Hevner, K. An experimental study of the affective value of sounds in poetry. *American Journal of Psychology*, 1937, *49*, 419–34. (b)

Hilgard, E. R., & Humphreys, L. G. The retention of conditioned discrimination in man. *Journal of General Psychology*, 1938, *19*, 111–25.

Hiller, L. A., Jr., & Isaacson, L. M. *Experimental Music*. New York: McGraw-Hill, 1959.

Hillman, J. *Emotion*. London: Routledge & Kegan Paul, 1960.

Hinde, R. A. Factors governing the changes in the strength of a partially inborn response, as shown by the mobbing behavior of the chaffinch (Fringilla coelebs): II. The waning of the response. *Proceedings of the Royal Society*, B, 1954, *142*, 331–58.

Hindemith, P. *A Composer's World: Horizons and Limitations*. Cambridge, Mass.: Harvard University Press, 1952.

Hippius, M. T. Experiment described in H. Rohracher, *Kleine Charakterkunde*. Wien & Innsbruck: Urban u. Schwarzenberg, 1959.

Hochberg, J. E. *Perception*. Englewood Cliffs, N.J.: Prentice-Hall, 1964.

Hochberg, J. E., & McAlister, E. A quantitative approach to figural "goodness." *Journal of Experimental Psychology*, 1953, *46*, 361–64.

Hochberg, J. E., & Silverstein, A. A quantitative index of stimulus similarity: proximity vs. differences in brightness. *American Journal of Psychology*, 1956, *69*, 456–58.

Hoffman, F. J. *Freudianism and the Literary Mind*. Baton Rouge: Louisiana State University Press, 1957.

Hofmann, W. *Die Plastik des 20. Jahrhunderts*. Frankfurt am Main: Fischer Bücherei, 1958.

Hofstätter, P. R. *Gruppendynamik*. Hamburg: Rowohlt, 1957.

Hofstätter, P. R., & Primac, D. W. Colors and the color blind. *Journal of General Psychology*, 1957, *57*, 229–40.

Holmes, D. S. Dimensions of projection. *Psychological Bulletin*, 1968, *69*, 248–68.

Holt, E. B. *Animal Drive and the Learning Process*. Vol. 1. New York: Holt, 1931.

Honkavaara, S. The psychology of expression. *British Journal of Psychology, Monograph Supplements*, 1961, no. 32.

Hopkins, G. M. *The Note-Books and Papers*. Edited by H. House. Oxford: Oxford University Press, 1937.

Hornberger, R. The projective effects of fear and sexual arousal on the ratings of pictures. *Journal of Clinical Psychology*, 1960, *16*, 328–31.

Hornbostel, E. M. v. Über Geruchshelligkeit. *Pflüg. Arch. ges. Physiologie*, 1931, *227*, 517–38.

Hornbostel, E. M. v. The unity of the senses. In W. D. Ellis, ed., *A Source Book of Gestalt Psychology*. New York: Harcourt, Brace, 1938. Pp. 210–16.

Horowitz, M. W., & Berkowitz, A. Structural advantage of the mechanism of spoken expression as a factor in differences in spoken and written expression. *Perceptual and Motor Skills*, 1964, *19*, 619–25.

Householder, F. W., Jr. On the problem of sound and meaning, and English phonesthemes. *Word*, 1946, *2*, 83–84.

Householder, F. W., Jr. From the viewpoint of linguistics: opening statement. In T. A. Sebeok, ed., *Style in Language*. Cambridge, Mass.: M.I.T. Press, 1960. Pp. 339–49.

Hovland, C. I. Reconciling conflicting results derived from experimental and survey studies of attitude change. *American Psychologist*, 1959, *14*, 8–17.

Hovland, C. I., Janis, I. L., & Kelley, H. H. *Communication and Persuasion*. New Haven, Conn.: Yale University Press, 1953.

Hovland, C. I., & Weiss, W. Transmission of information concerning concepts through positive and negative instances. *Journal of Experimental Psychology*, 1953, *45*, 165–82.

Howe, A. H. *Scientific Piano Tuning and Servicing*. New York: Alfred A. Howe, 1941.

Howe, I. *Politics and the Novel*. Meridian Books, New York: Horizon Press, 1957.

Howells, T. H. The experimental development of color-tone synesthesia. *Journal of Experimental Psychology*, 1944, *34*, 87–103.

Howes, D. H., & Osgood, C. E. On the combination of associative probabilities in linguistic contexts. *American Journal of Psychology*, 1954, *67*, 241–58.

Hřebiček, L. Aesthetic function of vocal harmony in the poetry of Abay Kunanbayef. *Archív Orientální*, 1964, *23*, 100–103.

Hrushovski, B. On free rhythms in modern poetry: preliminary remarks towards a critical theory of their structures and functions. In T. A. Sebeok, ed., *Style in Language*. Cambridge, Mass.: M.I.T. Press, 1960. Pp. 173–90.

Huber, K. *Der Ausdruck musikalischer Elementarmotive*. Leipzig: Barth, 1923.

Hudson, B. B. One-trial learning in the domestic rat. *Genetic Psychology Monographs*, 1950, *41*, 99–145.

Hull, C. L. *Principles of Behavior*. New York: Appleton-Century-Crofts, 1943.

Hulme, P. E. *Symbolism in Christian Art*. London: Sonnenschein, 1908.

Humboldt, W. v. *Über die Kawi-Sprache auf der Insel Java, nebst einer Einleitung über die Verschiedenheit des menschlichen Sprachbaues und ihren Einfluss auf die geistige Entwicklung des Menschengeschlechts*. Berlin, 1836; also published in *Wilhelm von Humboldt's Gesammelte Werke*. Vol. 6. Berlin, 1848. Pp. 1–425.

Humphrey, D. *The Art of Making Dances*. Ed. B. Pollack. New York: Holt, Rinehart and Winston, 1959.

Humphrey, G. *Thinking*. New York: Wiley, 1963.

Hunt, J. McV., Cole, M. W., & Reis, E. E. Situational cues distinguishing anger, fear and sorrow. *American Journal of Psychology*, 1958, *71*, 136–51.

Hunt, W. A. Anchoring affects in judgment. *American Journal of Psychology*, 1941, *54*, 395–403.

Hunt, W. A., & Volkman, J. The anchoring of an affective scale. *American Journal of Psychology*, 1937, *49*, 88–92.

Hunter, S. *Modern French Painting*. New York: Dell, 1956.

Hurvich, L. M., & Jameson, D. An opponent-process theory of color vision. *Psychological Review*, 1957, *64*, 384–404.

Huss, R., & Silverstein, N. *The Film Experience: Elements of Motion Picture Art.* New York: Harper and Row, 1968.

Hutchinson, A. *Labanotation.* New York: New Directions, 1954.

Huxley, A. *The Doors of Perception: Heaven and Hell.* Harmondsworth: Penguin Books, and London: Chatto & Windus, 1959.

Hyde, I. M. Effects of music upon electrocardiograms and blood pressure. In M. Schoen, ed., *The Effects of Music.* New York: Harcourt, Brace, 1927.

Hymes, D. H. Phonological aspects of style: some English sonnets. In T. A. Sebeok, ed., *Style in Language.* Cambridge, Mass.: M.I.T. Press. Pp. 109–31.

Inge, W. R. *Christian Mysticism.* New York: Meridian Books, 1956.

Inhelder, B., & Piaget, J. *The Growth of Logical Thinking.* New York: Basic Books, 1958.

Inhelder, E. Zur Psychologie einiger Verhaltensweisen—besonders des Spiels—von Zootieren. *Zeitschrift der Tierpsychologie*, 1955, *12*, 88–144.

Isenberg, A. Perception, meaning and the subject-matter of art. *Journal of Philosophy*, 1944, *41*, 561–75.

Jackson, G. The living dolls. In W. Sorell, ed., *The Dance Has Many Faces.* 2d ed. New York: Columbia University Press, 1966. Pp. 225–30.

Jacobi, J. *Complex, Archetype, Symbol in the Psychology of C. G. Jung.* London: Routledge & Kegan Paul, 1959.

Jacobs, B., Jr. A method for investigating the cue characteristics of pictures. In J. W. Atkinson, ed., *Motives in Fantasy, Action and Society.* Princeton, N.J.: Van Nostrand, 1958. Chap. 43, pp. 617–29.

Jacobson, E. *Progressive Relaxation.* Chicago: University of Chicago Press, 1929.

Jacobson, E. Electrical measurements of neuromuscular states during mental activities. *American Journal of Psychology*, 1930, *91*, 567–608; 1930, *94*, 22–34; 1930, *95*, 694–712; 1930, *95*, 703–12; 1931, *96*, 115–21; 1931, *96*, 122–25; 1931, *97*, 200–209.

Jaensch, E. Gefühl und Empfindung: Untersuchung ihres Verhältnisses am Beispiel des Farbsinnes. *Bericht des 15. Kongress der Deutschen Gesellschaft für Psychologie*, Jena, 1936. Pp. 65–70.

Jahoda, G. Sex differences in preferences for shapes: a cross-cultural replication. *British Journal of Psychology*, 1956, *47*, 126–32.

Jakobovits, L. A. The affect of symbols: towards the development of a cross-cultural graphic differential. *International Journal of Symbology*, 1969, *1*, 28–52.

Jakobson, R. *Kindersprache, Aphasie und allgemeine Lautgesetze.* Uppsala: Uppsala Universität, 1941.

Jakobson, R. Studies in comparative Slavic metrics. *Oxford Slavonic Papers*, 1952, *3*, 21–66.

Jakobson, R. From the viewpoint of linguistics: concluding statement: linguistics and poetics. In T. A. Sebeok, ed., *Style in Language.* Cambridge, Mass.: M.I.T. Press, 1960. Pp. 350–77.

Jakobson, R., Fant, G. M., & Halle, M. *Preliminaries to Speech Analysis: The Distinctive Features and Their Correlates.* Cambridge, Mass.: Acoustics Laboratory, M.I.T., Technical Report no. 13, 1952.

Jakobson, R., & Halle, M. *Fundamentals of Language.* The Hague: Mouton, 1956.

Jaques-Dalcroze, E. *Rhythm, Music, and Education.* New York: Putnam's 1921.

Jastrow, J. The popular aesthetics of color. *Popular Science Monthly,* 1897, *50,* 361–68.

Jeans, J. *Physics and Philosophy.* London: Cambridge University Press, 1943.

Jenkins, J. Affective processes in perception. *Psychological Bulletin,* 1957, *54,* 100–27.

Jenkins, J. J., & Palermo, D. S. Mediation processes and the acquisition of linguistic structure. *Monographs of the Society for Research in Child Development,* 1964, *29,* no. 1, 141–69.

Jespersen, O. *Language.* New York: Holt, 1922.

John, R. E. *Mechanisms of Memory.* New York: Academic Press, 1967.

Johns, E. H., & Sumner, F. C. Relation of the brightness difference of colors to their apparent distances. *Journal of Psychology,* 1948, *26,* 25–29.

Johnson, C., Suzecki, N. S., & Olds, W. K. Phonetic symbolism in an artificial language. *Journal of Abnormal and Social Psychology,* 1964, *69,* 233–36.

Johnson, H. M. The dynamogenic influence of light on tactile discrimination. *Psychobiology,* 1920, *2,* 351–74.

Johnson, M. G. Syntactic position and rated meaning. *Journal of Verbal Learning and Verbal Behavior,* 1967, *6,* 240–46.

Johnson, R. C., Thomson, C. W., & Frincke, G. Word values, word frequency, and duration threshold. *Psychological Review,* 1960, *67,* 332–42.

Johnson, W. *People in Quandaries.* New York: Harper, 1946.

Jones, A. Information deprivation in humans. In B. A. Maher, ed., *Progress in Experimental Personality Research.* Vol. 3. New York: Academic Press, 1966. Pp. 241–307.

Jones, E. *Hamlet and Oedipus.* Garden City, N.Y.: Doubleday, 1955.

Jones, L. Visual message presentation. Part I of *Final Contract,* AE 19 (122)–17 item I, Feb. 5, 1954.

Joyce, J. *Finnegans Wake.* New York: Viking Press, 1939.

Judd, D. B. *Color in Business, Science and Industry.* New York: Wiley, 1952.

Judd, D. B. Classic laws of color harmony expressed in terms of the color solid. *ISCC Newsletter,* 1955, *13,* no. 119.

Jung, C. G. *Contributions to Analytical Psychology.* New York: Harcourt, Brace, 1928.

Jung, C. G. "Psychology and literature," *Modern Man in Search of a Soul.* New York: Harcourt, Brace, 1933. Pp. 152–72.

Jung, C. G. *Psychology and Alchemy.* New York: Pantheon, 1953. (a)

Jung, C. G. *Psychological Types.* London: Routledge & Kegan Paul, 1953. (b)

Jung, C. G. *Symbols of Transformation.* London: Routledge & Kegan Paul, 1956. (a)

Jung, C. G. *Two Essays in Analytical Psychology.* New York: Meridian Books, 1956. (b)

Jung, C. G. *Psychology and Religion.* In *Collected Works,* Vol. II. London: Routledge & Kegan Paul, 1958.

Kaden, S. E., Wapner, S., & Werner, H. Studies in physiognomic perception: II. Effect of directional dynamics of pictured objects and of words on the position of the apparent horizon. *Journal of Psychology,* 1955, *39,* 61–70.

Kafka, F. *Der Prozess.* 3d ed. New York: Schocken Books, 1946.

Kagan, J. The concept of identification. *Psychological Review,* 1958, *65,* 296–305.

Kammann, R. Verbal complexity and preferences in poetry. *Journal of Verbal Learning and Verbal Behavior*, 1966, 5, 536–40.

Kandinsky, W. *Essays über Kunst und Künstler*. Teufen, Switzerland: Verlag Arthur Niggli und Willy Verkauf, 1955.

Kant, I. *Critique of Judgment*. London: Macmillan, 1931.

Kaplan, A. Referential meaning in the arts. *Journal of Aesthetics and Art Criticism*, 1954, 12, 457–74.

Kaplan, A. The aesthetics of the popular arts. In J. B. Hall & B. Ulanov, eds., *Modern Culture and the Arts*. New York: McGraw-Hill, 1967. Pp. 62–78.

Kaplan, E. An experimental study on inner speech as contrasted with external speech. M.A. thesis, Clark University, Worcester, Mass., 1952.

Kaplan, L. *Versuch einer Psychologie der Kunst*. Baden-Baden: Merlin Verlag, 1930.

Karwoski, T. F., & Odbert, H. S. Color-music. *Psychological Monographs: General and Applied*, 1938, 50, no. 2, 1–60.

Karwoski, T. F., Odbert, H. S., & Osgood, C. E. Studies in synesthetic thinking: II. The role of form in visual responses to music. *Journal of General Psychology*, 1942, 26, 199–222.

Karwoski, T. F., & Schachter, J. Psychological studies in semantics: III. Reaction times for similarity and difference. *Journal of Social Psychology*, 1948, 28, 103–20.

Karwoski, T. F., & Warrener, H. Studies in the peripheral retina: II. The Purkinje afterimage in the near foveal area of the retina. *Journal of General Psychology*, 1942, 26, 129–51.

Katz, D. *Der Aufbau der Tastwelt*. Leipzig: Barth, 1925.

Katz, D. *The World of Colour*. London: Kegan Paul, Trench, Trubner & Co., 1935.

Katz, D. *Gestalt Psychology: Its Nature and Significance*. New York: Ronald, 1950.

Katz, J. J., & Fodor, J. A. The structure of a semantic theory. *Language*, 1963, 39, 170–210.

Katz, R. L. *Empathy*. London: Collier-Macmillan, 1963.

Kellog, C. E. Alternation and interference of feelings. *Psychological Monographs*, 1915, 18, whole no. 79.

Kelly, G. A. *The Psychology of Personal Constructs*. Vol. 1. New York: Norton, 1955.

Kemp, W. Methodisches und Experimentelles zur Lehre von der Tonverschmelzung. *Archiv für die Gesammte Psychologie*, 1913, 29, 139–257.

Kendler, H. H., & Kendler, T. S. Vertical and horizontal processes in problem solving. *Psychological Review*, 1962, 69, 1–16.

Kennard, M. A. Autonomic interrelation with the somatic nervous system. *Psychosomatic Medicine*, 1947, 9, 29–36.

Kepes, G. *Language of Vision*. Chicago: Paul Theobald, 1944.

Kepes, G., ed., *Module, Proportion, Symmetry, Rhythm*. New York: Braziller, 1966.

Kerr, W. A. *Diplomacy Test of Empathy*. Chicago: Psychometric Affiliates, 1960.

Khozak, L. E. An attempt to change the verbal reactions of children by an experimental organization of their actions. *Na Putyakh k Izuch. vysshykh Form Neirodin. Reb.*, 1934, 405–14. In Russian.

Kido, M. Feeling manifestation in colors and tones. *Japanese Journal of Psychology*, 1926, 1, 433–52.

Kiell, N. *Psychiatry and Psychology in the Visual Arts and Aesthetics: A Bibliography.* Madison: University of Wisconsin Press, 1965. (a)

Kiell, N. *Psychoanalysis, Psychology, and Literature: A Bibliography.* Madison: University of Wisconsin Press, 1965. (b)

Kimura, T. Apparent warmth and heaviness of colours. *Japanese Journal of Psychology,* 1950, *20,* 33–36.

King, H. E. *Psychomotor Aspects of Mental Disease.* Cambridge, Mass.: Harvard University Press, 1954.

Kish, G. B., & Antonitis, J. J. Unconditional operant behavior in two homozygous strains of mice. *Journal of Genetic Psychology,* 1956, *88,* 121–29.

Klein, A., & Thomas, L. C. *Posture and Physical Fitness.* Washington: Children's Bureau Publications, no. 205, 1931.

Kleinsmith, L. J., & Kaplan, S. Interaction of arousal and recall interval in nonsense syllable paired-associate learning. *Journal of Experimental Psychology,* 1964, *67,* 124–26.

Klemm, O. Lokalisation von Sinneseindrücken bei disparaten Nebenreizen. *Psychologische Studien,* 1909, *5,* 73–162.

Klineberg, O. *Social Psychology.* New York: Holt, 1940.

Knapp, R. H. An experimental study of a triadic hypothesis concerning the source of aesthetic imagery. *Journal of Projective Techniques,* 1964, *28,* 49–54.

Knight, G. W. *The Wheel of Fire.* New York: Meridian Books, 1957.

Knowlton, K. C. Computer-produced movies. *Science,* 1965, *150,* 1116–20.

Koch, B. C. The apparent weight of colors. *Ohio State University Studies, Contributions to Psychology,* 1928, no. 9.

Koch, K. *Der Baumtest.* 2d ed. Bern and Stuttgart: Huber, 1954.

Koen, F. Polarization, m, and emotionality in words. *Journal of Verbal Learning and Verbal Behavior,* 1962, *1,* 183–87.

Koestler, A. *Insight and Outlook.* London: Macmillan, 1949. (a)

Koestler, A. The novelist deals with character. *Saturday Review of Literature,* 1 Jan. 1949. (b)

Koestler, A. *The Act of Creation.* New York: Macmillan, 1964.

Koffka, K. Experimentaluntersuchungen zur Lehre von Rhythmus. *Zeitschrift der Psychologie,* 1909, *52,* 1–109.

Koffka, K. Some problems of space perception. In *Psychologies of 1930.* Worcester, Mass.: Clark University Press, 1930. Pp. 161–87.

Koffka, K. *Principles of Gestalt Psychology.* New York: Harcourt, Brace, 1935.

Koffka, K. On problems of color perception. *Acta Psychologica,* 1936, *1,* 129–34.

Koffka, K. Problems in the psychology of art. In *Art: A Bryn Mawr Symposium.* Lancaster, Pa.: Lancaster Press, 1940. Chap. 3, pp. 180–275.

Koffka, K. *The Growth of the Mind.* London: Routledge & Kegan Paul, 1952.

Köhler, W. Akustische Untersuchungen. *Zeitschrift für Psychologie,* 1910, *54,* 241–89; 1911, *28,* 59–140; 1913, *64,* 92–105; 1915, *72,* 1–192.

Köhler, W. Zur Psychologie des Schimpansen. *Psychologische Forschung,* 1922, *1,* 2–46.

Köhler, W. *Gestalt Psychology.* New York: Liveright, 1929.

Köhler, W. *Psychologische Probleme.* Berlin: Springer, 1933.

Köhler, W. *The Place of Value in a World of Facts.* New York: Liveright, 1938.

Köhler, W. *Dynamics in Psychology.* New York: Liveright, 1940.

Kohut, H. Observations on the psychological functions of music. *Journal of the American Psychoanalytic Association*, 1957, 5, 389–407.

Kohut, H., Levarie, S. On the enjoyment of listening to music. *Psychoanalytic Quarterly*, 1950, 19, 64–87.

Kopfermann, H. Psychologische Untersuchungen über die Wirkung zweidimensionaler Darstellungen körperlicher Gebilde. *Psychologische Forschung*, 1930, 13, 293–364.

Kouwer, B. J. *Colors and Their Character: A Psychological Study*. The Hague: Martinus Nijhoff, 1949.

Kovsharova, V. A study in experimentally influencing the verbal choice reactions of children. *Na Putyakh k Izuch. vysshykh Form Neirodin. Reb.*, 1934, 415–35. In Russian.

Kraehenbuehl, D., & Coons, E. Information as a measure of the experience of music. *Journal of Aesthetics and Art Criticism*, 1959, 17, 510–22.

Kramrisch, S. *The Art of India Through the Ages*. 2d ed. London: Phaidon Press, 1955.

Kraus, K. Der Reim, *K. Kraus, Auswahl aus dem Werk*. Frankfurt am Main: Fischer Bücherei, 1961. Pp. 257–58.

Krauss, R. Über graphischen Ausdruck. *Zeitschrift für angewandte Psychologie*, 1930, 48, 1–141.

Kravkov, S. V. Changes of visual acuity in one eye under the influence of the illumination of the other or of acoustic stimuli. *Journal of Experimental Psychology*, 1934, 17, 805–12.

Kravkov, S. V. The influence of aural stimulation on photic and chromatic sensitivity of the eye. *Izv. Akademya Nauk SSSR, Seria Biolog.*, 1937, no. 1, 237–45. (a) In Russian.

Kravkov, S. V. Physiological optics in the USSR after twenty years. *Vestn. Oftalmologii*, 1937, 11, 468–78. (b). In Russian.

Kravkov, S. V. The influence of the loudness of the indirect sound stimulus on the color sensitivity of the eye. *Acta Ophthalmologica*, 1939, 17, 324–31. (a)

Kravkov, S. V. The influence of odours upon color-vision. *Acta Ophthalmologica*, 1939, 17, 425–41. (b)

Kravkov, S. V. Color vision and the autonomic nervous system. *Journal of the Ophthalmological Society of America*, 1941, 31, 335–37.

Kravkov, S. V. Physiological optics in the Soviet Union after twenty-five years. *Vestn. Oftalmologii*, 1942, 21, 42–55. In Russian.

Kravkov, S. V. On some principles of vision as a function of accessory stimuli. *Problemy fiziol. Optiki*, 1947, 4, 31–45. In Russian.

Kravkov, S. V. *The Interaction of the Sense Organs*. Moscow: Akademya Nauk SSSR, 1948. In Russian.

Kravkov, S. V., & Galochkina, L. P. The effect of direct current on vision. *Problemy fiziol. Optiki*, 1947, 4, 77–86. In Russian.

Kreindler, A. The role of the reticular formation in the conditioning process. In H. Jaspers & G. D. Smirnov, eds., *The Moscow Colloquium on Electroencephalogy of Higher Nervous Activity*. Montreal: EEG Journal, 1960.

Kreitler, H. Psychologische Grundlagen des Kunstgenusses. Unpublished doctoral dissertation, University of Graz, Austria, 1956.

Kreitler, H. The psychology of Dadaism. In W. Verkauf, ed., *Dada: Monograph of a Movement*. Teufen, Switzerland: Niggli, 1957. Pp. 74–88.

Kreitler, H. Bilder die der Beschauer malt. *Forum*, 1960, 7, 300–302. In Hebrew: On the psychology of Tachism. *Keshet*, 1960, 2, 85–88.

Kreitler, H., & Elblinger, S. Tension and relief of colors and color combinations. Unpublished manuscript, Tel Aviv University, 1961.

Kreitler, H. & Kreitler, S. Modes of action in the psychodramatic role test. *International Journal of Sociometry and Sociatry*, 1964, 4, 10–25.

Kreitler, H. & Kreitler, S. *Die weltanschauliche Orientierung der Schizophrenen.* Basel-München: Reinhardt, 1965.

Kreitler, H., & Kreitler, S. *Die kognitive Orientierung des Kindes.* Basel-München: Reinhardt, 1967.

Kreitler, H., & Kreitler, S. The validation of psychodramatic behavior against behavior in life. *British Journal of Medical Psychology*, 1968, 41, 185–92. (a)

Kreitler, H., & Kreitler, S. Unhappy memories of the happy past: studies in cognitive dissonance. *British Journal of Psychology*, 1968, 59, 157–66. (b)

Kreitler, H., & Kreitler, S. Cognitive orientation and defense mechanisms. Princeton, N.J.: Educational Testing Service, Research Bulletin no. 23, 1969.

Kreitler, H., & Kreitler, S. The cognitive antecedents of the orienting reflex. *Schweizerische Zeitschrift für Psychologie und ihre Anwendungen* (Meili Festschrift), 1970, 29, 94–105. (a)

Kreitler, H., Kreitler, S. Cognitive orientation, achievement motivation theory, and achievement behavior. Princeton, N.J.: Educational Testing Service, Research Momorandum no. 1, 1970. (b)

Kreitler, H., & Kreitler, S. Dependence of humor on cognitive strategies. *Merril-Palmer Quarterly*, 1970, 16, 163–77. (c)

Kreitler, H., & Kreitler, S. Perceptions of self and perceptions of others. In press. 1971. (a)

Kreitler, H., & Kreitler, S. The model of cognitive orientation: towards a theory of human behavior. *British Journal of Psychology*, 1972, 63, 9–30. (1971b)

Kreitler, H., & Kreitler, S. Cognitive orientation. In W. Arnold, H. J. Eysenck, & R. Meili, eds., *Lexikon der Psychologie*, Vol. 2. In six languages. Freiburg: Herder, 1971. (c)

Kreitler, H., & Kreitler, S. The cognitive determinants of defensive behavior. *British Journal of Social and Clinical Psychology*, 1972 (in press). (a)

Kreitler, H., & Kreitler, S. *Cognitive Orientation and Behavior.* New York: Springer, 1972. (b)

Kreitler, S. *Symbolschöpfung und Symbolerfassung: eine experimentalpsychologische Studie.* Basel-München: Reinhardt, 1965.

Kreitler, S., & Kreitler, H. Dimensions of meaning and their measurement. *Psychological Reports*, 1968, 23, 1307–29.

Kreitler, S., & Kreitler, H. Symbol and sign. In W. Arnold, H. J. Eysenck, & R. Meili, eds., *Lexikon der Psychologie*, Vol. 3. In six languages. Freiburg: Herder, 1971.

Kris, E. *Psychoanalytic Explorations in Art.* New York: International Universities Press, 1952.

Kris, E., & Kaplan, A. Aesthetic ambiguity. In E. Kris, *Psychoanalytic Explorations in Art.* New York: International Universities Press, 1952. Pp. 243–64.

Kris, J. von. Die Gesichtsempfindungen. In *Handbuch der Physiologie des Menschen.* Vol. 3. Braunschweig: Vieweg, 1905. Pp. 109–282.

Kultermann, U. *The New Sculpture: Environments and Assemblages*. New York: Praeger, 1968.

Kurth, E. *Musikpsychologie*. Bern: Krompholz, 1947.

Laban, R. *Modern Educational Dance*. London: MacDonald and Evans, 1948.

Laban, R. *The Mastery of Movement*. London: MacDonald and Evans, 1950.

Laban, R. The educational and therapeutic value of the dance. In W. Sorrell, ed., *The Dance Has Many Faces*. 2d ed. New York: Columbia University Press, 1966. Pp. 113–27.

LaBarre, W. The cultural basis of emotions and gestures. *Journal of Personality*, 1947, *16*, 49–68.

Lambert, W. E., & Jakobovits, L. A. Verbal satiation and changes in the intensity of meaning. *Journal of Experimental Psychology*, 1960, *60*, 376–83.

Langer, S. K. *Philosophy in a New Key: A Study in the Symbolism of Reason, Rite and Art*. Mentor Books. New York: The New York American Library, 1948.

Langer, S. K. *Feeling and Form*. New York: Scribner's, 1953.

Langer, S. K. *Mind: An Essay on Human Feeling*. Vol. 1. Baltimore: Johns Hopkins Press, 1967.

Langfeld, H. S. *The Aesthetic Attitude*. New York: Harcourt, Brace, 1920.

Lanier, L. H. An experimental study of "affective tone." *Journal of Psychology*, 1941, *11*, 199–217.

Lanier, S. *The Science of English Verse*. New York: Scribner's, 1920.

Lanson, G. *Histoire de la littérature française*. Paris: Hachette, 1952.

Lasagna, L., von Felsinger, J. N., & Beecher, H. K. Drug-induced mood changes in man: observations of healthy subjects, chronically ill patients, and "post-addicts." *Journal of the American Medical Association*, 1955, *157*, 1006–20.

Latané, B., & Rodin, J. A lady in distress: inhibiting effects of friends and strangers on bystander intervention. *Journal of Experimental Social Psychology*, 1969, *5*, 189–202.

Lawler, C. O., & Lawler, E. E. Color-mood associations in young children. *Journal of Genetic Psychology*, 1965, *107*, 29–32.

Lawler, M. Cultural influences on preference for designs. *Journal of Abnormal and Social Psychology*, 1955, *61*, 690–92.

Lazarus, R. S. *Psychological Stress and the Coping Process*. New York: McGraw-Hill, 1966.

Lazarus, R. S., & Alfert, E. The short-circuiting of threat by experimentally altering cognitive appraisal. *Journal of Abnormal and Social Psychology*, 1964, *69*, 195–205.

Lazarus, R. S., Opton, E. M., Jr., Nomikos, M. S., & Rankin, N. O. The principle of short-circuiting of threat: further evidence. *Journal of Personality*, 1965, *33*, 622–35.

Lazarus, R. S., Speisman, J. C., Mordkoff, A. M., & Davison, L. A. A laboratory study of psychological stress produced by a motion picture film. *Psychological Monographs*, 1962, *76* (34, whole no. 553).

Lee, H. B. On the esthetic states of mind. *Psychiatry*, 1947, *10*, 281–306.

Lee, H. B. The values of order and vitality in art. In G. Roheim, ed., *Psychoanalysis and the Social Sciences*. Vol. 2. New York: International Universities Press, 1950. Pp. 231–74.

Lee, V. *The Beautiful*. London: Cambridge University Press, 1913.

Lefkowitz, M. M., Blake, R. R., & Mouton, J. S. Status factors in pedestrian violation of traffic signals. *Journal of Abnormal and Social Psychology*, 1955, 51, 704–6.

Legowski, L. W. Beiträge zur experimentellen Ästhetik. *Archiv für die Gesammte Psychologie*, 1908, 12, 236–311.

Leijonhielm, C. *Colors, Forms and Art: Studies in Differential Aesthetic Psychology*. Stockholm: Almquist & Wiksell, 1967.

Lerner, M. J., & Matthew, G. Reactions to suffering of others under conditions of indirect responsibility. *Journal of Personality and Social Psychology*, 1967, 5, 319–25.

Lesser, S. O. *Fiction and the Unconscious*. Vintage Books. New York: Knopf, 1962.

Lessing, G. E. Laocoön, in *Laocoön, Nathan the Wise, Minna von Barnhelm*. New York: Dutton, 1930. Pp. 1–110.

Leuba, C. Toward some integration of learning theories: the concept of optimal stimulation. *Psychological Reports*, 1955, 1, 27–33.

Leuba, C., & Lucas, C. The effects of attitudes on descriptions of pictures. *Journal of Experimental Psychology*, 1945, 35, 517–24.

Leventhal, H., Singer, R., & Jones, S. The effects of fear and specificity of recommendation upon attitudes and behavior. *Journal of Personality and Social Psychology*, 1965, 2, 20–29.

Levin, S. R. *Linguistic Structures in Poetry*. The Hague: Mouton, 1962. (a)

Levin, S. R. Suprasegmentals and the performance of poetry. *Quarterly Journal of Speech*, 1962, 48, 366–72. (b)

Levin, S. R. Internal and external deviation in poetry. *Word*, 1965, 21, 225–37.

Levine, S. The role of irrelevant drive stimuli in learning. *Journal of Experimental Psychology*, 1953, 45, 410–16.

Levy, D. M. The hostile act. *Psychological Review*, 1941, 48, 356–61.

Lévy-Bruhl, L. *Les Fonctions mentales dans les sociétés inférieures*. Paris: Alcan, 1910.

Lewin, K. *Principles of Topological Psychology*. New York: McGraw-Hill, 1936.

Lewin, K. Intention, will and need. In D. Rapaport, *Organization and Pathology of Thought: Selected Sources*. New York: Columbia University Press, 1951. Chap. 5, pp. 95–153.

Lewin, K., Dembo, T., Festinger, L., & Sears, P. S. Level of aspiration. In J. McV. Hunt, ed., *Personality and the Behavior Disorders*. New York: Ronald, 1944.

Lewinski, R. T. An investigation of individual responses to chromatic illumination. *Journal of Psychology*, 1938, 6, 155–60.

Lewis, M. *Infant Speech: A Study of the Beginnings of Language*. New York: Harcourt, Brace, 1936.

Lieberman, P. *Intonation, Perception, and Language*. Cambridge, Mass.: M.I.T. Press, Research Monograph no. 38, 1967.

Lieberman, P., & Michaels, S. B. Some aspects of the fundamental frequency, envelope amplitude and the emotional content of speech. *Journal of the Acoustical Society of America*, 1962, 34, 922–27.

Lillie, A. A note on the nature of color associations. *Mind*, 1926, 35, 533–36.

Lindberg, B. J. Experimental studies of color and non-color attitude in school children and adults. *Acta Psychiatrica Kbh.*, 1938, supplement 16.

Lindner, R. M. An experimental study of anticipation. *American Journal of Psychology*, 1938, 51, 253–61.

Lindsley, D. B. Psychophysiology and motivation. In M. R. Jones, ed., *Nebraska*

Symposium on Motivation, 1957. Lincoln: University of Nebraska Press, 1957. Pp. 44–105.

Lipps, T. *Ästhetik: Psychologie des Schönen und der Kunst.* Hamburg & Leipzig: L. Voss, 1903–6.

Lipps, T. Das Wissen von fremden Ichen. *Psychologische Untersuchungen,* 1907, *1,* 694–722.

Lipps, T. *Psychological Studies.* Vol. 2 of Psychology Classics. Baltimore: Williams & Wilkins, 1926. Pp. 138–265.

Lipps, T. Empathy, inner imitation, and sense feelings. In M. Rader, ed., *A Modern Book of Esthetics: An Anthology.* 3d ed. New York: Holt, Rinehart and Winston, 1962. Pp. 374–82.

Lipps, T. Empathy and aesthetic pleasure. In K. Aschenbrenner & A. Isenberg, eds., *Aesthetic Theories: Studies in the Philosophy of Art.* Englewood Cliffs, N.J.: Prentice-Hall, 1965. Pp. 403–12.

Lipsky, A. Rhythm as a distinguishing characteristic of prose style. *Archives of Psychology,* 1907, *4,* 1–44.

Lissa, Z. On the evolution of musical perception. *Journal of Aesthetics and Art Criticism,* 1965, *24,* 273–86.

Lissner, K. Die Entspannung von Bedürfnissen durch Ersatzhandlungen. *Psychologische Forschung,* 1933, *18,* 218–50.

Lloyd, N. Composing for the dance. In W. Sorell, ed., *The Dance Has Many Faces.* 2d ed. New York: Columbia University Press, 1966. Pp. 137–50.

Lo, C. The affective value of color combinations. *American Journal of Psychology,* 1936, *48,* 617–24.

Loewenstein, A., & Donald, G. A color stereoscopic phenomenon. *Archives of Ophthalmology,* 1941, *26,* 551–64.

London, I. D. Research on sensory interaction in the Soviet Union. *Psychological Bulletin,* 1954, *51,* 531–68.

Lorenz, K. Die angeborenen Formen möglicher Erfahrung. *Zeitschrift der Tierpsychologie,* 1943, *5,* 235–49.

Lorenz, K. Plays and vacuum activities, in *L'Instinct dans le comportement de l'animal et de l'homme.* Paris: Masson et Cie., 1956.

Lorge, I. Predicting readability. *Teachers College Record,* 1944, *45,* 404–19.

Lotz, J. Metric typology. In T. A. Sebeok, ed., *Style in Language.* Cambridge, Mass.: M.I.T. Press, 1960. Pp. 135–48.

Löwenfeld, B. Systematisches Studium der Reaktionen der Säuglinge auf Klänge und Geräusche. *Zeitschrift für Psychologie,* Abt. 1, 1927, *104,* 62–96.

Lowenfeld, H. Psychic trauma and productive experience in the art. *Psychoanalytic Quarterly,* 1941, *10,* 116–30.

Lowenfeld, V. *The Nature of Creative Activity.* New York: Harcourt Brace, 1939.

Lowenfeld, V. *Creative and Mental Growth.* Rev. ed. New York: Macmillan, 1953.

Lowenfield, M. The mosaic test. *American Journal of Orthopsychiatry,* 1949, *19,* 537–550.

Lubbock, P. *The Craft of Fiction.* New York: Viking Press, 1957.

Luchins, A. S. Mechanization in problem-solving: the effect of Einstellung. *Psychological Monographs,* 1942, *54,* no. 248.

Luckiesh, M. *The Language of Color.* New York: Dodd Mead, 1918. (a)

Luckiesh, M. Retiring and advancing colors. *American Journal of Psychology,* 1918, *29,* 182–86. (b)

Luckiesh, M. *Light and Color in Advertising and Merchandising*. New York: Van Nostrand, 1923.

Luckiesh, M. *Color and Colors*. New York: Van Nostrand, 1938.

Lund, F. H., & Anastasi, A. An interpretation of aesthetic experience. *American Journal of Psychology*, 1928, *40*, 434–48.

Lundholm, H. The affective tone of lines. *Psychological Review*, 1921, *28*, 43–60.

Lundin, R. W. Toward a cultural theory of consonance. *Journal of Psychology*, 1947, *23*, 45–49.

Lynch, J. J. The tonality of lyric poetry: an experiment in method. *Word*, 1953, *9*, 211–24.

Lynn, R. *Attention, Arousal and the Orientation Reaction*. Oxford: Pergamon Press, 1966.

McAuley, J. Metrical accent and speech stress. *Balcony: The Sydney Review*, 1966, no. 4, 21–31.

McClelland, D. C., Atkinson, J. W., Clark, R. A., & Lowell, E. L. *The Achievement Motive*. New York: Appleton-Century-Crofts, 1953.

McDougall, R. The relation of auditory rhythm to nervous discharge. *Psychological Review*, 1902, *9*, 460–80.

McElroy, W. A. A sex difference in preferences for shapes. *British Journal of Psychology*, 1954, *45*, 209–216.

McGuire, W. J. Selective exposure: a summing up. In R. P. Abelson, E. Aronson, W. J. McGuire, T. M. Newcomb, M. J. Rosenberg, & P. H. Tannenbaum, eds., *Theories of Cognitive Consistency: A Sourcebook*. Chicago: Rand McNally, 1968. Pp. 797–800.

McKinney, J. P. Disappearance of luminous designs. *Science*, 1963, *140*, 403–4.

McLuhan, M. The medium is the message. In J. B. Hall & B. Ulanov, eds., *Modern Culture and the Arts*. New York: McGraw-Hill, 1967. Pp. 415–29.

McMurray, G. A. A study of "fittingness" of signs to words by means of the semantic differential. *Journal of Experimental Psychology*, 1958, *56*, 310–12.

McNeill, D. The origin of associations within the same grammatical class. *Journal of Verbal Learning and Verbal Behavior*, 1963, *2*, 250–62.

McReynolds, P. A restricted conceptualization of human anxiety and motivation. *Psychological Reports*, 1956, *2*, 293–312.

McWhinnie, H. J. Effects of a learning experience on preference for complexity and asymmetry. *Perceptual and Motor Skills*, 1966, *23*, 119–22.

Maccoby, E. E. Why do children watch television? *Public Opinion Quarterly*, 1954, *18*, 239–44.

Macdermott, M. M. *Vowel Sounds in Poetry*. London: Kegan Paul, 1940.

Mackworth, J. *Vigilance and Habituation*. Harmondsworth: Penguin Books, 1969.

Maclagan, E. *Italian Sculpture of the Renaissance*. Charles Eliot Norton Lectures, 1927–28. Cambridge, Mass.: Harvard University Press, 1935.

Maddi, S. R. Affective tone during environmental regularity and change. *Journal of Abnormal and Social Psychology*, 1961, *62*, 338–45.

Maddi, S. R. The pursuit of consistency and variety. In Abelson, R. P., Aronson, E., et al., eds., *Theories of Cognitive Consistency: A Sourcebook*. Chicago: Rand McNally, 1968. Pp. 267–94.

Magnus, H. *Die geschichtliche Entwicklung des Farbsinnes*. Leipzig: Veit, 1877.

Mahl, G. F. The lexical and linguistic levels in the expression of the emotions.

In P. H. Knapp, ed., *Expression of the Emotions in Man.* New York: International Universities Press, 1963. Chap. 5, pp. 77–105.

Mahler, W. Ersatzhandlungen verschiedener Realitätsgrade. *Psychologische Forschung,* 1933, *18,* 27–89.

Maier, B., Bevan, W., & Behar, I. The effect of auditory stimulation upon the critical flicker frequency for different regions of the visible spectrum. *American Journal of Psychology,* 1961, *74,* 67–73.

Major, B. S. On the affective tone of simple sense-impressions. *American Journal of Psychology,* 1895, *7,* 57–77.

Mallarmé, S. Crise de vers, in *Divagations.* Paris: Charpentier, 1935.

Malmberg, C. F. The perception of consonance and dissonance. *Psychological Monographs,* 1918, *25,* no. 108, 93–133.

Malmo, R. B. Activation: a neurophysiological dimension. *Psychological Review,* 1959, *66,* 367–86.

Maltzew, C. v. Das Erkennen sukzessiv gegebener musikalischer Intervalle in den äussern Tonregionen. *Zeitschrift für Psychologie,* 1913, *64,* 161–257.

Maltzman, I., Kantor, W., & Langdon, B. Immediate and delayed retention, arousal, and the orienting and defensive reflexes. *Psychonomic Science,* 1966, *6,* 445–46.

Maltzman, I., Morrisett, L., Jr., & Brooks, L. O. An investigation of phonetic symbolism. *Journal of Abnormal and Social Psychology,* 1956, *53,* 249–51.

Mandler, G., & Watson, D. L. Anxiety and the interruption of behavior. In C. D. Spielberger, ed., *Anxiety and Behavior.* New York: Academic Press, 1966. Pp. 263–88.

Marañon, G. Contribution à l'étude de l'activité émotive de l'adrénaline. *Revue Français d'Endocrinologie,* 1924, *2,* 301–25.

Marbe, K. *Über den Rhythmus der Prosa.* Giessen: Töpelmann, 1904.

Marchand, H. Phonetic symbolism in English word-formations. *Indogermanische Forschungen,* 1958–59, *64,* 146–68, 256–77.

Margolis, N. M. A theory on the psychology of Jazz. *American Imago,* 1954, *11,* 263–91.

Maritain, J. *Creative Intuition in Art and Poetry.* New York: Meridian Books, 1955.

Marshall, H. R. *Pain, Pleasure, and Aesthetics.* New York: Macmillan, 1894.

Marsicano, M. Thoughts on dance. In W. Sorell, ed., *The Dance Has Many Faces.* 2d ed. New York: Columbia University Press, 1966. Pp. 238–41.

Martin, J. *The Dance: The Story of the Dance Told in Pictures and Text.* New York: Tudor, 1946.

Martin, J. L. An experimental study of Fechner's principles of aesthetics. *Psychological Review,* 1906, *13,* 142–219.

Marx, M. H., Henderson, R. L., & Roberts, C. L. Positive reinforcement of the bar-pressing response by a light stimulus following dark operant pretests with no after effect. *Journal of Comparative and Physiological Psychology,* 1955, *48,* 73–76.

Maslow, A. H., & Mintz, N. L. Effects of esthetic surroundings: I. Initial effects of three esthetic conditions upon perceiving "energy" and "well-being" in faces. *Journal of Personality,* 1956, *41,* 247–54.

Masserman, J. H. A biodynamic psychoanalytic approach to the problems of feeling and emotion. In M. L. Reymert, ed., *Feelings and Emotions*. New York: McGraw-Hill, 1950. Pp. 40–75.

Masson, D. I. Synesthesia and sound spectra. *Word*, 1952, 8, 39–41.

Masson, D. I. Vowel and consonant patterns in poetry. *Journal of Aesthetics and Art Criticism*, 1953, 12, 213–27.

Masson, D. I. Sound-repetition terms. In *Poetics: Proceedings of the First International Conference of Work-in-Progress Devoted to the Problems of Poetics, Warsaw, August 18–27, 1960*. Warsaw and The Hague, 1961. Pp. 189–99.

Matoré, G. *L'Espace humain: l'expression de l'espace dans la vie, la pensée et l'art contemporains*. Paris: Editions de La Colombe, 1961.

Mauser, B., & Bloch, B. L. A study of the additivity of variables affecting social interaction. *Journal of Abnormal and Social Psychology*, 1957, 54, 250–56.

Max, L. W. An experimental study of the motor theory of consciousness: III. *Journal of Comparative Psychology*, 1935, 19, 469–86.

Mednick, S. A. The associative basis of the creative process. *Psychological Review*, 1962, 69, 220–32.

Mehler, J. Some effects of grammatical transformation on the recall of English sentences. *Journal of Verbal Learning and Verbal Behavior*, 1963, 2, 346–51.

Meili, R., & Tobler, E. Les mouvements stroboscopiques chez les enfants. *Archives de Psychologie, Genève*, 1931, 23, 131–57.

Melzack, R. Irrational fears in dogs. *Canadian Journal of Psychology*, 1952, 6, 141–47.

Mendel, G. Children's preferences for differing degrees of novelty. *Child Development*, 1965, 36, 453–66.

Menzel, E. W., Jr., Davenport, R. K., & Rogers, C. M. Some aspects of behavior toward novelty in young chimpanzees. *Journal of Comparative and Physiological Psychology*, 1961, 54, 16–19.

Mercer, F. M. Color preferences of 1,006 negroes. *Journal of Comparative Psychology*, 1925, 5, 109–46.

Merleau-Ponty, M. *Phénoménologie de la perception*. Paris: Gallimard, 1945.

Messer, S., Jakobovits, L. A., Kanungo, R., & Lambert, W. E. Semantic satiation of words and numbers. *British Journal of Psychology*, 1964, 55, 155–63.

Meyer, L. B. *Emotion and Meaning in Music*. Chicago: University of Chicago Press, 1956.

Meyer, L. B. Meaning in music and information theory. *Journal of Aesthetics and Art Criticism*, 1957, 15, 412–24.

Meyer, L. B. Some remarks on value and greatness in music. *Journal of Aesthetics and Art Criticism*, 1959, 17, 486–500.

Michael, D. N. A cross-cultural investigation of closure. *Journal of Abnormal and Social Psychology*, 1953, 48, 230–55.

Michaud, G. *La Doctrine Symboliste; documents*. Paris: Librairie Nizet, 1947.

Michels, K. M., & Zusne, L. Metrics of visual form. *Psychological Bulletin*, 1965, 63, 74–86.

Michotte, A. The emotions regarded as functional connections. In M. L. Reymert, ed., *International Symposium on Feelings and Emotions*. New York: McGraw-Hill, 1950. Pp. 50–93.

Michotte, A. *The Perception of Causality*. London: Methuen, 1963.

Milerian, E. A. Electrical activity of the cerebral cortex during attention to auditory stimuli. *Voprosy Psychologii*, 1955, 6, 101–12. In Russian.

Miles, J. *Eras and Modes in English Poetry.* Rev. ed. Berkeley: Univ. of California Press, 1964.

Miles, R. C. Learning in kittens with manipulatory, exploratory, and food incentives. *Journal of Comparative and Physiological Psychology,* 1958, *51,* 39–42.

Miller, G. A. *Language and Communication.* New York: McGraw-Hill, 1951.

Miller, G. A. The magical number seven, plus or minus two: some limits on our capacity for processing information. *Psychological Review,* 1956, *63,* 81–97.

Miller, G. A. From the viewpoint of psychology: closing statement. In T. A. Sebeok, ed., *Style in Language.* Cambridge, Mass.: M.I.T. Press, 1960. Pp. 386–95.

Miller, G. A. Some psychological studies of grammar. *American Psychologist,* 1962, *17,* 748–62.

Miller, G. A., & Selfridge, J. A. Verbal context and the recall of meaningful material. *American Journal of Psychology,* 1950, *63,* 176–85.

Miller, N. E., & Bugelski, R. Minor studies of aggression: II. The influence of frustrations imposed by the in-group on attitudes expressed toward out-groups. *Journal of Psychology,* 1948, *25,* 437–52.

Miller, R. E., Banks, J. A., Jr., & Ogawa, N. Communication of affect in "cooperative conditioning" of rhesus monkeys. *Journal of Abnormal and Social Psychology,* 1962, *64,* 343–48.

Miller, R. E., Banks, J. A., Jr., & Ogawa, N. Role of facial expression in "cooperative avoidance conditioning" in monkeys. *Journal of Abnormal and Social Psychology,* 1963, *67,* 24–30.

Miller, R. E., Caul, W. F., & Mirsky, I. A. Communication of affect between feral and socially isolated monkeys. *Journal of Personality and Social Psychology,* 1967, *7,* 231–39.

Miller, R. E., Murphy, J. V., & Mirsky, I. A. Nonverbal communication of affect. *Journal of Clinical Psychology,* 1959, *15,* 155–59.

Miron, M. S. *A Cross-Linguistic Investigation of Phonetic Symbolism.* Ann Arbor, Mich.: University Microfilms, No. 60–3961, 1960.

Miron, M. S. A cross-linguistic investigation of phonetic symbolism. *Journal of Abnormal and Social Psychology,* 1961, *62,* 623–30.

Mogensen, M. F., & English, H. B. The apparent warmth of colors. *American Journal of Psychology,* 1926, *37,* 427–28.

Moles, A. Informationstheorie der Music. *Nachrichtentechnische Fachberichte,* Band 3: *Informationstheorie,* 1956, 47–55.

Moles, A. *Information Theory and Esthetic Perception.* Urbana: University of Illinois Press, 1966.

Monroe, M. The apparent weight of color and correlated phenomena. *American Journal of Psychology,* 1925, *36,* 192–206.

Montgomery, K. C. Exploratory behavior as a function of "similarity" of stimulus situations. *Journal of Comparative and Physiological Psychology,* 1953, *46,* 129–33.

Montgomery, K. C. The role of the exploratory drive in learning. *Journal of Comparative and Physiological Psychology,* 1954, *47,* 60–64.

Montgomery, K. C. The relation between fear induced by novel stimulation and exploratory behavior. *Journal of Comparative and Physiological Psychology,* 1955, *48,* 254–60.

Montgomery, K. C., & Segall, M. Discrimination learning based upon the exploratory drive. *Journal of Comparative and Physiological Psychology,* 1955, 48, 225–28.

Moon, L. E., & Lodahl, T. M. The reinforcing effect of changes in illumination on lever-pressing in the monkey. *American Journal of Psychology,* 1956, 69, 288–90.

Moore, H. Notes on sculpture. In H. Read, *Henry Moore: Sculpture and Drawings.* 2d ed. New York: Valentin, 1946.

Moore, H. T. The genetic aspect of consonance and dissonance. *Psychological Monographs,* 1914, 17, no. 73, 1–68.

Morgan, D. N. Psychology and art today: a summary and critique. *Journal of Aesthetics and Art Criticism,* 1950, 10, 81–96.

Morgan, D. N. Must art tell the truth? *Journal of Aesthetics and Art Criticism,* 1967, 26, 17–27.

Morgan, S. S., & Morgan, J. J. B. An examination of the development of certain adaptive behavior patterns in infants. *Journal of Pediatrics,* 1944, 25, 168–77.

Moritz, R. E. On the variation and functional relation of certain sentence-constants in standard literature. *University of Nebraska Studies,* 1903, 3 (3), 229–53.

Morris, C. W. Science, art and technology. *Kenyon Review,* 1939, 1, 409–23.

Moul, E. R. An experimental study of visual and auditory "thickness." *American Journal of Psychology,* 1930, 42, 544–60.

Mount, G. E., Case, H. W., Sanderson, J. W., & Brenner, R. Distance judgment of colored objects. *Journal of General Psychology,* 1956, 55, 207–14.

Mowatt, M. H. Configurational properties considered "good" by naïve subjects. *American Journal of Psychology,* 1940, 53, 46–69.

Mowrer, O. H. *Learning Theory and Behavior.* New York: Wiley, 1960.

Moyles, E. W., Tuddenham, R. D., & Block, J. Simplicity/complexity or symmetry/asymmetry? A re-analysis of the Barron-Welsh art scales. *Perceptual and Motor Skills,* 1965, 20, 685–90.

Müller, G. E. Über die Farbenempfindungen. *Zts. Psychol. Physiol. Sinnesorgane,* 1930, 17, 1–430; 18, 435–647.

Munroe, T. *Toward Science in Aesthetics: Selected Essays.* New York: Liberal Arts Press, 1956.

Munsell, A. H. *A Color Notation.* 7th ed. Baltimore: Munsell Color Company, 1926.

Munsell Book of Color. Vol 1.: 2.5 BG–10 RP; Vol 2.: 2.5 R–10 G. Baltimore: Munsell Color Company, 1966.

Munsinger, H., & Kessen, W. Uncertainty, structure and preference. *Psychological Monographs,* 1964, 78, no. 9(whole no. 586).

Munsinger, H., Kessen, W., & Kessen, M. L. Age and uncertainty: Developmental variation in preference for variability. *Journal of Experimental Child Psychology,* 1964, 1, 1–15.

Münsterberg, H. *The Principles of Art Education.* New York: Prang Educational Co., 1905.

Murray, D. C., & Deabler, H. L. Colors and mood-tones. *Journal of Applied Psychology,* 1957, 41, 279–83.

Murray, H. A. In nomine diaboli. *New England Quarterly,* 1941, 24, 435–52.

Murray, J. M. *The Problem of Style.* London: Oxford University Press, 1922.

Mursell, J. *The Psychology of Music.* New York: Norton, 1937.

Murstein, B. I., & Pryer, R. S. The concept of projection: a review. *Psychological Bulletin,* 1959, *56,* 353–74.

Myers, A. K., & Miller, N. E. Failure to find a learned drive based on hunger; evidence for learning motivated by "exploration." *Journal of Comparative and Physiological Psychology,* 1954, *47,* 428–36.

Myers, C. S. A case of synesthesia. *British Journal of Psychology,* 1911, *4,* 228–38.

Myers, C. S. Two cases of synesthesia. *British Journal of Psychology,* 1914, *7,* 112–17.

Myers, C. S. Individual differences in listening to music. In M. Schoen, ed., *The Effects of Music.* New York: Harcourt, Brace, 1927. Chap. 2.

Napoli, P. Interpretative aspects of fingerpainting. *Journal of Psychology,* 1947, *23,* 93–132.

Neisser, U. *Cognitive Psychology.* New York: Appleton-Century-Crofts, 1967.

Neumann, E. *The Great Mother.* Bollingen Series, XLVII. New York: Pantheon Books, 1955.

Neumann, E. *The Archetypal World of Henry Moore.* Bollingen Series, LXVIII. New York: Pantheon Books, 1959.

Newcomb, T. M. Motivation in social behavior. In J. S. Brown, et al. *Current Theory and Research in Motivation: A Symposium.* Lincoln: University of Nebraska Press, 1953.

Newhall, S. M. Measurement of simultaneous contrast. *Psychological Bulletin,* 1940, *37,* 500. Abstract.

Newhall, S. M. Warmth and coolness of colors. *Psychological Record,* 1941, *4,* 198–212.

Newman, S. Further experiments in phonetic symbolism. *American Journal of Psychology,* 1933, *45,* 53–75.

Nisbett, R. E., & Schachter S. The cognitive manipulation of pain. *Journal of Experimental Social Psychology,* 1966, *2,* 227–36.

Nogué, J. *Esquisse d'un système des qualités sensibles.* Paris: Presses Universitaires de France, 1943.

Noll, A. M. Human or machine? A subjective comparison of Piet Mondrian's *Composition with Lines* (1917) with a computer-generated picture. *Psychological Record,* 1966, *16,* 1–10.

Noll, M. Computers and the visual arts. *Design Quarterly,* 1967, nos. 66–67, 65–71.

Norman, R. D., & Scott, W. A. Color and affect: a review and semantic evaluation. *Journal of General Psychology,* 1952, *46,* 185–223.

Noverre, J. G. *Letters on Dancing and Ballet.* London: Beaumont, 1951.

Obonai, T., & Matsuoka, T. *Manual of the Color Symbolism Personality Test.* Tokyo: Kobunshya, 1952.

Obonai, T., & Matsuoka, T. The color symbolism personality test. *Journal of General Psychology,* 1956, *55,* 229–39.

O'Connor, J. D. Recent work in English phonetics. *Phonetica,* 1957, *1,* 96–117.

Odbert, H. S., Karwoski, T. F., & Eckerson, A. B. Studies in synesthetic thinking: I. Musical and verbal associations of color and mood. *Journal of General Psychology,* 1942, *26,* 153–73.

Ogden, C. K., & Richards, I. A. *The Meaning of Meaning.* London: Routledge & Kegan Paul, 1949.

Ogden, C. K., Richards, I. A., & Wood, J. *The Foundations of Aesthetics*. London: International Publishers & George Allen and Unwin, 1922.

Ogden, R. M. *Hearing*. New York: Harcourt, Brace, 1924.

Ohmann, R. M. Generative grammars and the concept of literary style. *Word*, 1964, 20, 424–39.

Olds, J., & Olds, M. E. Drives, rewards and the brain. In F. Barron et al. *New Directions in Psychology*, Vol. 3. New York: Holt, Rinehart & Winston, 1965.

Ortega y Gasset, J. *Dehumanization of Art and Notes on the Novel*. Princeton, N.J.: Princeton University Press, 1948.

Ortmann, O. On the melodic relativity of tones. *Psychological Monographs*, 1926, 35, 1–47.

Ortmann, O. Types of listeners: genetic considerations. In M. Schoen, ed., *The Effects of Music*. New York: Harcourt, Brace, 1927, Chap. 3.

Ortmann, O. Tonal intensity as an aesthetic factor. *Musical Quarterly*, 1928, 14, 178–91.

Ortmann, O. Interval frequency as a determinant of melodic style. *Peabody Bulletin*, December 1937, pp. 3–10.

Osgood, C. E. *Method and Theory in Experimental Psychology*. New York: Oxford University Press, 1953.

Osgood, C. E. The cross-cultural generality of visual-verbal synesthetic tendencies. *Behavioral Science*, 1960, 5, 146–69.

Osgood, C. E. Studies on the generality of affective meaning systems. *American Psychologist*, 1962, 17, 10–28.

Osgood, C. E. Dimensionality of the semantic space for communication via facial expressions. *Scandinavian Journal of Psychology*, 1966, 7, 1–30.

Osgood, C. E. Speculations on the structure of interpersonal intensions. *Behavioral Science*, 1970, 15, 237–54.

Osgood, C. E., & Sebeok, T. A., eds., *Psycholinguistics: A Survey of Theory and Research Problems*. Bloomington: Indiana University Press, 1967.

Osgood, C. E., Suci, G., & Tannenbaum, P. *The Measurement of Meaning*. Urbana: University of Illinois Press, 1957.

Osgood, C. E., & Walker, E. Motivation and language behavior; a content analysis of suicide notes. *Journal of Abnormal and Social Psychology*, 1959, 59, 58–67.

Ostwald, W. *Color Science*. London: Winsor & Newton, 1931.

Otis, M. Aesthetic unity. *American Journal of Psychology*, 1918, 24, 291–315.

Otto, R. *Mysticism East and West*. New York: Macmillan, 1932.

Ovio, G. *La Vision des couleurs*. Paris: Alcan, 1932.

Ovsiankina, M. Die Wiederaufnahme von unterbrochener Handlungen. *Psychologische Forschung*, 1928, 11, 302–79.

Oyama, T., & Nanri, R. The effects of hue and brightness on the size perception. *Japanese Psychological Research*, 1960, 2, 13–20.

Oyama, T., Tanaka, Y., & Chiba, Y. Affective dimensions of colors: a cross-cultural study. *Japanese Psychological Research*, 1962, 4, 78–91.

Oyama, T., & Yamamura, T. The effect of hue and brightness on the depth perception in normal and color-blind subjects. *Psychologia*, 1960, 3, 191–94.

Paffmann, C. The pleasures of sensation. *Psychological Review*, 1960, 67, 253–68.

Page, M. M. Modification of figure-ground perception as a function of awareness of demand characteristics. *Journal of Personality and Social Psychology*, 1968, 9, 59–66.

Paget, R. *Human Speech*. New York: Harcourt, Brace, 1930.

Paine, R. T., & Soper, A. *The Art and Architecture of Japan*. 1st ed., reprinted with corrections. Pelican History of Art. Baltimore: Penguin Books, 1960.

Palermo, D. S., & Jenkins, J. J. *Word Association Norms: Grade School Through College*. Minneapolis: University of Minnesota Press, 1964.

Panofsky, E. *Meaning in the Visual Arts*. Garden City, N.Y.: Doubleday, 1955.

Parker, De W. H. *The Analysis of Art*. New Haven, Conn.: Yale University Press, 1924.

Parker, De W. H. The nature of art. *Revue Internationale de Philosopie*, 1939, *1*, 684–702.

Patrick, J. R. The effect of emotional stimuli on the activity of the white rat. *Journal of Comparative Psychology*, 1931, *12*, 357–64.

Patterson, W. M. *The Rhythm of Prose: An Experimental Investigation of Individual Differences in the Sense of Rhythm*. New York: Columbia University Press, 1916.

Payne, M. C., Jr. Apparent weight as a function of color. *American Journal of Psychology*, 1958, *71*, 725–30.

Pepper, S. C. *Principles of Art Appreciation*. New York: Harcourt, Brace, 1949.

Perkins, F. T. Symmetry in visual recall. *American Journal of Psychology*, 1932, *44*, 473–90.

Pervin, L. A. The need to predict and control under conditions of threat. *Journal of Personality*, 1963, *31*, 570–87.

Peters, G. A., & Merrifield, P. R. Graphic representation of emotional feelings. *Journal of Clinical Psychology*, 1958, *14*, 375–78.

Peters, H. N. Experimental studies of the judgment theory of feeling: V. The influence of set upon the affective values of colors. *Journal of Experimental Psychology*, 1943, *33*, 285–98.

Pevsner, N. *An Outline of European Architecture*. 5th ed. Harmondsworth: Penguin Books, 1957.

Pflederer, M. The responses of children to musical tasks embodying Piaget's principle of conservation. *Journal of Research in Music Education*, 1964, *12*, 251–60.

Philip, B. R. A method for investigating color preferences in fashions. *Journal of Applied Psychology*, 1945, *29*, 208–14.

Phillips, J. D. The reinforcing property of an aversive stimulus. Unpublished doctoral dissertation, Louisiana State University, 1963.

Piaget, J. *La Psychologie de l'intelligence*. Paris: Colin, 1947. English version: *The Psychology of Intelligence*. London: Routledge & Kegan Paul, 1950.

Piaget, J. *Language and Thought of the Child*. London: Routledge & Kegan Paul, 1948.

Piaget, J. *The Origins of Intelligence in Children*. New York: International Universities Press, 1952.

Piaget, J. *La Formation du symbole chez l'enfant*. Neuchâtel: Delachaux et Niestlé, 1959. English version: *Play, Dreams and Imitation in Childhood*. London: Routledge & Kegan Paul, 1951.

Piaget, J. *The Psychology of Intelligence*. Paterson, N.J.: Littlefield, Adams & Co., 1960.

Piaget, J., & Inhelder, B. *The Child's Conception of Space*. London: Routledge & Kegan Paul, 1956.

Pickford, R. W. *Individual Differences in Colour Vision*. London: Routledge & Kegan Paul, 1951.

Pierce, D. H., & Weinland, J. D. The effect of color on workmen. *Personality Journal*, 1934, 13, 34–38.

Pierce, E. Aesthetics of simple forms: (1) Symmetry. *Psychological Review*, 1894, 1, 483–95.

Pierce, E. Aesthetics of simple forms: (2) The functions of the elements. *Psychological Review*, 1896, 3, 270–85.

Pikas, A. *Abstraction and Concept Formation*. Cambridge, Mass.: Harvard University Press, 1966.

Pike, A. Perception and meaning in serial music. *Journal of Aesthetics and Art Criticism*, 1963, 22, 55–61.

Pike, K. L. *Phonetics: A Critical Analysis of Phonetic Theory and a Technic for the Practical Description of Sounds*. Ann Arbor: University of Michigan Press, 1943.

Pike, K. L. *The Intonation of American English*. Ann Arbor: University of Michigan Press, 1945.

Pike, K. L. *Phonemics: A Technique for Reducing Languages to Writing*. Ann Arbor: University of Michigan Press, 1947.

Pillsbury, W. B., & Schaefer, B. R. A note on "Advancing and Retreating" colors. *American Journal of Psychology*, 1937, 49, 126–30.

Pinkerton, R. C. Information theory and melody. *Scientific American*, 1956, 194, 77–87.

Pittenger, R. E., & Smith, H. L., Jr. A basis for some contributions of linguistics to psychiatry. *Psychiatry*, 1957, 20, 61–78.

Plato. Philebus, in *The Dialogues of Plato*. Translated by B. Jowett. Vol. 2. New York: Random House, 1937. (a)

Plato. Laws, Book II, in *The Dialogues of Plato*. Translated by B. Jowett. Vol. 2. New York: Random House, 1937. (b)

Plato. Cratylus, in *The Dialogues of Plato*. Translated by B. Jowett. Vol. 1. New York: Random House, 1937. (c)

Platt, J. R. Beauty: pattern and change. In D. W. Fiske & S. R. Maddi, eds., *Functions of Varied Experience*. Homewood, Ill.: Dorsey, 1961. Pp. 402–30.

Poffenberger, A. T., & B. E. Barrows. The feeling value of lines. *Journal of Applied Psychology*, 1924, 8, 187–205.

Portmann, A. Das Problem der Urbilder in biologischer Sicht. In O. Froebe-Kapteyn, ed., *Eranos Yearbook*. Vol. 18. Bollingen Series. New York: Pantheon Books, 1950.

Power, E. Elements of the beautiful in music. In E. Gurney, *The Power of Sound*. London: Smith, Elder, 1880.

Praagh, P. van, & Brinson, P. *The Choreographic Art: An Outline of its Principles and Craft*. New York: Knopf, 1963.

Prall, D. W. *Aesthetic Judgment*. New York: Crowell, 1929.

Pratt, C. C. Some qualitative aspects of bitonal complexes. *American Journal of Psychology*, 1921, 32, 490–515.

Pratt, C. C. Quarter-tone music. *Journal of Genetic Psychology*, 1928, 35, 286–92.

Pratt, C. C. *The Meaning of Music*. New York: McGraw-Hill, 1931.

Pratt, C. C. Interaction across modalities: simultaneous stimulation. *Proceedings of the National Academy of Science*, 1936, 22, 562–66.

Pratt, C. C. Aesthetics. In P. R. Farnsworth, ed., *Annual Review of Psychology*. Vol. 12. Palo Alto, Calif.: Annual Reviews, Inc., 1961. Pp. 71–92.

Pratt, C. C. *The Meaning of Music: A Study in Psychological Aesthetics*. New York: McGraw-Hill, 1968.

Pratt, W. S. ed., *The New Encyclopedia of Music and Musicians*. Revised edition. New York: Macmillan, 1944.

Pressey, S. L. The influence of color upon mental and motor efficiency. *American Journal of Psychology*, 1921, 32, 326–56.

Pritchard, R. M., W. Heron, & D. O. Hebb. Visual perception approached by the method of stabilized images. *Canadian Journal of Psychology*, 1960, 14, 67–77.

Puffer, E. D. Studies in symmetry. *Psychological Review, Monograph Supplements*, 1903, 4, 467–539.

Radner, M., & J. J. Gibson. Orientation in visual perception: the perception of tip-character in forms. *Psychological Monographs*, 1935, 46, 48–65.

Raeff, L. The effects of poetic and literal orientations on the meaning structure of words. Doctoral dissertation, Clark University, Worcester, Mass., 1955.

Rank, O., & Sachs, H. *Die Bedeutung der Psychoanalyse für die Geisteswissenschaften*. Wiesbaden: Bergmann, 1913.

Rank, O., & Sachs, H. Esthetics and psychology of the artist. In *The Significance of Psychoanalysis for the Mental Sciences*. Washington: Nervous and Mental Disease Publishing Co., 1916.

Rashevsky, N. Contribution to the mathematical biophysics of visual perception with special reference to the theory of aesthetic values of geometrical patterns. *Psychometrika*, 1938, 3, 253–71.

Razran, G. H. S. Studies in configural conditioning: III. The factors of similarity, proximity, and continuity in configural conditioning. *Journal of Experimental Psychology*, 1939, 24, 202–10.

Read, H. *English Prose Style*. London: G. Bell & Sons, 1931.

Read, H. *The Philosophy of Modern Art*. New York: Meridian Books, 1955.

Read, H. *The Art of Sculpture*. The A. W. Mellon Lectures in the Fine Arts, 1954, National Gallery of Art, Washington. Bollingen Series XXXV, 3. New York: Pantheon Books, 1956.

Redfield, J. *Music—A Science and an Art*. New York: Knopf, 1928.

Reimanis, G. Disparity theory and achievement motivation. *Journal of Abnormal and Social Psychology*, 1964, 69, 206–10.

Reitman, F. Lear's nonsense. *Journal of Clinical Psychopathology and Psychotherapy*, 1946, 7, 671–78.

Rensch, B., & Rahmann, H. Einfluss des Pervitins auf das Gedächtnis von Goldhamstern. *Pfluegers Archiv der Gesammten Psychologie*, 1960, 271, 693–704.

Révész, G. *Die Formwelt des Tastsinnes*. The Hague: Martinus Nijhoff, 1938.

Révész, G. *Introduction to the Psychology of Music*. Norman: University of Oklahoma Press, 1954.

Rich, S. The perception of emotion. Honors thesis, Radcliffe College, 1953.

Richards, I. A. *Principles of Literary Criticism*. London: Kegan, Paul, Trench, Trubner, 1926.

Richards, I. A. Poetic process and literary analysis. In T. A. Sebeok, ed., *Style in Language*. Cambridge, Mass.: M.I.T. Press, 1960. Pp. 9–23.

Richter, G. M. A. *The Sculpture and Sculptors of the Greeks*. New Haven: Yale University Press, 1930.

Rickers-Ovsiankina, M. Some theoretical considerations regarding the Rorschach method. *Rorschach Research Exchanges*, 1943, 7, 41–53.

Riemann, H. *Geschichte der Musiktheorie im 9.–19. Jahrhundert*. Edited by G. Becking. 2d ed. Berlin: M. Hesse, 1921.

Riesen, A. H., & Kinder, E. F. *Postural development of infant chimpanzees*. New Haven: Yale University Press, 1952.

Rigg, M. G. Speed as a determiner of musical mood. *Journal of Experimental Psychology*, 1940, 27, 566–71.

Rigg, M. G. The mood effects of music: a comparison of data from four investigators. *Journal of Psychology*, 1964, 58, 427–38.

Riggs, L. A., Armington, J. C., & Ratliff, F. Motions of the retinal image during fixation. *Journal of the Optical Society of America*, 1954, 44, 315–21.

Riggs, L. A., & Karwoski, T. Synaesthesia. *British Journal of Psychology*, 1934, 25, 29–41.

Riggs, L. A., Ratliff, F., Cornsweet, J. C., & Cornsweet, T. N. The disappearance of steadily fixated visual test objects. *Journal of the Optical Society of America*, 1953, 43, 495–501.

Rilke, R. M. *Auguste Rodin*. Leipzig: Insel Verlag, 1930.

Rimbaud, A. Alchimie du verbe. In *A. Rimbaud, Les Plus Belles Œuvres*, Vol. 3. London: Editions Bernard, Bernard and Westwood, 1943. P. 141.

Roblee, L., & Washburn, M. F. The affective values of articulate sounds. *American Journal of Psychology*, 1912, 23, 579–83.

Rodin, A. *Art*. Boston: Small, Maryland & Co., 1912.

Rodin, A. Die Kunst. In P. Gesell, ed., *Gespräche der Meister*. Leipzig: Kurt Wolff Verlag, 1918.

Roe, A. Painting and personality. *Rorschach Research Exchange*, 1946, 10, 86–100.

Rogers, C. R. *Client-Centered Therapy*. Boston: Houghton Mifflin, 1951.

Rogers, C. R. Toward a theory of creativity. In H. H. Anderson, ed., *Creativity and Its Cultivation*. New York: Harper, 1959, Pp. 69–82.

Rohracher, H. *Kleine Charakterkunde*. Wien u. Innsbruck: Urban & Schwarzenberg, 1959.

Rommetveit, R. *Words, Meanings, and Messages: Theory and Experiments in Psycholinguistics*. New York: Academic Press, 1968.

Rorschach, H. *Psychodiagnostics*. 5th ed. Bern and Stuttgart: Hans Huber, 1951.

Rosenbaum, M. E., & Tucker, I. F. The competence of the model and the learning of imitation and non-imitation. *Journal of Experimental Psychology*, 1962, 63, 183–90.

Ross, D. *The Theory of Pure Design*. New York: Houghton Mifflin, 1917.

Ross, R. T. Studies in the psychology of the theatre. *Psychological Records*, 1938, 2, 127–90.

Rothschild, H. Über den Einfluss der Gestalt auf das negative Nachbild ruhender visueller Figuren. *Archiv der Ophthalmologie*, 1923, 112, 1–24.

Rotter, J. B. *Social Learning and Clinical Psychology*. New York: Prentice-Hall, 1954.

Rowland, E. H. A study in vertical symmetry. *Psychological Review*, 1907, 14, 391–94.

Rowland, L. W. The somatic effects of stimuli graded in respect to their exciting character. *Journal of Experimental Psychology*, 1936, 19, 547–60.

Rubin, E. *Visuell wahrgenommene Figuren*. Copenhagen: Gyldendalske, 1921.

Ruckmick, C. A. A bibliography of rhythm. *American Journal of Psychology*, 1913, 24, 508–19; 1915, 26, 457–59; 1918, 29, 214–18.

Ruesch, J., & Kees, W. *Nonverbal Communication: Notes on the Visual Perception of Human Relations.* Berkeley: University of California Press, 1961.

Ryan, T. A. Interrelations of the sensory systems in perception. *Psychological Bulletin*, 1940, 33, 659–98.

Ryan, T. A. *Intentional Behavior: An Approach to Human Motivation.* New York: Ronald Press, 1970.

Sachs, C. *World History of the Dance.* New York: Norton, 1937.

Sachs, H. *The Creative Unconscious.* 2d ed. Cambridge, Mass.: Science-Art Publishers, 1951.

St. Denis, R. *My Unfinished Life.* New York: Harper, 1939.

St. George, M. W. Color preferences of college students with reference to chromatic pull, learning, and association. *American Journal of Psychology*, 1938, 51, 714–16.

Saintsbury, G. *A History of English Prose Rhythm.* London: Macmillan, 1912; reprinted 1922.

Sakurabayashi, H. Studies in creation: IV. The meaning of prolonged inspection from the standpoint of creation. *Japanese Journal of Psychology*, 1953, 23, 207–16, 286–88.

Sanders, A. F. Expectancy: application and measurement. *Acta Psychologica*, 1966, 25, 293–313.

Sanford, F. H. Speech and personality. *Psychological Bulletin*, 1942, 39, 811–45.

Sapir, E. A study in phonetic symbolism. *Journal of Experimental Psychology*, 1929, 12, 225–39.

Savin, H. B., & Perchonock, E. Grammatical structure and the immediate recall of English sentences. *Journal of Verbal Learning and Verbal Behavior*, 1965, 4, 348–53.

Schachtel, E. On color and affect; contributions to an understanding of Rorschach's test: II. *Psychiatry*, 1943, 6, 393–409.

Schachter, J. Pain, fear, and anger in hypertensives and normotensives: a psychophysiologic study. *Psychosomatic Medicine*, 1957, 19, 17–29.

Schachter, S. The interaction of cognitive and physiological determinants of emotional state. In L. Berkowitz, ed., *Advances in Experimental Social Psychology.* Vol. 1. New York: Academic Press, 1964. Pp. 49–80.

Schachter, S. Cognitive effects on bodily functioning: studies of obesity and eating. In D. C. Glass, ed., *Neurophysiology and Emotion.* New York: Rockefeller University Press and Russell Sage Foundation, 1967. Pp. 117–44.

Schachter, S., & Singer, J. E. Cognitive, social and physiological determinants of emotional state. *Psychological Review*, 1962, 69, 379–99.

Schachter, S., & Wheeler, L. Epinephrine, chlorpromazine, and amusement. *Journal of Abnormal and Social Psychology*, 1962, 65, 121–28.

Schaefer, H. H., & Hess, E. H. Color preferences in imprinting object. *Zeitschrift der Tierpsychologie*, 1959, 16, 161–72.

Schaefer-Simmern, H. *The Unfolding of the Artistic Activity.* Berkeley: University of California Press, 1948.

Schaie, W. K. Scaling the association between colors and mood-tones. *American Journal of Psychology*, 1961, 74, 266–73.

Schaie, W. K. The color pyramid test: a nonverbal technique for personality assessment. *Psychological Bulletin*, 1963, 60, 530–47.

Scharfstein, B. A. *The Artist in World Art* [Ha'oman be-tarbuyot ha'olam]. Tel Aviv: Am Oved, 1970. In Hebrew.

Scheerer, M., & Lyons, J. Line drawings and matching responses to words. *Journal of Personality*, 1957, 25, 251–73.

Schertel, E. Stilformen des Tanzes. *Frankfurter Zeitung*, no. 673, 10 Sept. 1926.

Schiffman, H. R. Golden section: preferred figural orientation. *Perception and Psychophysics*, 1966, 1, 193–94.

Schilder, P. Psychoanalytic remarks on Alice in Wonderland and Lewis Carroll. *Journal of Nervous and Mental Disease*, 1938, 87, 159–68.

Schiller, J. An alternative to "Aesthetic Disinterestedness." *Journal of Aesthetics and Art Criticism*, 1964, 22, 295–302.

Schiller, P. v. Die Rauhigkeit als intermodale Erscheinung. *Zeitschrift der Psychologie*, 1932, 127, 265–89.

Schiller, P. v. Interrelation of different senses in perception. *British Journal of Psychology*, 1935, 25, 465–69.

Schillinger, J. *The Mathematical Basis of the Arts*. New York: Philosophical Library, 1948.

Schlosberg, H. Stereoscopic depth from single pictures. *American Journal of Psychology*, 1941, 54, 601–5.

Schneider, D. E. *The Psychoanalyst and the Artist*. New York: Farrar Straus, 1950.

Schneirla, T. C. Aspects of stimulation and organization in approach-withdrawal processes underlying behavioral development. In D. L. Lehrman, R. Hinde, & E. Shaw, eds., *Advances in the Study of Behavior*. New York: Academic Press, 1965.

Schoen, M. *The Psychology of Music*. New York: Ronald, 1940.

Schönberg, A. *Harmonielehre*. 3d ed. Vienna: Universaledition, 1922.

Schönpflug, W. Paarlernen, Behaltensdauer und Aktivierung. *Psychologische Forschung*, 1966, 29, 132–48.

Schramm, W., Lyle, J., & Parker, E. B. *Television in the Lives of Our Children*. Stanford, Calif.: Stanford University Press, 1961.

Schramm, W. L. Approaches to a science of English verse. *University of Iowa Studies, Series on Aims and Progress of Research*, no. 46, 1935. Pp. 32–75.

Schroder, H. M., Driver, M. J., & Streufert, S. *Human Information Processing*. New York: Holt, Rinehart & Winston, 1967.

Schrödinger, E. Grundlinien einer Theorie der Farbenmetrik im Tagessehen. *Annalen der Physik*, 1920, 63, 397–456, 481–520.

Schueler, F. W. Discussion. In R. G. Heath, ed., *The Role of Pleasure in Behavior*. New York: Harper & Row, 1964. Pp. 167–70.

Schultz, D. P. *Sensory Restriction: Effects on Behavior*. New York: Academic Press, 1965.

Scott, F. N. The most fundamental differentia of poetry and prose. *Publications of the Modern Language Association of America*, 1904, 19, 250–69.

Scott, F. N. The scansion of prose rhythm. *Publication of the Modern Language Association of America*, 1908, 20, 707–28.

Scripture, E. W. The nature of verse. *British Journal of Psychology*, 1921, 11, 225–35.

Seashore, C. E. *Psychology of Music.* 1st ed. New York: McGraw-Hill, 1938.

Segal, J. Beiträge zur experimentellen Ästhetik; Über die Wohlgefälligkeit einfacher räumlicher Formen. *Archiv für die Gesammte Psychologie,* 1906, 7, 53–124.

Segall, M. H., Campbell, D. T., & Herskovits, M. J. *The Influence of Culture on Visual Perception.* Indianapolis: Bobbs-Merrill, 1966.

Selden, E. *Elements of the Free Dance.* New York: Barnes, 1930.

Selden, E. *The Dancer's Quest: Essays on the Aesthetic of Contemporary Dance.* Berkeley: University of California Press, 1935.

Selfridge, J. Investigations into the structure of verbal context. Honors thesis, Harvard University, 1949.

Selye, H. *The Physiology and Pathology of Exposure to Stress.* Montreal: Acta, Inc., 1950.

Semenovskaia, E. N. Modification of photic sensitivity of central and peripheral vision during acoustic stimulation. *Problemy fiziol. Optiki,* 1946, 3, 94–96. In Russian.

Semeonoff, B. Further developments in a new approach to the testing of musical ability, with special reference to groups of secondary school children. *British Journal of Psychology,* 1940, 30, 145–61.

Serrat, W. D., & Karwoski, T. An investigation of the effect of auditory stimulation on visual sensitivity. *Journal of Experimental Psychology,* 1936, 19, 604–11.

Seward, J. P. Secondary reinforcement as tertiary motivation: a revision of Hull's revision. *Psychological Review,* 1950, 48, 362–74.

Seward, J. P., & Seward, G. H. The effect of repetition on reaction to electric shock. *Archives of Psychology,* 1934, no. 168.

Shahn, Ben. *The Shape of Content.* New York: Vintage Books, 1957.

Shannon, C. E., & Weaver, W. *The Mathematical Theory of Communication.* Urbana: University of Illinois Press, 1949.

Sharpless, S., & Jasper, H. Habituation of the arousal reaction. *Brain,* 1956, 79, 655–80.

Sheets, M. *The Phenomenology of Dance.* Madison: University of Wisconsin Press, 1966.

Sheffield, F. D. A drive-reduction theory of reinforcement. In R. N. Haber, ed., *Current Research in Motivation.* New York: Holt, Reinhart & Winston, 1966.

Sheffield, F. D., & Roby, T. B. Reward value of a non-nutritive sweet taste. *Journal of Comparative and Physiological Psychology,* 1950, 43, 471–81.

Sheffield, F. D., Roby, T. B., & Campbell, B. A. Drive reduction versus consummatory behavior as determinants of performance. *Journal of Comparative and Physiological Psychology,* 1954, 47, 349–54.

Sheffield, F. D., Wulff, J. J., & Backer, R. Reward value of copulation without sex drive reduction. *Journal of Comparative and Physiological Psychology,* 1951, 44, 3–8.

Shepard, R. N. Production of constrained associates and the informational uncertainty of the constraint. *American Journal of Psychology,* 1963, 76, 218–28.

Sherif, M. An experimental study of stereotypes. *Journal of Abnormal and Social Psychology,* 1935, 29, 371–75.

Sherman, L. A. On certain facts and principles in the development of form in literature. *University of Nebraska Studies,* 1892, 1 (4), 337–66.

Sherrington, C. *The Integrative Action of the Nervous System.* 2d ed. New Haven, Conn.: Yale University Press, 1947.

Shimp, B. Reliability of associations of known and unknown melodic phrases with words denoting states of feeling. *Journal of Musicology*, 1940, *1*, 22–35.

Shirley, M. M. The sequential method for the study of maturing behavior patterns. *Psychological Review*, 1931, *38*, 507–28.

Shock, N. W., & Coombs, C. H. Changes in skin resistance and affective tone. *American Journal of Psychology*, 1937, *49*, 611–20.

Siegel, C. *Structure and Form in Modern Architecture*. New York: Reinhold, 1962.

Siegel, P. S., & Brantley, J. J. The relationship of emotionality to the consummatory response of eating. *Journal of Experimental Psychology*, 1951, *42*, 304–6.

Silberer, H. Über die Symbolbildung. *Jahrbuch für Psychoanalyse und Psychopathologische Forschungen*. Vol. 3. Vienna: Deuticke, 1912. Pp. 661–723.

Simon, C. R., & Wohlwill, J. F. An experimental study of the role of expectation and variation in music. *Journal of Research in Music Education*, 1968, *16*, 227–38.

Simpson, R. H., Quinn, M., & Ausubel, D. P. Synesthesia in children: association of colors with pure tone frequencies. *Journal of Genetic Psychology*, 1956, *89*, 95–103.

Singer, J. L. *Daydreaming*. New York: Random House, 1966.

Skaife, A. M. Role of deviation and complexity in changing musical taste. *Proceedings, 75th Annual Convention, APA, 1967*. Pp. 25–26.

Skinner, B. F. The alliteration in Shakespeare's sonnets: a study in literary behavior. *Psychological Record*, 1939, *3*, 186–92.

Slade, T. K. An inquiry into the nature of color associations. *Mind*, 1925, *34*, 455.

Small, A. M. An objective analysis of artistic violin performance. *University of Iowa Studies in the Psychology of Music*, 1937, *4*, 172–231.

Smith, A. A. An electromyographic study of tension in interrupted and completed tasks. *Journal of Experimental Psychology*, 1953, *46*, 32–36.

Smith, A. A., Malmo, R. B., & Shagass, C. An electromyographic study of listening and talking. *Canadian Journal of Psychology*, 1954, *8*, 219–27.

Smith, W. W. *The Measurement of Emotion*. New York: Harcourt, Brace, 1922.

Smock, C. D., & Holt, B. G. Children's reactions to novelty: an experimental study of "curiosity motivation." *Child Development*, 1962, *33*, 631–42.

Snell, A. L. F. *Pause: A Study of Its Nature and Its Rhythmical Function in Verse, Especially Blank Verse*. Ann Arbor, Mich.: Ann Arbor Press, 1918.

Snyder, E. D. *Hypnotic Poetry: A Study of Trance-Inducing Technique in Certain Poems and Its Literary Significance*. Philadelphia: University of Pennsylvania Press, 1930.

Sokolov, E. N. *Perception and the Conditioned Reflex*. Oxford: Pergamon Press, 1963.

Solarz, A. K. Perceived activity in Semantic Atlas words as indicated by a tapping response. *Perceptual and Motor Skills*, 1963, *16*, 91–94.

Solomon, P., Kubzansky, P. E., Leiderman, P. H., Mendelson, J. H., Trumbull, R., & Wexler, D. eds. *Sensory Deprivation: A Symposium at Harvard Medical School*. Cambridge: Harvard University Press, 1961.

Soltysik, S. Studies on avoidance conditioning: III. Alimentary conditioned reflex model of the avoidance reflex. *Acta Biologica Experimentalia*, 1960, *21*, 235–52.

Sorell, W. Two rebels, two giants: Isadora and Martha. In W. Sorell, eds., *The*

444 *Psychology of the Arts*

Dance Has Many Faces. 2d ed. New York: Columbia University Press, 1966. Pp. 27–39.
Sowa, J. *A Machine to Compose Music.* New York: Oliver Garfield Co., 1956.
Speiser, A. Symmetry in science and art. *Daedalus*, Winter, 1960, pp. 191–98.
Spence, K. W. *Behavior Theory and Conditioning.* New Haven, Conn: Yale University Press, 1956.
Spencer, H. *Principles of Psychology.* London, 1855.
Spiegel, R. Specific problems of communication in psychiatric conditions. In S. Arieti, ed., *American Handbook of Psychiatry.* Vol. 3. New York: Basic Books, 1959. Pp. 909–50.
Spinoza, B. *Ethics, Part III* (1675). Translated and edited by J. Gutman. New York: Hafner, 1957.
Spitz, R. A., & Wolfe, K. M. The smiling response: a contribution to the ontogenesis of social relations. *Genetic Psychology Monographs*, 1946, *34*, 57–125.
Spragg, S. D. S. Morphine addiction in chimpanzees. *Comparative Psychology Monographs*, 1940, *15*, no. 7.
Stagner, R., & Karwoski, T. F. *Psychology.* New York: McGraw-Hill, 1952.
Stamm, J. S. Fourier analyses for curves of affective value of color as functions of hue. *American Journal of Psychology*, 1955, *68*, 124–32.
Stankiewicz, E. Linguistics and the study of poetic language. In T. A. Sebeok, ed., *Style in Language.* Cambridge, Mass.: M.I.T. Press, 1960. Pp. 69–81.
Staples, R. The response of infants to colours. *Journal of Experimental Psychology*, 1932, *15*, 119–41.
Staples, R., & Walton, W. E. A study of pleasurable experience as a factor in color preference. *Journal of Genetic Psychology*, 1933, *43*, 217–23.
Stebbing, S. L. *Philosophy and the Physicists.* Harmondsworth: Penguin Books, 1937.
Stefanescu-Goanga, F. Experimentelle Untersuchungen zur Gefühlsbetonung der Farben. *Psychologische Studien*, 1911, *7*, 284–335.
Stein, L. Reciprocal action of reward and punishment mechanisms. In R. G. Heath, ed., *The Role of Pleasure in Behavior.* New York: Harper & Row, 1964. Pp. 113–39.
Stephenson, W. Correlating persons instead of tests. *Character and Personality*, 1935, *4*, 17–24.
Stern, E. Der Farbpyramidentest von Pfister-Heiss. In E. Stern, ed., *Die Tests in der klinischen Psychologie.* Zürich: Rascher Verlag, 1955. Pp. 462–85.
Stern, W. *Psychologie der frühen Kindheit.* Leipzig: Quelle u. Meyer, 1923.
Sternbach, R. A., & Tursky, B. Ethnic differences among housewives in psychophysical and skin potential responses to electric shock. *Psychophysiology*, 1965, *1*, 241–46.
Sterne, L. *Tristram Shandy.* Modern Library. New York: Random House, 1950.
Sterzinger, O. Rhythmische Ausgeprägtheit und Gefälligkeit musikalischer Sukzessintervalle. *Archiv für die Gesammte Psychologie*, 1916, *35*, 75–124.
Sterzinger, O. Rhythmische und ästhetische Charakteristik der musikalischen Sukzessintervalle und ihre ursächlichen Zusammenhänge. *Archiv für die Gesammte Psychologie*, 1917, *36*, 1–58.
Stetson, R. B. A motor theory of rhythm and discrete succession. *Psychological Review*, 1905, *12*, 250–70, 293–350.
Stevens, S. S., ed. *Handbook of Experimental Psychology.* New York: Wiley, 1951.

Stevens, S. S. The surprising simplicity of sensory metrics. *American Psychologist*, 1962, 17, 29–39.

Stevens, S. S., & Galanter, E. H. Ratio scales and category scales for a dozen perceptual continua. *Journal of Experimental Psychology*, 1957, 54, 377–411.

Stevenson, B. *Book of Quotations.* London: Cassell, 1934.

Stewart, G. R., Jr. *The Technique of English Verse.* New York: Holt, 1930.

Stolnitz, J. On the origins of "Aesthetic Disinterestedness." *Journal of Aesthetics and Art Criticism*, 1961, 20, 131–43.

Storms, M. D., & Nisbett, R. E. Insomnia and the attribution process. *Journal of Personality and Social Psychology*, 1970, 16, 319–28.

Stotland, E. Exploratory investigations of empathy. In L. Berkowitz, ed., *Advances in Experimental Social Psychology.* Vol. 4. New York: Academic Press, 1969. Pp. 271–314.

Straus, E. *The Primary World of Senses: A Vindication of Sensory Experience.* London: Collier-Macmillan, 1963.

Straus, E. W. Aesthesiology and hallucinations. In R. May, E. Angel, & H. F. Ellenberger, eds., *Existence.* New York: Basic Books, 1958. Pp. 139–70.

Street, R. F. *A Gestalt Completion Test.* Columbia University Press, 1931.

Stumpf, C. *Tonpsychologie.* Vol. 1. Leipzig, 1883.

Stumpf, C. Konsonanz und Dissonanz. *Beiträge zu Akustik und Musikwissenschaft*, 1898, 1, 91–107.

Stumpf, C. *Die Sprachlaute; experimentell-phonetische Untersuchungen, nebst einem Anhang über Instrumentalklänge.* Berlin: Springer, 1926.

Suci, G. J. A comparison of semantic structures in American Southwest culture groups. *Journal of Abnormal and Social Psychology*, 1960, 60, 25–30.

Sullivan, H. S. *The Interpersonal Theory of Psychiatry.* New York: Norton, 1953.

Sulzer, J. G. *Allgemeine Theorie der schönen Künste.* 2d revised ed. Vol. 4. Leipzig, 1794.

Sulzer, J. L., & Burglass, R. K. Responsibility attribution, empathy and punitiveness. *Journal of Personality*, 1968, 36, 272–82.

Sumner, F. C. Influence of color on legibility of copy. *Journal of Applied Psychology*, 1932, 26, 201–4.

Sutton, S., Braren, M., Peterson, P., Zubin, J., & John, E. R. Evoked potential correlates of guessing and its consequences. *Eastern Association of Encephalographers, EEG Society*, 1965.

Symmes, D. Anxiety reduction and novelty as goals of visual exploration by monkeys. *Journal of Genetic Psychology*, 1959, 94, 181–98.

Tagiuri, R. Movement as a cue in person perception. In H. P. David, & J. C. Brengelmann, eds., *Perspectives in Personality Research.* New York: Springer, 1960. Pp. 175–95.

Tanaka, Y., Oyama, T., & Osgood, C. E. A cross-cultural and cross-concept study of the generality of semantic space. *Journal of Verbal Learning and Verbal Behavior*, 1963, 2, 392–405.

Tatibana, Y. Color feelings of the Japanese: I. The inherent emotional effects of colors. *Tohoku Psychological Fol.*, 1937, 5, 21–46.

Taylor, C. D. Visual perception versus visual plus kinaesthetic perception in judging colored weights. *Journal of General Psychology*, 1930, 4, 229–46.

Taylor, I. K. Phonetic symbolism re-examined. *Psychological Bulletin*, 1963, 60, 200–209.

Taylor, I. K., & Taylor, M. M. Phonetic symbolism in four unrelated languages. *Canadian Journal of Psychology*, 1962, *16*, 344–56.

Taylor, I. K., & Taylor, M. M. Another look at phonetic symbolism. *Psychological Bulletin*, 1965, *64*, 413–27.

Taylor, I. L., & Sumner, F. C. Actual brightness and distance of individual colors when their apparent distance is held constant. *Journal of Psychology*, 1945, *19*, 79–85.

Taylor, W. L. "Cloze procedure": A new tool for measuring readability. *Journalism Quarterly*, 1953, *30*, 415–33.

Tennant, J. The psychological factor in color contrast. *British Journal of Psychology*, 1929–30, *20*, 1–26.

Terwilliger, R. F. Pattern complexity and affective arousal. *Perceptual and Motor Skills*, 1963, *17*, 387–95.

Thackray, R. I., & Michels, K. M. Externally-aroused drives in the racoon. *Animal Behavior*, 1958, *6*, 160–63.

Thompson, G. G. *Child Psychology*. Boston: Houghton Mifflin, 1952.

Thompson, G. S. The effect of chronological age on aesthetic preferences for rectangles of different proportions. *Journal of Experimental Psychology*, 1946, *36*, 50–58.

Thompson, R. F., Voss, J. F., & Brogden, W. J. Effects of brightness of simultaneous visual stimulation on absolute auditory sensitivity. *Journal of Experimental Psychology*, 1958, *55*, 45–50.

Thompson, W. R., & Solomon, L. M. Spontaneous pattern discrimination in the rat. *Journal of Comparative and Physiological Psychology*, 1954, *47*, 104–7.

Thomson, W. B. A. *The Rhythm of Speech*. Glasgow: Maclehose, 1923.

Thorndike, E. L. Individual difference in judgment of the beauty of simple forms. *Psychological Review*, 1917, *24*, 147–53.

Thouless, R. H. Individual differences in phenomenal regression. *British Journal of Psychology*, 1932, *22*, 216–41.

Thurstone, L. L. The problem of melody. *Musical Quarterly*, 1920, *6*, 426–29.

Tinbergen, N. *The Study of Instinct*. London: Oxford University Press, 1951.

Tinbergen, N. "Derived" activities: their causation, biological significance, origin, and emancipation during evolution. *Quarterly Review of Biology*, 1952, *27*, 1–32.

Tindall, W. J. *The Literary Symbol*. New York: Columbia University Press, 1955.

Tinker, M. A. Effect of stimulus-texture upon apparent warmth and affective values of colors. *American Journal of Psychology*, 1938, *51*, 532–35.

Tolman, E. C. *Purposive Behavior in Animals and Men*. New York: Appleton, 1932.

Tomada, T. The affective value of color combinations. *Japanese Journal of Psychology*, 1934, *9*, 489–569.

Trager, G. L., & Smith, H. L., Jr. *An Outline of English Structure*. Studies in Linguistics, Occasional Papers 3. Norman, Okla.: Battenberg Press, 1951.

Trier, E. *Form and Space: Sculpture of the Twentieth Century*. New York: Praeger, 1962.

Tsuru, S. Sound and meaning. Unpublished manuscript on file with G. W. Allport, Harvard University, 1934.

Ulam, S. Patterns of growth of figures: mathematical aspects. In G. Kepes, ed.,

Module, Proportion, Symmetry, Rhythm. New York: Braziller, 1966. Pp. 64–101.

Uldall, E. Attitudinal meanings conveyed by intonation contours. *Language and Speech*, 1960, *3*, 223–34.

Ullman, S. de. Romanticism and synaesthesia. *Publications of the Modern Language Association of America*, 1945, *60*, 811–27.

Usnadze, D. N. Ein experimenteller Beitrag zum Problem der psychologischen Grundlagen der Namengebung. *Psychologische Forschung*, 1924, *5*, 24–43.

Uznadze, D. N. *The Psychology of Set.* New York: Consultants Bureau, Plenum Publishing Corp., 1966.

Valentine, C. W. The aesthetic appreciation of musical intervals among school children and adults. *British Journal of Psychology*, 1913, *6*, 190–216.

Valentine, C. W. The colour perception and colour preference of an infant during its fourth and eight months. *British Journal of Psychology*, 1914, *6*, 363–86.

Valentine, C. W. *The Experimental Psychology of Beauty.* London: Methuen, 1962.

Valéry, P. *Poetry and Abstract Thought: Essays on Language and Literature.* Edited by J. L. Hevesi. London: Wingate, 1947.

Valins, S., & Ray, A. A. Effects of cognitive desensitization on avoidance behavior. *Journal of Personality and Social Psychology*, 1967, *7*, 345–50.

Van de Geer, J. P. *A Psychological Study of Problem Solving.* Haarlem: De Toorts, 1957.

Van de Geer, J. P., Levelt, W. J. M., & Plomp, R. The connotation of musical consonance. *Acta Psychologica*, 1962, *20*, 308–19.

Vanderplas, J. M., & Garvin, E. A. The association value of random shapes. *Journal of Experimental Psychology*, 1959, *57*, 147–54.

Verhoeff, F. H. An optical illusion due to chromatic aberration. *American Journal of Ophthalmology*, 1928, *11*, 898.

Verhoeff, F. H. A color stereoscopic phenomenon. *Archives of Ophthalmology*, 1941, *26*, 914.

Verinis, J. S., Brandsma, J. M., & Cofer, C. N. Discrepancy from expectation in relation to affect and motivation: tests of McClelland's hypothesis. *Journal of Personality and Social Psychology*, 1968, *9*, 47–58.

Vernon, P. E. The phenomenon of attention and visualization in the psychology of musical appreciation. *British Journal of Psychology*, 1930, *21*, 50–63.

Vernon, P. E. The apprehension and cognition of music. *Proceedings of the Musical Association Session*, 1933, *59*, 61–84.

Vernon, P. E. Auditory perception: I. The gestalt approach. *British Journal of Psychology*, 1934, *25*, 123–39.

Vernon, P. E. Auditory perception: II. The evolutionary approach. *British Journal of Psychology*, 1935, *25*, 265–83.

Vitz, P. C. Preferences for rates of information presented by sequences of tones. *Journal of Experimental Psychology*, 1964, *68*, 174–83.

Vitz, P. C. Preference for different amounts of visual complexity. *Behavioral Science*, 1966, *11*, 105–14. (a)

Vitz, P. C. Affect as a function of stimulus variation. *Journal of Experimental Psychology*, 1966, *71*, 74–79. (b)

Vivas, E. A natural history of the aesthetic transaction. In Y. H. Krikorian, ed., *Naturalism and the Human Spirit.* New York: Columbia University Press, 1944. Pp. 96–120.

Von Domarus, E. The specific laws of logic in schizophrenia. In J. S. Kasanin, ed., *Language and Thought in Schizophrenia*. New York: Norton, 1964. Pp. 104–14.

Waelder, R. *Psychoanalytic Avenues to Art*. Psychoanalytical Epitomes, no. 6. London: Hogarth Press and The Institute of Psychoanalysis, 1965.

Walker, C. M., & Bourne, L. E., Jr. Concept identification as a function of amounts of relevant and irrelevant information. *American Journal of Psychology*, 1961, *74*, 410–17.

Walker, E. L., & Tarte, R. D. Memory storage as a function of arousal and time with homogeneous and heterogeneous lists. *Journal of Verbal Learning and Verbal Behavior*, 1963, *2*, 113–19.

Wallerstein, H. An electromyographic study of attentive listening. *Canadian Journal of Psychology*, 1954, *8*, 228–38.

Wallin, J. E. W. Experimental studies of rhythm and time. *Psychological Review*, 1911, *18*, 100–131 (a); 1911, *18*, 202–22 (b); 1912, *19*, 271–98.

Wallis, W. D. *Religion in Primitive Society*. New York: Crofts, 1939.

Walsh, D. The cognitive content of art. In F. J. Coleman, ed., *Contemporary Studies in Aesthetics*. New York: McGraw-Hill, 1968. Pp. 282–97.

Walters, R. H., & Thomas, E. L. Enhancement of punitiveness by visual and audiovisual displays. *Canadian Journal of Psychology*, 1963, *17*, 244–55.

Walton, W. E., & Morrison, B. M. A preliminary study of the affective values of colored light. *Journal of Applied Psychology*, 1931, *15*, 294–303.

Wapner, S., Werner, H., & Chandler, K. A. Experiments on sensory-tonic field theory of perception: I. Effect of extraneous stimulation on the visual perception of verticality. *Journal of Experimental Psychology*, 1951, *42*, 341–45.

Wapner, S., Werner, H., & Krus, D. M. Studies in physiognomic perception: IV. Effect of muscular involvement on the dynamic properties of objects. *Journal of Psychology*, 1957, *44*, 129–32.

Warden, C. J., & Flynn, E. L. The effect of color on apparent size and weight. *American Journal of Psychology*, 1926, *37*, 398–401.

Warner, S. J. The color preferences of psychiatric groups. *Psychological Monographs*, 1949, *63*, no. 6.

Washburn, M. F. Über den Einfluss von Gesichtsassociationen auf die Raumwahrnehmungen der Haut. Doctoral dissertation, Cornell University, 1894. Abstract in *American Journal of Psychology*, 1895, *7*, 286–87.

Washburn, M. F. Note on the affective value of colors. *American Journal of Psychology*, 1911, *22*, 114–15.

Washburn, M. F. Emotion and thought: A motor theory of their relations. In M. L. Reymert, ed., *Feelings and Emotions: The Wittenberg Symposium*. Worcester, Mass.: Clark University Press, 1928. Pp. 104–15.

Washburn, M. F., & Dickinson, G. L. The sources and nature of the affective reaction to instrumental music. In M. Schoen, ed., *The Effects of Music*. New York: Harcourt, Brace, 1927. Chap. 6.

Washburn, M. F., & Grose, S. L. Voluntary control of likes and dislikes; the effects of an attempt voluntarily to change the affective value of colors. *American Journal of Psychology*, 1921, *32*, 284–89.

Washburn, M. F., Haight, D., & Regensburg, J. The relation of the pleasantness of color combinations to that of the colors seen singly. *American Journal of Psychology*, 1921, *32*, 145–46.

Washburn, M. F., MacDonald, M. T., & Van Alstyne, D. Voluntarily controlled likes and dislikes of color combinations. *American Journal of Psychology*, 1922, *33*, 426–28.

Washburn, M. F., McLean, K. G., & Dodge, A. The effect of area on the pleasantness of colors. *American Journal of Psychology*, 1934, *46*, 638–40.

Watson, K. B. The nature and measurement of musical meanings. *Psychological Monographs*, 1942, *54*, 1–43 (whole no. 244).

Weber, C. O. The aesthetics of rectangles and theories of affection. *Journal of Applied Psychology*, 1931, *15*, 310–18.

Weinstein, S. Intensive and extensive aspects of tactile sensitivity as a function of body part, sex, and laterality. In D. R. Kenshalo, ed., *The Skin Senses*. Springfield, Ill.: Charles C Thomas, 1968. Pp. 195–222.

Weiss, P. *The World of Art*. Carbondale: Southern Illinois University Press, 1961.

Weisskopf, E. A. A transcendence index as a proposed measure in the TAT. *Journal of Psychology*, 1950, *29*, 379–90.

Weitzenhoffer, A. M. *General Techniques of Hypnosis*. New York: Grune & Stratton, 1957.

Weld, P. H. An experimental study of musical enjoyment. *American Journal of Psychology*, 1912, *23*, 245–308.

Welker, W. I. Play and exploration in chimpanzees. Unpublished doctoral dissertation, University of Chicago, 1954.

Welker, W. I. Effects of age and experience on play and exploration of young chimpanzees. *Journal of Comparative and Physiological Psychology*, 1956, *49*, 23–226. (a)

Welker, W. I. Some determinants of play and exploration in chimpanzees. *Journal of Comparative and Physiological Psychology*, 1956, *49*, 84–89. (b)

Welker, W. I. Variability of play and exploratory behavior in chimpanzees. *Journal of Comparative and Physiological Psychology*, 1956, *49*, 181–85. (c)

Welker, W. I. "Free" vs. "forced" exploration of a novel situation by rats. *Psychological Reports*, 1957, *3*, 95–108, Monograph Supplement no. 2.

Welleck, A. Die Ganzheitspsychologischen Aspekte der Musikästhetik. *Bericht über den internationalen Musikwissenschaftlichen Kongress*, Wien, 1958. Pp. 678–88.

Wellek, R., & Warren, R. *Theory of Literature*. 3d ed. New York: Harcourt, 1956.

Wells, H. M. The phenomenology of acts of choice. *British Journal of Psychology, Monograph Supplement*, 1927, no. 11.

Wells, N. A. Description of the affective character of the colors of the spectrum. *Psychological Bulletin*, 1910, *7*, 181–95.

Wells, R. Nominal and verbal style. In T. A. Sebeok, ed., *Style in Language*. Cambridge, Mass.: M.I.T. Press, 1960. Pp. 213–20.

Wenzel, B. M. Tactile stimulation as reinforcement for cats and its relation to early feeding experience. *Psychological Reports*, 1959, *5*, 297–300.

Werner, H. Die melodische Erfindung in frühen Kindesalter. *Philosophisch-Historische Klasse. Sitzungsberichte*, 1917, *182*, 4. Abhandlung.

Werner, H. Untersuchungen über Empfindung und Empfinden: I. Das Problem des Empfindens und die Methode seiner experimentellen Prüfung. *Zeitschrift für Psychologie*, 1930, *114*, 152–66.

Werner, H. L'unité des sens. *Journal de Psychologie*, 1934, *31*, 190–205.

Werner, H. A psychological analysis of expressive language. In H. Werner, ed.,

On Expressive Language. Worcester, Mass.: Clark University Press, 1955. Pp. 11–18.

Werner, H. *Comparative Psychology of Mental Development*. New York: International Universities Press, 1957.

Werner, H., & Kaplan, B. *Symbol Formation: An Organismic-Developmental Approach to Language and the Expression of Thought*. New York: Wiley, 1963.

Werner, H., & Kaplan, E. The acquisition of word meanings: A developmental study. *Monographs of the Society for Research in Child Development*, 1952, no. 15.

Werner, H., & Wapner, S. Sensory-tonic field theory of perception. *Journal of Personality*, 1949, *18*, 88–107.

Werner, H., & Wapner, S. Toward a general theory of perception. *Psychological Review*, 1952, *59*, 324–38.

Werner, H., Wapner, S., & Bruell, J. H. Experiments on sensory-tonic field theory of perception: IV. Effect of the position of head, eye and of object on the position of the apparent median plane. *Journal of Experimental Psychology*, 1953, *46*, 293–99.

Wertheimer, M. *Productive Thinking*. New York: Harper & Bros., 1959.

Weston, J. L. *From Ritual to Romance*. Garden City, N.Y.: Doubleday, 1957.

Wever, E. G. Figure and ground in the visual perception of form. *American Journal of Psychology*, 1927, *38*, 194–226.

Wexner, L. B. The degree to which colors (hues) are associated with mood-tones. *Journal of Applied Psychology*, 1954, *38*, 432–35.

Weyl, H. *Symmetry*. Princeton, N.J.: Princeton University Press, 1952.

Wheeler, R. H., & Cutsworth, T. D. Synesthesia in judging and choosing. *Journal of General Psychology*, 1928, *1*, 497–519.

Whiting, J. W. M. Resource mediation and learning by identification. In I. Iscoe & H. W. Stevenson, eds., *Personality Development in Children*. Austin: University of Texas Press, 1960. Pp. 112–26.

Whorf, B. L. An American-Indian model of the universe. *Journal of American Linguistics*, 1950, *16*, 67–72.

Whorf, B. L. *Language, Thought, and Reality*. Cambridge, Mass.: Technology Press, 1956.

Wicker, F. W. A scaling study of synesthetic thinking. Princeton, N.J.: Educational Testing Service Research Bulletin, RB–66–25, 1966. (And ONR Technical Report NR 150–088, NR 151–174).

Wight, F. The revulsions of Goya. *Journal of Aesthetics and Art Criticism*, 1946, *5*, 1–28.

Wigman, M. *The Language of Dance*. Middletown, Conn.: Wesleyan University Press, 1966.

Wilcox, W. W., & Morrison, B. M. A psychological investigation of the relation of illumination to aesthetics. *Psychological Monographs*, 1933, *44*, 282–300.

Wiley, L. Some factors of pleasantness in visual design. *Psychological Bulletin*, 1940, *37*, 568. Abstract.

Williams, C. B. A note on the statistical analysis of sentence-length as a criterion of literary style. *Biometrika*, 1940, *31*, 356–61.

Williams, C. D., & Kuchta, J. C. Exploratory behavior in two mazes with dissimilar alternatives. *Journal of Comparative and Physiological Psychology*, 1957, *50*, 509–13.

Wilson, D. J. An experimental investigation of Birkhoff's aesthetic measure. *Journal of Abnormal and Social Psychology*, 1939, 34, 390–94.

Wilson, G. D. Arousal properties of red versus green. *Perceptual and Motor Skills*, 1966, 25, 947–49.

Wilson, N. P., & Wilson, W. P. The duration of human electroencephalographic arousal responses elicited by photic stimulation. *EEG Clinical Neurophysiology*, 1959, 11, 85–91.

Wimsatt, W. K., Jr. *The Prose Style of Samuel Johnson.* New Haven, Conn.: Yale University Press, 1941.

Wimsatt, W. K., Jr. One relation of rhyme to reason. *Modern Language Quarterly*, 1944, 5, 323–38.

Wimsatt, W. K., Jr. Poetry and morals: a relation reargued. *Thought*, 1948, 23, 281–99.

Wimsatt, W. K., Jr. *The Verbal Icon.* Lexington: University of Kentucky Press, 1954.

Wimsatt, W. K., Jr., & Beardsley, M. C. The concept of meter: an exercise in abstraction. *Publications of the Modern Language Association of America*, 1959, 74, 585–98.

Wimsatt, W. K., Jr., & Beardsley, M. C. A word for rhythm and a word for meter. *Publications of the Modern Language Association of America*, 1961, 76, 305–8.

Winterstein, A. *Zur Problematik der Einfühlung und des psychologischen Verstehens.* Wien: Internationaler Psychoanalytischer Verlag, 1932.

Wissemann, H. *Untersuchungen zur Onomatopoii: 1. Teil. Die sprachpsychologischen Versuche.* Heidelberg: Carl Winter Universitätsverlag, 1954.

Witasek, S. Zur psychologischen Analyse der ästhetischen Einfühlung. *Zeitschrift für Psychologie und Physiologie der Sinnesorgane*, 1901, 25, 1–49.

Witkin, H. A., Lewis, H. B., Hertzman, M., Machover, K., Meissner, P. B., & Wapner, S. *Personality Through Perception.* New York: Harper, 1954.

Witmer, L. Zur experimentellen Ästhetik einfacher räumlicher Formverhältnisse. *Philosophische Studien*, 1893, 9, I, 96–144; II, 209–263.

Wittgenstein, L. *Philosophical Investigations.* New York: Oxford University Press, 1953.

Wittkower, R. The changing concept of proportion. *Daedalus*, Winter 1960, pp. 199–215.

Wohlgemut, A. Pleasure-unpleasure: an experimental investigation on the feeling elements. *British Journal of Psychology, Monograph Supplement*, 1919, no. 6.

Wohlwill, J. F. Developmental studies of perception. *Psychological Bulletin*, 1960, 57, 249–88.

Wohlwill, J. F. Amount of stimulus exploration and preference as differential functions of stimulus complexity. *Perception and Psychophysics*, 1968, 4, 307–12.

Wolberg, L. R. *Hypnoanalysis.* New York: Grune & Stratton, 1945.

Wolf, K. M., & Fiske, M. The children talk about comics. In P. F. Lazarsfeld, & F. N. Stanton, eds., *Communications Research 1948–1949.* New York: Harper, 1949.

Wolfenstein, M., & Leites, N. *Movies: A Psychological Study.* Glencoe, Ill.: Free Press, 1950.

Wolff, W. Experimental self-analysis. *Ciba Symposia*, 1945, 7, 1–36.

452 *Psychology of the Arts*

Wolff, W. *The Personality of the Preschool Child.* New York: Grune & Stratton, 1946.

Wölfflin, H. *Classic Art.* New York: Phaidon Press, 1952.

Woods, W. A. Some determinants of attitude towards colors in combinations. *Perceptual and Motor Skills,* 1956, *6,* 187–93.

Woodworth, R. S. *Experimental Psychology.* New York: Holt, 1938.

Woodworth, R. S. *Contemporary Schools of Psychology.* Revised ed. New York: Ronald, 1948.

Worringer, W. *Abstraktion und Einfühlung.* München: R. Piper Verlag, 1948.

Wright, B. The influence of hue, brightness, and saturation on apparent warmth and weight. *American Journal of Psychology,* 1962, *75,* 232–41.

Wright, B., & Rainwater, L. The meanings of color. *Journal of General Psychology,* 1962, *67,* 89–99.

Wulf, F. Über die Veränderung von Vorstellungen (Gedächtnis und Gestalt). *Psychologische Forschungen,* 1922, *1,* 333–73.

Wunderlich, E. *Die Bedeutung der roten Farbe im Kultur der Griechen und Römer.* Giessen: Töpelman, 1925.

Wundt, W. *Völkerpsychologie: eine Untersuchung der Entwicklungsgesetze von Sprache, Mythen und Sitte.* 3 vols. Leipzig: Engelmann, 1900–1909.

Wundt, W. *Grundzüge der physiologischen Psychologie.* 5th revised ed. Vol. 2. Leipzig: Engelmann, 1902.

Yeats, W. B. *Essays.* London: Macmillan, 1924.

Yokoyama, M. Affective tendency as conditioned by color and form. *American Journal of Psychology,* 1921, *32,* 81–107.

Yoshida, M. Word-music in English poetry. *Journal of Aesthetics and Art Criticism,* 1952, *11,* 151–59.

Yoshii, N., & Tsukiyama, K. EEG studies on conditioned behavior of the white rat. *Japanese Journal of Physiology,* 1952, *2,* 186–93.

Young, P. T. Pleasantness and unpleasantness in relation to organic response. *American Journal of Psychology,* 1921, *32,* 38–54.

Young, P. T. The role of hedonic processes in motivation. In M. R. Jones, ed., *Nebraska Symposium on Motivation, 1955.* Lincoln: University of Nebraska Press, 1955. Pp. 193–238.

Youngblood, J. E. Music and language: some related analytical techniques. Unpublished doctoral dissertation, Indiana University, 1960.

Zagorul'ko, T. M., & Sollertinkaia, T. N. On the comparative analysis of the mechanisms of the orienting reflex. In L. G. Voronin et al., eds., *The Orienting Reflex and Exploratory Behavior.* Moscow: Academy of Pedagogical Sciences, 1958.

Zeaman, D. Response latency as a function of the amount of reinforcement. *Journal of Experimental Psychology,* 1949, *39,* 466–83.

Zeaman, D., & House, B. J. The growth and decay of reactive inhibition as measured by alternation behavior. *Journal of Experimental Psychology,* 1951, *41,* 177–86.

Zeigarnik, B. Über das Behalten von erledigten und unerledigten Handlungen. *Psychologische Forschung,* 1927, *9,* 1–85.

Zevi, B. *Architecture as Space: How to Look at Architecture.* Edited by J. A. Barry. New York: Horizon Press, 1957.

Zietz, K. Gegenseitige Beeinflussung von Farb- und Tonerlebnissen. *Zeitschrift der Psychologie,* 1931, *121,* 257–356.

Zigler, M. J., Cook, B., Miller, D., & Wemple, L. The perception of form in peripheral vision. *American Journal of Psychology,* 1930, *42,* 246–59.

Zimmer, H. *Philosophies of India.* Edited by J. Campbell. New York: Meridian Books, 1956.

Zimmer, H. *Myths and Symbols in Indian Art and Civilization.* Edited by J. Campbell. New York: Harper, 1962.

Zink, S. The moral effect of art. *Ethics,* 1950, *60,* 261–74.

Zipf, G. K. *The Psycho-Biology of Language.* Boston: Houghton Mifflin, 1935.

Zipf, G. K. The meaning-frequency relationship of words. *Journal of General Psychology,* 1945, *33,* 251–56.

Zipf, G. K. *Human Behavior and the Principle of Least Effort.* Cambridge, Mass.: Addison-Wesley, 1949.

Zucker, W. M. Inside and outside in architecture: a symposium. *Journal of Aesthetics and Art Criticism,* 1966, *25,* 7–13.

Zusne, L., & Michels, K. M. Geometricity of visual form. *Perceptual and Motor Skills,* 1962, *14,* 147–54. (a)

Zusne, L., & Michels, K. M. More on the geometricity of visual form. *Perceptual and Motor Skills,* 1962, *15,* 55–58. (b)

Name Index

Subject Index

478   *Psychology of the Arts*

Chromaticists, 78

Chromatism (in music), 138

Closure, 8, 84
expectation and, 97–99, 153
observation of image and of forms,
42, 84, 85–86, 88, 97–99
observation of sculpture and, 193, 275
plot and, 254
in reading, 273
in rhythm, 153
in symbols, 319

Cognitive contents, 8, 15, 23, 27, 28, 30
See also Beliefs, Cognitive Orientation, Meaning

Cognitive dissonance, 330–32

Cognitive elaboration, in concretization,
309, 310
in dance, 277
daydreams and, 291
determinants of, 27, 273, 277
emotion and, 24, 271
empathy and, 267–69, 271
fantasied reconstruction, 273–74, 277
feeling-into and, 271, 273–77
identification and, 291
identification with the author and,
273–74
incompleteness of artistic presentation and, 273–90
in literature, 273–74, 275
meaning and, 12, 271, 294
in music, 280–81
in painting, 277
projection and, 290
role, in catharsis, 293; in emotional
experiencing, 24, 255, 268–71, 273–
74, 277; in imitation, 269–71
in sculpture, 276–277
in theory of representation, 267–68

Cognitive orientation, abstraction and,
360
aesthetic distance and, 332–333, 357,
359, 360
arousal and, 23, 24
art experience and, 327, 330, 332–35,
355–58, 366
catharsis and, 293
changes in, 332, 356–57
changes in behavior and, 357–58
contribution of art realities to, 120,

336–39, 346–47, 349, 351, 353–54,
355, 356–58, 366
defined, 23, 328
effects of novelty and complexity, 26,
330–32, 337–39, 351, 357
expansion of, as a goal, 26, 329–30,
355; by learning, 26, 329, 334;
through art, 28, 330–35, 336–39,
354–57, 363, 366
expectation for, in art, 355
individual differences in, 365
primacy of striving for, 329–30, 355,
358
reflection in art realities, 333
relations with tension and relief, 24–
27, 203, 330, 356, 358
role, of beliefs in, 23, 24, 328–29, 357,
358; in determining behavior, 23–
24, 328–30, 332–33, 357–58; of intention in, 329, 357; of meaning in,
23–24, 26, 27, 328–29
set and, 357
symbols and, 323–24, 360
theory of, 23–24, 328–30, 357

Collative variables, 10, 371, 381

Collective unconscious, in archeological
reality, 340–44
archetypes in, 73–75, 322–23

Color discrimination, 39, 55, 56

Color mixing, 44

Color names, in other cultures, 56

Color solid, 34, 36, 41, 43, 46

Color vision theories, 40

Colored-light painting, 79, 353

Colors, abstractness and associations to,
54, 56
archetypes and, 73–75; in balance,
105
brightness, 377, 378; effect on tension, 37, 38, 42, 71
changes in meaning of, 60–62
climate and, 62–63
concepts and, 302, 304
culturally shared meanings, 60–62,
63, 297
cross-culturally shared meanings, 67–
75, 377
definitions, 33, 373
determinants of associations to, 54,
55, 56, 59, 60–63, 70, 73, 76
dimensions of, 34, 373

(Homeostasis, *ctd.*)
  pleasure and displeasure and, 12–16,
    17–18, 369
  role of expectations in, 15–16, 369–70
  striving for, 41
  tension and relief and, 12–16, 369–70
Human body, empathy in dance, 169,
    277; literature, 272; painting, 277;
    sculpture, 213, 275–76
  gravity and, 167
  habitual image as good gestalt, 173–
    75
  line of, 168–73, 386
  portrayal in sculpture, 210–12
  positions in dance, 158–61, 166–74,
    210
  remaining within potentialities, 169
  shapes in, 173–75
Hypnosis, and color reactions, 59, 68
  motoric patterns and emotions, 270
  slow rhythms, 148
  sound repetition, 244

Identification, analogizing and, 289–92,
    310
  cognitive elaboration and, 291, 310
  in concretization, 310
  cues for, 291-92
  culture and, 291
  in dance, 167
  of dance movements, 386
  defined, 28–29
  in drama, 280
  dynamization and, 118
  of emotions, 270, 271, 390
  of features in cartoons, 307
  feeling-into and, 28
  of forms, 392–93
  of individual figures and events, 308
  imitation and, 291
  latent contents, 7, 292
  with literary figures, 29, 273, 280, 321,
    347, 356
  meaning and, 26
  motives for, 290–91
  multiple, 287–88; and aesthetic dis-
    tance, 282, 359
  in music, 280
  of percepts and meaning, 393
  projection and, 290, 310, 366

of the reader with the author, 273,
    274–75
  role of in sublimation, 289–92, 310,
    392
  in sculpture, 280, 283
  wish fulfillment and, 289–92, 366
Illumination, effects of color, 379
  expanse colors and, 35
  gestalt perception and, 89
  motion and, 209
  of a painting, 35
  of surfaces, 51, 193, 209, 373, 374
Image, associations and, 57
  composite or average, 306
  concepts and, 302
  of future, 351
  generic, 305–8
  in meaning responses, 225–26
  multileveled, 292, 295
  to music, 278, 280
  of people in life and literature, 273
  percepts and, 333–34
  of reality, 305
  on retina, 379–80
  schema and, 306
  symbol and, 298, 313–18, 321
  the unconscious and, 342–43
  in visual arts, 254
Imitation, in adults, 268, 269
  arousal and, 271–72
  of aggressive models, 292–93
  in children, 117, 268, 269, 384
  cognitive elaboration and, 269–71,
    273–74, 276, 277
  commonness of, 269, 360
  culture and, 291
  in dance, of movement, 277
  dynamization and, 117
  emotion and, 268–69
  empathy and, 117, 268, 269, 293
  in film, 283
  of forms, 277–78
  identification and, 291
  inhibition of, 213, 276, 277
  kinesthetic, 117, 213, 268, 269, 277
  in Lipps's theory, 268–69, 277–78,
    391
  in literature of depicted movement,
    271–73, 275
  in observing paintings, 277–78

(Metaphor, *ctd.*)
origin of, 228
as science model, 21
in symbol formation, 316
as symbolic category, 56, 69, 73, 76, 78, 111, 226, 228, 288, 292, 311, 314–15, 342, 393
See also Meaning, Symbols
Meter, basic, 154–55, 240
as acoustic gestalt, 154–55, 240, 242, 243
in dance, 179
defined musical, 154; poetic, 239–40, 390; in prose, 236–37
expectation and, 237, 241, 246–47
expressive nature, 242–43
interactions with meaning rhythm, and syntax in poetry, 240–44, 246–47, 390–91
interactions with rhythm in music, 154–56
modulation and, 240–42
in music, 154–56; and poetry compared, 240
as norm, 239
pleasure of, 240
in poetry, 239–44, 390
in prose, 236–37
rhyme and, 239, 244, 246
rhythm and, 239–40, 242–43
set and, 247
stress in, 239–40, 390
temporal, 390
tension and relief, 155–56, 240–43, 390–91
types in poetry, 239–40, 243, 390
Mode (in music), defined, 133
meaning and associations, 143
in melody, 137–38
Modern dance, balance in, 167
gravity, 162, 175
line in, 171–73
movements of, 161–62, 164–65, 167, 175–76, 178–80
positions in, 173
Modulation, in atonal music, 133–34
cadence and, 133
defined, 133
developments in, 132–34, 138
key and, 132–34
in poetry, 240–42

tension and relief, 133–34, 138, 240–42
Module, 104
Motifs, in dance, 162, 175
in literature, 299
in music, 134, 141, 156, 253, 255, 344
in narrative-representational content, 319
in painting, 101
in rhythm, 156
role in multileveledness, 298–99
in sculpture, 211–13
Movement, in acrobatics, 167, 184
in balancing, 105
in ballet, 159, 161, 166, 168, 177
as category of symbols, 158, 181, 226, 298, 313–14, 315, 319, 393
classification, 184, 386–87
colors in, 78, 79
in communication, 180
concepts and, 302, 304
contrasts in, 177–78, 183
cross-culturally shared meanings, 179, 181
culturally shared meanings, 180, 297, 387
in dance, 158, 163, 166, 169, 171, 173, 174, 176, 177, 184, 277, 386
in different planes, 169, 177–78
direction of, 169, 177, 387
dynamization and, 116–18, 278
evocation of emotions by, 268–71, 273; of tension and relief by, 158, 163, 166–67, 169, 171–77, 180, 185, 207–8
expressive, 56, 157, 181, 184, 268–70, 272, 387; of emotions and personality, 158, 161, 180, 182–83, 268–70, 297–98, 301, 387
floor track of, 176, 182, 387
forms and, 116–18, 169, 171–77, 185
frequency of shifting and, 300
habituation and, 175, 300, 386
imitation of, 117, 181, 268, 270, 271, 272–73, 275–77, 391
in Indian dance, 168
of inanimate objects and human motives, 182–83
lability and, 166–69, 173, 184
in language, 383–84
learning of meaning of, 180–81, 387

(Theater, *ctd.*)
  emotional experiencing of, 264
  empathy in, 267, 271
  living, 284
  new information through, 331
  psychodramatic, 29
  set in, 262–63
  sublimation in, 288
  See also Drama
Theory of cognitive orientation, *see* Cognitive orientation
Theory of representation, 266–68, 271
Three-dimensionality, in architecture 187–88, 212
  bidimensional perception and, 299
  as characteristic of sculpture, 187
  development in sculpture, 198–203, 388
  form and space as aspects, 204, 387
  of human body, 169, 171–72
  in painting, 51–52, 78, 103, 107
  plasticity and, 51–52
  shape and, 171–72, 195–97
Thriller, 17, 132, 140, 252, 363
Timbre, 141, 143
Tones, articulation of within glissandi, 128, 136
  association to body movements, 136
  beats and, 124–25
  brightness, 71
  in chords, 121
  color, 279
  color brightness and, 378
  complexity of sequences, 373, 385
  concept and, 302, 304
  and context of music, 142–44
  effects on arousal, 16, 42, 136, 375
  frequency of vibrations, 125
  as gestalts, 130, 278
  habituation to, 375
  meaning of, 143
  movement and, 136
  perception of, 123, 384–85
  pitch of, 42, 136, 141–43, 378
  principles of choice, 127–29
  relative duration, 234
  similarity and tension, 130
  spatial localization, 378–79
  speech sounds and, 216–17
  synesthesia and, 9, 71, 142–43, 378
  tension and relief, 130, 136, 234–35

  timbre of, 141, 143
  tonal movement, 143–44
  in tone system, 126
  volume of, 143
Tone systems, 126–30
Tonic (in melody), 137–38, 140
Touch, *see* Tactility
Transformational grammar, 232–33
Tri-dimensionality, *see* Three-dimensionality
Twelve-tone music, *see* Atonality
Type, abstraction and, 306, 310
  perception of, 393

Uncertainty, complexity and, 381
  gestalt and, 89
  information and, 11, 18
  in listening to melody, 139
  orientation and, 330
  preference for, 26
  tension and, 330
  in tone sequences, 385
Unconscious, in archeological reality, 341–44
  associations and, 57–59, 76
  expression of, in art, 335
  Freud's concept of, 6, 7, 150, 288, 296, 322, 339–40, 344
  Jung's concept of, 322, 340
  consciousness and, 288, 323, 341
  rhythms, 150
  sublimation and, 288
Unpredictability, preferences of linguistic, 230
  work of art and, 18
Utopia, 351, 352

Variation, abstraction and, 102, 304–5
  in accidental or central features, 307–8
  context and, 102
  in dance, 177, 180
  defined, 101–2, 304
  development in, 103
  in drama, 305
  gestalt and, 101–2
  in intonational contour, 235
  in literary narrative, 304
  meaning and, 102
  modules, 104
  mythological heroes, 306